FORENSIC PSYCHOLOGY:

THE USE OF BEHAVIORAL SCIENCE IN CIVIL AND CRIMINAL JUSTICE

SECOND EDITION

HENRY F. FRADELLA, J.D., PH.D.
CALIFORNIA STATE UNIVERSITY, LONG BEACH

CENGAGE
Learning™

Australia • Brazil • Japan • Korea • Mexico • Singapore • Spain • United Kingdom • United States

CENGAGE
Learning™

FORENSIC PSYCHOLOGY: THE USE OF BEHAVIORAL SCIENCE IN CIVIL AND CRIMINAL JUSTICE, SECOND EDITION

HENRY F. FRADELLA, J.D., PH.D.
CALIFORNIA STATE UNIVERSITY, LONG BEACH

Executive Editors:
 Michele Baird

 Maureen Staudt

 Michael Stranz

Project Development Manager:
 Linda deStefano

Senior Marketing Coordinators:
 Sara Mercurio

 Lindsay Shapiro

Production/Manufacturing Manager:
 Donna M. Brown

PreMedia Services Supervisor:
 Rebecca A. Walker

Rights & Permissions Specialist:
 Kalina Hintz

Cover Image:
 Getty Images*

* Unless otherwise noted, all cover images used by Custom Solutions, a part of Cengage Learning, have been supplied courtesy of Getty Images with the exception of the Earthview cover image, which has been supplied by the National Aeronautics and Space Administration (NASA).

For product information and technology assistance, contact us at **Cengage Learning Customer & Sales Support, 1-800-354-9706**

For permission to use material from this text or product, submit all requests online at **cengage.com/permissions** Further permissions questions can be emailed to **permissionrequest@cengage.com**

ISBN-13: 978-1-4266-3064-4

ISBN-10: 1-4266-3064-6

Cengage Learning
5191 Natorp Boulevard
Mason, Ohio 45040
USA

Cengage Learning is a leading provider of customized learning solutions with office locations around the globe, including Singapore, the United Kingdom, Australia, Mexico, Brazil, and Japan. Locate your local office at: **international.cengage.com/region**

Cengage Learning products are represented in Canada by Nelson Education, Ltd.

For your lifelong learning solutions, visit **custom.cengage.com**

Visit our corporate website at **cengage.com**

Printed in the United States of America

FORENSIC PSYCHOLOGY:
THE USE OF BEHAVIORAL SCIENCE IN CIVIL AND CRIMINAL JUSTICE
SECOND EDITION

HENRY F. FRADELLA, J.D., PH.D.
CALIFORNIA STATE UNIVERSITY, LONG BEACH

Dedicated to my "little brother,"
Ryan A. Melendez

TABLE OF CONTENTS

ORGANIZATION OF THIS BOOK

PART I

This textbook is divided into three parts. Part I provides an overview of behavior science and law. Chapter 1 examines the unique problems created by the often incompatible alliance of psychology and the legal system by looking at the disciplinary differences in language, assumptions about human nature, and methodologies used. Chapter 2 is devoted to developing an understanding of the concepts of socialization and social control, and the roles of both law and behavioral science in both. Special attention is paid to sociological critiques of the medicalization of deviance and the role behavioral science plays in formal social control. Chapter 3 summarizes some basics concepts and tools of forensic psychological assessment. To help those unfamiliar with abnormal psychology, Appendix A contains brief descriptions and diagnostic criteria for a number of mental illnesses that are commonly seen in the forensic setting.

PART II

Part II of this textbook explores the specifics of psychology in the law by examining the specific questions the law poses to the behavioral sciences. Chapters 4 through 10 are concerned with the material that is at the heart of forensic psychology. Chapters 4 and 5 are concerned with important issues surrounding criminal competencies. Chapter 4 is a detailed study of the competency to stand trial, while Chapter 5 explores the remaining criminal competencies, such as the capacity to confess, plead guilty, waive counsel, be sentenced, and be punished. Chapter 6 is a detailed analysis of the insanity defense, starting with its early history in English common law, and tracing its evolution to the present. Chapter 7 is the final chapter concerned with forensic psychology in the criminal law setting, examining the diminished capacity defense and those defenses flowing from it, such as the infamous PMS defense and Twinkie defense, among others.

In Chapter 8, the focus of the book turns to the role of forensic psychology in the civil justice system. Chapter 8 examines one of the most important functions behavioral scientists play in American civil law—their role in the involuntary civil commitment process. Chapter 9 then examines the role of psychology and psychiatry in determining civil competencies. Included in the interdisciplinary examination are the civil capacities to testify, to make a will, to enter a binding contract, and to be a custodial parent. Chapter 9 concludes with a detailed look at guardianship and conservatorship—the legal proceedings used when someone lacks the capacity to manage his or her own affairs in terms of financial and health care matters.

Part II ends with Chapter 10. It explores some of the special rights and responsibilities that accompany forensic psychology from both the perspective of the client-patient and the practitioner. Accordingly, the right to refuse treatment, the right to treatment, the right to informed consent, and the complex rules governing confidentiality in the forensic psychological arena are all included in the chapter.

PART III

As Chapter 1 explains, the term forensic psychology is often used to refer to many areas in which law and psychology intersect that go beyond the clinical assessment of someone under the jurisdiction of a court of law for any of the purposes covered in Part II of this book. Part III provides an overview of some of these other areas in which behavioral science and the justice system intersect. Chapter 11 examines the psychology of policing. Chapter 12 is devoted to some specialized applications of empirical behavioral science to the law, including the reliability of eyewitness testimony, the reliability of confessions and interrogations, and the psychology of the jury and its decision-making role. Chapter 13 examined the American jury system, with special attention to the psychological assumptions inherent in the jury selection process as well as jury deliberations. Part III ends with a comprehensive interdisciplinary examination criminal punishment, focusing on the philosophy and psychology of sentencing in Chapter 14 and correctional psychology in Chapter 15.

PART I:
OVERVIEW OF BEHAVIORAL SCIENCE AND LAW

CHAPTER ONE
AN OVERVIEW OF THE TENUOUS RELATIONSHIP BETWEEN LAW AND THE BEHAVIORAL SCIENCES

I. AN OVERVIEW OF THE INTERSECTION OF LAW AND THE BEHAVIORAL SCIENCES

A. What Is Forensic Psychology?

Finding the appropriate title for this book was a difficult task. The intersection of psychology, psychiatry, and the legal system is broad and not particularly well defined. Only recently has the intersection of law and the behavioral sciences been recognized as its own discipline. In fact, most scholarship in the area has been written in the last twenty-five years or so.[1] Regardless, the field has grown and continues to do so.[2] And with such growth, definitions evolve, boundaries change, and areas of specialization and sub-specialization develop.[3] A number of specialized joint-degree programs provide for interdisciplinary training between law and the mental health fields.[4] Perhaps the rapid growth is what has given rise to disagreements about the appropriate definition of the term "forensic psychology."

Defining the first part of the term "forensic psychology" is the easy part. The word *forensic* comes from the Latin word *forensis*, which means "of the market or forum." The forum was an active place in ancient Rome. Trials, theatrical performances, and political debates all occurred in the forum. Accordingly, the word forensic is sometimes used to refer to rhetoric or debate skills today. More commonly, though, since trials occurred in the forum, the word forensic is typically used to mean "of or pertaining to the law," especially in terms of the application of science or technology in the investigation of facts or evidence relevant in a court of law. The term "psychology" refers to the science that deals with mental processes and behavior. Forensic psychology, then, at its core, is the use or application of psychology to the law. But such a generic definition is a bit misleading, for the field is more complicated than this simple definition would suggest.

Defining forensic psychology is difficult because the term is often used generically to encompass a diverse group of behavioral scientists who study and/or interact with the legal system. Behavioral scientists include medical doctors who are psychiatrists and neurologists, other medical professionals such as forensic nurses, clinical social workers and clinical psychologists, academics with degrees in social sciences who study human behaviors such as sociologists, criminologists, anthropologists, and many different types of psychologists.

---

[1] Gary B. Melton, *The Law Is a Good Thing (Psychology Is, Too): Human Rights in Psychological Jurisprudence*, 16 LAW & HUM. BEHAV. 381 (1992).

[2] *See* generally Kirk Heilbrun & Randy K. Otto, *The Practice of Forensic Psychology: A Look at the Future in Light of the Past*, 57 AM. PSYCHOLOGIST 5-18 (2002); Bruce D. Sales, *The Legal Regulation of Psychology: Scientific and Professional Interactions*, in 2 THE MASTER LECTURE SERIES: PSYCHOLOGY AND THE LAW (C. James Scheirer & Barbara L. Hammons eds., 1980).

[3] *E.g.*, Craig Haney, *Psychology and Legal Change: The Impact of a Decade*, 17 L. & HUM. BEHAV. 371, 375 (1993).

[4] Linda R. Crane, *Interdisciplinary Combined-degree and Graduate Law Degree Programs: History and Trends*, 33 J. MARSHALL L. REV. 47, 75 (1999); Janet Weinstein, *Coming of Age: Recognizing the Importance of Interdisciplinary Education in Law Practice*, 74 WASH. L. REV. 319, 362 (1999); Alan J. Tomkins & James R.P. Ogloff, *Training and Career Options in Psychology and Law*, 8 BEHAVIORAL SCI. & L. 205, 205 (1990).

Collectively, these behavioral scientists engage in a wide range of activities within their respective disciplinary fields that relate to the law. For example, social scientists conduct empirical research on the law and functioning of the legal system; psychiatrists, clinical psychologists, and clinical social workers all conduct clinical evaluations of patients who may be involved in a legal proceeding; and all of the aforementioned behavioral scientists may serve as expert witnesses, researchers, consultants, and even as the authors of court reports and briefs that may be used in both adjudicative and legislative processes.

Given the wide array of professionals who may be involved in different aspects of forensic psychological practice and research, the text uses two terms "behavioral sciences" or "behavioral scientists" both in the title and throughout this book. The reader should recognize that these terms may seem to some too broad since I use them primarily to refer to the work of those who engage in forensic clinical assessment (i.e., psychiatrists, clinical psychologists, neurologists, neuropsychologists, and clinical social workers). I nevertheless opt for this arguably overbroad term due to the participation of many professionals who are not psychologists.

In light of the broad and diverse areas in which the behavioral sciences intersect with the law, some use the term *forensic psychology* to refer collectively to any such interaction. Under such a broad definition, psychologists who evaluate people under court jurisdiction and academic researchers who empirically investigate some aspect of the relationship between the two disciplines, such as the reliability of eyewitness testimony, would all be forensic psychologists.[5] In recognition of this broad perspective, Dr. Joseph Davis offered the following definition of forensic psychology: "The scientific application of methods, procedures, and techniques that involve the investigation, consultation, and research into the psychological understanding of human behavior, mental processes, and the brain to the resolution of problems found in the criminal and civil law."[6]

As the intersections of the behavioral sciences and the law have become more defined, it would seem logical to narrow the definition of forensic psychology so the term is not too generic. I offer the following, more narrow definition of forensic psychology in an attempt to differentiate *forensic psychological assessment* from other subfields of forensic psychology: "the clinical assessment of patients under the jurisdiction of a court of law, whether criminal or civil, as part of the judicial process." In using this more narrow definition of forensic psychology, its practitioners can be distinguished from other mental health professionals who work with substantive or procedural law. These include *police psychologists*, researchers and clinicians who work with law enforcement; and *correctional psychologists*, who work with both officials and inmates in the correctional setting.[7]

This more narrow definition also allows us to differentiate those engaging in forensic clinical assessment from the host of researchers who study the law and its processes. Many of these people work in colleges or universities or in private industry, and not all of them are psychologists by training; they are behavioral scientists in the broad sense of the term. As social scientists, they seek "to amass enough knowledge about a phenomenon to be able to understand

---

[5]   *E.g.*, Randy K. Otto, Kirk Heilbrun, & Thomas Grisso, *Training and Career Options in Psychology and Law*, 8 BEHAVIORAL SCI. & L. 217, 217-31 (1990).

[6]   Joseph A. Davis, "Forensic Psychology and Law: A Contemporary Perspective" (Feb. 2003) (unpublished lecture given at San Diego State University, San Diego, CA); Joseph A. David, "Contemporary Perspectives in Psychology and Law: Theory, Application and Practice: A Clinical-Forensic Approach (1999) (unpublished manuscript on file with author).

[7]   CURT R. BARTOL & ANNE M. BARTOL, PSYCHOLOGY AND LAW 13 (2d ed. 1994).

and predict it with an accuracy rate substantially above chance."[8] Most of these researchers are *social or empirical psychologists* who specialize in empirical research concerning the law, such as juror understanding of jury instructions, the reliability of eyewitness testimony, suggestibility and coercion in interview tactics, etc. While many such researchers consider themselves to be forensic psychologists, we should attempt to differentiate researchers from the clinicians who are participants in judicially related proceedings with roles that are prescribed for them by applicable law.

Recognizing, however, that the behavioral sciences are used in many areas of the justice system beyond the courts, this text examines the intersection of law and the behavioral sciences from a broad perspective. Accordingly, Part II focuses on the more narrow definition of forensic psychology by examining how mental health professionals are used as parts of judicial processes. And Part III explores the intersection of the disciplines in research, investigations, policing, sentencing, and corrections.

B. The Ways in Which Psychology and Law Interact

In 1980, Craig Haney wrote one of the more thoughtful analyses of the ways in which psychology and law as disciplines interact.[9] He conceptualized three distinct realms of interaction. His approach has been praised and adopted by other psycho-legal scholars, and it is similarly adopted in this text.[10]

The first of the ways in which Haney saw the two disciplines relate he terms *psychology in the law*. It is in this relationship that forensic psychology, as defined above and used throughout this book, lies. It is also the intersection that "may be the source of much of the malaise within the discipline."[11] Psychology in the law refers to the way in which the law makes selective use of the behavioral sciences. Psychiatry and psychology are used by the law to answer legal questions posed by the law itself. In other words, the legal realm not only defines the question, but also limits the scope of the answer expected from the behavioral sciences. For example, is someone competent to stand trial? Is someone insane? Although the law is clearly the dominant discipline in this relationship, behavioral science plays a significant and important role in the specified legal contexts. In fact, as you will see in many contexts throughout this book, the law is often highly deferential to psychological or psychiatric expert opinion. Yet, it is clear that the decisions to be made are set by the law.

Unfortunately, when law defines the scope of the question to be answered, it often does not avail itself to the benefits of the body of knowledge that the behavioral sciences can offer. The second of Haney's relationships, *psychology **and** the law*, does this much better. Here, the two disciplines are balanced in a partnership. Experimental psychology, as its own discipline, examines legal processes and offers informed opinions about their operation. For example, instead of answering the question "what is in the best interest of the child" to determine which parent gets custody of a child upon divorce (a question in the realm of psychology in the law), psychology and the law might challenge the very assumption that there is a single "best interest" by empirically demonstrating (probably using quasi-experimental methods) differences in

---

[8]   *Id.*

[9]   Craig Haney, *Psychology and Legal Change: On the Limits of a Factual Jurisprudence*, 4 L. & HUM. BEHAV. 147 (1980).

[10]   *E.g.*, BARTOL & BARTOL, *supra* note 7, at 2.

[11]   *Id.*

placement outcomes. Ideally, the law then responds to the data offered by psychological research. The law is often slow to change in response to research, however. That is not necessarily a bad thing, though. Arguably, research needs to be replicated and theory subsequently refined before law and policy are changed rather than just because research suggests that something is or is not so.

The third of Haney's classifications is called *psychology of the law*. It lies more in the philosophical than practical realm. It seeks to address abstract questions regarding the role of law in society as a tool in regulating individual and collective behaviors. (Chapter Two on social control explores this relationship in some detail.) For example, does mandatory minimum sentencing of first-time drunk driving offenders lower recidivism for the crime? Such questions about how laws affect human behavior and vice versa lie beyond the scope of this book. We are primarily concerned with psychology in the law—how the law makes use of the behavioral sciences. But we will also critique the status of the law using data from psychology and the law.

II.   LAW: ITS SOURCES, CLASSIFICATIONS, AND OPERATION

A. <u>What Is Law?</u>

Defining law is no easy task. As Steven Vago has commented, "comprehensive reviews of the literature . . . indicate that there are almost as many definitions of law as there are theorists."[12] One of the most influential definitions of law comes from the sociologist Max Weber. Weber conceptualized *law* as a rule of conduct that is "externally guaranteed by the probability that coercion (physical or psychological), to bring about conformity or avenge violation, will be applied by a staff of people holding themselves specially ready for that purpose."[13] Weber's definition of law has been modified into three distinct elements: "(1) explicit rules of conduct, (2) planned use of sanctions to support the rules, and (3) designated officials to interpret and enforce the rules, and often to make them."[14]

Law can be categorized in many ways. In terms of content, it may be substantive or procedural. *Substantive law* sets forth legal prescriptions and proscriptions—the "rules" of what one must do, may do, and may not do. *Procedural law* sets forth the mechanisms through which substantive laws are administered. Homicide statutes are examples of substantive laws. The rules regulating trial procedures and the ways in which evidence may be introduced in a homicide trial are examples of procedural laws.

Another way of categorizing law is using the distinction between civil and criminal law. *Criminal law*, also referred to as penal law, is that body of law that defines conduct that is criminally punishable by the government as a wrong committed against the people in society as a whole. In contrast, wrongs committed against an individual, called torts, are the realm of *civil law*. But civil law encompasses more than just torts; it includes many areas that regulate the relationships between individuals such as business law (e.g., corporate and contract law); family law (e.g., marriage, divorce, child custody); and property/estate law (e.g., the law of wills, trusts, and inheritance; landlord/tenant relations).

---

[12]   STEVEN VAGO, LAW AND SOCIETY 9 (5th ed. Prentice Hall 1997).

[13]   *Id.* at 7 (citing MAX WEBER, LAW IN ECONOMY AND SOCIETY 5 (ed. and trans. by Max Rheinstein and Edwahard Shils) (Harvard Univ. Press 1954).

[14]   F. James Davis, *Law as a Type of Social Control*, in F. JAMES DAVIS, ET AL. (EDS.), SOCIETY AND THE LAW: NEW MEANINGS FOR AN OLD PROFESSION 39-63 (1962).

B. Sources of Law

Nearly all of criminal law applicable in the United States has its roots in what is known as English **common law**. Accordingly, it is often referred to as Anglo-Saxon or Anglo-American law. Common law is really nothing more than judge-made law. It first started to appear in feudal England in the eleventh century as means of settling disputes between the estates of Lords.[15] By the reign of King Henry II (1154–1189), the royal court system was established.[16] One of its primary purposes was to insure that the law applied in one part of England was not different from the law applied in another part of the kingdom. Hence, a set of "common" laws would prevail throughout the country.[17] The United States is in the minority in terms of following the history and tradition of the common law. Most countries follow the civil law codes of continental Europe as they developed from the Napoleonic Code.[18] Notable exceptions include other current or former territories of England, such as Canada, Australia, and New Zealand.

As the common law developed, judges were called upon to interpret the law as it existed in prior precedent and then apply it in each case that came before them. The method of reasoning they used, based in logical and analytic reasoning, is still used in the courts of England and the United States today. The decisions handed down by judges add to the prior body of judge-made law and subsequently serve as precedent for the next dispute. The collective body of judge-made law is "common law."

There are three other main sources of law. **Statutory law** are those laws enacted by a legislative body, such as the U.S. Congress or a state assembly. Today, these laws are codified into statutory compilations. U.S. federal laws are codified in the various titles of the United States Code. State laws are similarly codified into state codes. Local laws passed by county, city, or towns are a subtype of statutory law called municipal ordinances.

Both statutory law enacted by legislative bodies and common law made by judges are subject to limitations. The primary limitations on the creation of common and statutory law comes from the U.S. Constitution. **Constitutional law** is, therefore, that body of law which is set forth in the constitution of a government. It sets forth the structure of government and the laws limiting the power to be exercised by that government. In short, constitutional law governs the government.

Finally, there is **administrative law**. Administrative law consists primarily of regulations issued by administrative agencies given the power to enact regulations that carry the force of law by an act of a legislative body. For example, Congress empowers the Federal Trade Commission to make administrative law by issues regulations that govern trade and commerce.

C. The Social Objectives of Law

We often conceptualize law as the tool by which we control human behaviors. But such a conceptualization of law is naive, as the relationship between law and human behavior is complex and subject to debate.[19] Law can be both cause and effect; in the language of

---

[15] DAVID W. NEUBAUER, AMERICA'S COURT AND THE CRIMINAL JUSTICE SYSTEM 28 (6th ed. Wadsworth 2000).

[16] *Id.*

[17] *Id.*

[18] *Id.*

[19] *E.g.,* DONALD BLACK, SOCIOLOGICAL JUSTICE (1989); DONALD BLACK (ED.), TOWARD OF GENERAL THEORY OF SOCIAL CONTROL, Vol. 1 (1984).

psychology—both independent and dependant variable.[20] More often than not, sociologists of law view the opinions of society—especially strongly held social mores and customs—as being the guiding force of human behavior, with the law having to be in accordance with such beliefs in order for it to be effective.[21] Ehrlich went so far as to say that the "center of gravity of legal development lies not in legislation, nor in juristic science, nor judicial decision, but in society itself."[22] Yet, in spite of the limited role that positive law might have on human behavior, social control is one of the primary purposes of law: controlling the behaviors of members of society. Criminal law, designed to deter crime by threatening punishment and actually punishing those who commit offenses, is the primary tool of formal social control.

Social control is not the only purpose of law. Law exists for a variety of other reasons and is generally seen to have seven primary social objectives, the first of which is social control as described above. Carter set forth a typology that includes four additional problems that law is designed to address: to coordinate for the collective advantage of society (e.g., laws regulating radio and television broadcasting); to promote government itself (e.g., the IRS Code; elections laws); to promote health, safety, and welfare (e.g., building and sanitation codes); and remedial laws—those which seek to cure an ill that faces society as a whole (e.g., racial discrimination laws).[23] The final two social objectives of law come from the typology developed by Vago[24]: dispute settlement and social change.[25]

D. The Evolution of Law

We often hear of people refer to "the law." But "the law" is a bit of a misnomer because law is constantly changing. What the law might be on a given topic on Monday might not be the law on Tuesday due to legislative action (i.e., changes in statutory law); regulatory action (i.e., changes in administration law); or court action (i.e., changes in constitutional and/or common law).

As mentioned above, U.S. law is a product of the English common law tradition. Two important and highly related principles are the bedrock of that tradition: precedent and *stare decisis*. **Precedent** is the body of previously decided law "that serves as the legal guide for resolution of subsequent cases."[26] In other words, precedent sets the "rule of law" applicable to cases presenting a given legal issue. Judges are supposed to apply precedent to the facts of the case before them. In doing so, they follow the law as it evolved in the past under similar factual situations. The process of reasoning from precedent and applying it as the legal authority applicable to the case-at-hand is referred to as **stare decisis**, Latin for "let the decision stand."

---

[20] *See generally,* Michael Gottfredson and Michael Hindelang, *A Study of the Behavior of Law,* 44 AM. SOCIOLOGICAL REV. 3 (1979); Davis, *supra* note 14, at 39-63.

[21] EUGEN ERLICH, FUNDAMENTAL PRINCIPLES OF THE SOCIOLOGY OF LAW (1936) (W.L. Moll, trans., Arno Press: New York, 1975); EDWARD ALSWORTH ROSS, SOCIAL CONTROL: A SURVEY OF THE FOUNDATIONS OF ORDER (New York: MacMillian, 1901).

[22] ERLICH, *supra* note 21, at Foreword.

[23] LIEF H. CARTER, REASON IN LAW 12-13 (5th ed. Longman 1998).

[24] VAGO, *supra* note 12, at 17-18.

[25] For a comprehensive discussion on law and social change, *see* STEPHEN LIVINGSTONE AND JOHN MORISON (EDS.), LAW, SOCIETY, AND CHANGE (Dartmouth 1990).

[26] NEUBAUER, *supra* note 15, at 29.

Actually, the term *stare decisis* "is itself an abbreviation of the Latin phrase '*stare decisis* et non quieta movere' which translates as 'to stand by decisions and not to disturb settled matters.'"[27]

The principle of *stare decisis* allows for stability in law over time. Change in law, therefore, tends to be a slow, evolutionary process. Sometimes, this means the law in a particular area has grown old and stagnant. But the law allows for itself to be corrected, rather than following *stare decisis* blindly, a sentiment expressed in an often quoted statement of Justice Oliver Wendell Holmes:

> It is revolting to have no better reason for a rule of law than it was so laid down in the times of Henry IV. It is still more revolting if the grounds upon which is was laid down have vanished long since , and the rule simply persists from blind imitation of the past.[28]

Avoiding such stagnation in law is accomplished via the process of legal reasoning. **Legal reasoning** describes how a legal opinion combines four elements to persuade us that the judge has reached the "correct" decision.[29] The four elements are the facts of a case; the rules of law applicable to the case (precedent); the "facts, events, and other conditions that we observe in the world"; and "widely shared moral values and social principles."[30] When a judge combines these four elements persuasively, we tend to view the opinion as being "right" and well reasoned. When judges fail to fit these elements together in a coherent manner, we are often left unconvinced that the judge correctly reasoned the case to a proper decision.

Since good legal reasoning incorporates contemporary values and current events, with precedent and the principle of *stare decisis* being only one part of the legal reasoning process, the law is permitted to change with the times. When the evolution of law presents a conflict between precedent and the needs of changing times, old precedent may be overruled, leaving a new rule of law to act as precedent for subsequent cases.

E. The Adversary System

When we think of the judicial process in the United States, we often think of a courtroom in which lawyers for two sides of a dispute argue their points to a judge and jury. We call this battle the **adversary system**. Under this system, the parties to a legal dispute are each given an opportunity to "make their case." We assume, at least at the philosophical level, that pitting adversaries against each other in a "winner-take-all" courtroom battle will encourage both parties to gather the best evidence they can and make their best arguments.

The adversary process, of course, is guided by many rules of procedure. The judge is supposed to act as the interpreter and enforcer of these rules as a neutral, disinterested manner. Sometimes, the judge also serves as the **trier-of-fact**, that is, the decision-maker with regard to the factual issues in dispute in a case. More frequently, however, a jury serves as the trier-of-fact, and the judge is left to make purely legal decisions. This is especially true in criminal cases because in most criminal cases the right to a trial by a jury of one's peers is guaranteed by the Sixth Amendment to the U.S. Constitution. Such a right does not exist in civil law disputes or

---

[27] Paul Perell, *Stare decisis* and Techniques of Legal Reasoning and Legal Argument (orig. pub. 1987; retrieved July 20, 2000) <http://legalresearch.org/docs/perell.html>.

[28] OLIVER WENDELL HOLMES, COLLECTED LEGAL PAPERS 187 (Harcourt 1920).

[29] CARTER, *supra* note 23, at 8.

[30] *Id.*

with most minor criminal or quasi-criminal offenses (e.g, traffic violations) unless provided for by statutory law.

A common misperception of law is that the adversarial process will lead to the uncovering of "the truth." But the judicial process is not about uncovering truth. In fact, a number of evidentiary and procedural mechanisms applicable in the judicial process prevent the trier-of-fact from knowing the truth. The exclusionary rule is a good example of this. It operates to keep material out of evidence at trial (e.g., confessions or real evidence) that was obtained in violation of a defendant's constitutional rights. When such evidence is excluded on legal grounds, the jury will not get to know of its existence at trial, thereby impeding the jury from knowing the truth.

If not uncovering truth, then what is the goal of the adversarial process? While the answer to this question is open to debate, a good response would be to achieve resolution of a legal dispute using fair procedures. How the trier-of-fact does so may or may not concern the truth, but rather involves whether legal standards of knowledge, called "burdens of proof," were met. How the trier-of-fact comes to have sufficient knowledge to render its decision, however, is of direct relevance to us here. "Knowing," for legal decision-making purposes, is a far cry from "knowing" for scientific purposes.

The legal system asks the trier-of-fact to use the *a priori method* of knowledge. A priori is Latin for "it stands to reason." Using deductive reasoning skills, one draws a logical conclusion after analyzing the facts presented. But since the facts presented to the trier-of-fact may be incomplete or inaccurate, knowledge under this method is not about arriving at truth, but rather at a logical conclusion that may be right or wrong.

There are other ways of knowing that come into play in the law, some of which are more embraced than others. The *method of tenacity* is frowned upon by the law. It is when people claim to know not because of any fact or piece of evidence, but rather because of their personal belief system. The *method of authority* is when we come to know something because someone in authority has told us that something is so. The law often embraces this type of knowledge when expert testimony is used. The trier-of-fact learns that something is so from an expert in the relevant field. Of course, this method of knowledge is limited as well. If the expert is not a true authority, or is just plain wrong, then the so-called knowledge passed along is flawed. Finally, there is the *method of science*, the method used by the behavioral sciences. The scientific method involves formulating hypotheses from prior scientific knowledge and then testing those hypotheses using systematic experimentation and observation. Key to the method of science is the notion of falsifiability—the ability for something to be empirically disproved.

F. The Study and Practice of Law

Law is practiced by attorneys. Attorneys are lawyers who have been admitted to the practice of law in a given jurisdiction, usually by having taken and passed the bar exam, a test of various fields of law designed to ensure a minimum level of competency and knowledge before allowing someone to represent another as an attorney. One becomes a lawyer by going to law school. Traditionally, law school is a three-year, post-baccalaureate degree program which culminates in the award of the J.D. degree, short for Juris Doctor or Doctor of Jurisprudence. One does not become an attorney, however, until after passing the bar exam and being sworn-in as an officer of the court.

Although there are differing approaches to the study of law, law school education has historically been doctrinal and continues to be so today in large part, although broader perspectives are gaining acceptance.[31] Under this model, rather than studying legal skills (something that lawyers were supposed to gain in "practice," after law school), students learn legal theory and reasoning via the case method, "a method that combine[s] conceptions of legal reasoning and legal doctrine with a pedagogical technique."[32] Students are taught how to decipher the "rule of law" by extrapolating it from a published judicial opinion (a "case") using logical and analytical reasoning skills. Students then are asked to apply the rule of law to hypothetical fact patterns, both orally in class in Socratic dialogues, and in writing on exams. Historically, approach to the study of law was devoid of the study of legal processes and their relationship to law's impact on society via the lenses of sociology, philosophy, psychology, public policy, and other disciplines. At best, such disciplines were mentioned peripherally.

The goal of such an education is to make students learn to "think like a lawyer": acquire knowledge of specialized legal vocabulary; understand the operation of differing sets of legal rules; learn how to read various sources of law, such as cases, constitutions, statutes, and administrative regulations; and apply the law in a persuasive form of appropriate argumentation.[33] Today, however, although law schools still hold on to the doctrinal study of law via the case method, legal education has been broadening to encompass the interdisciplinary study of law and well as the practical skills of lawyering.[34]

Even in modern times with a more enlightened view toward legal education, law school often leaves its graduates with a highly doctrinal approach to law in which the unit of analysis is always the case. The participants in a case each have differing views of reality rather than a shared objective one. And the behavior of those participants is assumed to be a product of free-will guided by the principles of individual autonomy and rational decision-making.[35] As we will explore in Section III of this chapter, the view of those who are a product of law school—and arguably the view of the law itself—stands in sharp contrast to the views of those in the behavioral sciences.

III. BEHAVIORAL SCIENCE: ITS SOURCES, CLASSIFICATIONS, AND OPERATION

A. Defining the Behavioral Sciences and Exploring Education and Training in Them

As described earlier in this chapter, the term "behavioral sciences" is being used in this text to encompass a number of mental health professions: psychology, psychiatry, neuropsychology, forensic psychiatric nursing, counseling/clinical social work, and other fields related to the mental health professions. Defining these fields is much easier than defining law. We will focus, though, on psychology and psychiatry since they are the two fields primarily involved in forensic psychological assessment. As defined earlier, *psychology* is "the science that deals with mental

---

[31] *See generally* Jay M. Feinman, *The Future History of Legal Education*, 29 RUTGERS L. J. 475 (1998); David Hall, *Legal Education and the Twenty-First Century: Our Calling to Fulfill*, 19 W. NEW ENG. L. REV. 139 (1997); Richard A. Rosen, *Clinical Legal Education*, 73 N.C.L. REV. 749 (1995); John Mixon & Gordon Otto, *Continuous Quality Improvement, Law, and Legal Education*, 43 EMORY L.J. 393 (1994).

[32] Feinman, *supra* note 31, at 476.

[33] *Id.* at 478–79.

[34] *See sources supra* note 31.

[35] *See generally* Ronald L. Akers, *Criminology: Rational Choice, Deterrence, and Social Learning Theory in Criminology: The Path Not Taken*, 81 J. CRIM. L. & CRIMINOLOGY 653 (1990).

processes and behavior."[36] It is a social science dedicated to understanding human behavior at the level of the individual, as opposed to sociology or economics, both of which are also social sciences, but study human behavior at the aggregate/societal level.[37]

Psychology, as a field, has many sub-disciplines within it. ***Clinical psychology*** is devoted to the study of psychopathology and to providing psychological diagnostic and treatment services to patients.[38] Entry into the field normally requires between four and seven years of graduate study earning the Ph.D. (Doctor of Philosophy) or Psy.D. (Doctor of Psychology) degree. The Ph.D. in all areas of psychology "requires a heavy emphasis on laboratory work, research design, statistics, and the empirically based study of human and animal behavior."[39] Those specializing in clinical psychology, though, are also required to learn specific techniques while graduate students and as post-doctoral interns in a clinical setting. These include not only the assessment and diagnosis of mental illness, but also the treatment of psychopathology using psychotherapy. Additionally, clinical psychologists are usually well-trained in ***psychometrics***—the subfield of psychology concerned with the design, administration, and interpretation of tests that measure psychological variables such as intelligence, aptitude, and personality traits. The Psy.D. degree generally involves the same curriculum, but it has more of an emphasis on practical skills than on research. Some masters programs in social work and counseling psychology offer similar clinical education to that of the Ph.D. or Psy.D., but without the heavy emphasis on research.[40]

Psychiatry is the branch of medical science "that deals with the diagnosis, treatment, and prevention of mental and emotional disorders."[41] Psychiatry adheres to the medical model of deviance, a concept discussed in greater detail in Chapter Two. The study of psychiatry requires the earning of the M.D. (Doctor of Medicine) degree, followed by four to six years of post-graduate clinical training in a residency program. Although psychiatrists can diagnose and treat mental disorders in the same ways clinical psychologists do, they are usually not trained in psychometrics. Above all, though, the main difference in the two professions is that psychiatrists function in their full capacity as physicians by conducting physical examinations, ordering medically diagnostic tests, and prescribing drugs—three areas in which psychologists are not permitted to work given their lack of biochemical and physiological training.

B. The Empirical Methods of Behavioral Science Research

Unlike law, which is doctrinal, as described above, the behavioral sciences are ***empirical***. That is, they seek to identify "an objectifiable world of experience that can best be understood by unwavering adherence to the rules of science."[42] The experimental method of science is quite different from the case method used in law. First and foremost, rather than applying logical and analytical reasoning and reasoning by analogy, the experimental methods adheres to "systematic testing hypotheses by observation and experimental methodology."[43] In doing so, the goal is to

---

[36]   THE AMERICAN HERITAGE DICTIONARY 667 (3d ed. 1994).

[37]   BARTOL & ANNE M. BARTOL, *supra* note 7, at 14.

[38]   GERALD C. DAVISON & JOHN M. NEALE, ABNORMAL PSYCHOLOGY 9 (7th ed. Wiley 1998).

[39]   *Id.*

[40]   *Id.*

[41]   THE AMERICAN HERITAGE DICTIONARY 667 (3d ed 1994).

[42]   LAWRENCE S. WRIGHTSMAN, MICHAEL T. NIETZEL, AND WILLIAM H, FORTUNE, PSYCHOLOGY AND THE LEGAL SYSTEM 24 (4th ed 1998).

[43]   *Id.*

identify objective reality or "truth"—"not to choose between alternative views" the way the law does.[44] For something to have objective truth, it must be able to be empirically tested under conditions that allow for *falsification* (i.e., a way to disprove a hypothesis) and *replication* (i.e., repeated by others to verify the outcome of the research).[45]

In seeking objective knowledge using the scientific method, the behavioral sciences employ a number of research strategies that stand in sharp contrast to the law's adversarial process and its *a priori* method of knowing. Behavioral scientists conduct empirical studies using experimental designs and quasi-experimental designs that can be replicated.

1. <u>Variables and Experimental Design</u>

Experimental design requires the careful manipulation and controlling of variables in laboratory settings. Social scientists classify these variables into two categories. An *independent variable* is one that is manipulated in research so that it is either present or absent, or present to a particular degree. What makes it an independent variable is the fact that its existence is not what is sought to be explained by the research. Rather, the presence or absence (or level) of the variable is what may have some effect on another variable being studied, called the *dependent variable.* In other words, experimental research seeks to explore whether the dependent variable is in some way dependent on or caused by the independent variable. Suppose we wanted to know if men or women are more likely to be adjudicated "not guilty by reason of insanity." Gender would be the independent variable, while adjudication status would be the dependent one. A good experimental design to test this relationship would provide identical fact patterns to jurors, only have the defendant for one group of decision-makers be a male, and be a female defendant for the other group of decision-makers. If the verdicts differ to a statistically significant degree, we would conclude that gender does, in fact, have an effect on insanity adjudication decisions.

2. <u>Quasi-Experimental Design</u>

The careful control of variables in a laboratory setting required of true experimental design is not always possible, or even desirable. Sometimes, researchers want to study a phenomenon as it occurs—outside of a controlled setting under the conditions that were preexisting before the researcher's arrival or participation. This type of research is called *quasi-experimental design.* Using this type of design, we might look at actual jury verdicts for similar offenses to see if there were different rates of acquittals by reason of insanity between men and women. But see that doing so would require picking cases that were similar—say all homicide cases. And even then, the method of killing might be so different from one homicide to another that comparing the two cases is fundamentally unfair, akin to the proverbial comparison of apples and oranges. These other factors that influence the dependent variable—here, the verdict—are called *confounding variables.*

Obviously, experimental design is much better than quasi-experimental design for controlling confounding variables, although they are not always completely controlled for. And even if every possible variable were controlled for in a laboratory setting, generalizing the results from a

---

[44] *Id.* at 25.

[45] *See* KARL POPPER, CONJECTURES AND REFUTATIONS: THE GROWTH OF SCIENTIFIC KNOWLEDGE 37 (5th ed. 1989); *see also* Daubert v. Merrell Dow Pharm., Inc., 509 U.S. 579, 593 (1993) (citing and adopting Popper's view of science as that of the U.S. Supreme Court).

laboratory study to real world situations would still be a problem. Accordingly, be aware that even the empirical methods of social science have their limitations, just as legal methods have theirs.

3. Validity and Reliability

Knowledge is concerned with both the validity and reliability of the research design, execution, and interpretation. *Validity* is concerned with whether empirical evidence proves what it purports to prove. In other words, validity asks if we are measuring what we claim to be measuring.[46]

Validity has several subtypes, two of which are of particular importance to the intersection of law and psychology. First is internal validity. *Internal validity* is concerned with the particulars of a specific study. How well designed was the study? Did it follow proper data collection methodologies? Were confounding variables controlled for?[47] Does the performance on a test or measure correlate highly with behavior that it should? This is a concept known as *criterion validity*. Judges are more and more frequently being called upon to make assessments regarding the validity of a study before allowing an expert to testify in court regarding its findings and applicability to a given case,[48] even though their legal training may not equip them to do so.[49]

External validity, also referred to as ecological validity, is concerned with how the measurements obtained in a given research project and the conclusions drawn from them can be generalized to situations outside of (i.e., external to) the study. In other words, it is concerned with whether study results are consistent across time, place, and situation.

There are numerous other sub-types of validity. The extent to which a test includes materials from all relevant areas and does not include extraneous material is called *content validity.* If two tests are measuring the same thing, then they should be highly correlated—a principle known as *convergent validity.* In contrast, tests that are designed to measure different things should not be highly correlated, a concept known as *discriminant validity.*

Related to yet distinct from the concept of validity is reliability. *Reliability* is concerned with the accuracy and consistency of those measurements over time.[50] Something can be reliable, yet invalid. For example, suppose you used a ruler that had inaccurate markings for inches. Each time you used it, you would get the same result. Therefore, it is a reliable instrument. But it is not a valid one since real inches are not being measured by that defective ruler. In contrast, something cannot be invalid, yet reliable. How can something measure that which it is supposed to be measuring if it uses a tool that yields inconsistent results?

Good empirical research used valid and reliable procedures in research design, data collection, and data analysis. Moreover, it does so in a manner that allows for another researcher to replicate the study. These hallmarks of good science are necessary foundations under the rules of evidence for any evolution in law to take place based on behavioral science research (Haney's "psychology and the law" relationship), but the more narrow definition of forensic psychology

---

[46] Robert Rosenthal & Ralph L. Rosnow, Essentials of Behavioral Research 482 (1984) (glossary).

[47] For a detailed explanation of internal validity problems in empirical research, *see* 1 David L. Faigman, et al., Modern Scientific Evidence: the Law and Science of Expert Testimony (1997 & Supp. 1999), at 62-76 (Supp. 1999).

[48] *See* Daniel W. Shuman & Bruce D. Sales, *The Impact of Daubert and Its Progeny on the Admissibility of Behavioral and Social Science Evidence,* 5 Psych. Pub. Pol. & L. 3 (1999).

[49] William M. Grove & R. Christopher Barden, *Protecting the Integrity of the Legal System: The Admissibility of Testimony from Mental Health Experts under Daubert/Kumho Analyses,* 5 Psych. Pub. Pol. & L. 224-42 (1999).

[50] Rosenthal & Rosnow, *supra* note 46, at 479.

presented earlier in this chapter is primarily concerned with forensic clinical assessment. Empirical studies are not used to do such assessments; case studies are. And, although case studies use assessment instruments that should first be validated, case studies themselves often lack demonstrable validity, reliability, and replicability. Accordingly, "a significant portion of mental health-related social science testimony" (Haney's "psychology in the law" relationship) could be inadmissible under the newest evidentiary standards given "the limited scientific knowledge base in many areas of clinical psychology and psychiatry."[51] An exploration of case studies should show why.

C. Case Studies in Behavior Science Research and Clinical Evaluation

In addition to experimental and quasi-experimental designs, the *case study* method is often used to learn about a phenomenon. In contrast to empirical methodologies, however, the case study method uses the "case" as the unit of analysis, rather than the subject in some experimental or control group. In a traditional case study, the researcher conducts an in-depth analysis of a single event, entity, or phenomenon generically referred to as "the case." But identification of the case is not always easy because it means so many things in different research situations. What marks a case study is that it focuses on the "one among others" that are bounded in some way.[52] Stake illustrates this point by explaining that a single physician may be a case, but the way in which that physician goes about his doctoring lacks "the specificity and boundedness to be called a case."[53]

1. Types and Benefits of Case Study Research

Case studies are one of the most useful research designs for examining behaviors in their natural settings. The key strength of a case study is that it allows the researcher to go "directly to the social phenomenon under study and observ[e] it as completely as possible, . . . develop[ing] a deeper and fuller understanding of it."[54] Thus, it is the depth of understanding that can be gained from a case study that is the chief benefit to using a case study research design.

Lofland and Lofland list a number of social settings for which case studies, among other types of field research, are appropriate.[55] These include situation in which the researcher is seeking to get at meanings, behavioral practices, episodic events (crime, for example), encounters (interaction between people), and roles (within relationships, groups, organizations, neighborhoods, etc.). It is not that traditional quantitative research could not get at some of these things, but to the extant that it can, by administering a survey, for example, the meanings gained would be superficial due to the operationalization of real-world things into variables.

Flexibility is another advantage of case study research that may make it appropriate for certain research questions. One's research design can be modified as one progresses through

---

[51] Grove & Barden, *supra* note 49, at 238; *see also* Shuman & Sales, *supra* note 48, at 13.

[52] Robert E. Stake, *Case Studies*, in The Handbook of Qualitative Research 236 (Norman K. Denzin & Yvonna S. Lincoln, eds., 1994).

[53] *Id.*

[54] Earl Babbie, The Practice of Social Research 286 (6th ed. Wadsworth 1992).

[55] John Lofland & Lyn H. Lofland, Analyzing Social Settings (3d ed. Wadsworth 1995).

field research in response to understandings gained through the process of "emergence."[56] The same cannot be done once a survey is constructed.

Beyond these generalized benefits of case study research for certain types of research problems, a variety of sub-types of case studies are appropriate for different types of research problems. *Intrinsic case studies* "are undertaken because one wants better understanding of [a] particular case."[57] The case being studied presents the researcher with some interest both in the particularity and the ordinariness of the case. Stake claims that the purpose of an intrinsic case study is neither to study "some abstract construct or generic phenomenon," nor one of theory building. Rather, an intrinsic case study is undertaken because of interest in the case itself.

Instrumental case studies are those in which a particular case is examined "to provide insight into an issue or refinement of theory."[58] The case is secondary in such a study. It is, in essence, an example whose role is to facilitate understanding of something else. These types of case studies offer the advantage of in-depth analysis of a case that can be used to develop theory, illustrate the application of theory, and point out both the theory's strengths and weaknesses in explaining the data observed in the case.

Finally, there are *collective case studies.* In such a research design, a particular case is not of great import, but rather a collection of cases studies jointly shed light on some "phenomenon, population, or general condition" leading to a better understanding of the entire collection of cases.[59]

None of the above types of case studies should be confused with the "case method" often used by law, medicine, business, and other disciplines as a teaching tool. Case studies are concerned with a rigorous presentation of empirical data; the study of cases for pedagogical reasons is not. Materials may be invented or deliberately altered to make a point when a case is used as a teaching tool, something strictly prohibited in the social science definition of a case study.

2. Problems with Case Study Research in General

Case studies are of particular importance to our study of forensic psychology. First and foremost, forensic inquiries are usually focused on a particular person under court jurisdiction, the clinical evaluation of whom is the job of the forensic psychologist. The unit of analysis is, therefore, that one person. But case study research has limitations, both generally, and within the realm of clinical assessment in particular.

Two of the most frequently used lines of inquiry in case study research are direct observation and systematic interviewing.[60] Yet, several weaknesses in case study design often prevent them from receiving the respect in the social sciences that empirical research is traditionally accorded. First, case studies are perceived as lacking rigor due to biases of the researcher that "influence the direction of findings and conclusions."[61] For example, cases selected for study, cases excluded from consideration, and cases selectively highlighted as part of the analyses and

---

[56] Norman K. Denzin, *The Art and Politics of Interpretation*, in THE HANDBOOK OF QUALITATIVE RESEARCH 502-03 (Norman K Denzin & Yvonna S. Lincoln, eds., 1994).

[57] Stake, *supra* note 52, at 237.

[58] *Id.*

[59] *Id.*

[60] RoROBERT K. YIN, CASE STUDY RESEARCH: DESIGN AND METHODS 8 (2d. ed. Sage 1994).

[61] *Id.* at 9.

conclusions are all within the subjective control of the case study researcher. While this is undoubtedly true for a number of case studies, it should be noted that similar criticisms can be levied against even the most traditional of quantitatively empirical research methodologies. For example, Rosenthal illustrated the effect of researcher bias in the experimental setting.[62] And Sudman and Bradburn explored the same issues in questionnaire design.[63]

Even if separated from case selection issues, both validity and reliability issues can be problematic for case study research. In quantitative case studies, traditional tools for assessing these concerns are possible.[64] But in qualitative case studies, these statistical tools are not generally available. Yin, however, argues that validity can be achieved via the use of multiple sources of evidence, the establishment of a proper chain of evidence, and having key informants review the draft case study report.[65] He argues internal validity can be achieved through pattern matching, explanation building, and time-series analyses.[66] Yin further states that external validity can be achieved by follow-up studies that seek to replicate the original case study and by using a multiple-case study design. And finally, Yin argues that reliability can be achieved by using a case study protocol and by developing a case study database for data coding. Yin's suggestions are in accord with Guba and Lincoln's notion of "dependability."[67] To the extent that a *process* is: (1) established, (2) trackable, and (3) documentably followed so that data are stabile over time, then reliability concerns in case studies can be addressed.

Stake points out that validity concerns in case studies are directed toward the validity of communication. "Meanings do not transfer intact, but take on some of the conceptual uniqueness of the reader, but there is an expectation that the meaning of the situation, observation, reporting, and reading will have a certain correspondence."[68] To foster this type of validity, Stake, along the same lines espoused by Yin, argues we should used triangulation methodologies. Triangulation in this sense refers to using procedures like "redundancy in data gathering and procedural challenges to explanations."[69] In so using multiple perceptions to clarify meanings and to certifying the repeatability of an observation or interpretation, while acknowledging that no qualitative observation is interpretation is perfectly repeatable, serves to clarify meanings.

Finally, generalizability is also problematic for case studies. Whenever one attempts to generalize from the particular to the universal, one opens oneself up to the ***logical fallacy*** of generalizing from incomplete data. For example, if the first Martian you met had green skin, you might expect all Martians to have green skin. But see the error if the Martians reached a similar conclusion if the first Earthling they encountered was an albino. Case studies inherently run this risk of generalizing from incomplete information or focusing on the exceptional.

Defenders of case study research point out that generalizability is not the primary goal of such research. Case studies are used to give an in-depth understanding of an event or phenomenon that by its nature (e.g, a theory) is generalized to the particular in its application. The most effective way of doing so is by comparison. There are, of course, dangers in making

---

[62] ROBERT ROSENTHAL, EXPERIMENTER EFFECTS IN BEHAVIORAL RESEARCH (Appleton-Century 1966).

[63] SEYMOUR SUDMAN & NORMAN M. BRADBURN, ASKING QUESTIONS : A PRACTICAL GUIDE TO QUESTIONNAIRE DESIGN (Jossey-Bass 1982).

[64] BABBIE, *supra* note 54, at 127-135.

[65] YIN, *supra* note 60, at 33.

[66] *Id.*

[67] EGON G. GUBA & YVONNA S. LINCOLN, FOURTH GENERATION EVALUATION 242 (Sage 1989).

[68] Stake, *supra* note 52, at 241.

[69] *Id.*

arguments by analogy or even direct comparison. But by setting up a comparative framework for cases in which similarities are noted and differences are explored, the possibility for valid and/or credible generalization grows greater. Comparisons are necessarily driven by logical and analytic reasoning. Since a person's logic may be flawed, so may be the comparisons he makes. But to the extent that a researcher's comparisons are logically sound, comparison becomes "an epistemological function competing with learning about and learning from the particular case."[70] Moreover, generalizability is often problematic even in empirical research using experimental or quasi-experimental designs. What occurs in the controlled settings of a laboratory may or may not be generalizable to the external world. The fact that much psychological research is done on college students and is then generalized to the entirety of the population is a perfect example. And even when sampling is not an issue, a confounding variables may still also limit generalizability of any piece of empirical research. Arguably, these limitations may, at least in part, be responsible for the law's refusal to change in the face of empirical psychological evidence that challenges a tenet of the law. Whether true or not, though, it should be recognized that the methods of social scientific inquiry are all limited in some way or another. Moreover, some methods, like case studies, are more flawed than others.

3. Problems with Case Study Research in Clinical Assessment

In addition to the general problems with case study research, the use of this research method poses particular problems in the sphere of psychology in the law. The legal questions posed to forensic behavioral scientists require case study of an individual for an answer to be attempted. Clinical assessments, often called psychological evaluations, pose special methodological problems because of way in which such assessments are conducted.

Forensic psychological evaluation usually includes ***psychological testing*** of a person. This is accomplished using instruments whose validity and reliability are not at issue for the clinician. Empirical research should have already demonstrated the validity and reliability of the diagnostic tests administered to a patient, such as with certain well-respected tests of cognitive ability (e.g., the Stanford-Binet and the WAIS [Wechsler Adult Intelligent Scale]), and with objective personality tests (e.g., the MMPI-2 [Minnesota Multiphasic Personality Inventory]). But not all assessment instruments have been as vigorously validated as the three just mentioned. And even those that have been validated are not without criticism. For example, objective tests may ask questions that are scored based on a culturally, racially, or sexually based normative framework.[71]

Moreover, many psychological tests are not objective. Rather, they involve significant subjective interpretation by the clinician administering the test. Projective personality tests are perhaps the best example of this. ***Projective tests*** assume that personality characteristics are most likely to be revealed by someone when asked to respond to something ambiguous. The ***Rorschach*** test, which presents the subject with ten inkblots, is such a test. The clinician must interpret the subject's responses in making scoring determination. Although the test is now scored using a system designed to increase both its reliability and validity, critics still argue the Rorschach is too subjective. The same criticism is even more appropriate for the ***Thematic Apperception Test*** (TAT), a test in which the subject is asked to construct a story based on a

---

[70] Stake, *supra* note 52, at 242.

[71] *See generally* ROBERT M. KAPLAN & DENNIS P. SACCUZZO, PSYCHOLOGICAL TESTING: PRINCIPLES, APPLICATIONS, AND ISSUES (4th ed. 1997); ANNE ANASTASI & SUSANA URBINA, PSYCHOLOGICAL TESTING (7th ed. 1997).

picture presented to the subject. It should be evident that the level of subjectivity in evaluating and scoring responses on such tests gives rise to real concerns regarding the reliability and validity of projective tests.[72] Yet, they are a hallmark of clinical assessment.[73]

In addition to the limitations of psychological testing instruments, other components of a forensic case study are also problematic. First of all, most of the data gathered is *self-reported data.* A person may not be honest with a clinician. Of course, this is a limitation of all types of research that relies on self-reports, not just case study research. To counter this weakness, clinicians also obtain input from people other than the patient—family members, physicians, police, neighbors, teachers, friends, and so on. But these have limitations as well since all involve the interaction of the patient with others and these other people's corresponding evaluations of the patient. Subjective opinions, not valid and reliable objective data, are often gathered. This is even the case in circumstances that might otherwise appear to be scientifically objective. If a forensic neurological examination reveals organic brain dysfunction, that itself may be objective. But the impact of such pathology is dependent upon the neurologist's assessment of the patient. In other words, to answer the question "what effect did the brain damage have on the individual's behavior,"[74] the clinician must subjectively evaluate the functioning of the patient which, in turn, is also partially dependent on what the patient does and says to the evaluator.

The above problems associated with valid and reliable forensic evaluation is especially problematic for a clinician who is given limited time to evaluate a person in a given setting (in jail, for example) and at a particular point in time. Yet, from such an evaluation, they are often expected to offer explanations about past behaviors, as with the insanity defense, or future behaviors, such as dangerousness after release from a mental hospital. The legal system's continued use of psychology in law in light of these limitations on valid and reliable forensic assessment is a frequent criticism by researchers of law and psychology—a problem we will visit time and time again throughout this book.

IV. THE FORENSIC PSYCHOLOGIST AS EXPERT WITNESS

Earlier in this chapter, a distinction was made between the various sub-types of forensic psychologists. Regardless of whether a psychologist is a clinician evaluating a criminal defendant's competency to stand trial, or whether the psychologist is an empirical researcher explaining to a jury why false confessions occur, behavioral scientists have an important role to play as *expert witnesses* in the trial process. In this section, we will explore the legal standards governing the admissibility of expert testimony with special attention to how the rules affect forensic psychology.

---

[72] Grove & Barden, *supra* note 49), at 226-29 (reviewing literature on reliability and validity of Rorschach test); RICHARD I. LANYON & LEONARD D. GOODSTEIN, PERSONALITY ASSESSMENT 104 (3d. ed. 1997) (criticizing projective test for "lack of standardized procedures and formal normative data, low reliabilities, overenthusiastic and undercritical acceptance of intuitive hunches about the supposed meaning of certain responses").

[73] ANASTASI & URBINA, *supra* note 71, at 410 (stating, "projective techniques present a curious discrepancy between research and practice. When evaluated as psychometric instruments, the large majority make a poor showing. Yet their popularity in clinical use continues unabated.").

[74] BARTOL & BARTOL, *supra* note 7, at 39.

A. Background on the Admissibility of Scientific Evidence

1. The *Frye* General Acceptance Test

At common law, the *Frye* test governed the admissibility of scientific testimony. In *Frye v. United States*,[75] "the court rejected scientific testimony based on the use of a lie detector, stating that 'the thing from which the deduction is made must be sufficiently established to have gained general acceptance in the particular field in which it belongs' in order to be admissible."[76]

The purpose behind the *Frye* test was "to prevent . . . the introduction into evidence of specious and unfounded scientific principles or conclusions based upon such principles."[77] At the heart of *Frye* is the realization that the expert witness is a hired gun. "Whatever his credentials, publications, or affiliations, a scientist who becomes the alter ego of a lawyer is no longer a scientist . . . . So while a resume may be a necessary condition of expert competence, it is never a sufficient one. Science is defined by a community, not the individual, still less by a resume . . . . The cowl does not make a monk."[78]

Despite the uniformity its followers argue the *Frye* rule provides, it employs several terms that are open to differing interpretation. Who comprises the relevant scientific community? After all, "[m]any scientific techniques do not fall within the domain of a single academic discipline or professional field."[79] What is general acceptance? Is it "wide-spread, prevalent, and extensive, though not universal,"[80] or is it "agreement by a substantial section of the [relevant] scientific community?"[81] Perhaps, however, the biggest problem with the *Frye* test is "that it often results in excluding relevant, probative evidence, and thereby impedes the truth-seeking function of litigation."[82]

2. The Federal Rules of Evidence

Given the various problems associated with the *Frye* rule, it was intentionally not incorporated into the Federal Rules of Evidence.[83] Instead, the Federal Rules of Evidence opted for a more liberal approach to the admissibility of scientific evidence. This more liberal approach was adopted by some thirty-one states as of 1988.[84] Federal Rule of Evidence 702 provides, "If scientific, technical, or other specialized knowledge will assist the trier of fact to understand the evidence or to determine a fact in issue, a witness qualified as an expert by knowledge, skill,

---

[75] 293 F. 1013 (D.C. Cir. 1923).

[76] Denise M. Dunleavy, *Expert Testimony and the Charge of Junk Science*, 451 PLI/Lit 449, 451–452 (1992).

[77] Paul C. Giannelli, *The Admissibility Of Novel Scientific Evidence: Frye v. United States, A Half-Century Later*, 80 COLUM. L. REV. 1197, 1224 (1980) (citations omitted).

[78] Peter Huber, *Junk Science in the Courtroom*, 26 VAL. U. L. REV. 723, 742-43 (1992).

[79] Giannelli, supra note 77, at 1208.

[80] United States v. Zeiger, 475 F.2d 1280 (D.C. Cir. 1972).

[81] United States v. Williams, 443 F. Supp. 269, 273 (S.D.N.Y. 1977).

[82] N. Kathleen Strickland & Leah S. Elkins, *A Current Assessment of Frye in Toxic Tort Litigation*, 446 PLI/LIT. 321, 323 (1992) (citing United States v. Downing, 753 F.2d 1224, 1236 (3d Cir. 1985)); *see also* Jack B. Weinstein, *Improving Expert Testimony*, 20 U. RICH L. REV. 473, 476 (1976).

[83] *See* Weinstein's *Evidence*, §§ 702.36–702.44.

[84] Bert Black, *Evolving Legal Standards for the Admissibility of Scientific Evidence*, 239 Science 1508, 1512 n.1 (1988).

experience, training or education, may testify thereto in the form of an opinion or otherwise."[85] Rule 703 requires that the facts or data relied upon in the formulation of an expert opinion be of "a type reasonably relied upon by experts in the particular field in forming opinions or inferences upon the subject."[86] The role of the *Frye* test after the adoption of the Federal Rules of Evidence was unclear until 1993 when the U.S. Supreme Court decided *Daubert v. Merrill-Dow Pharmaceuticals, Inc.*[87] In it, the Court set a new standard for determining the admissibility of scientific evidence.

3. The Daubert Standard for Admissibility of Scientific Evidence

Daubert involved two children born with serious birth defects. Their parents brought suit alleging the defects were caused by Bendectin,® an anti-nausea drug produced by the predecessor companies to the Merrell-Dow Pharmaceutical Company in the early 1950s. The drug was approved by the Food and Drug Administration in 1956 as an antinausea drug.[88] Between 1957 and 1983, physicians frequently prescribed the drug for treatment of "morning-sickness" in pregnant women.[89] In well over a thousand cases since its availability in 1956, women have alleged that the combination of dicyclomine hydrochloride and doxylamine succinate in Bendectin® is teratogenic, that is, a substance that causes birth defects.[90]

Merrill-Dow moved for summary judgment of the *Daubert* case claiming Bendectin® did not cause birth defects and that the plaintiffs would not be able to proffer evidence to the contrary. To support their motion, Merrill-Dow introduced an affidavit by a well-credentialed epidemiologist with an expertise in chemical exposure risk. The physician cited 30 published studies on the subject, none of which concluded Bendectin® caused birth defects.

The plaintiffs countered with eight well-credentialed experts of their own who had conducted various studies, all of which demonstrated a causal link between the product and birth defects. The District Court granted Merrill-Dow's motion for summary judgment. Relying on the *Frye* standard, it concluded the plaintiff's expert testimony was inadmissible because it was not "sufficiently established to have general acceptance in the field to which it belongs."[91] The case was appealed, and the U.S. Court of Appeals for the Ninth Circuit affirmed the summary judgment, stating that the reliability of a scientific technique must be "generally accepted" by the relevant scientific community for it to be admissible.[92] The Supreme Court, however, vacated the judgment of the lower courts and accepted the plaintiff's argument that the Federal Rules of Evidence superseded the *Frye* test. The Court made clear that the critical concerns of Rule 702 are evidentiary reliability and relevancy.[93]

---

[85]   Fed. R. Evid. 702.

[86]   Fed. R. Evid. 703.

[87]   509 U.S. 579 (1993).

[88]   Lynch v. Merrell-Nat'l Lab., 830 F.2d 1190, 1191 (1st Cir. 1987).

[89]   *Id.*

[90]   *Id.*

[91]   727 F. Supp. 570, 572 (S.D. Cal. 1989) (quoting United States v. Kilgus, 571 F. 2d 508, 510 (9th Cir. 1978)).

[92]   951 F. 2d, at 1129–1130 (citing Frye v. United States, 54 App. D.C. 46, 47, 293 F. 1013, 1014 (1923)).

[93]   Daubert, 509 U.S. at 589.

The essence of the reliability standard lies within the Court's citation to philosopher of science Karl Popper's statement that "the criterion of the scientific status of a theory is its falsifiability, or refutability, or testability."[94]

> In order to best ensure relevant and reliable testimony and exclude "unsupported speculation," *Daubert* establishes a two-pronged test which requires a district court to determine "whether the expert is proposing to testify to (1) scientific knowledge that (2) will assist the trier of fact to understand or determine a fact in issue." This "gatekeeping" role calls for the trial judge to make a "preliminary assessment of whether the reasoning or methodology underlying the testimony is scientifically valid, i.e., whether it is reliable; and whether that reasoning or methodology properly can be applied to the facts in issue," i.e., whether it is relevant to the issue involved. Proffered scientific evidence must satisfy both prongs to be admissible.[95]

As gate-keepers, judges must first determine whether a witness is sufficiently qualified by "knowledge, skill, experience, training, or education" before being permitted to give expert testimony.[96] This means that a witness must be qualified in the specific subject for which the testimony is offered. "Just as a lawyer is not by general education and experience qualified to give an expert opinion on every subject of the law, so too a scientist or medical doctor is not presumed to have expert knowledge about every conceivable scientific principle or disease."[97] The evaluation of an alleged expert's qualification in his or her field is not a novel concept and is well within the abilities of our capable federal judiciary.

Once a judge has decided a witness is qualified to serve as an expert, *Daubert* requires the judge to then make an independent assessment to "ensure that any and all scientific testimony or evidence admitted is not only relevant, but reliable."[98] This involves an examination of the methodology underlying the expert opinion to determine whether it utilizes valid scientific methods and procedures. *Daubert* suggests several factors to aid federal judges in evaluating whether a particular scientific theory or study is reliable: (1) its empirical testability; (2) whether the theory or study has been published or subjected to peer review; (3) whether the known or potential rate of error is acceptable; and (4) whether the method is generally accepted in the scientific community. But these factors are neither exhaustive nor applicable in every case.[99]

> This gatekeeping role is simply to guard the jury from considering as proof pure speculation presented in the guise of legitimate scientifically-based expert opinion. It is not intended to turn judges into jurors or surrogate scientists. Thus, the gatekeeping responsibility of the trial courts is not to weigh or choose between conflicting scientific opinions, or to analyze and study the science in question in order to reach its own scientific conclusions from the material in the field. Rather, it is to assure that an expert's opinions are based on relevant scientific methods, processes, and data, and not on mere speculation, and that they apply to the facts in issue.[100]

---

[94] Daubert, 509 U.S. at 593 (quoting KARL POPPER, CONJECTURES AND REFUTATIONS: THE GROWTH OF SCIENTIFIC KNOWLEDGE 37 (5th ed. 1989))..

[95] Joiner v. General Electric Co., 78 F.3d 524, 529–530 (11th Cir. 1996).

[96] Fed. R. Evid. 702.

[97] Whiting v. Boston Edison Co., 891 F. Supp. 12, 24 (D. Mass. 1995).

[98] Daubert, 509 U.S. at 589.

[99] *See, e.g.,* In re Paoli R.R. Yard PCB Litigation, 35 F.3d 717, 750 (3d Cir. 1994).

[100] Joiner, 78 F.3d at 530.

The *Daubert* standard was criticized for a number of reasons. Even upon remand, the Ninth Circuit Court of Appeals wrote:

> [S]omething doesn't become "scientific knowledge" just because it's uttered by a scientist; nor can an expert's self-serving assertion that his conclusions were "derived by the scientific method" be deemed conclusive . . . . As we read the Supreme Court's teaching in *Daubert*, therefore, though we are largely untrained in science and certainly no match for any of the witnesses whose testimony we are reviewing, it is our responsibility to determine whether those experts' proposed testimony amounts to "scientific knowledge," constitutes "good science," and was "derived by the scientific method."
>
> The task before us is more daunting still when the dispute concerns matters at the very cutting edge of scientific research, where fact meets theory and certainty dissolves into probability. As the record in this case illustrates, scientists often have vigorous and sincere disagreements as to what research methodology is proper, what should be accepted as sufficient proof for the existence of a "fact," and whether information derived by a particular method can tell us anything useful about the subject under study.[101]

4. *Daubert* Expanded

In *General Electric Co. v. Joiner*, the U.S. Supreme Court made it clear that a trial court's determination on the admissibility of expert testimony under *Daubert* is to be given great deference on appeal. Admissibility decisions are to be overturned on appeal only if the trial court's decision was an abuse of discretion.[102] Initially, *Daubert* applied only to scientific evidence, but in *Kumho Tire Co. v. Carmichael*,[103] the Court held that all expert testimony that involves scientific, technical, or other specialized knowledge must meet the *Daubert* test for admissibility.

Several scholars have been praised *Kumho* for numerous reasons, but two in particular stand out. The first is that the case gives a plain-text meaning to Federal Rule of Evidence 702 since it does not differentiate between "scientific," "technical," or "other specialized" knowledge.[104] The second and more important reason is that *Kumho* "eliminated the trial judge's impossible task of differentiating between scientific and non-scientific evidence."[105] As Morsek has pointed out, this has particular applicability to the behavioral sciences.

---

[101] Daubert, 43 F.3d 1311, 1315–1316 (9th Cir.), *cert. denied*, 516 U.S. 869 (1995).

[102] General Electric Co. v. Joiner, 522 U.S. 136 (1997).

[103] 526 U.S. 137 (1999).

[104] Leslie Morsek, *Get on Board for the Ride of Your Life! The Ups, the Downs, the Twists, and the Turns of the Applicability of the "Gatekeeper" Function to Scientific and Non-Scientific Expert Evidence:* Kumho's *Expansion of* Daubert, 34 AKRON L. REV. 689, 721-22 (2001); C. WRIGHT & V. GOLD, FEDERAL PRACTICE AND PROCEDURE § 6266, at 285 (1997) ("Nothing in the language of the Rule suggests that scientific expert testimony should be treated differently from other expert testimony.").

[105] Morsek, *supra* note 104, at 728 (citing Patricia A. Krebs and Bryan J. De Tray, Kumho Tire Co. v. Carmichael: *A Flexible Approach to Analyzing Expert Testimony Under* Daubert, 34 TORT & INS. L.J. 989, 996 (1999)); *see also* Michelle Michelson, *Recent Development: The Admissibility of Expert Testimony on Battering and its Effects after Kumho Tire*, 79 WASH. U. L. Q. 367, 370 & n.13 (2001) (comparing, e.g., Watkins v. Telsmith, Inc., 121 F.3d 984, 990-91 (5th Cir. 1997) (finding application of *Daubert* not limited to scientific expert testimony), with Compton v. Subaru of America, Inc., 82 F.3d 1513, 1518-19 (10th Cir. 1996) (finding application of *Daubert* factors unwarranted "in cases where expert testimony is based solely upon experience or training"); Diana K. Sheiness,, *Out of the Twilight Zone: The Implications of Daubert v. Merrell Dow Pharmaceuticals, Inc.*, 69 WASH. L. REV. 481, 491 (1994); Timothy B. Dyk and Gregory A. Castanias, Daubert *Doesn't End Debate on Experts*, NAT'L L.J. 17, 20 (Aug. 2, 1993) 20 ("Who is a scientist? A political scientist? A "human factors expert'?").

Psychology is an example illustrating the difficulty in discerning between scientific and non-scientific testimony. By its very definition, psychology is the "science of mind and behavior." Psychologists conduct experiments and there are standard texts and accepted methods of analysis which evince that a psychologist's testimony is grounded in science. However, a psychologist may also utilize observations and experience to reach conclusions, which are not necessarily grounded in science. Henceforth, the totality of the psychologist's testimony should be subject to the rigorous scrutiny because it would be impossible for a judge to separate the testimony into scientific and non-scientific segments.[106]

B. *Daubert's* Implications for Behavioral Science

Daubert's adoption of Popper's view of what constitutes "science" is somewhat problematic for the social sciences in general. Many of the social sciences "rely predominantly on retrospective observational studies rather than on controlled experimentation, and do not necessarily meet the . . . standard of falsifiability."[107] That is not to say, however, that social science evidence ought to be inadmissible under *Daubert*. As several scholars have pointed out, the social sciences have their own standards for assessing validity and reliability. These standards include, but are not limited to, (1) replicability, (2) logic, (3) adherence to recognized methodologies, (4) construct validity (i.e., how well data analysis "fits" into preexisting theory); (5) adherence to proper statistical sampling and statistical procedures for data analysis, (6) avoidance of bias, and (7) qualifications of the researcher.[108]

In spite of these criteria, some continue to argue that social science on the whole should be more rigorously scrutinized under the traditional *Daubert* reliability standards using the Popperian notion of "science," warning that courts need to "protect jurors from 'worthless social science evidence.'"[109] If *Daubert's* focus on reliability were rigorously adhered to—whether reliability were "defined in its scientific sense to mean consistency of result or, in the sense the Court appeared to use it, to mean a measure of accuracy or validity—much behavioral science testimony [would] not fare well . . . ."[110] For example, mental health clinicians "disagree more than half the time even on major diagnostic categories such as schizophrenia and organic brain syndrome" and mood disorders.[111] Reliability is even lower for Axis II personality disorders in

---

[106] Morsek, *supra* note 104, at 729, n.130 (internal citations omitted).

[107] Erica Beecher-Monas, *Blinded by Science: How Judges Avoid the Science in Scientific Evidence,* 71 TEMPLE L. REV. 55 , 69 (1998).

[108] *Id.* at 70-71 (citing, inter alia, KARIN D. KNORR-CETINA, THE MANUFACTURE OF KNOWLEDGE: AN ESSAY ON THE CONSTRUCTIVIST AND CONTEXTUAL NATURE OF SCIENCE 21 (1981); Alvan R. Feinstein, *Scientific Standards in Epidemiologic Studies of the Menace of Daily Life,* 242 SCI. 1257, 1259-61 (1988); Richard Lempert, *The New Evidence Scholarship: Analyzing the Process,* 66 B.U. L. REV. 439, 442 (1986)).

[109] Harvard Law Review, *Confronting The New Challenges of Scientific Evidence Summary,* 108 HARV. L. REV. 1481, 1524-25 (1995) (citing David L. Faigman, *To Have and Have Not: Assessing the Value of Social Science to the Law as Science and Policy,* 38 EMORY L.J. 1005, 1009, 1083-84 (1989)). *But cf.* David McCord, *Syndromes, Profiles and Other Mental Exotica: A New Approach to the Admissibility of Nontraditional Psychological Evidence in Criminal Cases,* 66 OR. L. REV. 19, 94-107 (1987).

[110] Christopher Slobogin, *Doubts About* Daubert: *Psychiatric Anecdata as a Case Study,* 57 WASH & LEE L. REV. 919, 919 (2000).

[111] *Id.* at 920 (citing Samuel Fennig et al., *Comparison of Facility and Research Diagnoses in First Admission Psychotic Patients,* 151 AM. J. PSYCHIATRY 1423, 1426 (1994) (showing 57.1% agreement on schizophrenia); Paul B. Lieberman & Frances M. Baker, *The Reliability of Psychiatric Diagnosis in the Emergency Room,* 36 HOSP. & COMMUNITY PSYCHIATRY 291, 292 (1985) (showing 41% agreement on schizophrenia, 50% agreement on mood disorders, and 37% agreement on organic brain syndromes)); *see also* David Faust & Jay Ziskin, *The Expert Witness in Psychology and Psychiatry,* 241 SCI. 31 (1988) ("A number of subsequent studies showed that rate of disagreement of specific diagnostic categories often equals or exceeds rate of agreement.").

the clinical setting, with a high of 49% for antisocial personality disorder to a low of only 1% for schizoid personality disorder.[112]

Moreover, even if reliability were high, validity is often low because "many symptoms—such as whether a person is "depressed," "anxious," or suffering from "low self-esteem"—are unverifiable in the same way a physical fact is because the terms themselves are so amorphous and subjective."[113] And the problem worsens when not focusing on clinical diagnosis.

> Attempts to explain the causes of behavior (e.g., unconscious conflicts, chemical imbalances, abuse as a child, relationship with parents) are even more speculative. Most opinion testimony of this type is based on untested theories, or theories that have been subjected only to the most preliminary scientific inquiry. Paul Meehl's highly critical comment twenty years ago is still true today: "[M]ost so-called 'theories' in the soft areas of psychology . . . are scientifically unimpressive and technologically worthless." In many of these situations, forensic clinicians can at best offer only "anecdata": information obtained through experience in dealing with psychological problems, reading about case studies, and extrapolation from the theoretical speculations of others.[114]

In light of the aforementioned problems with psychological theories, methodologies, and diagnostic conclusions, several commentators have argued that behavioral science testimony should almost always fail the *Daubert* test.[115] But a recent study conducting a content analysis of federal cases applying *Daubert* to issues of forensic behavioral science found that *Daubert* was not being used to exclude the testimony of forensic psychologists, but rather, a specific jurisprudence appears to have developed with regard to various specialized forensic psychological issues.[116] While exploring the specifics of the ten distinct sub-areas of forensic behavioral science the study identified is beyond the scope of this book, the study concluded that in all ten areas "judges [were] applying *Daubert* vigorously when experts seek to offer opinions based on methodologies that are not generally accepted."[117] Accordingly, the importance of forensic behavioral scientists adhering to proper research methodologies appropriate for either empirical research or clinical assessment cannot be overstated.

V. CONCLUSION

Law and behavioral science intersect in many ways, some of which cause a number of problems that will be explored throughout the rest of this book. From this chapter, you should have a fundamental understanding of why there is often difficulty in fitting the disciplines together.

---

[112] Slobogin, *supra* note 110, at 920 (citing Graham Mellsop, *The Reliability of Axis II of DSM-III*, 139 AM. J. PSYCHIATRY 1360, 1361 (1982)).

[113] *Id.* at 921.

[114] *Id.* at 921-22 (citing Richard J. Bonnie & Christopher Slobogin, *The Role of Mental Health Professionals in the Criminal Process: The Case for Informed Speculation*, 66 VA. L. REV. 427, 461 (1980); Paul E. Meehl, *Theoretical Risks and Tabular Asterisks: Sir Karl, Sir Ronald, and the Slow Progress of Soft Psychology*, 46 J. CONSULTING & CLINICAL PSYCHOL. 806, 806 (1978)).

[115] *E.g.*, Michael J. Gottesman, *Admissibility of Expert Testimony After* Daubert: *The "Prestige" Factor*, 43 EMORY L.J. 867 (1996).

[116] Henry F. Fradella, Adam Fogarty & Lauren O'Neill, *The Impact of* Daubert *on the Admissibility of Behavioral Science Testimony*, 30 PEPPERDINE L. REV. 403 (2003).

[117] *Id.*

Here is a summary of the major differences between the legal and mental health professions that often make cooperation strained, even when accompanied by the best of intentions.[118]

Lawyers and behavioral scientists speak different languages, using the vocabularies that are native to their respective disciplines. They are educated differently, often without the benefit of interdisciplinary training. Moreover, their different fields involve socialization into very different worlds with value systems that are often in conflict. Lawyers tend to be concerned with doctrinal rules, civil rights, precedent, and helping their client achieve the desired outcome in a particular case. Behavioral scientists tend to be less concerned with such abstractions and focus instead on the therapeutic needs of the individual, often to the exclusion of macro-level considerations such as whether doing something might set an adverse precedent, or whether procedural due process protections were strictly adhered to in a particular case. As a result, while both professions ostensibly are there to help, they do so in very different ways from perspectives that are often at odds with each other.

Law asks very different types of questions than those asked by the behavioral sciences. What is established as a fact for one may not be sufficient for the other. Law determines fact by relevant evidence admissible under the rules of evidence. Credibility is often key to determining whether proffered evidence will be accepted by the trier-of-fact as fact. Psychological methods for determining the existence of a fact are quite different and are dependent on issues like the replicability of reliable and valid conclusions.

Moreover, in seeking to answer questions of fact, the two disciplines employ fundamentally different methods of acquiring knowledge. The behavioral sciences are concerned with contributions to scientific theory via the application of scientific methods. Statistical probabilities, and their corresponding uncertainties, are inherent to empirical methodologies. The law, however, does not concern itself with statistical probability but rather with levels of proof that are not only often arrived at in very nonscientific ways, but also are significantly beyond the limits of empirical design. Uncertainty requiring "further study" is simply not an option in a trial. So, the law asks experts to offer their conclusions to "a reasonable degree of scientific certainty." This inherently ambiguous standard[119] may cause behavioral scientists to overstate the level of certainty they have in their factual determinations in order to "fit" into the model the law may be unreasonably asking of them.[120]

Finally, behavioral science offers a number of theoretical models for explaining human behavior. The law is rarely concerned with the deterministic explanations of behavior. Quite the contrary, the law presumes behavior is a product of autonomous free-will guided by rational decision-making. This fundamental difference alone—a philosophical one that concerns the very basis of human nature—is significant enough to explain why the disciplines often have difficulty with each other.

---

[118] This section summaries the points made throughout this chapter, adding those made in GARY B. MELTON, ET AL., PSYCHOLOGICAL EVALUATION FOR THE COURTS 4-10; 12-13 (1987).

[119] Michael M. Martin, *The Uncertain Rule of Certainty: An Analysis and Proposal for a Federal Evidence Rule*, 20 WAYNE L. REV. 781, 804-05 (1974).

[120] *See* American Psychological Association, *Ethical Principles of Psychologists*, 36 AM. PSYCHOL. 633, principle 1 (1981) (requiring experts to state the uncertainty of their conclusions even if doing so translates into lower evidentiary weight being accorded to them and their testimony).

In spite of these many differences, law and the behavioral sciences intersect in ever-growing ways. As mentioned earlier in this chapter, this book is primarily concerned with examining the ways in which psychology in the law operates, but with an informed eye to what psychology and the law has to say about such operation.

CHAPTER TWO
LAW, SOCIAL CONTROL, AND THE MEDICALIZATION OF DEVIANCE

I.   SOCIAL CONTROL

A. An Introduction to Deviance

Deviance is a widely misunderstood concept. It is often confused with criminality. In reality, most crime is just one form of deviant behavior. *Deviance* can be conceptualized in three ways. In its most basic form, it means any departure from that which is typical. The strict social scientific definition of deviance concerns any significant departure from a statistical norm. But in terms of behavior, deviant behavior is that which departs from social norms.[1] We tend to refer to deviant behavior, however, with regard to one specific type: Those behaviors that are negatively viewed or condemned in society.[2]

Two points ought to be noted about the aforementioned definitions of deviance. First, what is considered deviant is dependent on which is typical or "the norm." *Norms*, however, are simply societal rules, whether *prescriptive*—telling us what we ought to do—or *proscriptive*—telling us what we ought not to do. Norms vary across both situation and time. What is appropriate behavior at school may be inappropriate at home. What was unacceptable, and therefore deviant to our grandparents—such as males piercing their ears—may be considered perfectly acceptable behavior today. The relative nature of norms is also evidence across cultures. For example, belching at the dinner table is considered rude in modern America but is a compliment to the host in some African countries.

Even within a given culture, subcultures might have their own set of norms. *Subcultures* are groups that share a set of norms that are different from those of the larger society. These norms are "deviant" because they differ from the norms of the larger culture, but they are not deviant within the subculture; rather, they are indicative of membership in it. Subcultures often exist based on race, ethnicity, religion, sexual orientation, and occupation. For example, members of certain professions, like police, have their own subculture in which their behaviors are quite different from those not in the subculture. Their behaviors, however, are not commonly thought of as deviant behaviors because they are not necessarily in conflict with the norms of society at large. When a subculture's behaviors (such as those of organized crime, street gangs, and drug addicts) are at odds with greater societal values, the subculture itself is often defined as a deviant one. But it is important to note that the behaviors of members of deviant subcultures may or may not be criminal; social identity in a subculture is not necessarily synonymous or coterminous with behaviors associated with that subculture. For example, the members of a biker gang may be deviant insofar as the way they act and dress, but may be law-abiding citizens. In contrast, "swingers" are members of a deviant subculture due to the nature of their sexual activities. Sex with multiple partners may be perfectly legal in your jurisdiction, while constituting the crimes of either fornication (if the participants are unmarried) or adultery (if the participants are married) in other jurisdictions.

---

[1] CHARLES MCCAGHY, DEVIANT BEHAVIOR 2-3 (McMillian, 1976).

[2] PETER CONRAD AND JOSEPH SCHNEIDER, DEVIANCE AND MEDICALIZATION: FROM BADNESS TO SICKNESS 3 (1980).

B. An Overview of Social Control

As discussed in Chapter One, one of the primary functions of law is social control. But law is not the only tool in society responsible for influencing human behavior. Psychology tends to be deterministic in its view of human behavior, viewing it as a function of innate drives, intra-psychic conflict, learned behaviors, or cognitive functioning. Psychiatry tends to view behavior as being a function of biochemistry. In this chapter, however, we focus on the discipline of sociology. Sociology, like psychology and psychiatry, examines human behavior as a product of person-in-environment interactions. Unlike the behavioral sciences, however, sociology tends to focus on macro- rather than micro-level causes of behavior. Its focus on "society" and "social forces" stands in sharp contrast to psychology's focus on the individual. This chapter is not meant to be a comprehensive guide to the sociology of human behavior. Instead, it is meant to expose the reader to various conceptualizations of human behavior from a discipline other than psychiatry or psychology—the focus throughout the rest of this text. Although a gross over-generalization, sociology views human behavior as a function of two related processes: socialization and social control.

1. Socialization and Deviance

Socialization can be defined as the process by which "people learn to conform to social norms; a process that makes possible an enduring society and the transmission of its culture between generations."[3] Two major conceptualizations explain how socialization works. The first is via internalization. A person learns social norms in such a way that they become a part of the individual's personality. That is to say, behavior is controlled via self-imposed regulation rather than externally.[4] In contrast, socialization can also be viewed as a part of social interaction in which people behave in accordance with social norms so that they gain "acceptance and status in the eyes of others."[5]

Traditionally, the three primary agents of socialization are the family, the educational system, and religion. But they are not the only institutions of socialization. The media, for example, is a major influence on the development of societal norms and values. And in today's secular society, some have argued the role of religion has been minimized, as other institutions, especially peers and media (e.g., television, cinema, music, the Internet) have become more important mechanisms of socialization.[6]

In the primary stage of socialization, one's family teaches social norms. Later in life, secondary socialization, both in school and via religion, plays a larger part. Interaction with one's teachers and peers which in school become the dominant institution of socialization in the

---

[3]NICHOLAS ABERCROMBIE, STEPHEN HILL, & BRYAN S. TURNER, DICTIONARY OF SOCIOLOGY 231 (2d ed., Penguin 1988).

[4]*Id.*

[5]*Id.*

[6]*See, e.g.,* George W. Dent, Jr., *Secularism and the Supreme Court*, 1999 B.Y.U.L. REV. 1, 41-45 (summarizing and evaluating claims of the decline of religion in America); AMITAI ETZIONE, A RESPONSIVE SOCIETY 140 (1991) (discussing decline of importance of religion and corresponding decay in values); Rebecca R. French, *Reconsidering Religion and Social Theory*, 10 YALE J.L. & HUMAN. 505 (1998) (discussing the "decline of religion"); THEODORE CAPLOW ET AL., ALL FAITHFUL PEOPLE: CHANGE AND CONTINUITY IN MIDDLETOWN'S RELIGION 34 (1983) (a study of the decline of religion). *But cf.* ANDREW M. GREELEY, UNSECULAR MAN: THE PERSISTENCE OF RELIGION (1972) (arguing against the decline of religion); ANDREW M. GREELEY, RELIGIOUS CHANGE IN AMERICA (1989) (same); JEFFREY K. HADDEN & ANSON SHUPE (EDS.), SECULARIZATION AND FUNDAMENTALISM RECONSIDERED 27 (1989) (predicting fall of secularization theory).

secondary stage. Finally, in the adult stage of socialization, other institutions—such as one's work environment—socialize a person into "roles for which primary and secondary socialization may not have prepared them fully."[7]

Sociology explains deviance in one of two ways. The first explanation of deviance is a failure of the normal socialization process.[8] Under this view, the institutions of socialization fail to properly "impart the knowledge and opportunities that result in rule-abiding behavior."[9] The second major sociological explanation for deviance is that people may be successfully socialized into a deviant subculture. In other words, by meaningful exposure to norms and values that are deviant in themselves, and then adhering to them (via both internalization of these deviant norms and externally conforming to them for social approval within the group teaching the deviant norms and values), one learns to be deviant. When socialization fails to produce a rule-abiding person, mechanisms of formal social control may be used to bring about behavioral conformity with societal norms.

2. Social Control of Deviance

Social control refers to the processes by which society controls behavior within itself at the individual and group levels. This definition is derived from the one originally set forth in 1901 by Edward A. Ross who used the term to refer to social regulation in the broadest sense, encompassing "virtually all of the human practices and arrangements that contribute to social order and . . . that influence people to conform.[10] Today, however, largely due to the work of Talcott Parsons,[11] and later Donald Black,[12] the term is used more narrowly to refer to the mechanisms by which deviant behaviors are controlled.

Social control of deviance operates in both formal and informal ways. Additionally, it accomplishes it ends both positively (through rewards) and negatively (through sanctions). *Informal social controls* are the tools used in the socialization process. They are both internal (often referred to as "self-control") and external (often referred to as "relational controls"). Internal or self-control is akin to one's conscience—one's "internalized norms, beliefs, morals, and self-concept."[13] Sociology explains the development of conscience via the socialization process, not unlike the way social, learning, and cognitive psychology explain its development. External or relational social control is dependent upon a person's interactions with others. Virtually any type of positive or negative reactions from others for one's behavior constitute informal social control, such as "ridicule, praise, gossip, smiles, disapproving glances and 'dirty looks,' mythmaking, [and] group ostracism and support."[14]

In contrast, law is the tool by which formal social control is exercised. And although the criminal law continues to be used by society as the *sine qua non* tool of *formal social control,* it is not the only form of formal social control; constitutional law, civil law, and administrative

---

[7]ABERCROMBIE, et. al., *supra* note 3, at 231.

[8]NANCY A. HEITZEG, DEVIANCE: RULEMAKERS & RULEBREAKERS 38 (West 1996).

[9]*Id.*

[10]EDWARD ALSWORTH ROSS, SOCIAL CONTROL: A SURVEY OF THE FOUNDATIONS OF ORDER (MacMillian 1901).

[11]TALCOTT PARSONS, THE SOCIAL SYSTEM 297-325 (1951); *see also* CONRAD AND SCHNEIDER, *supra* note 2, at 7.

[12]DONALD BLACK, SOCIOLOGICAL JUSTICE (1989); DONALD BLACK (ED.), TOWARD OF GENERAL THEORY OF SOCIAL CONTROL, Vol. 1 (1984).

[13]CONRAD & SCHNEIDER, *supra* note 2, at 7.

[14]*Id.*

regulatory law are all tools of formal social control. They operate through different agents and in different styles. We will first explore the different agencies of social control, and then turn to examine the styles in which they operate.

3. Institutions of Social Control

The institutions of social control are similar to those of socialization. Eitzen and Baca-Zinn classify the institutions of social control into two types of agents: agents of ideological social control, and agents of direct social control.[15]

Agents of ideological social control attempt to shape the consciousness of people in society. Such agents include the family, educational institutions, religion, organized sports, media, and the government. These agents influence ideas, attitudes, morals, and values. In doing so, they help to maintain the status quo by reinforcing governing ideologies and persuading citizens to comply willingly with laws. These goals are accomplished primarily via socialization, although both direct attacks on competing ideologies and governmental propaganda are also used by some of these agents.[16]

According to Eitzen and Baca-Zinn, the family teaches the child to "fit" into society.[17] Educational institutions uphold the behavioral standards of the community and indoctrinate their students in the correct attitudes about work, respect for authority, and patriotism.[18] Religion supports the status quo in American society by extolling the American way of life and teaching acceptance of an imperfect world because people are born sinners, but that they will be rewarded in the next life if they strive to achieve what is defined by society as "good."[19] Sports promote local, regional, and national pride; allow for a cathartic channeling of aggressive energies; provide an avenue for upward social mobility; and is supposed to build character, although they may simply encourage conformity.[20] The media similarly promotes adherence to the basic values of the status quo by shaping how we evaluate ourselves and others; by influencing, via advertising, what we view as desirable; and by molding how the public perceives and interprets events.[21] Finally, government sets educational standards; acts in the name of national security; and promotes solidarity and patriotism through public services and by the public appearances of elected leaders.[22] In acting as they do, these institutional agents of social control successfully promote social order in a manner that leads most Americans to accept the legitimacy of the social, political, and economic order. And even when the status quo is questioned, it tends to be done in a manner within the prescriptions of permissible dissent, such as through critical commentary and peaceful demonstrations.

---

[15]D. STANLEY EITZEN & MAXINE BACA ZINN (EDS.), IN CONFLICT & ORDER: UNDERSTANDING SOCIETY 130-51 (8th ed., Allyn & Bacon 1998).

[16]*Id.* at 132.

[17]*Id.* at 133.

[18]*Id.* at 133-34.

[19]*Id.* at 134-36. Of course, the level to which this statement is true will vary depending on the given religion, as some clearly perpetuate the status quo more than others.

[20]*Id.* at 136-38. It should be noted, however, that there is a body of psychological research that has questioned – perhaps even refuted the assumptions of sociology that sports allow for a cathartic channeling of aggressive energies. *See generally, e.g.,* Daniel L. Wann, Jeffrey D. Carlson, Lisa C. Holland, Bryan E. Jacob, Dale A. Owens & D. Dayne Wells, *Beliefs in Symbolic Catharsis: The Importance of Involvement with Aggressive Sports,* 27 SOCIAL BEHAV. & PERSONALITY 155-164 (1999).

[21]*Id.* at 138-39.

[22]*Id.* at 139.

The *agents of direct social control* attempt to punish or neutralize both organizations and individuals who deviate from society's norms.[23] These need not be "bad" people, just those who are deviant insofar as they are a departure from that which is expected of good citizens under the dominant paradigm, such as the poor, the mentally ill, criminals, and political dissidents. The agents of direct social control include welfare agencies, science and medicine, and government.

Welfare agencies provide and administer public assistance programs that function to defuse social unrest. Moreover, the stigmatization that is often associated with being on such public assistance programs reinforces and legitimizes the value of work and self-sufficiency.[24] Science and medicine have developed a number of devices that are aimed at controlling the behavior of some members of society that include neurochemical, physical, psychosocial, and biological devices.[25] The role of science and medicine in social control is discussed more fully in Section II of this chapter. Finally, the government acts an agent of direct social control, primarily through law as a tool of formal social control. Before exploring the four main subtypes or styles of formal social control the government exerts, it should be noted that the very existence of government under our paradigm of Classical Liberalism and the Social Contract is predicated on the necessity of government providing for the maintenance of societal order and stability. So, not only does the government directly exert social control in the following four way, but also, in doing so, government reinforces the ideological belief that it *should* be directly exercising social control.[26]

C. Styles of Formal Social Control

Donald Black, one of the leading scholars on law and society, has argued that law is used as a tool of formal social control in four related, yet distinct ways. He termed the four styles of formal social control penal, compensatory, therapeutic, and conciliatory.[27]

The *penal style of social control* views the violator of a codified social norm (i.e., a criminal law) as an offender who deserves official condemnation. Four main justifications are proffered for using criminal law as a tool of formal social control: retribution, deterrence, rehabilitation, and incapacitation.[28]

Retribution espouses the infliction of just punishment and suffering on a person deserving of it for having violated a societal norm that was deemed important enough to have been codified as a criminal law. In other words, it is a theory of just desserts exemplified in the "eye for an eye, tooth for a tooth" philosophy. It also justifies punishment as a means of *expatiation* (i.e., atoning for sin).

The rehabilitative view looks at the criminal as a "sick" person who needs treatment. *Rehabilitation* will help this sick person get better and thereby become a part of the norm—the nondeviant portion of society.

---

[23]*Id.* at 140; 177.

[24]*Id.* at 140-41.

[25]*Id.* at 141-44.

[26]*Id.* at 145-50.

[27]*See* Donald Black, *Social Control as a Dependent Variable*, in DONALD BLACK (ED.) 1 TOWARD A GENERAL THEORY OF SOCIAL CONTROL 8-12 (1984).

[28]*See generally* Louis M. Seidman, *Soldiers, Martyrs, and Criminals*, 94 YALE L.J. 315 (1984) (critically evaluating the four primary justifications).

At the heart of using criminal law as a tool of formal social control in a diversely heterogeneous society is the notion of simple *deterrence.*[29] Classical deterrence theory rejects the notion of retributive justice on the grounds that punishment as an end in and of itself cannot be justified.[30] Instead, deterrence theory is predicated on the utilitarian notion that the criminal law should be used as a tool to control rational decision-making.[31]

After a period in which the rehabilitative model, derived in large part from the works of Plato, St. Thomas Aquinas, and Hegel,[32] became the primary focus of the criminal justice system in the mid- to late 1960s through the early 1980s, the deterrence model reemerged as the significant driving philosophy in the criminal justice system. Punishment serves several goals under the deterrence model, two of which are particularly important to any general theory of social control. First, punishment acts as a tool of external social control by generally deterring the would-be criminal offender from committing the proscribed behaviors out of fear of punishment.[33] Second, along the lines of classical social control theory as set forth by Edward A. Ross,[34] it helps create a type of consensus regarding the immorality of the proscribed act, thereby assisting in the creation of both conscious and unconscious internal social controls.[35]

Finally, the incapacitative view rejects the other three justifications for penal social control, but still recognizes the need to do something with those who violate criminal law. The *incapacitation* approach simply posits that by incarcerating offenders (i.e., "lock 'em up and throw away the key"), criminals will be physically incapacitated from committing further deviant acts against society.

The *compensatory style of formal social control* focuses upon providing restitution to the victim of an act. In other words, it attempts to compensate a wronged or aggrieved person in such a manner as to restore them as closely as possible to the "status quo ante,"—the way they were before the deviant person wronged them. This is typically accomplished via the civil justice system. The victim sues the rule-breaker and is compensated for his or her injuries, usually financially.[36]

The *therapeutic style of formal social control* views the deviant person as someone who needs help to become nondeviant or "normal." This is often accomplished via science and medicine, especially psychology and psychiatry. Because of this fact, it is clear that science and medicine are major institutions of social control. Their role as direct agents of therapeutic social control is discussed more fully in Section II of this chapter.[37]

The *conciliatory style of formal social control* attempts to create and preserve social harmony via dispute resolution. Mediation is an example of conciliatory social control. The focus is on allowing both sides to express their displeasures and then work toward a compromise

---

[29]*E.g.,* H. Lawrence Ross, Limitations on Deterring the Drinking Driver: Legal Policy and Social Control 63 (1984).

[30]Caesare Beccaria, On Crimes and Punishment (H. Paolucci, trans., Bobbs-Merrill 1963).

[31]Jeremy Bentham, Principles of Penal Law (Russell & Russell 1962).

[32]Philip Bean, Punishment: A Philosophical and Criminological Inquiry (1981).

[33]Johannes Andenaes, Punishment and Deterrence (Univ. Mich. Press 1974).

[34]Ross, *supra* note 10.

[35]*See generally* Andenaes, *supra* note 33; *see also* Herbert L. Packer, The Limits of the Criminal Sanction (Stanford Univ. Press. 1968).

[36]Black, *supra* note 27, at 8-12.

[37]*Id.*

that allows not only the removal of the irritants in a relationship, but also perhaps even some semblance of social harmony.[38]

Black viewed the type and style of social control as a dependent variable. In other words, whether informal or formal social controls would be dominant, and if the latter, the style of formal social control being exercised would depend upon a number of factors. Black's theory postulates that law, as formal social control, has an inverse relationship with other forms of informal social control such as morality or close relations with family and community. The more significant these social relationships, the more informal social control we would expect to see. For example, in tightly knit, highly structured, homogeneous societies, the need for formal social control should be very low since both socialization and informal social control should be highly effective.

But as societies become more complex, close relationships with family and community become less important. Moreover, stratification increases. *Stratification* refers to relational differences between members of a society that are demarcated in some sort of hierarchical manner that results in levels of inequality, such as income, age, ethnicity, etc.[39] In homogeneous societies, where there is little stratification, socialization tends to be more effective in producing consensus. Correspondingly, informal social controls are highly effective in controlling deviant behavior. But when informal social controls fail in these homogeneous societies, then the formal mechanisms of social control used tend to be compensatory and/or conciliatory. In contrast, more heterogeneous societies in which there is more stratification produces a correspondingly lower degree of consensus. Accordingly, socialization is less complete, and informal social controls are much less effective in controlling deviance. Formal social controls in such complex societies tend to be more punitive and more therapeutic than in more simple ones.

Black's theory of law is far more complicated than the short overview above might suggest. But for our purposes, this highly abbreviated summary should suffice as a background to allow us to explore how deviance in our modern society has been increasingly medicalized and, correspondingly, how therapeutic social control of deviance came to have its strong foundation in America.

II. MEDICINE AND SOCIAL CONTROL

A. The Medicalization of Deviance

The *medical model of deviance* is, historically speaking, a relatively new way of explaining deviance. "The origin of the formal rule of law is in the 1500s, and informal social control has existed, in one form or another, since the beginning of human society."[40] Its emergence was predicated on the development of medicine as an established science. It views deviance as a disease. In doing so, it asserts itself as being objective and absolutist.[41] And, as such, the medical model of deviance advocates "treatment" of the underlying disease in accordance with the therapeutic style of formal social control.

---

[38] *Id.*

[39] ABERCROMBIE, ET AL., *supra* note 3, at 243.

[40] HEITZEG, *supra* note 8, at 219.

[41] *Id.* at 220.

Talcott Parsons was the first to conceptualize medicine as an institution of social control.[42] Parsons viewed illness as a form of deviance, primarily because the sick could not perform their normal roles in society (and thereby threatened the stability of the social order).[43] The sick person is viewed as ill through no fault of his own. He is viewed as being in need of treatment so he can get well. Such treatment is supposed to be sought out from a health care professional with whom the sick person is expected to cooperate. The health care professional, especially the physician, acts as a tool of social control, then, because the expert seeks to return the sick person to wellness, thereby removing the deviance and allowing the sick person to resume his normal role in society.

In 1980, one of the most comprehensive treatments on medicine as an institution of social control was given in a book by Peter Conrad and Joseph Schneider entitled *Deviance and Medicalization: From Badness to Sickness*. In it, they trace the history of changing "moral-criminal definitions of deviance to medical ones, what [they] call the medicalization of deviance."[44] Examples of the medicalization of deviance include the excessive consumption of alcohol, once considered sinful and/or immoral, is now understood as alcoholism; what was once thought of as an unruly child in need of discipline may now be diagnosed as hyperactive. Similar transformations have occurred for such "badness" as drug addiction, suicide, obesity, delinquency, homosexuality, and other forms of deviance.[45] The defining of deviant behavior as an illness or a symptom of an illness or underlying disease—and subsequent direct medical intervention as treatment of that illness or disease—is what Conrad and Schneider mean when they speak of the *medicalization of deviance*.

The medicalization of deviance is most evident in psychiatry and psychology. The social control function of the behavioral sciences is most evident in the sphere of institutionalization in the criminal setting, given the role the behavioral sciences play in determining criminal responsibility, such as with the insanity and diminished capacity defenses. The behavioral sciences are also powerful in the civil law arena for determinations regarding involuntary hospitalization, guardianship and conservatorship, child custody placements, and a host of civil competencies, all of which are explored in detail later in this book. It has even been argued that psychiatry and psychology are powerful tools of social control even when they operate independently of the civil and criminal justice systems because psychotherapy "reinforces dominant values and adjusts people to their life situations, . . . [thereby] support[ing] the status quo."[46]

B. Types of Medical Social Control

Theorists have conceptualized the ways medicine acts as social control in different ways. In spite of such differences, the typology developed by major scholars of medical social control have similar themes running through their assessments. For example, Clark and Robboy assert that medicine acts as a social control in three primary ways. First through physical treatments designed to "fix" deviant behaviors, such as surgery and psychotropic medication.[47] Second, via

---

[42]PARSONS, *supra* note 11, at 297-325.

[43]*Id.* at 428-79.

[44]CONRAD & SCHNEIDER, *supra* note 2, at 32.

[45]*Id.* at 34.

[46]CONRAD & SCHNEIDER, *supra* note 2, 242.

[47]CANDACE CLARK & HOWARD ROBBOY (EDS.), SOCIAL INTERACTION: READINGS IN SOCIOLOGY (4th ed., St. Martin's Press 1992).

labeling theory. By labeling groups as sick, we imply their illness can be cured, something seen historically with homosexuality.[48] And third, Clark and Robboy assert eugenics—manipulation of hereditary factors—as a powerful form of social control. This may be accomplished through sterilization, selective abortion, genetic therapy, gene splicing, cloning, or even genetic elimination (i.e., genocide) that removes a group from the population.[49]

Conrad and Schneider's typology asserts that medicine acts as a tool of social control in three distinct ways: though medical technology, medical collaboration, and medical ideology. *Medical technologies,* especially psycho-technologies, are common means of treating many forms of deviance. Psychotropic medications, for example, are routine treatments for mental illness. This classification of medical social control is akin to Clark and Robboy's category of physical control.

What is key to understanding the role of medical technology/physical social control is to see what gets medicalized so it can, in turn, be treated. Medicine, specifically through the American Medical Association (AMA) and the American Psychiatric Association (APA), control the definitions of sickness. The primary tool for defining deviance under the medical model is the *Diagnostic and Statistical Manual of Mental Disorder, Fourth Edition (DSM-IV)*. It was first created by the APA in 1952 and it identified sixty mental disorders.[50] Prior to its publication, its precursor was the *Statistical Manual for the Use of Institutions for the Insane*. It identified twenty-two illnesses in 1918. Since the first edition of the DSM, it has gone through four major revisions: the DSM-II (1968), the DSM-III (1980), the DSM-III revised edition (1987), and the current DSM-IV, published in 1994. The most recent edition of the DSM contains diagnostic criteria for 410 disorders.[51] This represents an increase of more than 580 percent in the number of recognized mental disorders over forty years! Appendix A contains an overview of the DSM-IV, as well as the diagnostic criteria for a number of mental disorders.

Moreover, medicine often holds the exclusive ability to treat what it defines as illness. Consider the examples Conrad and Schneider give: "tranquilizers such as chlordiazepoxide (Librium) and diazepam (Valium) for anxiety, nervousness, and general malaise; stimulant medications for hyperactive children; amphetamines for overeating and obesity; disuffiram (Antabuse) for alcoholism; methadone for heroin, and many others."[52] More radical forms treatment include "hospitalization, modifying environments, long-term psychotherapy," surgery (e.g., sterilization), psychosurgery (e.g., lobotomies), behavior modification, and even genetic manipulation.[53] While it should be recognized that some of Conrad and Schneider's examples are dated (e.g., psychosurgery is quite rare today; amphetamines are no longer the treatment of choice for obesity; and self-help groups like Alcoholics Anonymous are far more common for treating alcoholism than medical interventions are), their underlying point is still important. Medicine often holds the power to define and then treat deviant behaviors. By definition, that is the power of social control since medicine can modify or even eliminate the underlying behaviors.

---

[48] *Id.*

[49] *Id.*

[50] Steven I. Friedland, *on Treatment, Punishment, and the Civil Commitment of Sex Offenders*, 70 U. COLO. L. REV. 73, 134 & n.340-42 (1999) (citing Ariz Sharon Begley, Is Everybody Crazy?, NEWSWEEK, Jan. 26, 1998, 52).

[51] *Id.; see also* Jeanne Louise Carriere, *Reconstructing the Grounds for Interdiction*, 54 LA. L. REV. 1199, 1225 (1994); Phil Brown, *The Name Game: Toward a Sociology of Diagnosis*, 11 J. MIND & BEHAV. 385, 397-99 (1990).

[52] CONRAD & SCHNEIDER, *supra* note 2, at 243.

[53] *Id.*

Medical collaboration refers to how medicine works with other institutions of social control to reduce and/or eliminate deviance. "Such collaboration includes roles as information provider, gatekeeper, institutional agent, and technician."[54] Two examples offered by Conrad and Schneider illustrate well what they mean by medical collaboration. Work and school environments, both institutions of social control, require attendance of employees and pupils respectively. A physician's note, however, can excuse a person from those obligations. Halleck called this "the power of medical excuse."[55] Medical excuse works similarly in a wide-variety of settings, such as in workman's compensation claims, social security disability benefit claims, exemptions from military service, placement in prisons, and so on. Perhaps the most clear cut example of medical collaboration occurs in the legal system where an invocation of the insanity defense can excuse criminal liability. And although the determination of insanity is a legal one, it is made in great deference to medical experts and their opinions.

Medical ideology concerns "the social and ideological benefits accrued by conceptualizing [a behavior or condition] in medical terms."[56] This can work in two ways. First, by labeling something as disease, the moral blame is often shifted away from the individual. This may benefit the individual insofar as he or she can be thought of as "sick" and in need of treatment, rather than as "bad" and in need of punishment. On the other hand, such labeling can reinforce the interest of social institutions in repressive ways that support the dominant values and morality of society, making social change harder. The Victorian view of masturbation as an illness, and the Soviet labeling of dissidents as mentally ill are two such examples offered by Conrad and Schneider.

C. Social Consequences of Medicalizing Deviance

1. Positive Effects of Medicalization

Conrad and Schneider identify five beneficial consequences attributed to the medicalization of deviance. First, a rehabilitative focus, as opposed to a punitive one, is more humanitarian, leading to a more compassionate society.[57]

Second, the diminution of moral blame increases societal understanding towards the deviant, rather than contributing to condemnation of him. Doing so reduces both guilty and social stigma for the deviant person, making it easier for him to reintegrate into society after effective medical social controls have been administered.[58]

Third, the therapeutic ideology is an optimistic one. Optimism concerning improvement or even a "cure" through proper treatment can help the deviant person psychologically "by mobiliz[ing] hope . . . and even becom[ing] a self-fulling prophesy."[59]

Fourth, medicalization increases the power and prestige of those in the medical professional. Conrad and Schneider view this as a positive consequence since medical professionals are, for

---

[54]*Id.* at 244.

[55]*Id.*

[56]*Id.* at 245.

[57]*Id.* at 246.

[58]*Id.* at 246-47.

[59]*Id.* at 247. Note that Conrad and Schneider caution, however, that when we lack effective treatments, then pessimism can take over.

the most, "beneficent and honorable."[60] In support of this belief, they cite Pitts who contends that medical professionals are "more immune to corruption than are the judicial and para-judicial professions and relatively immune to political pressure."[61]

And fifth, they see medical social control as the most flexible and efficient form of formal social control since "medical controls are adjustable to fit the needs of the individual patient, rather than being a response to the deviant act itself."[62] As an example, they cite methadone treatment of heroin addicts as being more effective both clinically and in terms of cost when compared to incarceration in prisons or hospitals.

2. Negative Consequences of Medicalization

Conrad and Schneider also identify seven negative consequences to the medicalization of deviance. First, it has the effect of dislocating personal responsibility. If one is deemed not to be personally responsible for one's actions, that person becomes a "second-class citizen" who is dependent on society to take care of him or her.[63]

Second, medicalization masks the fact that medicine is not morally neutral. Although "cloaked in the mantle of science . . . [and therefore] assumed to be objective and value-free, . . . the very nature of medical practice involves value judgment."[64] They cite the former definition of homosexuality as mental illness as an example.

Third, allowing highly educated experts to control the definition of deviance and its treatment takes power out of the hands of the public. Defining something as scientific fact perpetuates that conceptualization of it since ordinary citizens are often unable to discuss the technicalities of the definition set by the experts. This has the practical effect of "decreasing the accessibility of public debate."[65]

Fourth, medical social control allows for things to be done in the name of "treatment" that would not ordinarily be socially acceptable. Forced administration of psychotropic medications and psychosurgery are two examples of social controls that would not be capable of use but for the involvement of medicine since they lie outside the realm of other institutions of social control.[66]

Fifth, Conrad and Schneider consider medicalization to be a "part of a larger phenomenon that is prevalent in our society: the individualization of social problems." Rather than looking at societal ills, such as poverty and inadequate educational systems, we look at the individual level. By treating the person or the family, we avoid the harder, more pressing problems that exist on a macro level that may well be the cause of the individualized deviance. In other words, individualized deviance may be a response to—or a symptom of—a larger social problem that goes untackled when we look at the individual, rather than the big picture.[67]

---

[60] *Id.* at 248.

[61] *Id.* (citing Jesse Pitts, *Social Control: The Concept*, in 14 INTERNATIONAL ENCYCLOPEDIA OF SOCIAL SCIENCES 391 (D. Sills ed., Macmillan 1968)).

[62] *Id.*

[63] *Id.* at 248-49.

[64] *Id.* at 249.

[65] *Id.*

[66] *Id.* at 250.

[67] *Id.*

Sixth, medicalization and the larger process of the individualization of social problems perpetuates the political status quo since they depoliticize deviance. By focusing on the individual, we fail to see the politics of the dominant culture that might be a cause of, or at least a contributing factor to, the particularized deviance at issue. They offer several examples, the most clear of which was when Soviets confined dissidents to mental institutions to avoid public criticism of their politics. But they offer other examples that strike closer to home despite it being more than twenty years since they wrote their text. For example, labeling children as hyperactive takes attention away from the educational system against which students may be rebelling. Similarly labeling the inner-city user of opiates as a drug addict takes away from the socio-economic pressures that might drive one to use drugs.[68]

Finally, Conrad and Schneider offer the "exclusion of evil" as an important negative effect of medicalization. Uncomfortable with notions of sin and evilness, that which is innately bad, deviance that might otherwise have been defined as evil is given medicalized explanations because it is easier for us to do so. But sometimes there are just "bad eggs" who do bad things. For example, defining Adolph Hitler as sick "portrays the horror of the Holocaust as a product of individual pathology."[69] Other times, bad consequences occur without any evil intent. Our ever-increasing cultural inability to distinguish the two "detracts from our ability to see and confront the evils that face our world."[70]

D. Some Public Policy Considerations

Conrad and Schneider ended their treatise on the medicalization of deviance by pointing out the impact the medicalization of deviance has had on social policy. They also offered some predictions about the future regarding the role of medical social control and the very nature of the medicalization of deviance.

1. Shifts in Forms of Social Control

Conrad and Schneider pointed to the ***deinstitutionalization/decarceration*** movement of the 1960s and 1970s as one of the more dramatic shifts in social control. People were released from mental hospitals and prisons in favor of community-based social controls. Social service agencies, diversion programs, halfway houses, and group homes are all examples of social control mechanisms that either grew stronger or were created in response to decarceration. In other words, the form and subtype of social control changed in response decarceration. This change, according to Conrad and Schneider, was an increase in medicalization via outpatient medical technologies and an increase in medical collaboration. They point to public drunkenness as an example. As it was widely decriminalized (i.e., taken out of the control of law as a tool of social control), medical treatment of alcoholism increased dramatically.

The shifting forms of social control that accompanied the decarceration movement was not only in response to a changed definition of what was legally controlled, but also was symbiotically responsible for it. In other words, "medicalization allows for the decriminalization

---

[68]*Id.* at 250-51.

[69]*Id.* at 251.

[70]*Id.* at 252.

of certain activities . . . because they remain defined as deviant . . . and an alternative form of social control is available (medicine)."[71]

It should be noted that the shifting from the legal to the medical can also work in reverse. Since the time Conrad and Schneider wrote, there has been a swing back to formal legal control of a number of behaviors that had previously been medicalized. Drug use is the clearest example. While rehabilitation programs may have been the primary treatment for drug addicts under the medical model, the 1980s brought a "war on drugs" that led to ever-increasing criminal sanctions for drug use and possession, even for some first-time offenders. Clearly, the form of formal social control varies with the political state of affairs at any given time.

2. Putative Backlash

What if medical social controls are not triggered upon the decriminalization of a given behavior? When something is both decriminalized and demedicalized, one of two things (or both) are likely to occur according to Conrad and Schneider. The first possibility is that the underlying behavior will become "vindicated." *Vindication* occurs when the behavior is no longer viewed as deviant. Alternatively, some *putative backlash* will occur that either recriminalizes the behavior or otherwise redefines the deviant nature of the behavior.

In support of this proposition, Conrad and Schneider used the example of homosexuality. At a time when reconceptualizations of the right to privacy led several states to decriminalize homosexuality, the medical community was correspondingly redefining homosexuality as a natural variant in human sexuality, as opposed to being the mental illness medicine once claimed it was. The consequences predicted by Conrad and Schneider have both come true. Without doubt, the arrival of the 21st century brought a new social perspective on homosexuality. No longer does it hold the social stigma that it once did. Homosexuality has been decriminalized. Thirty-four states had decriminalized sodomy between 1971 to 2000.[72] And, in 2003, the U.S. Supreme Court invalidated the remaining sodomy laws in the U.S. as unconstitutional violations of the right to privacy and personal liberty embodied in the Fourteenth Amendment's Due Process Clause.[73]

Moreover, a fair argument can be made that homosexuality has also been vindicated, at least in part. By the start of 2007, laws banning discrimination on the basis of sexual identity have been enacted in hundreds of counties and cities nationwide, as well as in seventeen states and the District of Columbia (only seven of these states, however, include gender identity in their non-discrimination laws);[74] 430 (86%) of the Fortune 500 companies have policies that prohibit discrimination on the basis of sexual orientation, 81 (16.2%) of which include gender identity;[75] 90% of the top 100 colleges and universities as ranked by *U.S. News and World Report* have written nondiscrimination policies that included sexual orientation, thirty-eight of which include

---

[71]*Id.* at 253.

[72]American Civil Liberties Union, Status of U.S. Sodomy Laws (retrieved July 17, 2000) <http://www.aclu.org/issues/gay/sodomy.html>.

[73]Lawrence v. Texas, 539 U.S. 558 (2003).

[74]Samir Luther & Daryl Herschaft, *The State of the Workplace for Gay, Lesbian, Bisexual, and Transgender Americans 2005-2006* (Washington, D.C.: Human Rights Campaign 2006), *available at* http://www.hrc.org.

[75]*Id.* at 10. The number of companies including non-discrimination policies on the basis of sexual orientation increases to 98% when looking at the Fortune 100 companies. *Id.* And, of the Fortune 100, 35% of companies include gender identity in their non-discrimination policies. *Id.*

gender identity in their policies;[76] thirty-three states and the District of Columbia have laws against hate crimes that include sexual orientation, eleven of which also include gender identity in their hate crime laws;[77] Massachusetts has legalized same-sex marriage, Vermont, Connecticut, and New Jersey offer civil unions, and California, Hawaii, Maine, and the District of Columbia offer legal recognition of domestic partnerships that confer many of the same state rights attendant to marriage to same-sex couples;[78] countless corporations, including 51% of the Fortune 500 companies and 77% of the Fortune 100, offer domestic partnership benefits;[79] more than 200 cities, counties, and municipalities, as well thirteen states and the District of Columbia offer domestic partnership benefits to their employees;[80] and gay and lesbian characters on television and in movies have become commonplace.[81]

On the other hand, there can also be no doubt that the putative backlash Conrad and Schneider predicted has also occurred. Anti-Gay violence, for example, is alive and well. While most media attention is focused on the tragic antigay killings of the likes of Gwen Araujo (California), Bill Clayton (Washington), Tyra Hunter (D.C.), Alan Schindler (a U.S. military base in Japan), Michael Sandy (New York), Matthew Shepard (Wyoming), Brandon Teena (Nebraska), Arthur "J.R." Warren (West Virginia), Barry Winchell (Kentucky), and Diane Whipple (California) to name a few,[82] more routine antigay violence in the form of assaults and batteries often goes unreported in the mainstream press even though they occur in significant numbers.[83] "Anti-Gay" initiatives, seeking to repeal hate crime laws, domestic partnership laws and ordinances, and non-discrimination laws that include homosexuality are one of the hottest topics in politics.[84] And the legal status of same-sex relationships has proven to be one of the most divisive issues of our time. For example, when the federal government enacted the Defense of Marriage Act ("DOMA") which refused federal recognition of same-sex marriages that might be recognized by any given state, forty-one states followed suit with similar state laws.[85] And, since then, both the federal government and those of many states have been attempting to enact constitutional amendments restricting the right to marry to heterosexuals.[86] Bolstered by the overwhelming success of these antigay marriage initiatives, as well as unsuccessful court challenges to a Florida law banning GLBT from adopting children, antigay forces have most

---

[76] *Id.* at 11.

[77] Human Rights Campaign, Hate Crime Laws: State by State, *available at* http://www.hrc.org/

[78] Luther & Herrschaft, *supra* note 74, at 4-5; *see also* National Gay and Lesbian Task Force, *The Issues: Marriage and Partnership Recognition*, *available at* http://www.thetaskforce.org/theissues/issue.cfm?issueID=14.

[79] Luther & Herrschaft, *supra* note 74, at 8.

[80] *Id.* at 13.

[81] Ellen Ann Anderson, *The Law and Politics of Antigay Initiatives*, in OUT OF THE CLOSET AND INTO THE COURTS: LEGAL OPPORTUNITY STRUCTURE AND GAY RIGHTS LITIGATION 143-174 (Ellen Ann Anderson, ed., 2005); CRAIG A. RIMMERMAN, KENNETH D. WALD, & CLYDE WILCOX, THE POLITICS OF GAY RIGHTS (2000); STEPHANIE L. WITT & SUZANNE MCCORKLE, ANTI-GAY RIGHTS: ASSESSING VOTER INITIATIVES (1997); V. Gay, *They're Out and About: Gay Characters Are More Prominent than Ever on TV, Which Is Set to Go Where the Medium Has Never Gone Before*, NEWSDAY, Nov. 26, 2000, at D-6.

[82] *See generally* http://www.HateCrime.org.

[83] National Coalition of Anti-Violence Programs, Anti-Lesbian, Gay, Bisexual and Transgender Violence in 2004. (New York 2005), *available at* http://www.cuav.org/docs/2004hvreport.pdf.

[84] *See, e.g.*, Lambda Legal Defense and Educational Fund, *Antigay Initiatives*, *available at* http://www.lambdalegal.org.

[85] National Conference of State Legislatures, *Same Sex Marriage*, *available at* http://www.ncsl.org/programs/cyf/samesex.htm

[86] Human Rights Campaign, Marriage/Relationship Recognition Laws: State by State (retrieved June 28, 2005) <http://www.hrc.org>.

recently turned their attention to banning GLBT people from adopting children or serving as foster parents nationwide.[87]

The backlash against GLBT rights is not limited to legislative or ballot initiatives on politically sensitive issues like same-sex marriage or parenting. Courts have been applying cases like *Romer v. Evans*[88] and *Lawrence v. Texas*[89]—cases that at first blush appeared to be major legal victories for GLBT rights[90]—in the most limited ways, often reading into their holdings legal constraints that restrict further expansion of GLBT rights.[91] For example:

> Several recent federal cases outline the possibility that *Romer* stands for three basic legal propositions: (1) homosexuals are not a suspect class; (2) there is no fundamental right to participate equally in the political process; and (3) rational basis is the appropriate standard of review for homosexuals' equal protection claims.[92]

Thus, using the lowest possible standard of review for Equal Protection Clause challenges, courts have continued to validate numerous laws discriminating against GLBT people, such as the military's "Don't Ask Don't Tell" policy and various employment discrimination cases.[93] Similar narrow constructions of Lawrence have been applied to the privacy rights arena. For example, consensual sodomy remains an offense under the Military Code of Justice despite challenges based on *Lawrence*,[94] and, as mentioned above, statutory laws banning gays and lesbians from adopting children have also been upheld by the courts in the post-*Romer* and *Lawrence* era.[95] These decisions give *Lawrence* a very narrow reading, making statements like: "[The Court] 'didn't locate [any] right directly in the Constitution . . . .' and that the opinion contained 'language and reasoning inconsistent with standard fundamental-rights analysis.'"[96]

---

[87] Andrea Stone, *Drives to Ban Gay Adoption Heat up in 16 States*, U.S.A. TODAY, Feb. 20, 2006), *available at* http://www.usatoday.com/news/nation/2006-02-20-gay-adoption_ x.htm; *see also* Elizabeth L. Maurer, *Errors That Won't Happen Twice: A Constitutional Glance at a Proposed Texas Statute That Will Ban Homosexuals from Foster Parent Eligibility*, 5 APPALACHIAN J.L. 171 (2006); Jenni Hetzel-Gaynor, Note, *What about the Children? The Fight for Homosexual Adoption after* Lawrence *and* Lofton, 51 WAYNE L. REV. 1271 (2005); Christopher D. Jozwiak, Lofton v. Secretary Dep't of Children & Family Servs: *Florida's Gay Adoption Ban under Irrational Equal Protection Analysis*, 23 LAW & INEQ. 407 (2005); Nicole M. Shkedi, Comment, *When Harry Met* <u>Lawrence</u>: *Allowing Gays and Lesbians to Adopt*, 35 SETON HALL L. REV. 873 (2005).

[88] 517 U.S. 620 (1996) (invalidating, on Equal Protection Clause grounds, an amendment to the Colorado state constitution that would have barred local, country, and state legislation banning discrimination on the basis of sexual orientation).

[89] 539 U.S. 558 (2003) (invalidating, on Due Process Clause grounds, sodomy laws in the United States that criminalized private acts of oral or anal sex between consenting adults).

[90] *E.g.*, K.M. Hamill, Romer v. Evans: *Dulling the Equal Protection Gloss on* Bowers v. Hardwick." 77 B.U. L. REV. 655 (1997); K.G. Walsh, *Throwing Stones: Rational Basis Review Triumphs over Homophobia*, 27 SETON HALL L. REV. 1064 (1997); A.R. Amar, *Attainder and Amendment 2:* Romer's *Rightness*, 95 MICH. L. REV. 203 (1996); A.M. Jacobs, Romer *Wasn't Built in a Day: The Subtle Transformation in Judicial Argument over Gay Rights*, 1996 WIS. L. REV. 893 (1996).

[91] *See generally* Henry F. Fradella, Lawrence v. Texas: *Genuine or Illusory Progress for Gay Rights in America*, 39 CRIM. L. BULL. 597 (2003) (predicting that the strained logic of the *Lawrence* decision was likely to produce both further backlash against gay rights, and courts applying the precedential value of the decision in the most limited of ways).

[92] M.E. Papadopoulos, *Inkblot Jurisprudence: Romer v. Evans as a Great Defeat for the Gay Rights Movement*, 7 CORNELL J.L. PUB. POL'Y, 165, 197 (1997).

[93] *Id.*; *see also* Richard D. Dodson, Homosexual Discrimination and Gender: Was Romer v. Evans Really a Victory for Gay Rights?, 35 CAL. W. L. REV. 271, 290 (1999).

[94] United States v. Marcum, 60 M.J. 198 (2004).

[95] Lofton v. Secretary of the Department of Children and Family Services, 358 F.3d 804 (11th Cir. 2004).

[96] John G. Culhane, *Writing On, Around, and Through* Lawrence v. Texas, 38 CREIGHTON L. REV. 493 (2005) (citing *Lofton*, 358 F.3d at 816).

Thus, as Conrad and Schneider predicted, putative backlash against rights that are not completely vindicated appears to be part and parcel of the process of social control.

III. THE SOCIALLY CONSTRUCTED MYTH OF MENTAL ILLNESS

A number of scholars in various disciplines have criticized the medicalized social control of deviant behavior. Numerous scholars who have studied the historical evolution of mental illness have argued that mental illness is nothing more than a "socially constructed phenomenon."[97] The most outspoken of these critics is Thomas Szasz, himself a medical doctor with a specialization in psychiatry. He is considered to be the father of the **anti-psychiatry movement** in the United States with the publication of his book *The Myth of Mental Illness: Foundations of a Theory of Personal Conduct* in 1961.[98] As the title of his book suggests, Szasz does not believe there is such a thing as mental illness. Rather, he believes that medicine, as a powerful institution of social control, has simply labeled everyday problems of living as mental illnesses and done so within the cloak of science that makes it nearly impossible for lay persons to understand what has truly transpired.

Szasz's writing is condemning of psychiatry as a discipline and is often caustic in its tone. Consider that in 1994, he wrote "Anyone with an ear for language will recognize that the boundary that separates the serious vocabulary of psychiatry from the ludicrous lexicon of psychobabble, and both from playful slang, is thin and permeable to fashion."[99] Given both the substance and style of his message, it is not surprising that psychology and psychiatry as disciplines have shunned him and his work. But his writings have been received "more favorably by philosophers, psychologists, sociologists, and civil libertarians, who recognized the merit of [his] cognitive challenge to the concept of mental illness, and the legitimacy of [his] questioning the morality of involuntary psychiatric interventions."[100]

Szasz does not dispute that there are organic illnesses, such as brain lesions, that cause behaviors that appear to be deviant to those without such organic diseases. Szasz recognizes that such organic diseases do, in fact, cause real suffering. Instead, he asserts that "most psychological disorders do not exist at all, and those that do are actually physical diseases with mental consequences."[101] In other words, Szasz takes issue with calling organic illnesses diseases of the mind when they are physical diseases of the brain. Moreover, labeling certain behaviors or misbehaviors as "mental illnesses" not only is an example of medical social control via medical collaboration and medical ideology, but also undercuts the severity of true organic disorders.

In support of Szasz's argument that mental illness is not real, but socially constructed, he points to the history and development of the DSM. Its evolution is largely political, with

---

[97]Jeanne Louise Carriere, *Reconstructing the Grounds for Interdiction*, 54 LA. L. REV. 1199, 1224 (1994); *see also* R.H.S. Mindham et al., *Diagnoses Are Not Diseases*, 161 BRIT. J. PSYCHIATRY 686 (1992); Joel Kovel, *A Critique of DSM-III*, 9 RES. L. DEV. & SOC. CONTROL 127, 135 (1988) ("The mental disorder is the object wrought by the objectifying gaze; it is not so much what the gaze sees as what it constructs"); NICHOLAS N. KITTRIE, THE RIGHT TO BE DIFFERENT; DEVIANCE AND ENFORCED THERAPY (1971).

[98]THOMAS S. SZASZ, THE MYTH OF MENTAL ILLNESS: FOUNDATIONS OF A THEORY OF PERSONAL CONDUCT (rev. ed. 1974) (1961); *see also* THOMAS S. SZASZ, THE MANUFACTURE OF MADNESS 209-41 (1970)

[99]Thomas Szasz, *Mental Illness Is Still a Myth*, 31 SOCIETY 34 (May-June 1994).

[100]*Id.*

[101]Ron Nichwolodoff, *Expert Psychological Opinion Evidence in the Courts*, 6 HEALTH L.J. 279, 286 (1998).

definitions being reached by consensus of committees and sub-committees comprised of representatives from various stake-holding groups. Accordingly, Szasz views the DSM

> not [as a] classification[] of mental disorders that "patients have," but [as] rosters of officially accredited psychiatric diagnoses. This is why in psychiatry, unlike in the rest of medicine, members of "consensus groups" and "task forces," appointed by officers of the APA, make and unmake diagnoses, the membership sometimes voting on whether a controversial diagnosis is or is not a disease. For more than a century, psychiatrists constructed diagnoses, pretended that they are diseases, and no one in authority challenged their deceptions. The result is that few people now realize that diagnoses are not diseases. [102]

There are any number of examples to which one could look to see the validity in Szasz's critique of the DSM. As one article in the *New York Times* put it, "a good percentage of any prison's criminal population would seem to fit the criteria for Antisocial Personality Disorder"; yet, "how could Hollywood or Sunday morning television media-punditry thrive without personalities who exhibit the symptoms of Histrionic Personality Disorder?"[103] The DSM lists "Caffeine Intoxication" as a substance-related disorder that diagnostically requires: "recent consumption of caffeine in excess of 259 mg (e.g. more than 2–3 cups of brewed coffee)" combined with any five symptoms that include the following, nearly all of which are biochemical reactions to caffeine consumption: restlessness, nervousness, excitement, difficulty sleeping, increased urination, increased heartbeat, and increased psychomotor behavior![104] And what of the classification and subsequent declassification of homosexuality as a mental illness discussed above in Section II of this chapter? Even premenstrual syndrome has been elevated to the level of mental illness in the DSM-IV with the creation of the disease "Premenstrual Dysmorphic Disorder."[105]

Szasz is not alone in his critique of the DSM. One scholar summarized the research on the DSM's reliability by saying "reliable progress in reliable diagnosis has been either non-existent or even negative."[106] Consider the landmark study conducted by Rosenhan that led to the publication of his famous article *Being Sane in Insane Places*.[107] In it, Rosenhan and seven colleagues, all of whom were ostensibly in good mental health, got admitted to psychiatric hospitals by complaining they heard voices. They did not exhibit any other signs of psychosis. And, once admitted, they behaved perfectly normally.

> Despite the lack of symptoms and abnormal behaviors, none of the pseudopatients were ever detected by hospital staff. The pseudopatients and all their behaviors were continually viewed in light of their original psychotic diagnoses. "One a person is designated abnormal, all of his other behaviors and characteristics are colored by that label. Indeed, the label is so powerful that many of the pseudopatients' normal behaviors were overlooked or profoundly misinterpreted."[108]

---

[102]Szasz, *supra* note 99, at 34.

[103]*Mental Illness: Defining the Line Between Behavior That's Vexing and Certifiable*, N.Y. TIMES, Dec. 19, 1999.

[104]AMERICAN PSYCHIATRIC ASS'N, DIAGNOSTIC AND STATISTICAL MANUAL OF MENTAL DISORDERS 213 (4th ed. 1994) (diagnostic code 305.90).

[105]*Id.* at 717.

[106]Nichwolodoff, *supra* note 101, at 285; *see also* STUART A. KIRK & HERB KUTCHINS, THE SELLING OF DSM: THE RHETORIC OF SCIENCE IN PSYCHIATRY (Aldine De Gruyter 1992); JAY ZISKIN & DAVID FAUST, COPING WITH PSYCHIATRIC AND PSYCHOLOGICAL TESTIMONY (4th ed., Law & Psych. Press 1988).

[107]David L. Rosenhan, *On Being Sane in Insane Places* 179 SCIENCE 250 (1973).

[108]HEITZEG, *supra* note 8, at 224 (citing Rosenhan, *supra* note 107, at 250-58).

In addition to definitional and reliability problems, the DSM has also been criticized for having medicalized informal deviance, much of which is both temporally and culturally related. For example, the term "magical thinking" is a diagnostic criterium for schizophrenia. Yet, "belief in clairvoyance, telepathy, or a 'sixth sense'" is viewed with esteem if not reverence in some cultures.[109]

The DSM has also been criticized because, over time, certain diagnoses appear to be highly correlated with socio-economic status, although these proposition remain in dispute. Heitzeg, for example, argues that minorities are over-represented in those diagnosed with psychoses, while wealthy Caucasians are rarely so diagnosed.[110] She also asserts that men are much more likely to be diagnosed with schizophrenia and anti-social personality disorder, while women are much more likely to be diagnosed with depression, manic-depression, and obsessive-compulsive disorder.[111] Finally, Heitzeg points out that those who are young are much more likely to be diagnosed with "an overwhelming array of psychiatric conditions."[112] To be fair, though, these sociological criticisms have been disputed in the psychological literature.[113]

Szasz argues that although maintaining social order requires both "treating the sick and punishing criminals," the former should be the role of medicine, while the latter left to the justice system. Moreover, in performing its treatment functions, medicine should limit itself to the treatment of bona-fide diseases, not social constructions of deviance that have been medicalized.

> Medicalizing interpersonal conflicts, that is, disagreements among family members, the members of society, and between citizens and the state, threatens to destroy not only respect for persons as responsible moral agents, but also for the state as an arbiter and dispenser of justice. Let us never forget that the state is an organ of coercion with a monopoly on force—for good or ill. The more the state empowers doctors, the more physicians will strengthen the state (by authenticating political preferences as health values), and the more the resulting union of medicine and the state will enfeeble the individual (by depriving him of the right to reject interventions classified as therapeutic). If that is the kind of society we want, that is the kind we shall get—and deserve.[114]

IV. CONCLUSION

There can be no real argument that medicine acts as a powerful institution of social control in a variety of ways. The medicalization of deviance has produced what *The New York Times* described as "a veritable epidemic of mental illness" when reporting that the U.S. Surgeon General had asserted that "22 percent of the population has a diagnosable mental disorder."[115] And that statistic is a conservative one when compared to other studies, one of which estimated that nearly *half* of the U.S. population suffered from mental illness.[116]

---

[109] *Id.* at 225.

[110] *Id.*

[111] *Id.*

[112] *Id.*

[113] *See, e.g.,* H.N. Garb, *Race Bias, Social Class Bias, and Gender Bias in Clinical Judgment*, 4 CLINICAL PSYCHOL.: SCI. & PRACTICE 99-120 (1997).

[114] Szasz, *supra* note 99.

[115] *Mental Illness: Defining the Line Between Behavior That's Vexing and Certifiable*, N.Y. TIMES, Dec. 19, 1999.

[116] *Survey: Mental Illness Strikes 48% of U.S. Population*, N.Y. TIMES, Jan. 14, 1994, at 1A.

As some critics have pointed out, as the DSM has continually broadened its definitions of what constitutes mental illness, a corresponding increase in the number of routine behaviors have been labeled as mental illness, including excessive drinking, over- and under-eating, and "compulsive gambling."[117] The medicalization of deviance in this manner has real consequences. The medical model of deviance is driven, in part, by a profit motive. As more behaviors qualify as sickness, the need for specialists to diagnose and then treat the sickness increases. More clients means more money. That is not to say that the members of the AMA or APA are not necessarily acting with the best of intentions, but there can be no doubt that the medicalization of deviance has been a major contributor to the ever-rising costs of health care.[118]

In addition to the economic consequences of medicalization on health care costs, putative backlash against medicalization has created many other problems with real cost—both economic and human. Consider the fact that in the last twenty years, we have heard repeated calls for people "taking responsibility" for their own actions as science has continually offered excuses for their deviant behavior.[119] In spite of the fact that insanity defenses rarely work, people get angry when they see criminal defendants like John Hinckley, Lorena Bobbit, Jeffery Dahmer, and Lyle and Eric Menedez, just to name a few, arguing that they should not be held responsible for their actions. This backlash against medicalization has endangered a significant change in the *legal* definitions of mental illness for a host of criminal and civil justice proceedings including insanity, diminished capacity, involuntary civil commitment, and guardianship and conservatorship.[120]

These definitional changes in what qualifies as a bona-fide mental illness in court impacts due process as well as our pocket books. People adjudicated to be sane, guilty, and then criminally incarcerated are now finding themselves labeled mentally ill upon their parole, resulting in their continued involuntary incarceration in a mental health setting in the name of incapacitative social control.[121]

An even more alarming consequences of medicalization as the DSM has broadened its scope of mental illness is the law's narrowing its definition for insanity defense purposes. Those who are truly insane now have a harder time than ever proving it, resulting in correctional populations filled with the mentally ill. The number of people under correctional supervision in the United State exceeds five million; nearly 1.7 million of these people are incarcerated in prisons and jails.[122] Estimates of the percentage of incarcerated people with serious mental disorders range from a conservative 7.2 percent[123] to 20 percent in certain metropolitan jails.[124]

---

[117]STANTON PEELE, THE DISEASING OF AMERICA: ADDICTION TREATMENT OUT OF CONTROL (Lexington Books 1990).

[118]*See* CONRAD & SCHNEIDER, *supra* note 2, at 254-55.

[119]*E.g.*, ALAN M. DERSHOWITZ, THE ABUSE EXCUSE AND OTHER COP-OUTS, SOB STORIES, AND EVASIONS OF RESPONSIBILITY (Little, Brown & Co., 1994).

[120]*See, e.g.*, Bruce J. Winick, *Ambiguities in The Legal Meaning And Significance of Mental Illness,* 1 PSYCH. PUB. POL. AND L. 534 (1995).

[121]*E.g.*, Robert D. Miller, *The Continuum of Coercion: Constitutional and Clinical Considerations in the Treatment of Mentally Disordered Persons*, 74 DENV. U.L. REV. 1169 (1997).

[122]BUREAU OF JUSTICE STATISTICS, U.S. DEP'T OF JUSTICE, CORRECTIONAL POPULATIONS IN THE UNITED STATES iii (1996).

[123]T. Howard Stone, *Therapeutic Implications of Incarceration for Persons with Severe Mental Disorders: Searching for Rational Health Policy*, 24 AM. J. CRIM. L. 283, 291 (1997) (citing E. FULLER TORREY, ET AL., CRIMINALIZING THE SERIOUSLY MENTALLY ILL: THE ABUSE OF JAILS AS MENTAL HOSPITALS 13 (1992)).

[124]Fox Butterfield, *Asylums Behind Bars: A Special Report; Prisons Replace Hospitals for the Nation's Mentally Ill*, THE N.Y. TIMES, Mar. 5, 1998, at A1; *see also* Stone, *supra* note 123, at 288-89 (*citing* Linda A. Teplin, *Psychiatric and Substance Abuse Disorders Among Male Urban Jail Detainees*, 84 AM. J. PUB. HEALTH 290, 292 (1994) (reporting range from 6.2% - 9.4%)).

The explanations proffered for the prevalence of mentally ill persons in correctional institutions are varied but most frequently are attributed to the "deinstitutionalization" movement of the 1960s and 1970s,[125] the economic shift from mental health spending to correctional spending in the 1980s and 1990s,[126] the lack of insurance coverage for the mentally ill,[127] and "aggressive prosecution and incarceration for drug-related offenses,"[128] the latter two of which are part of the putative backlash against medicalization.

Regardless of the causes of the high numbers of mentally ill persons in correctional institutions, both empirical research and common sense tell us that the mentally ill criminal offender often does not receive adequate treatment while incarcerated. "The lack of adequate mental health resources exacerbates existing serious mental conditions for inmates, resulting in decompensation in inmate mental and physical health, inmate suicides, and related complications in inmate management for correctional officials."[129] Scholars have repeatedly demonstrated that the mentally ill inmate fails to adapt to life in jail or prison on every measure of psychological adaptation.[130] This fact often manifests itself in significantly higher rates of disciplinary infractions[131] and suicide rates[132] for mentally ill inmates than for inmates who are not mentally ill.

Numerous books and articles have been published on the lack of treatment for mentally ill jail and prison inmates. Many such scholarly works not only point out the empirical evidence that we have a national crisis on our hands in dealing with mentally ill inmates, but also conduct a detailed examination of inmate's rights in their calls for reform, covering legal arguments from substantive and procedural due process rights and equal protection to the application of the American with Disabilities Act[133] and Section 504 of the Rehabilitation Act of 1973.[134] The calls for reform have largely gone unheeded while the conditions faced by inmates with untreated mental illness usually prevent them "from obtaining access to prison programs or rehabilitation plans which could facilitate release and improve post-release success. As a result, inmates with severe mental disorders are virtually condemned to a cycle of criminal offending."[135] Thus, mentally ill inmates may serve longer sentences because of their inability to qualify for early release, and, upon their release, are likely to find themselves yet again involved with the criminal justice system. We must recognize that this is a problem not only for the individual, but for society at large.

---

[125]Stone, *supra* note 123, at 291 (citing Mary L. Durham, *The Impact of Deinstitutionalization on the Current Treatment of the Mentally Ill,* INT'L J. L. & PSYCHIATRY 117, 123-24 (1989)); *see also* Butterfield, *supra* note 124.

[126]Stone, *supra* note 123 (citing Robert D. Miller, *Economic Factors Leading to Diversion of the Mentally Disordered Offender from the Civil to the Criminal Commitment Systems,* 15 INT'L J. L. & PSYCHIATRY 1 (1991)).

[127]Jeffrey Rubin, *Paying for Care: Legal Developments in the Financing of Mental Health Services*, 28 HOUS. L. REV. 143, 162-64 (1991).

[128]Stone, *supra* note 123, at 291.

[129]*Id.* at 285.

[130]*Id.* at 299 (citing Hans Toch, et al., COPING: MALADAPTATION IN PRISONS 42, 50-54 (1989)).

[131]*Id.* (citing Toch, et al., *supra* note 130, at xvii, xix).

[132]*Id.* (citing Torrey, et al., *supra* note 123, at 60-61).

[133]*E.g.*, Stone, *supra* note 123 (citing, *inter alia*, 42 U.S.C. §§ 12101-213 (1990)).

[134]*Id.* (citing 29 U.S.C. § 794 (1973)).

[135]Stone, *supra* note 123, at 357.

CHAPTER THREE
FORENSIC CLINICAL ASSESSMENT FOR THE JUSTICE PROFESSIONAL

I. OVERVIEW OF CLINICAL ASSESSMENT

In Chapter One, a narrow definition of forensic psychology was the clinical assessment of patients under the jurisdiction of a court of law, whether criminal or civil, as part of the judicial process.[1] At that time, however, we did not define clinical assessment. Within the realm of the forensic behavioral sciences, clinical assessment may be conceptualized as the formal and informal techniques used "to evaluate psychological functioning and to diagnose psychiatric disorders."[2] Clinical assessment may also be used to uncover the *etiology*—or causes—of a patient's problems. And it may even be used to determine both the appropriate course of treatment and the subsequent evaluation of that treatment. Clinical assessment combines all the knowledge obtained through objective tests and other clinical applications into a succinct, subjective image of mental condition. Accordingly, it should be considered both science and art.[3]

Scientifically speaking, *clinical assessment* can be defined "as the process of evaluating the characteristics, strengths, and weaknesses of an individual as a basis for informed decision making."[4] It is a process that involves planning, data collection, examination, and judgment on behalf of the individual clinician. The information gathered during the process of clinical evaluation is derived from both objective and subjective sources that will be explored in greater detail later in this chapter.

One of the primary goals of clinical assessment is to arrive at an appropriate diagnosis. A *diagnosis* is nothing more than a conclusion that a person is suffering from a particular disorder based upon the set of signs and symptoms exhibited during the course of assessment. *Signs* are objective manifestations of illness, like high blood pressure, sweating, temperature, etc. In contrast, *symptoms* are what patients describe as their "subjective experience, such as pain," something than cannot be objectively measured.[5]

> It is a process of inclusion and exclusion. By comparing the person's signs and symptoms with standard classifications of mental illnesses, the diagnostician decides which illnesses to consider as possibilities. By noting the absence of other manifestations, he or she decides which illnesses to exclude from further consideration. The latter part of the process is known as differential diagnosis.[6]

It is important to keep in mind that any particular diagnosis may be right or wrong since arriving at a diagnosis always involves some level of subjective interpretation by the clinician.

---

[1]*See* Chapter One.

[2]DONALD W. GOODWIN & SAMUEL B. GUZE, PSYCHIATRIC DIAGNOSIS 293 (4th ed. 1989).

[3]NORMAN TALLENT, THE PRACTICE OF PSYCHOLOGICAL ASSESSMENT (1992).

[4]Robert J. Gregory, *Clinical Assessment and Diagnosis*, 26 *in* FOUNDATIONS OF CLINICAL PSYCHOLOGY (Salvatore Cullari, ed., 1998).

[5]Jules B. Gerard, *An Overview of Clinical Evaluation, in* ALEXANDER D. BROOKS, LAW, PSYCHIATRY, AND THE MENTAL HEALTH SYSTEM 21 n.1 (1974).

[6]*Id.* at 21.

Clinical assessment usually also includes a ***prognosis***—an educated prediction regarding the likely course and outcome of an illness or disorder. And, finally, assessment often concludes with recommendations for the courses of action that should be taken to treat the individual in light of the diagnosis and prognosis.

II. SPECIFICS OF CLINICAL ASSESSMENT

Clinicians, both medical and psychological, gather information from an expansive pool of sources and information. Correct diagnoses and effective treatment plans can only be determined after reviewing many facets of a person. Assessment of behavior, both past and present, is only one part of the overall assessment of pathological conditions. A proper psychiatric evaluation therefore contains three parts: a medical examination; a personal history; and a mental status examination.[7] Psychological evaluation beyond a basic psychiatric evaluation requires even more in the way of clinical assessment.

A. Psychiatric Examination

Numerous physical causes can account for what might appear to be a mental illness. Physical illness such as "cardiovascular disease, endocrine abnormalities, metabolic disturbances, vitamin deficiency, drugs and toxins, infectious diseases, tumors, immune diseases, trauma, . . . neurological conditions," and organic brain injuries such as lesions must be ruled out before a psychiatric diagnosis is made.[8] Any number of apparent cognitive problems might be caused by "overmedication, inappropriate medication, poor diet, depression, environmental deficiency, sensory deprivation, poor eyesight, or impaired hearing."[9]

Conducting a thorough physical examination requires the use of a number of diagnostic tools and procedures. Of course, the first step would be a traditional physical examination. Keep in mind such an examination is performed by a physician (an M.D. or D.O.), not a clinical psychologist (a Ph.D. or a Psy.D.). A traditional physical includes an audio-visual inspection of the body and blood tests to screen for "anemia, infection, and malignancies; . . . syphilis; vitamin . . . and folate levels; and . . . abnormal liver, kidney, and thyroid function";[10] HIV; and Lyme disease. Beyond the usual visual evaluation, an electrocardiogram should be performed to assess heart functioning since it is related to the activities of the autonomic nervous system (ANS). Changes in autonomic nervous system functioning have been linked to many types of behavioral changes.[11]

---

[7]Gerard, *supra* note 5, at 21.

[8]Jan Ellen Rein, *Proceeding of the Conference on Ethical Issues in Representing Older Clients: Clients with Destructive and Socially Harmful Choices – What's an Attorney to Do?: Within and Beyond the Competency Construct*, 62 FORDHAM L. REV. 1101, 1123 (1994).

[9]*Id.* at 1121 (citing Gerald K. Goodenough, *The Lack of Objectivity of Physician Evaluations in Geriatric Guardianship Cases*, 14 J. CONTEMP. L. 53, 55 (1988)); *see also* Joan M. Krauskopf, *New Developments in Defending Commitment of the Elderly*, 10 N.Y.U. REV. L. & SOC. CHANGE 367 (1980).

[10]*Id.* at 1123.

[11]GERALD C. DAVISON & JOHN M. NEALE, ABNORMAL PSYCHOLOGY 91 (7th ed. 1998).

Brain imagining is an important part of a complete neurological examination. Electroencephalograms (EEGs), which measure brain wave activity, can be used to rule out epilepsy and other seizure disorders.[12] Using computerized axial tomography (CAT scans) and magnetic resonance imaging (MRIs), the structure and physical integrity of the brain can be assessed.[13] And using even more advanced diagnostic tools, such as positron emission tomography (PET scans), actual brain functioning can even be assessed,[14] something that has great potential as evidence in courts of law.[15]

Finally, a neurochemical assessment of the patient should be routinely completed as an important part of the physical examination . This should include toxicological screenings for drugs (both illicit and prescribed), as well as environmental toxins such as heavy metal, since many drugs and toxins can affect behavior to such a degree that they can mimic the symptoms of psychoses and mood disorders.[16]

As should be evidence from this short overview of the physical examination, the cooperation of health care professionals in several fields are necessary. Medical doctors, especially neurologists and psychiatrists, should work hand-in-hand with psychologists to ensure complete clinical assessment.

B. Case History

Obtaining a *case history* is important because present symptoms need to be put into a historical framework to make a proper diagnosis. Any number of factors can cause symptoms that, at any given point in time, appear to indicate mental illness. But psychopathological symptoms can be caused by any number of factors. The ingestion of psychedelic drugs, for example, can cause hallucinations. But if a clinician learns that hallucinations have existed over a period of time, that data allow the clinician to put the symptoms in context, allowing a more reliable diagnosis to be made.

It should be noted that clinical assessment (including the taking of a case history) is generally used to determine a course of treatment. Treatment, in the forensic setting, however, is often secondary, if a concern at all. Forensic assessment is primarily considered with arriving at a valid and reliable diagnosis, and then assessing functioning in light of that diagnosis within the confines of specific questions of capacity posed by the law. The general techniques of clinical assessment outlined herein are important to both forensic evaluation and general psychological assessment and treatment.

---

[12]WILLIAM A. MCKIM, DRUGS AND BEHAVIOR: AN INTRODUCTION TO BEHAVIORAL PHARMACOLOGY 33-34 (4th ed. 2000).

[13]Rein, *supra* note 8, at 1123 24; DAVISON & NEALE, *supra* note 11, at 87-88.

[14]*Id.* at 89.

[15]For an overview of how brain imaging techniques are used in courts of law, *see* Jennifer Kulynych, Note: *Psychiatric Neuroimaging Evidence: A High-Tech Crystal Ball?*, 49 STAN. L. REV. 1249 (1997).

[16]*See generally* MCKIM, *supra* note 12; KEN LISKA, DRUGS AND THE HUMAN BODY WITH IMPLICATIONS FOR SOCIETY (6th ed. 2000); R.E. FERNER, FORENSIC PHARMACOLOGY: MEDICINES, MAYHEM, AND MALPRACTICE (1996).

1. Identifying Data and Presenting Problem

A case history has four parts, although they overlap to a certain degree. A case history should always start with *identifying data:* the patient's name, age, sex, race, and the time, date, and place where the interview occurred. This is information should be summarized in a sentence or two. The case history should then specify the *presenting problem:* Why is the patient being seen now? What symptoms is the patient currently experiencing? When did these symptoms start? Was the onset of a symptom gradual or sudden? Since onset, have the symptoms been constant, chronic with some level of variability, or episodic? What changes in both behavior and daily activities (e.g., eating, sleeping, socializing, working) accompanied the onset of the symptoms?[17] Some of the information gained in this phase of the case history necessarily involves obtaining some past history, but the past history obtained in this section of the case history is limited to the onset of symptoms concerning the presenting problem. In contrast, a complete past history involves the obtaining of information that goes far beyond the scope of the presenting problem.

2. Medical History

A *medical history* contains as much information as possible about a person's past physical and mental health. Knowing about prior hospitalizations, whether for physical or psychiatric reasons, might allow a clinician to gather highly insightful information from other medical sources. A history of mental illness, for example, sheds light on the presenting problem—especially since the psychopharmacological treatment of some mental illness can cause other behavioral symptoms. Someone previously diagnosed with a tumor might be presenting current symptoms that are a function of that physical abnormality. A long-time drug or alcohol abuser might be experiencing toxic psychosis. Side-effects of cancer treatments might be responsible for symptoms. Nerve damage from a prior surgical procedure might be responsible for some presenting symptoms. A current diagnosis of a terminal illness can explain current depression and/or anxiety. Finding out about such information from the patient's past helps rule out certain diagnoses as well as treatments.

3. Social History

In addition to gathering information about a patient's medical history, a past history should also include information about the patient's social history and family history. A *social history* includes information such as the number of "years of education and how well the patient did in school from the standpoint of grades and adjustment; military and job history; marital history; . . . number and ages of children";[18] employment history; sexual history; developmental milestones (e.g., when person walked, talked, hit puberty, etc.); major turning points in the patient's life; recreational activities, hobbies, and other interests; number and stability of important friendships; and noted difficulties with authority, including a criminal history, if any.[19] The social history should also include the patient's self-description of how he or she sees himself/herself, the current situation, and the likely outcome of the presenting problem/situation.

---

[17]GOODWIN & GUZE, *supra* note 2, at 311-12; *see also* Gerard, *supra* note 5, at 22.

[18]*Id.* at 312.

[19]Gerard, *supra* note 5, at 23.

4. Family History

A *family history* concerns patient's upbringing and relationship with family members. Of particular importance are factors such a history of parental separation or divorce; substance and/or other types of abuse by family members; parents' age, educational, and vocational backgrounds; the number and age of siblings, as well as their educational, vocational, and social backgrounds; the individual's early memories of family interactions (something especially important for psychodynamic and cognitive clinicians); and the medical and mental health history of close family members.

5. A Word of Caution on Obtaining Case Histories

In a normal, non-forensic clinical setting, a case history is obtained during clinical interviews primarily to learn about the patient and his or her life experiences. For example, if a patient in psychotherapy tells a therapist that he or she had an "abusive" mother, that tells the clinician something important about how the patient sees himself or herself, the patient's mother, and the nature of the mother-child relationship. The value of that perception in a forensic evaluation, however, is quite different since therapeutic treatment of the patient is not the goal of forensic clinical assessment (although it ought to be the goal of correctional psychology). In a forensic setting, the veracity of case history information is arguably much more important than in non-forensic setting. From that standpoint, then, one of the shortcomings of obtaining a case history from a patient is that such data are self-reported. Accordingly, not only will much of the information be hearsay but also will be colored by the patient's own memory (which may be impaired) and psychological framework (which can be severely distorted by any number of mental illnesses). It is therefore critical from a legal/evidentiary standpoint to obtain case history information from additional sources, such as family members, coworkers, friends, law enforcement (if applicable), and other health care providers (such as the patient's primary care physician). Of course, obtaining a complete past history from such varied sources can be quite time consuming. Often, psychologists and psychiatrist rely on others to gather such information, such as psychiatric social workers or nurses, especially in inpatient and forensic settings.[20]

C. Clinical Interviews

A clinical interview is a face-to-face interaction in which the interviewer attempts to obtain information regarding an individual's current condition, feelings, beliefs, and/or opinions.[21] Clinical interviews go beyond obtaining a case history as discussed in the last section; they are designed to obtain an overview of an individual's general level of functioning at a given time. Information gathered during a clinical interview can lay the foundation for further evaluation and testing, as well as determining appropriate avenues for treatment or therapy.

---

[20] *E.g.*, Michael L. Lindsey, *Responses to the Conference: Ethical Issues in Interviewing, Counseling, and the Use of Psychological Data with Child and Adolescent Clients*, 64 FORDHAM L. REV. 2035, 2046 (1996).

[21] Arthur N. Wiens, *Structured Clinical Interviews for Adults in* GERALD GOLDSTEIN & MICHEL HERSEN (EDS.) HANDBOOK OF PSYCHOLOGICAL ASSESSMENT (2d ed. 1990).

Clinical interviews can be unstructured or structured. In *unstructured interviews,* a majority of the questions asked are open-ended (i.e., they cannot be answered with a simple yes or no response). This style allows the interviewer the freedom to explore topics that he or she might not have thought of previous to the interaction and find an appreciation for what the individual regards as important information. Most clinical interviews are unstructured. In *structured interviews,* the interviewer usually uses a rather stringent interview schedule and set of prepared questions. This style is optimal in reducing variations between interviewers but might be too inflexible and/or time consuming in a particular setting.

The most common and widely used type of clinical interview is the *mental status examination* (MSE). It is a semi-structured interview designed to broadly assess a patient's "mood, affect, thinking, behavior, and various aspects of cognitive function such as attention, concentration, memory, abstract thinking and judgment."[22] The purpose of such an exam is not only to determine an individual's current condition, but also to serve as a guide for further assessment or formal diagnosis.[23] The MSE is administered in its purest semi-structured form only under particular circumstances, such as upon admission to an inpatient unit or to determine the presence of psychotic symptoms. The information obtained in MSE is more often gathered during longer, unstructured interviews presuming that circumstances allow for such patient-clinician interaction.

Although the actual number of parts in a MSE varies depending on the authority one consults, the MSE is generally divided into six components: (1) general appearance, attitude, and behavior; (2) speech and language functioning as indicators of thought processes; (3) affect and emotional functioning; (4) thought content; (5) sensorium and cognitive functioning; and (6) insight and judgment.[24]

1. <u>General Appearance, Attitude, and Behavior</u>

A mental status examination usually begins by asking the patient's name, age, and marital status. Observation is the key to assessment in this category. The examiner should make careful observations regarding a person's general appearing, including how a patient is dressed and groomed. For example, are clothes clean? Is hair combed? Are there tattoos and body piercings? While any one piece of such data may not be significant in and of itself, how a patient presents himself/herself overall can be relevant to the diagnosis. Goodwin and Guze offer the following examples: schizophrenics and depressives are often poorly groomed or dirty; looking much older than one's age might indicate long-term abuse of alcohol or drugs; attempts to hide one's identity using hooded clothing, sunglasses, and the like might indicate paranoia.[25] Visibly notable scars or burns could indicate self-destructive behaviors.

Further observations should be made about an individual's attitude toward the examiner. Is the patient hostile, indifferent, suspicious, cooperative, relaxed, etc.? Like with appearance, one's attitude can also be a diagnostic indicator.

---

[22]Rein, *supra* note 8, at1123.

[23]*See generally* P.T. Trzapacz, & R.W. Baker, The Psychiatric Mental Status Examination (1993); Linda Denise Oakey, Psychiatric Primary Care (1997).

[24]Gerard, *supra* note 5, at 23.

[25]Goodwin & Guze, *supra* note 2, at 302.

Finally, the observable behaviors of the patient should be carefully scrutinized. Of particular importance is the patient's level of arousal. Are they "hyperalert," alert, drowsy, stuporous, or near comatose. Does the patient make eye contact? Do they have any odd mannerisms (e.g., pacing or hand-wringing) or motor agitation (e.g., ticks or tremors) or retardation (e.g., slow movement, slumping)? What types of facial expressions were used, if any. Certain behaviors are often tell-tale signs of particular disorders. For example, *"negativism,* doing the opposite of what is requested" or *echopraxia,* in which movements of another person are imitated, and *waxy flexibility* (also known as *posturing*) in which awkward positions are maintained for long periods of time without apparent discomfort are rare symptoms that are usually only seen in schizophrenics or other psychotics.[26]

2. Speech and Language Functioning as Indicators of Thought Processes

This category is concerned both with a patient's rate of speech and the manner in which speech is communicated. *Rate of speech* is obviously concerned with how slowly or quickly one talks. The period of time it takes for the patient to answer a question is also an important concern. Additionally important are a patient's tone and volume. Manics, for example, might speak very rapidly, loudly, and with great voice inflection. Depressives, in contrast, might speak slowly and without change in voice intonation.

Language skills are also a part of this assessment. Is the person fluent in the language being spoken? Does the person use words correctly? Vocabulary can be a sign of intelligence level. Can a person correctly name people, places, or objects, or is the person confused? Of course, if the person does not talk, a phenomenon referred to as *mutism,* it is likely to be a very short diagnostic interview.

Oddities in speech content should be noted here, as they indicate disturbances in thought processes. Do they *perseverate* in their speech (repeat the same word or phrase, referred to as the noun *perseveration*)? Are nonsensical or made-up words, called *neologisms*, used? Sometime a patient might give a commonplace word a special meaning or significance that is understood only by the patient, a phenomenon known as *metonymy*. *Echolalia* is the senseless, parrot-like repetition of another's words or phrases. Or perhaps the patient speaks in *clang associations*— groups of words that sound alike, but are not related to each other in meaning (i.e., rhyming and punning). Severely ill patients might talk in what is referred to as *"word salad,"* a collection of words and phrases that have nothing to do with each other.

Finally, abnormalities in the expression of thoughts and ideas should be noted in this area. *Blocking* occurs when there is an abrupt interruption in the middle of the expression of an idea, which is followed by an inability to recall what was being expressed. *Tangentiality* occurs when a person starts to make a point, but then fails to follow a logical form of expression to reach a conclusion. Care should be taken not to confuse tangentiality with "flight of ideas." *Flight of ideas* occurs when someone jumps from one idea to the next, but the ideas are connected in some circumstantial way. But when there is no association between the jump from one idea to the next so the patient is incoherent, the patient is said to suffer from *loose associations.* Finally, although somewhat more difficult to detect in a clinical interview, especially a brief or initial one, patients suffering from some impairment of memory might engage in *confabulation,* the fabrication of facts or events to fill in gaps in memory.

---

[26]*Id.* at 303.

3. Affect and Emotional Functioning

This category is concerned with the patients *affect* or mood and the manner in which it is displayed. Affect has four dimensions: range, stability, appropriateness, and intensity. In terms of range, the examiner attempts to discern if a constricted or full range of emotions are being displayed by the patient.

The stability of affect concerns how mood changes. At one extreme, a patient might display *flat affect* in which the person's apparent mood does not vary at all but is constant even when provided with stimuli that should change affect, such as failing to smile when a joke is told. *Blunted affect* is a severe reduction in the intensity of externalized feelings, but with minimal responsiveness in terms of changing moods. See that blunted affect is different from flat affect where there is no observable changes in mood. Being non-reactive to tragic news is an example of flat affect, while a minor frown accompanied by a shrug of the shoulders would be an example of blunted affect. Depressives can exhibit flat affect, showing little or no emotion whatsoever. At the other extreme, affect can be *labile,* meaning highly variable. Manics often shift rapidly between one mood and the next.

When trying to observe the manner in which an individual expresses his or her mood, an examiner also tries try to determine the appropriateness of affect. Simply stated, does an individual react appropriately to a certain stimulus? If not, the patient would be said to have *inappropriate affect.* Laughter while communicating that a loved parent or spouse just passed away is an example of inappropriate affect.

Finally, the intensity of affect is of concern. Does the mood appear to be mild, moderate, or severe? There are "normal" parameters for the expression of mood. Hysterical crying in front of a stranger is an example of an unusually intense expression of emotion.

4. Thought Content

Examination of thought content is concerned with whether the patient has irrational thoughts, thought fixations, or disturbances of thought that fall into one of four categories: illusions, delusions, hallucinations, and pathological suicidal ideations.

Illusions are misinterpretations of actual stimuli. As such, they are disturbances in perception that involve a real object that anyone can perceive being interpreted as something it is not. Seeing a paint spot on a wall as a poisonous spider, or seeing tree branches at night as a monster are both examples of illusions. Illusions are very common with delirium.

Delusions are fixed, false beliefs. They are contrary to reality insofar as evidence contrary to the belief will not cause a delusional person to change his or her belief. The most common types of delusions include: *persecutory delusions,* the belief that someone or something is "out to get" the patient; *delusions of grandeur,* the belief that the patient is someone of great or special importance; *delusions of nihilism,* the belief that the world or one's mind, body, or self does not exist; *somatic delusions,* the belief that one is suffering from a disease or some biological abnormality (which can include distortions of body image); *delusions of control,* the belief that someone or something (e.g., the devil, aliens) controls oneself; *erotic delusions,* the belief that one is loved by a famous person; *delusions of though insertion or withdrawal,* beliefs that thoughts are being implanted in or taken from one's mind by other people or forces; and *delusions of thought broadcasting,* the belief that one's own thoughts can be heard by others.

Hallucinations are false sensory perceptions. When one is hallucinating, one perceives something that is not really there. Hallucinations can affect all five senses, although those affecting the senses of hearing, sight, and touch are the most common forms. When one "hears" things that are not there, one is said to suffer from *auditory hallucinations.* These are most commonly associated with schizophrenia, chronic substance abuse, and serveral affective disorders.[27] When one "sees" things that are not there, one is said to suffer from *visual hallucinations,* something most frequently observed in patients that have either acquired some type of brain damage or using psychedelic drugs.[28] Hallucinations of touch (e.g., feeling that bugs are crawling on or under one skin called) are called *haptic* or *tactile hallucinations,* common in schizophrenia and with certain substance abuse.[29] False perceptions of taste are *gustatory hallucinations.* And false perceptions of smell are called *olfactory hallucinations,* commonly associated with seizure disorder of the temporal lobe.[30] Other common disturbances of perception include "*depersonalization,* the feeling one has changed in a bizarre way; *derealization,* the feeling the environment has changed; and *déjà vu,* a sense of familiarity with a new perception."[31]

The examiner should not just note when hallucinations are present but also should explore the content of the hallucinations. If the patient reports hearing voices, does he or she recognize the voice? How often is the voice heard? If heard only at certain times, when?[32] What does the voice say?[33] Where does the voice come from (e.g., inside the person's head or externally)?

Other types of major thought disturbances are obsessions and compulsions. *Obsessions* are intrusive and pervasive thoughts, images, or urges. They may be rational or irrational, even nonsensical. Clearly there are times when everyone cannot get a thought out of their head. But an obsession becomes the focus of a person's thought content, no matter how hard they might try to rid themselves of the thought. And true obsessions cause the person experiencing them great anxiety. In order to relieve that anxiety, the sufferer may engage in compulsive behaviors. *Compulsions* are the actions used to relieve the stress produced by obsessive thoughts. Moreover, they are something the experiencer feels compelled to do. If they do not engage in the compulsive behavior, they may believe that something horrible will occur. Sometimes compulsive behaviors are directly and logically tied to the underlying obsessive thought. For example, someone obsessed with germs might ritualistically wash their hands, even to the point of making their hands bleed. Other times, compulsions are magical, ritualistic behaviors that have little to do with the underlying obsessive thought. For example repetitive checking of major appliances or door locks might be related to obsessive sexual thoughts. The person experiencing obsessions and compulsions may realize how bizarre or irrational their thoughts and behaviors are, but they cannot change their behavior. They are driven to them, making the presence of these thought disturbances highly traumatic for the sufferer.

---

[27]GOODWIN & GUZE, *supra* note 2, at 305.

[28]*Id.*

[29]*Id.*

[30]*Id.*

[31]*Id.* at 305-06.

[32]Hallucinations experienced as one is trying to fall asleep are referred to hypnogogic hallucinations. They are common even in "normal" people. *Id.* at 305.

[33]If the voice tells the person to do or not to do something, the hallucination is referred to be an auditory hallucination of the command subtype.

Finally, there are **pathological ideations,** persistent thought content concerned with either killing oneself or someone else. The former is called a **suicidal ideation,** while the latter is called a **homicidal ideation.** If such ideations are passive, they manifest themselves from time to time, but a plan to carry out the thoughts combined with intent to follow through on the plan are not present. When such a plan and intent are present, however, the ideation is said to be an active one.

5. Sensorium and Cognitive Functioning

This category deals with brief assessment of cognitive functioning by exploring one's level of awareness, and one's ability to think in different ways. More extensive tests of cognition are carried out after a mental status exam is performed if cognitive impairment is indicated.

The awareness component of cognitive functioning is concerned both with sensorium and memory functioning. **Sensorium** is a term used to refer to four levels of orientation: person, place, time, and situation. A patient is "oriented times four" when he knows who he is, where he is, when it is (generally), and why he is there. Asking a series of questions to make sure the person is oriented with respect to each of the four dimensions (e.g., Do you know what day is it? Can you tell me where we are and why we are here?) is the way in which sensorium is tested.

Memory is also minimally assessed as part of a mental status exam. Remote memory is often assessed by asking things about the person's past that can then be verified (e.g., Where did you go to high school?), or if not, to put remote events in historical context (e.g., Who was the U.S. president during the civil war? In approximately what time frame did the Second World War occur?). Recent memory can be assessed by asking what the patient had for breakfast or did last night. And immediate recall memory is often tested by asking the patient to repeat three words (normally objects like a book, a airplane, and a comet) back to the examiner. After the passage of five to fifteen minutes, the patient is asked to repeat the three items again.

Current intellectual functioning can be assessed in a variety of ways. It is important, though, to be sure that any assessment of intellectual functioning be conducted via questions that are appropriate for the patient's age, background, and educational level. Attention and concentration is frequently tested by asking the person to do what is known as "serial sevens"—counting backward from 100 in increments of seven. Those who are cognitively impaired usually cannot do more than two or three in the series. If impairment is noted doing serial sevens, the patient might be asked to do the subtractions in increments of three or two to see if that makes any difference. Visual-spacial functioning is often tested by asking the patient to draw two intersecting pentagons. Intellectual functioning can also be assessed by asking the patient to write a sentence. If the sentence is not meaningful, or it is not a sentence at all (i.e., lacking a subject and a verb), cognitive impairment is indicated. The ability to process simple written commands is also a good indicator of cognitive functioning. For example, a patient might be given a card that reads, "close your eyes." If the patient fails to read (or reads but fails to do what was requested), cognitive impairment is evidenced (provided the person is simply just not being cooperative). Finally, vocabulary used during the course of the interview, already covered as part of the assessment of speech, language, and thought process, may also be a good indicator of intellectual functioning.

6. Insight and Judgment

This category is primarily concerned with whether an individual is aware of problems he is experiencing (***insight***), and whether he can adequately judge or assess situations in which the patient finds himself (***judgment***). It is arguably the most subjective section of the mental status exam. It will be very meaningful when dealing with seriously ill individuals but also may be helpful in assessing the extent to which even a non-serious mental disorder has impacted a person's overall functioning. For example, a patient might display good insight and judgment in one sphere (e.g., professionally), but lack insight and exercise poor judgment in another arena (e.g., in intimate associations).

Insight might be assessed by asking the patient if he knows why a clinical interview is being conducted. One who demonstrates some insight into a problem will acknowledge that he or she is mentally ill. A lack of awareness of mental dysfunction, in contrast, shows poor insight.

Judgment is more concerned with a person's ability to make reasonable decisions in spite of their illness and whatever level of insight into it they may have. Asking a person to explain a proverb (e.g., What does "the early bird catches the worm" mean?), an analogy (e.g., How are flies and dogs alike?), or to answer a question such as what the patient would do if he or she found a letter on the sidewalk that was stamped, addressed and sealed, are typical ways in which judgment is assessed.

D. The Mini-Mental Status Exam

Conducting a full mental status examination requires sufficient time to conduct a thorough clinical interview. In some situations there is insufficient time to conduct a full mental status examination, yet a quick assessment of functioning is needed, such as when law enforcement suspects someone is mentally ill and a determination needs to be made if that person should be taken into emergency protective custody.[34] Other times, it may be deemed desirable to quantify mental status function as a part of a larger full mental status examination. The primary tool for accomplishing either task is called the ***Mini-Mental Status Exam*** (MMSE). It was developed by Folstein et al. in 1975 and can be administered in approximately fifteen minutes.[35]

The MMSE measures cognitive functioning on a scale of 0 to 30. Performance on it varies by both age and educational level.

> There is an inverse relationship between MMSE scores and age, ranging from a median of 29 for those 18 to 24 years of age, to 25 for individuals 80 years of age and older. The median MMSE score is 29 for individuals with at least 9 years of schooling, 26 for those with 5 to 8 years of schooling, and 22 for those with 0 to 4 years of schooling.[36]

Some sample questions from the Folstein MMSE appear in Figure 4.1.

---

[34]*See* Chapter Eight.

[35]Folstein et al., *Mini Mental State*, 12 J. PSYCHIATRIC RES. (1975); *see also* R.M. Crum et al., *Population-Based Norms for the Mini-mental State Examination by Age and Educational Level*, 18 J.A.M.A. 2386-2391 (1993).

[36]The New England Medical Center Department of Psychiatry, *Normative Data on The Mini Mental State Examination* (2000) <http://www.nemc.org/psych/mmse.asp>.

Figure 4.1: Folstein Mini-Mental Status Exam

Time Orientation	"What is the year?"	1 point ___
	"What is the season of the year?"	1 point ___
	"What is the date of the month?" (+/- 1 day)	1 point ___
	"What is the day of the week?"	1 point ___
5 points	What is the month?"	1 point ___

Written Commands	Show the subject a page with "Close Your Eyes" at the top and say: "Read the words on this page, then do as it says."	
1 point	SUBJECT CLOSES EYES	1 point ___

Writing	Give the subject a blank piece of paper and pencil and say: "Write any complete sentence on this paper for me."	
1 point	SUBJECT WRITES SENTENCE WITH SUBJECT AND VERB.	1 point ___

Serial Sevens	Ask the patient to count backwards from 100 by 7. Stop after five answers.	
5 points	93 86 79 72 65	1 point each number ___
OR	OR	
Spelling	"Now I am going to give you a word and ask you to spell it forwards and backwards. The word is "WORLD." Spell "WORLD" forwards." If the subject is unable to spell the word, spell it out loud, and ask the subject to repeat the spelling. Continue until it has been spelled successfully or until you have spelled it for the subject three times.	
	W O R L D	no points
5 points	"Now spell the word "WORLD" backwards."	
	D L R O W	1 point each letter ___

Drawing	Give the subject a stimulus page on which two pentagons intersect. Then ask the subject to copy the figure. If the subject is not sure where to copy the design, point to the blank part of the page below the design and instruct to place the copy there.	
1 point	SUBJECT DRAWS A FIGURE WITH TEN CORNERS AND TWO INTERSECTING LINES	1 point ___

III. DIAGNOSTIC TESTS FOR PSYCHOLOGICAL ASSESSMENT

A wide variety of standardized psychological tests exist to gather information about various dimensions of an individual's psychological functioning. A test is a ***standardized test*** when it is administered under controlled conditions and the results are measured against norms set for achievement on the test that were established using a sample of people representative of the group for whom the test was designed.[37] Standardized psychological tests sample behaviors, attitudes, and/or knowledge; describe them through scores, scales, or categories; and compare and contrast them to the behaviors, attitudes, and/or knowledge of others. In this regard, psychological tests are crucial to uncovering information that might not be discovered through interviews, observation, or other form of clinical assessment.

The field of psychological assessment is called ***psychometrics.*** The most widely used psychometric instruments are those that evaluate intelligence, personality, or the ability to perform a specific task. Grisso has identified the following eight ways in which standardized tests are commonly used in the legal decision-making process: (1) criminal court issues; (2) correctional decisions; (3) mental health law decisions; (4) juvenile delinquency decisions; (5) family law matters; (6) law enforcement personnel selection; (7) examination of discriminatory practices; and (8) evaluations of disability claims.[38] Not every psychometric test, however, is appropriate for each purpose. "[A] test that reliably and validly assesses a particular construct (e.g., psychopathology) in one setting (e.g., psychiatric hospitals) may not be especially useful in another type of setting (e.g., custody evaluations).[39] Care should, therefore, be exercised in selecting an appropriate test in light of the ultimate goal.

> The use of psychological test data in court should provide, among other sources of information, a genuinely empirical basis for an expert's opinion. Psychological testing has the potential of providing objective support to the expert's opinion. A properly developed standardized test should provide the expert with data grounded in objective, empirical research. Furthermore, the use of psychological tests helps to balance the bias and potential errors inherent in clinical interview data with objective results. However, it is critical for the evaluator to understand that any test results provide only hypotheses that are subject to verification from alternative data sources.[40]

A. Intelligence Tests

Intelligence has been a central focus of research and testing for more than 100 years. It is difficult to specifically determine what exactly intelligence is, or what facets combine to constitute it. Intelligence has been defined as the ability to successfully reason and arrive at innovative solutions to problems, as well as the ability to apply knowledge in order to manipulate one's environment.

---

[37]LUDY T. BENJAMIN, JR. ET AL., PSYCHOLOGY (3d ed. 1994) (available on-line at http://www.tjhsst.edu/Psych/ch11/11.htm>.

[38]Thomas Grisso, *Psychological Assessment in Legal Context, in* FORENSIC PSYCHIATRY AND PSYCHOL. 103, 103-28 (William J. Curran et al., eds., 1986).

[39]Randy K. Otto et al., *The Use of Psychological Testing in Child Custody Evaluations*, 38 Fam. & Concil. Cts. Rev. 312, 318 (2000).

[40]Jonathan W. Gould & Philip M. Stall, *The Art and Science of Child Custody Evaluations: Integrating Clinical and Forensic Mental Health Models*, 38 FAM. & CONCIL. CTS. REV. 392, 403 (2000) (internal citations omitted).

Intelligence is a different construct than both achievement and aptitude. ***Achievement tests*** measure previous learning by evaluating an individual's level of mastery of certain materials. In other words, they test a subject's knowledge of a specific area by measuring current skills and performance.[41] ***Aptitude tests,*** in contrast, are used to forecast future success in academic and/or occupational arenas.[42] Examples of aptitude tests include the SAT, GRE, LSAT, and a host of tests regulating military admission or corporate employment. Neither achievement nor aptitude tests are measures of intelligence; although tautological, only "intelligence tests" measure intelligence. Out of the hundreds of intelligence tests, only a select few highly reliable and valid tests are individually administered. The two most popular of such IQ tests are the Stanford-Binet and Wechsler intelligence tests.

1. Stanford-Binet

Intelligence tests were first developed by Alfred Binet in France. Binet defined intelligence as the capacity (a) to find and maintain a definite direction or purpose; (b) to be self-critical and make adaptions accordingly (i.e., adjust to circumstances so direction or purpose can be maintained).[43] Binet worked with Theodore Simon and the Paris school board and developed a battery of tests to highlight individual differences in the ability to reason, judge, and solve problems so that children in need of special academic attention could be identified.

Lewis Terman of Stanford University translated the test into English. The modern English version of this test is therefore known as the ***Stanford-Binet Intelligence Test***. One's score on the test is known as an "intelligence quotient," or IQ. For years, IQ was determined by dividing a person's mental age as scored on the test by the subject's chronological age. An IQ of 100 is considered average, and the standard deviation is 16.[44] Today, IQ is established by comparing one's performance score to aged norms.[45]

The fourth edition of the Stanford-Binet IQ Test, released in 1986, consists of fifteen subtests. The vocabulary subtest consists of forty-six items, fourteen of which are pictures of objects the subject must identify, thirty-two of which are words the subject must define. The "bead memory" subtest asks the subject to reproduce a pattern of beads on a stick or locate them in a photograph. There are forty items on the quantitative subtest that require computational problem solving. The "memory for sentences" subtest seeks to have the subject repeat orally presented sentences of increasing length; a similar test of twenty-six items using digits is also included; "memory for objects" similarly tests the subject's ability to recall items pictured on cards in the order in which they were presented. In the "pattern analysis" area, the subject is asked to reproduce a design drawn on a card using blocks. The comprehension test poses questions dealing with social situations or involving judgment. The subject is asked to identify a problem in a picture in the "absurdities" subtest. The subject must copy geometric designs (e.g., line, circle, triangle) on a card onto a piece of paper in the "copying" subtest, complete patterns

---

[41] LUDY ET AL., *supra* note 37.

[42] *Id.*

[43] Alfred Binet & Theodore Simon, *New Methods for the Diagnosis of the Intellectual Level of Subnormal, in* ALFRED BINET AND THEODORE SIMON, THE DEVELOPMENT OF INTELLIGENCE IN CHILDREN: (Elizabeth S. Kite, trans., 1973) (original published in 1905 and reprinted in 1916).

[44] LUDY ET AL., *supra* note 37.

[45] Personal Communication with Jeanine Vivona, Ph.D., Professor of Clinical Psychology, The College of New Jersey (Sept. 1, 2000).

on a "matrix" subtest, and predict which numbers appear next in a "number series" sequence. The subject must choose among five alternatives to match how a folded, cut piece of paper looks when unfolded on the "paper folding" subtest. "Verbal relations" asks the subject how three items are alike and how they collectively differ from a fourth item. Finally, the "equation building" subtest seeks to have the subject arrange numbers and mathematical symbols into a meaningful series. These fifteen subtests provide valid and reliable measures of verbal, abstract/visual, quantitative, and short-term memory abilities.[46]

2. Wechsler Intelligence Scales

David Wechsler's family of intelligence tests has dominated the field of intelligence testing since the 1950s.[47] The three main versions are the Wechsler Preschool and Primary Scale of Intelligence–Revised (WPPSI-R); the Wechsler Intelligence Scale for Children-III (WISC-III); and the *Wechsler Adult Intelligence Scale* (WAIS) released in its newest edition as the WAIS-III in 1997. These tests were designed for preschool, school-aged, adolescent, and adult populations.

The WAIS was designed to be administered to subjects age sixteen and older. It consists of six or seven verbal subtests and five to seven performance subtests. The test yields summary scores for Verbal IQ, Performance IQ, and Full Scale IQ. The verbal IQ is derived from performance on the following seven subtests: vocabulary (sixty-six words of increasing difficulty such as "define 'hypnotize'"); information (twenty-eight items designed to test a range of general knowledge such as "What is the world's population?"); comprehension (eighteen items designed to test judgment using questions like "Why do people wear clothes?" or asking for the meaning of proverbs); arithmetic (twenty problems testing both concentration and mathematical skills with questions such as "If you have twenty pears and give seven away, how many are left?"); similarities (a nineteen item measure of abstract thinking, e.g., "In what ways are shoes and socks alike?"); digit span (by repeating numbers up to nine digits forward then backwards, concentration, immediate memory, and anxiety level are measured); and letter-number sequencing (an optional subtest containing combinations of letters and numbers, from two to nine letter–number combinations that first requires repetition of the numbers in ascending order, and then the letters in alphabetical order).

Performance IQ is derived from the following five subtests: block design (a test of non-verbal reasoning through arranging blocks to match patterns); object assembly (analysis of whole-part relationships via the arrangement of cut-up pieces so the resemble an object); picture arrangement (tests planning ability by having the subject arrange pictures so they depict a logical story); picture completion (by finding the missing part in increasingly complex pictures, attention to detail can be measured); and coding–digit symbol (visual-motor functioning is assessed by having the subject copy designs associated with digits one though nine as quickly as possible). Two additional performance subtests are optional: object assembly (a puzzle-like test requiring the taker to assemble the parts into a whole); and symbol search (requires matching of one or two symbols in one column with the same symbol[s] another column to measure organization accuracy and processing speed).

---

[46]*See generally* LEWIS R. AIKEN, PSYCHOLOGICAL TESTING AND ASSESSMENT (10th ed., Allyn & Bacon 2000) [hereinafter "AIKEN, TESTING"].; THOMAS GRISSO, EVALUATING COMPETENCIES: FORENSIC ASSESSMENTS AND INSTRUMENTS (1986).

[47]DAVID WECHSLER, THE WECHSLER INTELLIGENCE SCALE FOR CHILDREN (1949); DAVID WECHSLER, THE MEASUREMENT OF ADULT INTELLIGENCE (1939).

The raw scores on each subtest are converted to scales with a standard score of 10 and a standard deviation of 3. The scaled scores are then summed separately for the verbal and performance tests, and each IQ can then be determined from a table that converts the summed scale scores to a standard score with a mean of 100 and a standard deviation of 15. The identical process is followed for overall IQ. The forms of the Wechsler tests designed for children are similar in design and scoring, but they measure intelligence in age-appropriate manners.

B. Personality Tests

Gordon Allport, one of the leaders in the psychology of personality, once wrote that the "outstanding characteristic of man is his individuality."[48] This individuality is often referred to as our personality. ***Personality,*** like intelligence, is difficult to define but is generally conceptualized as "a stable set of tendencies and characteristics that determine those commonalities and differences in people's psychological behavior (thoughts, feelings, and actions) that have continuity in time and that may not be easily understood as the sole result of the social and biological pressures of the moment."[49] It should be self-evident that this definition of personality uses both cognitive and affective (emotional) components.[50]

Allport believed our personalities predisposed us to engage in certain behaviors across situations.[51] Other research in psychology has called the validity of this hypothesis into question. since "individual differences in social behaviors tend to be surprisingly variable across different situations."[52] But even researchers who reject the stability of personality traits across time and situations buy into the notion of a personality.

Psychological assessments of personality are attempts to understand both a range of normal emotional and behavioral functioning, as well as the abnormal behavior. The most common psychometric methods used to assess personality are structured personality inventories and projective tests.

Of course, as stated above, a clinician's theoretical orientation will influence how he or she conducts clinical assessment. A behavioral psychologist is not likely to be concerned with personality but rather with the behavioral reinforcers that might be responsible for maintaining maladaptive behaviors. In contrast, psychodynamic and cognitive psychologists would be interested in personality assessment, with the former particularly interested in those that use projective techniques.

1. Structured Personality Inventories

A ***structured personality inventory*** is a self-report questionnaire on which subjects respond "true or false," "yes or no," or "agree or disagree" to a series of statements about themselves.[53]

---

[48]GORDON W. ALLPORT, PERSONALITY – A PSYCHOLOGICAL INTERPRETATION 3 (1937).

[49]SALVATORE R. MADDI, PERSONALITY THEORIES: A COMPARATIVE ANALYSIS 8 (5th ed. 1989)

[50] LEWIS R. AIKEN, ASSESSMENT OF PERSONALITY 4 (1989) [hereinafter "AIKEN, ASSESSMENT"] (defining personality as including both cognitive and affective components but then focusing "on the assessment of affective characteristics, which encompass the traditional, albeit somewhat limited, conception of personality variables").

[51]*Id. pasim.*

[52]Walter Mischel & Yuichi Shoda, *A Cognitive-Affective System Theory of Personality: Reconceptualizing Situations, Dispositions, Dynamics, and Invariance in Personality Structure*, 102 PSYCHOL. REV. 246 (1995).

[53]AIKEN, ASSESSMENT, *supra* note 50, at 192.

Alternatively, some structured personality inventories ask subjects to choose between two or more statements by selecting the response most characteristic of themselves.[54]

The best known and most widely used structured personality inventory is the ***Minnesota Multiphasic Personality Inventory*** (**MMPI**), first released in 1943 by Starke Hathaway and J. Charnley McKinley. It was revised as the MMPI-2 in 1989.[55] Currently, although both versions can be used in the clinical setting dependent upon the individual clinician's preference (a debate still exists over whether one is more effective),[56] the clear clinical preference is for the MMPI-2. The MMPI is the most widely used personality inventory in forensic clinical assessment; "more than 12,000 research articles and books have been written about the MMPI since it was developed over 50 years ago."[57] Accordingly, it enjoys wide acceptance in courts of law.[58]

The traditional MMPI consists of 550 "true-false" or "cannot say" self-statements that are designed to assess dimensions of personality such as health concerns, mood, beliefs regarding religion, sex, and society, and possible symptoms of abnormality. The test is composed of ten clinical (or content) scales and four scales used to assess the validity of the test.

Content scale scores range from 0 to 120. If an individual scores above 70 on a certain scale, his or her functioning on the personality dimension measured by that scale is considered abnormal or deviant. The four validity scales are included because some people answer either affirmative or negative more often, regardless of the question; others purposefully try to skew their answers in ways they believe are socially acceptable; and others simply lie.

The L-scale, or lie scale, consists of fifteen items that indicate whether a person is answering truthfully to all questions, or trying to look too good. For example, a person who answers false to "I have never had a bad night's sleep," or true to "I read the newspaper editorials every night," would score unusually high on this scale, indicating dishonest test-taking. The assumption is that few people can completely endorse such statements honestly. The F scale consists of 64 infrequently endorsed items (60 on the MMPI-2) to pick out subjects who take an unusual or unconventional approach to testing by attempting to fake abnormality. The 30 item K-scale is included to detect whether an individual is defensive and trying to project a socially acceptable image. If individuals score high on either the L, F, or K scales, the test results are deemed invalid or inconclusive. They are, therefore, not used as part of the data from which clinical conclusions are made.

The MMPI-2 is a slightly modified version of the original personality inventory. This test contains 567 items; many are identical to the MMPI items, yet some are rewritten to reflect more modern, contemporary times. In addition to the ten basic scales, the MMPI-2 contains additional scales that are designed to measure personality dimensions such as vulnerability to eating disorders, drug or alcohol abuse, or poor occupational functioning.

---

[54]*Id.*

[55]YOSSEF S. BENPORATH ET AL. (EDS.), FORENSIC APPLICATIONS OF THE MMPI-2 (1995); JOHN ROBERT GRAHAM, MMPI-2 ASSESSING PERSONALITY AND PSYCHOPATHOLOGY (1993).

[56]Edward Helmes & John R. Reddon, *A Perspective on Developments in Assessing Psychopathology: A Critical Review of the MMPI and MMPI-2*, 113 PSYCHOL. BULL. 453-71 (1993).

[37]Andrew E. Taslitz, *Myself Alone: Individualizing Justice Through Psychological Character Evidence.* 52 MD. L. REV. 1, 37 (1993) (citing MARC J. ACKERMAN & ANDREW W. KANE, HOW TO EXAMINE PSYCHOLOGICAL EXPERTS IN DIVORCE AND OTHER CIVIL ACTIONS 196 (1990)).

[58]AIKEN, TESTING, *supra* note 50, at 433-36 (stating that the MMPI is perhaps the "most frequently administered of all psychometric instruments in legal Settings"); DANIEL SHUMAN, PSYCHIATRIC AND PSYCHOLOGICAL EVIDENCE 54 (1986) (stating that the MMPI is the "premier diagnostic and screening device in clinical psychology").

2. Projective Techniques

Projective personality assessment is so termed because projective techniques are employed to study personality.[59] These techniques consist of "unstructured stimuli that examinees are asked to describe, tell a story about, complete, or respond to in some other manner."[60] The central purpose of projective techniques is to discover underlying, unconscious aspects of an individual's personality from his or her responses to the ambiguous stimuli. Obviously, these techniques are favored by those with a psychodynamic theoretical orientation, and not particularly favored by those who subscribe to the medical or behavioral models of mental illness.

Psychodynamically oriented clinicians believe projective techniques are less amenable to conscious manipulation by the testtaker since what constitutes a "good" or a "bad" response is not readily apparent—especially in comparison to the types of questions asked on the MMPI. Yet, even fans of projective techniques concede that responses can be faked, "are very susceptible to the conditions under which they are administered, are scored and interpreted differently by different examiners, and have inadequate [norms], unrepresentative norms, or no norms at all."[61] In spite of these concerns, some projective techniques remain among the most used instruments of personality assessment.

One of the most commonly used projective techniques is the ***Rorschach Inkblot Test,*** introduced by Swiss psychiatrist Hermann Rorschach (1884–1922).[62] This test consists of a series of 10 inkblots created by dropping ink on paper, folding the paper in half, and then opening the paper to reveal roughly symmetrical designs. Half of the inkblots are black and white with shades of gray; two add red splotches; the remaining three are in pastel color. The projective method assumes that facets of the subject's personality and overall psychological condition are reflected in the responses. For example, it might be assumed that a subject may have aggressive and/or violent tendencies if fierce animals, warfare, or weapons are seen within the inkblots.

A subject is shown one inkblot at a time. In what is termed the free-association phase, the subject is asked to identify what is seen in the inkblot. During this phase, the subject is free to manipulate the picture. After giving the free-association response, the examiner conducts the inquiry phase to obtain sufficient information for scoring. To do so, the examiner asks the subject to identify what aspects of the inkblot (the color, shape, shading, etc.) were influential in forming the free-association response.

---

[59]*See* Lawrence K. Frank, *Projective Methods for the Study of Personality*, 8 J. PSYCHOL. 389-413 (1939).

[60]Taslitz, *supra* note 57, at 39 (citing AIKEN, ASSESSMENT, *supra* note 50, at 305).

[61]*Id.* (citing AIKEN, ASSESSMENT, *supra* note 50, at 306).

[62] HERMANN RORSCHACH, PSYCHODIAGNOSTICS; A DIAGNOSTIC TEST BASED ON PERCEPTION (Paul Lemkau & Bernard Kronenberg, eds. & trans., 1964).

Table 4.2: Overview of the MMPI

Scale	Purpose	Example
HS (Hypochondriasis)	Items indicating abnormal concern with health and bodily functions.	"I have chest pains several times a week."
D (Depression)	Items assessing pessimism and feelings of hopelessness.	"I often feel hopeless about the future."
Hy (Conversion Hysteria)	Items that suggest repression, denial, and the use of physical or mental symptoms as a way of avoiding conflicts or responsibilities.	"My heart frequently pounds so hard I can feel it."
Pd (Psychopathic Deviate)	Items that show disregard for social customs, emotional shallowness, and family conflict.	"My activities and interests are often criticized by others."
Mf (Masculinity-Femininity)	Items that differentiate between men and women (some that arguably do so in a sexist manner).	"I like to repair things."
Pa (Paranoia)	Items revealing abnormal suspicions, or delusions.	"There are evil people trying to influence my mind."
Pt (Psychastenia)	Items showing obsessions, compulsions, unusual fears, and guilt.	"I save nearly everything I buy, even after I have no use for it."
Sc (Schizophrenia)	Items indicating bizarre thoughts and behaviors, delusions, and hallucinations.	"Things around me do not seem real."
Ma (Hypomania)	Items reflecting overactivity, emotional excitement, and flight of ideas.	"My speech is faster than it used to be."
Si (Social Introversion)	Items that portray shyness, insecurity, and little interest in social activities.	"I like to go to parties."
L (Lie) Validity Scale	Items designed to test if a person is trying to make themselves look good by creating a falsely ideal personality.	"I never lose control of myself when I drive."
F (Infrequency) Validity Scale	Items seeking to uncover if the subject is trying to appear abnormal.	"I am aware of a special presence which others cannot perceive."
K (Correction) Validity Scale	Items showing that the subject is being guarded or defensive while taking the test, seeking to avoid appearing poorly adjusted.	"Things couldn't be going any better for me."
? (Cannot Say) Validity Scale	A count of the number of questions left unanswered, or marked as both true and false. A high score indicates evasiveness, reading difficulties, severe depression, or severe obsessive-compulsive tendencies.	

Adapted from: Robert M. Kaplan & Dennis P. Saccuzzo, *Psychol. Testing: Principles, Applications and Issues* 410 (4th ed. 1997).

Several systems were developed to administer, score, and interpret the Rorschach, raising significant reliability and validity concerns. Different examiners focused on different aspects of a subject's response when scoring the test. Does the subject use a lot or a little detail? Does the subject pay attention to color? To shading? Does the subject interpret the entire inkblot or only sections of it? Is attention focused on the inkblots themselves or on the white spaces between the inkblots?

John Exner's work brought standardization to the test in a manner that has revolutionized the use of the Rorschach.[63] The five major Rorschach scoring categories on Exner system are location (where), determinant (why), content (what), popular-original (frequency of occurrence), and form quality (correspondence of percept to stimulus properties of the inkblot). The Exner scoring system is considered to be the most reliable and valid and is therefore the preferred method for forensic assessment. Some clinicians have even moved to a modern computer-aided scoring and interpretive system based on the Exner system to further enhance reliability.

The **Thematic Apperception Test** (TAT) is another projective test for personality assessment. The TAT was developed by psychologist Henry A. Murray in 1930.[64] It consists of thirty black and white pictures and one blank card. The pictures usually depict one or more persons engaged in ambiguous conduct.[65] The first card, for example, shows a scene in which a boy, neatly dressed and groomed, is sitting at a table with a violin on the table.

Subjects are shown one picture at a time and instructed to make a story stating what is happening in the current scene; what events led up to this picture; what the characters are thinking and feeling; and what the outcome of the story will be. It is assumed that either the subjects will identify with the central character of each card and project their own circumstances, motivations, needs, and emotions into their created stories, or the examiner will be able to infer these things simply from story content and theme. As with the Rorschach, there is no standard method of response interpretation for the TAT in the clinical setting. However, several standardized scoring techniques are used in research that are not necessarily appropriate as diagnostic indicators.[66]

Sentence completion tests are another popular projective measure. Although there are several variations of this test, they are similar in design. The subject is provided with a series of unfinished sentences, (e.g., "My mother_____," or "I only wish_____,") and asked to provide an ending. It is assumed that underlying fears, concerns, emotions, or attitudes will be reflected in subject responses. Additionally, these tests are easily administered and used to pinpoint topics to be explored and expanded upon further.

Drawings constitute another popular group of projective tests. Some clinicians will have subjects draw their family, or a scene, or an object (e.g., a tree or house) and then evaluate the drawings. Most commonly used is the Draw-a-Person Test (DAP) in which subjects are given a blank piece of paper and instructed to first draw one person and then draw another person of the opposite sex.[67] Evaluations of these drawings are based on criteria such as size, style, and shape and other dimensions all based upon psychodynamic centered hypotheses. For example, a person

---

[63]*See* JOHN E. EXNER, THE RORSCHACH: A COMPREHENSIVE SYSTEM: VOL. I: BASIC FOUNDATIONS (3d ed. 1993); JOHN E. EXNER, THE RORSCHACH: A COMPREHENSIVE SYSTEM: VOL. II: INTERPRETATION (2d ed. 1991); John E. Exner, *But It's Only an Inkblot*, 44 J. PERSONALITY ASSESSMENT 562-577 (1980).

[64]HENRY A. MURRAY, EXPLORATIONS IN PERSONALITY (1938).

[65]*Id.*

[66]Vivona, *supra* note 45.

[67]KAREN MACHOVER, PERSONALITY PROJECTION IN THE DRAWING OF THE HUMAN FIGURE (1949).

drawn with a disproportionately large or small head is said to convey problems in intellectual functioning, or the graphic emphasis of neck features on a person is said to reflect lack of impulse control. The validity and reliability of these projective tests are even lower than for the Rorschach or the TAT.

Because of interpretation difficulties and the subjective nature of both subject responses and examiner scoring, many have questioned the validity of projective personality tests as diagnostic tools.[68] In fact, one study found a majority of clinical psychology faculty in universities viewed the Rorschach and the TAT negatively.[69] Yet, these two tests are widely used, and at least some modern studies have empirically demonstrated reliability and validity when the tests are properly used and scored.[70] Regardless of their shortcomings, there is no doubt that insight into personality can be gained using projective tests. While they should not be used as primary diagnostic tools, their use as secondary indicators can meaningfully contribute to appropriate diagnosis in both clinical and forensic settings.[71]

IV. CONCLUSION

This chapter should have provided a basic understanding of how patients are clinically evaluated. As stated several times in this chapter, one of the most important goals of clinical assessment is to arrive at an appropriate diagnosis. Although you are now familiar with several of the methods most frequently used to arrive at diagnoses, you may not be familiar with the diagnostic criteria for any of the major mental disorders. Doing so is beyond the scope of this book. However, recall from Chapter One that the bible of psychiatric diagnosis is the *Diagnostic and Statistical Manual* of the American Psychiatric Association, currently in its fourth edition with minor text revisions as of the writing of this text ("DSM-IV-TR"). It is a comprehensive and authoritative text that presents the diagnostic criteria for hundreds of recognized mental disorders. Although Appendix A contains information on select DSM-IV diagnoses, justice professionals should always consult the latest version of the DSM, along with an appropriate text in abnormal psychology, to make sure they understand the disorder(s) relevant to any particular case.

---

[68]James M. Wood et al., *The Rorschach Test in Clinical Diagnosis: A Critical Review*, 56 J. CLINICAL PSYCHOL. 395-420 (2000).

[69]AIKEN, ASSESSMENT, *supra* note 50, at 307.

[70]Irving B. Weiner, *Using the Rorschach Properly in Practice and Research*, 56 J. CLINICAL PSYCHOL. 453-58 (2000); Irving B. Weiner, *Some Observations on the Validity of the Rorschach Inkblot Method*, 8 PSYCHOL. ASSESSMENT 206-13 & n.20 (1996).

[71]Donald J. Viglione, *A Review of Recent Research Addressing the Utility of the Rorschach*, 11 PSYCHOL. ASSESSMENT 251-65 (1999).

PART II:
PSYCHOLOGY IN THE LAW

CHAPTER FOUR
ISSUES REGARDING COMPETENCY TO STAND TRIAL

I. INTRODUCTION

Evaluating the legal concept of competency ranks among the greatest challenges in criminal justice. A vague concept that varies from one situation to another, competency may involve more than 30 different legal actions and imposes numerous burdens on defendants and the courts.[1]

This chapter is concerned with the notion of competency to stand trial. "*Incompetency* is a mental disability that impairs a defendant to the extent that he cannot grasp the nature of the charges against him nor assist counsel in his defense."[2]

Historically, *competency to stand trial* was viewed quite differently from other types of competencies, both civil and criminal.[3] In recent years, however, the lines between the various types of competencies have been blurred, largely as a result of the U.S. Supreme Court's decision in *Godinez v. Moran*,[4] in which the Court rejected the contention that courts should apply a higher standard of incompetency for determining competency to plead guilty than for determining competency to stand trial. The *Godinez v. Moran* case will be discussed in detail later in this chapter. For now, we should define competency to stand trial and explore the justifications for the doctrine.

II. THE DOCTRINE OF COMPETENCY TO STAND TRIAL

The U.S. system of criminal justice requires that one be competent or "fit" to stand trial before one's guilt or innocence is assessed at a criminal trial. Accordingly, when the fitness of a particular criminal defendant to stand trial becomes an issue in a case, his or her competency to stand trial must be determined before a trial can proceed.

A. Justifications for the Competency to Stand Trial Doctrine

1. Historical Justifications

The legal bar against trying incompetent defendants dates back to common law England.

> Blackstone wrote that a defendant who becomes "mad" after the commission of an offense should not be arraigned "because he is not able to plead . . . with the advice and caution that he ought," and should not be tried, for "how can he make his defense?" The ban on trial of an incompetent defendant stems from the common law prohibition on trials in absentia, and from the difficulties

---

[1] Marcia J. Weiss, *A Legal Evaluation of Criminal Competency Standards: Competency to Stand Trial, Competency to Plead Guilty, and Competency to Waive Counsel*, 13 J. CONTEMP. CRIM. JUST. 213 (1997).

[2] Alaya B. Meyers, *Supreme Court Review: Rejecting the Clear and Convincing Evidence Standard for Proof of Incompetence*, 87 J. CRIM. L. & CRIMINOLOGY 1016 (1997) (citing HENRY WEIHOFEN, MENTAL DISORDER AS A CRIMINAL DEFENSE 429 (1954)).

[3] *Id.*

[4] 509 U.S. 389 (1993).

the English courts encountered when defendants frustrated the ritual of the common law trial by remaining mute instead of pleading to charges. Without a plea, the trial could not go forward.[5]

At this point in the history of English common law, a person rarely had the right to counsel; in fact, counsel was prohibited in many cases. A defendant, therefore, usually had to represent himself or herself.[6] As a result, "the defendant stood alone before the court, and trial was merely 'a long argument between the prisoner and the counsel for the Crown.' Thus, it was imperative that defendants be competent because they were required to conduct their own defense."[7]

2. Modern Justifications

Unlike under English common law, the right to counsel is guaranteed to nearly all criminal defendants today.[8] As a result, the common law rationale underlying the doctrine of incompetence to stand trial is no longer applicable. But there are still important justifications for the doctrine in modern times.

According to Professors Wayne R. LaFave and Austin W. Scott, Jr., the courts, most notably the U.S. Supreme Court in cases like *Dusky v. United States*,[9] *Drope v. Missouri*,[10] *Pate v. Robinson*,[11] and *Medina v. California*,[12] have reasoned that the Constitution's guarantee of due process prohibits the trying of an incompetent defendant for several reasons.[13]

> First, it increases the accuracy and reliability of the trial since an incompetent defendant cannot, for example, adequately testify on his behalf. The requirement also enhances fairness, since an incompetent defendant cannot make decisions regarding the course and nature of his defense. In addition, it maintains the "dignity" of the trial, in that an incompetent defendant may behave in an offensive or inappropriate manner. Finally, a competent defendant's comprehension of why he is being punished makes the punishment more just.[14]

B. Competency to Stand Trial vs. Insanity

Competency to stand trial is often confused with insanity. Although the two doctrines are related insofar both as they are both concerned with the mental status of a criminal defendant, they are quite different in terms of their goals, justifications, and processes.

---

[5]Bruce J. Winick, *Criminal Law: Reforming Incompetency to Stand Trial and Plead Guilty: A Restated Proposal and a Response to Professor Bonnie*, 85 J. CRIM. L. & CRIMINOLOGY 571, 574 (Winter, 1995) (quoting, *inter alia*, WILLIAM BLACKSTONE, COMMENTARIES *24 (9th ed. 1783); 1 MATTHEW HALE, THE HISTORY OF THE PLEAS OF THE CROWN 34-35 (1736)).

[6]Faretta v. California, 422 U.S. 806, 823 (1975).

[7]Winick, *supra* note 5, at 575.

[8]U.S. CONST. amend. VI; *see* Gideon v. Wainwright, 372 U.S. 335 (1963) (guaranteeing right to counsel to all indigent persons in felony trials); Argersinger v. Hamlin, 407 U.S. 25 (1972) (extending *Gideon* to all misdemeanor trials in which defendants face a potential jail sentence); *cf.* Scott v. Illinois, 440 U.S. 367 (1979) (holding that so long as an indigent defendant is not actually sentenced to imprisonment, then the state is not required to appoint counsel).

[9]362 U.S. 402, 402 (1960).

[10]420 U.S. 162 (1975).

[11]383 U.S. 375 (1986).

[12]505 U.S. 437, 452 (1992).

[13]WAYNE R. LaFAVE & AUSTIN W. SCOTT, JR., SUBSTANTIVE CRIMINAL LAW 4.4(a) (2d ed. 1986).

[14]Meyers, *supra* note 2 at1017 (citing *id.*).

1. Timing

Competency to stand trial concerns itself with a criminal defendant's mental state *at the time of trial*. The central focus of a hearing on competency is to see if the trial court should be deprived of jurisdiction over the defendant due to his or her lack of capacity to stand trial. In contrast, insanity is concerned with the defendant's state of mind at the time the criminal offense is alleged to have taken place. The issue of insanity is litigated over the course of a criminal trial in which the defendant's alleged insanity serves as a defense to the crime with which the defendant has been charged. Accordingly, timing is a critical distinction between the two doctrines.[15]

2. When and How the Issue May Be Raised

Because insanity is a criminal defense, it must be timely asserted by the defendant, usually through counsel, in order to be used at trial. Only the defendant can assert insanity. It cannot be forced upon the defendant by the state or the court.

Insanity is not a defense that the defendant can spring on the court in the middle of trial. Proper notice must be given by the defense that they insanity defense is going to be used.

> If a defendant intends to rely upon the defense of insanity at the time of the alleged offense, the defendant shall, within the time provided for the filing of pretrial motions or at such later time as the court may direct, notify the attorney for the government in writing of such intention and file a copy of such notice with the clerk. If there is a failure to comply with the requirements of this subdivision, insanity may not be raised as a defense. The court may for cause shown allow late filing of the notice or grant additional time to the parties to prepare for trial or make such other order as may be appropriate.[16]

Thus, if a plea of not guilty by reason of insanity or (its equivalent) is not pled in a timely manner, the defense is deemed to be waived.[17]

Competency to stand trial, however, may be raised at any time in the criminal process, even after conviction.[18] While the issue of competency to stand trial is usually raised by the defense, the prosecution can raise the issue, as can the court on its own.[19]

3. Burdens of Proof

Historically, the defendant only bore the burden of production on the insanity defense and the prosecution had to prove the sanity of a criminal defendant beyond a reasonable doubt after the defense raised the issue of insanity. Today, however, largely in response to the not guilty by reason of insanity verdict in the case against John Hinckley for his assassination attempt against President Ronald Reagan, insanity is an affirmative defense. Accordingly, in the federal system and in most U.S. jurisdictions, the defense now bears both the burden of production and the

---

[15]*See generally* Stephanie M. Herseth, *Competency to Stand Trial*, 84 GEO. L.J. 1066, 1076 n.1418 (1996).

[16]Fed. R. Crim. Pro. 12.2(a).

[17]*Id.; see also, e.g.,* Bakic v. United States, 971 F. Supp. 697, 700 (N.D.N.Y. 1997) (denying petition to set aside conviction and sentence on alleged due process grounds due to insanity since insanity defense was not timely pled); People v. Low, 732 P.2d 622 (Colo. 1987) (holding insanity defense not pled at arraignment as required by Colorado statute is deemed waived).

[18]Winick, *supra* note 5, at 572.

[19]Pate v. Robinson, 383 U.S. 375 (1966).

burden of persuasion on the issue of insanity.[20] In the federal system and in many states that have followed the federal government's lead, the defense must prove insanity by clear and convincing evidence, although a handful of jurisdictions require the defendant to prove his or her insanity by only a preponderance of the evidence.

In contrast, there is no burden of production when dealing with the issue of incompetency to stand trial. As stated above, the issue of competency can be raised by either the prosecution or the defense, or even by the court on its own. Most requests for a clinical determination of competency go unopposed by opposing counsel and are routinely granted by judges.[21] Once granted the opportunity to have such a determination made, the process of determining competency to stand trial is quite different from the trial process used to determine insanity: Clinical evaluations followed by an evidentiary hearing on the issue of competency is the norm.

As a general rule, the prosecution must show at the competency hearing that the defendant is competent to proceed with the criminal trial.[22] This showing must be by a preponderance of the evidence.[23] However, some states have shifted the burden of persuasion to the defense who must show the incompetency of the defendant by a preponderance of the evidence. The Supreme Court specifically approved this allocation of the burden of persuasion over a due process challenge in *Medina v. California.*[24] The Court, however, stuck down Oklahoma's attempt to require the defendant to show his or her competence by clear and convincing evidence, finding it violates the guarantee of due process.[25] In doing so, it invalidated the laws of the four states— Connecticut, Oklahoma, Pennsylvania, and Rhode Island—that had set the burden unconstitutionally high.[26]

Regardless of whether the prosecution or defense bears the burden of persuasion at the competency hearing, the process unfolds in the manner set forth in the next section of this chapter. Before moving on to the technicalities of the competency hearing, it is necessary to consider what happens when a competency hearing should take place, but does not. As stated above, once requested by either side, judges normally grant a competency determination. But if a judge refuses to order a competency hearing, that refusal can have consequences on the ultimate outcome of a case.

If there are no objective grounds for a judge to order a competency determination, it is highly unlikely that the judge's refusal will have any outcome on a case. On the other hand, if there were grounds upon which the competency of the defendant had been called into question and the judge refused to order a competency hearing, then serious constitutional concerns can be raised that could invalidate a conviction on appeal or via some post-conviction relief mechanism such as a habeas corpus proceeding. The law is clear on this latter point: A failure to conduct an evidentiary hearing where evidence before a trial court raises a "bona fide doubt" about the

---

[20]The burden of production means the burden of coming forward. It "announces" to the court and all concerned parties that something will be at issue in a case. In contrast, the burden of persuasion is the actual level of proof that must be introduced at trial to prevail on a claim.

[21]Ronald Roesch & Stephen L. Golding, *Defining and Assessing Competency to Stand Trial, in* IRVING B. WEINER & ALLEN HESS (eds.), HANDBOOK OF FORENSIC PSYCHOLOGY (1987); GARY B. MELTON, ET AL., PSYCHOLOGICAL EVALUATION FOR THE COURTS 71 (1987).

[22]18 U.S.C. § 4241(d); *see also* United States v. Teague, 956 F.2d 1427, 1431 n.10 (7th Cir. 1992); United States v. Frank, 956 F.2d 872 (9th Cir. 1991), *cert. denied*, 506 U.S. 932 (1992).

[23]*See* sources *id.*

[24]505 U.S. 437, 452 (1992).

[25]Cooper v. Oklahoma, 517 U.S. 348, 369 (1996).

[26]*Id.* at 360.

defendant's competency to stand trial violates due process.[27] While a concise rule, what constitutes a "bona fide doubt" is ambiguous, and reasonable people can offer differ with respect to whether such a doubt exists given the facts of any particular case.[28]

C. The Competency Hearing

1. Clinical Assessment

Once a bona fide issue regarding the defendant's competency to stand trial has been raised, the defendant must be clinically assessed. The assessment of a criminal defendant for competency to stand trial is one of the most important roles mental health professionals play in the criminal process. The assessment of the defendant is normally conducted by clinicians appointed by the court. "These clinical evaluators examine the defendant and then submit written reports to the court. The court then decides the issue, sometimes following a hearing at which the examiners testify and are subject to cross-examination."[29]

Although the determination of competency to stand trial is a purely legal determination—not a clinical one—the importance of the role of the evaluating clinician(s) cannot be overstated. First and foremost, the overwhelming number of competency determinations are based on the clinical assessment of a single clinician.[30] Second, although "state statues typically call for a court hearing in the issue of competency, . . . in reality hearings are often not held and defendants are frequently adjudicated incompetent after the parties stipulate to the results of the clinical evaluation."[31] And arguably most important, even when a hearing is held, "it is likely to be perfunctory. . . . [W]homever examining mental health professionals characterize as incompetent is likely ultimately to be found incompetent."[32]

2. Psycho-Legal Focus of the Inquiry into Competency

According to the Supreme Court's landmark decision in *Dusky v. United States*,[33] to be competent to stand trial, a defendant must have (1) "a rational as well as factual understanding of the proceedings against him" and (2) "sufficient present ability to consult with his lawyer with a reasonable degree of rational understanding." This formulation is followed in nearly all U.S. jurisdictions and has been reaffirmed by the Supreme Court quite recently (in constitutional terms).[34]

The first question—can the defendant understand the proceedings against him or her—is not directed at whether the defendant understands the intricacies of the criminal process. Rather, it is

---

[27]*Pate,* 383 U.S. at 378; *Medina,* 505 U.S. at 452.

[28]*Compare, e.g.,* United States v. Jacobo Loyola-Dominguez, 125 F.3d 1315 (9th Cir. 1997), *with* Blazak v. Ricketts, 1 F.3d 891 (9th Cir. 1993).

[29]Winick, *supra* note 5, at 572.

[30]CURT R. BARTOL & ANNE M. BARTOL, PSYCHOLOGY AND LAW 124 (2d ed. 1994) (citing MELTON, ET AL., *supra* note 21, at 72).

[31]MELTON, ET AL., *supra* note 21, at 72 (citing RONALD ROESCH & STEPHEN L. GOLDING, COMPETENCY TO STAND TRIAL 50-52 (1980)).

[32]*Id.* (citing various studies reporting judge-clinician agreement on the issue of competency to stand trial to be greater than 90% in numerous jurisdictions).

[33]362 U.S. 402, 402 (1960).

[34]*See* Medina v. California, 505 U.S. 437, 452 (1992).

concerned with whether the defendant has a basic understanding of the circumstances in which he or she finds himself or herself. More simply, does the defendant understand that he or she has been charged with a crime and faces government-imposed punishment if convicted?[35]

Although not technically a requirement of the test for competency, mental health professionals often consider whether the defendant is orientated with respect to time, place, and situation as part of their inquiry in this phase of the competency evaluation.[36] In other words, does the defendant know who and where he or she is? Without such orientation, it is unlikely that a defendant understands, even in a basic way, the proceedings against him or her.

The second of the criteria is whether the defendant is capable of assisting in his or her own defense. If the defendant cannot communicate with his or her attorney in a manner that permits the defense lawyer the ability to formulate a defense, there is little likelihood that the defendant will be found competent.[37]

The competency standard as applied in any particular case tends to be flexible.[38] Flexible means there are no set of "fixed" diagnostic criteria that, if satisfied, renders a person either competent or incompetent. A federal court in 1961 set forth the following factors to explain how it might determine if a defendant were competent to stand trial. The court stated one would be competent to stand trial if the defendant:

(1) has the "mental capacity to appreciate his presence in relation to time, place and things";

(2) has "elementary mental processes are such that he apprehends (i.e., seizes and grasps with what mind he has) that he is in a Court of Justice, charged with a criminal offense";

(3) understands "there is a Judge on the Bench";

(4) understands there is "a prosecutor present who will try to convict him of a criminal charge";

(5) understands "he has a lawyer (self-employed or Court-appointed) who will undertake to defend him against that charge";

(6) understands "he will be expected to tell his lawyer the circumstances, to the best of his mental ability, (whether colored or not by mental aberration) the facts surrounding him at the time and place where the law violation is alleged to have been committed";

(7) understands "there is, or will be, a jury present to pass upon evidence adduced as to his guilt or innocence of such charge"; and

(8) has "memory sufficient to relate those things in his own personal manner."[39]

While helpful guidelines, applying such criteria to the facts of any one case can be difficult, especially in where there is conflicting opinions between different mental health professionals.

---

[35] *See generally* ABA Criminal Justice Mental Health Standards 7-4.1 (1989); *see also* Richard J. Bonnie, *The Competence of Criminal Defendants: Beyond Dusky and Drope*, 47 U. Miami L. Rev. 539, 578 (1993) (criticizing the requirement of "basic understanding" – the ability to understand the nature and consequences of the decision, and arguing for a requirement of "basic rationality" – the ability to express plausible, rather than grossly irrational, reasons for the decision – but not "the ability to make a reasoned choice among alternatives.").

[36] Thomas Grisso, Evaluating Competencies: Forensic Assessments and Instruments 95 (1986) ("Although psychopathological symptoms are by themselves not synonymous with legal incompetency, they are certainly relevant for pretrial competency determinations").

[37] *Id.* The ability to assist in one's own defense has been criticized as an outdated requirement left over from the time when the right to counsel was not guaranteed to all criminal defendants. *See* Bruce J. Winick, *Restructuring Competency to Stand Trial*, 32 UCLA L. Rev. 921, 957-58 (1985). While that is a matter open to debate, *see, e.g.,* Bonnie, *supra* note 35, it remains the requirement of the law for now.

[38] Melton, et al., *supra* note 21, at 67 (citing Note, *Incompetency to Stand Trial*, 81 Harv. L. Rev. 454, 457-58 (1967)).

[39] Wieter v. Settle, 193 F. Supp. 318, 321-22 (W.D. Mo. 1961). For an extensive discussion of the various forensic psychological lines of inquiry a mental health professional might use to conduct a competency evaluation, *see* Melton, et al., *supra* note 21, at 68-92.

3. Assessment Instruments

The mental health sciences have developed a number of competency assessment instruments. *The Competency Screening Test* (CST) requires a defendant to complete twenty-two sentences. The appropriateness of the defendant's completion of each sentence is rated a 0 (incompetent), 1 (questionable competency), and 2 (competent). A total score of 20 or less raises issues of the defendant's competency to stand trial and suggests further evaluation. Melton, et al., in reviewing several studies on the CST, point out that there are significant questions regarding the validity and reliability of the CST as an instrument.[40] But since the measurement and assessment concerns center around false positives (more likely to produce a low score raising the issue of incompetence), and since additional evaluation would be necessary for a determination of incompetency, the CST is not particularly problematic given its use.

A second instrument, the *Competency Assessment Instrument* (CAI), is often used as a follow-up to the CST when additional evaluation is indicated. It is designed not only to determine competency to stand trial, but all types of legal competencies.[41] It consists of thirteen "'ego functions' or observable groups of behaviors related to a defendant's ability to cope with and understand the trial process."[42] It is administered using a structured interview format. Like the CST, the defendant's responses are rated by the evaluator, but the CAI uses a scale of 1 (total incapacity) to 5 (no incapacity).[43] There is no recommended minimal score on the CAI, although it suggests that "'a majority of substantial accumulation'" of score of 3 or less may be cause for inpatient observation."[44] The validity and reliability of the CAI are arguably more questionable than that of the CST, therefore, since assessors are left "to make their own recommendations about the defendant's capacity."[45]

The *Interdisciplinary Fitness Interview* (IFI) is one of the more promising tools of assessment in this area, as the reliability of the assessment tool has been demonstrated to be quite high.[46] Using a structured interview format, the IFI is unique in that it is designed to be jointly administered by both a clinician and a lawyer.[47] It has three sections: one consisting of five items targeting the quality of the defendant's appreciation of the legal issues involved in a criminal trial (e.g., appreciating the consequences of various legal options); another on psychopathological items (e.g., disturbances in thought, communication, or affect); and a third that interdisciplinarily assesses the competency of the defendant's fitness to stand trial.[48]

The *Georgia Court Competency Test* (GCCT) consists of twenty-one questions and "has been found to be a highly reliable instrument that taps three dimensions: general legal knowledge (e.g., the job of the judge, your lawyer, etc.), courtroom layout (e.g., where the judge and jury are located in the courtroom), and specific legal knowledge (e.g., how to interact with defense

---

[40]MELTON ET AL., *supra* note 21, at 81-84.

[41]Keep in mind that the distinctions between the different types of legal competencies have been blurred as a result of the Supreme Court's decision in *Gordinez v. Moran*, 509 U.S. 389 (1993) (rejecting requirement of a higher standard of incompetency for determining competency to plead guilty than for determining competency to stand trial).

[42]BARTOL & BARTOL, *supra* note 30, at 125.

[43]*Id.*

[44]MELTON, ET AL., *supra* note 21, at 84.

[45]BARTOL & BARTOL, *supra* note 30, at 125.

[46]MELTON, ET AL, *supra* note 21, at 85.

[47]BARTOL & BARTOL, *supra* note 30, at 125.

[48]MELTON, ET AL., *supra* note 21, at 85.

counsel)."[49] One of the major drawbacks of this tool, however, is its focus on cognition (i.e., "knowing") rather than on an affective and other psychopathological issues.[50]

4. Concluding Remarks on the Competency Hearing Process

In spite of the fact that it may seem the various criteria used to assess competency is complex, the overall determination on competency is not all that complicated. The threshold for finding a defendant to be competent to stand trial is quite low.[51]

> It is estimated that 25,000 defendants are evaluated for competency in the United States each year, and that the number is increasing. Perhaps because the threshold for requiring a competency hearing is low, a large percentage of defendants evaluated are found competent—as many as ninety-six percent or more in some jurisdictions, and probably no less than seventy-five percent in most jurisdictions.[52]

Even if a defendant suffers from a mental illness that might impair his or her ability to both cognitively know and affectively appreciate the circumstances in which he or she finds himself or herself, that does not necessarily render the defendant incompetent. Significant correlates among defendants found incompetent to stand trial were not demographic characteristics, but rather clinical ones. They share the following criteria: they (1) "performed poorly on tests specifically designed to assess legally relevant functional abilities; (2) were diagnosed psychotic; and (3) had psychiatric symptoms indicating severe psychopathology."[53] It therefore appears that given the very low threshold for competency to stand trial, mental impairment has to be quite substantial before incompetency to stand trial is found.

D. The Quandary Presented by Synthetic Competency

The issue of competency has been greatly impacted by the advent of psychotropic medications. Drugs such as Thorazine, Mellaril, Prolixin, Haldol, and Stelazine[54] are frequently used, often in an inpatient setting, on those defendants competent to stand trial in order to restore the person to competency.[55] By altering brain chemistry, often through regulation of neurotransmitters, these antipsychotic drugs (sometimes called *neuroleptics*), "enable the incompetent individual affected by psychosis to possibly think more clearly or control his emotions in such a way as to prevent them from interfering with his rational thinking process."[56]

---

[49]LAWRENCE S. WRIGHTSMAN, ET AL., PSYCHOLOGY AND THE LEGAL SYSTEM 290 (4th ed. 1998).

[50]*Id.*

[51]MELTON, ET AL., *supra* note 21, at 67; BARTOL & BARTOL, *supra* note 30, at 122-25.

[52]Winick, *supra* note 5, at 578 (citing Bruce J. Winick, *Presumptions and Burdens of Proof in Determining Competency to Stand Trial: An Analysis of Medina v. California and the Supreme Court's New Due Process Methodology in Criminal Cases*, 47 U. MIAMI L. REV. 817, 847-48 (1993) (citing studies)); *see also* BARTOL & BARTOL, *supra* note 30, at 124 (stating roughly 80% of all criminal defendants evaluated are ultimately found to be competent to stand trial) (citing Grisso, *supra* note 36).

[53]BARTOL & BARTOL, *supra* note 30, at 125.

[54] Steve Tomashefsky, Note, *Antipsychotic Drugs and Fitness to Stand Trial: The Right of the Unfit Accused to Refuse Treatment*, 52 U. CHI. L. REV. 773, 773 n.3 (1985).

[55]Winick, *supra* note 5, at 578 (citing Ronald Roesch & Stephen L. Golding, *Treatment and Disposition of Defendants Found Incompetent to Stand Trial: A Review and a Proposal*, 2 INT'L J.L. & PSYCHIATRY 349, 349 (1979)).

[56]Keith Alan Byers, *Incompetency, Execution, and the Use of Antipsychotic Drugs*, 47 ARK. L. REV. 361, 376 (1994).

For most patients treated with these drugs, competency is restored, but for some, it never is.[57] It is generally agreed that such drugs do not cure mental illness, but rather only treat it—and only temporarily—so long as continuously administered under carefully monitored doses.[58] This process of using drugs to restore competency has been termed "*synthetic sanity*" by some[59] and "*artificial competency*" by others.[60] This process of restoring competency raises clinical,[61] ethical,[62] and constitutional issues,[63] most of which are beyond the scope of this book.

After being duly convicted and sentenced (which, of course, presumes competency at the time of trial and sentencing), "given the requirements of the prison environment, the Due Process Clause permits the State to treat a prison inmate who has a serious mental illness with antipsychotic drugs against his will, if the inmate is dangerous to himself or others and the treatment is in the inmate's medical interest."[64] Similarly, in *Youngberg v. Romeo*, the Supreme Court permitted the forced medication of the civilly committed, provided that the judgment to do so was exercised by a qualified professional.[65] But the scope of a pre-trial detainees's right to be free from unwanted medication is not entirely clear.

The federal Court of Appeals for the Fourth Circuit Columbia directly addressed the issue and held that an incompetent defendant can be forced to take psychotropic medications to restore sanity.[66] While directly challenging the holding of that case, the Supreme Court cast some doubt on its rationale when it decided *Riggins v. Nevada*[67] in 1992.

Riggins involved a defendant who had been found mentally competent to stand trial after being treated with Mellaril (an antipsychotic) and Dilantin (an anticonvulsant). The case did not address his synthetic sanity directly, though. Rather, it was concerned with the fact that Riggins

---

[57]Winick, Restructuring Competency, *supra* note 37, at 936 (finding the ordinary defendant hospitalized for incompetency in Dade County, FL spent seven months in the state hospital).

[58]Michelle K. Bachand, Note, *Antipsychotic Drugs and the Incompetent Defendant: A Perspective on the Treatment and Prosecution of Incompetent Defendants*, 47 WASH. & LEE L. REV. 1059, 1059-61 (1990).

[59]E.g., BARTOL & BARTOL, *supra* note 30, at 127; Linda C. Fentiman, *Whose Right Is It Anyway?: Rethinking Competency To Stand Trial in Light of the Synthetically Sane Defendant*, 40 U. MIAMI L. REV. 1109, 1111 (1986); M. Catherine Healy, *Comments: Riggins v. Nevada: Are "Synthetically Sane" Criminal Defendants Competent to Stand Trial?*, 20 N.E. J. CRIM. & CIV. CON. 385 (1994).

[60]Ptolemy H. Taylor, Comment, *Execution of the "Artificially Competent;" Cruel and Unusual?* 66 TUL. L. REV. 1045, 1059 (1992).

[61]For example, "while the therapeutic benefits of antipsychotic drugs are well documented, it is also true that the drugs can have serious, even fatal, side effects." Washington v. Harper, 494 U.S. 210, 229 (1990). For a basic summary of the acute and long-term effects of neuroleptic drugs, *see* Byers, *supra* note 56, at 378-80; for a more complete albeit complex one, *see* Gerald J. Schaefer, *Drug-Induced Alteration of Psychotic Behavior: Who Benefits?*, 9 J.L. & HEALTH 43 (1994-1995).

[62]*See generally* Fentiman, *supra* note 59; Rochelle G. Salguero, *Medical Ethics and Competency To Be Executed*, 96 YALE L.J. 167, 167 (1986).

[63]Bruce J. Winick, *Psychotropic Medication in the Criminal Trial Process: The Constitutional and Therapeutic Implications of Riggins v. Nevada*, 10 N.Y.L. SCH. J. HUM. RTS. 637 (1993).

[64]Harper, 494 U.S. at 221-22. Note that *Harper* recognized that a prison inmate possesses a significant due process liberty interest in avoiding the unwanted administration of psychotropic medication, but found that the prison's penological interest in protecting such an inmate from himself and others outweighed the individual's liberty interest.

[65]457 U.S. 307, 321-22 (1982). Interestingly, following its decision in *Youngberg*, the Court vacated a judgment of the Third Circuit Court of Appeals that had recognized the right of involuntarily confined mental patients to refuse psychotropic medication and remanded it for further consideration in light of *Youngberg*. Rennie v. Klein, 458 U.S. 1119 (1982), *vacating* 653 F.2d 836 (3d Cir. 1981) (en banc). For a critique of the professional judgment standard, *see* Susan Stefan, *Leaving Civil Rights to the "Experts": From Deference to Abdication Under the Professional Judgment Standard*, 102 YALE L.J. 639 (1992).

[66]*See, e.g.*, United States v. Charters, 151 829 F.2d 479 (4th Cir. 1987).

[67]504 U.S. 127 (1992).

did not want to be on any psychotropic medication during his trial because he had asserted the insanity defense.

The Supreme Court ruled that the trial court's denial of Riggins' motion to stop being forcibly medicated during his trial violated his Sixth Amendment fair trial rights and his Fourteenth Amendment due process rights because the trial court had not considered a less drastic alternative.

"The Court reasoned that Riggins' rights at trial possibly were impaired because the side effects of the medication may have impacted his outward appearance, the content of his testimony, his ability to follow the proceedings, or the substance of his communication with counsel."[68] In order to forcibly medicate someone in light of such interests on the part of the defendant, the Court explained that two criteria had to be established. First, the state would have to show that medicating someone under such circumstance was medically appropriate to ensure his or her own safety or that of others during trial. Second, the state would have to show that forcibly medicating a defendant when medically appropriate to do so served a compelling state interest.[69]

Given the stringent requirements of *Riggins*, the ability to synthetically create competency to stand trial is in doubt from a constitutional perspective. The Court made clear due process would be satisfied if forced medication "medically appropriate and, considering less intrusive alternatives, essential for the sake of [the defendant's] own safety or the safety of others."[70] Morris suggests that due process might also be satisfied "if the compelled treatment is medically appropriate and an adjudication of guilt or innocence cannot be obtained by using less intrusive means."[71] What "less intrusive means" might keep a psychotic person "competent" to stand trial without running afoul of the due process concerns raised in *Riggins*, however, is unclear at best, and, more accurately, "mired in controversy"[72] that may take years to unravel.

III. CONCLUSION

After evaluation and a hearing, if the defendant is found competent, then the case proceeds to trial. Such a determination of competency does not prevent the defendant from asserting the insanity defense for many of the reasons discussed above, the most important of which is the issue of timing since competency deals with the defendant's state of mind at the time of trial and insanity deals with the defendant's state of mind at the time of the alleged offense.

The more difficult scenario is when a defendant is found to be incompetent. The normal course of events in such a case is that the court "suspends the criminal proceedings and remands the defendant for treatment, typically on an inpatient basis. Treatment is designed not to cure the defendant, but to restore competency."[73]

---

[68]Elizabeth A. Schmidtlein, *Notes: Riggins V. Nevada: The Accused's Right to "Just Say No" to Antipsychotic Drugs?*, 10 J. CON. H. L. & POL'Y 541 (1994).

[69]Riggins, 504 U.S. at 136.

[70]*Id.*

[71]Grant H. Morris, *Judging Judgment: Assessing the Competence of Mental Patients to Refuse Treatment*, 32 SAN DIEGO L. REV. 343, 356 (1995).

[72]Bruce J. Winick, *New Directions in the Right to Refuse Mental Health Treatment: The Implications of Riggins v. Nevada*, 2 WM. & MARY BILL OF RTS. J. 205, 206 (1993).

[73]Winick, *supra* note 5, at 572.

After a period of evaluation often set by statute, if the psychiatric staff feels the defendant can be respired to competency, then the defendant will remain for treatment and the government must report to the court on the defendant's progress at regular intervals, often every six months. Assuming the psychiatric staff's original evalution was correct and the defendant recovers (i.e., is restored to competency), he or she will then face trial.

If, however, the defendant's condition is fixed, and the psychiatric staff does not believe the defendant's condition will improve, the defendant may not be held indefinitely. This was not always the case, though. Until the Supreme Court's decision in *Jackson v. Indiana*,[74] defendants found incompetent to stand trial were routinely kept hospitalized indefinitely, often for a period of time that was in excess of the maximum sentence that could have been imposed had they been convicted (a fact especially so for defendants charged with misdemeanors). And in some cases, such defendants were kept hospitalized for the remainder of their lives.[75] *Jackson* changed that by holding a defendant committed after a finding of incompetency to stand trial could not "be held more than a reasonable period of time necessary to determine whether there is a substantial probability that he will attain that capacity in the foreseeable future."[76]

Since *Jackson*, then, a defendant found incompetent to stand trial can only be kept confined if the treatment he or she is receiving while committed is likely to restore capacity "in the foreseeable future"—not at some distant point-in-time. If the treatment being provided to the defendant either does not advance the defendant toward competency, or does so, but without a fair probability that competency will be restored in the foreseeable future, "then the state must either institute customary civil commitment proceedings to detain the defendant, or release the defendant."[77] To prevent such a person from being released, the state must show that a person poses a danger to himself or herself, or to others. Without proving such danger, a person cannot be civilly committed and must therefore be released.[78]

---

[74] 406 U.S. 715 (1972).

[75] *See, e.g.,* James J. Gobert, *Competency to Stand Trial: A Pre-and-Post Jackson Analysis*, 40 TENN. L. REV. 659, 660 (1973).

[76] Jackson, 406 U.S. at 738.

[77] Winick, *supra* note 5, at 580.

[78] *See generally* David B. Wexler, *The Structure of Civil Commitment: Patterns, Pressures, and Interactions in Mental Health Legislation*, 7 LAW & HUM. BEHAV. 1, 11-12 (1983).

CHAPTER FIVE
ISSUES REGARDING OTHER CRIMINAL PROCESS COMPETENCIES

I. INTRODUCTION

In the previous chapter, the issue of competence to stand trial was addressed in some detail. However, the legal system has other types of competencies, all of which potentially, if not necessarily, involve mental health professionals. The issues regarding civil competencies will be addressed in a subsequent chapter. In this chapter, we explore the remaining competencies in the criminal process: the competency to plead guilty; the competency to waive one's Sixth Amendment right to counsel; the competency to confess; the competency to testify; the competence to refuse an insanity defense; the competency to be sentenced; and the competency to be executed.

II. AUTONOMY AND THE STATE

A. Philosophical and Political Roots

As respect for individual **autonomy** in decision-making was one of the justifications for the competency to stand trial, so is it also one of the most important justifications for other criminal competencies.[1] The constitution guarantees certain rights to people, and as autonomous creatures of free will, they should be free to control their own decisions.[2] (This is the perspective taken by the law—one that you may recall from Chapter One is incongruous with the deterministic perspective of the mental health sciences.) The notion of autonomy has been expressed differently by philosophers and political theorists who have written on the subject, but its embodiment in American jurisprudence stems largely from the Enlightenment writings of John Locke.[3] To Locke, "liberty was freedom from restraint, and the exercise of coercive power by the sovereign was always suspect."[4] Isaiah Berlin, interpreting Locke's writings, summarized autonomy as the notion that "there ought to exist a certain minimum area of personal freedom which must on no account be violated."[5]

Thomas Jefferson, relying largely on the writings of John Locke, viewed autonomy as a "natural right."[6] Jefferson expressed this viewpoint in the Declaration of Independence when he declared "life, liberty, and the pursuit of happiness" to be "inalienable rights."[7] And the notion of

---

[1]*See generally* Bruce J. Winick, *On Autonomy: Legal and Psychological Perspectives*, 37 VILL. L. REV. 1705, 1747-53 (1992) [hereinafter "Winick, On Autonomy].

[2]*See, e.g.,* JOHN STUART MILL, ON LIBERTY 97 (C. Shields ed., 1956) ("leaving people to themselves is always better, caeteris paribus [meaning "all things being equal"], than controlling them").

[3]*See generally* Rogers M. Smith, *The Constitution and Autonomy*, 60 TEX. L. REV. 175, 176-80 (1982).

[4]Winick, On Autonomy, *supra* note 1, at 1708 (citing, *inter alia,* DANIEL A. FARBER & SUZANNA SHERRY, A HISTORY OF THE AMERICAN CONSTITUTION 5-6, 9-12, 39, 259 (1990)).

[5]*Id.* (CITING ISAIAH BERLIN, FOUR ESSAYS ON LIBERTY 124 (1969)).

[6]*Id.* at 1709 (citing GARRETT W. SHELDON, THE POLITICAL PHILOSOPHY OF THOMAS JEFFERSON 9, 12, 42-45 (1991)).

[7]THE DECLARATION OF INDEPENDENCE para. 2 (U.S. 1776).

autonomy as a natural right is evident in the Bill of Rights to the U.S. Constitution.[8] "Individual autonomy is thus a value that infuses the Constitution."[9]

Although another ardent supporter of the notion of autonomy, John Stuart Mill did not approach the concept from a natural rights perspective the way the Locke and Jefferson did. Rather, he viewed autonomy as justified from a utilitarian viewpoint, based largely on the work of Jeremy Bentham.[10] Mill believed the government ought to allow its citizens to exercise their own discretion in make individual choices that were right for them, even if doing so meant that some people would make choices that were foolish. He reasoned that, on the whole, individuals know better than government what their own needs and desires are. Moreover, with such knowledge, Mill further reasoned that individuals would then make decisions that were in their own best interests.

It should be obvious that Mill's beliefs were predicated on rational, self-interested decision-making. Much of the basis of American jurisprudence and law is based upon that same premise. If accepted, the autonomy principle is a logical philosophical principle upon which to limit governmental power. But what if the premise is incorrect? What are the limits of the autonomy principle? Even Mill himself acknowledged that "those who are still in a state to require being taken care of by others must be protected from their own actions as well as against external injury."[11]

B. Limits on Autonomy

Justifying autonomy as he did, Mill thought the law, in respect for autonomy, should adhere to the "*harm principle.*" Simply stated, the harm principle posits that "'the only purpose for which power can be rightfully exercised over any member of a civilized community, against his will, is to prevent harm to others. . . .' With few exceptions, Mill would regard paternalistic interventions to be beyond the government's authority. Mill argued that the individual's 'own good, either physical or moral, is not a sufficient warrant' for governmental intrusion."[12]

The law has never followed Mill's harm principle in the way he set it forth, although the concept has been highly influential. The Supreme Court has conceptualized autonomy as a matter of "self-determination,"[13] but has stated on numerous occasions that the government may constrain or restrain an individual's autonomy and right of self-determination when compelling

---

[8]Winick, On Autonomy, *supra* note 1, at 1710 (citing 1 JONATHAN ELLIOT, THE DEBATES IN THE SEVERAL STATE CONVENTIONS ON THE ADOPTION OF THE FEDERAL CONSTITUTION 328 (2d ed. 1836); BERNARD SCHWARTZ, THE GREAT RIGHTS OF MANKIND: A HISTORY OF THE AMERICAN BILL OF RIGHTS 119-59 (1977); GERALD GUNTHER, CONSTITUTIONAL LAW 406 (11th ed. 1985); JOHN E. NOWAK ET AL., CONSTITUTIONAL LAW 315 (3d ed. 1986); LAURENCE H. TRIBE, AMERICAN CONSTITUTIONAL LAW § 1-2, at 3-4 (2d ed. 1988); Leonard W. Levy, *Bill of Rights*, in ESSAYS ON THE MAKING OF THE CONSTITUTION 258, 260, 266-67, 277 (2d ed. 1987)).

[9]Winick, On Autonomy, *supra* note 1, at 1712.

[10]*Id.* at 1713-14. Utilitarianism, somewhat oversimplified, is a moral theory that defines "good" in terms of what produced the greatest amount of happiness for the greatest number of people. *See id.* (citing JOHN STUART MILL, UTILITARIANISM (O. Piest ed., 1957); JEREMY BENTHAM, A COMMENT ON THE COMMENTARIES AND A FRAGMENT ON GOVERNMENT (J. Burns & H. Hart eds., 1977)).

[11]Robert D. Miller, "Symposium on Coercion: An Interdisciplinary Examination of Coercion, Exploitation, and the Law: Coerced Confinement and Treatment: *The Continuum of Coercion: Constitutional and Clinical Considerations in the Treatment of Mentally Disordered Persons*," 74 DENV. U.L. REV. 1169, 1170 (1997) (citing JOHN STUART MILL, ON LIBERTY 9 (Elizabeth Rapapport ed., 1978) (1859)).

[12]*Id.* at 1713 (citing MILL, ON LIBERTY, *supra* note 2, at 9).

[13]*E.g.,* Planned Parenthood v. Casey, 112 S. Ct. 2791 (1992).

state interests are at issue.[14] One of the times when the government has such a compelling state interest is when someone is incompetent to make specific types of decisions.[15]

C. *Parens Patriae*

When someone is mentally ill such that they are incapable of rational decision-making, the justification of respect for the autonomy right of the person dwindles significantly. When this occurs, the government acts on behalf of the person under a doctrine known as ***parens patriae***—meaning "the state as parent." "Historically, the *parens patriae* power was premised on the presumed incapacity of minors and mentally disabled persons to protect or care for themselves."[16] Under the *parens patriae* doctrine, the government may impinge upon the autonomy rights of an incompetent person, in the name of beneficence, because he or she is incapable of engaging in the rational decision-making process in which the law presupposes people engage.[17]

Using the doctrine of *parens patriae,* the courts have upheld the involuntary civil commitment of individuals to mental institutions[18] and the forced medication of a state prison inmate.[19] But the doctrine has limits. For example, as discussed in the previous chapter, *Riggins v. Nevada*[20] invalidated the conviction of a man who was tried and convicted while forcibly medicated during his criminal trial at which he had unsuccessfully attempted to assert the insanity defense.

Parens patriae is the doctrine underlying many types of civil and criminal competencies. Additional justifications for the doctrine apply to the competency to stand trial, such as the historical prohibition on trials *in absentia* and the fact that the right to counsel was not available in many, if not most, criminal prosecutions at common law. Since these justifications do not apply to some of the criminal competencies addressed in this chapter or the civil ones addressed later in this book, the importance of *parens patriae* as a justification for competencies other than the competency to stand trial is quite important.[21]

---

[14]*Id.; see also, e.g.,* Roe v. Wade, 410 U.S. 113, 155-56 (1973) (holding any restraint on a woman's right of self-determination over her body in terms of regulating abortion must advance a "compelling state interest," and "must be narrowly drawn to express only the legitimate state interest at stake.").

[15]*See, e.g.,* Addington v. Texas, 441 U.S. 418, 426 (1979) ("The state has a legitimate interest under its *parens patriae* powers in providing care to its citizens who are unable because of [mental] disorders to care for themselves."); Washington v. Harper, 494 U.S. 210 (1990) (recognizing a compelling state interest in providing treatment to further the best interests of mentally ill prisoners unable to meaningfully participate in their treatment decisions).

[16]Winick, On Autonomy, *supra* note 1, at 1772.

[17]*See, e.g.,* Addington v. Texas, 441 U.S. 418, 426 (1979) (discussing parens patriae power); O'Connor v. Donaldson, 422 U.S. 563, 583 (1975) (Burger, C.J., concurring) (noting historical roots of parens patriae power).

[18]*Addington,* 441 at 432 (holding that if a state produces "clear and convincing" evidence that a person is mentally ill and dangerous, he or she may be involuntarily committed).

[19]Washington v. Harper, 494 U.S. 210, 221-22 (1990) (upholding a prison regulation authorizing the involuntary administration of psychotropic medication if the treating psychiatrist determined the prisoner was both mentally disordered and dangerous to either himself or others without the need for a judicial determination of incompetency).

[20]504 U.S. 127 (1992).

[21]*See generally* Daniel B. Griffith, *The Best Interests Standard: A Comparison of The State's Parens Patriae Authority And Judicial Oversight in Best Interests Determinations For Children And Incompetent Patients,* 7 Issues L. & Med. 283 (1991).

III. SPECIFIC CRIMINAL COMPETENCIES

A. Overview

Until 1993, courts had developed specific rules regarding different criminal competencies. In 1993, however, the viability of these various standards of competency was called into question by the Supreme Court's decision in *Godinez v. Moran.*[22] A discussion of *Godinez* appears later in this chapter when we cover the specifics of competencies to plead guilty and to waive counsel. For background purposes, we will now briefly explore the standards of competency governing competency to confess, competency to refuse an insanity defense, competency to testify, and competency to be sentenced. Before embarking on that endeavor, however, a few generalities regarding criminal competencies should be noted since, even after *Godinez*, the standards for each competency remain important in practice, if not in law.

The vast majority of the literature on criminal process competencies is both applied and "largely descriptive, depicting characteristics of persons found incompetent, factors associated with findings of incompetence by clinicians and courts, and the consequences of being found incompetent."[23] We have little empirical data on what it means to be incompetent for a particularized standard because the determination of competence is "open-textured."[24] The determination, albeit a legal one, is often deferred to the expertise of mental health clinicians who are free to use much discretion in making determinations regarding criminal competencies.[25] Accordingly, forensic competency evaluations are "functional in nature, context-dependent, and pragmatic in orientation."[26] In other words, whether someone is found competent or not will depend on a number of factors that are often left to the discretion of the evaluating clinician.

Most clinicians evaluate competency with an eye towards what is expected of the criminal defendant under the particular competency standard. As one scholar put it, "competency . . . cannot be determined without reference to the activity for which it is required."[27] For example, waiving one's constitutional rights—regardless of the right involved—requires a "knowing, intelligent, and voluntary waiver."[28] But knowing the consequences of one's actions and understanding them in an intelligent manner logically should vary depending upon what, specifically, one is waiving.

> The different levels of competence are related in that a higher level generally includes all lesser ones. Thus a defendant who is competent to plead guilty will normally also be competent to stand trial or participate in non-trial proceedings. A defendant who is competent to stand trial will usually be competent to participate in a non-trial proceeding. The converse is not true. This is

---

[22]509 U.S. 389 (1993).

[23]Richard J. Bonnie, *The Competence of Criminal Defendants: Beyond Dusky and Drope*, 47 U. Miami L. Rev. 539, 540 (1996) (citing Thomas Grisso, *Five-Year Research Update (1986-1990): Evaluations for Competence to Stand Trial*, 10 Behav. Sci. & L. 353, 360-62 (1992).

[24]*Id.* at 449 (citing Ronald Roesch & Stephen L. Golding, Competency to Stand Trial 10-13 (1980)).

[25]*E.g.,* Stephen D. Hart & Robert D. Hare, *Predicting Fitness to Stand Trial: The Relative Power of Demographic, Criminal and Clinical Variables*, 5 Forensic Reports 53, 56, 59 (1992) (reporting over 96% concurrence rate by courts in a study with competency finding of clinicians).

[26]ABA Criminal Justice Mental Health Standards 7-4.1 commentary at 175 (1986).

[27]Barbara A. Ward, *Competency for Execution: Problems in Law and Psychiatry*, 14 Fla. St. U.L. Rev. 35, 59 (1985).

[28]*See, e.g.*, Boykin v. Alabama, 395 U.S. 238, 242 (1969); Johnson v. Zerbst, 304 U.S. 458, 465 (1938).

where most difficulties arise. A defendant who is competent to stand trial is not necessarily competent to plead guilty.[29]

Using a rationale similar to the one offered by the court in the quote above, clinicians often tailor their inquiries into competency based on the tasks that might be required of a defendant.[30] Yet, the law does not always recognize such a functional difference as best illustrated by the *Godinez* opinion. In spite of *Godinez,* clinicians often evaluate a defendant's cognitive abilities to "(1) communicate a choice; (2) understand information; (3) appreciate the significance of information in relation to one's own situation; and (4) engage in a process of rational manipulation, or reasoning, about the information."[31] With this in mind, we proceed to the specifics of the other criminal competencies.

B. Competency to Confess

Before turning to the specifics of **competency to confess,** a brief discussion of the law of confessions is in order. Pursuant to the Supreme Court's decision in *Miranda v. Arizona,*[32] a person subject to "custodial interrogation" by police must be given certain warnings. The meaning of custodial interrogation is complex, but for our purposes, we can make two generalizations. **Custody,** for *Miranda* purposes means when a suspect is not "free to leave."[33] **Interrogation,** for *Miranda* purposes, does not necessarily involve direct questioning; interrogation occurs when the police engage in words or actions that the police should know is "likely to elicit an incriminating response" from the suspect.[34]

When someone is in custody and subject to police interrogation, *Miranda* requires that the suspect be informed of his or her right to remain silent. Further, the suspect must be told that if the right to remains silent is waived (i.e., "given up"), then anything the suspect says can and will be used against the suspect in a court of law. The suspect must be told he or she has a right to have an attorney present during questioning, and if the suspect cannot afford an attorney, one will be appointed for him or her at the expense of the government.[35]

The purpose of *Miranda* warnings is to guard against infringement of the suspect's rights against self-incrimination under the Fifth Amendment.[36] In requiring these warnings to so protect a suspect's Fifth Amendment right, the Supreme Court acknowledged that custodial interrogations are inherently coercive from a psychological point of view.[37] Thus, the warnings

---

[29]Chavez v. United States, 656 F.2d 512, 519 n.3 (9th Cir. 1981).

[30]Bonnie, *supra* note 23, at 540.

[31]*Id.* at 570 (citing Paul S. Appelbaum & Thomas Grisso, *Assessing Patients' Capacities to Consent to Treatment*, 319 NEW ENG. J. MED. 1635 (1988)).

[32]384 U.S. 436 (1966).

[33]*See, e.g.,* Oregon v. Mathiason, 429 U.S. 492 (1977).

[34]*See. e.g.,* Rhode Island v. Innis, 46 U.S. 291 (1980), Brewer v. Williams, 430 U.S. 387 (1977). For a detailed exploration of the meaning of "custodial interrogation" and other specific issues with *Miranda* and the cases that followed in its progeny, *see* JOEL SAMAHA, CRIMINAL PROCEDURE 291-344 (3d ed. 1996) [hereinafter "Samaha"].

[35]384 U.S. 436 (1966).

[36]*Id.* at 448; see also Samaha, *supra* note 34, at 302.

[37]*Miranda*, 384 U.S. at 448-55.

are supposed to alert a suspect that he or she does not have to talk to the police, thereby avoiding the psychological pressure tactics that police often use during interrogations. [38]

After *Miranda* warnings have been given to a suspect being subjected to custodial interrogation, a suspect may waive his or her *Miranda* rights either expressly or implicitly.[39] But the **waiver** will be a matter of proof for the government to show that the suspect waived voluntarily, knowingly, and intelligently.[40] This three-prong standard is further protection to make sure that a suspect did not waive his or her rights due to coercive police tactics.[41] In applying this standard to see if *Miranda* rights were waived voluntarily, knowingly, and intelligently, courts evaluate the ***totality of the circumstances*** surrounding the waiver.[42] Circumstances that are frequently evaluated are suspects' "age, education, whether suspects gave an explicit waiver, language barriers, whether suspects initiated contact with the police, suspects' prior experience with the criminal justice system, and suspects' physical condition."[43]

In examining the totality of the circumstances as part of a determination of whether a waiver was voluntary, knowing, and intelligent, a suspect's mental condition can be a significant issue. *Miranda* warnings require meaningful advice in language the suspect can comprehend and on which the suspect can knowingly act. The crucial test is whether the words used by the police conveyed a clear understanding of all the suspect's rights under the totality of the circumstances. Thus, for example, non-English speaking suspects must have the warnings administered to them in a language they understand.

The level of comprehension of one's rights that is required in order to find a valid waiver is very low. One need only basically comprehend that one need not speak, and that if one chooses to speak, what is said can be used against the person, and, finally, that the suspect the right to counsel regardless of the suspect's ability to afford an attorney.

Mental health professionals might get involved in a hearing to determine if a waiver was "knowing, intelligent, and voluntary." To do so, a clinician needs to examine a defendant's cognitive abilities and assess if the defendant understood that he or she was giving up rights. Moreover, even if such a fundamental understanding is present, for a waiver to be intelligent, it must be the "product of a rational reasoning process."[44] Finally, to determine voluntariness of a waiver, a clinician must inquire as to whether the interrogation setting was sufficiently coercive that the defendant did not feel he or she could refuse to make the confession. In other words, was the defendant's will over "overborne?"[45]

Psychological inquiry into each of the three prongs is difficult because, absent mental retardation or some severe psychosis that was evident at the time of custodial interrogation, "in most cases, the waiver and confession occur months before the professional's evaluation, requiring many assumptions about the defendant's psychological condition at the time. As a result of these difficulties, professional evaluation of competence to confess are given less

---

[38]Miranda warnings must be given in a clear and unambiguous manner so that the individual understands his/her rights and feels free to exercise them. The police do not need to quote the exact words of the Miranda, but their rendition of the warnings must communicate the total of the substance of the decision. California v. Prysock, 453 U.S. 355 (1981).

[39]North Carolina v. Butler, 441 U.S. 369 (1979).

[40]*Id.*

[41]*Id.*

[42]Moran v. Burbine, 475 U.S. 412 (1986).

[43]Samaha, *supra* note 34, at 325.

[44]GARY B. MELTON, ET AL., PSYCHOLOGICAL EVALUATION FOR THE COURTS 95 (1987).

[45]*Id.*

weight than evidence about the police methods used to obtain the confession."[46] Accordingly, even expert testimony to the effect that a particular suspect did not really "understand" his or her rights or the fact that the suspect was waiving them is not likely to have any effect on the determination.[47]

C. Competency to Refuse an Insanity Defense

The **competency to refuse an insanity defense** is a "relatively uncommon variant of competency."[48] This competence is concerned with a situation in which the defendant refuses to go forward with an insanity defense when, in fact, the defendant is insane and would likely be acquitted on the grounds of his or her insanity. If such a situation arises, the question becomes whether due process imposes a duty on a court to compel the defendant to use the insanity defense, even though the defendant doesn't want to use the defense. There is no simple answer to this question. Courts are divided. Some courts take the view that since society is only justified in punishing the morally culpable (i.e., those who are "guilty" because they are responsible for their actions), then the court must impose the insanity defense on an unwilling defendant.[49] Other courts view this competency as any other. If the defendant understands the consequences of rejecting an insanity, then he or she should be free to do so.[50]

Both approaches are problematic. The former is paternalistic and invades the autonomy/self-determination rights of the defendant. Yet, if a defendant does not recognize that he or she was mentally ill (or the severity of such an illness), then serious doubts about the person's competency to stand trial are likely to exist. In forcing the insanity defense on such a defendant under the government's *parens patriae* power, the *Whalen* standard serves to protect such a defendant from criminal punishment when it is not warranted. Yet, there is a paradox in this. Why is such a defendant—someone a court feels should be *required* to raise an insanity defense to avoid criminal punishment but refuses to do so—competent to stand trial in the first place? That being said, there are logical reasons why a competent person who was legally insane at the time of the commission of an offense (but who no longer is) would not want to assert the insanity defense: "factual innocence"[51]; "the waiver of the constitutional rights associated with a fair trial; the deprivation of liberty; the stigma of being found to be mentally ill; and the invasive regimen of mental health treatment"[52]; long periods of confinement for terms "far in excess of that which would have been meted out for criminal punishment";[53] and the loss of collateral civil rights, such as a drivers license.[54] If any of these seemingly rational explanations are applicable, then the *Whalen* standard might well operate to the detriment of the defendant. The other approach,

---

[46]LAWRENCE S. WRIGHTSMAN, ET AL., PSYCHOLOGY AND THE LEGAL SYSTEM 280 (4th ed. 1998) [hereinafter "Wrightsman, et al."]; *see also* Melton, et al., *supra* note 44, at 96.

[47]THOMAS GRISSO, JUVENILES' WAIVER OF RIGHTS: LEGAL AND PSYCHOLOGICAL COMPETENCE (1981).

[48]MELTON, ET AL., *supra* note 44, at 98.

[49]*E.g.,* Whalen v. United States, 346 F.2d 812 (1965).

[50]*E.g.,* Frendak v. United States, 408 A.2d 364 (D.C. 1979).

[51]Justine A. Dunlap, *What's Competence Got to Do with It: the Right Not to Be Acquitted by Reason of Insanity*, 50 OKLA. L. REV. 495, 496 n.1008 (1997).

[52]*Id.* at 507.

[53]*Id.* at 510.

[54]MELTON, ET AL., *supra* note 44, at 98.

taken by *Frendak* and cases in its progeny, protect a competent defendant's autonomy and thereby allows him or her to avoid an insanity defense for one of the above stated reasons.

But the *Frendak* approach only works if a defendant, who was legally insane at the time of the commission of the criminal offense, has truly been restored to competency such that he or she can raise the insanity defense for one of the aforementioned seemingly logical reasons. If, on the other hand, a defendant fails to recognize the validity of a bona-fide insanity defense in his or her case when one of the above stated reasons why it might be preferable to be criminally convicted than to be found not guilty by reason of insanity are not applicable, then serious doubts are raised about that defendant's competency to stand trial.

D. Competency to Testify

Of all the competencies, the **competency to testify** is the least exacting. Of course, it applies not only to a defendant, but to any witness in either a civil or criminal proceeding at which testimony might be given. Note that the requirement that all witnesses who testify be competent to do so is different from the right to testify. A criminal defendant has a right to testify in his or her own defense; other witnesses have no such right but may be compelled to do so via subpoena.[55] But whether testifying as a right or not, a witness must meet a number of requirements under the Federal Rules of Evidence and most state's analogous evidence codes. These requirements apply to the competency to testify at the time the witness is called to give testimony.

First, the witness must be able to communicate either directly or through a qualified interpreter.[56] Second, unless a witness is properly qualified as an expert, a witness is only competent to testify about matters about which he or she "has personal knowledge,"[57] something usually gained via the witness' own senses (such as sight, smell, or hearing). Information a witness has learned from someone else is considered hearsay. Third, the witness must be capable of testifying truthfully—something he or she is required to do by an oath or affirmation that is "calculated to awaken the witness' conscience and impress the witness' mind with the duty to do so."[58] The inability to tell truth from non-truth (e.g., someone who is totally out of touch with reality) can therefore render someone incompetent to testify.

These requirements raise particular problems for child witnesses and the mentally ill. As a rule in the federal system, children, regardless of their age, are competent to testify if the judge finds the child possesses the ability to observe, recollect, and communicate. Some states follow the old common law rule that sets a rebuttable presumption that children over a certain age (e.g., eight or ten) are competent to testify, while the competency of younger children must be determined by the trial court. Of course, just because a child is competent to testify does not mean that he or she will be believed. A child's age and the beliefs that the child holds all goes towards the credibility of the child's testimony, not its admissibility. To cast doubt on the credibility of a child, cross-examination tends to explore things that a child believes, partially as

---

[55]Rock v. Arkansas, 483 U.S. 44 (1987).

[56]Fed. R. Evid. 604.

[57]Fed. R. Evid. 602.

[58]Fed. R. Evid. 603.

a function of his or her age, to be "true" such as the existence of imaginary friends, Santa Claus, the Easter Bunny, the tooth fairy, and so on.[59]

In terms of mental illness, the existence of such an illness does not, per se, render a witness incompetent to testify. To rise to the level of incompetency to testify under the rules of evidence, the mental illness would have to be of such severity as to render the witness' ability to perceive, know, and recall unreliable. The law of evidence in some states creates a rebuttable presumption that someone civilly committed, adjudicated insane, or determined to be incompetent in a judicial proceeding is also incompetent to be a witness.

Two old limitations on competency to testify are no longer in effect in the United States, but bear mentioning for historical purposes. At one time, a convicted felon was deemed incompetent to testify as a matter of law (i.e., without regard to cognitive functioning) just because he or she was a felon. Today, the prior felony conviction may serve as a basis for impeachment going to the weight and credibility of testimony, but not its admissibility. And, finally, unlike at common law when atheists, agnostics, or persons of certain religious beliefs would not have been competent to testify as a witness, today "evidence of the beliefs or opinions of a witness on matters of religion is not admissible for the purpose of showing that by reason of their nature the witness' credibility is impaired or enhanced."[60]

E. Modern Competencies to Plead Guilty and to Refuse Counsel

Competency to plead guilty and competency to refuse counsel (i.e., act as one's own attorney) are quite similar to each other and to the competency to confess. All three require that a waiver of the respective constitutional rights be knowing, intelligent, and voluntary.[61]

1. Constitutional Foundation of the Rights

The Sixth Amendment to the United States Constitution provides that "[i]n all criminal prosecutions, the accused shall enjoy the right . . . to have the assistance of counsel for his defen[s]e." This **right to counsel** is so fundamental to American jurisprudence that the criminal justice system must provide an indigent defendant with an attorney to represent him or her in all critical stages of a criminal prosecution.[62] The rationale underlying *Gideon* was that qualified counsel can navigate the procedural and substantive complexities of criminal prosecutions in a meaningful manner, while the layperson is not likely to be able to do so.[63]

As fundamental a right as the Sixth Amendment right to the assistance of counsel is, like other constitutional rights, it can be waived. In *Faretta v. California*,[64] the Supreme Court held

---

[59]For an excellent summary of the psychological research on children's testimony, including research on children's memories, cognitive development, and moral development (relevant because a morally understanding between right and wrong for the purpose of telling the truth as opposed to lying), and their suggestibility, *see* MELTON, ET AL., *supra* note 44, at 101-06.

[60]Fed. R. Evid. 610.

[61]*See* North Carolina v. Butler, 441 U.S. 369 (1979) (to confess); Johnson v. Zerbst, 304 U.S. 458, 463-64 (1938) (to waive counsel); Brady v. United States, 397 U.S. 742, 748 (1970) (to plead guilty).

[62]Gideon v. Wainwright, 372 U.S. 335, 342-44 (1963) (felony cases); Argersinger v. Hamlin, 407 U.S. 25, 32-33 (1972) (extending *Gideon* to any criminal trial where the defendant faces imprisonment, even misdemeanors). *But see* Scott v. Illinois, 440 U.S. 367, 369, 373-74 (1979) (holding an indigent's right to counsel does not include prosecutions in which imprisonment is authorized, but not actually imposed).

[63]*Gideon*, 372 U.S. at 345.

[64]422 U.S. 806, 819-20 (1975).

that the state cannot force a defendant to accept the representation of counsel if the defendant does not want it. In so reasoning, the Court held that a criminal defendant has a right to represent himself or herself "for it is he who suffers the consequences if the defense fails."[65]

In much the same way, the Fifth Amendment guarantees that "no person shall ... be compelled in any criminal case to be a witness against himself." When one pleads guilty, one is required to waive this right by admitting one's guilt and providing a factual basis for the guilty plea. Additionally, when pleading guilty, one waives three other important Sixth Amendment rights as well, including the right to a trial by jury, the right to confront and cross-examine witnesses, and the right to compel others to testify on behalf of one's defense.[66]

2. Waiver of the Rights

Any **waiver of the right to counsel** under either the Fifth or Sixth Amendment rights must be knowing, intelligent, and voluntary. Thus, many of the same problems that arise when determining the competency to confess also arise when determining competency to waive these rights.

As mentioned several times before in this book, the proper standards for determining the various criminal competencies was altered by the Supreme Court's decision in *Godinez v. Moran*.[67] In it, the Court attempted to resolve a split among the circuit courts of appeals regarding the appropriate standard for determining different competencies. At the court of appeals level, the Ninth Circuit held that a higher level of competency was required to allow someone to waive counsel and proceed *pro se* (representing himself as his own counsel) than was required for a finding of competency to stand trial.[68] The Supreme Court reversed, holding the Constitution did not require states to use a heightened level of competency for waiving counsel. It stressed that the inquiring was on the competency to waive a constitutional right, not the competency to perform well as one's own counsel (the specific right at issue). The Court reasoned that "there is no reason to believe that the decision to waive counsel requires an appreciably higher level of mental functioning than the decision to waive other constitutional rights."[69] The Court did note, however, that states were free to employ heightened competency standards if they wished, but the Due Process Clause does not require them to do so.[70]

The Court's decision in *Godinez* has received much criticism from scholars of the law and behavioral science.[71] In fact, some mental health scholars, urged "psychologists to employ a functional approach to competency determinations, argu[ing] that following the unitary *Godinez*

---

[65]*Id.* at 819-20.

[66]Boykin v. Alabama, 395 U.S. 238, 243 (1969).

[67]509 U.S. 389 (1993).

[68]Moran v. Godinez, 972 F.2d 263 (9th Cir. 1992).

[69]*Godinez*, 509 U.S. at 399.

[70]*Id.* at 402.

[71]*See, e.g.,* Bruce J. Winick, *Reforming Incompetency to Stand Trial and Plead Guilty: A Restated Proposal and a Response to Professor Bonnie*, 85 J. CRIM. L. & CRIMINOLOGY 571 (1995); Ronald L. Kuby & William M. Kunstler, *So Crazy He Thinks He Is Sane: The Colin Ferguson Trial and the Competency Standard*, 5 CORNELL J.L. & PUB. POL'Y 19 (1995); Alan R. Felthous, *The Right to Represent Oneself Incompetently: Competency to Waive Counsel and Conduct One's Own Defense Before and After Godinez*, 18 MENTAL & PHYSICAL DISABILITY L. REP. 105, 110 (1994) ("The Supreme Court in Godinez missed an opportunity to promote reason, logic, and justice in American jurisprudence...."); Luke Stephen Vadas, *Godinez v. Moran: An Insane Rule for Competency?*, 39 LOY. L. REV. 903, 919-20 (1994); Sheila Taub, *Competency Standard Clarified: Mental Capacity to Stand Trial Is at Issue*, NAT'L L.J., Oct. 18, 1993, at 25.

standard would 'represent a substantial deviation from the accepted standard of care in conducting such evaluations.'"[72] Unfortunately, the *Godinez* opinion has left the approach to various criminal competencies in a state of disarray, with each state opting for one of three approaches.

> Some states . . . do not require a heightened competency standard, or even a separate competency hearing, before determining whether a defendant is competent to waive counsel. Rather, they construe *Godinez* as requiring only a voluntary and knowing waiver of Sixth Amendment rights, without regard to a defendant's mental capacity. Other courts, after *Godinez*, assert that the constitutional right to waive counsel mandates using only the *Dusky* test to determine competence to choose self-representation, in spite of [the Court's] express invitation to adopt enhanced standards. Other states . . . have followed [the] suggestion, employing a standard for determining a defendant's competency to waive counsel that is higher than the standard for determining competency to stand trial.[73]

F. Competency To Be Sentenced

Mental illness that arises after guilt is established does not affect the judgment of guilt. It does, however, affect whether someone can be sentenced. Both at common law and under the statutory law of nearly every U.S. jurisdiction, a criminal defendant has to possess the requisite ***competency to be sentenced.***[74]

Several rationales underlie the requirement of competency to be sentenced. The usual concerns regarding competency of autonomy and *parens patriae* are, of course, at issue. But at common law, Blackstone reasoned that madness was punishment enough in itself.[75] A theological reason was offered in the 1700s and continues to be discussed by courts today.[76] It espoused that an incompetent person could not atone for his sin through punishment, thereby undercutting the notion of expatiation used to justify retributive punishment.[77] And today, concerns about an incompetent person not being able to assist counsel on his or her own behalf arguing mitigating factors at sentencing also are offered as rationales for the competency, a justification that also has its roots in English common law.[78]

The standard for competency to be sentenced is lower than the competency to stand trial, to plead guilty, or to waive counsel. After all, there are no constitutional rights for a criminal defendant to waive knowingly, intelligently, and voluntarily at a sentencing hearing. Accordingly, the test for competence has been quite low, asking only if "the defendant is able to understand the nature of the proceedings and participate intelligently to the extent participation is

---

[72]Jennifer W. Corinis, *Note: A Reasoned Standard for Competency to Waive Counsel after Godinez v. Moran*, 80 B.U.L. Rev. 265, 280 (2000) (citing David L. Shapiro, *Ethical Dilemmas for the Mental Health Professional: Issues Raised by Recent Supreme Court Decisions*, 34 CAL. W. L. REV. 177, 182 (1997).

[73]*Id.* at 282.

[74]Bonnie, *supra* note 23, at 556; *see also* Saddler v. United States, 531 F.2d 83, 86 (2d Cir. 1976) (per curiam).

[75]4 W. BLACKSTONE, COMMENTARIES *395-96.

[76]Ward, *supra* note 27, at 50-51 (citing Solesbee v. Balkcom, 339 U.S. 9, 17-19 (1950) (Frankfurter, J., dissenting, and citing J. Hawles, *Remarks on the Tryal of Charles Bateman, in* 3 STATE TRYALS 651, 652-53 (1719)).

[77]*See* Hazard & Louisell, *Death, the State, and the Insane: Stay of Execution*, 9 UCLA L. Rev. 381, 387 & n.21 (1962) (analyzing St. Thomas Aquinas, *Treatise on Angels, in* SUMMA THEOLOGICA (c. 1250-70); ST. THOMAS AQUINAS, SUMMA CONTRA GENTILES, bk. 3, ch. 146 (c. 1250-70)).

[78]*See* 1 M. Hale, Pleas of the Crown, 35 (1736) ("if after judgment he became of non sane memory, his execution shall be spared; for were he of sound memory he might allege somewhat in stay of judgement or execution").

called for."[79] The former requires a defendant to understand the nature of the sentencing hearing, specifically that he or she has previously been convicted of a crime and is now about to have a criminal punishment pronounced that could result in the loss of life, liberty, or property. It does not require an "affectively based appreciation" of the crime, nor must a defendant "demonstrate [an] understanding of why he is to be punished. He must merely understand the nature . . . that he must pay for his crime."[80]

The second part of the test requiring intelligent participation, is somewhat more complicated in light of the right of allocution. Allocution means a formal speech. In legal parlance, though, *allocution* is the formal inquiry of a criminal defendant by the court as to whether there is "any legal cause why the sentence of conviction should not be pronounced upon the verdict of conviction."[81]

The right to allocution existed at common law for two important reasons. First, there was no right to counsel at common law.[82] Second, a defendant was not competent to testify on his own behalf at common law. Given these restrictions, allocution was important because it may have been the only time a criminal defendant was permitted to address the court.[83] But since all criminal defendants facing the possibility of incarceration are guaranteed the right to counsel under the Sixth Amendment to the U.S. Constitution,[84] and further since a criminal defendant has the right to testify on his or her own behalf,[85] allocution is much less important today.

Although not constitutionally required, allocutions are required by most state's laws and under the Federal Rules of Criminal Procedure when someone pleads guilty[86] and when someone is sentenced.[87] Since a defendant must speak on his or her own behalf when allocution is required, it should be self-evident why some minimal understanding of what is transpiring is required of criminal defendants at sentencing.

G. Competency To Be Executed

In 2007, there are roughly 3,350 prisoners in the United States who sit on death row awaiting execution.[88] Up to as many as 70 percent of these death-row inmates suffer from schizophrenia or some other form of psychosis. These prisoners were found competent to stand trial and to be sentenced, but have either suffered "a relapse of a pre-existing mental illness or due to the

---

[79]Chavez v. United States, 656 F.2d 512, 518 (9th Cir. 1981).

[80]Ward, *supra* note 27, at 65.

[81]STEVEN H. GIFIS, BARRON'S LAW DICTIONARY 19 (2d. ed. 1984).

[82]*See* Gideon v. Wainwright, 372 U.S. 335, 342-44 (1963) (felony cases); Argersinger v. Hamlin, 407 U.S. 25, 32-33 (1972) (extending *Gideon* to any criminal trial where the defendant faces imprisonment, even misdemeanors). *But see* Scott v. Illinois, 440 U.S. 367, 369, 373-74 (1979) (holding an indigent's right to counsel does not include prosecutions in which imprisonment is authorized, but not actually imposed).

[83]Daniel L. Owel , *Clarifying Trial Courts' Obligation to Conduct Sua Sponte Inquiries into a Defendant's Competence to Stand Trial and Defendants' Right to Allocution,* 53 MD. L. REV. 793, 797 (1994).

[84]*See* cases cited *supra* note 82.

[85]Rock v. Arkansas, 483 U.S. 44 (1987).

[86]Fed. R. Crim. P. 11(f).

[87]Fed. R. Crim. P. 32(c)(3)(C).

[88]Raymond Bonner & Sara Rimer, *Executing the Mentally Retarded Even as Laws Begin to Shift,* N.Y. TIMES, Aug. 7, 2000, at A14 (estimating death row population); Rhonda K. Jenkins, *Comment: Fit to Die: Drug-Induced Competency for the Purpose of Execution,* 20 S. ILL. U. L. J. 149 (1995) (estimating percentage of death row inmates who are psychotic).

circumstances of their prison existence," have developed one.[89] What should be done with these condemned inmates who are mentally ill? This question is answered by the law regarding the ***competency to be executed.***

According to the Supreme Court, "no one disputes the need to require that those who are executed know the fact of their impending execution and the reason for it."[90] It therefore held in *Ford v. Wainwright* that under the Constitution, no "insane" person could be executed given the Eighth Amendment's restriction on cruel and unusual punishment. Even at the time *Ford v. Wainwright* was decided, every state that had a death penalty barred its application to mentally incompetent prisoners.[91] The Court did not define what they meant by "insane," but clearly it did *not* mean the term to be used in the same way it is used in the insanity defense since the defense is concerned with the defendant's state of mind at the time the offense was committed, and *Ford v. Wainwright* was concerned with the defendant who was convicted at trial, but subsequently became mentally ill.[92]

Because the very determination regarding whether to impose a death sentence requires a weighing of aggravating and mitigating factors in a particular case,[93] "psychiatric opinion concerning the impact of a defendant's background and the likelihood of future dangerousness may play an important part in jurors' decisions about whether to impose the death penalty."[94] This continues unabated, even though renowned legal scholars, psychologists, psychiatrists, and even the American Psychiatric Association (APA) have urged the Supreme Court that mental health clinicians have no expertise in predicting future dangerousness, and moreover, when such predictions are made, they are unreliable.[95] In spite of such protestations, the Supreme Court has continued to require case-specific evaluations on the imposition of the death penalty, thereby virtually assuring "routine participation by mental health professionals, especially psychiatrists, in the sentencing phase of capital murder trials."[96]

1. The Standard for Competency To Be Executed

The standard for competency to be executed is not very different from that regarding the imposition of any other criminal sentence. The person has to understand that he is being put to death by the state and must further understand the state is doing so as punishment for the crime of which the defendant was convicted. The technicalities of how this standard is defined from state to state, however, varies greatly. Some states follow the language in *Ford v. Wainwright* and simply prohibit the execution of "insane" prisoners without defining insanity for this

---

[89]*Id.* at 149 (citing Keith A. Byers, *Incompetency, Execution, and the Use of Antipsychotic Drugs*, 47 ARK. L. REV. 361, 362 n.2 (1994)).

[90]Ford v. Wainwright, 477 U.S. 399, 421 (1986) (Powell, J., concurring in part and concurring in the judgment).

[91]Mark A. Small & Randy K. Otto, *Evaluations of Competency to be Executed*, 18 CRIM. JUST. & BEHAV. 146, 148 (1991).

[92]Matthew S. Collins, *Involuntarily Medicating Condemned Incompetents for the Purpose of Rendering Them Sane and Thereby Subject to Execution*, 70 WASH. U. L.Q. 1229, 1234 n.32 (1992).

[93]Lockett v. Ohio, 438 U.S. 586, 600 (1978).

[94]Douglas Mossman, *The Psychiatrist and Execution Competency: Fording Murky Ethical Waters*, 43 Case W. Res. 1, 3 & n.8 (1992) (citing Jurek v. Texas, 428 U.S. 262, 276 (1976)).

[95]*Id.* at 4 & n.10 (citing Brief *Amicus Curiae* for the American Psychiatric Association, at 14, Barefoot v. Estelle, 463 U.S. 880 (1983) (No. 82-6080) ("stating long-term predictions of dangerousness should be based on 'predictive statistical or actuarial information that is fundamentally non-medical in nature'").

[96]Richard J. Bonnie, *Psychiatry and the Death Penalty: Emerging Problems in Virginia*, 66 VA. L. REV. 167, 174 (1980).

purpose.[97] Some states have attempted to flesh out a more defined standard by adopting the language Justice Powell used in his concurring opinion in *Ford v. Wainwright,* which required an understanding of the punishment and the reason for its imposition.[98] The federal government follows this standard as well.[99] And at least one state—Oklahoma—appears to have embraced the old "wild beast" standard for insanity when it prohibited the execution of inmates who are in "a state of general insanity, the[ir] mental powers being wholly obliterated."[100] The lack of uniformity in the approach to competency to be executed, coupled with the inherent ambiguities of clinical assessment has led the process of determining competency for execution to be called "a game of chance" by some commentators.[101]

The American Bar Association has attempted to set a national standard for determining competency to be executed. It rejected the use of the term "insanity" as used by the Supreme Court in *Ford v. Wainwright,* and recommended someone be found incompetent to be executed if:

> as a result of mental illness or mental retardation, the convict cannot understand the nature of the pending proceedings, what he or she was tried for, the reason for the punishment, or the nature of the punishment[, or cannot] recognize or understand any fact . . . which would make the punishment unjust or unlawful, or lacks the ability to convey such information to counsel or to the court.[102]

The first prong of the ABA standard is based on the definition of incompetency offered by Justice Powell in his concurring opinion in *Ford v. Wainwright.*[103] It also mirrors the generalized standard for competency to be sentenced. It focuses on cognition—knowing what is transpiring. The second prong, however, embodies the old common notion that one who cannot effectively communicate with counsel and assist in his own defense is not competent to be executed.[104] It therefore provides more protection than afforded by the Supreme Court in *Ford v. Wainwright,* or by the statutes of most states. One can only hope that the Supreme Court acts to offer "a unifying definition."[105]

2. Special Problems with Execution of Juveniles and the Mentally Retarded

The number of mentally retarded people on death row in the United States is not known, but experts estimate it is approximately 10 percent of the condemned population, or 360 inmates.[106]

---

[97]Ward, *supra* note 27, at 60-61.

[98]*Id.* (citing 477 U.S. at 422 (Powell, J., concurring)).

[99]18 U.S.C. § 3596 (c) (" . . . . A sentence of death shall not be carried out upon a person who, as a result of mental disability, lacks the mental capacity to understand the death penalty and why it was imposed on that person).

[100]*Id.* (citing Bingham v. State, 169 P.2d 311, 314 (Okla. Crim. App. 1946)).

[101]Jenkins, *supra* note 88, at 167 (citing Byers, *supra* note 89, at 366; Ward, *supra* note 27, at 61-62; Kristen W. Crosby, *Comment, State v. Perry: Louisiana's Cure-to-Kill Scheme Forces Death-row Inmates to Choose Between a Life Sentence of Untreated Insanity and Execution,* 77 MINN. L. REV. 1193 (1993)).

[102]AMERICAN BAR ASS'N, ABA CRIMINAL JUSTICE MENTAL HEALTH STANDARDS, Standard 7-5.6 at 290, 293 (1989).

[103]477 U.S. at 422 (Powell, J., concurring).

[104]Jenkins, *supra* note 88, at 168.

[105]*Id.* at 168 (citing Byers, *supra* note 89, at 366).

[106]Bonner & Rimer, *supra* note 88, at A14.

Since the death penalty was reinstated by the Supreme Court in 1976, thirty-four mentally retarded prisoners have been executed.[107]

The constitutionality of executing a mentally retarded offender was unsuccessfully challenged on Eighth Amendment grounds in *Penry v. Lynaugh*.[108] Mr. Penry had an IQ of approximately 60 and "the mental ability of a 7-year-old."[109] The Supreme Court ruled that mental retardation does not automatically preclude execution but rather is one factor that must be taken into account by jurors when weighing mitigating factors as a part of their deliberations on whether to impose the death penalty.[110]

As the standard quoted in the previous section states, the ABA has taken the position that a mentally retarded person who cannot understand the nature of punishment of death and why it is being imposed should be found incompetent to be executed. A federal law barring the imposition of the death penalty on the mentally retarded was enacted during the term of President Ronald Reagan.[111] But of the thirty-eight states that imposed capital punishment at the dawn of the twenty-first century, only thirteen prohibit the execution of someone who is mentally retarded.[112] In August of 2000, the Supreme Court voted 6-3 to deny an emergency application for a stay of execution for Oliver David Cruz. Texas then proceeded to execute the death row inmate who had an IQ that tested as low as 63.[113] But in the summer of 2002, the Supreme Court had a change of heart and overruled *Penry* when it decided *Atkins v. Virgina*.[114] In it, the Court declared the imposition of the death penalty against someone who was mentally retarded was cruel and unusual punishment and thus in violation of the Eighth Amendment. Key to the Court's reasoning was the fact that in the time since *Penry* had been decided, more and more states barred the execution of the mentally retarded.

> It is not so much the number of these States that is significant, but the consistency of the direction of change. Given the well-known fact that anticrime legislation is far more popular than legislation providing protections for persons guilty of violent crime, the large number of States prohibiting the execution of mentally retarded persons (and the complete absence of States passing legislation reinstating the power to conduct such executions) provides powerful evidence that today our society views mentally retarded offenders as categorically less culpable than the average criminal. The evidence carries even greater force when it is noted that the legislatures that have addressed the issue have voted overwhelmingly in favor of the prohibition. Moreover, even in those States that allow the execution of mentally retarded offenders, the practice is uncommon. . . . The practice, therefore, has become truly unusual, and it is fair to say that a national consensus has developed against it.[115]

Three years after barring the execution of the mentally retarded, the Supreme Court extended the rationale of *Atkins v. Virginia* by barring the execution of people who committed their crimes

---

[107]*Id.*

[108]492 U.S. 302 (1989).

[109]Bonner & Rimer, *supra* note 88, at A14.

[110]*Penry*, 492 U.S. at 320-30.

[111]*Id.* at A1; *see also* 18 U.S.C. § 3596 (c) ("A sentence of death shall not be carried out upon a person who is mentally retarded. . .)

[112]Bonner & Rimer, *supra* note 88, at A1 & A14 (citing Arkansas, Colorado, Georgia, Indiana, Kansas, Kentucky, Maryland, Nebraska, New Mexico, New York, South Dakota, Tennessee, and Washington).

[113]*Man Said to Be Retarded Is 1 of 2 Killers Executed*, N.Y. TIMES, Aug. 10, 2000, at A14.

[114]536 US 304 (2002).

[115]*Id.* at 2249.

while under the age of eighteen in *Roper v. Simmons*.[116] Until that case was decided, of the thirty-eight states with capital punishment laws, nineteen allowed for its use against juvenile offenders, down from twenty-five in 1989. The decrease in consensus about the propriety of executing juvenile offenders, coupled with strong international condemnation of the practice, were important parts of the Court's rationale in deciding that the execution of minors violated the Eighth Amendment's ban on cruel and unusual punishment.

3. Ethical and Practical Considerations

Not only do clinicians who are called upon to make determinations regarding competency to be executed face the normal complexities of evaluating any criminal competency, but they also face a particular ethical issue when making this determination. The consequences of finding someone to be competent practically translate into giving the green light for an execution to take place. This ethical dilemma is especially problematic for psychiatrists who, as physicians, have taken the Hippocratic Oath to "do no harm."[117] In addition to the principles of beneficence toward patients and respect for their autonomy embodied in Hippocratic Oath, there are also other reasons psychiatrists argue their evaluation of death-row inmates for competency to be executed is unethical.

First, the APA's ethical guidelines for psychiatrists prohibit a psychiatrist from being "a participant in a legally authorized execution."[118] If a competency evaluation is considered "participating" in an execution, then such clinical evaluation is not ethically permissible.[119] Both the American Medical Association and the APA, however, do not consider clinical evaluation to be participation barred by the guidelines.[120] Yet, a "substantial number of professionals believe that 'this arena is no place for a psychiatrist to function, that it downgrades the profession, and that all psychiatrists should refuse to participate' in such proceedings."[121]

Second, there are concerns about informed consent. The doctrine of informed consent, stemming from respect for autonomy and privacy rights, requires "full notice as to that which is being consented to" before one consents to medical treatment or participation in research.[122] But, someone who is incompetent is unable to give informed consent; the incompetent "will not

---

[116]543 U.S. 551 (2005).

[117]"I swear by Apollo the physician, by Aesculapius, Hygeia, and Panacea, and I take to witness all the gods, all the goddesses, to keep according to my ability and my judgment the following Oath: . . . I will prescribe regimen for the good of my patients according to my ability and my judgment and never do harm to anyone. To please no one will I prescribe a deadly drug, nor give advice which may cause his death . . . I will preserve the purity of my life and my art . . . In every house where I come I will enter only for the good of my patients, keeping myself far from all intentional ill-doing. . . ." Hippocrates (c.460-400 B.C.), *in* STEDMAN'S MEDICAL DICTIONARY 647 (4th Unabridged Lawyer's Ed. 1976). For a critique of interpreting this provision of the Hippocratic Oath as requiring physicians to preserve life, *see* ROBERT M. VEATCH, A THEORY OF MEDICAL ETHICS 166 (1981) ("Hippocratic Oath does not require a physician to use his skill to preserve life").

[118]AMERICAN PSYCHIATRIC ASSOCIATION, THE PRINCIPLES OF MEDICAL ETHICS WITH ANNOTATIONS ESPECIALLY APPLICABLE TO PSYCHIATRY § 1, P4, (1989).

[119]*See. e.g.,* Donald H. Wallace, *Incompetency for Execution: The Supreme Court Challenges the Ethical Standards of the Mental Health Professions,* 8 J. LEGAL MED. 265, 272 (1987).

[120]Mossman, *supra* note 94, at 31 (citing Brief for the AMA and APA as *Amici Curiae* in Perry v. Louisiana, 498 U.S. 38 (1990) (arguing a state cannot medicate an inmate only for the purposes of capital punishment since administration of such medication is "treatment" of the inmate that would be unethical in light of the consequences of such treatment).

[121]Mossman, *supra* note 94, at 9 (citing Michael L. Radelet & George W. Barnard, *Ethics and the Psychiatric Determination of Competency to be Executed,* 14 BULL. AM. ACAD. PSYCHIATRY & L. 45 (1986)).

[122]STEVEN H. GIFIS, BARRON'S LAW DICTIONARY 231 (2d. ed. 1984).

understand the process, nature, purpose, or consequences of an . . . evaluation."[123] Of course, someone who is not competent to give informed consent is probably not competent to be executed,[124] so the problem may be more of a theoretical than practical one.

In addition to the ethical issues involved, there also remains a host of other problems in this area of determinating competency, summarized by Mossman as follows:

> the method for selecting competency evaluators, the method and detail with which evaluators should examine prisoners, the nature of adequate representation for prisoners undergoing competency evaluations, the proper forum for hearing evaluators' findings, the proper scope of mental health expert testimony, and the procedure for initiating treatment of prisoners found incompetent.[125]

4. The Quagmire of Treatment to Restore Competency

As if all of the practical, clinical, and ethical problems outlined above were not enough, the realm of competency to be executed has another snag that raises even more ethical problems. If someone is determined to be incompetent to be executed, what do we do with such a person? Do we restore them to competency so we can execute them? If clinicians use psychotherapies and psychopharmacology do restore competency, are they acting within the ethical boundaries of their respective disciplines? From a legal standpoint, this issue was addressed, in part, by the case of *Perry v. Louisiana*.[126]

Perry concerned a death-row inmate who was found incompetent to be executed. Perry was diagnosed as a schizophrenic at age sixteen.[127] He was in and out of mental hospitals when not living with his family. While home, and clearly in a delusional state, he killed five family members, including his parents. At first, his psychosis led to a determination that he was unfit to stand trial.[128] After eighteen months of inpatient treatment which included administration of the powerful antipsychotic drug Haloperidol (marketed under the trade name Haldol®), he was found competent to stand trial.

Over the objections of his lawyers, Perry refused to go forward with an insanity plea. Having been found competent to waive an insanity defense, his lawyers futilely argued he was not guilty. He was convicted and sentenced to death. On direct appeals, his conviction and sentence were affirmed, but his competency to be executed was called into question.[129] It was determined that Perry was incompetent to be executed unless he remained medicated. The trial court ordered the continued administration of antipsychotic drugs to Perry over his objection. He appealed to the U.S. Supreme Court who vacated Perry's death sentence and remanded the case for reconsideration in light of its decision in *Washington v. Harper*.[130] The *Harper* Court held that constitutionally an inmate could be forcibly medicated with psychotropic medications against his

---

[123]Ward, *supra* note 27, at 77.

[124]*Id.* at 78.

[125]*Id.*

[126]498 U.S. 38 (1990).

[127]State v. Perry, 610 So. 2d 746, 748 (La. 1992).

[128]State v. Perry, 502 So.2d 543, 547 (La. 1986) *cert. denied*, 484 U.S. 872 (1987).

[129]State v. Perry, 502 So.2d 543, 564 (La. 1987).

[130]494 U.S. 210 (1990).

will if in the best medical interest of the inmate, and for the safety of the inmate and those around him.

On remand, the trial court determined *Harper* had no relevance in the competency to be executed sphere. *Harper* was limited to consideration of maintaining the mental health of an inmate while incarcerated, as well as the legitimate penological goals of preserving the safety of other inmates and correctional personal from the mentally ill prisoner. Dismissing *Harper*, the court ordered Perry to be forcibly medicated and his sentence to be carried out when he was competent.

Perry appealed to the Supreme Court of Louisiana who ultimately held that Perry could not be restored to competency via forcible administration of psychotropic medications solely so the state could proceed with his execution.[131] The state supreme court agreed with the lower court's reading of *Harper*, but concluded *Harper* was applicable precedent insofar as it could not be used to support the forcible administration of antipsychotic medication for the purposes of punishment. *Harper,* it reasoned, permitted forcible administration of medication for treatment purposes only. The court also found that Perry had valid privacy and autonomy interests against being forcibly medicated, which also weighed heavily in its determination that one cannot be synthetically restored to competency against one's will so that an execution may be carried out.[132] But key to the *Perry* court's decision was respect for the dignity and ethics of the medical professions. Its reliance on psychiatrist's ethical opposition to treating condemned inmates so they can be executed once restored to competency has been praised by clinicians and legal scholars alike.[133]

Perry carries no precedential value outside the state of Louisiana. Accordingly, other states may decide a prisoner may be forcibly medicated to synthetic competency so he can be executed. To date, only one state appellate court has published an opinion on the same issue, *Singleton v. State.*[134] In that case, the South Carolina Supreme Court cited *Perry* with favor and adopted its holding. However, the Eighth Circuit Court of Appeals reached the opposite conclusion in *Singleton v. Norris.*[135] In that case, the defendant had been restored to *Ford v. Wainwright* competency under a *Harper* order of involuntary medication. When the order expired, he continued taking his medication voluntarily to avoid renewed bouts of active psychosis. But once the state of Arkansas scheduled his execution, he sought a stay of execution arguing that, if he voluntarily ceased taking his medicine, he would return to a state of psychosis, and then be incompetent to be executed under *Ford*. Faced with two unacceptable consequences— "medication followed by execution and no medication followed by psychosis and imprisonment," Singleton sought a permanent stay of execution that would allow him to continue to receive medical treatment for his psychosis while incarcerated.[136] The Eighth Circuit rejected his request, finding it was constitutionally appropriate to forcibly medicate him and then execute

---

[131]610 So. 2d 746 (La. 1992).

[132]*Id.* at 755-58.

[133]*See, e.g.*, Bruce Arrigo & Jeffrey Tasca, *Right to Refuse Treatment, Competency to be Executed, and Therapeutic Jurisprudence: Toward A Systematic Analysis*, 24 L. & PSYCHOL. REV. 1, 1-47 (1999); Alfred M. Freedman & Abraham L. Halpern, *Professionalism, Mental Disability, and the Death Penalty: the Erosion of Ethics and Morality in Medicine: Physician Participation in Legal Executions in the United States*, 41 N.Y.L. SCH. L. REV. 169 (1996); Crosby, *supra* note 101.

[134]437 S.E.2d 53 (S.C. 1993).

[135]319 F.3d 1018, 1020 (8th Cir. 2003), *cert. denied*, 540 U.S. 832 (2003).

[136]Amir Vonsover, 7 U. PA. J. CONST. L. 311, 326 (2004).

him. Central to the court's reasoning was that Singleton preferred to be medicated than be in a psychotic state. Thus, his medication was "'unwanted' only in the shadow of an impending execution."[137]

After concluding that Singleton "suffered no substantial side effects" from his medication, the court decided that "'the State's interest in carrying out its lawfully imposed sentence [was] . . . superior' to Singleton's interest in being free from unwanted medication."[138] While conceding that forcible medication was not in Singleton's best long-term medical interests since it would result in his being executed, the court found it was in his short-term medical interest to be medicated. Following a denial of a petition for a writ of certiorari, Singleton was executed by lethal injection.[139]

It cannot be disputed that the result in *Singleton v. Norris* comports with the requirements of *Ford v. Wainwright* because, even when an inmate is synthetically competent, he or she is able to relate their impending punishment with the crime for which they were convicted. However, substantial room for disagreement exists with the court's conclusion that the forcible medication of a capital inmate to restore competency to be executed comports with the requirements of *Sell v. United States*.[140] *Sell* clarified the union of *Harper* and *Riggins* by stating:

> The Constitution permits the Government involuntarily to administer antipsychotic drugs to a mentally ill defendant facing serious criminal charges in order to render that defendant competent to stand trial, but only if the treatment is medically appropriate, is substantially unlikely to have side effects that may undermine the fairness of the trial, and, taking account of less intrusive alternatives, is necessary significantly to further important governmental trial-related interests.[141]

Sell made it clear that specific findings on all four factors (i.e., important governmental interests in trying the person; a substantial likelihood that competency can be restored using medicines; an absence of less intrusive alternative treatments; and a determination of the medical appropriateness of administering antipsychotics) are required before medicines can be forcibly administered within the confines of constitutional law. Singleton argued that it was not in his best medical interested to be forcibly medicated since that would lead to his death. The court reasoned the "best medical condition" language was not concerned with its effects on any criminal competencies, but rather was only concerned with treating a mental illnesses. While this may be a plausible construction of *Sell's* constitutional mandate, it is an arguable point whether focusing on the short-term medical interests of an inmate in the fact of death is the appropriate lens through which to assess the constitutionality of the underlying governmental actions.

Moreover, separate and apart from the constitutional questions raised by synthetic competency to be executed, professional ethical standards of the medical and behavioral scientific community cast doubt on the practicality of the approach taken in *Singleton v. Norris*.[142]

---

[137]*Id.* at 326 n. 134.

[138]*Id.* at 325–26 (citing *Singleton*, 319 F.3d at 1025).

[139]*Id.* at 327 n. 144.

[140]539 U.S. 166 (2003).

[141]*Sell*, 539 U.S. at 181.

[142]*See* Jennifer E. Lloyd, *Primum Non Nocere:* Singleton v. Norris *and the Ethical Dilemma of Medicating the Condemned*, 58 Ark. L. Rev. 225 (2005).

But even if the approach taken by *Perry v. Louisiana* were adopted as the nationwide standard, such an approach is not without shortcoming. *Perry* leaves open the possibility of executing someone who subsequently is restored to competency without having been forced to take psychotropic medication. By failing to automatically commute a death sentence to one of life imprisonment without the possibility of parole upon a determination that one is not competent to be executed (the way some states, like Maryland, do),[143] one of three bizarre situations is created. Either (1) an inmate is forcibly medicated in violation of the holding and well-reasoned rationale of *Perry*; (2) the condemned prisoner can avoid execution by refusing voluntary medication and be left to suffer with untreated mental illness; or (3) the inmate can voluntarily accept medical treatment of his or her mental illness which could then lead to the prisoner's execution. "Such a choice is an atrocity and repugnant to every life-affirming, dignity-preserving tenet of American law."[144]

IV. CONCLUSION: CRIMINAL COMPETENCIES AFTER *GODINEZ*

In the wake of the varying approaches to competency that have evolved as a result of the *Godinez* opinion, legal and mental health scholars have repeatedly urged states to contextualize their competency evaluations.[145] This is largely because the very issue of competency is supposed to be concerned with the capacity to do something in particular. Logic dictates that what the particular thing is ought to determine whether one is competent to do it. In other words, to properly assess a criminal process competency, we must make a contextualized inquiry into "whether the individual possesses the mental faculties relevant to the task at hand."[146] When we fail to make a proper contextualized inquiry regarding competency for a particular purpose— something that arguably occurred in the illustrative case of *State v. Camacho*[147] that appears below—such a failure may not rise to level of a due process violation according to the Supreme Court's opinion in *Godinez*. But such a failure is certainly antithetical to the therapeutic jurisprudential direction in which many scholars believe our nation's laws ought to be headed.[148]

---

[143] *See* Paul S. Appelbaum & Steven K. Hoge, *Psychiatrists and Capital Punishment: Evaluation and Restoration of Competence to be Executed*, 20 NEWSL. AM. ACAD. PSYCHIATRY & L. 14, 15 (1995) (praising Maryland's approach of commuting an incompetent prisoner's death sentence to life imprisonment without parole so that psychiatrists can ethically care for prisoners without the risk that competence for execution will be restored);

[144] Jenkins, *supra* note 88, at 177.

[145] *Id.* at 284-88 (citations omitted).

[146] Taub, *supra* note 71, at 28.

[147] 561 N.W.2d 160 (Minn. 1997).

[148] *See generally* Winick, supra note 71, at 575-76; David B. Wexler, *An Orientation to Therapeutic Jurisprudence*, 20 N.E. J. ON CRIM. & CIV. CON. 259 (1994); Robert F. Schopp, *Therapeutic Jurisprudence and Conflicts Among Values in Mental Health Law*, 11 BEHAVIORAL SCI. & L. 31 (1993); David B. Wexler, *Justice, Mental Health, and Therapeutic Jurisprudence*, 40 CLEV. ST. L. REV. 517 (1992); DAVID B. WEXLER & BRUCE J. WINICK (eds.), ESSAYS IN THERAPEUTIC JURISPRUDENCE, 1991); DAVID B. WEXLER (ed.), THERAPEUTIC JURISPRUDENCE: THE LAW AS A THERAPEUTIC AGENT (1990).

CHAPTER SIX
THE INSANITY DEFENSE

I. INTRODUCTION

A. Overview

In several places earlier in this book, the law's view of free will and autonomy have been explored in some detail. While the mental health sciences have challenged these notions,[1] it cannot be disputed that the law, and the criminal law in particular, holds these concepts to be central to the American jurisprudence. Perhaps the area of criminal law in which this is most evident is in dealing with the insanity defense.

Insanity is a legal term—not a psychological or medical one. Unlike competency to stand trial, which examines the state of mind of the defendant at the time of the criminal prosecution of a case, insanity refers to the defendant's state of mind *at the time of the offense.* Thus, the very nature of the defense is retrospective. The law requires the trier-of-fact (usually a jury) to go back in time to evaluate the defendant's state of mind in the past. Accordingly, mental health experts are used to assist the trier-of-fact in reconstructing the defendant's past mental state. This task is complicated at best, because "[t]he longer the interval between the offense and the administration of [psychological] test, the less representative any current appraisal is likely to be of the previous mental state."[2]

B. Justifications for the Insanity Defense

Why do we have an insanity defense? While answers to this question can take volumes of writing, an oversimplified answer can be given in three parts. First, it is unfair to punish people for acts that result from mental illness. Why? The rational decision-making model of a person of free-will is inapplicable when dealing with someone who is severely mentally ill. With the very premise of human action taken by the criminal law undercut or totally gone, the criminal law's reasons for imposing a sanction are no longer applicable.[3]

Second, in terms of the major theoretical justifications for punishment, all seem inapplicable to the mentally ill criminal offender. From the standpoint of retribution theory, what evil is there to punish if someone acted not out of criminal intent, but rather out of a delusionary or otherwise psychotic thought process? Punishment of the mentally ill also cannot be justified under deterrence theory because it is nearly impossible to deter acts resulting from mental illness. Deterrence as a theory is predicated on the utilitarian notion of rational choice, a presupposition that is not applicable to the insane defendant. Since the treatment of the mentally ill in the correctional setting leaves much to be desired, charitably speaking, rehabilitation is better

---

[1] *See generally* Chapter 1.

[2] GARY B. MELTON, ET AL., PSYCHOLOGICAL EVALUATION FOR THE COURTS 155 (1987).

[3] *See* MICHAEL S. MOORE, LAW AND PSYCHIATRY 65-66 (1984) (punishment applied only to those who "are in full possession of their facilities"); *see also* Morrissette v. United States, 342 U.S. 246, 250 n.4 (1952) (quoting Roscoe Pound, *Introduction,* in F. SAYRE, CASES ON CRIMINAL LAW (1924) ("criminal law is based upon . . . punishing the vicious will. It postulates a free agent confronted with a choice between doing right and doing wrong . . . .").

accomplished through the mental health system, not in jails or prisons. Substantially the same argument applies to incapacitation theory.

Third, those who commit criminal acts as a result of their mental illness do not fit nicely into the criminal law's doctrinal definitions of *mens rea*. *Mens rea* is "a guilty mind; a guilty or wrongful purpose; a criminal intent."[4] With the exception of a small number of crimes, *mens rea* is an essential element of all crimes.[5] But those who are mentally ill may or may not form *mens rea*, and even if they do, it may be formed defectively. This was recognized as early as the thirteenth century in English common law when the courts excused a "madman" who lacked "mind and reason."[6]

C. Common Misperceptions Regarding the Insanity Defense

In a two-year research study on insanity defense, Professor Michael Perlin found much evidence to support two propositions regarding public perceptions of the insanity defense. First, he found that people believed the defense was much more widely used than it really is, and second, he found that public sentiment toward the defense was overwhelmingly negative.[7]

> According to the news media, the allegedly "popular" insanity defense—nothing more than a "legalistic slight of hand" and a "common feature of murder defenses"—is a reward to mentally disabled defendants for "staying sick," a "travesty," a "loophole," a "refuge," a "technicality," one of the "absurdities of state law," perhaps a "monstrous fraud." It is used—again, allegedly—in cases involving "mild disorders or a sudden disappointment or mounting frustrations . . . or a less-than-perfect childhood." It is reflected in "pseudoscience that can only obfuscate the issues," and is seen as responsible for "burying the traditional Judeo-Christian notion of moral responsibility under a tower of psychobabble."[8]

In fact, the insanity defense is used quite rarely. It is raised in approximately 1 percent of all felony cases, and when invoked, it is successful less than 25 percent of the time.[9] It is used nearly twice as much for non-homicide offenses than it is for those offenses involving a human death.[10] Thus, contrary to popular misperceptions, the insanity defense is infrequently raised and, even when it is raised, it is unsuccessful three-quarters of the time.[11]

---

[4]BLACK'S LAW DICTIONARY (6th ed. 1990).

[5]JOEL SAMAHA, CRIMINAL LAW 114-17 (4th ed. 1993); *see also* Williamson v. Norris, 1 Q.B. 7, 14 (1899) ("the general rule of English law is, that no crime can be committed unless there is *mens rea*"); Duncan v. State, 26 Tenn. (7 Hum.) 148, 150 (1846) ("It is a sacred principle of criminal jurisprudence that the intention to commit the crime is of the essence of the crime, and to hold that a man shall be held criminally responsible for an offense of the commission of which he was ignorant at the time would be intolerable tyranny.").

[6]Brian E. Elkins, *Idaho's Repeal of the Insanity Defense: What Are We Trying to Prove?*, 31 IDAHO L. REV. 151, 162 (1994) (internal citations omitted).

[7]Michael L. Perlin, *"The Borderline Which Separated You From Me": The Insanity Defense, the Authoritarian Spirit, the Fear of Faking, and the Culture of Punishment*, 82 IOWA L. REV. 1375, 1380 (1997) [hereinafter, "Perlin, The Fear of Faking"].

[8]*Id.* at 1403 (internal citations omitted).

[9]*Id.* at 1404 (citing Lisa A. Callahan et al., *The Volume and Characteristics of Insanity Defense Pleas: An Eight-State Study*, 19 BULL. AM. ACAD. PSYCHIATRY & L. 331, 334 (1991); Joseph H. Rodriguez et al., *The Insanity Defense Under Siege: Legislative Assaults and Legal Rejoinders*, 14 RUTGERS L.J. 397, 401 (1983)).

[10]*Id.* (citing Rodriguez, et al., *supra* note 9 at 402).

[11]*See also* Jeffrey S. Janofsky et al., *Defendants Pleading Insanity: An Analysis of Outcome*, 17 BULL. AM. ACAD. PSYCHIATRY & L. 203, 205 (1989) (reporting that 143 (1.2%) of 11,497 defendants in Baltimore County initially pled insanity, but after forensic evaluation, only 16 defendants (.001%) maintained the plea to the trial stage. Of these 16, the parties stipulated to

There is also much public concern about defendants who fake mental illnesses in order to escape a conviction, and who simply hire clinicians to engage in an expert battle with the prosecution at trial.[12] While these cases make for good media play, they are the rare exception and not the rule. In fact, there is overwhelming agreement on a clinical diagnosis between clinicians on both sides of the criminal dispute. One study put the clinician agreement rate at 88 percent[13]; another at 92 percent.[14] Moreover, the media and Hollywood—in films like *Primal Fear*—exacerbate the fears of a defendant feigning mental illness to avoid criminal punishment. However, such fears are ill founded. "Recent carefully crafted empirical studies have clearly demonstrated that malingering among insanity defendants is, and traditionally has been, statistically low."[15] In practice, modern diagnostic instruments and procedures allow clinicians to distinguish correctly those who are truly mentally ill and those who are faking between 92 and 95 percent of the time.[16] Thus when defendants fake mental illness, it is extraordinarily difficult for them to "get away with" it.

II. EVOLUTION OF THE INSANITY DEFENSE

A. The Wild Beast Defense

The insanity defense has a long history, having roots in Moslem, Hebrew, and Roman law.[17] It dates back to thirteenth century England.[18] Justice Tracy, a judge in King Edward's court, formulated what became known as the "***wild beast test***" in a case referred to today as Arnold's case.[19] In the case:

> the defendant shot and wounded a British Lord in a homicide attempt. Justice Tracy instructed the jury that it should acquit by reason of insanity if it found the defendant to be a madman which he described as 'a man that is totally deprived of his understanding and memory, and doth not know what he is doing, no more than an infant, than <u>a brute, or a wild beast</u>, such a one is never the object of punishment.'[20]

---

the defendants' insanity in 13 cases, leaving only 3 cases contested. One of the three cases was dropped, one resulted in acquittal, and one resulted in a conviction.).

[12]Perlin, The Fear of Faking, *supra* note 7, at 1404.

[13]*Id.* at 1405 (citing Jeffrey L. Rogers et al., *Insanity Defenses: Contested or Conceded?*, 141 AM. J. PSYCHIATRY 885, 885-86 (1984)).

[14]*Id.* (citing Kenneth Fukunaga et al., *Insanity Plea: Interexaminer Agreement and Concordance of Psychiatric Opinion and Court Verdict*, 5 LAW & HUM. BEHAV. 325, 326 (1981)).

[15]*Id.* (citing Dewey G. Cornell & Gary L. Hawk, *Clinical Presentation of Malingerers Diagnosed by Experienced Forensic Psychologists*, 13 LAW & HUM. BEHAV. 375, 380-81 (1989) (discussing a study in which "clinicians diagnosed 8% of criminal defendants as malingering psychotic symptoms"); Linda S. Grossman & Orest E. Wasyliw, *A Psychometric Study of Stereotypes: Assessment of Malingering in a Criminal Forensic Group*, 52 J. PERSONAL. ASSESSMENT 549, 549 (1988) (finding a minority of defendants clearly malingered)).

[16]*Id.* (citing David Schretlen & Hal Arkowitz, *A Psychological Test Battery to Detect Prison Inmates Who Fake Insanity or Mental Retardation*, 8 BEHAV. SCI. & L. 75, 75 (1990)).

[17]Moore, *supra* note 3, at 65-66.

[18]DONALD. T. LUNDE, MURDER AND MADNESS (1975).

[19]Rex v. Arnold, Y.B. 10 Geo. 1 (1724), *reprinted in* 16 A COMPLETE COLLECTION OF STATE TRIALS 695 (T. Howell ed. 1812).

[20]Michael L. Perlin, *Unpacking The Myths: The Symbolism Mythology of Insanity Defense Jurisprudence*, 40 CASE W. RES. 599, 632 n.142 (1990) [hereinafter, "Perlin, Unpacking the Myths"]; *see also* RITA JAMES SIMON, THE JURY AND THE DEFENSE OF INSANITY 17 (1967). Professor Perlin goes on to explain that the word "brute" as used in Arnold's case referred to "farm animals such as 'badgers, foxes, deer, and rabbits.' Thus, the emphasis was apparently meant to focus on a lack of *intellectual*

Justice Tracy's wild beast test, although rejected for a short while by the decision in the Hadfield case (discussed in the next paragraph), "set the standard which would be applied in English courts throughout the eighteenth century."[21] Yet, there are few records about how the wild beast test was actually applied, but "commentators of the period consistently spoke of a requirement that the defendant lack understanding of good and evil or be devoid of all reason, and often equated the insane with animals or infants."[22] Interestingly, there was no separate or special verdict that excused a defendant on the basis of his insanity. Rather, after conviction, an appeal was made to the king for a pardon.[23]

The defense evolved significantly in 1800 when James Hadfield shot King George III because Hadfield believed he had acted on orders from God.[24] At his trial for treason, defense counsel argued that Hadfield's delusions, stemming from head trauma suffered during battle, caused his actions.[25] Several physicians offered testimony corroborating Hadfield's head trauma claims.[26] The jury acquitted Hadfield because "the prisoner appear[ed] to be under the influence of insanity at the time the act was committed."[27]

The Hadfield case represented a departure from the wild beast test in two ways. First, "it rejected the argument that the defendant 'must be totally deprived of all mental faculty before acquitt[al].'"[28] Second, it was the first time that a verdict of not guilty by reason of insanity (NGBI) "became a separate verdict of acquittal."[29] However, within a few years of the Hadfield decision, English jurisprudence reverted to using Justice Tracy's wild beast test, which did require a near complete deprivation of mental faculties for an acquittal.[30]

---

ability, rather than the savage beast-like image the phrase calls to mind." Perlin, Unpacking the Myths, *supra* note 20, at 632 n.142.

[21] Anne C. Gresham, *The Insanity Plea: A Futile Defense For Serial Killers*, 17 LAW & PSYCHOL. REV. 193, 194 (1993) (citing SIMON, *supra* note 20, at 18-19).

[22] Christopher Slobogin, *An End to Insanity: Recasting the Role of Mental Disability in Criminal Cases*, 86 VA. L. REV. 1199, 1208 (2000). Slobogin states: "In medieval times, the insanity finding was implemented not through a formal verdict after judicial instructions, but via pardon from the king. There are several accounts of pardons before the sixteenth century, but the precise grounds for these actions are not clear." *Id.* at 1208 n.32.

[23] *Id.* (quoting THOMAS MAEDER, CRIME AND MADNESS: THE ORIGINS AND EVOLUTION OF THE INSANITY DEFENSE 5 (1985) ("There was no need for tests of exculpatory insanity because the only criteria for a pardon were those dictated by the king's opinion and conscience.")).

[24] Gerald Robin, *The Evolution of the Insanity Defense*, 13 J. CONTEMP. CRIM. JUST. 224, 226 (1997).

[25] *Id.* at 226.

[26] *Id.*

[27] *Id.*; *see generally* Richard Moran, *The Origin of Insanity as a Special Verdict: The Trial for Treason of James Hadfield*, 19 LAW & SOC'Y REV. 487 (1985).

[28] Gresham, *supra* note 21, at 194 (quoting SIMON, *supra* note 20, at 19).

[29] Robin, *supra* note 24, at 226 (citing B. Caesar, *The Insanity Defense: The New Loophole*, 16 PROSECUTOR 19 (1982)).

[30] Gresham, *supra* note 21, at 194 (citing SIMON, *supra* note 20, at 19).

B. The M'Naghten Test

1. Background of the M'Naghten Case

In 1843, the *M'Naghten* case[31] set forth a legal standard for insanity that many U.S. jurisdictions still use today.[32] Daniel M'Naghten was indicted for the first-degree murder of Edward Drummond, the secretary to the English Prime Minister Sir Robert Peel.[33] M'Naghten had intended to kill Peel, but mistook Drummond for him.[34] He explained to the police that he wanted to kill the Prime Minister "because the Tories in my city follow and persecute me wherever I go, and have entirely destroyed my peace of mind. They do everything in their power to harass and persecute me; in fact, they wish to murder me."[35]

At M'Naghten's trial, his defense attorneys argued that he suffered from paranoid persecutory delusions.[36] To support this defense, "[M'Naghten] had the assistance of four of the most able barristers in Britain and nine prominent medical experts."[37] In contrast, the prosecution put on no experts.[38] Lord Chief Justice Tindal charged the jury as follows:

> The question to be determined is whether at the time of the act in question was committed, the prisoner had or had not the use of his understanding, so as to know that he was doing a wrong or wicked act. If the jurors should be of opinion that the prisoner was not sensible at the time he committed it, that he was violating the laws of both God and man, then he would be entitled to a verdict in his favor; but if, on the contrary, they were of opinion that when he committed the act he was in a sound state of mind, then their verdict must be against him.[39]

The jury found M'Naghten not guilty by reason of insanity.[40] M'Naghten was committed to Bedlam, the notorious asylum, "where he remained until his death twenty-two years later."[41] Much public outrage over the acquittal followed, including condemnation of the case from Queen Victoria who herself had be the target of assassination attempts.[42] The House of Lords subsequently set down what became known as the **M'Naghten test** for insanity.[43] Under this test:

---

[31] *M'Naghten*, 8 Eng. Rep. 718 (H.L. 1843). There are at least twelve different spellings of M'Naghten's last name, something that he himself likely contributed to since he spelled his own name differently on several occasions. RICHARD MORAN, KNOWING RIGHT FROM WRONG: THE INSANITY DEFENSE OF DANIEL M'NAGHTEN xi (1981).

[32] Public Broadcasting Service, Frontline: State Insanity Defense Laws (2005), *at* http://www.pbs.org/wgbh/pages/frontline/ shows/crime/trial/states.html (last visited Feb. 22, 2007).

[33] Robin, *supra* note 24, at 226.

[34] *Id.*

[35] SANFORD H. KADISH AND STEPHEN J. SCHULHOFER, CRIMINAL LAW AND ITS PROCESSES: CASES AND MATERIALS 969 (5th ed. 1989) (citing MORAN, *supra* note 31, at 90).

[36] Robin, *supra* note 24, at 226 (citing J. BIGGS, THE GUILTY MIND 97 (1955)).

[37] KADISH & SCHULHOFER, *supra* note 35, at 969 n.20 (citing MORAN, *supra* note 31, at 90).

[38] *Id.*

[39] *M'Naghten*, 8 Eng. Rep. at 718, *quoted in* KADISH & SCHULHOFER, *supra* note 35, at 969,

[40] Robin, *supra* note 24, at 226.

[41] *Id.*

[42] *Id.* (citing J. BIGGS, THE GUILTY MIND 97 (1955)).

[43] *See* M'Naghten's Case, 8 Eng. Rep. 718 (H.L. 1843).

It must be clearly proved that, at the time of the committing of the act, the party accused was labouring under such a defect of reason, from a disease of the mind, as not to know the nature and quality of the act he was doing; or, if he did know it, that he did not know he was doing what was wrong.[44]

2. The Elements of the M'Naghten Test

The *M'Naghten* "right-wrong" test for insanity can be stated in terms of elements:

1) A person is not responsible for criminal conduct if, at the time of the offense

2) the defendant suffered from of a mental disease or defect

3) that caused the defendant either:

   (a) not to know the nature and quality of the act he or she committed;
   or
   (b) knowing the quality or nature of the act, nonetheless not to know that the act was wrong.

As discussed above, the first element sets forth the fact that the insanity defense is not concerned with the time of trial, but rather with the defendant's state of mind at the time the criminal act is alleged to have taken place. The second element required that the defendant suffer from a "mental disease or defect." What constitutes a mental disease or defect for the purposes of the insanity defense is somewhat complicated matter that will be addressed later in this chapter. The third part of the test concerns the legal doctrine of *causation.* As discussed in some detail in Part I of this book, the question of what causes a person's behavior is not only the subject of psycho-legal ontological debates in terms of free-will and determinism, but also the subject of debate even within the field, as illustrated by the many different psychological approaches to the study and treatment of psychopathology.[45]

The doctrine of causation applicable in criminal law requires two distinct types of causation: cause-in-fact and proximate cause.[46] The *M'Naghten* test is concerned with the former type of causation. Cause-in-fact is what we normally think of as causing; if a person does some act that directly brings about a particular result, then the person is said to have caused the result.[47] In other words, would the result have occurred "but for" the defendant's conduct? If so, the conduct is not cause-in-fact of the result since it would have occurred anyway. In contrast, though, if the answer to the question is no, then conduct is the cause-in-fact of the result since the result would not have occurred "but for" the act.

It is important to distinguish legal causation from the way causation is used in the mental health sciences. As far as the law is concerned, the relevant question concerning causation is

---

[44]*Id.* at 722.

[45]*See generally* Ronald J. Rychlak and Joseph F. Rychlak, *Mental Health Experts on Trial: Free Will and Determinism in the Courtroom*, 100 W. Va. L. Rev. 193, 200 (1997) (citing Aristotle, *Physics*, in Robert M. Hutchins (ed.), 8 Great Books of the Western World, 257, 271 (1952)).

[46]*See generally* Model Penal Code § 2.03 (1963).

[47]*Id.* cmt. 258 ("The Code thus poses an initial factual inquiry, asking whether the conduct of the defendant is an antecedent but for which the result in question would not have occurred.").

"But for the mental disease or defect, would the criminal act have occurred?"[48] If the answer to that question is "yes," then the mental illness was not the cause-in-fact of the crime; only if the answer to the question is "no" is there causation for insanity purposes. In conducting this inquiry, courts "make no distinction between 'conscious' and 'unconscious' causes of behavior. . . ."[49] Thus, "even if one assumes that a person's behavior is 'caused' by unconscious beliefs, the environment, or some other factor, that person is nonetheless 'responsible' for his or her behavior" unless the specific legal requirements of the insanity defense are met.[50]

Under the *M'Naghten* test, the mental disease or defect that existed at the time of the offense, must have caused one of two things: *cognitive incapacity*, the inability to know the nature and quality of the act committed; or *moral incapacity*, the inability to know that the act committed was wrong.[51] The cognitive incapacity part of the test relieves the defendant of liability when the defendant is incapable of forming *mens rea*. For example, if a man strangled another person believing that he was squeezing the juice out of a lemon, he did not understand the nature and quality of his act.[52] Finding cognitive incapacity is rare because it requires that a person suffer from a psychotic disorder of such severity so as to be removed from reality and not know what he or she is doing.[53] For example, in *M'Naghten*, the defendant knew the nature and quality of his act. He wanted to kill the Prime Minister, and attempted to do so. He was, therefore, not cognitively incapacitated under the first prong of this formulation of the insanity test.

Given the rarity of someone not knowing the nature and quality of his or her acts, the second part of the *M'Naghten* test—the moral incapacity to distinguish right from wrong—is usually at the crux of an insanity defense.[54] This part of the insanity test relieves a defendant from criminal liability even if the person forms the requisite *mens rea* (as Daniel M'Naghten formed intent to kill) as long as the actor does not understand that his act, even though committed with specific intent, is wrong.[55]

C. Shortcomings of the Cognitive Focus of the *M'Naghten* Test

For years, scholars criticized the *M'Naghten* test because it only looked at the cognitive aspect of the defendant's actions.[56] The test had no affective element that evaluated the volition of the defendant.[57] *M'Naghten*'s focus on the cognitive, to the full exclusion of the affective and volitional elements of human behavior, failed to consider "that mentally ill offenders might be aware that their behavior is wrong, yet nonetheless be emotionally unable to restrain themselves or control their conduct."[58] Thus, to many scholars and practitioners of the mental health sciences, the test was incomplete and "scientifically outdated."[59]

---

[48]*See, e.g.*, Carter v. United States, 252 F.2d 608, 616 (D.C. Cir. 1957).

[49]MELTON, ET AL., *supra* note 2, at 122.

[50]*Id.*

[51]*See* Clark v. Arizona, 126 S. Ct. 2709, 2719 (2006). It should be noted that the Supreme Court had never used these terms for the two prongs of the *M'Naghten* test before its decision in *Clark*. Moreover, there were no law review articles that used these terms in relation to the prongs of *M'Naghten* at the time the Supreme Court elected to use in *Clark*. Thus, it is fair to say that the terms referencing moral and cognitive incapacity were not widely used or accepted prior to 2006.

[52]Marc Rosen, *Insanity Denied: Abolition of the Insanity Defense in Kansas*, 8 KAN. J.L. & PUB. POL'Y 253, 261 (1999).

[53]*Id.* at 261.

[54]*Id.* at 261-62.

[55]*Id.* at 261; *see also* M'Naghten's Case, 8 Eng. Rep. 718 (H.L. 1843).

[56]The distinction between pure cognitive knowledge of something and an understanding of that same thing can be illustrated using Einstein's classic equation $E=MC^2$. Nearly all people have heard of the equation. And many people may even know

Practitioners and scholars also criticized the *M'Naghten* test for being too rigid. "Even if one accepts the premise that cognitive dysfunction is the only appropriate focus of the insanity defense, the *M'Naghten* [test] . . . did not fairly pose the question. . . . '[I]f the test language were taken seriously . . . it would excuse only those totally deteriorated, drooling hopeless psychotics of long-standing and congenital idiots.'"[60]

And, finally, scholars criticized the *M'Naghten* test for its focus on "right" and "wrong," a standard that often required clinicians to make moral judgments about defendants.[61] These problems with the *M'Naghten* test led to the development of other formulations of the insanity defense that included an affective component.

D. The Short-Lived *Durham* Rule

Dissatisfied with the *M'Naghten* test, the U.S. Court of Appeals for the District of Columbia Circuit formulated a new insanity test in *Durham v. United States*.[62] In it, the court announced what came to be known as the **Durham Product Test** or the **Durham Rule**. It held that "an accused is not criminally responsible if his unlawful act was the product of a mental disease or defect."[63]

While the *Durham* rule did away with both the cognitive focus of the *M'Naghten* test and the moral judgments involved in determinations of right and wrong embedded in *M'Naghten*, it proved to be an unworkable standard. It led to an "influx of psychiatrists and clinical psychologists into the courtroom as expert witnesses . . . [whose] testimony . . . usurp[ed] the jury's fact-finding function."[64] Additionally, the number of criminal acquittals on the basis of the *Durham* rule rose.[65] While this increase was not necessarily problematic in and of itself, some viewed it as having the effect of doing away with the notion of insanity as a limited excuse and having judicially legislated a rule that basically excused all mentally ill persons from criminal responsibility, regardless of either the type or degree of impairment.[66] The *Durham* rule was not

what the formula represents: energy = mass multiplied by the speed of light, squared. Few, however, understand the equation well enough to explain what it means or how it can be applied. Thus, they have cognitive knowledge, but not true understanding.

[57] *See, e.g.*, Gov't of Virgin Islands v. Fredericks, 578 F.2d 927, 937 (3d Cir. 1978) (Adams, J., dissenting); *see also* Durham v. United States, 214 F.2d 862 (D.C. Cir. 1954) (rejecting *M'Naghten* test), *overruled by* United States v. Brawner, 471 F.2d 969, 981 (D.C. Cir. 1972).

[58] Robin, *supra* note 24, at 227.

[59] Joshua Dressler, Understanding Criminal Law 321 (2d ed. 1995).

[60] Melton, et al., *supra* note 2, at 116 (citing Gregory Zilboorg, Mind, Medicine, & Man 273 (1943)).

[61] Durham v. United States, 214 F.2d 862 (D.C. Cir. 1954) (rejecting M'Naghten Rule), *overruled*, United States v. Brawner, 471 F.2d 969, 981 (D.C. Cir. 1972); *see also* Robin, *supra* note 24, at 228.

[62] 214 F.2d 862, 874-75 (D.C. Cir. 1954), *overruled*, United States v. Brawner, 471 F.2d 969, 981 (D.C. Cir. 1972).

[63] *Durham*, 214 F.2d at 874-75.

[64] Lawrence S. Wrightsman, et al., Psychology and the Legal System 297 (4th ed. 1998); *see also* Robin, *supra* note 24, at 229 ("psychiatric witnesses were prone to testify in conclusory terms that the defendant was or was not suffering from a mental disease and that the criminal act was or was not the product of the illness. By doing so, expert witnesses were essentially deciding the ultimate issue of the defendant's criminal responsibility . . . .").

[65] Simon, *supra* note 20, at 203 (reporting a 0.24% success rate for the insanity defense at trials in Washington, D.C. in the four years preceding Durham, and a 2.29% rate of trials in the six years following Durham); Richard Arens, The Insanity Defense 17, 71 (1974) (reporting 0.4% success rate for insanity defense in trials in Washington, D.C. in 1954, the year proceeding Durham, and a 7.2% success rate in the twelve years following the Durham decision).

[66] *See, e.g.*, Frigillana v. United States, 307 F.2d 665, 668 (D.C. Cir. 1962) ("If our objective is to excuse all mentally or emotionally disturbed persons from criminal responsibility we should frankly and honestly say that and proceed accordingly,

widely accepted and was eventually overruled by the D.C. Court of Appeals in 1972 in *United States v. Brawner,*[67] which adopted a formulation of the insanity defense based on the one suggested by the American Law Institute (ALI) in its 1962 Model Penal Code.

E. The ALI/MPC Affective Test

The ALI, a prestigious, nonpartisan group of judges, lawyers, and scholars from both law and related disciplines, developed a Model Penal Code (MPC) in 1962. Its formulation of the insanity defense is usually referred to as the ***ALI/MPC Affective Test.*** It provides that "a person is not responsible for criminal conduct if, at the time of such conduct as of a result of a mental disease or defect, [the defendant] lacks the substantial capacity to appreciate the criminality [wrongfulness] of his conduct or to conform his conduct to the requirements of law."[68] Although the ALI/MPC formulation of the insanity defense did not define what a mental disease or defect was (just as the *M'Naghten* test failed to do), it did include a provision purposefully excluding those who were suffering from antisocial personality disorder from being considered to have a mental disease or defect.[69] For the sake of being able to make element-by-element comparisons among the various formulations of the insanity defense, the ALI/MPC Affective test can be expressed in this way:

1) A person is not responsible for criminal conduct if, at the time of the offense;

---

for that is precisely where our rule, as applied, it taking us."). *See generally* Wechsler, *The Criteria of Criminal Responsibility,* 22 U. CHI. L. REV. 367, 373 (1955) (The *Durham* rule constituted "a legal principle beclouded by a central ambiguity, both unexplained and unsupported by its basic rationale.").

[67]471 F.2d 969, 981 (D.C. Cir. 1972).

[68]AMERICAN LAW INSTITUTE, MODEL PENAL CODE § 4.01(1) (1962).

[69]According to the DSM-IV-TR, antisocial personality disorder is a:

> [P]ervasive pattern of disregard for and violation of the rights of others occurring since age 15 years, as indicated by three or more of the following: (1) failure to conform to social norms with respect to lawful behaviors as indicated by repeatedly performing acts that are grounds for arrest; (2) deceitfulness, as indicated by repeated lying, use of aliases, or conning others for personal profit or pleasure; (3) impulsivity or failure to plan ahead; (4) irritability and aggressiveness, as indicated by repeated physical fights or assaults; (5) reckless disregard for safety of self or others; (6) consistent irresponsibility, as indicated by repeated failure to sustain consistent work behavior or honor financial obligations; and (7) lack of remorse, as indicated by being indifferent to or rationalizing having hurt, mistreated, or stolen from another.

Id. at 687, 702-06. The person being diagnosed with this disorder must be at least eighteen years of age, and, prior to age fifteen, must have exhibited evidence of a conduct disorder such as aggression to people and animals (bullying, threatening, initiating fights, using a weapon, robbery, forcing sexual activity); destruction of property (including by fire); deceitfulness or theft (including breaking & entering, shoplifting); and serious rule violations (truancy or running away). *Id.* at 706. Finally, to qualify for the diagnosis, the person cannot have exhibited such behaviors exclusively during an active psychosis, such as one prompted by schizophrenia or a manic episode. *Id.*

2) the defendant suffered from of a mental disease or defect (other than antisocial personality disorder and/or any other abnormality manifested only by repeated criminal or otherwise antisocial conduct);

3) that caused the defendant either:

    (a) to lack the substantial capacity to appreciate the criminality [wrongfulness] of his or her conduct;

or

    (b) [having substantial capacity to appreciate the criminality of his or her conduct], to lack the substantial capacity to conform his conduct to the requirements of law.[70]

The first two elements of the ALI/MPC formulation of the insanity defense are the same as those required under the *M'Naghten* test. Both look at the defendant's conduct at the time of the offense, and both require a mental disease or defect. The only difference in the mental disease or defect requirement between the *M'Naghten* and ALI formulations of the insanity defense is that the latter specifically excludes antisocial personality disorder.[71] The principal difference between the two formulations is in the third element.

As discussed earlier in this chapter, the *M'Naghten* test focused on the cognitive aspects of behavior: Did the defendant know what he or she was doing, and if so, did the defendant know it was wrong. It was an all-or-nothing-at-all test that required total (or near total) impairment. The ALI/MPC formulation avoided a purely cognitive focus by a volitional element. Further, the ALI/MPC test replaced the M'Naghten test's focus on pure cognitive knowledge of the wrongfulness of one's acts with a less stringent test requiring that the defendant lack the "substantial capacity to appreciate" the wrongfulness of his actions.[72] As a result, mental health experts and, ultimately, juries, were permitted to "consider the defendant's moral, emotional, and legal awareness of the consequences of his or her behavior. . . [in recognition that] there are gradations of criminal responsibility and that the defendant need not be totally impaired to be absolved of such responsibility."[73]

Additionally, the ALI/ MPC test is less strict than the *M'Naghten* test since it allows even those who both know and appreciate that their acts were wrong to assert the insanity defense by claiming they were unable to abide by the law. This aspect is known as the ***irresistible impulse test.*** Its inclusion in the MPC was an explicit recognition of the evolving state of behavioral science knowledge that one's volition (i.e., free will) is often impacted by mental illness.[74] Thus, with the implementation of the ALI/MPC insanity test, "defendants' inability to control their actions [became] an independent criterion for insanity."[75]

The ALI/MPC formulation of the insanity defense was repeatedly criticized by scholars, lawyers, and psychiatrists for the inclusion of the irresistible impulse test.[76] These critics argued

---

[70]*See* MODEL PENAL CODE § 4.01(1) (1962).

[71]*See supra* note 69.

[72]MODEL PENAL CODE § 4.01(1) (1962).

[73]Robin, *supra* note 24, at 230 (citing United States v. Freeman, 357 F.2d 606 (1966)).

[74]*Id.*

[75]WRIGHTSMAN, ET AL., *supra* note 64, at 298.

[76]*See, e.g.,* Stephen J. Morse, *Culpability and Control*, 142 U. PA. L. REV. 1587, 1600 (1994) (distinguishing an "impulse" from a bona-fide "compulsion," thereby criticizing the notion of an irresistible impulse).

that an irresistible impulse was really just an impulse that was not, in fact, resisted.[77] For example, would a criminal defendant have committed the crime if a policeman had been next to him? Since the answer to this hypothetical question would in all likelihood be a resounding "no" for nearly all offenders, it suggests that the impulse was not truly irresistible, but rather one that was simply not resisted. Even the American Bar Association and the American Psychiatric Association joined in this criticism of the volitional aspect of the ALI/MPC test[78] because allowing volitional impairment to qualify as the basis of a defense of excuse was inconsistent "with a criminal justice system premised on free will."[79] In spite of the criticisms, a majority of the states and all but one federal circuit[80] eventually adopted the ALI/MPC formulation of the insanity defense.[81]

F. The Modern Federal Formulation of the Insanity Defense

1. Background of the John Hinckley Case

In the late 1970s John Hinckley became obsessed with the characters in the movie *Taxi Driver*, and, in particular, Jodie Foster, one of the stars of the film.[82] He made several attempts to woo Jodie Foster while she was a first-year student at Yale University in New Haven, Connecticut, including sending her love letters, poems, and having two "awkward" phone conversations with her.[83] When Foster rebuffed his overtures, Hinckley decided he needed to do something that would make an impression on her—some "historic deed [that would] finally gain her respect and love for him."[84] On March 30, 1981, he carried out his plan by attempting to assassinate then-President Ronald Reagan as he was leaving the Washington Hilton Hotel in Washington, D.C.[85]

At his trial for attempted murder, Hinckley asserted the insanity defense.[86] Under the decision in *United States v. Brawner*,[87] the ALI/MPC formulation of the insanity defense governed his trial. Moreover, under *Brawner*, once the issue of insanity was raised by the defense, the government had to prove that Hinckley was sane, beyond a reasonable doubt, at the time he made his assassination attempt on Reagan.[88]

"After weeks of conflicting testimony by defense and prosecution psychiatrists—testimony that struck some as an affront to common sense—the jury found Hinckley not guilty by reason of insanity. One juror felt trapped by the substantial capacity test: 'My conscience had me voting

---

[77]*Id.* at 1599-1602; *see also, e.g.,* ABRAHAM S. GOLDSTEIN, THE INSANITY DEFENSE 67 (1967); Michael Moore, *Responsibility and the Unconscious*, 53 S. CAL. L. REV. 1563 (1980) (distinguishing causation of behavior from compulsion).

[78]MELTON, ET AL., *supra* note 2, at 117 (citing AMERICAN BAR ASSOCIATION, CRIMINAL JUSTICE MENTAL HEALTH STANDARDS, standard 7-6.1 (1984), at 329-32; AMERICAN PSYCHIATRIC ASSOCIATION, STATEMENT ON THE INSANITY DEFENSE 12 (1982)).

[79]Christopher Slobogin, *The Interactionist Alternative to the Insanity Defense: Reflections on the Exculpatory Scope of Mental Illness in the Wake of the Andrea Yates Trial*, 30 AM. J. CRIM. L. 315, 320 (2003).

[80]Robin, *supra* note 24, at 231 (citing United States v. Torniero, 735 F.2d 725 (1984), *cert. denied*, 469 U.S. 1110 (1995)).

[81]*Id.; see also* MELTON, ET AL., *supra* note 2, at 117.

[82]PETER LOW, ET AL., THE TRIAL OF JOHN W. HINCKLEY, JR.: A CASE STUDY IN THE INSANITY DEFENSE 23-24 (1986).

[83]*Id.* at 25.

[84]*Id.* at 32.

[85]*Id.* at 27.

[86]United States v. Hinckley, 525 F. Supp. 1342 (D.D.C. 1981).

[87]471 F.2d 969, 981 (D.C. Cir. 1972).

[88]*Id.*

one way, but the law would not allow me to vote that way.'"[89] Hinckley's acquittal using the insanity defense sparked a furor over the defense and focused critical, national attention on it.[90] "Within days [of the verdict], the most 'celebrated' insanity trial in American history had instantly become the most 'outrageous' verdict."[91]

In the wake of the *Hinckley* verdict, the insanity defense underwent sweeping reforms in both the federal system and in many states.[92] After twenty-six different pieces of legislation were introduced in Congress to either abolish or restrict the insanity defense at the federal level,[93] Congress enacted the ***Insanity Defense Reform Act of 1984 (IDRA)***.[94] In doing so, Congress codified the federal insanity defense for the first time and legislatively overruled the application of the ALI/MPC formulation of the insanity defense in all federal cases.[95]

2. The Provisions of the IDRA

The modern federal formulation of the insanity defense as enacted in IDRA provides: "At the time of the commission of the acts constituting the offense, the defendant, as of a result of a severe mental disease or defect, was unable to appreciate the nature and quality or the wrongfulness of his acts. Mental disease or defect does not otherwise constitute a defense."[96] Again, for comparative purposes, it is helpful to consider the requirements of this formulation of the insanity defense in terms of elements.

1) A person is not responsible for criminal conduct if, at the time of acts constituting the offense;

2) the defendant suffered from a <u>severe</u> mental disease or defect

3) that caused the defendant to be unable to appreciate either:

   (a) the nature and quality of his or her acts;
   or
   (b) the wrongfulness of his or her acts [which presumes being able to appreciate the nature and quality of his or her acts].[97]

---

[89]Robin, *supra* note 24, at 231 (quoting *Insane on All Counts: Is the System Guilty?*, TIME, July 5, 1982, at 26-27); *see also* Stuart Taylor, Jr., *Hinckley Cleared But Is Held Insane in Reagan Attack*, N.Y. TIMES, June 22, 1982, at A1, D27.

[90]George L. Blau & Richard A. Pasewark, *Statutory Changes And The Insanity Defense: Seeking The Perfect Insane Person,* 18 LAW & PSYCHOL. REV. 69, 70 n.6 (1994) (citing Valerie P. Hans & Dan Slater, *John Hinckley, Jr. and the Insanity Defense: The Public's Verdict*, 47 PUB. OPINION Q. 202, 203 (1983); Valerie P. Hans & Dan Slater, *"Plain Crazy": Lay Definitions of Legal Insanity*, 7 INT'L J. OF L. & PSYCHIATRY 105 (1984); Nightline: Insanity Plea on Trial (ABC Television Broadcast, 1982); Otto F. Wahl, *Post-Hinckley Views of the Insanity Defense*, 8 AM. J. FORENSIC PSYCHOL. 3, 5-7 (1990)).

[91]Perlin, Unpacking The Myths, *supra* note 20, at 637.

[92]*E.g.,* Lisa A. Callahan et al., *Insanity Defense Reform in the United States Post-Hinckley*, 11 MENTAL & PHYS. DISABILITY L. REP. 54, 54-59 (1987).

[93]Michael L. Perlin, *The Things We Do For Love: John Hinckley's Trial and the Future of the Insanity Defense in the Federal Courts* (Book Review), 30 N.Y.L. SCH. L. REV. 857, 860 (1985).

[94]Pub. L. No. 91-190, 98 Stat. 1837 (1984) (codified as amended at 18 U.S.C. § 17 (2000)).

[95]Perlin, Unpacking the Myths, *supra* note 20, at 638; Elkins, *supra* note 6, at 155.

[96]18 U.S.C. § 17.

[97]*See id.*

In effect, the IDRA returned the law of insanity to being very close to where it was at the time the *M'Naghten* test was adopted. As with all of the other insanity defense formulations, the first element looks at the mental state of the defendant at the time of the commission of the offense. The second element, just like the *M'Naghten* and ALI/MPC formulations of the insanity defense, requires a mental disease or defect. But the IDRA added the requirement that the mental disease or defect be severe. This requirement of severity effectively limited the applicability of the defense to people suffering from psychoses and mental retardation, thereby eliminating neurosis, disabilities, and personality disorders from qualifying as predicate mental diseases or defects.[98]

The third element is similar to all prior formulations of the insanity defense insofar as there must be, as always, a causal nexus between the mental illness and the crime committed. But the third element changed the insanity defense as it existed in the federal courts quite significantly in two important ways. For one thing, the third element effectively abolished the volitional aspect of the ALI/MPC insanity defense as expressed in the irresistible impulse test. Thus, under the IDRA, no longer will an inability to conform one's conduct to the requirements of law allow one to use the insanity defense. Second, the third element of the IDRA effectively reinstated the *M'Naghten* test for insanity with a slight modification. Instead of requiring a lack of "knowledge" that one's conduct is wrong to qualify as legally insane, the IDRA requires an inability to "appreciate" the wrongfulness of one's conduct. This leaves the slightest door open for some affective component to the defense, rather than having to focus exclusively on the defendant's cognitive incapacities in the way that the *M'Naghten* test originally did.

In addition to changing the elements of the insanity defense and standardizing the defense for the federal system, the IDRA also made a critical change in procedure regarding the way the insanity defense is litigated. Up until the time of the IDRA, once the defense announced its intention to use the insanity defense (i.e., once the defense met its burden of production), the prosecution bore the burden of persuasion to prove a defendant was legally sane at the time of a criminal offense beyond a reasonable doubt. But the IDRA shifted both the burden of production and the burden of persuasion to the defense by making insanity an affirmative defense. Accordingly, the defense must now prove that the defendant was insane at the time of the criminal offense by clear and convincing evidence. Whether this shift in the burden of proof has had a significant impact on case outcomes is questionable in light of the few studies that have failed to demonstrate "any consistent relationship between the imposition of the burden of proof and the acquittal rate."[99]

Finally, the IDRA triggered a change to the law of evidence with regards to expert witnesses.

> No expert witness testifying with respect to the mental state or condition of a defendant in a criminal case may state an opinion or inference as to whether the defendant did or did not have the mental state or condition constituting an element of the crime charged or of a defense thereto. Such ultimate issues are matters for the trier of fact alone.[100]

---

[98] *See* Perlin, Unpacking Myths, *supra* note 20, at 639 (stating that the word "severe" was added as a qualifier "to ensure that relatively minor disorders such as nonpsychotic behavior disorders or personality defects would not provide the basis for an insanity defense") (citing HANDBOOK ON THE COMPREHENSIVE CRIME CONTROL ACT OF 1984 AND OTHER CRIMINAL STATUTES ENACTED BY THE 98TH CONGRESS 59 (1984)).

[99] Renee Melançon, Note: *Arizona's Insane Response to Insanity*, 40 ARIZ. L. REV. 287, 297 (1998) (citing GARY B. MELTON ET AL., PSYCHOLOGICAL EVALUATIONS FOR THE COURTS 202 (2d ed. 1997)).

[100] FED. R. EVID. 704(b).

However, at least two studies using simulated trials have demonstrated that this change in the law of evidence regarding the "ultimate issue" has had no significant effects on jury verdicts.[101]

3. The Impact of the IDRA on the States

By 1985, thirty-three states had followed the lead of Congress and evaluated the insanity defense as it applied in their respective jurisdictions.[102] Many states followed the IDRA and made insanity an affirmative defense, thereby shifting the burden of persuasion from the prosecution to the defense to prove the defendant's insanity, usually by a preponderance of the evidence.[103] Other states left the burden of persuasion with the government to show the defendant's sanity, but tightened the substantive test for insanity by requiring a "severe" mental disease or defect or some equivalent.[104] Twelve states replaced the insanity defense with a "guilty, but mentally ill" verdict.[105] And four states—Utah, Montana, Idaho, and Kansas—abolished the insanity defense altogether.[106]

G. Alternative Verdicts for Defendants Claiming Mental Illness

1. Michigan's "Guilty But Mentally Ill" Verdict

In August of 1975, Michigan was the first U.S. state to add a third possible verdict in criminal cases in which the defendant was mentally ill. Up until that time, using the traditional insanity defense, a jury had to find a defendant either guilty or NGBI. Michigan did not abolish the NGBI verdict, but instead supplemented it by adding another alternative it termed ***"guilty but mentally ill"*** (***GBMI***).[107] The impetus for enacting the new verdict came largely from the case of John Bernard McGee.[108] McGee was found NGBI in a murder trial and committed to a mental institution. While institutionalized, he admitted to twenty-five additional killings.[109] Two months later, in a civil commitment hearing mandated for NGBI acquittees by an unrelated Michigan Supreme Court case,[110] McGee was found "not presently insane" and was released.[111] He was arrest a month later for beating his wife to death.[112] Public outcry led the state legislature to

---

[101]*See* Richard Rogers et al., *Effects of Ultimate Opinions on Juror Perceptions Of Insanity*, 13 INT'L J. L. & PSYCHIATRY 225 (1990); Solomon M. Fulero & Norman J. Finkel, *Barring Ultimate Issue Testimony: An "Insane" Rule?* 15 LAW & HUM. BEHAV. 495 (1991).

[102]Callahan, et al., *supra* note 92, at 54-56.

[103]*Id.; see also* Melançon, *supra* note 99, at 297.

[104]*Id.*

[105]*Id.*

[106]*Id.* The abolition of the insanity defense is discussed later in this chapter, *infra* at Part IV.

[107]MICH. COMP. LAWS § 768.36(1) (1992) (initially enacted Aug. 6, 1975).

[108]Ira Mickenberg, *A Pleasant Surprise: The Guilty But Mentally Ill Verdict Has Both Succeeded in Its Own Right and Successfully Preserved the Traditional Role of the Insanity Defense,* 55 U. CIN. L. REV. 943, 973 (1987).

[109]*Id.*

[110]*See* People v. McQuillan, 221 N.W.2d 569 (1974).

[111]Mickenberg, *supra* note 108, at 973.

[112]*Id.*

adopt the GBMI verdict in an effort to "to reduce the number of successful NGBI pleas and insure lengthy confinement for those defendants who are found insane."[113]

Under the Michigan GBMI law, a verdict of GBMI is supposed to be returned by the trier-of-fact if the following three criteria are found beyond a reasonable doubt: "(a) That the defendant is guilty of an offense[;] (b) That the defendant was mentally ill at the time of the commission of the offense [; and] (c) That the defendant was *not* legally insane at the time of the commission of the offense."[114] This verdict was, in effect, a "compromise."[115] It allowed a jury to completely acquit those defendant who were clearly legally insane under a tradition NGBI verdict, but gave jurors a "middle ground" verdict to convict those who were not clearly legally insane, but did suffer from a mental illness at the time of the commission of a criminal offense.

Under the Michigan GBMI schema, someone so adjudicated was to be sentenced just as if he or she had been found guilty of the crime with one exception: the court must make a determination if the GBMI defendant needs treatment.[116] If a court finds the defendant does need treatment, then the defendant is supposed to be remanded either into the custody of the department of corrections or the state's department of mental health services for treatment.[117] Interestingly, though, after treatment, the defendant must serve whatever time remains on his or her sentence in a correctional facility.[118] The law, however, provides that a judge can order the remainder of the term to be served on probation if the defendant continues with mandatory mental health treatment.[119]

2. Other States Follow Michigan's Lead

Michigan adopted the GBMI verdict before the *Hinckley* case. Three other states "adopted the GBMI verdict during the period of the *Hinckley* case, and eight adopted it shortly after his June 1982 acquittal."[120] These changes were largely in response to a combination of two factors: NGBI verdicts in those states that brought public outcry over the insanity defense and Dan White's successful "Twinkie Defense" in 1979 (a version of the diminished capacity defense discussed in the next chapter of this book). White killed San Francisco Mayor George Moscone and fellow City Supervisor Harvey Milk. His trial for two counts of first degree murder resulted only in convictions for voluntary manslaughter after the jury ostensibly found White, a hypoglycemic, to have suffered from diminished capacity in a sugar and caffeine induced

---

[113]*Id.* at 974.

[114]MICH. COMP. LAWS § 768.36(1) (1992) (initially enacted Aug. 6, 1975) (emphasis added).

[115]Perlin, Fear of Faking, *supra* note 7, at 1379.

[116]MICH. COMP. LAWS § 768.36(1) (1992) (initially enacted Aug. 6, 1975).

[117]MICH. COMP. LAWS § 768.36(3) (1992) (initially enacted Aug. 6, 1975).

[118]*Id.*

[119]*Id.*

[120]HENRY J. STEADMAN, ET AL., BEFORE AND AFTER HINCKLEY: EVALUATING INSANITY DEFENSE REFORM 38 (1993); *see also* ALASKA STAT. 12.47.040 (1990); DEL. CODE ANN. tit. 11, 401(b), 408 (1990); GA. CODE ANN. 17-7-131 (1985); ILL. ANN. STAT. ch. 38, para. 115-2(b) (Smith-Hurd 1990); Ind. Code 35-36-2-3 (Supp. 1982); KY. REV. STAT. ANN. 504.120 (Michie/Bobbs-Merrill 1990); MONT. CODE ANN. 46-14-312 (1993); N.M. STAT. ANN. 31-9-3 (Michie 1984 & Supp. 1994); 18 PA. CONS. STAT. 314 (1983); S.C. CODE ANN. 17-24-20 (Law. Co-op. Supp. 1993); S.D. CODIFIED LAWS ANN. 23A-26-14 (1988). Utah, although adopting a GBMI verdict also abolished the NGBI verdict when it enacted UTAH CODE ANN. 77-16a-102 (Supp. 1993).

reactive psychosis brought about by a combination of depression and having gorged himself on Twinkies and Coca-Cola.[121]

In most of the jurisdictions that adopted the GBMI verdict, all three elements (i.e., the defendant (1) is guilty of the offense charged; (2) was mentally ill at the time of the commission of the offense; and (3) was not legally insane at the time of the commission of the offense) must be proven by the government beyond a reasonable doubt. Some states, however, require the state only to prove the first element—the guilt of the defendant—beyond a reasonable doubt, and then shift the burden to the defendant to prove that he or she was mentally ill at the time of the offense by a preponderance of the evidence.[122]

Regardless of the allocation of burden of persuasion, it is clear that "mental illness" for the purposes of a GBMI verdict, is quite different from a mental disease or defect that rises to level of insanity. Consider, for example, Kentucky's statute. It defines "insanity" using a variation of the ALI/MPC formulation. Under it, one is NGBI if, "as a result of mental incapacitation, [one] lack[s the] substantial capacity either to appreciate the criminality of one's conduct or to conform one's conduct to the requirements of the law."[123] In contrast, "mental illness" for GBMI purposes includes self-control problems, disturbances in judgment, and maladaptive behaviors.[124]

3. Critique of Guilty But Mentally Ill Statutes

The very phrase "guilty, but mentally ill" is an oxymoron. It allows jurors to affix guilt, while simultaneously allowing a finding of excuse for that guilt. The contradiction of a lack of moral blameworthiness due to mental illness, coupled with a determination of factual guilt, should be intellectually unreconcilable. But supporters argued that it will have a twofold benefit. It allows jurors to feel better about returning NGBI verdicts when someone is truly mentally ill. On the flip side, it allows jurors to convict those who are mentally ill, but not insane while still recognizing mental illness as a contributing factor that mitigates the need for punishment. [125]

The GBMI verdict received much criticism from scholars.[126] Notably, empirical research demonstrated that the verdict had little if any effect on the NGBI adjudication rate. For example, Smith and Hall found that NGBI acquittals represented .026 percent of all arrests before the GBMI law went into effect and .024 percent of all arrests in the six years after the new verdict was available.[127] They concluded the new GBMI verdict "merely substituted a new name for certain defendants who, in the absence of the new statute, probably would have been found guilty."[128]

Moreover, while one of the primary objectives of the GBMI verdict was to get treatment for those defendants who, although mentally ill, did not have their cognitive abilities so impaired as to be rendered legally insane. But "in reality, GBMI prisoners are treated like any other

---

[121]*See generally* Kenneth W. Salter, The Trial of Dan White (1991).

[122]*E.g.,* S.C. Code Ann. 17-24-20(B) (Supp. 1994).

[123]Ky. Rev. Stat. Ann. 504.060 (6) (1990).

[124]*Id.*

[125]Mickenberg, *supra* note 108, at 988-89.

[126]*See generally, e.g.,* Christopher Slobogin, *The Guilty But Mentally Ill Verdict: An Idea Whose Time Should Not Have Come,* 53 Geo. Wash. L. Rev. 494 (1985) (summarizing and analyzing critiques of the GBMI verdict).

[127]Gare A. Smith & James A. Hall, *Evaluating Michigan's Guilty But Mentally Ill Verdict: An Empirical Study,* 16 J. L. Reform 77, 109 (1982).

[128]*Id.* at 80.

prisoners; they will get extra treatment if they need it, but that's the same treatment we give everyone else."[129] In fact, Smith and Hall report that 75 percent of GBMI in Michigan received no psychiatric treatment at all, usually due to financial constraints.[130] Of all the states using a GBMI verdict, only Alaska, Kentucky and South Carolina actually guarantee treatment.[131] But whether treatment in these three states is any more effective than in the others is quite questionable. Consider that in 1991, the chair of the Parole Board in Kentucky stated: "From psychological evaluations and treatment summaries, the Board can detect no differences in treatment or outcome for [inmates adjudicated GBMI] from those who have been adjudicated as simply 'guilty.'"[132]

4. Guilty Except Insane

Not all states structured their variations on the GBMI verdict the way that Michigan originally did. Consider Arizona's approach. Under it, a person may be found ***"guilty except insane"*** if:

(1) at the time of the commission of the criminal act

(2) the person was afflicted with a mental disease or defect of such severity

(3) that the person did not know the criminal act was wrong.

(4) A mental disease or defect constituting legal insanity is an affirmative defense. The defendant shall prove the defendant's legal insanity by clear and convincing evidence.

(5) Mental disease or defect does not include disorders that result from acute voluntary intoxication or withdrawal from alcohol or drugs, character defects, psychosexual disorders or impulse control disorders. Conditions that do not constitute legal insanity include but are not limited to momentary, temporary conditions arising from the pressure of the circumstances, moral decadence, depravity or passion growing out of anger, jealousy, revenge, hatred or other motives in a person who does not suffer from a mental disease or defect or an abnormality that is manifested only by criminal conduct.[133]

The GEI verdict abolished the NGBI verdict in its entirety. Instead, it holds the person responsible (i.e., "guilty"), but simultaneously exempts the legally insane (under the narrow definition set forth in the statute) from criminal punishment. But as at least one critic of the statute has said, "the 'guilty but insane verdict' is a contradiction in terms. . . . [O]ne cannot be both guilty from a legal standpoint and insane from a legal standpoint."[134] This ostensible

---

[129]Smith & Hall, *supra* note 127, at 105 n.138 (quoting Dr. John Prelesnick, Superintendent of the Reception and Guidance Center at Michigan's Jackson State Penitentiary).

[130]*Id.* at 105 n.137.

[131]For two excellent critiques of the GBMI verdict, *see generally* Mark A. Woodmansee, Note, *The Guilty But Mentally Ill Verdict: Political Expediency at the Expense of Moral Principle*, 10 ND J. L. ETHICS & PUB POL'Y 341 (1996), Christopher Slobogin, *supra* note 126, *passim*.

[132]WRIGHTSMAN, ET AL., *supra* 64, at 309.

[133]ARIZ. REV. STAT. ANN. § 13-502 (West Supp. 1997) (broken out into elements above not specified in the statute for pedagogical purposes).

[134]Melançon, *supra* note 99, at 313.

oxymoron aside, the statute is one of the most restrictive insanity-related ones in the United States in some aspects, while being arguably the most progressive in other ways.

Arizona's statute returns to the *M'Naghten* concept of defining insanity as not knowing right from wrong. As a result, it suffers from the same criticisms levied at the *M'Naghten* test for its exclusive focus on cognitive aspects of thought and behavior to the exclusion of affective elements.[135] But Arizona's guilty except insane statute is more restrictive than both *M'Naghten* and the modern federal variation of the old *M'Naghten* test for two reasons.

First, like the modern federal formulation of the insanity defense under the IDRA, a "severe" mental disease or defect is required.[136] Also, like the modern federal formulation of the insanity defense, Arizona's GEI statute makes the defense an affirmative one, placing the burden of persuasion on the defendant to prove his or her insanity by clear and convincing evidence.[137] But, unlike previous formulations of the insanity defense, Arizona's formulation contains the most restrictive exclusions of mental disorders from qualifying as a "mental disease or defect" for insanity purposes. These restrictions range from antisocial personality disorder, psychosexual disorders, and impulse control disorders, to "disorders that result from acute voluntary intoxication or withdrawal from alcohol or drugs, character defects, . . . momentary, temporary conditions arising from the pressure of the circumstances, moral decadence, depravity or passion growing out of anger, jealousy, revenge, hatred or other motives."[138]

The second major change to the traditional *M'Naghten* test under the Arizona law is the elimination of the cognitive incapacity prong of the test (i.e., not knowing the nature and quality of one's acts) from the definition of legal insanity. The omission of this prong narrows the *M'Naghten* test's definition of insanity. This change appears to be one merely in form over substance since the first part of the *M'Naghten* test was the much more stringent part of the test.[139] Indeed, the U.S. Supreme Court recognized the overlap between the two prongs of the *M'Naghten* test in *Clark v. Arizona*, noting that "[i]n practical terms, if a defendant did not know what he was doing when he acted, he could not have known that he was performing the wrongful act charged as a crime."[140] Thus, while slightly more restrictive than the *M'Naghten* test, Arizona's narrowing of the test for insanity may be of little practical consequence.

While Arizona's GEI approach may seem harsher than the GMBI approach taken by other states, the treatment of the offender after a GEI verdict is actually more humane that in other jurisdictions. A defendant found GEI of a crime involving a death or physical injury does not go to a correctional institution under Arizona law but rather is remanded into the custody of a state-run mental health facility.[141] A person remains confined until it is shown by clear and convincing evidence that he or she no longer suffers from the mental disease or defect. However, a conditional release is available if the person is still mentally ill, but the illness is under control

---

[135] *Supra* at Part II, § C.

[136] 18 U.S.C. § 17 (2000).[Need cite to statute].

[137] *Id.*[Need cite to statute].

[138] ARIZ. REV. STAT. ANN. § 13-3994(A) (1997). For a critique of many of these restrictions, see Melançon, *supra* note 99, at 306-12 (including a discussion of the potential convictions of those suffering from brief reactive psychoses under the statute).

[139] *See, e.g.,* MELTON ET AL., *supra* note 99, at 123 ("[p]resumably, an accused who does not meet the first test [under *M'Naghten*] will not meet the second."). *But cf.* Melançon, *supra* note 99, at 305-06 (arguing that the omission of the first part of the *M'Naghten* test could lead to absurd results).

[140] Clark v. Arizona, 126 S. Ct. 2709, 2722 (2006).

[141] ARIZ. REV. STAT. ANN. § 13-3994(A) (Supp. 1997).

and the person poses no danger to himself or herself or to others.[142] Additionally, if the person's crime did not involve a death or physical injury, then a court must release the person upon a judicial determination that he or she poses no risk of danger to himself and herself or to others.[143] If, on the other hand, there is a risk of dangerousness, civil commitment proceedings, with its strict due process supervision requirements, are instituted.

These post-verdict procedures are among the most progressive in the United States. Arizona's statute is clearly designed to ensure those who need mental health care actually get it—quite a different result than appears to occur in GBMI jurisdictions. Equally important, the length of any period of detention in the mental health facility is not tied to any potential criminal sentence, but rather to the person's recovery. And finally, some adjudicated GEI convicts do not serve any time in correctional institutions, even if a fast recovery is made. Thus, although the law labels someone "guilty," its aim is clearly not to punish someone who is insane under its definition of insanity, a fact further established by the provision of the law which states, "A guilty except insane verdict is not a criminal conviction for sentencing enhancement purposes [for future crimes, if any]. . . ."[144]

III. AMBIGUITIES COMMON TO ALL VERSIONS OF THE INSANITY DEFENSE

A. What Is a Mental Disease or Defect?

1. Generally

What constitutes a mental disease or defect for the purposes of the insanity defense? Unfortunately, the question is difficult to answer. Rarely is there an answer to this question that turns on a pure matter of law. Courts have consistently refused to define the term "mental disease or defect" precisely. Instead, they have held that the issue of whether a person is suffering from a mental disease is a question of fact to be decided at trial.[145]

When deciding the factual question of which mental illnesses will qualify as the basis for an insanity plea, courts reluctantly guide themselves by the medical categories of mental illnesses as defined by the psychiatric community in the DSM-IV-TR.[146] However, it is clear that courts do not rely on medical labels exclusively. "[W]hat definition of 'mental disease or defect' is to be employed by courts enforcing the criminal law is, in the final analysis, a question of legal, moral and policy — not of medical judgment."[147] While the law does not recognize every psychiatric condition in the DSM as a qualifying mental disease or defect for insanity defense purposes, it

---

[142]Ariz. Rev. Stat. Ann. § 13-3994(F) (Supp. 1997).

[143]Ariz. Rev. Stat. Ann. §§ 13-3994(B)-(C) (1997).

[144]Ariz. Rev. Stat. Ann. § 13-502(E) (Supp. 1997).

[145]United States v. Jackson, 19 F.3d 1003, 1006 (5th Cir.), *cert. denied*, 513 U.S. 891 (1994); United States v. Prescott, 920 F.2d 139, 146 (2d Cir. 1990); United States v. Steil, 916 F.2d 485, 487-88 (8th Cir. 1990); United States v. Smeaton, 762 F.2d 796, 798 (9th Cir. 1985).

[146]*See* American Psychiatric Ass'n, Diagnostic and Statistical Manual of Mental Disorder (4th ed., text rev. 2000) [hereinafter DSM-IV-TR]; *see also, e.g.*, United States v. Cantu, 12 F.3d 1506, 1509, n.1 (9th Cir. 1993) (taking judicial notice that a condition listed in the DSM is a recognized psychiatric condition); United States v. Johnson, 979 F.2d 396, 401 (6th Cir. 1992) (taking judicial notice of an earlier edition of the DSM).

[147]United States v. Murdoch, 98 F.3d 472, 478 (9th Cir. 1996), *cert. denied*, 521 U.S. 1122 (1997) (quoting United States v. Lyons, 731 F.2d 243, 246 (5th Cir.), *cert. denied*, 469 U.S. 930 (1984)).

does usually require the condition being offered as a qualifying mental disease or defect at trial to be recognized in DSM.[148] And without a bona-fide psychiatric diagnosis, courts rarely allow defendants to plead insane.[149]

A literal reading of the insanity defense would mean that any "mental disease or defect" would qualify.[150] Such a reading, however, is not warranted, as neither courts nor clinicians read the insanity defense literally.[151] For one thing, "courts and juries pay more attention to the degree of impairment than to the specific mental disability suffered by the defendant."[152] In support of this proposition, Melton, et al., cite the fact that the overwhelming number of successful insanity defenses involve one of only two types of mental conditions: psychosis and mental retardation.[153]

Bruce Winick, one of the foremost scholars on the intersection of law and mental health, suggests that courts view mental diseases and defects within the framework of "a traditional medical model of illness" — one that may be limited to conditions that until recently were labeled psychoses. These major mental disorders—schizophrenia, major depressive disorders, and bipolar disorder—seem to be the paradigmatic cases of mental illness."[154] In support of the proposition that the modern conceptualization of mental illness involves psychoses, Winick cites the American Psychiatric Association's *American Psychiatric Glossary,* which defines a psychosis as follows:

> A major *mental disorder* of *organic* or *emotional* origin in which a person's ability to think, respond emotionally, remember, communicate, interpret reality, and behave appropriately is sufficiently impaired so as to interfere grossly with the capacity to meet the ordinary demands of life. Often characterized by *regressive* behavior, inappropriate *mood,* diminished impulse control, and such abnormal mental content as *delusions* and *hallucinations.* The term is applicable to conditions having a wide range of severity and duration. See also *schizophrenia, bipolar disorder, depression, organic mental disorder,* and *reality testing.*[155]

While there can be no doubt that courts accept psychoses as "mental diseases or defects," it is important to keep in mind that the existence of a psychosis is not, in and of itself, sufficient to

---

[148]Judith E. Macfarlane, *Neonaticide and the "Ethos of Maternity": Traditional Criminal Law Defenses and the Novel Syndrome,* 5 Cardozo Women's L.J. 175, 239 (1998) ("[T]he requirement that there be medical recognition of the disorder 'lends the necessary credibility to this objectively unconfirmable claim of abnormality.' The presence of the 'abnormality' in the DSM-IV as an authoritative source for mental disorders may help to satisfy the disability requirement in all insanity formulations.") (internal citations omitted).

[149]*See, e.g.,* United States v. Torniero, 570 F. Supp. 721 (D. Conn. 1983), *aff'd,* 735 F.2d 725 (1984), *cert. denied,* 469 U.S. 1110 (1995) (refusing to recognize compulsive gambling disorder as a qualifying mental disease or defect). *See also Murdoch,* 98 F.3d at 472, in which the concurring judge specifically explained his reliance on the DSM as not being "in contradiction with the position . . . that the definition of mental disease or defect is a matter of legal and not medical judgment," but rather was necessary because "the law must ultimately be applied to the facts, but the facts can only be determined by trying to understand what evaluating doctors [see] when . . . examin[ing defendant-patients]. Those observations [are] recorded in the diagnosis which can only be understood through reference to the DSM." *Id.* at 479 n.5.

[150]*E.g.,* McDonald v. United States, 312 F.2d 847, 850-51 (D.C. Cir. 1962) (explaining "a mental disease or defect includes any abnormal condition of the mind which substantially affects mental or emotional processes and substantial impairs behavior controls.").

[151]Melton, et al., *supra* note 2, at 123.

[152]*Id.* at 119.

[153]*Id.*

[154]Bruce Winick, *Ambiguities in the Legal Meaning and Significance of Mental Illness,* 1 Psych. Pub. Pol. & L. 534, 558-59 (1995).

[155]*Id.* (citing Am. Psychiatric Ass'n, American Psychiatric Glossary 139 (6th ed. 1988)).

establish legal incompetency or insanity.[156] The other criteria, notably the psychosis causing the defendant's inability to distinguish right from wrong, for example, must also be satisfied.

Psychoses, however, are easily handled by the legal system given its orientation toward the medical model of deviance. The more problematic situations for the law is deciding if other psychiatric disorders qualify as a "mental disease or defect" for insanity purposes. Perhaps the most challenging of these other diagnoses concern personality disorders.

2. Personality Disorders

Some federal circuit courts of appeals have specifically held that personality disorders are not "mental diseases or defects" within the meaning of the insanity defense.[157] Other federal circuit courts have determined that although personality disorders are mental diseases or defects, they are not "severe enough" under the modern federal formulation of the insanity defense to serve as the basis for an insanity defense.[158] And it appears that at least one federal circuit (the Ninth) refuses to have a rule covering personality disorders as a class of psychiatric diagnoses, considering instead the specific diagnosis on a case-by-case basis.[159] In fact, the concurring justice in *Murdoch* wrote "[a]lthough I agree that mere personality quirks or characteristics cannot be construed as mental diseases or defects for purposes of determining legal sanity, I conclude that a personality disorder such as that suffered by Appellant is much more than a mere quirk. It is a systemic, enduring, and severe condition resulting in an extremely abnormal perception of and reaction to everyday events. In short, Appellant's condition is so encompassing and impairing that it rises to the level of a disease or defect."[160] Regardless of the different approaches taken by the various federal circuits, it is clear that under federal law, antisocial personality disorder is not a qualifying a mental disease or defect for insanity defense purposes.[161]

There is a similar split of authority at the state level regarding whether personality disorders qualify as mental diseases or defects for insanity defense purposes. At least two states exclude personality disorders from the definition of mental disease or defect.[162] Other states exclude certain types of personality disorders, most notably antisocial personality disorder.[163] Alaska, on

---

[156]*See* PAUL S. APPELBAUM & THOMAS G. GUTHEIL, CLINICAL HANDBOOK OF PSYCHIATRY AND THE LAW 218, 220 (1991).

[157]*See* United States v. Bilyk, 29 F.3d 459, 46061 (8th Cir. 1994) (concluding that a severe antisocial personality disorder is not evidence of present mental illness); United States v. Prescott, 920 F.2d 139 (2d Cir. 1990) (upholding finding of no mental disease or defect where experts testified that personality disorder was not considered a mental disease or defect in the mental health community); United States v. Rosenheimer, 807 F.2d 107 (7th Cir. 1986) (upholding, without discussion, a trial court decision that personality disorders are not mental diseases or defects for purposes of an insanity plea).

[158]*See* United States v. Salava, 978 F.2d 320 (7th Cir. 1992) (holding non-psychotic behaviors or neuroses are not severe mental diseases or defects); United States v. Shlater, 85 F.3d 1251 (7th Cir. 1996).

[159]*E.g.*, United States v. Murdoch, 98 F.3d 472, 478 (9th Cir. 1996), *cert. denied*, 117 S. Ct. 2518 (1997).

[160]*Id.* at 479 (Wilson, J., concurring).

[161]Foucha v. Louisiana, 504 U.S. 71 (1992) (dicta).

[162]*See* CAL. PENAL CODE § 25.5 (Supp. 1997); OR. REV. STAT. § 161.295 (Supp. 1997).

[163]*E.g.*, ALA. CODE § 13A-3-1 (Supp. 1997), ARIZ. REV. STAT. ANN. §§ 13-501-02 (Supp. 1997) (distinguishing mental "disorders" from "character and personality disorders characterized by lifelong and deeply ingrained antisocial behavior patterns, including sexual behaviors which are abnormal and prohibited by statute unless the behavior results from a mental disorder"); ILL. ST. CH. 720 § 5/6-2; FLA. STAT. § 394.455(3) (1991) (excluding "conditions manifested only by antisocial behavior or drug addiction" from the definition of mental disease or defect); IND. ST. 35-41-3-6 (Supp. 1997); ME. REV. STAT. AM. Tit., 17-A, § 39 (Supp. 1997); OHIO REV. CODE § 5122.01(A) (Supp. 1992) (defining "mental illness" as "a substantial disorder of thought, mood, perception, orientation, or memory that grossly impairs judgment, behavior, capacity to recognize

the other hand, has an extraordinarily broad definition of mental disease or defect that seemingly encompasses all personality disorders.[164] Kentucky specifically excludes antisocial personality disorder, but appears to allow all other types of personality disorders to qualify as the basis of an insanity defense.[165]

As mentioned above, both the federal system and that of several states refuse to consider antisocial personality disorder as qualifying mental disease or defect for the purposes of the insanity defense. Prior to the third edition of the DSM, people suffering from antisocial personality disorder were called sociopaths, psychopaths, or moral imbeciles.[166] Winick suggests three issues concerning the diagnosis might justifying the law's refusal to treat it as a mental disease or defect. First, he reasons that antisocial personalty disorder is "exclusively behavioral in nature, involving certain behavioral manifestations and personality traits."[167] Second, unlike psychoses, antisocial personality disorder does not appear "to be biochemical in etiology."[168] And third, the disorder is not treatable in any predictable way.[169]

Using these same three criteria, Winick also explains why other personality disorders once labeled neuroses, as well as impulse control disorders like kleptomania, pyromania, and "the sexual disorders known as paraphilias (such as pedophilia, sexual sadism, exhibitionism, voyeurism, and frotteurism), also do not seem to be" mental diseases or defects for insanity purposes.[170] While Winick's explanations why these nonpsychotic disorders are not mental diseases or defects for insanity purposes are subject to debate, they are well reasoned and consistent with logic, precedent, and clinical evidence.

3. Alcohol and Drug Addiction

DSM-IV-TR classifies alcoholism and numerous drug addictions as Axis I "substance related disorders."[171] Involuntary intoxication on drugs or alcohol was a complete defense to a crime at common law and continues to be in most U.S. jurisdictions today.[172] Voluntary intoxication, however, has never been a complete defense under the criminal law.[173] At common law, voluntary intoxication was a partial defense that mitigated a crime of specific intent down to one

---

reality, or ability to meet the ordinary demands of life."); Tenn. Code Ann. § 39-11-501 (Supp. 1997); Utah Code Ann. § 76-2-305 (Supp. 1997).

[164] *Murdoch*, 98 F.3d at 479 (citing Alaska Stat. § 12.47.130 (3) ("mental disease or defect means a disorder of thought or mood that substantially impairs judgment, behavior, capacity to recognize reality, or ability to cope with the ordinary demands of life").

[165] Ky. Rev. Stat. Ann. § 504.060(6) (West 2005) (defining "mental illness" as "substantially impaired capacity to use self-control, judgment, or discretion in the conduct of one's affairs and social relations, associated with maladaptive behavior or recognized emotional symptoms where impaired capacity, maladaptive behavior, or emotional symptoms can be related to physiological, psychological, or social factors").

[166] Winick, *supra* note 154, at 566.

[167] *Id*. at 560.

[168] *Id*.

[169] *Id*.

[170] *Id*. at 573-74.

[171] *See* DSM-IV-TR, *supra* note 146, at 16-19, 192.

[172] Meghan Paulk Ingle, *Law on the Rocks: The Intoxication Defenses Are Being Eighty-Sixed*, 55 Vand. L. Rev. 607, 616 (2002) ("[T]he involuntary intoxication defense enjoyed early recognition in Anglo-American common law. . . . Currently, American courts generally recognize the defense when the defendant's intoxication is the result of coercion, fraud, an unexpected effect from prescription medication, or 'pathological intoxication.'").

[173] *Id*.

of general intent if the defendant was so intoxicated that he or she could not form specific intent.[174] Today, some jurisdictions still follow this old common law approach, while other jurisdictions have abolished the defense of voluntary intoxication totally.[175]

Separate and apart from the criminal defense of intoxication, however, two issues regarding intoxication and insanity continue to divide U.S. courts. The first is whether an addiction to drugs or alcohol can qualify as a mental disease or defect for the purposes of an insanity defense. The second is whether a drug- or alcohol-induced psychosis (when unaccompanied by some other mental illness) is a qualifying mental disease or defect for an insanity defense—so called *settled insanity.* The overwhelming number of U.S. jurisdictions answer both questions in the negative in spite of the fact that psychiatry recognizes a host of substance abuse disorders as mental illnesses in the DSM.[176] This is true even for iatrogenically caused addictions (those that result from medical treatment).

> [W]hat definition of "mental disease or defect" is to be employed by courts enforcing the criminal law is, in the final analysis, a question of legal, moral and policy—not of medical—judgment. Among the most basic purposes of the criminal law is that of preventing a person from injuring others or, perhaps to a lesser degree, himself. This purpose and others appropriate to law enforcement are not necessarily served by an uncritical application of definitions developed with medical considerations of diagnosis and treatment foremost in mind.[177]

Alcohol and/or drug addictions are not mental illnesses for insanity defense purposes for several reasons, but the primary justification for their not rising to the level of a qualifying mental disease or defect is the voluntariness of the person's addiction.[178] People cannot choose to not be schizophrenic. But people can choose whether they will drink or take drugs. Biological predispositions to alcoholism and/or addiction aside, the law takes the view that one should seek treatment for an illness brought upon one's self, not seek excuse from the harm caused by failing to control one's own behavior.[179]

4. Summary of the Meaning of Mental Illness

Three generalizations can be made that might clarify the "mental disease or defect" requirement of the insanity defense. First, neither intoxication nor addiction to drugs or alcohol, without more, constitute a "mental disease or defect" for insanity defense purposes. Second, DSM-IV Axis I clinical disorders (i.e., "psychoses") nearly always qualify as bona-fide mental diseases or defects for the purposes of the insanity defense. And third, DSM-IV Axis II personality disorders rarely qualify as bona-fide mental diseases or defects for insanity purposes unless the etiology of the given personalty disorder can be fit into the medical model of deviance (i.e., it is not purely behavior in nature; it has some organic cause and is treatable in some predicable fashion). The

---

[174]*Id.*

[175]*Id.*

[176]*See, e.g.,* People v. Bieber, 856 P.2d 811, 815-17 (Colo. 1993).

[177]*See Special Issue: Intoxication and Criminal Responsibility,* 13 INT'L J.L. & PSYCHIATRY 1 (1990).

[178]*Bieber,* 856 P.2d , 856 P.2d at 816 (stating that the defendant's settled insanity "resulted from his use of amphetamines and, as such, may be regarded [as voluntary, self-induced] intoxication . . . .")

[179]*See, e.g.,* United States v. Lyons, 731 F.2d 243 (5th Cir.), *cert. denied,* 469 U.S. 930 (1984).

reason for this distinction appears to be "a desire to guard against turning every personality quirk into a 'mental disease or defect' through the imprimatur of a psychiatric category."[180]

B. What is "Wrong"?

What is right, just, good, moral, and so on is a question that has perplexed philosophers for eons. The counter-question, what is bad, wrong, or immoral is not much easier to answer.[181] The law, however, often avoids complex philosophical issues leaving it to scholars to debate.[182] It certainly does so in defining what is meant by "wrong" for the purposes of the insanity defense requirement that a mental disease or defect render a defendant unable to "know right from wrong" or to "appreciate the wrongfulness" of his or her acts. The law simply looks at whether the defendant knew the act was wrong by societal standards. Imagine the consequences if one could argue "as Satanic worshiper, it is not wrong for me to kill, but rather offering human sacrifice is required under the tenets of my religion."[183] An objective societal standard of right and wrong is used to avoid all such arguments defendants could make that they thought what they were doing was "right."

IV. ABOLITION OF THE INSANITY DEFENSE: THE *MENS REA* APPROACH

Montana, Idaho, Utah, and Kansas have abolished the insanity defense in their states.[184] These four states currently allow the introduction of mental illness evidence only to show that the level of *mens rea* the state is required to prove as an element of a crime was not possessed by the defendant due to his or her mental condition.

The constitutionality of a state abolishing the insanity defense was first challenged in Montana. In *State v. Korell,*[185] the Montana Supreme Court rejected the challenge, relying primarily on the U.S. Supreme Court's decision in *Leland v. Oregon.*[186] In *Leland,* the Court upheld an Oregon statute requiring the defendant to prove insanity beyond a reasonable doubt.[187] The *Leland* Court reasoned this was constitutionally permissible because the burden to prove the requisite *mens rea* remained with the prosecution.[188] Relying on this holding, the Montana Supreme Court in *Korell* upheld the abolition of the insanity defense since the state still had to

---

[180]United States v. Murdoch, 98 F.3d 472, 479 (9th Cir. 1996) (citing *Criminal Procedure: Insanity Plea—Inadmissible Mental Conditions*, 26 PAC. L.J. 254, 255 (1995)). For a more detailed analysis of this issue, see Ralph Slovenko, *The Meaning of Mental Illness in Criminal Responsibility*, 5 J. LEGAL MED. 1 (1984).

[181]*See generally* Robert J. Lipkin, *The Moral Good Theory of Punishment*, 40 U. FLA. L. REV. 17 (1988) (exploring moral philosophy as applied to criminal punishment and excuse).

[182]*See, e.g.,* Peter Arenella, *Convicting the Morally Blameless: Reassessing the Relationship Between Legal And Moral Accountability,* 39 UCLA L. REV. 1511 (1992).

[183]*See* State v. Crenshaw, 659 P.2d 488 (Wash. 1983) (upholding first-degree murder conviction of a man who claimed he was insane when he killed his wife because he believed she was having an affair since his religion allowed such a killing).

[184]*See* IDAHO CODE § 18-207 (Supp. 1982); KAN. STAT. ANN. § 22-3220 (Supp. 1995); MONT. CODE ANN. §§ 46-14-101, 102, 103 (1981); UTAH CODE ANN. § 76-2-305(1) (Supp. 1986). Note that Utah initially phrased its abolition of the insanity defense in terms of adopting a GBMI verdict. *See* UTAH CODE ANN. § 77-35-21 (Supp. 1986).

[185]690 P.2d 992, 994 (Mont. 1984).

[186]343 U.S. 790 (1952).

[187]*Id.* at 798-99.

[188]*Id.* at 799; *see also* In Re Winship, 397 U.S. 358, 368 (1970) (holding the prosecution must prove beyond a reasonable doubt every element constituting the crime charged).

prove the state of mind element of the underlying criminal offense beyond a reasonable doubt.[189] The highest courts of Idaho, Utah, and Kansas all reached similar conclusions,[190] although the Nevada Supreme Court reached the opposite conclusion when it invalidated the state legislature's abolition of the insanity defense on due process grounds.[191]

Normally, the insanity defense would apply to the same types of cases as the *mens rea* approach. However, the technicalities of a true insanity defense function quite differently than the *mens rea* approach when dealing with a delusional defendant. For example, suppose a defendant killed another person because he delusionally believed that God had ordered him to kill that person. Under a traditional insanity defense, the psychosis responsible for such a delusionary belief system would likely excuse the defendant's criminal act because the defendant did not know that what he did was wrong if he believed he was doing God's will.[192] But under the *mens rea* approach, the defendant could be convicted of premeditated murder since he acted purposefully when killing his victim. The fact that a serious mental illness was responsible for forming the defendant's specific intent to kill would be irrelevant for determining his guilt. It would, however, be relevant in sentencing.[193]

Numerous articles have critiqued the abolition of the insanity defense, both pro[194] and con.[195] There can be, however, no "right" or "wrong" answer (to use the lingo of the insanity defense) since how one feels toward the defense is largely a matter of philosophy toward crime, punishment, and mental illness. Empirical research has shown, however, that in the states that have abolished the insanity defense, there has been a "statistically significant increase in the number of defendants found permanently incompetent to stand trial."[196] So, perhaps, insanity is with us to stay in one way, shape, or form.

V. AFTER A VERDICT OF NOT GUILTY BY REASON OF INSANITY

The disposition of defendants under Arizona's "guilty except insane" statue and under those states that have adopted GBMI verdicts was discussed above. But what happens to those persons in the majority of U.S. states upon a verdict of NGBI? Contrary to popular believe, most insanity acquittees are confined to secure mental institutions for many years following their trials, often for the balance of their natural lives. Take John Hinckley, for example. He was acquitted via a NGBI verdict in 1981. As of the writing of this text in 2007, he is still institutionalized in St.

---

[189]*Korell*, 690 P.2d at 994.

[190]*See* State v. Searcy, 798 P.2d 914 (Idaho 1990); State v. Bethel, 66 P.3d 840 (Kan. 2003); State v. Herrera, 895 P.2d 359 (Utah 1995).

[191]Finger v. State, 27 P.3d 66 (Nev. 2001).

[192]*See, e.g.*, Andrew J. Demko, Note, *Abraham's Deific Defense: Problems with Insanity, Faith, and Knowing Right from Wrong*, 80 NOTRE DAME L. REV. 1961 (2005); Grant H. Morris & Ansar Haroun, *"God Told Me to Kill": Religion or Delusion?*, 38 SAN DIEGO L. REV. 973 (2001).

[193]*See, e.g.*, UTAH CODE ANN. § 76-2-305(1)(b) (2006) ("Mental illness is not otherwise a defense, but may be evidence in mitigation of the penalty in a capital felony . . . and may be evidence of special mitigation reducing the level of a criminal homicide or attempted criminal homicide. . . .").

[194]*See, e.g.*, WILLIAM J. WINSLADE & JUDITH WILSON ROSS, THE INSANITY PLEA (1983).

[195]*See, e.g.*, Elkins, *supra* note 6; Mclançon, *supra* note 99.

[196]*See* Rita Buitendorp, *A Statutory Lesson from "Big Sky Country" on Abolishing the Insanity Defense*, 30 VAL. U. L. REV. 965, 993-96 (1996) (discussing the research reported in Henry J. Steadman et al., *Maintenance of an Insanity Defense Under Montana's "Abolition" of the Insanity Defense*, 146 AM. J. PSYCHIATRY 357, 359-60 (1989))."

Elizabeth's Hospital in the wing for the criminally insane.[197] And if Teddy Roosevelt's would-be assassin, who served 31 years in a mental hospital, serves as any indicator, Hinckley is likely to be at St. Elizabeth's for many years to come.

States differ markedly on how long an insanity acquittee may be incarcerated.[198] Some states limit the period of confinement in a mental health facility to no longer than what the maximum potential sentence could have been if the defendant had been convicted of the offense.[199] But other states impose an indefinite period of treatment,[200] sometimes referred to as a sentence of "one day to life."[201] Under this standard, the defendant who is committed as mentally ill and posing a risk of danger to himself or herself or to others remains committed in that mental institution until he or she is no longer mentally ill or no longer dangerous.[202] Normally, state law presumes a person so committed remains both mentally ill and dangerous and places the burden of proving otherwise on the person committed.

Only a small minority of states do not automatically commit someone to a mental facility upon a NGBI verdict. New Jersey's statute is representative of this minority approach:

2C:4-8. Commitment of a Person by Reason of Insanity

a.   After acquittal by reason of insanity, the court shall order that the defendant undergo a psychiatric examination by a psychiatrist of the prosecutor's choice. . . . The defendant, pursuant to this section, may also be examined by a psychiatrist of his own choice.

b.   The court shall dispose of the defendant in the following manner:

(1)   If the court finds that the defendant may be released without danger to the community or himself without supervision, the court shall so release the defendant; or

(2)   If the court finds that the defendant may be released without danger to the community or to himself under supervision or under conditions, the court shall so order; or

(3)   If the court finds that the defendant cannot be released with or without supervision or conditions without posing a danger to the community or to himself, it shall commit the defendant to a mental health facility approved for this purpose by the Commissioner of Human Services to be treated as a person civilly committed. In all proceedings conducted pursuant to this section and pursuant to section N.J.S.2C:4-6

---

[197]Douglas Mossman, *Is Prosecution "Medically Appropriate"?*, 31 NEW ENG. J. ON CRIM. & CIV. CONFINEMENT 15, 57-58 & n. 188 (2005).

[198]*See generally*, Joanmarie Ilaria Davoli, *Reconsidering the Consequences of an Insanity Acquittal*, 31 NEW ENG. J. ON CRIM. & CIV. CONFINEMENT 3 (2005).

[199]**[Need cite].***See* Maura Caffrey, *A New Approach to Insanity Acquittee Recidivism: Redefining the Class Of Truly Responsible Recidivists*, 154 U. PA. L. REV. 399, 423 & n.127 (2005) (citing RALPH REISNER, CHRISTOPHER SLOBOGIN, & ARTI RAI, LAW AND THE MENTAL HEALTH SYSTEM, CIVIL AND CRIMINAL ASPECTS 842 (4th ed. 2004)

[200]Caffrey, *supra* note 199, at 423 & n. 127 ("The length of . . . commitment will not depend on the severity of the crime . . . committed. Rather, it will rest on . . . continuing illness and dangerousness.").

[201]*See, e.g.*, Jessica Butterfield, *Blue Mourning: Postpartum Psychosis and the Criminal Insanity Defense, Waking to the Reality of Women Who Kill Their Children*, 39 J. MARSHALL L. REV. 515, 531 & n.111 (2006) (citing Christopher Slobogin, Symposium on the ABA Criminal Justice Mental Health Standards: *The Guilty But Mentally Ill Verdict: An Idea Whose Time Should Not Have Come*, 53 GEO. WASH. L. REV. 494, 500 (1985)). [Need cite].

[202]*Id.* [Need cite].

concerning a defendant who lacks the fitness to proceed, including any periodic review proceeding, the prosecuting attorney shall have the right to appear and be heard. The defendant's continued commitment, under the law governing civil commitment, shall be established by a preponderance of the evidence, during the maximum period of imprisonment that could have been imposed, as an ordinary term of imprisonment, for any charge on which the defendant has been acquitted by reason of insanity. Expiration of that maximum period of imprisonment shall be calculated by crediting the defendant with any time spent in confinement for the charge or charges on which the defendant has been acquitted by reason of insanity.

c.   No person committed under this section shall be confined within any penal or correctional institution or any part thereof.

VI. CONCLUSION

Whether the changes that occurred in the aftermath of the Hinckley case have had any significant impact on the rate of acquittals on the basis of insanity is questionable. Empirical research on the actual effects of the IDRA is woefully lacking. From the few studies conducted examining this issue, however, it would appear the changes in the law have had little impact.

One study by Normal J. Finkel that compared insanity acquittals in California under the ALI/MPC formulation of the insanity defense with the rate following the state's return to the *M'Naghten* test after the Hinckley case found the acquittal rate to be approximately 40 percent both before and after the legislative change.[203] Using an experimental design in which undergraduate students were presented with scripts in which five female defendants, each with a unique diagnosis, had been charged with a homicide and pled insanity in her defense, Finkel found that the particular version of the insanity defense the evaluating students were told to apply did not significantly alter the proportion of defendants found to be insane in each diagnostic category.[204] In a simulated trial study in which not only the actual insanity test used was altered as an experimental condition, but also the level of proof required and the side bearing the burden of persuasion, James R.P. Ogloff found no significant differences for the acquittal rate among the experimental conditions.[205] On the other hand, in contrast to those studies examining acquittal rates, at least one study found that the post-*Hinckley* statutory changes to the insanity defense in Georgia and New York resulted in fewer defendants entering insanity pleas in both jurisdictions.[206]

The lack of empirical evidence to support the proposition that the IDRA and state changes modeled after it, either in whole or in part, have actually had an effect on the incidence and success rates of the insanity defense is not surprising for a few reasons. First, "generally, in the absence of either exceptionally persuasive or 'objective' evidence, jurors reject the notion that an

---

[203]Margaret A. McGreevy et al., *The Negligible Effects of California's 1982 Reform of the Insanity Defense*, 148 AM. J. PSYCHIATRY 744, 745-47 (1991).

[204]Norman J. Finkel, *The Insanity Defense Reform Act of 1984: Much Ado About Nothing*, 7 BEHAV. SCI. & L. 403 (1989).

[205]James R.P. Ogloff, *A Comparison of Insanity Defense Standards on Juror Decision Making*, 15 LAW & HUM. BEHAV. 509, 516 (1991).

[206]STEADMAN, ET AL., *supra* note 120.

alleged mental disorder is severe enough to excuse criminal behavior."[207] Thus, regardless of the actual formulation of the insanity defense, juries tend to view the defense with skepticism.

Second, when faced with evidence of insanity, it appears jurors use their own views or constructs of what insanity is, such as:

> [P]erceptions of the defendant's incapacity, awareness, clarity of thinking, ability to control behavior, capability of evil motive, and whether any other person or persons were at fault for the criminal act. Essentially, jurors resorted to their own common sense definition of insanity, one that seemed much more complex than the simplistic conceptualization of the insane person embodied in the major rules.[208]

Finally, and perhaps most importantly, jurors bring to their insanity defense deliberations "their own personal sense of justice". . . including "attitudes about the morality of the insanity defense and the punishment of mentally ill offenders."[209] If so, perhaps there are crimes so heinous that it offends one's sense of justice to the point where one cannot excuse criminal responsibility even in the face of strong evidence of insanity. Consider the sensational criminal prosecutions of Jack Ruby, Sirhan Sirhan, John Wayne Gacy, Jeffery Dahmer, Charles Manson, Colin Ferguson, and John Salvi. All pled insanity; all were convicted.[210]

Wrightsman, et al., in discussing Jeffery Dahmer's case, wrote that the careful manner in which Dahmer killed his victims so as to reduce his chances of being caught must have left the jury unconvinced that he suffered from a mental disease or defect sufficiently severe to rise to the level of insanity. "This cautiousness suggested that he appreciated the wrongfulness of his behavior and could control it when it was opportune for him to do so."[211] While this explanation of Dahmer's conviction is plausible, it is equally plausible that the jury found what Dahmer did to be so heinous that they refused to acquit him using one of the most liberal of all the formulations of the insanity defense—the one that included the irresistible impulse test. Consider one commentator's summary of Dahmer:

> [A]ssuming that there might be degrees of insanity, I do not find it hard to accept that a jury might distinguish between Dahmer and Gacy. Gacy was an otherwise industrious, capable businessman, who carefully prepared in advance to commit numerous murders in secrecy, successfully hiding the bodies and his crimes for years. On the other hand, Dahmer was a maladjusted weirdo who drilled holes in the heads of his living victims for his own scientific purposes, killed a man after police responded to his apartment building and confronted him and his naked and bleeding victim, kept body parts in his closet and refrigerator for extended periods of time, and cannibalized his victims.[212]

---

[207]Perlin, Unpacking the Myths, *supra* note 20 at 721 (citing Arens, et al., *Jurors, Jury Charges and Insanity,* 14 CATH. U. L. REV. 1, 9 (1965); STEADMAN, ET AL., *supra* note 120, at 44 (finding that severe psychosis "almost became a prerequisite for success.")).

[208]Blau & Pasewark, *supra* note 90; *see also* WRIGHTSMAN, ET AL., *supra* note 64, at 298-99.

[209]WRIGHTSMAN, ET AL., *supra* note 64, at 298-99; *see also* Caton F. Roberts & Stephen L. Golding, *The Social Construction of Criminal Responsibility and Insanity,* 15 LAW & HUM. BEHAV. 349, 359-360 (1991); Norman J. Finkel, *De Facto Departures from Insanity Instructions,* 14 LAW & HUM. BEHAV. 105 (1990).

[210]For interesting explorations of the particular problems with proving insanity in postpartum depression cases, see Jessica Butterfield, Comment, *Blue Mourning: Postpartum Psychosis and the Criminal Insanity Defense, Waking to the Reality of Women Who Kill Their Children,* 39 J. MARSHALL L. REV. 515 (2006); Jessie Manchester, Comment, *Beyond Accommodation: Reconstructing the Insanity Defense to Provide an Adequate Remedy for Postpartum Psychotic Women,* 93 J. CRIM. L. & CRIMINOLOGY 713 (2003).

[211]WRIGHTSMAN, ET AL., *supra* note 64, at 299.

[212]William J. Kunkle, Jr., *Counter-Point: Gacy v. Dahmer: An Informed Response,* 30 J. MARSHALL L. REV. 331, 335 (1997).

Keep in mind, for comparison purposes, that John Hinckley was acquitted after being found insane under the same formal test for insanity. The resultant harm in the two cases, however, was quite different. Although Hinckley tried to kill the president, he did not succeed. His trial was, therefore, one of attempted murder. In contrast, Dahmer killed and dismembered fifteen victims, often had sex with their corpses, and, in some cases, ate parts of their bodies.[213] In spite of the bizarre behaviors exhibited by Dahmer, he was convicted. But if Jeffery Dahmer was not insane, then who is?

---

[213]Maureen O'Donnell, *Jury Hears of Dahmer's Gruesome Past*, CHI. SUN-TIMES, Feb. 5, 1992, at 5.

CHAPTER SEVEN
DIMINISHED CAPACITY AND BEYOND

I. INTRODUCTION

As explored several places in this book, the criminal law generally punishes only those offenders who are morally culpable for their criminal acts. The insanity defense, for example, demonstrates one way in which the law operates to relieve criminal responsibility from those who do not act with the requisite *mens rea* as a result of mental illness. But as you also know from the chapter on insanity, there are significant restrictions on the availability of the insanity defense. Consider people who are mentally ill but not "severely" enough to qualify as legally insane under IDRA and its progeny.[1] What about those people who are severely mentally ill, but still knew both the nature and quality of their acts and the difference between right and wrong? Although the law generally does not recognize such conditions as qualifying for a total defense of excuse, such defendants may not be as culpable as those who are not mentally ill in some way. The defense of ***diminished capacity*** might be available to such persons to either mitigate their criminal responsibility, their sentence, or in some circumstances, even excuse their criminal responsibility altogether.

II. THE "DEFENSE" OF DIMINISHED CAPACITY

A. Attempting a Definition of Diminished Capacity

Unfortunately, the doctrine of diminished capacityt does not have a standard definition. The doctrine exists, either statutorily or in case law, in more than half of all U.S. jurisdictions.[2] Although diminished capacity is often referred to as a defense, doing so is somewhat inappropriate. As commentators have often pointed out, it is not a defense at all, but rather deals with the admissibility of evidence concerning the accused's mental state.[3] It is most frequently invoked in first-degree murder cases to negate premeditation.[4]

Although there are clearly "differing views regarding the meaning and application of the diminished capacity concept," the favored view of diminished capacity is that it is "a type of evidence . . . admitted to rebut the specific intent required to convict the defendant of the crime charged."[5] In other words, a defendant invoking the diminished capacity doctrine asserts that his or her mental state prevented him or her from forming the requisite *mens rea* for the crime. Without proof of the required *mens rea* element, the defendant should not be convicted of that crime.[6] But the use of diminished capacity evidence to negate the existence of *mens rea* "is not

---

[1] *See generally* Chapter Six.

[2] Lucy Noble Inman, *Mental Impairment and Mens Rea: North Carolina Recognizes the Diminished Capacity Defense in* State v. Shank *and* State v. Rose, 67 N.C. L. REV. 1293, 1308-09 (1989).

[3] *See, e.g.*, Stephen J. Morse, *Undiminished Confusion in Diminished Capacity*, 75 J. CRIM. L. & CRIMINOLOGY 1, 44 (1984) (explaining that diminished capacity is usually not a true defense in its own right); Gayle Cohen, Johnson v. State — *Diminished Capacity Rejected as a Criminal Defense*, 42 MD. L. REV. 522 (1983) (same).

[4] Inman, *supra* note 2, at 1293.

[5] Chesney E. Falk, Comment, *Criminal Law —* State v. Phipps*: The Tennessee Court of Criminal Appeals Accepts "Diminished Capacity" Evidence to Negate Mens Rea*, 26 U. MEM. L. REV. 373, 383 (1995).

[6] Inman, *supra* note 2, at 1298.

an affirmative defense and does not result in an acquittal unless there is a failure to establish intent for the offense and for all of its lesser-included counterparts."[7] Thus, the burden of persuasion to prove intent remains with the prosecution when a defendant argues diminished capacity;[8] the defendant only needs to create a reasonable doubt with regard to state of mind in order to be acquitted.[9] Accordingly, diminished capacity is not only easier to use, but also is much "more likely to succeed than the insanity defense."[10]

The term diminished capacity is often used to encompass the related concept of ***diminished responsibility***, but they are technically distinct concepts in the criminal law. Diminished responsibility is concerned not with capacity to form intent, but rather with the propriety of punishment.[11] Diminished responsibility allows either a jury or a judge "'to mitigate the punishment of a mentally disabled but sane offender in any case where the jury believes that the defendant is less culpable than his normal counterpart who commits the same criminal act.'"[12] Diminished responsibility has not been embraced by the courts of the United States but has been in England.[13] However, a number of U.S. jurisdictions, the Model Penal Code, and the Federal Sentencing Guidelines allow for the admission of mental abnormality evidence in sentence mitigation.[14]

B. Applying Diminished Capacity

Jurisdictions that recognize diminished capacity vary greatly in the ways in which they permit the doctrine to be used. Some jurisdictions restrict the use of diminished capacity evidence to specific intent crimes.[15] Other states further limit its use to cases where evidence of diminished capacity might negate the specific intent requirement for murder only.[16] Still other jurisdictions have adopted the MPC's approach, which allows diminished capacity evidence in any case where the defendant's mental state is at issue.[17] The Model Penal Code approach has been

---

[7]State v. Phipps, 883 S.W.2d 138, 143 (Tenn. Crim. App. 1994) (citing United States v. Pohlot, 827 F.2d 889 (3d Cir. 1987), *cert. denied*, 484 U.S. 1011 (1988)).

[8]*Id.* at 143.

[9]*Id.*; *see also* J. Thomas Sullivan, *The Culpability, or Mens Rea, "Defense" in Arkansas*, 53 ARK. L. REV. 805, 816 (2000) (stating that diminished capacity actually serves as a means for rebutting the prosecution's proof on the essential element of the culpable mental state, rather than as an independent rationale either justifying or excusing the accused's behavior).

[10]Inman, *supra* note 2, at 1299.

[11]*See, e.g.*, Stephen J. Morse, *Diminished Rationality, Diminished Responsibility*, 1 OHIO ST. J. CRIM. L. 289 (2003).

[12]Jonas Robitscher & Andrew Ky Haynes, *In Defense of the Insanity Defense*, 31 EMORY L.J. 9, 26 n.66 (1982) (quoting Peter Arenella, *Diminished Capacity and Diminished Responsibility Defenses: Two Children of a Doomed Marriage*, 77 COLUM. L. REV. 827, 828-29 (1977)).

[13]Jennifer Kunk Compton, Note, *Expert Witness Testimony and the Diminished Capacity Defense*, 20 AM. J. TRIAL ADVOC. 381, 386-87 (1997).

[14]MODEL PENAL CODE § 210.6(4)(g) (1980); U.S. SENTENCING GUIDELINES MANUAL 5K2.13 (1998); *see also* Deborah E. Dezelan, *Departures from the Federal Sentencing Guidelines after* Koon v. United States: *More Discretion, Less Direction*, 72 NOTRE DAME L. REV. 1679, 1688-89 (1997) (recognizing diminished capacity as a mitigating factor to punishment).

[15]Inman, *supra* note 2, at 1309 (citing Wagner v. State, 687 S.W.2d 303 (Tex. Crim. App. 1984); State v. Holcomb, 643 S.W.2d 336 (Tenn. Crim. App. 1982)).

[16]*Id.* (citing Commonwealth v. Garcia, 479 A.2d 473 (Pa. 1984); Commonwealth v. Gould, 405 N.E.2d 927 (Mass. 1980)).

[17]*See, e.g.*, COLO. REV. STAT. § 18-1-803 (2006) (evidence of mental impairment admissible to negate mental element of any offense). Section 4.02(1) of the Model Penal Code reads: "[E]vidence that the defendant suffered from a mental disease or defect is admissible whenever it is relevant to prove that the defendant did or did not have a state of mind which is an element of the offense." MODEL PENAL CODE § 4.02(1) (1962).

endorsed by the American Bar Association[18] and is the one most frequently followed in the United States in those states recognizing diminished capacity.[19]

Before the defense may introduce any evidence of diminished capacity, the defendant must meet a burden of production by providing sufficient evidence of a mental disease or defect that would causally interfere with the ability to form the requisite *mens rea*.[20] Once the burden of production is met, the evidence used to show diminished capacity is essentially the same as the evidence that would be used to show insanity. Generally, the testimony of a mental health clinician is offered at trial to show that the defendant's capacity to form the requisite *mens rea* was "diminished" at the time of the crime due to some mental disease or defect.[21] Such expert testimony must not only be offered by a properly qualified expert but also must conform to the other applicable rules of evidence with regard to expert testimony.[22]

C. What Counts as a Predicate Mental Disorder for Diminished Capacity Purposes?

What qualifies as a "mental disease or defect" for insanity defense purposes is often quite different from what qualifies as a mental disorder for diminished capacity purposes. In light of IDRA and the majority of states that adopted its approach, it is clear that in most U.S. jurisdictions today, cognitive impairment is necessary to find insanity.[23] What qualifies for diminished capacity is significantly broader. For example, a learning disability generally does not constitute a "mental disease or defect" for insanity purposes.[24] But if a learning-disabled person strikes someone but as a result of his or her disability is unable to know that the blow could kill, he or she might be able to assert diminished capacity to negate the *mens rea* of intent to kill if charged a crime.[25]

The broad scope of what can qualify as diminished capacity is illustrated by *United States v. McBroom*.[26] The defendant in *McBroom* pled guilty to possessing child pornography.[27] At sentencing, he argued for mitigation in his sentence because "he suffered from a significantly reduced mental capacity due to the sexual abuse he had endured as a child, and that this reduced capacity compelled him to possess child pornography."[28] Although the trial court agreed that the defendant had fallen victim to repeated sexual abuse and suffered from bipolar disorder and multiple impulse control disorders, the circuit court determined that neither the abuse nor the

---

[18] AMERICAN BAR ASS'N, STANDARDS FOR CRIMINAL JUSTICE, CRIMINAL JUSTICE MENTAL HEALTH STANDARDS § 7-6.2 (1984).

[19] Compton, *supra* note 13, at 388.

[20] *See, e.g.*, Patterson v. New York, 432 U.S. 197, 230-31 (1977) (Powell, J., dissenting) (stating that even when the state has the burden of persuasion, a defendant may have the burden of producing evidence sufficient to raise a reasonable doubt about the issue); *see also* PAUL H. ROBINSON, CRIMINAL LAW DEFENSES § 64(a) (1984).

[21] *See, e.g.*, Henry F. Fradella, Adam Fogarty & Lauren O'Neill, *The Impact of* Daubert *on the Admissibility of Behavioral Science Testimony*, 30 PEPP L. REV. 403, 421-23 (2003) (discussing use of expert testimony as part of defendants' attempts to rebut *mens rea*).

[22] *Id.* at 421-23; *see also, e.g.*, State v. Weeks, 367 S.E.2d 895, 904 (N.C. 1988) (holding psychiatric testimony about a murder suspect's mental state was inadmissible because it used legal terms of art that were not readily understood by the expert).

[23] Recent Case, *Criminal Law and Criminal Procedure: Criminal Law — Federal Sentencing Guidelines — Third Circuit Holds that Volitional Impairments Can Support a Claim of Diminished Mental Capacity*, 111 HARV. L. REV. 1122 (1998).

[24] *See* Chapter Six.

[25] *See* State v. Breakiron, 532 A.2d 199 (N.J. 1987).

[26] 124 F.3d 533 (3d Cir. 1997).

[27] *Id.* at 534.

[28] *Id.* at 539.

disorders impacted the defendant's cognitive ability (i.e., knowing right from wrong).[29] Therefore, the Court held that a downward departure in sentencing was unwarranted.[30] The Third Circuit Court of Appeals reversed, holding that volitional impairment (including impulse control personality disorders) should be considered as evidence of diminished capacity under the U.S. Sentencing Guidelines when determining the appropriateness of sentence mitigation.[31]

Some jurisdictions have adopted such broad definitions of diminished capacity that a qualifying "mental disease or defect" need not even be recognized by the DSM. One of the leading cases in this area is the New Jersey Supreme Court's opinion in *State v. Galloway*.[32] In *Galloway*, the Court stated that "[f]orms of psychopathology other than clinically defined mental diseases or defects may affect the mental process and diminish cognitive capacity, and therefore may be regarded as a mental disease or defect in the statutory or legal sense."[33] As such, whether a mental disease or defect works to impair cognitive function is decided on a case-by-case basis in New Jersey.

It is somewhat ironic that the standard for qualifying a mental disease or defect for insanity defense purposes is rather stringent, while simultaneously being so much broader for diminished capacity purposes. This is especially true because of how much easier it is to get an acquittal by creating reasonable doubt, using a diminished capacity argument by reason of insanity — something the defendant must prove, often by clear and convincing evidence. Moreover, those found not guilty by reason of insanity rarely go free; in contrast, those who successfully assert diminished capacity evidence are found not guilty and are therefore set free. Given the benefits of diminished capacity, it is not surprising that defendants have attempted to extend the doctrine in a multitude of ways. The next section of this chapter is devoted to examining the ways in which defendants have tried to do just that.

III. BEYOND DIMINISHED CAPACITY

The rationale underlying diminished capacity has been extended to a variety of situations. By its use, defendants share the common goal to reduce criminal liability "due to some extenuating circumstance that allegedly rendered the defendant unable to form the requisite *mens rea* of a crime, or led to it being formed defectively—as a result of some mental condition rather than out of 'normal' criminal intent."[34] Accordingly, these "defenses" are really just extensions of diminished capacity.

---

[29] *Id.* at 540.

[30] *Id.*

[31] *McBroom*, 124 F.3d at 547-48; *see also* United States v. Pullen, 89 F.3d 368, 370-71 (7th Cir. 1996). *But see* United States v. Edwards, 98 F.3d 1364, 1371 (D.C. Cir. 1996) (requiring cognitive impairment); United States v. Johnson, 979 F.2d 396, 401 (6th Cir. 1992) (requiring cognitive impairment).

[32] 628 A.2d 735 (N.J. 1993). In *Galloway*, the defendant was convicted of murder and endangering the welfare of a child when he caused the death of his girlfriend's baby by shaking the baby (i.e., "Shaken Baby Syndrome"). *Id.* at 738. The intermediate appellate court upheld the conviction, holding that the defendant's borderline personality disorder, even though it rendered the defendant unable to control his impulses, was not a sufficient "mental disease or defect" for diminished capacity purposes. *Id.* at 739 (citing 611 A.2d 651 (1992)). The high court reversed, holding that "all mental deficiencies, including conditions that cause a loss of emotional control, may satisfy the diminished-capacity defense if the record shows that experts in the psychological field believe . . . that kind of mental deficiency can affect a person's cognitive faculties. . . ." *Id.* at 743.

[33] *Id.* at 741 (citing Slovenko, *supra* note 268, at 16).

[34] Henry F. Fradella, Key Cases, Comments, and Questions on Substantive Criminal Law 217 (2000).

At the outset, it should be noted that some extensions of diminished capacity have led to a backlash against the use of such evidence. The best example of this might be when California abolished the use of diminished capacity evidence after the successful use of the Twinkie Defense. Other high-profile examples include Lorena Bobbit and the Menendez brothers, all of whom argued their formation of *mens rea* was defective in light of their respective histories of abuse. Professor Alan Dershowitz of Harvard Law School termed these defenses "abuse excuses."[35] He defined an abuse excuse as "the legal tactic by which criminal defendants claim a history of abuse as an excuse for violent retaliation."[36] Such defenses have met with varying success, working for Lorena Bobbit, for example, but being unsuccessful for Lyle and Eric Menendez.[37]

A. The Twinkie Defense

The 1979 case of *People v. White*[38] was one of the most high-profile cases in which diminished capacity was extended. The defendant, Dan White, had been a member of the San Francisco Board of Supervisors.[39] He resigned his position on the Board, but then sought to be reinstated by San Francisco Mayor George Moscone who was responsible for filling vacancies on the Board.[40] Initially, Moscone had assured White that he would be reappointed, but he subsequently wrote White to inform him that "he had made no commitment of any kind to reappoint [White]."[41] Apparently, Moscone changed his mind because one of the other members of the Board of Supervisors, Harvey Milk, opposed White's reappointment.[42] Shortly thereafter, Moscone made arrangements to hold a press conference announcing the appointment of someone else to fill the vacancy created by White's resignation.[43] But Moscone never had to chance to make the announcement because, less than one hour prior to the time the press conference was scheduled to occur, White repeatedly shot and killed both Mayor Moscone and Supervisor Milk.[44] He was charged with two counts of murder in the first-degree.[45]

At White's trial, three psychiatrists and a psychologist testified that White had become clinically depressed.[46] As part of White's depression, he gorged himself on Twinkies® and Coca-Cola.®[47] But White was hypoglycemic (a low blood-sugar condition).[48] The sugar and caffeine he ingested caused a brief reactive psychosis that rendered White unable to control his

---

[35]*See, e.g.*, ALAN M. DERSHOWITZ, THE ABUSE EXCUSE AND OTHER COP-OUTS, SOB STORIES, AND EVASIONS OF RESPONSIBILITY (1994).

[36]*Id.* at 3.

[37]*See generally* Karla K. Leeper & Jon Bruschke, *The Prevalence of the Abuse Excuse: Media Hype or Cause for Concern?*, 17 COMM. & L. 47, 49 (1995).

[38]People v. White, 117 Cal. App.3d 270, 172 Cal. Rptr. 612 (1981).

[39]*White*, 117 Cal. App. 3d at 275.

[40]*Id.*

[41]*Id.*

[42]*Id.*

[43]*Id.*

[44]*Id.*

[45]*Id.* at 278.

[46]*Id.* at 276-77.

[47]*See Getting Off? Depression as a Defense*, TIME, May 28, 1979, at 57.

[48]*Id.*

actions.[49] His defense was dubbed the "***Twinkie Defense***" and it worked![50] The jury did not convict White of murder, but rather of manslaughter, apparently believing that his capacity was, in fact, diminished as a result of his hypoglycemic reaction to the sugar and caffeine.[51] The public outrage at the successful extension of diminished capacity in the *White* case eventually led California to statutorily abolish the diminished capacity doctrine in that state.[52]

B. Posttraumatic Stress Disorder Defense

Extreme cases of ***Posttraumatic Stress Disorder*** (PTSD) may serve as the qualifying "mental disease or defect" for an insanity defense.[53] Of course, to do so effectively in the overwhelming majority of U.S. courts, the disorder would have to render the defendant unable to substantially appreciate the wrongfulness or criminality of his or her actions. But if the level of impairment does not rise to the level of insanity, the disorder may still be used as the predicate for a finding of diminished capacity.

PTSD was first noted in America after the Civil War, though little was known about it then.[54] Subsequent wars, especially the two World Wars (during which time it was often referred to as "shell shock" and "combat fatigue")[55] and the Vietnam War,[56] led to study of the condition. PTSD was recognized as a mental disorder in 1980 by the American Psychiatric Association.[57] The condition originally applied only to veterans of wars who experienced intense "flashbacks" to times of combat.[58] During these flashbacks, individuals were known to have violent outbreaks, but PTSD evolved to encompass almost any individual who experienced extreme trauma or violence.[59] Such exposure remains a "necessary, but not sufficient, condition for the development of PTSD."[60] Because PTSD can affect one's perception of reality—including the circumstances in which one finds oneself even in "normal" situations—PTSD can interfere with the formation of *mens rea* and therefore serve as a predicate for introducing diminished capacity evidence.[61]

---

[49]*Id.*

[50]*Id.*

[51]*Id.*; *cf.* Commonwealth v. Mulcahy, No. 460-464 (Phila. Ct. C.P. Pa. Dec. 1978) (murder reduced to manslaughter based on diminished capacity).

[52]Inman, *supra* note 2, at 1309 (citing CAL. PENAL CODE § 28(a)-(b) (West 1988)).

[53]Debra D. Burke & Mary Anne Nixon, *Post-Traumatic Stress Disorder and the Death Penalty*, 38 HOW. L.J. 183 (1994); Michael J. Davidson, Note, *Post-Traumatic Stress Disorder: A Controversial Defense for Veterans of a Controversial War*, 29 WM. & MARY L. REV. 415 (1988).

[54]Davidson, *supra* note 53, at 417-18.

[55]*Id.*; *see also* Michael J. Pangia, *Posttraumatic Stress Disorder: Litigation Strategies*, 64 J. AIR L. & COM. 1091, 1093 (1999).

[56]Davidson, *supra* note 53, at 415.

[57]Eric H. Marcus, *Post-Traumatic Stress Disorder: Facts and Myths*, 32 TRAUMA 49 (1990).

[58]John E. Helzer et al., *Post-Traumatic Stress Disorder in the General Population*, NEW ENG. J. MED., Dec. 24, 1987, at 1630.

[59]*See* Edgar Garcia-Rill & Erica Beecher-Monas, *Gatekeeping Stress: The Science and Admissibility of Post-Traumatic Stress Disorder*, 24 U. ARK. LITTLE ROCK L. REV. 9 (2001).

[60]Patricia J. Falk, *Novel Theories of Criminal Defense Based Upon the Toxicity of the Social Environment: Urban Psychosis, Television Intoxication, and Black Rage*, 74 N.C. L. REV. 731, 761 (1996).

[61]Davidson, *supra* note 53, at 422.

Since its acceptance as a bona-fide medical condition,[62] courts have been more accepting of the PTSD defense than other excuse defenses since it appears to be the very type of disorder diminished capacity is designed to encompass. For example, in *State v. Phipps*,[63] the defendant was a Gulf War veteran who was on trial for murder.[64] On the day in question, Phipps went to his wife's home, where he got into an argument with his wife's lover who threatened Phipps with a stick.[65] Phipps took the stick and hit the wife's lover repeatedly with it, eventually killing him.[66] At trial, the defense presented expert testimony that Phipps suffered from depression and posttraumatic stress disorder.[67] Even the prosecution's expert testified that his impairment was "of a sufficient level to significantly affect his thinking, reasoning, judgment, and emotional well-being."[68] Moreover, his PTSD "may have lessened his threshold or made him more sensitive to defending himself and protecting himself and increased the likelihood of him over-reacting to a real or perceived threat."[69]

The trial court judge refused to give a jury instruction that would have allowed the jury to consider the evidence of mental disorders in relation to whether Phipps possessed the required *mens rea* for first-degree murder. The appeals court reversed the decision, holding that evidence of the defendant's mental state at the time of the offense is admissible to refute elements of specific intent in first-degree murder cases.[70]

But the acceptance of PTSD as a form of diminished capacity has not been universal, in spite of the generally accepted proposition that PTSD impairs an individual's mental functioning. Some critics have challenged the diagnosis of the disorder as being overly subjective, largely due to the fact that a PTSD diagnosis is based on patient testimonials and personal observations.[71] These critics fear that the disorder is often contrived just for the purposes of criminal defense.[72] Efforts are underway to provide a physiological basis for PTSD diagnosis, rather than relying on the patient's subjective assertions.[73] As of yet, no physiological evidence has been presented to a court. For now, in those jurisdictions that allow the use of diminished capacity evidence, mental health professionals are generally allowed to testify not only as to whether the defendant has PTSD, but also whether the disorder influenced the defendant's capacity to form the requisite criminal intent at the time of the offense.[74]

---

[62]*See generally* PETER CONRAD & JOSEPH SCHNEIDER, DEVIANCE AND MEDICALIZATION: FROM BADNESS TO SICKNESS (1980).

[63]883 S.W.2d 138 (Tenn. Crim. App. 1994).

[64]*Id.* at 139.

[65]*Id.* at 141.

[66]*Id.*

[67]*Id.*

[68]*Id.*

[69]*Id.*

[70]*Id.* at 1479.

[71]*E.g.*, Roger K. Pittman & Scott P. Orr, *Psychophysiologic Testing for Post-Traumatic Stress Disorder: Forensic Psychiatric Application*, 21 BULL. AM. ACAD. PSYCHIATRY L. 37, 39 (1993).

[72]*Id.* at 39-40.

[73]*Id.* at 40.

[74]*See, e.g.*, Alberto M. Goldwaser, *A Forensic Psychiatrist's Viewpoint Post-traumatic Stress Disorder*, 229 N.J. LAW. Aug. 2004, at 28-33.

C. Battered Women's Syndrome Defense

1. Battered Women's Syndrome

Dr. Lenore Walker first coined the term "***Battered Women's Syndrome***" (BWS) in her 1979 book, *The Battered Woman*.[75] In it, Walker put forth a theory that attempted to explain why abused women stayed in abusive relationships, and what finally triggers them to strike back.[76] Walker's research has been criticized as "little more than a patchwork of pseudo-scientific methods employed to confirm a hypothesis that its author and participating researchers never seriously doubted."[77] Such criticisms aside, there can be no doubt that Walker's work had a significant impact on the law, even if not on psychology. Her theory of BWS has been accepted in many U.S. courts and continues to enjoy widespread acceptance.[78]

As conceptualized by Walker, BWS develops as a result of exposure to a three-phase ***cycle of violence*** that typifies abusive relationships.[79] The first phase is called the "tension-building phase," which is characterized by arguments and ever-increasing tensions and may include minor acts of violence, such as slapping.[80] Eventually, however, an event triggers the second phase, which Walker calls the "acute battering incident." During this phase, the abuser explodes in a fit of rage and batters the victim.[81] Walker hypothesized that the acute battering incident causes the abuser to feel and express remorse, apologize profusely, and engage in loving, caring, and helpful behaviors to promote reconciliation.[82] In spite of the abuser's promises that it will "never happen again," the cycle inevitably repeats itself.[83]

Walker also offered an explanation as to why the cycle repeats itself, borrowing from behavioral psychology's notion of ***learned helplessness*** as espoused by noted psychologist Martin Seligman.[84] Seligman conducted experiments on dogs during which the animals were placed in harnesses and electrically shocked at random intervals.[85] At first, the dogs tried to escape, but given that the physical restraints in which they were placed made it impossible, the dogs eventually stopped.[86] In other words, they eventually accepted the fact that they were helpless to prevent the shocks. More importantly, though, after the dogs passively acquiesced to the shocks without resistance, Seligman changed the set up of the experiment by giving the dogs

---

[75]LENORE E. WALKER, THE BATTERED WOMAN (1979) [hereinafter WALKER I].

[76]Walker's theory was based on her clinical observations of abused women, not on empirical research. Walker's second book followed in 1984, offering empirical data in support of her theory. LENORE E. WALKER, THE BATTERED WOMAN SYNDROME (1984) [hereinafter WALKER II].

[77]David L. Faigman & Amy J. Wright, *The Battered Woman Syndrome in the Age of Science*, 39 ARIZ. L. REV. 67, 68 (1997).

[78]*Id.; see also* Regina Schuller & Patricia A. Hastings, *Battered Woman Syndrome and Other Effects of Domestic Violence Against Women, in* MODERN SCIENTIFIC EVIDENCE: THE LAW AND SCIENCE OF EXPERT TESTIMONY ch. 8 (David L. Faigman et al. eds., 1997); Stephen J. Morse, *The Misbegotten Marriage of Soft Psychology and Bad Law: Psychological Self-Defense as a Justification for Homicide*, 14 LAW & HUM. BEHAV. 595 (1990).

[79]WALKER II, *supra* note 76, at 95-96.

[80]*Id.*

[81]*Id.* at 95.

[82]*Id.* at 96.

[83]*Id.*

[84]*See* Martin E.P. Seligman et al., *Alleviation of Learned Helplessness in the Dog*, 73 J. ABNORMAL PSYCHOL. 256 (1968).

[85]*Id.* at 259-60.

[86]*Id.* at 260.

an opportunity to escape.[87] However, the dogs failed to avail themselves of the opportunity. Seligman concluded that the dogs viewed themselves as helpless and simply accepted their fate accordingly.[88] Some dogs were actually physically dragged out of the environment to show them how to escape the shocks.[89] Of these dogs, only some "unlearned" their learned helplessness; others never learned they could escape.[90]

Walker used the theory of learned helplessness to explain why battered women do not leave abusive relationships, building on the work of other researchers who had attempted to show how learned helplessness develops in humans.[91] According to Walker, a woman stays for a number of psycho-social reasons. She may have old-fashioned notions that "a woman's proper place is in the home."[92] She may be economically dependent on the abuser.[93] They may have children and the woman may not want to separate them from their father.[94] The stigma attached to a woman who leaves the family without her children undoubtedly also acts as a further deterrent to moving out.[95] Some women may even perceive the battering cycle as normal, especially if they grew up in a violent household.[96] And even when battered women want to leave, they are typically unwilling to reach out and confide in their friends, family, or the police, either out of shame and humiliation, fear of reprisal by their husband, or the feeling they will not be believed.[97] But one of the most important factors for Walker in a woman's decision to stay with her abuser is the loving and caring behavior the batterer exhibits during the reconciliation phase.[98] For Walker, the abuser's contrite behavior acts as a "positive reinforcement for [the victim] remaining in the relationship."[99]

The combination of the above factors leads an abuse victim to feel powerless to leave. Moreover, as she stays and tries to prevent the cycle of violence from repeating, she learns that it is not really within her power to control the abuser's feelings and temper. Her repeated failures to prevent tension from building up to an acute battering incident mirrors the learning of the dogs in Seligman's research. The repeated, failed attempts "to control the violence would, over time, produce learned helplessness and depression as the repeated batterings, like electrical shocks, [would] diminish the woman's motivation to respond."[100]

---

[87]*Id.* at 260-61.

[88]*Id.* at 261.

[89]*Id.* at 261-62.

[90]*Id.* at 260-61.

[91]MARTIN E.P. SELIGMAN, HELPLESSNESS: ON DEPRESSION, DEVELOPMENT, AND DEATH (1975); Lyn Y. Abramson et al., *Learned Helplessness in Humans: Critique and Reformulation*, 87 J. ABNORMAL PSYCHOL. 49, 50 (1978).

[92]WALKER II, *supra* note 76, at 31, 33-34.

[93]*Id.* at 127-44; *see also* Victoria Mikesell Mather, *The Skeleton in the Closet: the Battered Woman Syndrome, Self-Defense, and Expert Testimony*, 39 MERCER L. REV. 545, 552 (1988).

[94]Mather, *supra* note 93, at 552 (citing WALKER II, *supra* note 76, at 127-44).

[95]*Id.* at 552; WALKER II, *supra* note 76, at 167; *see also* State v. Kelly, 478 A.2d 364, 372 (N.J. 1984).

[96]*Kelly*, 478 A.2d at 371-72 (citing BATTERED WOMEN, A PSYCHOLOGICAL STUDY OF DOMESTIC VIOLENCE 60 (M. Roy ed. 1977)).

[97]Mather, *supra* note 93, at 547-60.

[98]WALKER II, *supra* note 76, at 95-96.

[99]*Id.* at 96.

[100]WALKER II, *supra* note 76, at 87 (internal quotation marks and citations omitted).

The cycle of violence tends to worsen as time passes. Not only may acute battering incidents become more frequent but also may become more severe.[101] Eventually, however, the woman endures "so much frustration, despair, and isolation that her perceptions of violence are altered. The woman may strike back violently against the batterer in an effort to free herself from the cycle of abuse that she may believe will ultimately lead to her death."[102] When the woman's strike-back leads to the filing of criminal charges against her for aggravated assault or homicide because the elements of the traditional defense of self-defense appear to be missing, BWS evidence will normally become the foundation of the woman's defense.[103]

2. Emergence of a Battered Women's Syndrome Defense

Whether there is actually a Battered Women's Syndrome Defense (BWSD) is actually a matter of some controversy. "The defense of battered women who kill their mates is slowly developing a distinct style or technique called the abused spouse defense," which is a hybrid of "the more familiar and established defenses of self-defense and diminished capacity."[104] Others insist it is not a defense in and of itself, but rather a psychological theory offered in support of the traditional defense of self-defense.[105]

The purpose of offering evidence of BWS is to fill a gap left by the law of self-defense and by the PTSD. BWSD is most frequently used in courts to explain the behavior of women who turn on their abusers and, in turn, to reduce their criminal responsibility.[106] BWSD is similar to PTSD in that the defendant's prior history or experience triggers a violent response. Battered women were frequently unable to assert PTSD, however, because they could not fulfill all of the diagnostic requirements of PTSD.[107]

The traditional self-defense doctrine recognizes the legitimacy of the use of force only when *necessary* to prevent an *imminent* attack from unlawful force.[108] As such, when a battered woman uses force to defend herself from such an unlawful, imminent attack, there is no problem in using the defense of self-defense. But in many cases, battered women act against their abusers when they are not in "imminent danger" and, therefore, are not acting within the technical requirements of the law of self-defense.[109] Alternatively, battered women may use deadly force

---

[101] *See* Lamis Ali Safa, *The Abuse Behind Closed Doors and the Screams That Are Never Heard*, 22 T. MARSHALL L. REV. 281, 294 n.121 (1997) (citing WALKER I, *supra* note 75, at 43).

[102] Tosha Yvette Foster, Note, *From Fear to Rage: Black Rage as a Natural Progression from and Functional Equivalent of Battered Woman Syndrome*, 38 WM. & MARY L. REV. 1851, 1859 (1997) (citing WALKER I, *supra* note 75, at 69-70).

[103] *See, e.g.*, State v. Stewart, 763 P.2d 572 (Kan. 1988).

[104] Elizabeth Vaughn & Maureen L. Moore, *The Battered Spouse Defense in Kentucky*, 10 N. KY. L. REV. 399, 399 (1983).

[105] Roberta K. Thyfault, Comment, *Self-Defense: Battered Woman Syndrome on Trial*, 20 CAL. W. L. REV. 485, 495 (1984).

[106] *See generally* John W. Roberts, *Between the Heat of Passion and Cold Blood: Battered Woman's Syndrome As an Excuse for Self-defense in Non-confrontational Homicide*, 27 LAW & PSYCHOL. REV. 135, 136-37 (2003).

[107] *See* Mary Ann Dutton, *Understanding Women's Responses to Domestic Violence: A Redefinition of Battered Woman Syndrome*, 21 HOFSTRA L. REV. 1191, 1199-1200 (1993); *see generally* Brett C. Trowbridge, *The Admissibility of Expert Testimony in Washington on Post Traumatic Stress Disorder and Related Trauma Syndromes: Avoiding the Battle of the Experts by Restoring the Use of Objective Psychological Testimony in the Courtroom*, 27 SEATTLE U. L. REV. 453, 517-18 (2003).

[108] Jane Campbell Moriarty, *"While Dangers Gather": The Bush Preemption Doctrine, Battered Women, Imminence, and Anticipatory Self-Defense*, 30 N.Y.U. REV. L. & SOC. CHANGE 1, 20 (2006) (citing WAYNE R. LaFAVE, CRIMINAL LAW § 10.4, at 539 (4th ed. 2003)).

[109] *E.g.*, Trowbridge, *supra* note 107, at 495; Joshua Dressler, *Battered Women and Sleeping Abusers: Some Reflections*, 3 OHIO ST. J. CRIM. L. 457 (2006) (arguing against allowing BWS evidence to be used to expand traditional notions of self-defense).

when they were confronted only with physical force, another requirement of the law of self-defense.[110] BWS evidence can help to explain why a woman might reasonably believe, in light of her history of abuse, her life was in danger, even though to the lay person, she was not facing what objectively looked like a threat of imminent, unlawful force.[111]

Interestingly, the use of BWS evidence has not been confined to cases where an abused woman strikes out against her abuser. Where the state of mind of the defendant at the time of the crime is at issue, BWS evidence can be offered to show that the defendant did not possess the required mental state—a diminished capacity argument in its purest form.[112] For example, the family court in *In re Glenn G.* relieved a mother of liability for child abuse after evidence of BWS was offered.[113] The mother, however, was still held liable for child neglect, a strict liability offense.[114] In *United States v. Marenghi,* the defendant offered BWS evidence to show she lacked the intent necessary for a conviction on possession and distribution of controlled substances.[115] The *Marenghi* court reasoned that the evidence was not being offered as a defense to the charges themselves, but rather as part of an attempt to show that the defendant's capacity was diminished in such a way that she did not entertain the requisite *mens rea.*[116]

3. Validity of the BWS Defense

As noted above, Walker's research suffered from serious methodological flaws. In fact, the research fails to demonstrate that abused women experience the cycle of violence as explained by Walker, or that abused women learn they are helpless to prevent it.[117] Consequently, some courts have excluded BWS evidence as unreliable.[118] However, in spite of these shortcomings, many courts continue to embrace BWS testimony in BWS cases.[119] Some believe this is driven by political motivation (i.e., not wanting to seem unsympathetic to the plight of the battered woman), while others see it as blind adherence to precedent established in the wake of Walker's initial research without critically examining the questionable reliability and validity of the BWS as elucidated by contemporary research.[120] Regardless of the reasons underlying its continued

---

[110]Moriarty, *supra* note 108, at 20; *see also* Faigman & Wright, *supra* note 77, at 81.

[111]State v. Kelly, 478 A.2d 364, 377 (N.J. 1984) (allowing BWS testimony because it aided juries "in determining whether, under the circumstances, a reasonable person would have believed there was imminent danger to her life."); Ibn-Tamas v. United States, 407 A.2d 626, 634 (D.C. 1979) (same).

[112]Faigman & Wright, *supra* note 77, at 95.

[113]*In re Glenn G.*, 587 N.Y.S.2d 464 (Fam. Ct. 1992), *aff'd*, 630 N.Y.S.2d 348 (N.Y. App. Div.), *leave to app. denied*, 662 N.E.2d 791 (N.Y. 1995).

[114]*Id.* at 470.

[115]United States v. Marenghi, 893 F. Supp. 85, 90 (D. Me. 1995).

[116]*Id.* at 89-91.

[117]OLA W. BARNETT & ALYEE D. LAVOLETTE, IT COULD HAPPEN TO ANYONE: WHY BATTERED WOMEN STAY 105-07 (1993); Regina A. Schuller & Neil Vidmar, *Battered Woman Syndrome Evidence in the Courtroom: A Review of the Literature*, 16 LAW & HUM. BEHAV. 273, 280 (1992); JULIE BLACKMAN, INTIMATE VIOLENCE: A STUDY OF INJUSTICE 192 (1989); RICHARD J. GELLES & CLAIRE PEDRICK CORNELL, INTIMATE VIOLENCE IN FAMILIES 77 (1985).

[118]*See, e.g.*, Hill v. State, 507 So. 2d 554, 555 (Ala. Crim. App. 1986); Buhrle v. State, 627 P.2d 1374, 1377 (Wyo. 1981) (criticizing not only Walker's methodology, but also finding that the defendant's case did not mirror that of the typical battered woman and, therefore, Walker inadequately explained and apparently ignored many of the troubling facts in the case "in arriving at an opinion").

[119]*See, e.g.*, United States v. Brown, 891 F. Supp. 1501 (D. Kan. 1995) (finding BWS evidence to satisfy the *Daubert* test).

[120]*See generally* Faigman & Wright, *supra* note 77.

acceptance, it is clear that many states continue to allow BWS evidence.[121] The presentation of psychological evidence concerning both the syndrome itself and the application of it to the facts of any particular case, therefore, remains an important function of forensic psychologists and psychiatrists.

D. Black Rage Defense

The **Black Rage Defense** is arguably the most controversial extension of the diminished capacity doctrine. Although discussed in the literature from time to time, the defense was brought into the spotlight during the trial of Colin Ferguson.[122] Ferguson had opened fire on a Long Island railroad car full of passengers, killing six people and injuring nineteen more.[123] After his arrest for the 1994 shooting, police discovered writings in which Ferguson wrote of his hatred for "whites, Asians and Uncle Tom Negroes," which led his lawyer, the late, celebrated civil rights attorney William Kunstler, to formulate a variant of the PTSD defense predicated upon "black rage."[124] Before trial, however, Ferguson fired Kunstler and was granted permission to represent himself *pro se*.[125] When acting as his own attorney (his competence to do so being highly questionable), Ferguson did not argue Black Rage. Instead, and in spite of a train-car full of eyewitnesses, he argued that he had fallen asleep on the train and someone else stole his gun from his bag and committed the shootings.[126] The Black Rage defense, therefore, was never tested in court. It did, however, provoke national debate over the legitimacy of such a defense.[127]

The first case to assert something akin to the Black Rage defense in the United States occurred in 1846 in the trial of William Freeman.[128] Freeman, the son of an ex-slave, was wrongly convicted and incarcerated for stealing a horse.[129] He escaped from jail, was recaptured, and was then sentenced to a prison term of hard labor.[130] During his prison sentence, Freeman suffered extensive psychological and physical abuse that included whipping and beatings of such severity that he was rendered nearly completely deaf.[131] After his release from prison, Freeman

---

[121]*See* People v. Aris, 264 Cal. Rptr. 167 (Ct. App. 1989); Knock v. Knock, 621 A.2d 267 (Conn. 1993); Ibn-Tamas v. United States, 407 A.2d 626 (D.C. 1979); Hawthorne v. State, 408 So. 2d 801 (Fla. Ct. App. 1982); Smith v. State, 277 S.E.2d 678 (Ga. 1981); People v. Minnis, 455 N.E.2d 209 (Ill. App. Ct. 1983); State v. Green, 652 P.2d 697 (Kan. 1982); State v. Anaya, 438 A.2d 892 (Me. 1981); State v. Hennum, 441 N.W.2d 793 (Minn. 1989); State v. Kelly, 478 A.2d 364 (N.J. 1984); State v. Gallegos, 719 P.2d 1268 (N.M. 1986); State v. Leidholm, 334 N.W.2d 811 (N.D. 1983); Commonwealth v. Stonehouse, 555 A.2d 772 (Pa. 1989); State v. Wilkins, 407 S.E.2d 670 (S.C. 1991); State v. Furlough, 797 S.W.2d 631 (Tenn. 1990); Fielder v. State, 756 S.W.2d 309 (Tex. 1988); State v. Allery, 682 P.2d 312 (Wash. 1984).

[122]*See* Deborah L. Goldklang, *Post-Traumatic Stress Disorder and Black Rage: Clinical Validity, Criminal Responsibility*, 5 Va. J. Soc. Pol'y & L. 213 (1997).

[123]John T. McQuiston, *Jury Finds Ferguson Guilty of Slayings on the L.I.R.R.: Families of the Dead and the Survivors Cheer the Verdict*, N.Y. Times, Feb. 18, 1995, at A1.

[124]Goldklang, *supra* note 122, at 214.

[125]*See* John T. McQuiston, *In the Bizarre L.I.R.R. Trial, Equally Bizarre Confrontations*, N.Y. Times, Feb. 5, 1995, at 13-LI.

[126]*Id.*

[127]*Compare* Kimberly M. Copp, Note, *Black Rage: The Illegitimacy of a Criminal Defense*, 29 J. Marshall L. Rev. 205 (1995) (arguing against recognition of the defense), *with* Foster, *supra* note 102, at 1865-75 (arguing for recognition of defense).

[128]Goldklang, *supra* note 122, at 217 (citing Freeman v. People, 4 Denio 9 (N.Y. Sup. Ct. 1847)); *see generally* Paul Harris, "Black Rage" Confronts the Law (1997).

[129]Goldklang, *supra* note 122, at 239.

[130]*Id.*

[131]Falk, *supra* note 62, at 749 n.99; Jennifer L. Larkin, *The Insanity Defense Founded on Ethnic Oppression: Defending the Accused in the International Criminal Tribunal for the Former Yugoslavia*, 21 N.Y.L. Sch. J. Int'l & Comp. L. 91, 102 (2001).

unsuccessfully sought employment from a Caucasian couple.[132] Freeman killed the couple and other members of their family.[133]

> Freeman's attorney, William Henry Seward, argued an early version of the insanity defense to the jury, contending that mistreatment by whites left his client with a life "'so filled with neglect, injustice, and severity, with anxiety, pain, disappointment, solicitude, and grief, [that it] would have its fitting conclusion in a madhouse.'" Although the jury rejected Freeman's insanity defense, the appellate court reversed and ordered a new trial, in part due to the trial court's limitation of expert testimony concerning Freeman's sanity. Before the retrial commenced, however, Freeman died in jail of tuberculosis.[134]

The theoretical underpinning of the Black Rage defense is clearly the diminished capacity doctrine. Psychiatrists William H. Grier and Price M. Cobbs first advanced the notion of Black Rage in 1969 when they asserted that African-Americans, as an insular racial minority in the United States, have endured years of discrimination starting in colonial days with slavery and continuing to the present.[135] This discrimination resulted in inadequate educational and employment opportunities for African-Americans as a group and thus disproportionate suffering from poverty and high unemployment.[136] As a result of this significant inequality, African-Americans suffer both "pent-up frustration" and "'cultural paranoia' in which every member of the white race is a possible enemy."[137] The frustration and the paranoia eventually builds to a point of "blind rage, hatred, and, ultimately, lethal violence" when someone suffering from Black Rage retaliates against one or more of the perceived oppressors, namely members of the white race.[138]

The notion of building frustration leading to violence embodied in the concept of Black Rage is referred to as *frustration–aggression*.[139] The Black Rage defense does not seek to excuse conduct along the lines of the insanity defense. Rather, it seeks to explain the evolution of anger so intense that it can impair someone's capacity to form *mens rea* in a normal way.[140]

The Black Rage defense has been criticized as an invalid extension of other forms of diminished capacity. PTSD, for example, seeks to explain the conduct of a single person that arose in connection with an identifiable, traumatic event that is generally outside the range of usual human experience, such as "military combat, violent personal assault, being kidnapped, being taken hostage, terrorist attack, torture, [and] incarceration as a prisoner of war or in a concentration camp."[141] Although there is no doubt that African-Americans have endured invidious discrimination, it is highly questionable whether discrimination in the post-Civil Rights era would qualify as a trauma of such magnitude that it could cause something akin to PTSD.[142]

---

[132]Larkin, *supra* note 131, at 102.

[133]*Id.*; Goldklang, *supra* note 122, at 239.

[134]Goldklang, *supra* note 122, at 239 (internal citations omitted).

[135]WILLIAM H. GRIER & PRICE M. COBBS, BLACK RAGE (1968)

[136]*Id.*; *see also* Copp, *supra* note 127, at 223.

[137]Copp, *supra* note 127, at 228 (citing ALEXANDER THOMAS & SAMUEL SILLEN, RACISM & PSYCHIATRY 54-55 (1972)).

[138]*Id.* at 229 (citing THOMAS J. SCHEFF & SUZANNE M. RETZINGER, EMOTIONS AND VIOLENCE: SHAME AND RAGE IN DESTRUCTIVE CONFLICTS 65-66 (1991)).

[139]*Id.* at 228 (citing SCHEFF & RETZINGER, *supra* note 138, at xix).

[140]*Id.* at 229.

[141]Copp, *supra* note 127, at 233-34.

[142]*Id.*

Moreover, to the extent that it might qualify, even harsh discrimination is quite different from a traumatic occurrence. For example, if one witnessed a family member as the victim of a racially motivated lynching, such an experience would be well within the diagnostic predicate for PTSD and its associated defense based on diminished capacity. However, blanket assertions of racism over one's lifetime do not demonstrate the same clear, requisite trauma. Other groups have faced intense forms of racism and oppression, including women, Jews, homosexuals, and certain ethnicities at various points in history.[143] Yet no significant movement has attempted to classify any such groups as candidates for a variant of PTSD sufficient to diminish the capacity to form *mens rea*.

Some might argue that Black Rage is more similar to the development of BWS, since a cycle of mistreatment over time is allegedly responsible for both, and the victim feels helpless to overcome or escape from that which inflicts the suffering. Copp pointed out, however, that when a battered woman strikes back, she does so at her abuser.[144] In doing so, she insulates herself from future abuse at his hands. In contrast, someone with Black Rage has no readily identifiable person at the root of his or her oppression nor will striking out against someone eliminate racism or discrimination.[145]

To date, the debate about the propriety of using Black Rage as a criminal defense has been mostly academic. It is feasible that forensic mental health professionals might be called upon to assess someone suffering from Black Rage. But in light of the fact that it is not recognized as a mental disorder in the DSM-IV-TR, it is questionable whether it would be accepted in court as a bona-fide defense. This conclusion is further bolstered in light of the *Daubert* requirements concerning the reliability of expert testimony and the methods they use.[146] Since Black Rage is more a sociological construct than a disorder validated by any reliable empirical support, the debate over Black Rage is likely to remain academic.

E. XYY Syndrome

Behavioral genetics is one of the driving forces in the medical model of deviance. One of the more interesting debates involving behavioral genetics concerns the ***XYY Syndrome Defense.***[147] Normal females have two X chromosomes, while normal males have one X chromosome and one Y chromosome.[148] In a genetic abnormality, some males are born with an extra Y chromosome.[149] In 1968, scientists searching for a genetic cause for criminal behavior discovered that three percent of the inmates at a psychiatric hospital for the criminally insane had the extra Y chromosome.[150] This was of particular interest to behavioral geneticists, lawyers, and

---

[143] *Id.*

[144] *Id.* at 234.

[145] *Id.*

[146] *See generally* Fradella et al., *supra* note 21 (reviewing judicial application of *Daubert* to expert testimony from behavioral scientists).

[147] *See generally* Sana Halwani & Daniel Brian Krupp, *The Genetic Defense: The Impact of Genetics on the Concept of Criminal Responsibility*, 12 HEALTH L.J. 35 (2004).

[148] *See, e.g.*, Herman A. Witkin et al., *Criminality in XYY and XXY Men*, 193 SCIENCE 547, 547-55 (1976); *see also, e.g.*, Matthew Jones, *Overcoming the Myth of Free Will in Criminal Law: the True Impact of the Genetic Revolution*, 52 DUKE L.J. 1031, 1042 (2003) (summarizing genetic research on XYY Syndrome and its purported link to aggressive behavior).

[149] *Id.*

[150] Witkin, et al., *supra* note 148, *passim*; Patricia A. Jacobs, Muriel Brunton, Marie M. Melville, R.P. Brittain & W.F. Mcclemont, *Aggressive Behaviour, Mental Sub-normality and the XYY Male*, 208 NATURE 1351, 1352 (1965); *see also* Jones,

mental health professionals since the extra Y chromosome "suggested the possibility of exaggerated maleness, aggressiveness, and violence."[151] As study of the genetic abnormality progressed, it was discovered that XYY males "were more than four times as likely to have criminal records than were XY males."[152] Studies also showed the percentage of XYY males in correctional institutions both in the United States and abroad were disproportionately high.[153]

In spite of such evidence, there has been no clear link between the presence of the extra Y chromosome and aggressive behavior.[154] The largest problem with the research supporting the link concerns the methodology of such studies. Researchers sampled exclusively from prison populations and therefore failed to have control groups for comparison.[155] Other reasons to doubt the XYY "supermale" theory include:

> First, evidence that some XYY individuals have impaired intellectual and physiological functioning, or developmental difficulties, such as speech, learning, or attention disorders, suggests that these intervening factors, and not "supermaleness" alone, may be associated with crime. Second, severe sample size and methodological limitations may lead to inconsistent results in many XYY studies. Third, a large and methodologically sophisticated study conducted on the relationship between the XYY disorder and crime reported that XYY males did exhibit a higher rate of criminality that was not explained by their subnormal intelligence; however, these males showed no disproportionate tendency toward violence. In light of the extremely low incidence of the XYY syndrome and other kinds of genetic abnormalities in the general population, as well as the inconsistent links between these conditions and crime, it is questionable whether there is a true association between the XYY chromosome abnormality and crime.[156]

Given the problems with the research on XYY syndrome, coupled with courts' "general reluctance to accept . . . 'genetic excuses,'" it is rarely asserted in court.[157] In fact, in only five reported U.S. cases have defendants attempted to introduce evidence of XYY. In four of them, the courts refused to admit any evidence of XYY syndrome.[158] And in the one case in which the

---

supra note 148, at 1039; Cecilee Price-Huish, Comment, *Born to Kill? "Aggression Genes" and their Potential Impact on Sentencing and the Criminal Justice System*, 50 SMU L. REV. 603, 625 (1997) (citing Deborah W. Denno, *Legal Implications of Genetics and Crime Research*, in GENETICS OF CRIMINAL AND ANTISOCIAL BEHAVIOUR 249 (Gregory R. Bock & Jamie A. Goode eds., 1996)).

[151] Sarnoff Mednick, *Biological Factors in Crime Causation: The Reactions of Social Scientists*, in INTRODUCTION TO THE CAUSES OF CRIME: NEW BIOLOGICAL APPROACHES 1, 2 (Sarnoff Mednick, Terrie E. Moffitt & Susan A. Stack eds., 1987).

[152] Marcia Johnson, *Genetic Technology and Its Impact on Culpability for Criminal Actions*, 46 CLEV. ST. L. REV. 443, 460-61 (1998).

[153] *Id.* at 461; *see also* Susan Horman, *The XYY Supermale and the Criminal Justice System: A Square Peg in a Round Hole*, 25 LOY. L.A. L. REV. 1343, 1346 (1992); *see also* Witkin et al., *supra*, note 148, at 547-55.

[154] Jones, *supra* note 148, at 1039.

[155] *See, e.g.*, Denno, *supra* note 150, at 249.

[156] Deborah W. Denno, *Gender Issues and the Criminal Law: Gender, Crime, and the Criminal Law Defenses*, 85 J. CRIM. L. & CRIMINOLOGY 80, 127-28 (1994) (internal citations omitted).

[157] Jones, *supra* note 148, at 1039-40 (citing *e.g.*, "People v. Yukl, 372 N.Y.S.2d 313, 319 (N.Y. Sup. Ct. 1975) (rejecting a motion for the appointment of a genetic expert because 'in New York an insanity defense based on chromosome abnormality should be possible only if one establishes with a high degree of medical certainty an etiological relationship between the defendant's mental capacity and the genetic syndrome'); State v. Roberts, 544 P.2d 754, 758-59 (Wash. Ct. App. 1976) (examining the use of genetic defenses in the criminal context and rejecting their future application))." Jones, *supra* note 148, at 1040 n.44.

[158] People v. Tanner, 91 Cal. Rptr. 656, 657-59 (Ct. App. 1970); Millard v. State, 261 A.2d 227, 231-32 (Md. Ct. Spec. App. 1970); People v. Yukl, 372 N.Y.S.2d 313, 315-20 (Sup. Ct. 1975); State v. Roberts, 544 P.2d 754, 758 (Wash. Ct. App. 1976).

court admitted the evidence, it was "rejected by the jury who found the defendant guilty of murder."[159]

Given the rejection of the XYY syndrome as a criminal defense, one might wonder why it is discussed in this book. The answer concerns not its present usefulness, but the potential for adaptation in the future. "If an individual's genetic composition is such that, when stimulated by certain environmental factors, he becomes more likely to exhibit aggressive behavior, it becomes difficult to define his behavior as being completely 'free.'" [160] In other words, the critical assumption of criminal law—the notion of a person with autonomy over himself/herself who acts through free-will, often guided by rational decision-making—might be flawed, if not totally inapplicable, when applied to a person who is genetically programmed to act (or react) violently.[161]

The XYY cases illustrate how a genetic abnormality might be used to establish a "mental disease or defect" within the meaning of the law. Making a diminished capacity claim using a diathesis–stress argument from behavioral genetics may very well be the future of much expert testimony in light of the continuing developments in genetic research such as the Human Genome Project.[162] Claims about the genetic component of alcoholism and drug addiction, for example, have already received credence in both forensic scholarship and practice.[163] As evidence of genetic components of behavior grows, so will the corresponding use of behavioral genetics in courts. For example, one's genetic predisposition has already begun to be used in a number of cases not as a defense, but as a basis for mitigation in sentencing, especially in death penalty cases.[164]

The future may hold genetic redefinitions of criminal responsibility in both determinations of guilt and in sentencing. Behavioral genetics might be used to increase the validity and reliability of predictions of dangerousness, screenings for employment, and academic admissions.[165] It may be used as part of rehabilitative therapy, perhaps even in the correctional setting.[166] Forensic mental health professionals must not only keep current of developments in this area for the sake of their clients, but also for their own sake when they are subjected to cross-examination on the witness stand.

---

[159]Carol A. Gaudet, Note, *Linking Genes with Behavior: The Social and Legal Implications of Using Genetic Evidence in Criminal Trials*, 24 FORDHAM URB. L.J. 597, 604 (1997).

[160]Jones, *supra* note 148, at 1041.

[161]*See, e.g.*, Steven I. Friedland, *The Criminal Law Implications of the Human Genome Project: Reimagining a Genetically Oriented Criminal Justice System*, 86 KY. L.J. 303, 324-41 (1998).

[162]*See id.*; Johnson, *supra* note 152, at 462-70; Richard Lowell Nygaard, *Free Will, Determinism, Penology and the Human Genome: Where's a New Leibniz When We Really Need Him?*, 3 U. CHI. L. SCH. ROUNDTABLE 417, 421-22 (1996).

[163]Kenneth Blum et al., *Allelic Association of Human Dopamine D_2 Receptor Gene in Alcoholism*, 263 J. AM. MED. ASS'N 2055, 2055 (1990) (finding dopamine D_2 receptor gene "is significantly associated with alcoholism").

[164]Halwani & Krupp, *supra* note 147, at 339.

[165]Friedland, *supra* note 161, *passim*.

[166]*Id.*

F. The PMS Defense

1. Background on PMS

Premenstrual syndrome (PMS) was first described in medical literature in 1931 by endocrinologist Robert Frank.[167] Frank described personality changes in women that corresponded to changes in hormone levels in the time period prior to menstruation.[168] The syndrome was defined in 1965 as "any combination of emotional or physical features which occurs cyclically in a female before menstruation, and which regresses and disappears during menstruation."[169]

In spite of the fact that PMS has been clinically studied for more than seven decades, there is no consensus with regard to its most common symptoms. Some physicians focus on the behavioral symptoms, the most common of which include irritability, anger, confusion, and mood swings. Others focus on the physical signs of PMS, such as headaches, bloating, and breast tenderness. Other symptoms of PMS include:

> [A]bdominal bloating, abdominal cramping, absentmindedness, accident-proneness, acne, alcohol intolerance, anger, anxiety, asthma, backpain, breast swelling and pain, cardiac arrhythmias (irregular heartbeats), confusion, crying, depression, dizziness, eating disorders, edema, eye difficulties, fainting, fatigue, food binges, hand tingling and numbness, headaches, hemorrhoids (flairups), herpes (oral, skin, genital), hives, indecisiveness, infections, insomnia, irritability, joint swelling and pain, lack of coordination, lactation difficulties, lethargy, muscle aches, nausea, noise sensitivity, palpitations, panic states, paranoia, pimple eruptions, rashes, salt cravings, seizures, (lack of) self-esteem, sex-drive changes, slurred speech, smell sensitivity, spaciness, stiff neck, sties, suicidal thoughts, sweet cravings, tension, tiredness, touch sensitivity, urinary difficulties, violence, weight gain, and withdrawal. PMS is commonly typified by behavioral symptoms, which include irritability, anger, confusion, and mood swings,[170] and physical symptoms such as headaches, bloating, and breast tenderness.[171]

Experts cannot agree on the cause of PMS.[172] Some believe an excess of estrogen in relation to progesterone causes the syndrome.[173] Other theories include: "the rise and fall of both estrogen and progesterone; the rapid decline in a metabolite of a neurotransmitter; yeast overgrowth in the intestines; [progesterone] allergies; . . . psychological stress,"[174] as well as

---

[167]Lee Solomon, *Premenstrual Syndrome: The Debate Surrounding Criminal Defense*, 54 MD. L. REV. 571, 573 (1995) (citing Robert T. Frank, *The Hormonal Causes of Premenstrual Tension*, 26 ARCHIVES NEUROLOGY & PSYCHIATRY 1053 (1931)).

[168]*Id.*; *see also* Joseph H. Morton, *Chronic Cystic Mastitis and Sterility*, 6 J. CLINICAL ENDOCRINOLOGY 802 (1946).

[169]Solomon, *supra* note 167, at 573 (citing Hamish Sutherland & Iain Stewart, *A Critical Analysis of the Premenstrual Syndrome*, 1 LANCET 1180, 1182 (1965)).

[170]*Id.*

[171]*Id.*

[172]*Id.* at 573 (citing Robert Mark Carney & Brian D. Williams, *Premenstrual Syndrome: A Criminal Defense*, 59 NOTRE DAME L. REV. 253, 267 (1983)); *see also* Robert L. Reid & S.C. Yen, *Premenstrual Syndrome*, 139 AM. J. OBSTETRICS & GYNECOLOGY 85, 86 (1981) ("Efforts to compare epidemiologic data on PMS are likely to be misleading because of variable interpretation of the clinical manifestations and the obvious difficulties encountered in quantitating [sic] the severity of symptoms.").

[173]Solomon, *supra* note 167, at 573.

[174]*Id.* at 574 (internal citations omitted).

fluid retention, vitamin deficiencies, hypoglycemia, nutritional deficiencies, endometrial toxins, and endogenous opiate excess or withdrawal.[175]

Studies on the prevalence of PMS are equally unsatisfying in the reliability of their conclusions. Some studies show that between 5 percent and 20 percent of women experience some form of PMS, while other assert incidence levels of up to 90 percent of all women.[176]

2. Recognition of PMDD in the DSM-IV

The 1994 publication of the DSM-IV brought official recognition to a new mental disorder called *Premenstrual Dysmorphic Disorder* (PMDD), formerly known as Late Luteal Phase Dysphoric Disorder (LLPDD).[177] It is a more severe form of PMS that affects an estimated 2 to 5 percent of menstruating women.[178] One commentator explained the difference between PMS and PMDD by analogizing the former to a cold, while the latter to full-blown pneumonia.[179] The diagnostic criteria for PMDD is presented in Table 7.1.

---

[175]Nicole R. Grose, Note, *Premenstrual Dysphoric Disorder as a Mitigating Factor in Sentencing: Following the Lead of English Criminal Courts*, 33 VAL. U.L. REV. 201, 203-08 & n.33 (1998) (citing, inter alia, William R. Keye, Jr. & Eric Trunnell, *Premenstrual Syndrome: A Medical Perspective*, 9 HAMLINE L. REV. 165, 170-73 & n.23 (1986)).

[176]*Id.* at 204 n.20 (citing Keye & Trunnell, *supra* note 175, at 167); *see also* Barbara L. Parry, *Psychobiology of Premenstrual Dysphoric Disorder*, 15 SEMINARS IN REPROD. ENDOCRINOLOGY 55 (1997) (reporting that 20% to 80% of menstruating women suffer from PMS); Meir Steiner, *Premenstrual Syndromes*, 48 ANN. REV. MED. 447, 448 (1997) (reporting that up to 75% of menstruating women suffer PMS).

[177]Solomon, *supra* note 167, at 577.

[178]Grose, *supra* note 175, at 209 n.54 (citing Meir Steiner, *supra* note 176; Parry, *supra* note 176).

[179]Jamie Talan, *Are Monthly Blues a Mental Disorder?*, NEWSDAY, July 10, 1993, at 10.

Table 7.1: Diagnostic Criteria for Premenstrual Dysmorphic Disorder

A. In most menstrual cycles during the past year, five (or more) of the following symptoms were present for most of the time during the last week of the luteal phase, began to remit within a few days after the onset of the follicular phase, and were absent in the week postmenses, with at least one of the symptoms being either (1), (2), (3), or (4):

  (1) markedly depressed mood, feelings of hopelessness, or self-depreciating thoughts
  (2) marked anxiety, tension, feelings of being "keyed up," or "on edge"
  (3) marked affective lability (e.g., feeling suddenly sad or tearful or increased sensitivity to rejection)
  (4) persistent and marked anger or irritability
  (5) increased interpersonal conflicts
  (6) decreased interest in usual activities (e.g., work, school, friends, hobbies)
  (7) subjective sense of difficulty in concentrating
  (8) lethargy, easy fatigability, or marked lack of energy
  (9) marked change in appetite, overeating, or specific food cravings
  (10) hypersomnia or insomnia
  (11) a subjective sense of being overwhelmed or out of control
  (12) other physical symptoms, such as breast tenderness or swelling, headaches, joint or muscle pain, a sensation of "bloating," weight gain

B. The disturbance markedly interferes with work or school or with usual social activities and relationships with others (e.g., avoidance of social activities, decreased productivity and efficiency at work or school).

C. The disturbance is not merely an exacerbation of the symptoms of another disorder, such as Major Depressive Disorder, Panic Disorder, Dysthymic Disorder, or a Personality Disorder (although it may be superimposed on any of these disorders).

D. Criteria A, B, and C must be confirmed by prospective daily ratings during at least two consecutive symptomatic cycles. (The diagnosis may be made provisionally prior to this confirmation.)

Source: DSM-IV-TR, *supra* note 141, at 771–774.

3. The PMS Defense

PMS has been used in Great Britain as a mitigating factor to reduce, not excuse, criminal culpability. Accordingly, it is recognized in England as a variant of diminished responsibility. For example, in *Regina v. Craddock,*[180] the defendant, Ms. Craddock, was on trial for killing a server in a bar in which she also was a server.[181] She had more than thirty prior convictions and several suicide attempts.[182] In preparing the case, Ms. Craddock's attorney reviewed her

---

[180]1 C.L. 49 (1980).

[181]Grose, *supra* note 175, at 212 (citing *Id.*).

[182]*Id.* (stating that "[r]ecords described the defendant as pleasant and a law-abiding citizen, but once every 29 days she would attempt arson in her cell, try to drown or strangle herself, or smash windows." *Id.* at 212 n.76 (citing Nadine Brozan, *Premenstrual Syndrome: A Complex Issue*, N.Y. TIMES, July 12, 1982, at C16.) "She had been in prison on and off for about 10 years and, in that time, showed 26 episodes of violence every 29 days." *Id.* at 212 n.76 (citing Brozan, *supra* note 182, at C16).

diaries.[183] The attorney noticed that her criminal activities and suicide attempts corresponded with her menstrual cycle.[184] Ms. Craddock was examined by Dr. Katherina Dalton, one of the world's leading experts on PMS.[185] Dr. Dalton testified that Ms. Craddock suffered from severe PMS and further testified that she had positively responded to progesterone therapy.[186] The court reduced the murder charge to manslaughter and released Ms. Craddock on probation, one of the terms of which was for her to continue on progesterone therapy.[187]

Interestingly, Ms. Craddock ran into the same trouble again some time later as Dr. Dalton had decreased her progesterone treatments.[188] Now living under the name Sandie Smith, she was tried for threatening a police officer and carrying a concealed weapon.[189] She was convicted, but her sentenced was mitigated to probation with continuing progesterone treatments as a result of her PMS.[190]

A similar mitigation of a murder charge down to manslaughter also occurred in *Regina v. English*, a case in which the defendant killed her boyfriend by pinning him to a pole and crushing him using her car.[191] And in *Regina v. Reynolds*,[192] an appeals court ordered the reduction of a murder conviction to manslaughter and sentenced the defendant to probation with psychiatric counseling due to its finding that PMS led the defendant to bludgeon her mother to death with a hammer.[193]

In the United States, defendants have attempted to use PMS as a type of diminished capacity defense to wholly excuse their conduct. In *People v. Santos*,[194] one of first cases to attempt such a use of the PMS defense, the legitimacy of the defense was not tested at trial because the parties negotiated a plea bargain after the defendant gave notice of her intent to use the defense.[195] Other cases attempting to use PMS as a defense were rejected in the years following *Santos*.[196]

---

[183]Grose, *supra* note 175, at 212.

[184]*Id.*

[185]*Id.* at 212-13.

[186]*Id.* at 213.

[187]*Id.*

[188]*Id.*

[189]*Id.* (citing Regina v. Smith, No. 1/A/82 (C.A. Crim. Div. 1982), (LEXIS, Enggen Library, Cases File at * 1)).

[190]*Id.*

[191]*Id.* at 213-14.

[192]*Id.* at 214 (citing Norwich Crown Ct. 1981 (unreported)).

[193]*Id.* at 214 (citing Crim. L.R. 679 (C.A. 1988), (LEXIS, Enggen Library, Cases File, at * 1)).

[194]People v. Santos, No. 1K046229 (Crim. Ct. Kings. County, N.Y. 1982) (unpublished opinion).

[195]Grose, *supra* note 175, at 215.

[196]*Id.* at 216 (citing Lovato v. Irvin, 31 B.R. 251 (Bankr. D. Colo. 1983) (refusing to accept PMS, due to its questionable scientific validity and reliability, as a means of discharging a debt in a bankruptcy proceeding when the debt was a judgment obtained in an intentional tort action); State v. Lashwood, 384 N.W.2d 319 (S.D. 1986) (refusing to set aside a plea entered into while the defendant was suffering from PMS)).

In 1991, however, the first successful PMS defense in the United States was used in a Virginia trial in *Commonwealth v. Richter*.[197] The defendant was a physician who was stopped for erratic driving.[198] She had her children in the car with her.[199] The state trooper who pulled her over noticed a strong smell of alcohol on her breath. The defendant:

> refused to take field sobriety tests, tried to kick the officer in the groin, used offensive language, and threatened the officer by saying, "You son of a [expletive]; you [expletive] can't do this to me; I'm a doctor. I hope you [expletive] get shot and come to my hospital so I can refuse to treat you . . . ."[200]

At her trial for driving under the influence, the defendant's attorney successfully used a dual line of defense. First, the defense argued the results of the breathalyzer test, which yielded a 0.13 percent blood alcohol concentration, were invalid.[201] The defense then attempted to explain her hostile conduct was due to PMS, not intoxication.[202] The defendant was found not guilty.[203] Given the unique facts of this case, it is important to note that the PMS defense was not specifically accepted or rejected in *Richter*. Rather, it was used to explain the defendant's hostile and combative behavior, thereby assisting in the creation of reasonable doubt with respect to whether she had been driving while intoxicated.

In the years since *Richter,* PMDD was officially recognized in the DSM-IV. Whether it will be accepted as a qualifying mental disease or defect for insanity or for diminished capacity purposes has not yet been determined. Critics argue that medical disagreement about its cause, symptoms, and treatment makes it very difficult for PMS to gain legal recognition as a complete defense.[204] Even if allowed, using the defense successfully might prove very difficult in light of the fact that the diagnosis is almost completely dependent on self-reported data from an obviously interested party (i.e., a criminal defendant) and other biased witnesses who are close to her.[205]

Other critics of the PMS defense argue that it is a dangerous precedent that can be used to encroach upon women's rights. Its use could lead to the societal labeling of women as "deficient" or being "mentally and physically unstable."[206] Such arguments, if accepted, could be used to justify keeping women out of certain executive and military roles and could even be used against women in divorce or custody proceedings.[207] In spite of these concerns, supporters of the

---

[197] *See* Solomon, *supra* note 167, at 586 (citing DeNeen L. Brown, *PMS Defense Successful in Va. Drunken Driving Case*, WASH. POST, June 7, 1991, at A1).

[198] Grose, *supra* note 175, at 216.

[199] *Id.*

[200] Solomon, *supra* note 167, at 586 n.146 (alterations and omission in original).

[201] *Id.* at 586 n.147.

[202] *Id.* at 588-87.

[203] Grose, *supra* note 175, at 217.

[204] *Id.* at 220 (citing Carney & Williams, *supra* note 172, at 267).

[205] Elizabeth Holtzman, *Premenstrual Symptoms: No Legal Defense*, 60 ST. JOHN'S L. REV. 712, 714-15 (1986); Kay A. Heggestad, *The Devil Made Me Do It: The Case Against Using Premenstrual Syndrome as a Defense in a Court of Law*, 9 HAMLINE L. REV. 155, 161 (1986).

[206] Grose, *supra* note 175, at 224 (citing, inter alia, Holtzman, *supra* note 205, at 715; Linda L. Castle, *PMS as a Defense in Criminal Cases*, 70 A.B.A. J. 211 (1984)).

[207] *Id.* at 225 (citing Candy Pahl-Smith, *Premenstrual Syndrome as a Criminal Defense: The Need for a Medico-Legal Understanding*, 15 N.C. CENT. L.J. 246, 256 (1984); Carney & Williams, *supra* note 172, at 268).

defense feel it should be used as a tool to mitigate punishment and to provide for therapeutic sentencing.[208] Whatever its future, it is clear that forensic behavioral scientists will play an important role in the evolution of the PMS defense.

G. Media Intoxication

A number of cases have asserted claims of insanity based on "*media intoxication*" from television, movies, pornography, and music. These cases have all been unsuccessful. For example, in the case of *Florida v. Zamora,* a fifteen-year-old boy was accused of killing an eighty-two-year-old woman after breaking into her house and stealing a gun and money.[209] Zamora's attorney pled insanity on his behalf.[210] In support of the insanity claim, the defense offered evidence that Zamora acted under a state of pseudo-intoxication resulting from watching hours of violent television programs which, in turn, drove the boy to kill the woman.[211] The trial court refused to allow testimony on television intoxication, finding it to be irrelevant to the question of Zamora's insanity.[212]

Media intoxication, however, could meet with more success in the diminished capacity realm, although to date, such attempts have been generally unsuccessful. In a provocative article, Patricia Falk reviewed the extensive body of literature addressing the nature and effects of media intoxication and addiction.[213] She noted: "[t]he primary, and almost unanimous, finding common to this extensive body of research is that a positive correlation exists between viewing violent television programs and subsequent aggressive behavior."[214] Similar research findings have linked violence against women to the viewing of pornography.[215] Serial killer Bobby Joe Long asserted in the sentencing phase of his murder trial that his addiction to violent pornography should have constituted a mitigating factor against the death penalty.[216] This argument was rejected by the jury, and he was sentenced him to death.[217]

In *Schiro v. Clark,*[218] the defendant "argued that he was a sexual sadist and that his extensive viewing of rape pornography and snuff films rendered him unable to distinguish right from wrong."[219] The defendant produced the testimony of two leading experts on the link between

---

[208]*Id.* at 220-30; Solomon, *supra* note 167, at 598-99; Ruth Macklin, *The Premenstrual Syndrome (PMS) Label: Benefit or Burden,* in PREMENSTRUAL SYNDROME 17, 23 (Benson E. Ginsberg & Bonnie Frank Carter eds., 1987).

[209]Zamora v. State (Dade County Cir. Ct. 1977), *aff'd,* 361 So. 2d 776 (Fla. Dist. Ct. App. 1978), *cert. denied,* 372 So. 2d 472 (Fla. 1979).

[210]*Zamora,* 361 So. 2d at 778.

[211]*Id.* at 778-79.

[212]*Id.* at 780-81. In *State v. Quillen,* the Court specifically stated that evidence of television intoxication did not support a plea of insanity. *See also* Falk, *supra* note 62, at 745 (citing State v. Quillen, No. S-87-08-0118, 1989 Del. Super. LEXIS 129 (Del. Super. Ct. Mar. 28, 1989)); *see also* State v. Molina, No. 84-2314B (11th Judicial Dist., Fla. 1984) (discussed in Juliet Lughbough Dee, *Media Accountability for Real-Life Violence: A Case of Negligence or Free Speech?,* 37 J. COMM. 106 (1987)).

[213]Falk, *supra* note 62, at 758-81.

[214]*Id.* at 767.

[215]*See, e.g.,* CATHARINE A. MACKINNON, TOWARDS A FEMINIST THEORY OF THE STATE 195-214 (1989); *see* Ron Hayes, *Attorney Knows How to Represent Himself,* CHI. TRIB., Sept. 9, 1991, at C1.

[216]Hayes, *supra* note 215, at C1.

[217]Long v. State, 517 So. 2d 664 (Fla. 1987), *cert. denied,* 486 U.S. 1017 (1988); Long v. State, 610 So. 2d 1276 (Fla. 1992).

[218]963 F.2d 962 (7th Cir. 1992), *aff'd,* 510 U.S. 222 (1994).

[219]*Id.* at 971.

violence and pornography and sought to have it used as evidence of insanity and as a type of intoxication, which the applicable state law recognized as a mitigating factor.[220] The defendant was convicted and his subsequent appeals were all denied on the rationale that allowing a criminal defense based on exposure to materials protected by the First Amendment would be incongruous.[221] Similar reasoning resulted in the unsuccessful assertion of an analogous argument using music lyrics in the case of Ronald Ray Howard.[222] The nineteen-year-old defendant killed a police officer and sought to avoid the death penalty by arguing that his addiction to "gangsta rap" was a mitigating factor.[223] The argument was rejected by the jury who sentenced Howard to death.[224]

The link between violence depicted in different media forms and actual violence will continue to be an important part of expert testimony in both civil and criminal cases. Whether media intoxication is eventually is accepted as a form of either diminished capacity or diminished responsibility remains to be seen. Either way, defense attorneys will undoubtedly call upon forensic mental health clinicians to assess defendants who assert such a defense in guilt and sentencing phases of criminal trials.

H. Summary of Diminished Capacity Evidence

Criminal defendants have attempted to expand the notion of diminished capacity into a multitude of defenses with varying degrees of success. Diminished capacity arguments based on bona fide mental illnesses that interfere with sensation, perception, and cognition tend to fare well. In contrast, attempts to cast defendants as less culpable because they were victims of abuse or neglect generally do not succeed.[225] This ever-increasing trend towards disease-based explanations for criminal behavior has clearly taken a toll on public attitudes towards excuse defenses based on mental illness.[226] While defendants and their lawyers who seek to avoid punishment are partially to blame, behavioral scientists also share in the responsibility for this trend.

"'The abuse excuse,' 'battered woman syndrome,' 'child sexual abuse accommodation syndrome,' 'false memory syndrome,' 'television intoxication,' 'urban survival syndrome,' 'XYY chromosome abnormality'[227]—these are just a few of the colorful appellations used to describe claims that mental health professionals have bolstered with their testimony over the years. . . . From reading the popular press, one could easily come to the conclusion that such testimony is spurious 'psychobabble' that will eventually swallow up our justice system."[228]

---

[220]*Id.* at 971-72.

[221]*Id.*

[222]Falk, *supra* note 62, at 747-48 (citing Michele Munn, Note, *The Effects of Free Speech: Mass Communication Theory and the Criminal Punishment of Speech*, 21 AM. J. CRIM. L. 433, 476-78 (1994); Janet Elliott, *Slain Trooper's Family Seeks Damages From Rapper: Round 2 in Gangsta Rap Case*, LEGAL TIMES, July 26, 1993, at 10; Chuck Phillips, *Rap Defense Doesn't Stop Death Penalty*, L.A. TIMES, July 15, 1993, at F1; Pamela Ward & Scott W. Wright, *Howard Gets Death Sentence*, AUSTIN AM.-STATESMAN, July 15, 1993, at B1).

[223]Ward & Wright, *supra* note 222, at B1.

[224]*Id*

[225]*See, e.g.*, Richard J. Bonnie, *Excusing and Punishing in Criminal Adjudication: A Reality Check*, 5 CORNELL J.L. & PUB. POL'Y 1 (1995); Stephanie B. Goldberg, *Fault Lines*, 80 A.B.A. J., 40 (1994).

[226]DERSHOWITZ, *supra* note 35, at 3 (1994); *see also* JAMES Q. WILSON, MORAL JUDGMENT (1997).

[227]Christopher Slobogin, *Psychiatric Evidence in Criminal Trials: To Junk or Not to Junk?*, 40 WM. & MARY L. REV. 1, 1-2 (1998).

An overwhelming number of psychologists and psychiatrists do not take part in sensational trials that attempt to extend diminished capacity into the realm of questionable scientific practice.[229] Media attention on the few cases that are the exception to this rule, however, has had real and palpable effects on the jurisprudence of defenses of excuse.[230] The perception that these defenses undermine legal notions of autonomy, free-will, and personal responsibility has led legislatures, judges, and juries to "define the grounds of excuse too narrowly."[231] The abolition of the insanity defense in favor of the *mens rea* approach is one of the best examples of the efforts to narrow legitimate criminal excuse. Other examples include the move towards "guilty except insane" formulations of the insanity defense, and the elimination of diminished capacity evidence altogether—even when offered to challenge the defendant's alleged formation of *mens rea*.[232] Sadly, the Supreme Court's decision in *Clark v. Arizona* upheld this last approach over a schizophrenic defendant's due process challenge.[233] While the next section of this chapter is devoted to critiquing the decision in that case, the true tragedy of *Clark* lies in the majority's distrust of forensic psychiatric and psychological evidence, and the effects that mistrust caused not only to the defendant in that case, but also to our notions of criminal responsibility. The Court's distrust of forensic psychiatric and psychological evidence is no doubt due, in part, to the behavioral sciences' complicity in supporting empirically and clinically questionable criminal defenses that seek to displace responsibility from a criminal actor onto a victim or society at large.[234]

IV. THE FUTURE OF DIMINISHED CAPACITY IN LIGHT OF *CLARK V. ARIZONA*

A. Factual Background

In the summer of 2000, a police officer was killed in the line of duty by seventeen-year-old Eric Clark.[235] Clark had been driving his pickup truck around a residential neighborhood with the

---

[228]*Id.* at 2.

[229]*Id.* at 7.

[230]*Id.* at 2 n.9 (citing, inter alia, Niko Price, *The "Abuse Excuse": Threat to Justice?; More and More Lawyers Using Trauma as Defense to Crimes*, Legal Intelligencer, May 31, 1994, at 3 (referring to "two decades of pop psychology and afternoon talk shows that have convinced society . . . that there is an explanation — and possibly a justification — for almost any act").

[231]Donald A. Dripps, *Fundamental Retribution Error: Criminal Justice and the Social Psychology of Blame*, 56 Vand. L. Rev. 1383, 1389 (2003).

[232]*See, e.g.*, State v. Mott, 931 P.2d 1046 (Ariz. 1997), *cert. denied*, 520 U.S. 1234 (1997).

[233]Clark v. Arizona, 126 S. Ct. 2709 (2006).

[234]*See generally* Henry F. Fradella, *A Content Analysis of Federal Judicial Views of the Social Science "Researcher's Black Arts,"* 35 Rutgers L.J. 103, 169 (2003).

> Abuse excuses run counter to retributive and deterrence based sentencing ideals. Testimony of sociologists and psychologists in particular that seek to justify criminal behavior or mitigate its seriousness on the basis of diminished capacity, other than that stemming from a bona-fide DSM-IV Axis I mental disorder, serves to alienate judges (and perhaps juries) from these disciplines. Moreover, since these excuses are premised on a deterministic view of human nature (i.e., something in someone's past caused someone to break the law), it is at odds with the law's assumption that behavior is a product of free will.

Id.

radio "blaring" loud music.[236] A police officer pulled-over Clark's truck in response to complaints.[237] Less than a minute after having approached Clark and having told him to "stay where he was," Clark shot the officer and ran away.[238] Before he died, the officer contacted the police dispatcher for help. Clark was apprehended later that day "with gunpowder residue on his hands."[239] The gun used to kill the officer was subsequently found close to where Clark had been arrested.[240]

At Clark's trial, friends, family, classmates, and school officials all testified about his "increasingly bizarre behavior over the year before the shooting."[241]

> Witnesses testified, for example, that paranoid delusions led Clark to rig a fishing line with beads and wind chimes at home to alert him to intrusion by invaders, and to keep a bird in his automobile to warn of airborne poison. There was lay and expert testimony that Clark thought Flagstaff was populated with "aliens" (some impersonating government agents), the "aliens" were trying to kill him, and bullets were the only way to stop them. A psychiatrist testified that Clark was suffering from paranoid schizophrenia with delusions about "aliens" when he killed Officer Moritz, and he concluded that Clark was incapable of luring the officer or understanding right from wrong and that he was thus insane at the time of the killing. In rebuttal, a psychiatrist for the State gave his opinion that Clark's paranoid schizophrenia did not keep him from appreciating the wrongfulness of his conduct, as shown by his actions before and after the shooting (such as circling the residential block with music blaring as if to lure the police to intervene, evading the police after the shooting, and hiding the gun).[242]

Although the trial court determined that Clark "was indisputably afflicted with paranoid schizophrenia at the time of the shooting," it found him guilty nonetheless, concluding that his mental illness "did not . . . distort his perception of reality so severely that he did not know his actions were wrong."[243] Clark, however, was sentenced to twenty-five years to life in prison.[244] His attorney then moved to vacate the judgment and sentence on the grounds that both the exclusion of psychiatric evidence to disprove *mens rea* and Arizona's narrow formulation of the insanity defense both violated Clark's due process rights.[245] The trial court denied this motion; the Arizona Court of Appeals affirmed in an unpublished disposition; and the Arizona Supreme Court denied discretionary review.[246] The U.S. Supreme Court granted Clark's petition for *certiorari* on two separate due process issues, each of which will now be separately explored.

---

[235]Clark v. Arizona, 126 S. Ct. 2709, 2716 (2006).

[236]*Id.*

[237]*Id.*

[238]*Id.*

[239]*Id.*

[240]*Id.* at 2716.

[241]*Id.* at 2717.

[242]*Id.* at 2717-18.

[243]*Id.* at 2718.

[244]*Id.*

[245]*Id.*

B. Issue 1: The Narrowing of *M'Naghten*

Clark asserted that Arizona's GEI formulation of the insanity defense violated due process because it lacked the first prong of the *M'Naghten* test, which evaluated the cognitive capacity to know the nature and quality of one's acts.[247] While Arizona had used the true *M'Naghten* test in the past, the state omitted inclusion of the cognitive incapacity prong when it enacted its Guilty Except Insane formulation of the insanity defense.[248] It appears, however, that the statutory change was not intended to alter substantively the test for insanity, but rather that the state legislature determined that "a streamlined standard with only the moral capacity part would be easier for the jury to apply."[249]

Clark argued that the new statutory language deprived him of his due process rights because the *M'Naghten* test for insanity represented a "principle of justice so rooted in the traditions and conscience of our people as to be ranked as fundamental."[250] Indeed, such an argument had worked before the Nevada Supreme Court in *Finger v. State,*[251] although it had been rejected in Utah, Idaho, and Montana.[252] The U.S. Supreme Court sided with the weight of state authority on the issue. The Court dismissed Clark's fundamental right argument outright, stating that "[h]istory shows no deference to *M'Naghten* that could elevate its formula to the level of fundamental principle, so as to limit the traditional recognition of a State's capacity to define crimes and defenses."[253] In support of this conclusion, the Court pointed to the many variations in the insanity defense (which are discussed in Chapter Six). States are therefore free to define insanity as they see fit without running afoul of the Due Process Clause of the Fourteenth Amendment.

While seemingly unnecessary to do so, the Court took issue with Clark's underlying logic, noting that, in practice, the cognitive incapacity prong of the *M'Naghten* test and its moral incapacity prong are intertwined:

> [C]ognitive incapacity is itself enough to demonstrate moral incapacity. Cognitive incapacity, in other words, is a sufficient condition for establishing a defense of insanity, albeit not a necessary one. As a defendant can therefore make out moral incapacity by demonstrating cognitive incapacity, evidence bearing on whether the defendant knew the nature and quality of his actions is both relevant and admissible. In practical terms, if a defendant did not know what he was doing when he acted, he could not have known that he was performing the wrongful act charged as a crime.[254]

---

[246]*Id.*

[247]*Id.*

[248]*Id.* at 2719 (citing 1993 Ariz. Sess. Laws ch. 256, §§ 2-3).

[249]*Clark*, 126 S. Ct. at 2723 (citing Ariz. House of Rep. Judiciary Comm. notes 3 (Mar. 18, 1993); 1 R. GERBER, CRIMINAL LAW OF ARIZONA 502-11 (2d ed. 1993 & Supp. 2000)).

[250]*Id.* at 2737 (citing Patterson v. New York, 432 U.S. 197 (1977)).

[251]27 P.3d 66, 80 (Nev. 2001).

[252]*Herrera*, 895 P.2d at 365-66; State v. Searcy, 798 P.2d 914, 919 (Idaho 1990); State v. Korell, 690 P.2d 992, 1002 (Mont. 1984).

[253]*Clark*, 126 S. Ct. at 2719.

Accordingly, the Court felt that the first prong of the *M'Naghten* test somewhat duplicated the second prong, and, therefore, the statutory omission of the cognitive incapacity test had little, if any, effect on the overall fairness of an insanity case.[255]

C. Issue 2: Due Process Challenge to Arizona's *Mott* Rule

The second of Clark's due process challenges concerned the rule set forth by the Arizona Supreme Court in *State v. Mott*.[256] *Mott* involved the conviction of a woman for "child abuse under circumstances likely to produce death or serious bodily injury" and for the murder of her daughter.[257] The mother knew that her daughter was being physically abused by the mother's boyfriend; yet, she not only failed remove her daughter from the abusive environment, but also, she failed to take her daughter for medical necessary car after her boyfriend severely injured her daughter.[258] At her trial, the mother sought to introduce evidence through expert testimony that she lacked the capacity to have acted to save her daughter because her own mental status was significantly impaired due to the Battered Woman Syndrome.[259] The defense tried to use such evidence to rebut the prosecution's argument that the child abuse via omission had been either purposeful or knowing within the meaning of these terms as *mens rea* for criminal liability.[260] The trial court refused to allow such evidence, however, ruling that "the testimony regarding the battered-woman syndrome was an attempt to establish a diminished capacity defense" that was inadmissible under Arizona law.[261] The defendant was convicted and appealed.[262] The Arizona Court of Appeals reversed, holding that "trial court's preclusion of defendant's proffered testimony regarding battered-woman syndrome violated due process."[263] The Arizona Supreme Court vacated the decision of the intermediate appellate court and reinstated the defendant's conviction and sentence.[264] The court reasoned that the proffered expert testimony was, in fact, diminished capacity evidence that was inadmissible because "Arizona does not allow evidence of a defendant's mental disorder short of insanity either as an affirmative defense or to negate the *mens rea* element of a crime."[265] But the *Mott* court's broad holding was not required by state law. The court could have strictly interpreted the state legislature's failure to adopt a diminish capacity defense as a limitation on using diminished capacity as an affirmative defense[266] without having barred the admissibility of psychological testimony shy of insanity to negate *mens rea*.[267] The dissent in *Mott* explained this critical distinction as follows:

---

[254]*Id.* at 2722.

[255]*Id.* at 2723-24.

[256]931 P.2d 1046, 1054-55 (Ariz. 1997), *cert. denied*, 520 U.S. 1234 (1997).

[257]*Mott* at 1049.

[258]*Id.* at 1048-49.

[259]*Id.* at 1049.

[260]*Id.*

[261]*Id.*

[262]*Id.*

[263]*Id.* (citing State v. Mott, 901 P.2d 1221, 1225 (Ariz. Ct. App.1995)).

[264]*Id.* at 1057.

[265]*Id.* at 1051 (citing A.R.S. § 13-502(A)).

[266]*See, e.g., id.* at 1050 ("The Arizona legislature . . . declined to adopt the defense of diminished capacity when presented with the opportunity to do so."); *see also* State v. Schantz, 403 P.2d 521, 529 (Ariz. 1965), *cert. denied*, 382 U.S. 1015 (1966) (refusing to judicially-recognize the diminished capacity defense on the grounds that the legislature is responsible for

The evidence of defendant's history of being battered and of her limited intellectual ability was . . . offered . . . as evidence to negate the *mens rea* element of the crime. The majority further acknowledges that "[s]uch evidence is distinguishable from an affirmative defense that excuses, mitigates, or lessens a defendant's moral culpability due to his psychological impairment." Yet, despite recognizing this distinction, the majority takes the inconsistent position that use of psychiatric evidence to negate *mens rea* is the same as an attempt to prove diminished capacity.[268]

The result in *Mott*, which is interpreted as barring the admissibility all evidence of mental illness to disprove *mens rea* if not offered as part and parcel of an insanity defense.[269] The *Mott* rule thus prevented the defendant in *Mott* from arguing that she did not entertain the requisite *mens rea* for child abuse and murder in the same way that the *Mott* rule's reach prevented Eric Clark from introducing evidence tending to show that he did not entertain the *mens rea* for murder.[270] In spite of *Mott*'s significant impingement on criminal defendant's ability to demonstrate that his mental illness interfered with the ability to form a culpable *mens rea*, *Clark* upheld *Mott*'s limitation on diminished capacity evidence over Clark's due process challenge.[271]

The Supreme Court felt that resolution of Clark's challenge to the constitutionality of *Mott* required an exploration of three categories of evidence that affect *mens rea* within the *Mott* framework. The first of these categories was termed "observational evidence" by the Court.[272] This category of evidence concerns the observations of experts and laypersons alike regarding someone's behavior—what someone said, how they behaved, their "tendency to think in a certain way."[273] Such evidence may be offered to support a clinical diagnosis, or as evidence of an actor's state of mind at the time of the commission of an offense.[274] The testimony of Clark's family and schoolmates about his bizarre behavior in the year leading up to the shooting falls under this category of evidence.[275] The second type of relevant proof of *mens rea* is "mental disease evidence"—opinion testimony, usually by a qualified expert based on clinical assessment, that an actor fits the criteria for a particular mental illness diagnosis.[276] The testimony of mental health professionals stating that Clark suffered from paranoid schizophrenia is an example of such evidence.[277]

The third subtype of evidence the Supreme Court felt was relevant to prove *mens rea* is "capacity evidence"—that which demonstrates a "defendant's capacity for cognition and moral judgment (and ultimately also his capacity to form *mens rea*)."[278] The Court explained that such

---

promulgating the criminal law and that it "ha[d] not recognized a disease or defect of mind in which volition does not exist ... as a defense to a prosecution for [a crime.]").

[267] *See Mott*, 931 P.2d at 1058 (Zlacket, C.J., concurring) ("I am unprepared to agree that expert testimony must be strictly limited to *M'Naghten* insanity under all circumstances in any and every case, or that psychological evidence tending to negate an essential element of the crime charged can never be admitted. Such an expansive holding seems both unwise and unnecessary.").

[268] *Id.* at 1061 (Feldman, J., dissenting) (internal citations omitted).

[269] *Id.* at 1054.

[270] *Clark*, 126 S. Ct. at 2737.

[271] *Id.*

[272] *Id.* at 2724.

[273] *Id.*

[274] *Id.*

[275] *See Clark*, 126 S. Ct. at 2717-18.

[276] *Id.* at 2725.

[277] *See id.* at 2717-18.

evidence, like mental disease evidence, is usually offered in the form of expert opinion testimony.[279] In *Clark,* the mental health experts proffered by the defense opined that Clark lacked the capacity to know his actions were wrong, while the opinions of the prosecution's experts were that Clark had such capacity in spite of his psychotic state.[280]

The Court's tripartite evidentiary structure in *Clark* does not appear anywhere in *Mott.* Moreover, the "razor-thin distinction[s]" drawn by the Court did not get to the crux of Clark's due process challenge.[281] *Mott*'s holding was not restricted to mental-disease evidence. The Arizona Supreme Court did not refer to any distinction between observation and mental-disease evidence, or lay and expert testimony. Its holding was stated in broad terms: "Arizona does not allow evidence of a defendant's mental disorder short of insanity either as an affirmative defense or to negate the *mens rea* element of a crime."[282]

It was precisely the exclusion of mental illness evidence from being used to determine whether Clark had acted with the requisite underlying *mens rea* of purpose or knowledge that formed the basis of his second due process challenge. His defense at trial centered on his diagnosis of paranoid schizophrenia.[283] Separate and apart from whether this debilitating psychotic disorder rendered him legally insane, he asserted that his mental illness made him delusional.[284] Of particular relevance was his belief that government workers, including municipal personnel in Flagstaff, like Officer Moritz, were aliens.[285] If he delusionally thought Officer Mortiz was an alien, and not a police officer, then he did not "knowingly" shoot another human being, much less knowingly shoot an officer of the law.[286] He would, therefore, not be guilty under the Arizona first-degree murder statute, an important point that the majority failed to comprehend.

The Court seems to have unnecessarily created its own narrow evidentiary scheme based upon its reading of the way *Mott* distinguished another Arizona case, *State v. Christensen:*[287]

> *Christensen* is distinguishable from the present case because the evidence offered by the defendant in that case was not evidence of his diminished mental capacity. Rather, the defendant merely offered evidence about his behavioral tendencies. He attempted to show that he possessed a character trait of acting reflexively in response to stress. The proffered testimony was not that he

---

[278]*Id.* at 2725.

[279]*Id.*

[280]*Clark*, 126 S. Ct. at 2725. It should be noted that although Arizona permits testimony on capacity evidence as defined by the Supreme Court, many jurisdictions do not allow testimony on the "ultimate issue" to be decided in a case. *See* Ariz. R. Evid. 704 (allowing otherwise admissible evidence on testimony "embrac[ing] an ultimate issue to be decided by the trier of fact."). *But see, e.g.*, Fed. R. Evid. 704(b).

> No expert witness testifying with respect to the mental state or condition of a defendant in a criminal case may state an opinion or inference as to whether the defendant did or did not have the mental state or condition constituting an element of the crime charged or a defense thereto. Such ultimate issues are matters for the trier of fact alone.

Id.

[281]*Clark*, 126 S. Ct. at 2741 (Kennedy, J., dissenting).

[282]*Id.* (quoting *Mott*, 931 P.2d, at 1051 ("The legislature's decision ___ evidences its rejection of the use of psychological testimony to challenge the *mens rea* element of a crime.") (omission in original)).

[283]*Id.* at 2716.

[284]*Id.* at 2717. (Part of his delusional belief system was that his town was inhabited by aliens. *Id.*)

[285]*Id.* at 2717, 2724-25.

[286]*Id.* at 2743.

was *incapable*, by reason of a mental defect, of premeditating or deliberating but that, because he had a tendency to act impulsively, he did not premeditate the homicide. Because he was not offering evidence of his diminished capacity, but only of a character trait relating to his lack of premeditation, the defendant was not precluded from presenting the expert testimony.[288]

The distinction made by the *Mott* court was plainly wrong. Evidence of a "character trait" that causes someone's "behavioral tendencies" to act impulsively is diminished capacity evidence. Such a "character trait" is part and parcel of an impulse control disorder, defined as "the failure to resist an impulse, drive or temptation to perform an act that is harmful to the person or to others."[289]

In fact, testimony concerning "character traits" and "behavioral tendencies" may well fall under the *Clark* majority's definition of "observational evidence," because labeling such traits and behaviors with the appropriate clinical diagnosis would be "mental disease evidence" under *Clark*'s evidentiary rubric. The admissibility of the evidence, however, should not turn on such a definitional distinction, as both work together to help jurors understand human behavior. Regardless of the definitional label, nothing changes the fact that both the observed behaviors and the diagnosis which flows from them are, in fact, evidence of diminished capacity as attested to by the facts of *Christensen*.[290]

In *Christensen*, the defendant's impulse control disorder led him to commit a murder under stress.[291] The Arizona Supreme Court reversed the defendant's conviction because he was not permitted to offer the testimony of a psychologist that the defendant's killing under stressful circumstances was more "reflexive" than "reflective."[292] The outcome in *Christensen* is surprising, since, as explained in Chapter Six, impulse control disorders, both historically and today, do not qualify as the basis for excusing criminal conduct. In fact, several years after the *Christensen* decision, Arizona changed its insanity statutes to specifically exclude impulse control disorders as qualifying mental diseases or defects for insanity defense purposes[293]—a change not mentioned in *Mott* or in *Clark*. Thus, the fact that *Mott* relied upon *Christensen* is somewhat befuddling.

Moreover, like the defendant in *Christensen*, the defendant in *Mott* offered diminished capacity evidence not as an affirmative defense, but as evidence to negate *mens rea*. Yet, such evidence was permitted in *Christensen* and not in *Mott*, apparently because the Arizona Supreme Court simply decided not to label the evidence proffered by the defense in *Christensen* diminished capacity evidence, while it decided that the evidence proffered in *Mott* was diminished capacity evidence. Specifically, the defendant in *Mott* sought to introduce BWS evidence, not to excuse her conduct, but to show that she did not neglect her children knowingly, intentionally, recklessly, or with criminal negligence.[294]

The inconsistency in *Christensen* and *Mott* appears to be due, in part, to the confusing nature of diminished capacity evidence. Some jurisdictions permit diminished capacity to be an

---

[287] 628 P.2d 580, 583-84 (Ariz. 1981).

[288] *Mott*, 931 P.2d at 1054.

[289] DSM-IV-TR, *supra* note 141, at 663.

[290] *Christensen*, 628 P.2d at 581-82.

[291] *Id.* at 582.

[292] *Id.* at 583.

[293] Ariz. Rev. Stat. Ann. § 13-502(A) (1997) ("Mental disease or defect does not include disorders that result from acute voluntary intoxication or withdrawal from alcohol or drugs, character defects, psychosexual disorders or impulse control disorders.").

affirmative defense, which excuses a defendant's conduct based on mental incapacity that does not rise to the level of insanity. Other jurisdictions, like Arizona, do not recognize diminished capacity as its own affirmative defense.[295] Regardless of whether diminished capacity evidence is accepted as a complete or partial defense of excuse, the separate factual question of whether a defendant actually entertained a particular level of *mens rea* necessary for a criminal conviction may well depend on whether the defendant's mental illness interfered with his or her ability to act with the requisite *mens rea*. The dissent in *Mott*[296] and Justice Kennedy's dissent in *Clark* both make this distinction clear.[297] The majority opinions in both cases, however, conflate the issue.

Mott's flawed understanding of both the psychological evidence at issue in *Christensen* and the nature of diminished capacity evidence notwithstanding, the Supreme Court's reliance on *Mott*'s interpretation of *Christensen* is still problematic. Assuming, *arguendo*, that the "character trait" at issue in *Christensen* did not concern "mental disease evidence" (which it did), using *Mott*'s reasoning, the outcome of *Clark* should still be different. The *Mott* court accepted that the defendant in *Christensen* was offering evidence of his inability to control his impulses as evidence that he did not entertain the requisite *mens rea* for murder. Specifically, the *Christensen* court held that denying the defendant the ability to argue that his mental status interfered with his ability to act deliberately or with premeditation violated due process.[298] Why, then, was Eric Clark denied the ability to argue that his mental status interfered with his ability to act knowingly? This inconsistency is exacerbated by the fact that the defendant in *Christensen* was not psychotic, and Eric Clark was. Accordingly, Clark had a much stronger case for demonstrating why his mental illness interfered with his ability to form *mens rea* than did the defendant in *Christensen*.

The U.S. Supreme Court should have discerned the inconsistencies in *Mott* and *Christensen*. It did not. It accepted *Mott* as settled state law without regard to the due process arguments that Eric Clark advanced. Moreover, the majority in *Clark* distilled a triad of types of evidence tending to establish *mens rea* from the illogical web of strained reasoning evidenced in both *Christensen* and *Mott*. These evidentiary distinctions were unnecessary. Moreover, they are so

---

[294]The defense in *Mott* wanted its expert to address the personality and character traits shared by women who suffer from domestic violence, and show how these could lead someone in the defendant's position to fail unintentionally to take action to protect her children from her boyfriend who physically abused both her and her children. She was denied the ability to do so. *Mott*, 931 P.2d at 1050.

[295]*See, e.g.*, State v. Schantz, 403 P.2d 521, 529 (Ariz. 1965), *cert. denied*, 382 U.S. 1015 (1966) (refusing to judicially-recognize the diminished capacity defense on the grounds that the legislature is responsible for promulgating the criminal law and that it "ha[d] not recognized a disease or defect of mind in which volition does not exist ... as a defense to a prosecution for [a crime.]").

[296]*Mott*, 931 P.2d at 1060, *cert. denied*, 520 U.S. 1234 (1997) (Feldman, J., dissenting).

> [W]e deal here with evidence "not offered as a defense to excuse [Defendant's] crimes, but rather [with] evidence to negate the *mens rea* element of the crime." In other words, the evidence was offered to help the jury determine whether Defendant acted knowingly, intentionally, recklessly, or with criminal negligence — the only real issues in the case.

Id.

[297]Clark v. Arizona, 126 S. Ct. 2709, 2738-39, 2747 (2006) (Kennedy, J., dissenting) ("Criminal responsibility involves an inquiry into whether the defendant knew right from wrong, not whether he had the *mens rea* elements of the offense.").

misleading that Justice Kennedy called them an "evidentiary framework that . . . will be unworkable in many cases."[299]

The U.S. Supreme Court is undoubtedly correct that laymen and experts alike have insights into a person's behavior, especially when it is bizarre, and, therefore, their testimony concerning their personal observations of a defendant's behavior is both relevant and admissible.[300] Presumably, this led the Court to interpret *Mott* as having no effect on "observational evidence" regardless of whether it was offered by a layperson or a qualified expert.[301] In contrast, the Court viewed *Mott* as limiting expert testimony with regard to both "mental disease evidence" and "capacity evidence."[302] But mental disease evidence is not a distinct construct from either observational evidence or capacity evidence. Forensic clinical assessment involves not only the administration of cognitive and personality tests but also observations of human behavior.[303] Moreover, a person's capacity to understand right from wrong is dependent not only upon a particular diagnosis, but also on how the disorder manifests itself in a given person—something deduced from observation of the patient. Thus, the *Clark* Court's evidentiary triad creates a false trichotomy, as all three types of evidence are intertwined with each other. Justice Kennedy points out this truism in his dissent:

> The mental-disease evidence at trial was also intertwined with the observation evidence because it lent needed credibility. Clark's parents and friends testified Clark thought the people in his town were aliens trying to kill him. These claims might not be believable without a psychiatrist confirming the story based on his experience with people who have exhibited similar behaviors. It makes little sense to divorce the observation evidence from the explanation that makes it comprehensible.[304]

Having unnecessarily created these three confusing and misleading categories of behavioral evidence, the Court construed Clark's due process challenge to *Mott* as being one limited to its prohibition on mental disease evidence from being used to establish diminished capacity.[305] The Court held that such a prohibition does not violate due process.[306] But the majority is wrong on two counts. Not only did Clark argue that barring diminished capacity evidence was a due process violation, but he also argued that even if it were constitutionally permissible to bar diminished capacity evidence, it would nonetheless be unconstitutional to apply that rule in a manner that prohibited a criminal defendant from attempting to prove that he lacked *mens rea*.[307] Thus, by construing Clark's claim so narrowly, the majority missed the gravamen of his second issue. To compound matters, the majority's substantive holding on its narrow interpretation of Clark's challenge to *Mott* is critically flawed for a number of other reasons. Justice Souter's opinion offers several bases for the Court's upholding of the *Mott* rule. All of them are related to the possible effects of confusion over mental illness expert testimony. First, the Court reasoned

---

[298]*Christensen*, 628 P.2d at 584 ("[I]t is inconsistent with fundamental justice to prevent a defendant from offering evidence to dispute the charge against him.").

[399]*Clark*, 126 S. Ct. at 2738 (Kennedy, J., dissenting).

[300]*See, e.g.*, State v. Bay, 722 P.2d 280, 284 (Ariz. 1986).

[301]*Clark*, 126 S. Ct. 2726

[302]*Id.*

[303]*See generally* DAVID L. SHAPIRO, FORENSIC PSYCHOLOGICAL ASSESSMENT: AN INTEGRATIVE APPROACH (1991).

[304]*Clark*, 126 S. Ct. at 2739 (Kennedy, J., dissenting).

[305]*Id.* at 2729 (majority opinion).

[306]*Id.* at 2737.

that by confining such evidence to the ultimate question of insanity, it preserves the full force of a state's allocation of the burden of persuasion to overcome the presumption of sanity.[308]

> [T]he presumption of sanity would then be only as strong as the evidence a factfinder would accept as enough to raise a reasonable doubt about *mens rea* for the crime charged; once reasonable doubt was found, acquittal would be required, and the standards established for the defense of insanity would go by the boards. Now, a State is of course free to accept such a possibility in its law. After all, it is free to define the insanity defense by treating the presumption of sanity as a bursting bubble, whose disappearance shifts the burden to the prosecution to prove sanity whenever a defendant presents any credible evidence of mental disease or incapacity. In States with this kind of insanity rule, the legislature may well be willing to allow such evidence to be considered on the *mens rea* element for whatever the factfinder thinks it is worth. What counts for due process, however, is simply that a State that wishes to avoid a second avenue for exploring capacity, less stringent for a defendant, has a good reason for confining the consideration of evidence of mental disease and incapacity to the insanity defense.[309]

Thus, when a state makes a policy judgment—as Arizona, many other states, and the federal government have done—to place the burden on a defendant to prove his insanity by clear and convincing evidence, allowing expert testimony on the defendant's mental illness could usurp that allocation of the burden of persuasion by allowing such evidence to cast reasonable doubt on the defendant's *mens rea*. The practical effect of the *Clark* Court's reasoning is twofold. First, it reaffirms the right of any U.S. jurisdiction to refuse to allow a defendant to introduce diminished capacity evidence.[310] Second, as Justice Kennedy's dissent makes clear, it undercuts the basic principle of due process that the prosecution must prove *mens rea* beyond a reasonable doubt.

The insanity defense merely allows the law to excuse the criminal conduct of someone who commits a criminal act due to significant mental impairment. Thus, the insanity defense separates "nonblameworthy from blameworthy offenders."[311] The insanity defense does not, however, have any effect on a determination of the actor's underlying guilt—a question that turns on whether the government can prove all elements of a criminal offense, including *mens rea*, beyond a reasonable doubt.[312]

A defendant, like Daniel M'Naghten, may well have formed specific intent to commit a crime but did so under morally blameless circumstances as a result of psychosis. It is an entirely separate question whether a defendant formed *mens rea*. The *Mott* rule, therefore, interferes with a defendant's fundamental right to present evidence that calls into question whether he entertained *mens rea*—an element on which the prosecution bears the burden of persuasion beyond a reasonable doubt.[313]

---

[307] *Id.* at 2739 (Kennedy, J., dissenting.

[308] *Id.* at 2732 (majority opinion).

[309] *Clark*, 126 S. Ct. at 2732-33.

[310] *Id.* at 2733 (citing Fisher v. United States, 328 U.S. 463, 466-76 (1946) (upholding a refusal to instruct a jury that it could consider the defendant's mental deficiencies, which did not rise to the level of insanity, in determining the elements of premeditation)).

[311] *Id.* at 2731 (citing DONALD H. HERMANN, THE INSANITY DEFENSE: PHILOSOPHICAL, HISTORICAL AND LEGAL PERSPECTIVES 4 (1983)).

[312] *See* Patterson v. New York, 432 U.S. 197, 210-11 (1977); *In re* Winship, 397 U.S. 358, 361-64 (1970).

While states have latitude to exclude relevant evidence offered by a criminal defendant,[314] they are constrained from doing so when it interferes with a criminal defendant's "meaningful opportunity to present a complete defense."[315] The deprivation of Eric Clark's constitutional right to present a defense as to the element of *mens rea* was at the heart of his due process challenge to *Mott*. Yet, the majority decision in *Clark* dismissed this essential point because it found that mental disease or capacity evidence was efficiently unreliable to warrant a rule of evidence excluding it in spite of its relevance, much like is done for hearsay evidence:

> While the Constitution prohibits the exclusion of defense evidence under rules that serve no legitimate purpose or that are disproportionate to the ends that they are asserted to promote, well-established rules of evidence permit trial judges to exclude evidence if its probative value is outweighed by certain other factors such as unfair prejudice, confusion of the issues, or potential to mislead the jury.[316]

The *Clark* Court found that mental disorder evidence and moral capacity evidence both suffer from sufficient reliability issues and that Arizona was justified in limiting such evidence exclusively to the question of insanity.[317] In support of this conclusion, the Court made three related arguments. First, it relied on language in the American Psychiatric Association's *Diagnostic and Statistical Manual of Mental Disorders*[318] that its diagnostic classifications reflect a "consensus" about mental disorders at the time of publication that may change as "[n]ew knowledge generated by research or clinical experience" becomes available.[319] The Court construed the APA's admission that consensus regarding diagnoses may change over time masked "vigorous debate" within the psychiatric community.[320] While the Court was careful to state that the consequence of this masking was not to "condemn mental-disease evidence wholesale," it concluded that "this professional ferment is a general caution in treating psychological classifications as predicates for excusing otherwise criminal conduct."[321]

Second, the Court cautioned that, even when the diagnostic criteria is "broadly accepted" and "uncontroversial," mental disease evidence still has the potential "to mislead jurors" by suggesting "that a defendant suffering from a recognized mental disease lacks cognitive, moral, volitional, or other capacity, when that may not be a sound conclusion at all."[322] This, according to the Court, is "because of the imperfect fit between the questions of ultimate concern to the law and the information contained in a clinical diagnosis."[323] But this is an absurd line of reasoning because forensic psychological/psychiatric testimony concerning a defendant's cognitive, moral, or volitional capabilities not only remains admissible to prove insanity but also to prove a host of other criminal competencies ranging from a mentally ill defendant's competency to stand trial,

---

[313]*Cf.*, Sandstrom v. Montana, 442 U.S. 510, 524 (1979) (holding jury instruction that had the effect of placing the burden on the defendant to disprove that he had the requisite mental state violates due process).

[314]*See, e.g.*, United States v. Scheffer, 523 U.S. 303, 308 (1998).

[315]Holmes v. South Carolina, 126 S. Ct. 1727, 1731 (2006) (quoting Crane v. Kentucky, 476 U.S. 683, 690 (1986)).

[316]*Clark*, 126 S. Ct. at 2731-32 (quoting Holmes v. South Carolina, 126 S. Ct. 1727, 1732 (2006) (citing Crane v. Kentucky, 476 U.S. 683 (1986); Montana v. Egelhoff, 518 U.S. 37 (1996); Chambers v. Mississippi, 410 U.S. 284 (1973)).

[317]*Clark*, 126 S. Ct. at 2734-35.

[318]DSM-IV-TR, *supra* note 141, at xxxiii.

[319]*Clark*, 126 S. Ct. at 2734 (citing DSM-IV-TR, *supra* note 141, at xxxiii).

[320]*Id.*

[321]*Id.*

[322]*Id.*

competency to waive *Miranda* rights, to act as his/her own attorney, to a defendant's competency to be sentenced and punished.[324]

Finally, the *Clark* Court asserted that there are "particular risks inherent in the opinions of the experts who supplement the mental-disease classifications with opinions on incapacity":[325]

> Unlike observational evidence bearing on *mens rea,* capacity evidence consists of judgment, and judgment fraught with multiple perils: a defendant's state of mind at the crucial moment can be elusive no matter how conscientious the enquiry, and the law's categories that set the terms of the capacity judgment are not the categories of psychology that govern the expert's professional thinking. . . . And even when an expert is confident that his understanding of the mind is reliable, judgment addressing the basic categories of capacity requires a leap from the concepts of psychology, which are devised for thinking about treatment, to the concepts of legal sanity, which are devised for thinking about criminal responsibility.[326]

This argument is not novel. It has been made by courts and scholars alike insofar as it posits that a mental health professional is no more qualified than anyone else to decide whether a particular defendant falls within the legal definition of insanity.[327] While an arguable position, it nonetheless misses the point in *Clark,* as the evidence was not being restricted in the consideration of insanity; such "ultimate issue" evidence is permissible under Arizona law.[328] Rather, the evidence was being restricted under *Mott* for the purposes of establishing *mens rea*—an entirely different line of analysis.[329]

All three arguments offered by the majority in support of its conclusion that Arizona may constitutionally limit the introduction of mental disease evidence and capacity evidence to disprove *mens rea* collectively demonstrate a deep distrust of forensic psychiatric and psychological clinical assessment. Do laypeople understand that clinical depression can be so severe as to cause psychotic breaks with reality?[330] Would the common juror understand that the auditory hallucinations experienced by schizophrenics often cause them to play music loudly to drown out the voices in their heads—something particularly relevant in *Clark?*[331] Who, if not mental health professionals, are more qualified to give an opinion regarding whether a particular mental illness interferes with a person's ability to act with specific intent? Justice Kennedy's dissent makes this point quite eloquently:

> The existence of . . . functional psychosis [in this case] is beyond dispute, but that does not mean the lay witness understands it or that a disputed issue of fact concerning its effect in a particular instance is not something for the expert to address. . . . [T]he opinion that Clark had paranoid schizophrenia—an opinion shared by experts for both the prosecution and defense—bears on

---

[323]*Id.* at 2735.

[324]*See generally* HENRY F. FRADELLA, FORENSIC PSYCHOLOGY: THE USE OF BEHAVIORAL SCIENCE IN CIVIL AND CRIMINAL JUSTICE (2006); RALPH REISNER, CHRISTOPHER SLOBOGIN, & ARTI RAI, LAW AND THE MENTAL HEALTH SYSTEM, CIVIL AND CRIMINAL ASPECTS (4th ed. 2004)).

[325]*Clark*, 126 S. Ct. at 2735.

[326]*Id.* at 2735-36.

[327]*Id.* at 2736 (citing DSM-IV-TR, *supra* note 141, at xxxii-xxxiii; PAUL GIANNELLI & EDWARD IMWINKELRIED, SCIENTIFIC EVIDENCE § 9-3(B), at 286 (1986); RALPH SLOVENKO, PSYCHIATRY AND CRIMINAL CULPADILITY 55 (1995)).

[328]State v. Sanchez, 573 P.2d 60, 64 (Ariz. 1977); ARIZ. R. EVID. 704 (2006) (allowing otherwise admissible evidence on testimony "embrac[ing] an ultimate issue to be decided by the trier of fact").

[329]Mullaney v. Wilbur, 421 U.S. 684, 706 (1975) (Rehnquist, J., concurring) ("[T]he existence or nonexistence of legal insanity bears no necessary relationship to the existence or nonexistence of the required mental elements of the crime.").

[330]*See* DSM-IV-TR, *supra* note 141, at 369-76.

> efforts to determine, as a factual matter, whether he knew he was killing a police officer. The psychiatrist's explanation of Clark's condition was essential to understanding how he processes sensory data and therefore to deciding what information was in his mind at the time of the shooting. Simply put, knowledge relies on cognition, and cognition can be affected by schizophrenia.[332]

Justice Kennedy's assessment is thoughtful and displays an understanding of the often complicated nuances of human behavior. His point that mental disease evidence works hand-in-hand with observational evidence demonstrates why the Court's tripartite evidentiary structure is nonsensical.

Not being able to offer all relevant evidence of the defendant's inability to have knowingly killed Officer Mortiz interfered with Clark's due process right to present evidence that could have cast significant doubt on the state's ability to meet its burden to prove *mens rea* beyond a reasonable doubt.[333] While states are free to shift the burden of proof to the defendant to prove his own insanity,[334] the *Mott* rule has the practical effect of being unconstitutional by placing a burden of disproving *mens rea* on the defendant while simultaneously limiting the defendant's ability to do so.[335]

Having shown why the exclusion of forensic psychiatric and psychological evidence on the issue of *mens rea* in *Clark* was a due process violation, Justice Kennedy's dissent then takes issue with the majority's arguments about the propriety of the exclusion of such evidence due to its potential to mislead or confuse the jury. First, a per se ruling banning certain types of evidence as unreliable cannot be constitutionally applied when the evidence at issue "may be reliable in an individual case."[336] Arizona has specialized rules of evidence dealing with the admissibility of expert testimony, including provisions to bar unreliable or speculative testimony as offered in a particular case.[337]

These rules have been held by state courts to allow a variety of types of psychological evidence to be used in cases varying from "the psychological characteristics of molestation victims"[338] to "psychiatric testimony regarding neurological deficits."[339] Courts across the nation

---

[331] *Clark*, 126 S. Ct. at 2739 (Kennedy, J., dissenting).

[332] *Id.*

[333] *See, e.g.*, Patterson v. New York, 432 U.S. 197, 210-11 (1977); *In re* Winship, 397 U.S. 358, 361-364 (1970).

[334] *See* Leland v. Oregon, 343 U.S. 790 (1952).

[335] *Clark*, 126 S. Ct. at 2747 (citing Sandstrom v. Montana, 442 U.S. 510, 524 (1979) ("jury instruction that had the effect of placing the burden on the defendant to disprove that he had the requisite mental state violates due process")); Cool v. United States, 409 U.S. 100, 103 (1972) (per curiam) (jury instruction that allowed jury to consider accomplice's testimony only if it was true beyond a reasonable doubt "place[d] an improper burden on the defense and allow[ed] the jury to convict despite its failure to find guilt beyond a reasonable doubt"); Martin v. Ohio, 480 U.S. 228, 233-34 (1987) (State can shift the burden on a claim of self-defense, but if the jury were disallowed from considering self-defense evidence for purposes of deciding the elements of the offense, it "would relieve the State of its burden and plainly run afoul of Winship's mandate")). Arizona attempted to justify doing so by relying on *Montana v. Egelhoff*, which upheld Montana's statutory ban on presenting evidence of voluntary intoxication to rebut *mens rea*. Montana v. Egelhoff, 518 U.S. 37 (1996). But this reliance on *Egelhoff* is misplaced. Egelhoff chose to become intoxicated; Clark did not choose to have paranoid schizophrenia. The difference is a critical one, as Egelhoff's purposeful decision to become intoxicated can serve as the basis of criminal liability, while Clark is devoid of any responsibility for having a mental state that renders him unable to distinguish reality from a world filled with delusions and hallucinations. *Id.* at 44 (citing 1 M. HALE, PLEAS OF THE CROWN, at *32-*33 ("the intoxicated defendant 'shall have no privilege by this voluntary contracted madness, but shall have the same judgment as if he were in his right senses'"); 4 W. BLACKSTONE, COMMENTARIES, at *25-*26 (the law viewed intoxication "as an aggravation of the offence, rather than as an excuse for any criminal misbehaviour")).

[336] *Clark*, 126 S. Ct. at 2744-45 (citing Rock v. Arkansas, 483 U.S. 44, 61 (1987)).

[337] *Id.* at 2745 (citing ARIZ. R. EVID. 403, 702 (West 2005)).

apply similar rules of evidence to behavioral science testimony with surprising consistency.[340] Thus, having a per se rule against all forms of forensic psychological testimony other than "observational evidence" is unnecessary.

Moreover, even if it were not unnecessary, a state's interest in excluding potentially unreliable evidence in courts of law must be balanced against an individual defendant's due process rights.[341] Ironically, it is observational evidence that is the least scientifically valid and reliable form of forensic mental health evidence. Consider that the diagnostic criteria in the DSM-IV-TR—the basis for forming an opinion with regard to "mental disease evidence"—has been validated to varying degrees,[342] while the individual observations of a layperson or a particular clinician cannot be validated empirically. The *Mott* rule, therefore, bizarrely allows "unexplained and uncategorized tendencies to be introduced while excluding relatively well-understood psychiatric testimony regarding well-documented mental illnesses."[343]

Justice Kennedy's dissent in *Clark* also criticizes the majority's contention that forensic behavioral science runs too high a risk of jury confusion. He begins his attack on this faulty premise by noting that "[w]e have always trusted juries to sort through complex facts in various areas of law."[344] Justice Kennedy concedes that there are numerous psychiatric diagnoses that might be confusing or misleading to a jury.[345] The one at issue in *Clark,* however, is not one such diagnosis. Schizophrenia "is a well-documented mental illness, and no one seriously disputes either its definition or its most prominent clinical manifestations."[346] The experts proffered both by Clark and the prosecution agreed that Clark suffered from paranoid schizophrenia, and they further agreed that Clark "was actively psychotic at the time of the killing."[347] Kennedy therefore concludes that if there were any jury confusion issue at all in the case, it was "the result of the Court's own insistence on conflating the insanity defense and the question of intent."[348]

> Considered on its own terms, the issue of intent and knowledge is a straightforward factual question. A trier of fact is quite capable of weighing defense testimony and then determining whether the accused did or did not intend to kill or knowingly kill a human being who was a police officer. True, the issue can be difficult to decide in particular instances, but no more so than many matters juries must confront.[349]

---

[338]*Id.* (citing State v. Lindsey, 720 P.2d 73, 74-75 (Ariz. 1986)).

[339]*Id.* (citing Horan v. Indus. Comm'n, 806 P.2d 911, 914-915 (Ariz. Ct. App. 1991)).

[340]*See* Fradella et al., *supra* note 21, at 443 ("First, although critics of *Daubert* have suggested that having judges evaluating scientific methodologies would lead to inconsistent results, it appears that inconsistencies are the exceptions, rather than the rule.").

[341]*Clark*, 126 S. Ct. at 2744 (citing Holmes v. South Carolina, 126 S. Ct. 1727, 1734 (2006) ("rule excluding, in certain cases, evidence that a third party may have committed the crime 'even if that evidence, if viewed independently, would have great probative value and even if it would not pose an undue risk of harassment, prejudice, or confusion of the issues'")); *Rock*, 483 U.S. at 56 (rule excluding all hypnotically refreshed testimony "operates to the detriment of any defendant who undergoes hypnosis, without regard to the reasons for it, the circumstances under which it took place, or any independent verification of the information it produced"); Washington v. Texas, 388 U.S. 14, 226, (1967) (rule excluding accomplice testimony "prevent[s] whole categories of defense witnesses from testifying on the basis of a priori categories that presume them unworthy of belief").

[342]*See generally* ALLEN FRANCES ET AL., DSM-IV-TR GUIDEBOOK 3-85 (2004).

[343]*Clark*, 126 S. Ct. at 2749 (Kennedy, J., dissenting).

[344]*Id.* at 2745 (citing United States v. Booker, 543 U.S. 220, 289 (2005) (Stevens, J., dissenting in part)).

[345]*Id.*

[346]*Id.* at 2746.

[347]*Id*

[348]*Clark*, 126 S. Ct. at 2746 (Kennedy, J., dissenting).

V. CONCLUSION

Defining and applying the parameters of diminished capacity evidence is difficult due to the amorphous nature of the doctrine and its ever-changing boundaries. As defendants have attempted to extend diminished capacity to cover PMS, media intoxication, and the like, there has clearly been a corresponding backlash against the use of diminished capacity evidence. Consider the following commentary:

> The acceptance of abuse defenses has transformed America into a nation of victims. This victimization has led to increased assertions of novel abuse defenses. America's new culture asserts an instinctive readiness to blame someone for every misfortune. Explanations for disadvantages are based on theories of sexism, racism, illness, rotten childhood, poor education, or anything else which can project guilt onto others.[350]

Even when diminished capacity is not extended into the realm of an abuse excuse, courts still dislike the doctrine. Judicial hostility to diminished capacity evidence may "reflect the traditional judicial distrust of the vagaries, uncertainties, and mysteries of psychiatric explanations, particularly when invoked to assess varying shades of capacity to perform such basic functions as intending and believing."[351]

In spite of this backlash, diminished capacity receives very little media coverage unless the case is exceptional, like Dan White's "Twinkie Defense." Outrage over the *Hinckley* verdict led to massive curtailment of the insanity defense, yet, insanity is used very rarely and, even when asserted, is unsuccessful nearly three-quarters of the time. In contrast, the ease with which diminished capacity can be used in most jurisdictions makes it much more appealing than insanity, with the added benefit of what ought to be a much higher likelihood of success.[352]

We must consider the impact of the continued narrowing of the insanity defense and our growing reliance on diminished capacity evidence—whether offered to disprove *mens rea* or as a mitigating factor at sentencing. As the insanity defense grows narrower (or, in some jurisdictions, nonexistent), the number of mentally ill people in prisons has sharply increased.[353] Given how the *Clark* Court further limited criminal defendants' ability to argue excuse defenses, there is every reason to believe the sad trend of incarcerating mentally ill people in prisons, rather than hospitals, will continue to increasing.

In upholding the overbroad *Mott* rule, the *Clark* Court allows states to severely limit a mentally ill criminal defendant from offering some of the most probative evidence concerning his or her guilt. To prove that Clark committed murder, the prosecution in the *Clark* case introduced evidence that the defendant spoke of wanting to kill police and then argued that to carry out this plan, the defendant lured police to the scene by blaring music from his truck while circling a block in a residential neighborhood. The defendant, however, was barred from introducing largely undisputed evidence about the nature of paranoid schizophrenia and how the disease caused or could have caused his actions:

---

[349]*Id.*

[350]Copp, *supra* note 127, at 221-22 (citing CHARLES J. SYKES, A NATION OF VICTIMS: THE DECAY OF AMERICAN CULTURE 11-12 (1992); DERSHOWITZ, *supra* note 35, at 339).

[351]Sanford H. Kadish, *Fifty Years of Criminal Law: An Opinionated Review*, 87 CAL. L. REV. 943, 956 (1999).

[352]*But see* Neil P. Cohen et al., *The Prevalence and Use of Criminal Defenses: A Preliminary Study*, 60 TENN. L. REV. 957, 972-73 (1993) (reporting use in only 0.01% of cases with 25% success rate).

For example, as Clark's expert testified during the insanity-defense phase of his trial, schizophrenics often play music loudly to drown out the voices in their heads and not to lure police officers to their cars. But in the first phase of the trial, the judge hearing the case (Clark waived his right to a jury) couldn't consider that evidence in deciding whether the prosecution had proved first-degree murder.[354]

One can only hope that since *Clark* upheld the *Mott* rule under Arizona law, the decision will have little impact beyond the state of Arizona. But both the language used in *Clark* and the underlying rationale do not bode well for the future of excuse defenses based on mental illness. Indeed, the decision calls into question the future admissibility of, or weight to be accorded to, forensic behavioral science evidence. And while that is a shame since the behavioral sciences have much to offer the law, the real tragedy concerns Eric Clark and those like him. With such a sorry state of affairs being the sad reality in present times, mentally ill inmates who do not belong in prisons will likely continue to burden the correctional system, inmates who instead should be treated and cared for in secure mental hospitals. Worse yet, more defendants like Clark may find themselves in a confusing web of unworkable evidentiary frameworks that prevent them from arguing what should be a "straightforward defense: [that they] did not commit the crime with which [they were] charged" because they lacked the requisite *mens rea*.[355]

---

[353] *See, e.g.*, Gilbert Geis, *Pathological Gambling and Insanity, Diminished Capacity, Dischargeability, and Downward Sentencing Departures*, 8 GAMING L. REV. 347 (2004).

[354] Emily Bazelon, *Crazy Law: The Supreme Court Beats Up on the Insanity Defense*, SLATE, July 6, 2006, http://www.slate.com/id/2145139 (last visited Dec. 3, 2006).

CHAPTER EIGHT
CIVIL COMMITMENT

I. INTRODUCTION

> The next time you attend a small gathering of about ten or twelve people, look around the room carefully. If the group is statistically average, one of the people there has been, is, or will be mentally ill and a patient in a mental hospital, perhaps involuntarily committed. . . . Ten percent of all Americans have a personal brush with mental disturbance so serious as to require hospitalization. Far greater numbers endure lesser degrees of mental illness.[1]

The process of hospitalizing a mentally ill person against his or her will is known as ***civil commitment.*** The term "civil" is used because the procedures for committing someone are civil procedures, not criminal ones. The government's authority to civilly commit a person stems from its *parens patriae* power and its police power.[2] The doctrine of ***parens patriae*** was summarized in the previous chapter. As you may recall, it is the doctrine that allows the government to substitute its judgment for that of its citizens who are not competent to make rationale decisions for themselves.[3] Although the exercise of this power is presumably beneficent (i.e., in the best interest of the person), it is an inherently coercive power.[4]

The state's ***police power*** is different. The police power of the state allow it to confine those who endanger society.[5] The exercise of this power has a long history of due process protections when used in the criminal setting, such a trials and the associated protections afforded the criminal defendant both statutorily and constitutionally. The same, however, cannot be said for the exercise of a state police power in the area of civil commitment, where judicial deference to legislative judgments (which, in turn, often defer to psychiatric judgments) have been the rule.[6]

II. HISTORICAL BACKGROUND OF CIVIL COMMITMENT

Civil commitment is a fairly unique tool of social control. It permits the involuntary hospitalization of someone in the name of benevolence—medically treating those who are mentally ill and dangerous.[7] But because it involves the deprivation of liberty, civil commitment raises socio-philosophical concerns of autonomy[8] as well as legal concerns under the Fourteenth Amendment's Due Process Clause. In fact, some critics of civil commitment have argued

---

[1]Douglas S. Stransky, Comments: *Civil Commitment and the Right to Refuse Treatment: Resolving Disputes from a Due Process Perspective*, 50 U. MIAMI L. REV. 413, 413-14 (1996).

[2]SAMUEL JAN BRAKEL, ET AL., THE MENTALLY DISABLED AND THE LAW 24 (1985).

[3]*See, e.g.,* Addington v. Texas, 441 U.S. 418, 426 (1979) (discussing *parens patriae* power).

[4]*E.g.,* Michael Shapiro, *Legislating the Control of Behavior Control: Autonomy and the Coercive Use of Organic Therapies*, 47 S. CAL. L. REV. 237, 270 (1974). *See generally* COERCION IN MENTAL HEALTH CARE, 11 BEHAV. SCI. & L. 237-345 (1993) (symposium issue interdisciplinarily addressing coercive hospitalization and mental health care).

[5]BRAKEL, ET AL., *supra* note 2, at 24.

[6]*See, e.g.,* Brian J. Pollock, *Note*: Kansas v. Hendricks: *A Workable Standard for "Mental Illness" or a Push Down the Slippery Slope Toward State Abuse of Civil Commitment?*, 40 ARIZ. L. REV. 319, 320-21 (1998).

[7]Paul Chodoff, *The Case for Involuntary Hospitalization of the Mentally Ill*, 133 AM. J. PSYCHIATRY 496 (1976).

[8]Bruce A. Arrigo's *Paternalism, Civil Commitment and Illness Politics: Assessing The Current Debate And Outlining a Future Direction*, 7 J.L. & HEALTH 131 (1992/1993).

"mental illness is manufactured, that civilly confined persons are in fact prisoners, and that the 'preciousness of liberty' doctrine demands that the practice of involuntary hospitalization be abolished."[9]

The early history of civil commitment can, at best, be described as one of loose protections for the person sought to be confined. Some jurisdictions statutorily authorized civil commitment for those persons defined as being a "social menace" or "a fit and proper candidate for institutionalization."[10] Under this broad and amorphous standard, much discretion was built into the system to involuntarily confine people. And this broad authority was frequently used, as is illustrated by the statistic that more than a half a million people were so confined in 1955.[11]

The social movements of the 1960s brought reforms to many areas of social life, including the law. The area of civil commitment was one of the areas in desperate need of reform. Conditions for those confined in mental hospitals were inhumane. In his classic text, *Asylums,* sociologist Erving Goffman detailed the squalid conditions in mental institutions, nearly all of which were dangerously understaffed.[12] The deinstitutionalization movement of the era brought many reforms.[13] Legal reforms that began to recognize the liberty interests of the mentally ill included "community-situated treatment, due process procedural protections, the right to treatment, medical and Constitutional minimal standards in treatment, and the right to refuse treatment."[14] By the mid 1970s, many states had moved to what became known as the "dangerousness" standard for civil commitment, the standard used by nearly all U.S. jurisdictions today.[15]

Before moving on to discuss the dangerousness standard in detail, it should be noted that the reforms that followed the deinstitutionalization movement of the 1960s and 1970s did not cure all of the problems they were designed to address. In fact, deinstitutionalization brought about a host of new problems that some would argue have yet to be meaningfully addressed by society. Consider the critique by law and psychology scholar Bruce Arrigo:

> Community support was not immediately forthcoming. To this day, many mentally disordered persons find themselves unwelcomed residents or guests of board-and-care homes, single room occupancies, welfare hotels and flophouses. Others filter through the criminal justice system, somehow surviving in local lock-up and detention centers or security prisons. And still other psychiatrically disabled persons marginally exist on the streets where they sometimes die homeless. These disturbing realities are exacerbated by bouts of involuntary re-hospitalization or multiple hospitalization for the chronically mentally ill. Even when

---

[9]*Id.* at 132 (citing Thomas S. Szasz, The Manufacture of Madness: A Comparative Study of the Inquisition and the Mental Health Movement 1-15 (1970); Bruce J. Ennis, Prisoners of Psychiatry: Mental Patients, Psychiatry and the Law 2 (1972); Stephen J. Morse, *A Preference For Liberty: The Case Against Involuntary Commitment of the Mentally Disordered,* 70 Cal. L. Rev. 54, 106 (1982)).

[10]*Id.* at 136 (citing John E.B. Myers, *Involuntary Civil Commitment of the Mentally Ill: A System in Need of Change,* 29 Vill. L. Rev. 367, 381 (1983-84)).

[11]*Id.* (citing Howard H. Goldman et. al., *Deinstitutionalization: The Data Demythologized,* 34 Hosp. & Community Psychiatry, 129 (1983)).

[12]Erving Goffman, Asylums Essays on the Social Situation of Mental Health Patients and Other Inmates 47 (1961).

[13]*See generally* Gerald N. Grob, *Historical Origins of Deinstitutionalization,* in Leona L. Bachrach (ed.), Deinstitutionalization, 121 (1983).

[14]Arrigo, *supra* note 8, at 139-40 (citing *See* Lake v. Cameron, 364 F.2d 657 (D.C. Cir.1966), *cert. denied,* 382 U.S. 863 (1966); Lessard v. Schmidt, 349 F. Supp. 1078 (E.D. Wis.1972), *vacated and remanded for a more specific order,* 414 U.S. 743, *ordered on remand,* 379 F. Supp. 1376 (E.D. Wis. 1974), *vacated and remanded on other grounds,* 421 U.S. 957 (1975), *order reinstated on remand,* 413 F. Supp. 1318, 1319 (E.D. Wis.1976); Rouse v. Cameron, 373 F.2d 451 (D.C. Cir.1966); Wyatt v. Stickney, 344 F. Supp. 373, 375 (M.D. Ala. 1972)).

[15]*See* David B. Wexler, Mental Health Law: Major Issues (1981).

community placements are secured, the results are not always rewarding. The clinical, controlled and predictable delivery of psychiatric services in these environments often echoes the familiar regimen of asylum practices.[16]

III. CIVIL COMMITMENT CRITERIA

A. Overview

Civil commitment proceedings are largely a matter of state law. Yet, federal constitutional law, primarily in the area of due process, is inextricably intertwined with the process. It is therefore necessary to devote coverage in this chapter not only to the state law mechanisms used in the civil commitment process that varies from state to state, but also to both procedural and substantive due process concerns under federal law.

In spite of the variations from jurisdiction to jurisdiction, a few generalizations can be made about the civil commitment process. First, all states require that to be civilly committed a person must suffer from a mental illness. Second, all states require proof that the person whose civil commitment is being sought presents a danger to himself/herself or to others.[17] Third, a causal link between the mental illness and the behavior complained of must be shown (i.e., the person's dangerousness is caused by or is a result of his/her mental illness). And finally, every state requires these three criteria to be proven, at minimum, by clear and convincing evidence.[18]

Additionally, approximately thirty states allow for the involuntary civil commitment of someone is not dangerous, but who is ***"gravely disabled"***—a condition defined by the American Psychiatric Association as follows:

> [The person] . . . is substantially unable to provide for some of his basic needs, such as food, clothing, shelter, health, or safety or [the person] will, if not treated, suffer or continue to suffer severe mental and abnormal mental, emotional, or physical distress, and this distress is associated with significant impairment of judgement, reason, or behavior causing a substantial deterioration of his previous ability to function on his own.[19]

Research has demonstrated that although the elderly are, as expected, frequently civilly committed as gravely disabled, surprisingly, the gravely disabled "consist mostly of disturbed young persons, 21–35 years old."

---

[16]Arrigo, *supra* note 8, at 141 (citing, *inter alia*, Nancy K. Rhoden, *The Right to Refuse Psychotropic Drugs*, 15 HARV. C.R.-C.L.L. REV. 363, 431 (1980); John A. Talbott, *Toward A Public Policy On The Chronic Mentally Ill Patient*, 50 AM. J. ORTHOPSYCHIATRY 43, 47 (1980); CHARLES HOCH & ROBERT A. SLAYTON, NEW HOMELESS AND OLD: COMMUNITY AND THE SKID ROW HOTEL, 189 (1989); Darold A. Treffert, *Legal "Rites" Criminalizing the Mentally Ill*, 3 HILLSIDE J. CLINICAL PSYCHIATRY 123, 123-25 (1982); H. Richard Lamb, *Deinstitutionalization and the Homeless Mentally Ill*, 35 HOSP. & COMMUNITY PSYCHIATRY, 899, 903 (1984); H. Richard Lamb, *Involuntary Treatment for the Homeless Mentally Ill*, 4 NOTRE DAME J.L., ETHICS & PUB. POL'Y, 269, 269 (1989); LEONA L. BACHRACH, DEINSTITUTIONALIZATION, 73-91 (1983))

[17]*See, e.g.,* H. Richard Lamb & M.J. Mills, *Needed Changes in Law and Procedure for the Chronically Mentally Ill*, 37 HOSP. & COMMUNITY PSYCHIATRY, 475, 475 (1988).

[18]Addington v. Texas, 441 U.S. 418 (1979).

[19]Winsor C. Schmidt, *Critique of the American Psychiatric Association's Guidelines For State Legislation on Civil Commitment of the Mentally Ill*, 11 NEW ENG. J. ON CRIM. & CIV. CONFINEMENT 13, 29 (1985).

B. Defining Mental Illness for Civil Commitment Purposes

As with the areas of competency and insanity, defining mental illness for the purpose of civil commitment is no easy task.[20] One commentator wrote, "Usually the use of the phrase 'mental illness' effectively masks the actual norms being applied; and, because of the unavoidably ambiguous generalities in which the [APA] describes its diagnostic categories, the diagnostician has the ability to shoehorn into the mentally diseased class almost any person he wishes, for whatever reason, to put there."[21] In the thirty years since that was written, we still have no clear-cut definitions of what will qualify as a mental illness for civil commitment purposes.[22] In fact, after the Supreme Court's 1997 decision in *Kansas v. Hendricks*[23] (which will be addressed later in this chapter), the waters may be even more muddy.

1. Sample Statutory Definitions

Vermont defines mental illness as "a substantial disorder of thought, mood, perception, orientation, or memory, any of which grossly impairs judgment, behavior, capacity to recognize reality, or ability to meet the ordinary demands of life, but shall not include mental retardation."[24]

New Jersey defines mental illness as:

> a current, substantial disturbance of thought, mood, perception or orientation which significantly impairs judgment, capacity to control behavior or capacity to recognize reality, but does not include simple alcohol intoxication, transitory reaction to drug ingestion, organic brain syndrome or developmental disability unless it results in the severity of impairment described herein. The term mental illness is not limited to "psychosis" or "active psychosis," but shall include all conditions that result in the severity of impairment described herein.[25]

And Texas, which until quite recently tautologically defined a mentally ill person as someone "whose mental health is substantially impaired,"[26] now defines mental illness as follows:

> "Mental illness" means an illness, disease, or condition, other than epilepsy, senility, alcoholism, or mental deficiency, that:
>> (A) substantially impairs a person's thought, perception of reality, emotional process, or judgment; or
>> (B) grossly impairs behavior as demonstrated by recent disturbed behavior.[27]

---

[20] *See* Bruce J. Winick, *Ambiguities in The Legal Meaning And Significance of Mental Illness,* 1 Psych. Pub. Pol. and L. 534 (1995).

[21] Joseph M. Livermore et al., *On the Justifications for Civil Commitment*, 117 U. Pa. L. Rev. 75, 80 (1968).

[22] Winick, *supra* note 21, at 554-70; *see also* Robert I. Simon, Concise Guide to Clinical Psychiatry and the Law 73 (1988) (mental illness is "loosely defined" in civil commitment statutes).

[23] 521 U.S. 346 (1997).

[24] Vt. Rev. Stat. § 18-7101 (Supp. 1998).

[25] N.J. Stat. Ann. § 30:4-27.2(r) (Supp. 1998).

[26] Tex. Rev. Civ. Stat. art. 5547-4(k) (Supp. 1983).

[27] Texas Code Ann. tit. 7C § 571.003(14) (Supp. 1998).

As these three state statutes should make clear, Axis I DSM-IV major mental disorders, such as schizophrenia, major depressive disorders, and bipolar disorder, clearly qualify "as the paradigmatic cases of mental illness" just as they do with the issues of competency and insanity.[28] And, as with competency and insanity, neither drug nor alcohol abuse qualify.[29] But unlike competency and insanity, mental retardation does not usually qualify as a mental illness for civil commitment purposes.[30] "Most states have enacted separate statutory provisions for the commitment of the mentally retarded which, on the whole, provide less procedural protection than commitment statutes for the mentally ill and are less explicit with respect to commitment criteria (often merely requiring a finding of mental retardation and need for treatment or habilitation)."[31] Other states have done away with this distinction and now afford the mentally retarded the same rights and protections afforded to all civilly committed persons.[32]

Whether personality disorders qualify as mental illnesses for civil commitment purposes differs from state to state. The New Jersey statute reproduced above makes clear that personality disorders *do* qualify by specifically stating "mental illness is not limited to 'psychosis' or 'active psychosis,' but shall include all conditions that result in the severity of impairment described" in the statute.[33] The statutes of Vermont and Texas are silent on the issue, presumably leaving the determination to be made on a case-by-case basis depending on the level of impairment.

Minnesota is quite specific on what qualifies as a mental illness, not only including Axis I clinical syndromes and Axis II personality disorders and mental retardation, but also Axis III medical conditions:

> "Mental illness" means an organic disorder of the brain or a clinically significant disorder of thought, mood, perception, orientation, memory, or behavior that is listed in the clinical manual of the International Classification of Diseases (ICD-9-CM), current edition, code range 290.0 to 302.99 or 306.0 to 316.0 or the corresponding code in the American Psychiatric Association's Diagnostic and Statistical Manual of Mental Disorders (DSM), current edition, Axes I, II, or III, and that seriously limits a person's capacity to function in primary aspects of daily living such as personal relations, living arrangements, work, and recreation.[34]

In contrast, other jurisdictions specifically exclude certain personality disorders. Kansas, for example, excludes: "alcohol or chemical substance abuse; antisocial personality disorder; mental retardation; organic personality syndrome; or an organic mental disorder."[35] Arizona excludes: "conditions which are primarily those of drug abuse, alcoholism or mental retardation . . . ; and character and personality disorders characterized by lifelong and deeply ingrained antisocial behavior patterns, including sexual behaviors which are abnormal and prohibited by statute. . . ."[36]

---

[28]Winick, *supra* note 21, at 558-59.

[29]A minority of jurisdictions, however, permit the involuntary commitment of someone "suffering from substance abuse" if he or she is "imminently dangerous to self or others, [or] is gravely disabled or is obviously ill" as a result of the addiction. HAW. REV. STAT. § 334-60.2(2)-(3) (1997) .

[30]*See* statues reproduced in text above; *see also, e.g.,* ARK. STAT. ANN. § 20-47-202 (1997).

[31]GARY B. MELTON, ET AL., PSYCHOLOGICAL EVALUATION FOR THE COURTS 242 (1987).

[32]*E.g.,* MINN. STAT. ANN. § 245.462(20)(a).

[33]N.J. STAT. ANN. § 30:4-27.2(r) (Supp. 1998).

[34]MINN. STAT. ANN. § 245.462(20)(a) (Supp. 1997).

[35]KAN STAT. ANN. § 59-2946 (Supp. 1997).

[36]ARIZ. REV. STAT. § 36-501 (Supp. 1997).

2. The Impact of Foucha

In *Foucha v. Louisiana*,[37] the Supreme Court held that even if an insanity acquittee is predicted to remain dangerous, constitutionally they cannot be kept committed after they have recovered from mental illness. Terry Foucha had been acquitted on insanity grounds due to a drug-induced psychosis.[38] Not surprisingly, after treatment he "recovered" from that illness. He sought to be released accordingly.

Louisiana law used procedures for the continued confinement of insanity acquittees not unlike the procedures for involuntary commitment. But there was an interesting quirk of state law that made the *Foucha* case unique. Louisiana law authorized the continued commitment of insanity acquittees if they were "dangerous," even if not mentally ill.

At his release hearing, there was no dispute that Foucha did not suffer any longer from a psychosis. He was, however, diagnosed with antisocial personality disorder. At the hearing, physicians testified Foucha was dangerous, but no longer mentally ill. "One of the doctors testified . . . that he evidenced no signs of psychosis or neurosis and was in 'good shape' mentally [but] that he had, however, an antisocial personality, a condition that is not a mental disease and that is untreatable."[39] The trial court, relying on the fact that he was dangerous, denied Foucha's petition for release. The Supreme Court ultimately ruled in Foucha's favor, holding that his continued involuntary hospitalization violated due process because he was no longer mentally ill—a necessary prerequisite to involuntary hospitalization. The Court specifically relied on the testimony at the trial: "According to the testimony given at the hearing in the trial court, Foucha is not suffering from a mental disease or illness."[40]

When the Court rejected Louisiana's rationale that it could hold an insanity acquittee who was dangerous, even though not mentally ill, the Court said such logic "would permit the state to hold indefinitely any other insanity acquittee not mentally ill who could be shown to have a personality disorder that may lead to criminal conduct."[41] This sentence is troubling because it suggests that "the Court regarded personality disorder and mental illness as being two mutually exclusive categories."[42]

According to Professor Bruce Winick, the language used by the Court

> suggests that the Court may have treated antisocial personality disorder, and indeed all personality disorders, as not being mental illnesses sufficient to justify commitment as a constitutional matter. Because the Court provided no explanation or analysis of the issue, precisely what it was deciding in this regard remains unclear.[43]

Winick goes on in his article critiquing *Foucha* to state that antisocial personality disorder, among other personality disorders, *should not* qualify as a mental illnesses for legal purposes—

---

[37] 504 U.S. 71 (1992).

[38] Louisiana is one of the very few states that allow a drug or alcohol induced psychosis to qualify as a predicate mental disease or defect for insanity purposes.

[39] Foucha, 504 U.S. at 75 .

[40] *Id.* at 79.

[41] *Id.* at 82.

[42] Winick, *supra* note 21, at 543.

[43] *Id.* at 548.

as opposed to clinical ones.[44] Instead, he argues that a medical model of deviance ought to guide the legal definition of mental illness. Thus, he asserts that mental illness, for the purposes of law, ought to be limited to those disorders that meet three criteria: (1) their etiology is organic in nature (rather than psycho-social); (2) their treatment follows some reasonably predicable course; and (3) they render the individual incapable of rational decision making or behavior control.[45] Since antisocial personality disorder fails to meet these criteria, he argues it should not be considered a mental illness. Nearly all states and the American Law Institute agree with him when it comes to the definition of mental illness for the purposes of the insanity defense. But as the statutes cited above in this chapter illustrate, the states are divided on that matter when it comes to civil commitment.

Before leaving our discussion of *Foucha,* it should be noted that the Supreme Court's treatment of antisocial personality disorder as *not* being a mental illness for civil commitment purposes in *Foucha* does not necessarily mean it will not ever qualify as a mental illness for civil commitment purposes. For one thing, neither Foucha nor was the state of Louisiana was claiming he was mentally ill. The matter, therefore, was not truly at issue in this case and the Supreme Court's handling of the disorder may therefore be regarded as dicta. Secondly, the decision was only a plurality one, meaning only four justices joined in the majority opinion. Justice O'Connor voted with the majority in terms of the result, but did not join its opinion. She filed a separate concurring opinion in which she equated the constitutional standard for "mental illness" with a "medical justification" for confinement.[46] The Louisiana statute did not meet this standard since it allowed the continued commitment of insanity acquittees who were no longer mentally ill. Thus, the diagnosis at issue in *Foucha* was not relevant to her rationale. Accordingly, *Foucha* should be read narrowly given the limited confines of the unique facts of the case and its plurality status.

3. The Impact of Hendricks

In 1997, the Supreme Court upheld a Kansas statute that provided for the civil commitment of "sexually violent predators" upon the completion of their period of criminal incarceration.[47] The Kansas statute authorized the civil commitment of:

> any person who has been convicted of or charged with a sexually violent offense and who suffers from a mental abnormality or personality disorder which makes the person likely to engage in the predatory acts of sexual violence, if not confined in a secure facility.[48]

Hendricks, a diagnosed pedophile, was committed under the act. He challenged his involuntary commission using the broad language in *Foucha* quoted above, arguing that even though he might be dangerous, he was not mentally ill under *Foucha* and therefore could not be constitutionally detained under *Foucha's* holding. The Kansas Supreme Court sided with Hendricks, finding that the law permitted the involuntary commitment of persons who were not

---

[11]*Id.* at 570-71.

[45]*Id.* at 558-59.

[46]Foucha, 504 U.S. at 88 (O'Connor, J., concurring) ("Insanity acquittees could not be confined as mental patients absent some medical justification for doing so . . . .").

[47]Kansas v. Hendricks, 521 U.S. 346 (1997).

[48]KAN. STAT. ANN. § 59-29a02(a) (Supp. 1996).

mentally ill within the meaning of *Foucha,* but rather unconstitutionally authorized the commitment of people with mere mental abnormalities or personality disorders.[49]

The Supreme Court reversed. It reasoned that the "mental abnormality" requirement of the Kansas statute that required a finding that a person could not control his or her behavior, coupled with a finding of dangerousness, was constitutionally sufficient to involuntarily commit a person. The Court distinguished the case from *Foucha* stating that the additional factor of mental abnormality in the statute effectively limited "involuntary civil confinement to those who suffer from a volitional impairment rendering them dangerous beyond their control."[50] Under *Hendricks,* we now know that civil commitment statutes for sexually violent predators are constitutionally permissible if they combine the traditional "dangerousness" criterium with some mental illness or "mental abnormality" that impairs, at minimum, volition (i.e., the ability to control oneself). For Hendricks, that disorder was his pedophilia.

In the wake of *Hendricks*, other states have followed the lead of Kansas by passing civil commitment laws for sexually dangerous offenders upon their parole from prison.[51] Some critics have argued that the civil commitment of sexual dangerous persons have "the topsy-turvy conversion of mental hospitals into prisons."[52] Others have pointed out that it makes little sense to incarcerate someone in prison for years during which time they are often not treated, and then expect the mental health community to treat them upon involuntary incarceration in a hospital.[53]

Where does the holding in *Hendricks* leave a definition of mental illness for civil commitment purposes, especially in light of *Foucha?* Brian J. Pollock wrote a thoughtful and provocative article aimed at answering that perplexing question.[54] He concluded the *Hendricks* majority dispensed with the need for a formal medical diagnosis so long as there is some deviant behavior that poses some danger that a person is unable to control—a type of impulsivity.[55] There need not even exist a medical treatment for whatever the condition might be.[56] He noted, however, that Justice O'Connor's concurring opinion offering the standard of "some medical justification" was somewhat more objective but still very deferential.

> For instance, the statute at issue in *Hendricks* did require some proof of a "condition" that affected volitional capacity to find a "mental abnormality"—mere impulsiveness was not enough. Hendricks suffered from pedophilia, a disorder recognized by the DSM-IV. Therefore, although

---

[49]In re Hendricks, 912 P.2d 129, 137-38 (Kan. 1996), *rev'd* Kansas v. Hendricks, 521 U.S. 346 (1997).

[50]*Hendricks*, 521 U.S. at 358.

[51]Steven I. Friedland, *on Treatment, Punishment, and the Civil Commitment of Sex Offenders*, 70 U. Colo. L. Rev. 73, 84-85 & n.50 (1999) (citing ARIZ. REV. STAT. ANN. 13-4601 to -4613 (West Supp. 1997); CAL. WELF. & INST. CODE 6600 to 6609.3 (West 1997); FLA. STAT. ANN. 775.21 (West 1997 & Supp. 1998); MINN. STAT. ANN. 253B.01-.23 (West 1997); WASH. REV. CODE ANN. 71.09.01-09.120 (West 1992 & Supp. 1998); WIS. STAT. ANN. 980.01-.13 (West Supp. 1997)).

[52]*Id.* at 76 (citing Rael Jean Isaac, Editorial, *Put Sex Predators Behind Bars, Not on the Couch*, WALL ST. J., May 8, 1998, at A14).

[53]*Id.* (citing statement of psychologist John Morin, *in* Francis Robles, *Sex Offender Bills Stir Debate: Proposals Would Keep Inmates Locked up Indefinitely*, MIAMI HERALD, Apr. 6, 1998, at 1B).

[54]Pollock, *supra* note 6, at 345-48 (some internal footnotes omitted; the footnotes cited in the indented quotation were in the original article).

[55]*Id.* at 345 (citing *Hendricks*, [521 U.S. at 358,] 117 S. Ct. at 2080).

[56]*Id.* at 345 (citing *Hendricks*, [521 U.S. at 366,] 117 S. Ct. at 2084. This conclusion is logical since Kansas confined sexual predators under its police power rather than under its *parens patriae* power. *See* Hendricks, 521 U.S. 357, 117 S. Ct. at 2079-80)).

the Court in *Hendricks* conceived of a new "impulsiveness" standard, the facts are more in line with Justice O'Connor's standard of "some medical justification."[57]

Pollack also argued that antisocial personality disorder fits within the impulsivity standard the *Hendricks* court appeared to adopt.[58] If that turns out to be so, states will be able to involuntarily commit many violent offenders under the *Hendricks* standard.[59] But Pollack doubts states will do so, opting instead for ever-increasing criminal sentences for violent offenders. His reason is simple. It is expensive to keep someone civilly committed in a hospital, often costing four to five times as much as the cost of incarceration in a penal setting.[60]

Practitioners and scholars of both law and mental health have criticized *Hendricks* standard of "mental abnormality" as being "much broader than any conceivable contemporary psychiatric diagnosis of mental disorder or mental illness. The definition is too... elastic. . . ."[61] The *Harvard Law Review* wrote the standard was "too broad, vague, and manipulable to function meaningfully in the civil commitment context."[62] It provides no guidance to lower courts seeking to determine if constitutional due process protections have been met in a given case, thereby invite abuse.[63] Some fear the nebulous standard could create a new class of people—"the uncontrollably dangerous, who can be detained indefinitely."[64] Others are concerned with the limited resources state mental health facilities have being overburdened by criminals at the expense of the mentally ill who need treatment.[65]

Kansas v. Hendricks did not address an evidentiary issue that became evident as the Kansas courts began to apply their statute within the framework of the Supreme Court's decision. The Court's focus on someone's inability to control himself left open the question of whether that was a necessary precondition to involuntary civil commitment for dangerous sexual predators. And, if it was, what levels of proof would be required for due process mandates to be satisfied? The Court addressed these questions in *Kansas v. Crane*.[66] In that case, the petitioner had been committed after a trial court had determined he suffered from a mental abnormality that made it likely he would reoffend. Crane, however, insisted that was an insufficient basis under *Kansas v. Hendricks* since the state had not proven that he lacked volitional control. The Kansas Supreme Court sided with Crane in light of the emphasis the Supreme Court had placed on volitional

---

[57]*Id.* at 346 (citing *Hendricks*, [521 U.S. at 359], 117 S. Ct. at 2081 (stating that legal definitions of terms of a medical nature do not have to fit precisely with the medical community's definitions).

[58]*Id.* at 348 (citing *Hendricks*, [521 U.S. at 358,] 117 S. Ct. at 2080).

[59]*Id.* at 348 (citing John Q. LaFond, *Washington's Sexually Violent Predator Law: A Deliberate Misuse of the Therapeutic State for Social Control*, 15 U. PUGET SOUND L. REV., 655, 701 (1992) (discussing the high cost of Washington's sexually violent predator commitment system); *see also* John Kip Cornwell, *Protection and Treatment: The Permissible Civil Detention of Sexual Predators*, 53 WASH. & LEE L. REV. 1293, 1334-35 (1996)).

[60]*E.g.*, Friedland, *supra* note 52, at 130-31 (citing annual costs of $100,000 per patient vs. $17,530 inmate in Florida, and $68,000 per patient vs. $15,331 per inmate in Washington) (internal citations omitted).

[61]Robert M. Wettstein, *A Psychiatric Perspective on Washington's Sexually Violent Predators*, 15 U. PUGET SOUND L. REV. 597, 602 (1992); Friedland, *supra* note 52, at 116; Richard I. Lanyon, *Scientific Status of the Concept of Continuing Emotional Propensity for Sexually Aberrant Acts*, 25 J. AM. ACAD. PSYCHIATRY L. 59, 60 (1997).

[62]*The Supreme Court, 1996 Term - Leading Cases*, 111 HARV. L. REV. 259, 267 (1997).

[63]Friedland, *supra* note 52, at 117; James D. Reardon, *Sexual Predators: Mental Illness or Abnormality? A Psychiatrist's Perspective*, 15 U. PUGET SOUND L. REV. 849, 851 (1992).

[64]*Id.* at 129.

[65]*Id.* at 132 (quoting California Superior Court Judge Harold Shabo, saying "You are diverting very scarce mental health resources to what is basically a criminal population," *in* Isaac, *supra* note 53, at A14).

[66]534 U.S. 407 (2002).

control in the *Hendricks* opinion.[67] On appeal, the U.S. Supreme Court constitutionalized the requirement of proof of volitional impairment on due process ground. The Court specifically rejected preventative civil detention based on dangerousness alone, thereby reaffirming the holding in *Foucha v. Louisiana*. But the Court noted that the state need not prove a "total or complete" lack of control since such a standard would be unworkable.[68] But the *Crane* opinion provides little guidance for understanding what quantum of proof is necessary.

> In recognizing that [lack of control is required], we did not give to the phrase "lack of control" a particularly narrow or technical meaning. And we recognize that in cases where lack of control is at issue, "inability to control behavior" will not be demonstrable with mathematical precision. It is enough to say that there must be proof of serious difficulty in controlling behavior. And this, when viewed in light of such features of the case as the nature of the psychiatric diagnosis, and the severity of the mental abnormality itself, must be sufficient to distinguish the dangerous sexual offender whose serious mental illness, abnormality, or disorder subjects him to civil commitment from the dangerous but typical recidivist convicted in an ordinary criminal case.[69]

The ambiguity of the Supreme Court's standard for proving volition impairment was quickly criticized. Stephen J. Morse, one of the leading scholars of the intersection of law and psychology, commented "there will be much legislative and judicial activity in the states about the definition of lack of control . . . ; the Supreme Court will ultimately have to provide more precise guidance."[70]

The full impact of *Hendricks* and *Crane* might take years to be felt. It is clear, however, that *Hendricks* has transformed the civil commitment terrain in a palpable way. The basis of civil commitment statutes in the pre-*Hendricks* era was treatment. After *Hendricks*, it has shifted to "the prevention of dangerousness, with treatment permissibly becoming an incidental and secondary objective."[71] Accordingly, we shift now to examine the meaning of dangerousness within the civil commitment context.

C. Defining Dangerousness

1. Dangerousness Generally

As mentioned earlier in this chapter, approximately thirty states provide for the involuntary commitment of the gravely disabled. All states, however, provide for the commitment of those who are mentally ill and "***dangerous.***" Dangerousness under the law comes in two forms: danger to self and danger to others. But from a clinical perspective, dangerousness is a classification that is highly problematic. "Dangerousness is the one characteristic of mental illness that [clinicians] are unable to predict with reasonable scientific certainty."[72] In fact, in reviewing the empirical literature on predicting dangerousness, Faust and Ziskin cite numerous studies that indicate

---

[67]In re Crane, 7 P.3d 285 (Kan. 2000).

[68]*Crane*, 534 U.S. at 411.

[69]*Id.*

[70]Stephen J. Morse, *Uncontrollable Urges and Irrational People*, 88 Va. L. Rev. 1025, 1033 (2002).

[71]Friedland, *supra* note 52, at 112.

[72]Joseph T. Carney, Note, *America's Mentally Ill: Tormented Without Treatment* 3 Geo. Mason U. Civ. Rts. L.J. 181, 198 (1992).

clinicians are incorrect in their predictions of dangerousness in more than two of every three cases.[73]

Advocates of the mentally ill have repeated called for replacement of the dangerousness standard with one that examines the severity of the person's mental illness.[74] But such calls for reform have had little effect on the law governing civil commitment, as the dangerousness standard is deeply ingrained in American jurisprudence on this issue of law.[75]

Dangerousness is universally concerned with physical harm to oneself or to others.[76] Nearly all states require that proof of dangerousness, whether specifically directed at harm to self or harm to others, be concerned with the immediate future, not at some time down the road. This time requirement is usually expressed in statutes of necessitation of showing that the person is "*imminently* dangerous."[77] Much to the dismay of civil rights activists, testimony satisfies this requirement in most U.S. jurisdictions.[78] But in a handful of states, a finding of imminent dangerousness requires some ***overt act*** as evidence that the person to be committed presents a "clear and present danger" to self or others.[79] This overt act requirement usually requires some demonstrable homicidal, suicidal, or assaultive behavior, or threats to the same effect.[80]

Additionally, many states limit the involuntary commitment of persons to those who are in need of treatment. This requirement, however, may be somewhat hollow.[81] The need for treatment, whether incorporated into the definition of mental illness, the definition of gravely disabled, or made a separate criterium for civil commitment, may be tautological given the other commitment criteria, specifically the requirements of both a mental illness and of dangerousness. To ensure that the lack of an effective treatment for a particular clinical disorder (i.e., "treatability") does not stand in the way of committing those who pose a danger to themselves or to others, some states have specifically provided that the need and availability of treatment should not impact the judicial determination to commit someone who otherwise meets commitment criteria.[82]

---

[73]David Faust & Jay Ziskin, *The Expert Witness in Psychology and Psychiatry*, 241 SCI. 31, 32 (1988); *see also* Joseph J. Cocozza & Henry J. Steadman, *The Failure of Psychiatric Predictions of Dangerousness: Clear and Convincing Evidence*, 29 RUTGERS L. REV. 1084, 1094-1101 (1976); Bruce J. Ennis & Thomas R. Litwack, *Psychiatry and the Presumption of Expertise: Flipping Coins in the Courtroom*, 62 CAL. L. REV. 693, 711-16 (1974) (arguing, as implied by the title of the article, that predictions of future dangerousness are analogous to a coin flip in terms of their accuracy).

[74]Carney, *supra* note 73, at 198-200.

[75]*See, e.g.,* O'Connor v. Donaldson, 422 U.S. 563, 575 (1975) (holding "dangerousness" is a prerequisite for indefinite civil confinement); Jackson v. Indiana, 406 U.S. 715 (1972) (holding that incapacity to stand trial, without dangerousness, is not a constitutionally sufficient ground for indefinite commitment).

[76]A few states include "substantial damage to property" in their definition of dangerousness if the harm is "of such a value and extent that the state's interest in protecting the property from such harm outweighs the person's interest in personal liberty." KAN. STAT. ANN. § 59-2946(f)(3) (Supp. 1997); *see also* N.D. Century Code § 25-03.1-02(11)(d) (Supp. 1997).

[77]*E.g.,* HAW. REV. STAT. § 334-60.2(2) (1997) .

[78]*See, e.g.,* In re Melton, 597 A.2d 892, 894-95 (D.C. 1991) (upholding commitment based on psychiatric prediction of dangerousness that relied almost exclusively on hearsay information supplied by family members, not a clinical evaluation).

[79]*See* Reed Groethe, Comment, *Overt Dangerous Behavior as a Constitutional Requirement for Involuntary Civil Commitment of the Mentally Ill*, 44 U. CHI. L. REV. 562, 576-79 (1977); John Q. La Fond, *An Examination of the Purposes of Involuntary Civil Commitment*, 30 BUFF. L. REV. 499, 502 (1981); *see also, e.g.,* Wyatt v. King, 781 F. Supp. 750, 753 (M.D. Ala. 1991); In re Harris, 654 P.2d 109, 113 (Wash. 1982) (en banc); Doremus v. Farrell, 407 F. Supp. 509, 514-15 (D. Neb. 1975).

[80]*See, e.g.,* ARK. STAT. ANN. § 20-47-207(c)(1) (Supp. 1997); PA. CONS. STAT. § 7301(1) (Supp. 1997).

[81]*See* A. LOUIS MCGARRY, ET AL., CIVIL COMMITMENT AND SOCIAL POLICY: AN EVALUATION OF THE MASSACHUSETTS MENTAL HEALTH REFORM ACT OF 1970 50-53 (1981).

[82]*See, e.g.,* ALA. CODE § 22-52-10.4(b) (Supp. 1997).

2. Things Clinicians Look for When Determining Dangerousness

Overall, clinicians tend to err on the side of caution when making predictions of dangerousness. An extensive review of the criteria clinicians often use when assessing a potential commitment for dangerous is beyond the scope of this text. However, a few generalizations might be useful to students of forensic psychology in coming to understand the scope of the label "dangerous."

The best predictor of future dangerousness is prior behavior (i.e., past dangerousness).[83] Other important criteria is lack of family stability; high impulsivity; alcohol or drug use; impaired cognition or affect that predisposes the person to cope with stress in a violent matter; impaired judgment; the adequacy of defense mechanisms; emotional withdrawal; hallucinatory behavior; current circumstances and stressors, including the presence or lack of a family network; whether the person has a "plan" to carry-out the actions/desires expressed; and the "means" the person intends to use in implementing the "plan" of action.[84]

3. Specifics of *Parens Patriae* Dangerousness: Danger to Self

As discussed above, involuntarily committing someone because he or she poses a danger to himself or herself stems from the state's *parens patriae* authority. But what constitutes being a danger to oneself? Some states do not define the term at all, simply stating one is a danger to oneself if he or she is "likely to injury himself."[85] In an attempt to clarify this ambiguous statement, Idaho has added a definition of the phase to its statutes:

> Likely to injure himself . . . shall mean . . . a substantial risk that physical harm will be inflicted by the proposed patient upon his own person, as evidenced by threats or attempts to commit suicide or inflict physical harm on himself. . . . [86]

Other states set forth more descriptive criteria, although in doing so, they are not necessarily more definitive. Consider Pennsylvania's statute:

> Clear and present danger to [self] shall be shown by establishing that within the past 30 days:
> (i) the person has acted in such manner as to evidence that he would be unable, without care, supervision and the continued assistance of others, to satisfy his need for nourishment, personal or medical care, shelter, or self-protection and safety, and that there is a reasonable probability that death, serious bodily injury or serious physical debilitation would ensue within 30 days unless adequate treatment were afforded under this act; or
> (ii) the person has attempted suicide and that there is the reasonable probability of suicide unless adequate treatment is afforded under this act. For the purposes of this subsection, a clear and present danger may be demonstrated by the proof

---

[83]Bartol & Bartol, *supra* note 20, at 158 (citing John Monahan, *Risk Assessment of Violence: The MacArthur Research*, 24 CORRECTIONAL PSYCHOLOGIST 1, 2 (1992); John Monahan, *Mental Disorder and Violent Behavior*, 47 AM. PSYCHOLOGIST 511, 512 (1992)); *see also* Deidre Klassen & William A. O'Connor, *A Prospective Study of Predictors of Violence in Adult Male Mental Health Admissions*, 12 LAW & HUM. BEHAV. 143, 147 (1988); Randy K. Otto, *Prediction of Dangerous Behavior: A Review and Analysis of "Second-Generation" Research*, 5 FORENSIC REP. 103, 118 (1992).

[84]*See* MELTON, ET AL., *supra* note 32, at 235-38.

[85]*E.g.,* UTAH CODE ANN. § 62A-12-232(1)(a)(ii) (Supp. 1997). Most states that used to use this term, like Alaska, Florida, and West Virginia, have modernized their statutes and now use language more like the Pennsylvania statute reproduced in this sub-section.

[86]IDAHO CODE § 66-317(L) (Supp. 1997).

that the person has made threats to commit suicide and has committed acts
which are in furtherance of the threat to commit suicide; or
(iii) the person has substantially mutilated himself or attempted to mutilate
himself substantially and that there is the reasonable probability of mutilation
unless adequate treatment is afforded under this act. For the purposes of this
subsection, a clear and present danger shall be established by proof that the
person has made threats to commit mutilation and has committed acts which are
in furtherance of the threat to commit mutilation.[87]

Nearly all of the "danger to self" provisions of civil commitment statutes include: contemplate suicide; severe, self-inflicted bodily harm; and attempts to harm oneself by provoking others to induce or inflict the harm. Some states, as illustrated by the Pennsylvania statues reproduced above, also include criteria regarding the inability to care for one's basic needs in their definition of dangerousness to self. The jurisdictions that include such nonsuicidal behavior in their danger-to-self statutes tend to be those states that do not specifically have "grave disability" civil commitment criteria.[88] The self-neglect criteria always targets the inability to provide for one's survival needs (e.g., food, clothing, shelter, etc.).[89] Sometimes, it also provides for the commitment of persons who are presently able to provide for their survival needs, but show a level of inattention to their deteriorating mental and physical health such that, if not committed now, commitment in the future might be too late.[90]

Of course, whether under a "gravely disabled" or a nonsuicidal "danger-to-self" statutory provision, those who are homeless present special problems in the civil commitment arena. A certain level of self-neglect is inevitable when someone is homeless. For a homeless person to be involuntarily committed, though, it must be shown that he or she is "gravely disabled" or presents an imminent danger to self *as a result of a mental illness*. This determination, however, is not always clear or easy. Before considering the complications these abstract legal standards often raise when being applied, though, a brief discussion of the danger to others standard is in order.

4. Specifics of Police Power Dangerousness: Danger to Others

Civil commitment on the basis of danger to self is rooted in the states' police power. It concerns preventive detention of the mentally ill—confinement based on a prediction of antisocial behavior rather than conviction of crime.[91] It usually requires a showing similar to that required by this Pennsylvania statute:

---

[87]PA. CONS. STAT. § 7301(2) (Supp. 1997).

[88]MELTON, ET AL., *supra* note 32, at 223.

[89]*E.g.,* Cal. Code § 5800(h)(2)-(3) ("gravely disabled" means a condition in which a person, as a result of impairment by chronic alcoholism, is unable to provide for his or her basic personal needs for food, clothing, or shelter, [but] . . . does not include mentally retarded persons by reason of being mentally retarded alone).

[90]*E.g.,* ALA. CODE § 22-52-10.4(a) (Supp. 1997); ALASKA STAT. § 47.30.915(7)(b) (Supp. 1997); KAN. STAT. ANN. § 59-2946(f)(3) (Supp. 1997); MINN. STAT. ANN. § 253B.065(5)(b)(3)(ii) (Supp. 1997); MONT. CODE. ANN. § 53-21-126(d); WASH. REV. CODE § 71.05.020(8) (Supp. 1997).

[91]*See generally* O'Connor v. Donaldson, 422 U.S. 563 (1975).

> Clear and present danger to others shall be shown by establishing that within the past 30 days the person has inflicted or attempted to inflict serious bodily harm on another and that there is a reasonable probability that such conduct will be repeated.[92]

As this statute illustrates, danger to others can require both a showing of some demonstrable behavior (an "overt act") that is homicidal or assaultive in nature, or, at minimum, a showing of threats to the same effect.[93] But the requirement of an overt act varies from state to state.[94] In addition to factors such as the magnitude of the potential harm to others, relevant factors include the probability that the harm will occur (most states only require proof that the person is "likely" or "probable" or "more likely than not" to be a danger to others); the frequency with which the harm may occur (if frequency is relevant); and the imminence of the harm.

When a person has engaged in conduct that may be interpreted as harmful to others (even in jurisdictions that do not require overt acts), even if such a causal determination is weak as illustrated by alternative explanations for such behaviors, the courts are likely to err on the side of safety and uphold a civil commitment.

D. The Least Restrictive Alternatives Requirement

Nearly all states authorize civil commitment of one who is mentally ill and dangerous only if involuntary hospitalization is the ***"least restrictive means"*** of protecting the person from himself or herself, or protecting society from the person. Nevada's statute well illustrates this point:

> Before issuing an order for involuntary admission or a renewal thereof, the court shall explore other alternative courses of treatment within the least restrictive appropriate environment as suggested by the evaluation team who evaluated the person, or other persons professionally qualified in the field of psychiatric mental health, which the court believes may be in the best interests of the person.[95]

What is meant by "least restrictive environment" is rarely defined. Generally, it means "acquiring or providing services, including protective services, for the shortest duration and to the minimum extent necessary to remedy or prevent situations of actual mistreatment or self-neglect."[96] Inpatient hospitalization is considered to be the most restrictive environment, but alternatives that fall short of hospitalization may fail to meet the medical needs of a person who is mentally ill and either dangerous or gravely disabled.[97]

IV. DUE PROCESS IN CIVIL COMMITMENT PROCEEDINGS

Due process of law is a flexible, perhaps even impalpable, concept.[98] *Black's Law Dictionary* defines it as "[a] course of legal proceedings according to those rules and principles which have

---

[92]PA. CONS. STAT. § 7301(1) (Supp. 1997).

[93]*Id; see also, e.g.,* ARK. STAT. ANN. § 20-47-207(c)(1) (Supp. 1997); MONT. CODE. ANN. § 53-21-126(d).

[94]*See, e.g.,* In re Albright, 836 P.2d 1, 5-6 (Kan. Ct. App. 1992) (upholding commitment without recent, overtly dangerous act); Hatcher v. Wachtel, 269 S.E.2d 849, 852 (W. Va. 1980) (same).

[95]NEV. REV. STAT. ANN. § 433A-137 (Supp. 1997).

[96]COLO. REV. STAT. § 26-3.1-101 (3) (Supp. 1997).

[97]*See. e.g.,* MELTON, ET AL., *supra* note 32, at 224-25.

[98]*E.g.,* Morrissey v. Brewer, 408 U.S. 471, 481 (1972).

been established in our systems of jurisprudence for the enforcement and protection of private rights."[99] More simply stated, it is a guarantee of fairness in judicial proceedings. Given the deprivation of liberty that is associated with an involuntary civil commitment, those subjected to the process are entitled to procedural safeguards to ensure their rights are being honored.

A. Minimal Procedural Processes That Are Due

Due process requires, at minimum: (1) notice of the commitment hearing given in sufficient time to allow the person to prepare for the hearing;[100] (2) the right to assistance of counsel;[101] (3) the opportunity to be heard, to present testimony, and confront witnesses; [102] (4) the right to periodic review of one's commitment;[103] and (5) the right to be placed in the least restrictive environment.[104]

At the hearing, the state must prove that the person is mentally ill and either dangerous or gravely disabled (if applicable) before someone may be involuntarily committed. As part of due process, the Supreme Court mandated in *Addington v. Texas*[105] that the quantum of proof necessary on both criteria (i.e., mental illness and dangerous and/or grave disability) is clear and convincing evidence.[106]

Some notable rights, however, do not generally apply unless specifically guaranteed by the provisions of a particular state's law, such as the right to a jury determination. In fact, most jurisdictions allow a judge to make the determination and the Supreme Court has hinted that even less formal procedures might be constitutionally sufficient, especially if a minor is the one to be committed.[107] To protect the privacy rights of the person whose commitment is being sought, though, most states do not allow commitments proceedings to be open to the public.

Unlike in criminal trials where the accused's right to be present is only abridged if he or she is too disruptive to the proceedings, the person to be committed may have his or her presence at the hearing denied if it is shown, by clear and convincing evidence, that his or her presence would be harmful to his or her person.[108]

Unless state laws provide otherwise, most legally recognized privileges do not apply in the civil commitment arena. For example, despite the fact that the privilege against self-

---

[99]BLACK'S LAW DICTIONARY 500 (6th ed. 1990).

[100]Vitek v. Jones, 445 U.S. 480, 494 (1980).

[101]*Id.*

[102]*Id.*

[103]Lessard v. Schmidt,, 349 F. Supp. 1078 (E.D. Wis. 1972), *vacated and remanded on procedural grounds*, 414 U.S. 473 (1974).

[104]*Id.*

[105]441 U.S. 418 (1979).

[106]*Id.* at 431-33; *see also* In re Irwin, 529 N.W.2d 366, 374 (Minn. Ct. App. 1995) (citing statutory requirement of clear and convincing evidence); *cf.* Heller v. Doe, 113 S. Ct. 2637, 2644 (1993) (upholding Kentucky's higher burden of proof standard for commitment of the mentally ill than for the mentally retarded). A defendant acquitted of a criminal charge on the basis of an insanity defense, however, may be committed to a psychiatric facility on that basis, even though the defense was established by a "preponderance of the evidence," rather than by "clear and convincing" evidence. Jones v. United States, 463 U.S. 354, 366-68 (1983).

[107]*See Parham v. J.R.*, 442 U.S. 584, 607 (1979) (upholding commitment of children under the orders of a psychiatrists, not judges, so long as the clinician was free to evaluate the child "independently"). *But cf.,* In re R.M., 889 P.2d 1201, 1204 (Mont. 1995) (finding violation of due process where the same person who filed the commitment petition also conducted the patient's examination).

[108]*See generally* Davidson, *Mental Hospitals & The Civil Liberties Dilemma*, 51 MENTAL HYGIENE 371, 374 (1967).

incrimination "not only permits a person to refuse to testify against himself at a criminal trial in which he is the defendant, but also privileges him not to answer official questions put to him in any other proceeding, civil or criminal, formal or informal, where the answers might incriminate him in future criminal proceedings," the Supreme Court held in *Allen v. Illinois* that it does not apply in civil commitment proceedings.[109] Similarly, many states allow hearsay at civil commitment proceedings, but other states have held the formal rules of evidence apply.

B. Preservation of Other Rights: Commitment Not Linked to Competency

In the great majority of jurisdictions, involuntary commitment is not determinative of competency in a wide variety of areas.[110] Thus, until the person is adjudicated to be incompetent in separate proceedings and has a guardian appointed, he or she is usually competent to manage affairs; contract; hold professional, occupational, or vehicle licenses; marry or divorce; register and vote; make a will. In many states, though, an involuntarily hospitalized person does lose the right to refuse treatment.[111]

C. Emergency Detentions and Screening Mechanisms

Nearly all states permit, under appropriate circumstances, the emergency hospitalization of an individual without any prior formal legal hearing. Most jurisdictions only require the decision maker (usually a police officer or a clinician) to have probable cause to believe the person is mentally ill and is a danger to self or to others.[112]

Although the lack of procedural due process associated with an initial emergency admission may appear to be problematic, such minimal processes are rarely challenged since anything more restrictive would be counter-productive in emergency situations. The formal due process protections described above do not attach until a person is hospitalized or until more than a temporary, emergency commitment is being sought. But, even still, a person detained on an emergency basis still has due process rights to more formal adjudication proceedings, usually within a very short period of time such as forty-eight or seventy-two hours.[113]

V. CONCLUSION

Not surprisingly, the scope of one's substantive due process rights in the civil commitment area is unclear. We know from *Jackson v. Indiana*[114] that mental illness alone, without some showing of dangerousness to self or others, is constitutionally insufficient to involuntarily commit someone in violation of their liberty rights under the Fourteenth Amendment's Due Process Clause. Conversely, from *Foucha v. Louisiana*,[115] we thought we knew that if one is dangerous,

---

[109]478 U.S. 364 (1986)

[110]*E.g.,* HAW. REV. STAT. § 334-61 (1997).

[111]*See generally* Stransky, *supra* note 1.

[112]*See, e.g.,* FLA. STAT. 394.463(2)(a)(2) ("A law enforcement officer shall take a person who appears to meet the criteria for involuntary examination into custody . . . for examination.").

[113]FLA. STAT. 394.463(2)(c) (Supp. 1997) (72 hours).

[114]406 U.S. 715 (1972).

[115]504 U.S. 71 (1992).

but not mentally ill, that one cannot be involuntarily committed. But *Kansas v. Hendricks*[116] created a great uncertainly somewhere in between the two extremes of *Jackson* and *Foucha,* allowing for the involuntary civil commitment of dangerous people who have some sort of "mental abnormality"—the precise definition of which has yet to be defined. But from *Kansas v. Crane,*[117] it appears a qualifying mental abnormality alone, even coupled with dangerousness, may be insufficient without also showing some sort of volition control impairment that contributes to the likelihood of future dangerousness, at least when civil commitment proceedings are instituted against dangerous sexual predators. Moreover, some proof of volition impairment will be necessary as well, although it remains an open question whether such impairment will be able to be inferred from diagnosis alone, or whether some quantum of independent proof will be necessary to satisfy the due process mandates of *Crane.*[118]

In addition to the constitutional due process guarantee that one cannot be deprived of one's liberty via civil commitment proceedings without the requisite showing of a mental illness and dangerousness, some states have enacted other rights. These include: (1) the right to treatment while in custody; (2) the right to a clean and safe environment; and (3) the right to communicate with the outside world.[119]

Finally, we know from *Addington v. Texas* that proof of mental illness and dangerousness must rise to the level of clear and convincing evidence before one can be involuntarily committed. But as discussed in some detail earlier in this chapter, what constitutes a mental illness and what constitutes dangerousness are matters that are without clear legal resolution to date.

---

[116]521 U.S. 346 (1997).

[117]*See* Kansas v. Crane, 534 U.S. 407 (2002).

[118]*Id.*

[119]For a thoughtful examination of some of these rights, *see, e.g.,* Stransky, *supra* note 1; *see also* Grant H. Morris, *Judging Judgment: Assessing the Competence of Mental Patients to Refuse Treatment,* 32 SAN DIEGO L. REV. 343 (1995).

CHAPTER NINE
CIVIL COMPETENCIES

I. INTRODUCTION TO THE NOTION OF CIVIL COMPETENCY

Much of this textbook has been devoted to the intersection of the mental health professions with the criminal law. In the last chapter, however, we addressed one of the most important areas of forensic psychology in the civil law area: civil commitment. In this chapter, we explore the concept of *civil competency*—the legal capacity to decide or to perform certain functions. Psychologists and psychiatrists are likely to play a significant role in a variety of areas of civil law when someone's competency is called into question.

It should be noted that the very notion of civil capacity exists for reasons of social control. "Unlike other policing mechanisms, however, the capacity doctrine requires courts to identify the abilities that are necessary for the exercise of contractual and donative choices."[1] Some would argue this form of formal social control violates the principles of autonomy and self-determination.[2] Others see the social control functions of civil capacity as being paternalistic, yet necessary to protect impaired persons from economically harming themselves.[3]

The law defines competency in different ways. Nearly all state statutes are modeled on one of the two following model statutes, both of which emphasize the nature and quality of the cognitive processes.

The Uniform Probate Code defines an *incompetent person* as:

> Any person who is impaired by reason of mental illness, mental deficiency, physical illness or disability, advanced age . . . or other cause (except minority) to the extent that he lacks sufficient understanding or capacity to make or communicate responsible decisions concerning his person.[4]

In contrast, the American Bar Association Model Statute on Incompetency authorizes guardianship only for

> [A]dults whose ability to receive and evaluate information effectively and/or to communicate decisions is impaired to such an extent that they lack the capacity to manage their physical health or safety.[5]

As with other areas of the law defining competency, neither formulation is particularly clear. Somewhat more refined definitions exist in particular areas of civil competency (e.g., definition

---

[1]Alexander M. Meiklejohn, *Contractual and Donative Capacity*, 39 CASE W. RES. 307, 308 (1989).

[2]*E.g.*, Alexander & Szasz, *From Contract to Status via Psychiatry*, 13 SANTA CLARA L. REV. 537 (1973).

[3]*E.g.*, Melvin Eisenberg, *The Bargain Principle and Its Limits*, 95 HARV. L. REV. 741, 748 (1982); Melvin Eisenberg, *Donative Promises*, 47 U. CHI. L. REV. 1, 5 (1979).

[4]Uniform Probate Code § 5 (4th ed. 1975) (Nat'l Conf. Comm'rs on Uniform State Law); *see, e.g.,* ARIZ. REV. STAT. § 14-5101(1).

[5]RALPH REISNER & CHRISTOPHER SLOBOGIN, LAW AND THE MENTAL HEALTH SYSTEM: CIVIL AND CRIMINAL ASPECTS 830 (2d ed. 1990) (citing American Bar Ass'n, Ch. 1, § 3); *see, e.g.,* N.J. STAT. ANN. § 3B:1-2 ("lacks sufficient capacity to govern himself and manage his affairs").

of testamentary capacity), but in general, the criteria for evaluating most civil competencies are quite ambiguous, leaving much latitude for the exercise of judicial discretion.

II. CAPACITY TO CONTRACT

A. Lack of Voluntary Assent Generally

To the layperson, the notion of a contract often involves signatures on formally prepared papers. But a contract is, in essence, very simple. It is nothing more than a bargained-for exchange of promises. Contrary to popular belief, contracts need not be in writing; oral contracts are as legally binding as written ones. Proving the terms of an oral contract in a court of law, however, is quite difficult compared to proving the terms of a written contract. But whether oral or written, what really differentiates a contract from any set of promises is the law's willingness to enforce the promises.[6] Of course, for the law to enforce a promise, one must have had the legal *capacity to contract* at the time the promise was made.

Defining a contract as a legally enforceable set of promises should, by necessary implication, allow one to deduce that there are sets of promises the law will not enforce. The law, for example, would not enforce a contract procured by fraud[7] or entered into under duress (e.g., at gunpoint).[8] Nor would the law enforce a murder-for-hire contract (a "hit") since the terms of the contract require the performance of a crime.[9] Illegal contracts, however, are only one example of contracts that are not enforceable at law. The class of contracts that are not legally enforceable that generally involve the mental health community are those contract which lack *voluntary assent*.

Voluntary assent is a precondition to all contracts.[10] It is based, in part, on the autonomy principle—"the sense that people should be free to order their own affairs by agreement. It is because the promisor has freely and voluntarily bound himself by agreement that the commitment should be given the force of law."[11] It is the premise of knowingly, freely, and voluntarily binding oneself to a contract that forms the basis of numerous defenses to a charge of breach of contract. Since one must have the mental capacity to contract knowingly, freely, and voluntarily in order to legally enter into contractual obligations, a lack of such mental capacity can negate a contract on the grounds that a promise was tainted by a lack of voluntary assent.[12]

The Second Restatement on Contracts provides:

> Section 12 - Capacity to Contract
> (2) A natural person who manifests assent to a transaction has full legal capacity to incur contractual duties thereby unless he is:
> (a) under guardianship;
> (b) an infant;

---

[6]Restatement (Second) of Contracts § 1 (1979).

[7]Arthur Rosett, Contract Law and Its Application 140-43 (4th ed. 1988).

[8]*Id.* at 111-19.

[9]Lawrence Kalevitch, *Contract, Will & Social Practice*, 3 J.L. & Pol'y 379, 388 (1995).

[10]1 E. Allan Farnsworth, Contracts, § 3.1, at 160 (2d ed. 1990).

[11]Rosett, *supra* note 7, at 94-95.

[12]*Id.* at 95.

(c) mentally ill or defective; or

(d) intoxicated.

The Restatement goes on to define a "mental illness or defect" as interfering with one's ability "to understand in a reasonable manner the nature and consequences of the transaction, or . . . is unable to act in a reasonable manner in relation to the transaction and the other party has reason to know of his condition."[13]

Unlike in the areas of criminal capacities in which there is great judicial deference to the opinions of mental health experts,[14] determinations regarding the capacity to contract do not unduly rely on or defer to expert testimony.[15] Instead, courts tend to assess the capacity to contract based on everyday notions of disability impairment, such as "forgetfulness, particularly of recent events, . . . disorientation with respect to time or place, . . . confusion, . . . [and] rambling or fragmented conversation. . . . Alcoholism is relevant, as is erratic or imprudent behavior. [And] while an occasional opinion indicates that eccentricity is evidence of incapacity . . . eccentric behavior per se is irrelevant."[16] Similarly, low intelligence, in and of itself, is not relevant, but "evidence of severely impaired intellect is probative" of incapacity to contract.

B. Contracts for those Under Guardianship/Conservatorship

"A person has no capacity to incur contractual duties if his property is under guardianship by reason of an adjudication of mental illness or defect."[17] Accordingly, if one's property is under guardianship/conservatorship, one is presumed to lack the capacity to contract.[18] Guardianship is discussed more fully later in this chapter.

C. Infancy and Contracts

Infancy is the term contact law uses to refer to minors. At common law, those under the age of twenty-one were considered minors, but today, virtually all states define infants as those under the age of eighteen.[19] Since the thirteenth century, the doctrine of infancy has allowed minors to legally avoid performance on most contracts they might make. The doctrine is based on the notion that "children are naive and unsophisticated, especially in the marketplace."[20] It also protects children from "foolishly squandering their wealth through improvident contracts with crafty adults."[21] These underlying rationales are likely more paternalistic towards children than

---

[13]RESTATEMENT (SECOND) OF CONTACTS § 15(1)(a)-(b).

[14]*See generally* Chapter Five.

[15]Meiklejohn, *supra* note 1, at 318-32; *see also* Milton Green, *Proof of Mental Incompetency and the Unexpressed Major Premise*, 53 YALE L.J. 271 (1944).

[16]*Id.* at 342 (internal string citations to caselaw omitted).

[17]RESTATEMENT (SECOND) OF CONTRACTS § 13 (1979).

[18]Meiklejohn, *supra* note 1, at 379.

[19]Larry A. DiMatteo, *Deconstructing the Myth of the "Infancy Law Doctrine": From Incapacity to Accountability*, 21 OHIO N.U.L. REV. 481, 484 n.2 (1994) (citing, *inter alia*, ROBERT NEIL CORLEY, ET AL., THE LEGAL AND REGULATORY ENVIRONMENT OF BUSINESS (9th ed. 1993)).

[20]Robert E. Richardson, *Children and the Recorded-Message Industry: The Need for a New Doctrine*, 72 VA. L.R. 1325, 1332-33 (1986).

[21]DiMatteo, *supra* note 19, at 487.

they ought to be. Research in developmental psychology suggests that minors are more competent to make a variety of decisions than the law gives them credit for.[22]

Historically, the infancy doctrine render all contracts entered into by minors *void ab initio*—"null from the beginning . . . ."[23] By the turn of the twentieth century, however, the infancy doctrine was softened to ease the harshness of the rule.[24] Under modern law's formulation of the infancy doctrine, if an adult enters into a contract with a minor, that adult must perform on the contractual obligation. But it does not go both ways; the minor need not perform on the contract because the contract is *voidable* by the minor only. In other words, to protect those who might enter into contractual obligations who, by reason of their lack of maturity, might not have a full understanding of the nature of the obligation, they are able to "back out" at any time while they are still under the age of majority, or within a reasonable time of reaching age of majority.[25]

There are limits on the general rule of voidability of contracts for minors, such as when a minor fraudulently misrepresents his or her age, or when the law imposes certain contractual duties upon minors. Although the technicalities of these exceptions to the infancy doctrine are beyond the scope of this textbook, two such exceptions bear brief mention since they potentially in theory, albeit rarely in practice, involve forensic clinical opinion. The first of these two is called the "rule of necessaries."

This *necessaries* doctrine requires minors to pay for goods or services that are necessary for life. For example, if a fourteen-year-old walked into a diner, ordered a meal, and then sought to leave without paying under the infancy doctrine, that minor would be unsuccessful in avoiding the contractual obligation to pay for the food order since food is a necessity for life. While items as such as food, clothing, medical services, and education might easily be classified as necessaries,[26] what is a necessary is a question of fact that often leaves courts struggling with determinations regarding that which is necessary for a minor. Is a car a necessary for a teenager who is dependent on it to go to work and school?[27] Although rare, forensic mental health expert testimony assessing the minor's views on the necessity of something could potentially be used in a civil action for breach of contract or restitution.

The other exception to the infancy doctrine where forensic mental health practitioners might be called upon to conduct an evaluation of a minor concerns the "benefits rule."[28] Some courts have taken to a case-by-case determination regarding the voidability of contracts entered into by minors, examining the benefits the minor received from having entered into the given contract. This extension of the necessaries doctrine posits that it is unfair to allow minors to bestow upon themselves certain benefits via the operation of the infancy doctrine. Accordingly, although the

[22]*See, e.g.,* Gary B. Melton, *Taking* Gault *Seriously: Toward a New Juvenile Court*, 68 NEB. L. REV. 146, 153 (1989) ("Piagetian theory implied that adolescents, at least by age fourteen, would not differ from adults on average in their ability to comprehend and weigh risks and benefits of personal decisions"); Andrew Walkover, *The Infancy Defense in the New Juvenile Court*, 31 UCLA L. REV. 502 (1984).

[23]*Id.* at 486 (citing Hall v. Butterfield, 59 N.H. 354 (1879); BLACK'S LAW DICTIONARY 1574 (6th ed. 1990)).

[24]*Id.*

[25]*See* RESTATEMENT (SECOND) OF CONTRACTS § 14.

[26]DiMatteo, *supra* note 19, at 489.

[27]*See id.* (*comparing* Harwell Motor Company v. Cunningham, 337 S.W.2d 765 (Tenn. Ct. App. 1959); Rodrigeuz v. Northern Auto Auction, Inc., 225 N.Y.S.2d 107 (Sup. Ct. 1962); Creer v. Active Automobile Exchange, 121 A. 888 (Conn. 1923); and Drennen Motorcar Co. v. Smith, 160 So. 761 (Ala. 1935); *with* Dodson by Dodson v. Shrader, 824 S.W.2d 545 (Tenn. 1992)).

[28]*Id.* at 490-92.

minor may technically still avoid performance on a contract, the minor may still be liable in an action for restitution.

In an action for restitution, the minor may have to minimize the economic damage he or she caused the other party to the contract by repaying the fair value of the benefit received by the minor when he or she entered into the contract. The rationale for doing so is not only to "protect the innocent adult who enters into a fair and reasonable transaction with a minor[, but also because] . . . a given minor may possess the maturity, experience, and sophistication that would render the application of the voidability rule an injustice.[29] Forensic clinical evaluation of these factors as applied to a particular minor might be helpful for either side in an action for restitution brought against the minor. They are, however, rare, given the expense of clinical evaluation in comparison to the amount of restitution that might be at issue in a given case.

D. Contracting With The Mentally Ill

The law generally allows one who lacks the mental capacity to contract to avoid (i.e., "get out of") his or her contractual obligations. There are exceptions to this rule that involve intricacies of contract law that are beyond the scope of this textbook. For our purposes, though, it is important to know that mental health professional may be called upon by lawyers to assess a person's capacity to contract.

As the Restatement specifies, this capacity involves both cognitive and affective components insofar as one must "understand . . . the nature and consequences" of the contractual obligation. If one does not so understand, he or she may void a contract, even if the other party did not know (nor had reason to know) of the mental illness.[30] Such understanding goes beyond cognitive knowledge; it even goes beyond basic cognitive understanding. If a mental illness or defect precludes a person from making a reasonable decision under the circumstances, a contract may be deemed voidable under this doctrine.[31] Using this reasonability standard, courts looks to whether the person entered into a transaction that "a reasonably competent person might have made."[32] In applying this objective standard, issues of fairness, especially business fairness, are quite important to the determination of reasonability.[33]

As a caveat to the reader, you should know there are other doctrines of contract law beyond the scope of this text that act to mitigate the harshness of this rule when the non-impaired party to the contract did not have reason to know of the mental illness or defect, and performed his or her obligation in reliance on the existence of the contract.[34] Therefore, caution should be taken

---

[29]*Id.* at 487-88 (internal citations omitted).

[30]RESTATEMENT (SECOND) OF CONTRACTS § 15(1)(a) (1979); *see also* Rosett, *supra* note 7, at 96-88.

[31]Rosett, *supra* note 7, at 98-108 (*citing and analyzing* Ortelere v. Teachers' Retirement Board of New York, 25 N.Y.2d 196, 303 N.Y.S.2d 362, 250 N.E.2d 460 (1969)).

[32]RESTATEMENT (SECOND) OF CONTRACTS § 15, comment b (1979).

[33]Meiklejohn, *supra* note 1, at 316; *see also* Green, *supra* note 15, at 305. The role of fairness has been criticized by some who attack this part of the competency doctrine as a paternalistic invasion of personal freedom. *See* Alexander & Szasz, supra note 2, at 547 (arguing self-determination has been "swallowed up in the battle between protecting transactions and protecting incompetents").

[34]*See, e.g.*, RESTATEMENT (SECOND) OF CONTRACTS § 15(2) (1979) ("Where the contract is made on fair terms and the other party is without knowledge of the mental illness or defect, the [incompetent person's power to avoid the contract] terminates to the extent that the contract has been so performed in whole or in part or the circumstances have so changed that avoidance would be unjust. In such a case a court may grant relief as justice requires).

not to presume the entirety of the law on voidable contracts when dealing with mental illness is presented in this short section of this text.

E. Intoxication and Contracts

Because the decision to become intoxicated is a voluntary one, courts are generally hostile to allowing one to escape contractual obligations based on intoxication.[35] "A court will grant relief in this context only where the intoxicated person is unable to understand the nature and consequences of the transaction (i.e., is cognitively impaired) and the other partly has reason to know of this inability."[36] In other words, if someone is visibly intoxicated on alcohol or drugs (whether prescription or illicit), and the intoxication is apparent (i.e., the other party to the contract either knew or should have known of the incapacity due to the apparent intoxication), no contract will be deemed to exist. If, on the other hand, the intoxication is not apparent, the intoxicated person will usually be held to his or her contractual relations.

These rules regarding capacity to contract in the intoxication sphere exist for basic reasons of public policy. It would not be fair to allow people to take advantage of someone whom they know to be impaired. On the other hand, if the impairment is not evident so that it is improbable that anyone is knowingly taking advantage of someone who is impaired, then there is no reason why the innocent party should not benefit from the terms of a contract.[37]

III. TESTAMENTARY CAPACITY

When someone dies, he or she often leaves a will disposing of his or her property. But one must be competent to make a will. One who is competent to make a will is said to have **testamentary capacity**. Testamentary capacity requires that the person making the will (known as the **testator**) be of sound mind and of a requisite age at the time of making the will.

There are three reasons justifying the requirement of testamentary capacity. First, a will should be given effect only if it represents the testator's true desires. Second, it protects the testator from: (1) his or her own actions when not in control of his or her faculties; and (2) exploitation of others who would exercise undue influence in the creation of a will. And finally, it protects the testator's family, the normal beneficiary's of a will.[38]

A. General Requirements for Testamentary Capacity

Testamentary capacity requires that all four of the following criteria be met:

(1)   the testator knows and understands the nature and extent of his or her property;
(2)   the testator knows and understands who are the natural objects of his or her bounty (i.e., who are the apparent heirs);

---

[35] RESTATEMENT (SECOND) OF CONTRACTS § 6; *see also* E. ALLAN FARNSWORTH, CONTRACTS 4.6 (3d ed. 1999).

[36] Paul L. Regan, *Great Expectations? A Contract Law Analysis for Preclusive Corporate Lock-ups*, 21 CARDOZO L. REV. 1, 41 (1999).

[37] *Id.*

[38] *See* JESSE DUKEMINIER & STANLEY M. JOHANSON, WILLS, TRUSTS, & ESTATES 129-31 (4th ed. 1990).

(3)   the testator understands the nature of the testamentary act; and

(4)   the testator understands the foregoing elements in relation to each other and how this interrelationship affects the disposition of his or her property.[39]

The threshold of knowledge and understanding is low. Knowing that one has approximately $500,000 in property and stocks is enough; the testator need not know the percentages of each, the names of the stocks, mutual funds, etc.[40] Eccentricities, prejudices, and unusual religious beliefs, even moral depravity by themselves, do note disqualify a person from having testamentary capacity.[41] Similarly, neither illiteracy, old age, great weakness, blindness, deafness, nor severe illness necessarily disqualifies the testator from being of sound mind for the purposes of testamentary capacity.[42] All such factors, however, may be relevant to determining overall mental capacity.[43] To illustrate how minimal the test for testamentary capacity is, Professors Dukeminier and Johanson cite and discuss *Estate of Wright*.[44]

In *Estate of Wright,* the testator lived in a shack filled with dirt and junk, gave a friend a fish marinated in kerosene to eat, was frequently drunk, picked articles from garbage cans to keep around his house, and even held his breath to trick the neighbors into believing he was dead. These bizarre activities and eccentricities aside, the court upheld his will since he did know who his relatives were and was mindful of the property he possessed.

Unlike in contract law where a guardianship or conservatorship usually renders a person without the capacity to contract, neither necessarily render a person to lack testamentary capacity. This is due to the fact that a different level of legal competency is required for making a will than is required for contractual obligations.[45]

B. Mental Incapacity

Even if one meets the four general criteria for testamentary capacity, a testator may be incapacitated due to a mental illness. There are two areas in particular in which the cognitive abilities of a person might be called into question so as to render the person incompetent to have made a valid will: insane delusions and undue influence.

1. Insane Delusions

An ***insane delusion***, also referred to as "***monomania***" (an unfortunate legal term since it has nothing whatsoever to do with clinical mania), is a technical term from the language of wills, trusts, and estate law; neither an insane delusion nor monomania are clinical terms. They refer to

---

[39]*Id.* at 132.

[40]*Id.*

[41]Warren F. Gorman, *Testamentary Capacity in Alzheimer's Disease*, 4 Elder L.J. 225, 231 (1996) (citing Jane B. Baron, *Empathy, Subjectivity, and Testamentary Capacity*, 24 SAN DIEGO L. REV. 1043 (1987)).

[42]DUKEMINIER & JOHANSON, *supra* note 38, at 132.

[43]*Id.*

[44]*Id.* (citing 7 Cal. 2d 348, 60 P.2d 434 (1936)).

[45]*Id.* at 133 (citing, *inter alia,* Lee v. Lee, 337 So. 2d 713 (Miss. 1976) (testator had been placed under a conservatorship due to his age and physical incapacity. On the same day, he executed both a will and a deed conveying real property. The court held the deed void, but upheld the will.). For a summary of clinical evaluation of testamentary capacity of those with dementia such as Alzheimer's Disease, *see* John C. Morris, *The Clinical Dementia Rating (CDR): Current Versions & Scoring Rules*, 43 NEUROLOGY 2412, 2412-13 (1993).

belief in facts "to which the testator adheres against all evidence and reason to the contrary."[46] Whether a person was suffering from an insane delusion is a question of law, not psychology or psychiatry. But expert testimony from the mental health professions is important to establishing not only if the person suffered from a mental illness that produced an insane delusion, or otherwise deprived the testator of testamentary capacity.

In order for an insane delusion to invalidate a will, it must not only exist, but also must *cause* the will to suffer from some defect that is a product of the insane delusion. For example, if one makes a will leaving all of one's money to one's cat, believing that the cat is the reincarnation of one's childhood sweetheart, the will could be invalidated due to the insane delusion. More frequently, however, insane delusions concern false beliefs about one's family members. Professors Dukeminier and Johanson illustrate that point using the case of *In re Honigman*.[47] In that case, approximately one month before he died and after nearly 40 years of a happy marriage, the testator executed a will in which he left his surviving wife only the minimum he had to under the law. He did so because he believed she was having an affair. She contested to will, claiming her late husband's belief that she was having an affair was an insane delusion. The court explained that the issue was *not* whether the wife had actually been unfaithful, but rather was whether there was sufficient evidence to support the testator's belief that his wife was unfaithful. Finding there was not, the court upheld the invalidation of Mr. Honigman's will.

It is important to differentiate between an insane delusion and a bona-fide mistake, such as believing one's spouse or child was killed, when, in fact, such an heir was actually alive, but unknown to be so by the testator. The law invalidates wills on the basis of insane delusions; it generally does not on the basis of a mistake.[48]

2. Undue Influence

A will can be invalidated if it is shown that the testator executed the will while under **undue influence.** The doctrine is suppose to safeguard both the testator and the natural objects of the testator's bounty by refusing to give legal effect to a will that reflects the intentions of someone other than the testator personally—someone who had so much influence on the testator at the time of the execution of the will that the "will of the person exercising [undue influence] is substituted for the will of the testator"[49] due to trickery, coercion, duress, importunity, or even flattery.[50] Undue influence is, by far, the most common basis upon which wills are challenged, up to 74 percent in one study of will contests.[51]

When determining if undue influence was exercised, courts use what is known as the "will substitution test." It requires the person challenging the validity of a will on undue influence grounds "to prove the following four elements: opportunity, naturalness of disposition, motive and susceptibility."[52] A number of factors are relevant to a determination if these elements are

---

[46]*Id.*; *see also* 79 AM. JUR. 2D *Wills* 87 (1975).

[47]*Id.* at 134-41 (citing In re Honigman, 8 N.Y.2d 244, 168 N.E.2d 676, 203 N.Y.S.2d 859 (1960)).

[48]*Id.* at 140.

[49]Melanie B. Leslie, *The Myth of Testamentary Freedom*, 38 Ariz. L. Rev. 235, 244 (1996).

[50]Kurt Wanless, *Comment: Rethinking Oregon's Law of Undue Influence in Will Contests*, 76 Or. L. Rev. 1027 n.1 (citing Ormsby v. Webb, 134 U.S. 47, 66 (1890)).

[51]Jeffrey A. Schoenblum, *Will Contests – An Empirical Study*, 22 REAL PROP., PROB. & TR. J. 607, 648 (1987).

[52]Ronald Chester, *Less Law, but More Justice?: Jury Trials and Mediation*

proven. The ones most likely to be taken into account, according to a 1996 study by Leslie[53] in which all reported cases in a randomly selected five-year period dealing with undue influence were examine, included:

> whether a "confidential relationship" existed between the alleged influence and the testator[54]; whether the influence was actively involved in procuring the will[55]; whether and to what extent the testator was susceptible to influence[56]; whether and the extent to which the testator obtained advice from other than the alleged influence, either from a disinterested attorney or from other friends and family members[57]; the degree to which the business or financial affairs of the testator were controlled by the alleged influence[58]; and the length of the relationship between the testator and the beneficiary.[59]

Both lay opinion testimony and expert opinion from mental health clinicians are admissible to explore any of these questions.

C. Lucid Intervals

A person suffering from mental illness that interferes with testamentary capacity, including insane delusions, may experience periods of lucidity during which he or she may execute a valid will. Such a period is called a ***lucid interval.*** "The lucid interval, which has been likened to an interval of sunshine during a storm, is an interval of apparent health between attacks or periods of a disease."[60] Someone who would otherwise lack testamentary capacity may be competent during a lucid interval. Both lay and expert testimony about the testator's ability to judge his or her testamentary acts during apparent lucid intervals are admissible and helpful to establish testamentary capacity.

D. Post-Mortem Competency Determinations

Unfortunately, a clinician may be called upon to make an evaluation of testamentary capacity after the death of a testator. This is problematic since the testator, now dead, cannot be clinically evaluated. The testator's mental state might have to be reconstructed post-mortem, using evidence from any source that can shed light on his or her mental state. This after-the-fact reconstruction led one commentator to label it the "'worst evidence principle' of American probate law "[61]

[as] *Means of Resolving Will Contests*, 37 DUQ. L. REV. 173, 175-76 (1999) (citing Trent J. Thornley, *The Caring Influence: Beyond Autonomy as the Foundation of Undue Influence*, 71 IND. L. J. 513, 517 (1996)).

[53] *Id.*

[54] *Id.* at n.47 (citing Jones v. Walker, 774 S.W.2d 532, 534 (Mo. Ct. App. 1989)).

[55] *Id.* at n.47 (citing Succession of Hamiter, 519 So. 2d 341, 344-45 (La. Ct. App. 1988); Walker, 774 S.W.2d at 534; Gaines v. Frawley, 739 S.W.2d 950, 952-53 (Tex. Ct. App. 1987)).

[56] *Id.* at n.47 (citing Heinrich v. Silvernail, 500 N.E.2d 835, 840 (Mass. App. Ct. 1986); Pace v. Richmond, 343 S.E.2d 59, 64 (Va. 1986)).

[57] *Id.* at n.47 (citing *Heinrich*, 500 N.E.2d at 842-43).

[58] *Id.* at n.47 (citing *Hamiter*, 519 So. 2d at 344-45; *Heinrich*, 500 N.E.2d at 842).

[59] *Id.* at n.47 (citing *Hamiter*, 519 So. 2d at 344-45).

[60] Gorman, *supra* note 41, at 234.

[61] John H. Langbein, *Will Contests: Undue Influence: The Epic Battle for the Johnson & Johnson Fortune*, 103 YALE L.J. 2039, 2046 (1994) (*reviewing* David Margolick, Undue Influence: The Epic Battle for the Johnson & Johnson Fortune (1993))

The preferred route, of course, is to establish the testator's testamentary capacity at the time the will is executed. Doing so, however, involves foresight on the part of the estate-planning attorney. Whenever questions of testamentary capacity might be an issue, it is a good idea to have the person seeking to make a will clinically evaluated so that a record of his or her mental state at the time the will was executed will exist. Videotaping the execution of the will, which includes the attorney asking certain questions relevant to establishing testamentary capacity, is another way of preserving credible evidence of sound mind.[62]

IV. COMPETENCY AND FITNESS IN CHILD CUSTODY CASES

Contrary to popular belief, mental health professionals are not involved in the great majority of divorce and child custody proceedings.[63] This is primarily due to the fact that upwards of 90 percent of all child custody decisions are negotiated between a divorcing couple.[64] That being said, mental health professionals can and often do play important roles in child custody cases.

A. Views on the Role of the Mental Health Professional in Custody Evaluations

> Psychiatrists and psychologists are important to the resolution of child custody and visitation disputes as well because they can 1) Assist parties in exploring the "real" reasons for disputes, i.e. power plays, value differences, revenge, economic question, etc., 2) Provide the subject child with a non-threatening environment to voice their preferences and explore their feelings, 3) Assist the court in the application of non-legal concepts that are useful in implementing the spirit and intent of the statutes and public policy regarding the placement of children: for example what does best interest of the child mean in developmental terms? Does the child understand what his preferences may mean? and 4) Provide assessments and uncover things which might otherwise be overlooked by the other parties involved and their attorney. This is especially true in abuse cases because all parties have usually been in some state of denial.[65]

In spite of the potential benefits mental health professionals might bring to the child custody decision-making process, their involvement has been criticized more than it has been praised.[66] In a summary of such critical literature, McBurney lists the following ten reasons as the main sources of discontent:

1. custody evaluations are an invasion of the family's right to privacy;
2. evaluations are based on limited contact and information;
3. evaluations often extend the length of the custody dispute;
4. evaluations are often confused with therapy;
5. evaluations are often costly;

---

[62]For an analysis of the various problems that arise when wills are challenged and potential solutions to these problems, see generally Schoenblum, *Will Contests – An Empirical Study*, 22 REAL. PROP., PROB. & TR. J. 607 (1987).

[63]GARY B. MELTON, ET AL., PSYCHOLOGICAL EVALUATION FOR THE COURTS 329 (1987).

[64]*Id.*

[65]Fay H. Williams, *The Role of Psychiatrist/Psychologist in Child Custody and Visitation Disputes: Hired Guns or Objective Professionals?*, 7 NAT'L B.A. MAG. 20 (1993).

[66]*E.g.*, LOIS A. WEITHORN (ed.), PSYCHOLOGY AND CHILD CUSTODY DETERMINATIONS vii (1987); Randy K. Otto, *Bias and Expert Testimony of Mental Health Professionals in Adversarial Proceedings: A Preliminary Investigation*, 7 BEHAV. SCI. 267 (1989).

6. evaluations may be used as a weapon against an opposing parent to the detriment of the child involved;
7. mental health professionals may be nonobjective or biased;
8. much of the information mental health professionals receive is tainted;
9. mental health professionals cannot predict the long range efficacy of parenting skills and the effect of those skills on the children involved; and
10. both parents and children are being observed at a time of unusually high stress, therefore, their behavior may be atypical, and the resultant evaluations are "potentially unreliable."[67]

McBurney offers the following list of counterpoints that illustrate the benefits of mental health professionals being involved with custody evaluations: (1) mental health professionals are generally trained in talking with, and gathering information from, children and families in crisis; (2) mental health professionals are generally knowledgeable in areas such as child development, psychological functioning, interpersonal relationships and interactions, and the current and possible future effect of certain situations and conditions on the child; and (3) the mental health professional will be able to discern feelings, attitudes, personality traits, and family interaction patterns not readily apparent to the court.[68]

B. Legal Standards for Child Custody and Visitation

Until the 1900s, the English common law doctrine of *pater familius* held that the male, as the head of household, had complete control over children.[69] In the event of divorce, the father maintained custody of the children. Largely as a result of the feminist movement, the doctrine eventually gave way to one known as the *tender years doctrine.* It posits that, absent some showing of unfitness, a mother is best-suited to care for young children—those of "tender years."[70] Implicit in this assumption was that fathers were unable to provide the "tender, loving care" that young children need for proper development.[71] But the maternal preference embodied in the tender years doctrine was generally limited to children under the age of seven years.

Since the 1950s and 1960s, however, the tender years doctrine has given way to *"the best interests of the child"* standard.[72] Although the overwhelming standard today, the best interests of the child standard is inherently ambiguous and leaves much room for the exercise of judicial discretion that often involves stereotypes and prejudices.[73] And it cannot be truly separated from the maternal preference embodied in the tender years doctrine since conventional wisdom continues to presume it is in the best interests of a young child to be with his or her mother.[74]

---

[67]Alison Richey McBurney, *Bitter Battles: The Use of Psychological Evaluations in Child Custody Disputes in West Virginia*, 97 W. Va L. Rev. 773, 775-78 (1995).

[68]*Id.* at 779.

[69]*E.g.*, Mary Ann Mason, From Father's Property to Children's Rights: The History of Child Custody in the United States (1994).

[70]*Id.*

[71]*E.g.*, Margaret F. Brinig & F.H. Buckley, Symposium on Law and the New American Family: *Joint Custody: Bonding and Monitoring Theories*, 73 Ind. L.J. 393, 394 (1998).

[72]*See* Mason, *supra* note 69; *see also, e.g.*, Lois E. Hawkins, *Comment: Joint Custody in Louisiana*, 43 La. L. Rev. 85, 90-91 (1982).

[73]*See* David Miller, *Joint Custody*, 13 Fam. L.Q. 345, 353-54 (1979).

[74]Hawkins, *supra* note 72, at 91.

In recent years, however, awarding sole custody to one parent has increasingly been viewed as something that is not in the best interests of a child—a legal development spurred, in large part, by psychological research.[75] As a result, the overwhelming number of U.S. jurisdictions have statutorily created rules favoring *joint custody.* In fact, as of 1998, "courts in virtually all states are authorized to consider joint-custody arrangements, and nearly a quarter presume that this will be in the child's best interests."[76]

> The distinguishing feature of joint custody is that both parents retain legal responsibility and authority for the care and control of the child, much as in an intact family. Joint custody upon divorce is defined here as an arrangement in which both parents have equal rights and responsibilities regarding major decisions and neither parent's rights are superior. Joint custody basically means providing each parent with an equal voice in the children's education, upbringing, religious training, nonemergency medical care, and general welfare. The parent with whom the child is residing at the time must make immediate and day-to-day decisions regarding discipline, grooming, diet, activities, scheduling social contacts, and emergency care.[77]

Whether joint custody, as an abstract concept, is truly in the best interests of the child is subject to debate; in the applied realm, it will, of course, vary from case to case depending on the situational factors of the parents and children involved in the given dispute. On the positive side, research suggests children adapt better to divorce when they maintain regular contact with both parents.[78] Research also suggests that joint custody arrangements significantly lower the amount of relitigation of custody status.[79] Other studies demonstrate that fathers who share joint custody with mothers are more than twice as likely to consistently pay their child support obligations than those who do not share in the custody of children.[80]

On the other hand, joint custody may require continued contact between two parents who ought not have anything further to do with each other. For example, it may allow for continued controlling or manipulative behaviors to go on between the parents, and, in the worse case scenario, for continued abuse.[81] Courts should be vigilant in assessing the particulars of each case to insure the "best interests of the child" are met by the custody decree. To assist them in this goal, judges often turn to mental health professionals.

C. Child Custody Evaluations

Courts often order evaluations by mental health professionals whose reports are used to assist judges in determining what is in the best interests of children in a given child custody dispute. Even when not ordered by a court, parties may proffer such evidence on their own. "To do justice under the 'best interests' standard, courts must endeavor to learn what the actual interests

---

[75]*See, E.g.,* JOSEPH GOLDSTEIN, ANNA FREUD, & ALBERT J. SOLNIT, BEYOND THE BEST INTERESTS OF THE CHILD, 37-38 (1973).

[76]Brinig & Buckley, *supra* note 71, at 395-96 (citations omitted).

[77] JAY FOLBERG (ed.), CUSTODY OVERVIEW, IN JOINT CUSTODY AND SHARED PARENTING 7 (1984).

[78]Jana B. Singer & William L. Reynolds, *A Dissent on Joint Custody*, 47 MD. L. REV. 497, 500 (1988) (summarizing and citing studies so concluding).

[79]*See, e.g.*, Deborah Anna Luepnitz, *A Comparison of Maternal, Paternal, and Joint Custody: Understanding the Varieties of Post-Divorce Family Life*, 9 J. DIVORCE 1, 5 (1986).

[80]*Id.* at 6; Joan B. Kelly, *Longer-Term Adjustment in Children of Divorce: Converging Findings and Implications for Practice*, 2 J. FAM. PSYCHOL. 119, 133 (1988).

[81]Luepnitz, *supra* note 79, at 10.

of the child are rather than rely on various presumptions regarding those interests."[82] But the benefit of expert testimony in child custody evaluations continues to be a point of contention in the literature on the subject. Some, like Faust and Ziskin, have argued that psychologists and psychiatrists rarely provide the legal system with any helpful insights that are any more valid or reliable than lay-witnesses can provide.[83] In contrast, others maintain that such testimony can be helpful if the focus of the psychological inquiry is limited to relevant data.[84] Most authorities agree that psychological testing is not helpful in making parental fitness determinations, except for ruling out psychopathology.[85]

Whatever the shortcoming of forensic child custody evaluations, they are used in 10 percent or so of child custody cases that are contested in court. Campbell reviewed the relevant literature of such evaluations in 1992 and concluded the following issues should explored by mental health professionals conducting forensic custody evaluations:

1. "The love, affection, and other emotional ties existing between the competing parties and the child,"[86] with a focus not only on the bonds between the child and the primary caretaker as they existed before the divorce, but also with an examination "which parent will most likely relate to their children as the primary caretaker on a post-decree basis."[87]
2. "The capacity and disposition of the parties involved to give the child love, affection, and guidance, and continuation of the educating and raising of the child in its religion or creed, if any."[88]
3. The capacity of either party to provide the child not only with basic necessities, but also with a relatively level or stable economic existence after the divorce such as existed before the divorce.[89]
4. The capacity of either party to provide a stable family life in terms of a day-to-date routine, rather than one that is characterized by "unpredictability and chaos."[90]
5. "The mental and physical health of the competing parties,"[91] with particular attention being paid to substance abuse and psychopathology since both tend to compromise the attention and care given to children.
6. A review of the "child's school record, the significance of sibling relationships, and participation in community activities" as part of "assessing the desirability of maintaining continuity and stability in the child's physical and/or custodial environment."[92]

[82]Kim H. McGavin, *Child Custody and Visitation in Maryland: in the Best Interests of the Child*, 26 U. BALT. L.F. 3, 5 (1995) (citing ROBERT M. HOROWITZ & HOWARD A. DAVIDSON, LEGAL RIGHTS OF CHILDREN 416 (1984)).

[83]David Faust & Jay Ziskin, *the Expert Witness in Psychology and Psychiatry*, 241 SCI., 31 (1988).

[84]*E.g.,* Terence W. Campbell, *Child Custody Evaluations and Appropriate Standards of Psychological Practice*, MICH. BAR. J., March 1992, at 278; *see also* Thomas Grisso, *The Economic and Scientific Future of Forensic Psychological Assessment*, 42 AMER. PSYCHOLOGIST 831 (1987).

[85]Campbell, *supra* note 84 (citing, *e.g.,* Grisso, *supra* note 84; Lois Weithorn, *Psychological Evaluations in Divorce Custody: Problems, Principles, and Procedures, in* PSYCHOLOGY AND CHILD CUSTODY DETERMINATIONS: KNOWLEDGE, ROLES, AND EXPERTISE. (Lois Weithorn, ed., U. Neb. Press 1987)).

[86]*Id.* at 278.

[87]*Id.* at 278-79.

[88]*Id.* at 279.

[89]*Id.*

[90]*Id.*

[91]*Id.* at 280.

[92]*Id.*

7. The preference of the child, taking into account both "chronological age and psychological maturity"[93] since children under nine years of age rare possess the ability to view parents critically.
8. The willingness of the parties "to facilitate and encourage a close and continuing parent-child relationship between the child and the other parent" since children adjust better to divorce when "positive relationships with both parents" are maintained.[94]
9. The availability of an extended family network that provides "support and assistance" without "excessive involvement [that] undermine[s] the parental authority of single parents."[95]

In contrast, Campbell points out that some traditional foci of parental fitness evaluations are questionable, at best. For example, "most attempts at inferring parental fitness from impressions of moral fitness are contraindicated by . . . research."[96] In particular, behaviors such as adultery, promiscuity, cohabitation, and homosexuality do not appear to have any relationship on parental fitness unless they "significantly influence[] how they function as parental figures."[97]

D. Conclusion

In an era when more than half of all marriages end in divorce, courts called upon to decide what is in a child's best interest often have little objective data upon which to base such a judgment other than the testimony of either parent and their witnesses (including the children themselves who are easily manipulated into providing unreliable data). Mental health professional can help to fill that void. But research on forensic child custody evaluations has produced evidence that should give us pause for thought on their usefulness as evidence. In spite of the mixed results research on the efficacy of forensic child custody evaluations has produced, it appears, at least for now, they are here to stay. Accordingly, mental health professionals should make clear that they have a limited ability to predict what will be in a child's best interests. And legal professionals, especially judges, must be vigilant not to give too much weight to the opinions of mental health professionals in this sphere—especially when candor on the limits of such evaluations is not forthcoming from a mental health clinician in a case.

V. GUARDIANSHIP AND CONSERVATORSHIP

A. Introduction

All states have procedures that allow someone to be appointed to take care of another's legal and personal affairs when that person becomes incompetent to do so for himself or herself. This procedure is usually referred to as **guardianship.** Legally speaking, it is the delegation of the government's *parens patriae* power to another person, usually a close family member. Some

---

[93] *Id.*

[94] *Id.*

[95] *Id.* For another extensive review of the factors that should be considered in forensic child custody evaluations, see McBurney, *supra* note 67, at 796-99.

[96] *Id.*

[97] *Id.*

jurisdictions differentiate between the delegation of *parens patriae* power over the person and the delegation of the power over the person's estate. The former (concerned mostly with a person's health, safety, and welfare needs) is nearly always referred to as *guardianship;* the latter (concerned with managing the incapacitated person's money, property, contractual obligations, and the like) is sometimes called a ***conservatorship.*** "In spite of differences in terminology, the substantive law governing these arrangements is similar or identical in most U.S. jurisdictions."[98]

Regardless of the often inconsistent terminology that may be applied, guardianship and conservatorship are authorized only for those who are not competent to make decisions for themselves. Most state statutes define such persons as "incapacitated individuals,"[99] although some still use the older term "ward." While the particular definition of an incapacitated person differs from jurisdiction to jurisdiction, nearly all statutes include language to the effect that an incapacitated individual is one who lacks the mental capacity (1) to appreciate the nature and implications of decisions regarding his or her own care or the care of his or her property; (2) to make a choice regarding his or her alternatives; or (3) to communicate his or her choice in an unambiguous fashion.

Normally, one thinks of the elderly when talking about guardianship and conservatorship, especially those suffering from some form of delirium or dementia. And with the "aging of America," these procedures may come to play an even more important role in everyday life for many people who have older family members for whom they care. But guardianships and conservatorships are not designed for the exclusive use of the aged; they are appropriate tools to care for any incapacitated individual—regardless of age—if other mechanisms were not put into place before the onset of the disability, such as durable powers of attorney. And minors are presumed to need guardianship and conservatorship, powers vested by law in their parents, although a "legal guardian" who is not the parent of a minor can be appointed for a minor if circumstances so require. And because those who are civilly committed are usually also deemed incompetent to manage their own affair, most state's commitment statutes contain provisions which allow an agent of the state to act as the guardian and/or conservator of a civilly committed person.[100]

B. A Historical Look at Guardianship and Conservatorship

The modern roots of guardianship and conservatorship can be traced back to English common law.

> In medieval England, the Lord Chancellor had responsibility for appointing a person or committee to protect persons with mental disabilities and their property. Later, the London judiciary established a separate Court of Orphans "which had the care and guardianship of minor children of deceased citizens of London." During the colonial period, England exported its judicial organization along with the common law to the American colonies, where jurisdiction over guardianship generally fell to the courts exercising probate jurisdiction. By the late nineteenth

---

[98] Paula L. Hannaford & Thomas L. Hafemeister, *The National Probate Court Standards: The Role of the Courts in Guardianship and Conservatorship Proceedings*, 2 ELDER L.J. 147, 149-50 (1994) (citing the Uniform Guardianship and Protective Proceedings Act as the "widely emulated model"; *see* Unif. Prob. Code §§ 5-501 to 5-505 (1983 & Supp. 1997)).

[99] *See, e.g.,* ARIZ. REV. STAT. § 14-5101(1) (Supp. 1997); N.J. STAT. ANN. § 3B:1-2 (Supp. 1997).

[100] MELTON, ET AL., *supra* note 63, at 247.

century, most of the American states had codified their procedures for imposing guardianships and delineated the rights and duties of guardians with respect to their wards.[101]

Although these legal devices have been, without doubt, important tools for caring for those who cannot care for themselves, in the late 1970s guardianship and conservatorship began to come under heavy criticism for a number of reasons. Some argued there were often insufficient due process protections for the incapacitated individual since advance notice of the hearing to determine competency and the right to appointed counsel were rare.[102] Other criticized the lack of evidentiary standards for assessing when guardianships and/or conservatorships were necessary.[103] For example, after a 1987 Associated Press investigation in which approximately 2200 guardianship case files were examine, "reporters found that the evidence introduced to prove incapacity was often no more than a one-sentence conclusion by a physician that the person was "unable to care for self or property.""[104] And even when duly warranted, the powers often granted to guardians over an incapacitated person often constituted an intrusion over the ward's autonomy that was more intrusive than necessary under particularized circumstances.[105] And since the power entrusted to the guardian or conservator was not sufficiently monitored by courts, it was often abused.[106]

C. Modern Reforms

As a result of many of the aforementioned problems having been brought to light by legal scholars, social commentators, groups such as the American Association of Retired Persons and the American Bar Association's Commissions on the Mentally Disabled and Commission on Legal Problems of the Elderly, and, most notably, the investigative report by the Associated Press,[107] there have been several notable reforms in recent years to the law in this area. Many of these reforms are specifically attributable to the recommendations of: (1) ABA's Commission on Legal Problems of the Elderly's Statement of Recommended Judicial Practices of 1986; and (2) the National College of Probate Judges and the National Center for State Courts (NCPJ/NCSC) as issued in their National Probate Court Standards of 1994.

---

[101]Hannaford & Hafemeister, *supra* note 98, at 150 (citing, *inter alia*, Lewis M. Simes & Paul E. Basye, *The Organization of the Probate Court in America*, 42 MICH. L. REV. 965, 979-80 (1942); John Parry, *Incompetency, Guardianship, and Restoration*, in SAMUEL J. BRAKEL ET AL. (eds.), THE MENTALLY DISABLED AND THE LAW 369 (1985). (Other internal citations omitted).

[102]*See, e.g.,* Alison P. Barnes, *Florida Guardianship and the Elderly: The Paradoxical Right to Unwanted Assistance*, 40 U. FLA. L. REV. 949, 974-87 (1988) (discussing traditional "all-or-nothing" guardianship arrangements).

[103]*Id.* at 957-67; *see also* George J. Alexander, *Premature Probate: A Different Perspective on Guardianship for the Elderly*, 31 STAN. L. REV. 1003 (1979); Forrest Scogin & James Perry, *Guardianship Proceedings with Older Adults: The Role of Functional Assessment and Gerontologists*, 10 LAW & PSYCH. REV. 123, 124-27 (1986).

[104]Hannaford & Hafemeister, *supra* note 98, at 150 (citing, Fred Bayles & Scott McCartney, *Diagnosing Incompetence Is Tricky, Ill-Defined Job*, in FRED BAYLES & SCOTT MCCARTNEY, GUARDIANSHIP OF THE ELDERLY: AN AILING SYSTEM 9 (Associated Press Special Report, Sept. 1987).

[105]*See, e.g,* Jan E. Rein, *Preserving Dignity and Self-Determination of the Elderly in the Face of Competing Interests and Grim Alternatives: A Proposal for Statutory Refocus and Reform*, 60 GEO. WASH. L. REV. 1818 (1992); Jamie L. Leary, *Note: A Review of Two Recently Reformed Guardianship Statutes: Balancing The Need to Protect Individuals Who Cannot Protect Themselves Against The Need to Guard Individual Autonomy*, 5 VA. J. SOC. POL'Y & L. 245 (1997).

[106]Hannaford & Hafemeister, *supra* note 98, at 150 (citing, *inter alia*, Lawrence A. Frolik, *Abusive Guardians and the Need for Judicial Supervision*, TR. & EST., July 1991, at 41).

[107]*See* Sally Balch Hurme, *Current Trends in Guardianship Reform*, 7 MD. J. CONTEMP. LEGAL ISSUES 143, 145-46 (1996) (attributing a "wave of guardianship reform" to the AP report).

To address the problems associated with evidentiary determinations of competency, the CPJ/NCSC Standards, which included many of the 1986 ABA Commission's recommendations,

> support "an appraisal of the functional limitations of the respondent" as the relevant criteria for adjudging incapacity. The Standards specifically observe that "incapacity is a multifaceted issue" and suggest that the court consider evidence from professionals other than physicians (e.g., nurses, psychologists, social workers, physical and occupational therapists, community mental health workers) who may possess special insights into whether the respondent is incapacitated. Finally, if the respondent to a guardianship petition objects to written documents containing expert opinions concerning his or her purported incapacity, the Standards endorse mandating the expert's appearance at the hearing and availability for cross-examination. If the expert is unavailable, the Standards note that "traditional rules of evidence may limit the ability of the fact finder to rely on the written report."[108]

The assessment of competency for guardianship/conservatorship purposes should include evaluation of the putative ward's judgment; ability to acquire and manage money; clarity of thought; ability to communicate; memory; sensation and perception; ability to care for his/her daily needs (diet, mobility, hygiene, etc.); ability to care for his/her medical needs, and the ability to utilize transportation to meet any and all of the aforementioned needs.[109]

The NCPJ/NCSC Standard's including the following due process protections: advance notice of the hearing "in plain language and large type"; a follow-up to such written notice by a court "visitor" who is supposed to explain the notice to the respondent; court-appointed counsel in most situations; and the right to be present at and participate in the hearing—even if that means the court needs to move the place for hearing to somewhere more accessible than the courthouse for the respondent.

To address the overbreadth of general or plenary guardianships and conservatorships, especially in the cases of temporary or only partial incapacity, forms of both are now available in which only limited, specific powers over the ward and/or the estate of the ward are granted. For example, a temporary guardianship limited to medical decisions following some accident or similar emergency medical situation might be granted for a fixed, short period of time (e.g., 30 days). Or a conservatorship over limited assets to care for only certain types of expenses might be granted. Both the NCPJ/NCSC Standards and the newer Uniform Guardianship and Protective Proceedings Act (UGPPA) advocate the "least restrictive alternative" form of guardianship/conservatorship.[110]

To confront the issue of the guardian or conservator's abuse of power, especially in terms of financial misconduct, most statutes now require a guardian to post a bond, be free of any criminal record, and participate in a state-sanctioned training course on the powers and duties entrusted to a guardian or conservator."[111] Further, the NCPJ/NCSC Standards advocate the monitoring of guardianships and conservatorships using court-appointed "visitors," as well as by direct court supervision though the filing of period reports, including full accountings.

---

[108]Hannaford & Hafemeister, *supra* note 98, at 150 (citing COMMISSION ON NAT'L PROBATE COURT STANDARDS, NATIONAL COLLEGE OF PROBATE JUDGES & NATIONAL CTR. FOR STATE COURTS, NATIONAL PROBATE COURTS STANDARDS (1994)).

[109]MELTON, ET AL., *supra* note 63, at 248.

[110]*See, e.g.*, R.I. GEN. LAWS 33-15-4(a)(1) (Supp. 1998) ("Absent a finding, based on a decision making assessment tool, that an individual is totally incapacitated, the court shall limit the scope of powers and duties of a guardian to the terms best suited to allow the individual found partially incapacitated to participate as fully as possible in decisions affecting him or her").

[111]*See, e.g.*, Jenni Bergal & Nancy McVicar, *Bills Would Toughen Laws on Guardians: Plans Vary in Protection for Elderly*, SUN-SENTINEL (Ft. Lauderdale, Fla.), Mar. 10, 1997, at 1A.

Monitoring reforms also include period hearings on the continued need for the guardianship and/or conservatorship.

D. Conclusion

In most states, proof of one's incapacitation must be shown by clear and convincing evidence. It also must be demonstrated by clear and convincing evidence that no available alternative resource plan is suitable to safeguard the proposed ward's health, safety, or habilitation which could be used instead of a guardianship or conservatorship. And even then, the modern preference in this area of the law is to grant only limited powers that constitute "the least restrictive form of intervention consistent with the ability of the ward for self-care."[112]

Guardianship and/or conservatorship is often the least restrictive alternative available to ensure that someone who does not meet the criteria for involuntary civil commitment (i.e., mental illness and dangerousness to self or others) still receives some assistance. On the other hand, drawing the line between the criteria needed to satisfy guardianship/conservatorship statutes and the criteria under which a court would find someone to be a danger to himself or herself, or be "gravely disabled" is not always clear.

---

[112]*E.g.,* N.D. CIV. CODE § 30.1-28-04(2)(b).

CHAPTER TEN
LEGAL RIGHTS AND RESPONSIBILITIES IN FORENSIC PSYCHOLOGY

I. INFORMED CONSENT

Throughout this book, the concept of autonomy has been explored as a principle underlying the rationale for many different areas of the law. Respect for individual autonomy and self-determination is a bedrock of classical Liberalism, the philosophical school of thought upon which Western politics is based.[1] Autonomy includes the concept of self-determination over one's body.[2] In the often quoted words of the great jurist Benjamin Cardozo, "every human being of adult years and sound mind has a right to determine what shall be done to his body."[3] The doctrine of *informed consent* stems from this right to self-determination, reflecting "the belief that an individual has the right to be free from non-consensual interference with his or her person."[4] In the health care context, including the realm of mental health, these principles have become embodied in the law of informed consent requiring the provider to make certain disclosures to a patient before administering treatment or evaluation.[5]

Informed consent can be enforced in tort law via actions for battery and/or negligence.[6] The use of battery statutes stems from actions when physicians removed body parts or organs without the patient's consent.[7] But when patients were inadequately informed, battery actions were difficult to sustain given their requirements of intent to do harm.[8] The shift to theories of negligence began with *Salgo v. Leland Stanford, Jr. Univ. Bd. of Trustees*.[9] "The concept developed that it was a doctor's duty to disclose sufficient information so that a patient could 'form the basis of an intelligent consent . . . .'"[10]

---

[1] *See, e.g.*, Cathy J. Jones, *Autonomy and Informed Consent in Medical Decisionmaking: Toward a New Self-Fulfilling Prophecy*, 47 WASH. & LEE L. REV. 379, 379-80 (1990); CHARLES FRIED, RIGHT AND WRONG, 146-147 (Harv. Univ. Press 1978) ("What a person is, what he wants, the determination of his life plan, of his concept of the good, are the most intimate expressions of self-determination, and by asserting a person's responsibility for the results of this self-determination we give substance to the concept of liberty"); Charles Fried, Correspondence, 6 PHIL. & PUB. AFF. 288-289 (1977) (the concept of privacy embodies the "moral fact that a person belongs to himself and not others nor to society as a whole"); *cf. Planned Parenthood of Southeastern Pa. v. Casey*, 505 U.S. 833, 928 (1992) (reasoning right to self-determination prohibits state from unduly burdening a woman's ability to terminate a pregnancy).

[2] Jones, *supra* note 1, at 385.

[3] Schloendorff v. Society of New York Hosp., 105 N.E. 92, 93 (1914).

[4] Paula Walter, *The Doctrine Of Informed Consent: To Inform Or Not To Inform?*, 71 ST. JOHN'S L. REV. 543, 545-56 (1997) (internal citations omitted).

[5] Arnold J. Rosoffs, 25 AM. J. L. AND MED. 367, 372 (1999) (citing Peter H. Schuck, *Rethinking Informed Consent*, 103 YALE L. J. 899 (1994); Jon F. Merz & Baruch Fischhoff, *Informed Consent Does Not Mean Rational Consent: Cognitive Limitations on Decision-Making*, 11 J. LEGAL MED. 321 (1990); ARNOLD J. ROSOFF, INFORMED CONSENT: A GUIDE FOR HEALTH CARE PROVIDERS (1981)).

[6] *See* Dorothy Derrickson, Note, *Informed Consent to Human Subject Research: Improving the Process of Obtaining Informed Consent from Mentally Ill Persons*, 25 FORDHAM URB. L.J. 143, 148 (1997); RUTH R. FADEN & TOM L. BEAUCHAMP, A HISTORY AND THEORY OF INFORMED CONSENT 29 (1986).

[7] Lisa Napoli, *the Doctrine of Informed Consent and Women: the Achievement of Equal Value and Equal Exercise of Autonomy*, 4 AM. U. J. GENDER & LAW 335, 342 (1996).

[8] *Id.*

[9] 317 P.2d 170 (Cal. Ct. App. 1957).

[10] Napoli, *supra* note 7, at 343 (citing Salgo v. Leland Stanford, Jr. Univ. Bd. of Trustees, 317 P.2d 170 (Cal. Ct. App. 1957)).

In order for legally valid informed consent to be give, a patient must be informed of "the diagnosis, the nature and purpose of the treatment, the risks of the treatment, . . . the probabilities of the risks occurring," and the risks and associated probabilities of not going forward with treatment.[11] But informed consent goes beyond the mere disclosure of information. It requires "competency, understanding, voluntariness, and decision-making."[12] Yet, evaluation of these criteria are devoid of specific legal guidance and are therefore often left to the judgment of the clinician who may wind up acting at his or her own peril.[13] As Merz and Fischoff have pointed out, "informed consent does not mean rational consent."[14] To prevent problems for both the patient and the clinician, criteria such as competency, voluntariness, and understanding should be evaluated in the informed consent contexts using the standards applicable to these same criteria in the waiver of other constitutional rights as more fully explained in Chapters Four and Five.

The doctrine of informed consent presents numerous problems when dealing with a mentally ill or mentally retarded patient.[15] Until recently, the doctrine was not even deemed applicable in the forensic assessment context since, by definition, such assessments were designed to be disclosed to other people for use in the context of some legal proceeding.[16] But after the Supreme Court's decision in *Estelle v. Smith,*[17] it is clear both informed consent and confidentiality have application to forensic clinical assessment.

In *Estelle v. Smith,* the testimony of a psychiatrist who evaluated a criminal defendant for competency to stand trial was later used in the penalty phase of his murder trial after which he was sentenced to death.[18] In upholding a lower court's decision to vacate his sentence, the Supreme Court found that neither the defendant nor his counsel had been properly informed about the scope of the forensic assessment and how its results could be used in other phases of the criminal process.[19] The Court held this deprivation to unconstitutionally violate the defendant's self-incrimination rights under the Fifth Amendment and his rights to effective assistance of counsel under the Sixth Amendment.[20]

Estelle v. Smith and cases in its progeny have had a palpable impact on both the forensic patient and clinician. In the wake of *Estelle*, the APA adopted new ethical standards to help ensure proper informed consent is obtained. Under Standard 5.01, at the beginning of the clinician–patient relationship, the clinician not only must disclose the purpose of the forensic evaluation and "the relevant limitations on confidentiality," but also must disclose the reasonably foreseeable consequences of the evaluation, including how any and all of the information generated through the clinician-patent interaction might be subsequently used in court.[21]

---

[11]Derrickson, *supra* note 6, at 148 (citing Williams v. Cordice, 418 N.Y.S.2d 995, 996-97 (App. Div. 2d Dept. 1979)).

[12]Bruce J. Winick, *Competency To Consent To Treatment: The Distinction Between Assent and Objection*, 28 HOUS. L. REV. 15, 16 (1991).

[13]*See id.; see also* GARY B. MELTON, ET AL., PSYCHOLOGICAL EVALUATION FOR THE COURTS 250-52 (1987).

[14]Merz & Fischoff, *supra* note 5, at 340.

[15]*See generally, e.g.,* Kathy Faulkner Yates, *Therapeutic Issues Associated With Confidentiality and Informed Consent In Forensic Evaluations*, 20 N.E. J. ON CRIM. & CIV. CON. 345 (1994).

[16]*See, e.g.,* David L. Shapiro, *Informed Consent in Forensic Evaluations*, 9 PSYCHOTHERAPY IN PRIVATE PRAC. 145 (1991).

[17]451 U.S. 454 (1981).

[18]*Id.* at 456-57.

[19]*Id.* at 471.

[20]*Id.* at 468, 471.

[21]American Psychological Ass'n, *Ethical Principles of Psychologists and Code of Conduct*, 47 AM. PSYCHOLOGIST 1597-1611 (1992).

This suggests that if a psychologist enters into a treatment contract with an individual who has been either a victim of or a witness to a criminal offense, then the psychologist must, as part of the Informed Consent to Treatment, discuss the fact that under certain limited circumstances the psychologist may be required to reveal part or all of the records of treatment. Of course, the client should also be made aware of the fact that the psychologist will make every effort to protect such an intrusion into the privilege from occurring. Nevertheless, the client must be made aware of it and never be given the assurance that "everything you say is confidential."[22]

The right to informed consent belongs to the patient. Unless proper informed consent is obtained, the trial process might be deemed constitutionally defective.[23] And for the clinician, a failure to obtain informed consent has both ethical and legal malpractice implications.[24]

II. THE RIGHT TO TREATMENT

In the civil rights era and the accompanying deinstitutionalization movement,[25] "a number of actions were brought to enforce patients' 'right-to-treatment,' on the theory that due process of law is violated if a person is deprived of liberty for purposes of treatment but does not actually receive such treatment."[26] Although such cases were met with moderate degrees of success, a constitutional right to treatment was not specifically held to exist by a federal court until the 1971 decision *Wyatt v. Stickney*.[27] *Wyatt* held that mental patients involuntarily committed to state institutions have a "constitutional right to receive such individual treatment as will give each of them a realistic opportunity to be cured or to improve his or her mental condition."[28] Additionally, *Wyatt* recognized "a right of mentally ill and mentally retarded persons to have such treatment in the least restrictive conditions necessary for that purpose, . . . the right to dignity and privacy, and the right to be free from unnecessary or excessive medication and restraint."[29]

In the 1974 case of *Donaldson v. O'Connor*,[30] a federal circuit court of appeals directly addressed the right to treatment. The petition, Keith Donaldson, had been involuntary committed for over fifteen years. After repeated requests to be released, he finally sued. The Fifth Circuit

---

[22]David L. Shapiro, *Law and Psychology: Ethical Dilemmas for the Mental Health Professional: Issues Raised by Recent Supreme Court Decisions*, 34 CAL. W. L. REV. 177, 190 (1997).

[23]*Id.*

[24]*See generally* Committee on Ethical Guidelines for Forensic Psychologists, *Speciality Guidelines for Forensic Psychologists*, 15 LAW & HUM. BEHAV. 655 (1991).

[25]*See generally* Nancy K. Rhoden, *Law and Psychiatry Part II - The Limits of Liberty: Deinstitutionalization, Homelessness, and Libertarian Theory*, 31 EMORY L.J. 375 (1982).

[26]*Id.* at 385 (citing Morton Birnbaum, *The Right to Treatment*, 46 A.B.A. J. 499 (1960)).

[27]325 F. Supp. 781 (M.D. Ala. 1971, *aff'd sub nom.*, Wyatt v. Aderholt, 503 F.2d 1305 (5th Cir. 1974). It should be noted, however, that the D.C. Circuit Court of Appeals did acknowledge, in dicta, the *possibility* that a constitutional right to treatment may exist in 1966. *See* Rouse v. Cameron, 373 F.2d 451 (D.C. Cir. 1966) (per Bazelon, J.). The right to treatment in *Rouse* was based on a D.C. statute, but the court noted that such a right *might* also exist under the Eighth and/or Fourteenth Amendments. *Id.* at 453.

[28]*Id.* at 784. Shortly after the *Wyatt* decision, another federal court issued an opnion agreeing with *Wyatt's* holding and analysis. *See* Welsch v. Likins, 373 F. Supp. 487 (D. Minn. 1974), *aff'd*, 525 F.2d 987 (8th Cir. 1975).

[29]Phyllis Podolsky Dietz, Note, *The Constitutional Right to Treatment in Light of Youngberg v. Romeo*, 72 GEO. L.J. 1785, 1802 (1984).

[30]493 F.2d 507 (5th Cir. 1974), *vacated and remanded*, 422 U.S. 563 (1975).

held "that a person involuntarily civilly committed to a state mental hospital has a constitutional right to receive such individual treatment as will give him a reasonable opportunity to be cured or to improve his mental condition."[31] It reasoned this was so because "there must be a *quid pro quo* extended by the government to justify" the involuntary civil commitment of a person.[32]

The Fifth Circuit's decision was appealed to the Supreme Court which vacated the Fifth Circuit's opinion on other grounds. Finding that Donaldson posed no danger to himself or to others, the Supreme Court held confinement of a nondangerous patient who is not receiving treatment is an unconstitutional exercise of state's *parens patriae* authority.[33] It did not, therefore, consider whether a properly civilly committed person had a right to treatment. Accordingly, the Fifth Circuit's formulation of the right to treatment remained viable for some time thereafter[34] and played an important role in the first U.S. Supreme Court case that directly addressed a constitutional right to treatment, *Youngberg v. Romero*.[35]

In *Youngberg,* the Supreme Court held that those involuntarily committed to a mental facility were entitled to "minimally adequate or reasonable training to ensure safety and freedom from undue restraint." Note, however, that this is not the same formulation or recognition of a "right to treatment" as was announced by the lower federal courts in either *Wyatt* or *Donaldson*. It specifically refused to consider whether there was a constitutional basis for right to treatment, finding that consideration of that issue was not required to resolve the narrow dispute raised by the facts in the *Youngberg* case.[36]

Where does a constitutional right to treatment stand after *Youngberg?* The only accurate answer is that we really do not know. The matter is even further complicated by the Supreme Court's decision in *Kansas v. Hendricks*.[37] As you may recall, *Hendricks* upheld a statute that civilly commitmented sexually dangerous predators after their release from prison upon a finding of any "mental abnormality."[38] The Court specifically stated that such confinement was constitutionally permissible, even if the abnormality at issue was not treatable.[39] In light of that statement, albeit *in dictum,* a constitutionally recognized right to treatment seems even more doubtful.

Given the uncertainty of a right to treatment as a matter of constitutional law, activists have successfully lobbied for passage of statutory laws dealing with the right to treatment. The *Youngberg* Court granted the states "considerable discretion in determining the nature and scope of its responsibilities" in the treatment of those mentally ill persons who are confined.[40] Accordingly, many states have guaranteed the right to treatment via legislative action.[41]

---

[31]*Id.* at 520.

[32]*Id.* at 522.

[33]O'Connor v. Donaldson, 422 U.S. 563, 581-83 (1975).

[34]*See* Joseph T. Carney, Note, *America's Mentally Ill: Tormented Without Treatment*, 3 GEO. MASON U. CIV. RTS. L.J. 181, 190 (1992).

[35]457 U.S. 307, 319 (1982).

[36]*Id.* at 318.

[37]521 U.S. 346 (1997).

[38]*Id.* at 358.

[39]*Id.* at 366; *see also* Brian J. Pollock, *Note*: Kansas v. Hendricks: *A Workable Standard for "Mental Illness" or a Push Down the Slippery Slope Toward State Abuse of Civil Commitment?*, 40 ARIZ. L. REV. 319, 345 (1998).

[40]*Id.* at 317.

[41]*See, e.g.,* West's Ann. Cal. Welf. & Inst. Code S 5325.1(a); Col. Rev. Stat. Ann. § 27-10-116; Fla. Stat. Ann. § 394.459(2); Mont. Code Ann. § 53-21-168; N.M. Stat. Ann. § 43-1-7; N.C. Gen. Stat. §§ 122C-51, 122C-57; R.I. Gen. Laws § 40.1-5-9.

III. THE RIGHT TO REFUSE MEDICAL TREATMENT

"[A] competent person has a constitutionally protected interest in refusing unwanted medical treatment."[42] This constitutional rights stems from the Fourteenth Amendment Due Process Clause, which provides, in relevant part, that no state shall deprive any person of life, liberty, or property without due process of law."[43] But when an incompetent person is under the control of the government via *parens patriae* or police power, there are clearly limitations on such a person's right to refuse unwanted treatment.[44]

Even after a person is committed, criminally or civilly, a person retains certain privacy/autonomy rights to remain free from unwanted physical intrusions.[45] But the state, under both its *parens patriae* power and its police power, may intrude upon the personal freedoms of a lawfully committed person to forcibly "treat" a person without his or her consent under certain circumstances.[46] The liberty interests of the confined individual must be weighed against the state's interest in protecting the individual from himself or herself and/or protecting others from the individual.[47]

While the precise limits on the state's authority are not clearly defined, it is now well established that "antipsychotic drugs may be constitutionally administered to an involuntarily committed mentally ill patient whenever, in the exercise of professional judgment, such an action is deemed necessary to prevent the patient from endangering himself or others."[48] The same holds true for a convicted prisoner who is mentally ill.[49] In cither scenario, for the state's interests to outweigh the individual's liberty interests, there must be both an "overriding justification" for such treatment and "a determination of medical appropriatenesss" of doing so.[50]

Notably, in either setting, a judicial determination that forcibly medicating the confined person does not appear to be constitutionally necessary. Rather, the due process liberty interest in avoiding unwanted treatment using antipsychotic drugs seems "adequately protected, and perhaps better served, by allowing the decision to medicate to be made by medical professionals rather than a judge."[51] Some have criticized this as violative of a patient's procedural due process rights[52] and as being inconsistent with "long-standing disparagement of the judgment of psychiatrists and psychologists and its concern about their ability to make reliable and valid decisions."[53] Others have criticized these informal procedures as "antitherapeutic and detrimental

---

[42]Cruzan v. Director, Mo. Dep't of Health, 497 U.S. 261, 278 (1990); Washington v. Harper, 494 U.S. 210, 221-22 (1990).

[43]U.S. Const. amend XIV.

[44]*See* Youngberg v. Romeo, 457 U.S. 307, 315-16 (1982); Hutto v. Finney, 437 U.S. 678, 683 (1978).

[45]*Youngberg*, 457 U.S. at 315-16 (1982); Vitek v. Jones, 445 U.S. 480, 491-94 (1980).

[46]*See* Youngberg, 457 U.S. at 315-16; Hutto v. Finney, 437 U.S. 678, 683 (1978).

[47]Jessica Litman, Note, *A Common Law Remedy for Forcible Medication of the Institutionalized Mentally Ill*, 82 COLUM. L. REV. 1720, 1738 (1982).

[48]Rennie v. Klein, 720 F.2d 266, 269 (3d Cir. 1983) (en banc).

[49]Washington v. Harper, 494 U.S. 210 (1990).

[50]Riggins v. Nevada, 504 U.S. 127, 135 (1992).

[51]*Id.* at 231. *But see* Riggins v. Nevada, 504 U.S. 127 (1992) (holding the state cannot forcibly medicate a criminal defendant during his or her trial).

[52]Douglas S. Stransky, Comments: *Civil Commitment and the Right to Refuse Treatment: Resolving Disputes from a Due Process Perspective*, 50 U. MIAMI L. REV. 413, 435-36 (1996).

[53]*Id.* at 439-440 (quoting O'Connor v. Donaldson, 422 U.S. 563, 584 (1975) (Burger, C.J., concurring) ("there can be little responsible debate regarding the uncertainty of diagnosis in this field and the tentativeness of professional judgment").

to the population of mentally disabled persons."[54] But to date, the Supreme Court has not so held. In fact, the court has stated that requiring judicial oversight of the decision to forcibly medicate is unnecessary because "there certainly is no reason to think judges or juries are better qualified than appropriate professionals in making [treatment] decisions."[55] That being said, the states are roughly divided in half on this issue with some using a judicial decision-maker model and the others using a medical decision-maker one.[56]

As the foregoing discussion should make clear, the "right to refuse treatment," although not illusory, is rather weak as a matter of federal constitutional law. Even if a person does not want treatment, his or her desires are secondary to the legitimate interests of the state in at least three circumstances: (1) if the patient poses a danger to self or others; (2) if the patient is not competent to make an informed decision to refuse treatment; or (3) if there were an emergency situation that necessitated forcible treatment from a medical perspective.[57] As a practical matter, "few patients refuse medication over a long period of time and those who persistently refuse typically will have their decisions ultimately overridden."[58]

IV. CONFIDENTIALITY

Normally, when a person "consults a physician, psychiatrist, or clinical psychologist, he or she is assured . . . that what goes on in the session will remain confidential . . . [meaning] that nothing will be revealed to a third party, except only to other professions and those intimately involved in the treatment, such as a nurse or medical secretary."[59] The law even protects certain confidential communications from disclosure by recognizing them as being "privileged."[60]

There are general limitations on the doctrines of *confidentiality* and *privilege* that apply in many settings, not just the forensic one. For example, if a client accuses his or her physician, therapist, or attorney of malpractice, the professional being accused can divulge whatever information is necessary to defend himself or herself against the malpractice charge.[61] Similarly, if a medical or mental health professional has reason to believe that a child client has been the victim of either physical or sexual abuse, many jurisdictions *require* the professional to contact the police and reveal the bases of their beliefs.[62]

Beyond these two general limitations, other limitations on the doctrines of confidentiality and privilege in the forensic setting would not necessarily exist in other settings. The most obvious of these limitations is that a forensic assessment is taking place for the very purpose of disclosure to

---

[54]*Id.* (citing DAVID B. WEXLER & BRUCE J. WINICK, ESSAYS IN THERAPEUTIC JURISPRUDENCE 75-79 (1991); DAVID B. WEXLER, THERAPEUTIC JURISPRUDENCE: THE LAW AS A THERAPEUTIC AGENT (1990)).

[55]*Youngberg*, 457 U.S. at 322-23; *see also* United States v. Charters, 829 F.2d 479, 498-99 (4th Cir. 1987) ("judicial approval of forcible medication imposes a needless and unwieldy obstacle to proper and prompt treatment"). For a critique of this deference to professional judgment, see Susan Stefan, *Leaving Civil Rights to the "Experts": From Deference to Abdication Under the Professional Judgment Standard*, 102 YALE L.J. 639 (1992).

[56]Catherine E. Blackburn, *The "Therapeutic Orgy" and the "Right to Rot" Collide: The Right to Refuse Antipsychotic Drugs Under State Law*, 27 HOUS. L. REV. 447, 479, 493 (1990).

[57]LAWRENCE S. WRIGHTSMAN, ET AL., PSYCHOLOGY AND THE LEGAL SYSTEM 462 (4th ed. 1998).

[58]*Id.* at 463 (citing, *inter alia,* Paul S. Appelbaum & Stephen K. Hoge, *The Right to Refuse Treatment: What the Research Reveals*, 4 BEHAV. SCI. & L. 279, 291 (1986)).

[59]GERALD C. DAVISON AND JOHN M. NEALE, ABNORMAL PSYCHOLOGY 621 (7th ed. 1998).

[60]*See* Jefferey A. Klotz, Limiting the Psychotherapist-Patient Privilege: The Therapeutic Potential, 27 Crim. L. Bull. 416 (1991).

[61]Davison and Neale, *supra* note 59, at 621.

[62]*Id.*

others involved in a judicial process.[63] *Estelle v. Smith,*[64] (discussed above in the section dealing with informed consent) made it clear that confidentiality issues must be addressed with a forensic patient in order to gain informed consent. But the law of confidentiality, and the limits on it, are quite complex in a mental health setting, going far beyond a disclosure regarding confidentiality (or more precisely, a lack thereof) in order to obtain informed consent. And there is no clearer example of the legal limitations on these doctrines that the case of *Tarasoff v. Regents of the University of California.*[65]

Tarasoff was a civil case brought by the parents of a girl named Tatiana Tarasoff. She was killed on October 27, 1969, by Prosenjit Poddar. Poddar had apparently told his psychologist, employed by the University of California at Berkeley, of his intention to kill Tatiana. In response to that disclosure, the psychologist informed campus police that Poddar might be dangerous. He was detained, but released by the police after a short interview during which time the police thought Poddar was "rational." He subsequently befriended Tatiana's brother, and persuaded him to become his roommate in an apartment close to where Tatiana lived. Tatiana was away in Brazil during this time, but upon her return to the United States, Poddar killed her.

Tatiana's parents sued the psychologist and the university arguing that Tatiana should have been warned of the danger Poddar presented to her. The psychologist argued he owed no duty of care to Tatiana since she was never his patient. The court sided with the family, holding that a therapist must take reasonable steps to protect an intended victim if the clinician feels the patient poses a real risk of danger to another person. Living up to this obligation will depend upon the nature of the particular case, but it always requires the clinician to take "whatever steps are reasonably necessary under the circumstances." Under the facts of the *Tarasoff* case, the court found that the psychologist's notification to the police was legally insufficient to meet his duty. The psychologist should have ordered Poddar confined because he was mentally ill and posed a danger to Tatiana, and/or the psychologist should have warned the Tarasoffs.

In finding this duty to protect third-parties, the court recognized the difficulties its holding could pose for therapists, especially since predicting dangerousness is so difficult. The court wrote:

> Obviously, we do not require that the therapist, in making that determination, render a perfect performance; the therapist need only exercise that reasonable degree of skill, knowledge, and care ordinarily possessed and exercised by members of that professional specialty under similar circumstances. Within the broad range of reasonable practice and treatment in which professional opinion and judgment may differ, the therapist is free to exercise his or her own best judgment without liability; proof, aided by hindsight, that he or she judged wrongly is insufficient to establish negligence.

Because the *Tarasoff* decision was issued by the California Supreme Court, it technically had no binding precedential authority outside of the state. But the decision has had an overwhelming effect in many states. "The concept of a duty to protect by warning, albeit limited in certain circumstances, has met with virtually universal approval"[66]—so much so that it is generally

---

[63]*See* Paul S. Appelbaum, *Confidentiality in the Forensic Evaluation,* 7 INT'L J.L. & PSYCHIATRY 285, 291, 296 (1984) (recommending the forensic clinician keep all information obtained during forensic evaluation confidential unless revealing the information is required to fulfill the purpose of the examination).

[64]451 U.S. 454 (1981).

[65]17 Cal. 3d 425, 551 P.2d 334, 131 Cal. Rptr. 14 (1976).

[66]Emerich v. Philadelphia Center for Human Development, Inc., 720 A.2d 1032, 1037 (Pa. 1998) (citing Naidu v. Laird, 539 A.2d 1064 (Del.1988); Bardoni v. Kim, 390 N.W.2d 218 (Mich. Ct. App. 1986); Bradley v. Ray, 904 S.W.2d 302 (Mo. Ct.

accepted as "a national standard of practice."[67] In spite of the acceptance of such a broadly sweeping statement, the reality of *Tarasoff*'s impact is that it has varied greatly. As Professor Perlin has pointed out, some states "have adopted its holding, some have extended its reach, others have limited it, while yet others have simply declined to follow it."[68]

In the jurisdictions following *Tarasoff,* empirical research has not borne out the fears the dissenting judges raised that this limitation on confidentiality would destroy the therapist-client relationship.[69] But research has, at least in part, validated the dissenting judges' fears regarding over-commitment to avoid *Tarasoff*-like liability. For example, one study found that approximately one-third of the therapists surveyed admitted they were more willing to initiate civil commitment proceedings in light of the *Tarasoff* decision.[70] And at least one commentator has urged clinicians to lower their decision-making threshold for determinations of dangerousness in civil commitments to avoid *Tarasoff* liability.[71] More empirical research is needed on this issue before a pronouncement is made regarding *Tarasoff*'s impact on civil commitment.[72]

While the duty to warn under *Tarasoff* may not exist at the moment in any particular jurisdiction, on many fronts courts have grown comfortable with a notion of a protective duty in the years since *Tarasoff* was decided.[73] For example, some scholars have contemplated how a *Tarasoff*-like duty to warn might play out in the medical community with patients who have tested positive for AIDS.[74] Thus, *Tarasoff*'s persuasive precedential value cannot be underestimated and its duty to warn should be a concern for all medical and mental health professionals.

App.1995); Lipari v. Sears, Roebuck & Co., 497 F. Supp. 185 (D. Neb.1980); McIntosh v. Milano, 403 A.2d 500 (N.J. Super. Ct. 1979); Leedy v. Hartnett, 510 F. Supp. 1125 (M.D. Pa.1981); Peck v. Counseling Service of Addison Co., Inc., 499 A.2d 422 (Vt.1985); Petersen v. Washington, 671 P.2d 230 (Wash. 1983); Schuster v. Altenberg, 424 N.W.2d 159 (Wis. 1988). *Accord,* Hamman v. County of Maricopa, 775 P.2d 1122 (Ariz. 1989); Bradley Center, Inc. v. Wessner, 287 S.E.2d 716 (Ga. Ct. App.), *aff'd,* 296 S.E.2d 693 (Ga. 1982); Perreira v. State, 768 P.2d 1198 (Colo.1989); Littleton v. Good Samaritan Hospital and Health Center, 529 N.E.2d 449 (Ohio 1988); Limon v. Gonzaba, 940 S.W.2d 236 (Tex. Ct. App. 1997). *But see,* Boynton v. Burglass, 590 So.2d 446 (Fla. Dist. Ct. App.1991)).

[67]James Beck, *The Psychotherapist and the Violent Patient,* in THE POTENTIALLY VIOLENT PATIENT AND THE TARASOFF DECISION IN PSYCHIATRIC PRACTICE 9, 33 (James Beck ed. 1985); *see also* Michael L. Perlin, *Tarasoff and the Dilemma of the Dangerous Patient: New Direction for the 1990's,* 16 LAW & PSYCHOL. REV. 29, 35 (1992).

[68]Perlin, *supra* note 67, at 33.

[69]*See, e.g.,* Mark J. Mills, et al., *Protecting Third Parties: A Decade After Tarasoff,* 144 AM. J. PSYCHIATRY 68, 72 (1987).

[70]Daniel J. Givelber et al., *The Tarasoff Controversy: A Summary of Findings From an Empirical Study of Legal, Ethical and Clinical Issues,* in THE POTENTIALLY VIOLENT PATIENT AND THE TARASOFF DECISION IN PSYCHIATRIC PRACTICE 477-78 (James Beck ed. 1985).

[71]Linn T. Greenberg, *The Psychiatrist's Dilemma,* 17 J. PSYCHIATRY & L. 381 (1989).

[72]*See* Perlin, *supra* note 67, at 46.

[73]*Id.* at 42 ("while the characterization of *Tarasoff* as a 'national standard' may be somewhat overblown, it is clear that most courts are comfortable with some sort of protective duty, and it is likely that courts in "new" jurisdictions will generally agree with this principle of law.).

[74]*Id.* at 44 (citing, *e.g.,* Kenneth E. Labowitz, *Beyond Tarasoff: AIDS and the Obligation to Breach Confidentiality,* 9 ST. L.U. PUB. L. REV. 495 (1990); Kimberly Waldron, Note, *AIDS: Establishing A Physician's Duty to Warn,* 21 RUTGERS L.J. 645 (1990); William J. Curran et al., *AIDS: Legal and Policy Implications of the Application of Traditional Disease Control Measures,* 15 L. MED. & HEALTH CARE 27 (1987); Charles D. Weiss, *AIDS: Balancing the Physician's Duty to Warn and Confidentiality Concerns,* 38 EMORY L.J. 299 (1989)).

PART III:
PSYCHOLOGY AND THE LAW

CHAPTER ELEVEN
POLICE PSYCHOLOGY

As stated in Chapter One, this text is primarily concerned with psychology in the law—how the behavioral sciences operate within the confines of the civil and criminal justice systems to answer questions posed within a doctrinal legal framework.[1] There are, however, many instances where law and psychology intersect outside of the judicial framework. Unit IV is devoted to the study of these situation. We begin doing so in this chapter by examining police psychology.

I. THE ROLE OF THE POLICE OFFICER

Police officers have a number of duties, each of which requires different skills. Movies and television often capitalize on the police role of law enforcement—the investigation of crime to apprehend suspected offenders. Yet, this part of law enforcement officers' role only occupies about 10 percent of police activity.[2] The great bulk of police time is spent maintaining order in and providing services to the community. In addition to the traditional law enforcement role of detecting criminal activity, the National Advisory Commission on Criminal Justice Standards and Goals identified eight other major police responsibilities that collectively take up the remaining 90 percent of police activity: (1) apprehension of criminal offenders; (2) participation in court proceedings; (3) protection of constitutional guarantees; (4) assistance to those who cannot care for themselves or who are in danger of physical harm; (5) traffic control; (6) resolution of day-to-day conflicts among family, friends, and neighbors; (7) creation and maintenance of a feeling of security in the community; and (8) promotion and preservation of civil order.[3] It takes a special person to balance all of these responsibilities while simultaneously remaining professional and in control while managing the stress law enforcement brings. Is there a "police personality" that is particularly well suited meeting these challenges?

II. THE "POLICE PERSONALITY"

Police perform one of the most important roles in society. They are entrusted with power that ordinary citizens do not have and are expected to exercise that power within the bounds of the law. For example, the police are the only segment of society permitted to use force to resolve problems. Police must often make split-second decisions under highly stressful circumstances, informed, hopefully, not only by knowledge of the law, but also of the behavioral sciences. It takes a special type of person to carry out the police role effectively while avoiding the omnipresent temptations police work can present, ranging from police wrongdoings like bribery

---

[1]Craig Haney, *Psychology and Legal Change: On the Limits of a Factual Jurisprudence*, 4 L. & HUM. BEHAV. 147 (1980).

[2]E.g., A.C. Germann, *Community Policing: An Assessment*, 60 J. CRIM. L., CRIMINOLOGY, & POLICE SCI. 84-96 (1969); Robert J. Meadows, *Beliefs of Law Enforcement Administrators and Criminal Justice Educators Toward the Needed Skill Competencies in Entry-Level Police Training Curriculum*, 15 J. POLICE SCI. & ADMIN. 1-9 (1987).

[3]NATIONAL ADVISORY COMMISSION ON CRIMINAL JUSTICE STANDARDS AND GOALS, REPORT ON THE COURTS 392 (Washington, DC: U.S. Department of Justice, Law Enforcement Assistance Administration 1973); *see also* HARRY P. HATRY ET AL., SERVICE EFFORTS AND ACCOMPLISHMENTS REPORTING: ITS TIME HAS COME 186 (Washington, D.C.: Governmental Accounting Standards Board 1990).

and corruption, to police brutality incidents such as those seen in the cases of Rodney King,[4] Abner Louima,[5] and Tyisha Miller,[6] just to name a few of the more notable cases.[7]

A number of scholars have conducted research into discovering if there is a "police personality." While no such core personality has been validly identified in any research, it does appear that law enforcement officers often do share certain values and belief systems. One of the leading researchers into the police personality is Joel Lefkowitz.[8] He asserts that police do not differ from the general population in terms of intelligence or psychopathy, but they do manifest certain groups of personality traits that he termed **Police Trait Syndrome Cluster I** and **Police Trait Syndrome Cluster II.**

Lefkowitz asserts that Cluster I develops as a result of police largely keeping to themselves, interacting with each other, often as a result of being misunderstood by society at large. Interestingly, surveys of citizens do not reveal negatives attitudes towards the police to the degree that law enforcement officer tend to believe.[9] Yet, their view that the public mistrusts them leads police to feel isolated, defensive, suspicious, and cynical.

Cluster II centers around **authoritarianism** and police status as enforcers of the law. They come to see themselves as the societal embodiment of the authority of the state (i.e., "I am the law."). This often can lead to both a rejection of anything different as "abnormal" and a corresponding belief in the need for punishment and discipline for norm-breakers. Cluster II also involves a near-blind acceptance of authority figures; a high pressure for conformity (i.e., to "fit in"); and a tendency to think rigidly and in oversimplified ways (i.e., seeing things as black or white).

While the personality traits identified by Lefkowitz have been found in other studies,[10] it is generally accepted that "the existence of a pervasive authoritarianism in most law enforcement officers has not been substantiated."[11] Most scholars agree there is no "single, unitary 'cop personality.'"[12] Moreover, to the extent that law enforcement personnel do share some of the traits identified by Lefkowitz, it remains unclear if people develop the traits as a result of their job experiences, or if people "predisposed to this sort of outlook naturally self-selected to become police officers."[13]

---

[4]*See, e.g.*, Janny Scott, *Violence Born of the Group*, L.A. TIMES, Mar. 28, 1991, at A1, A26.

[5]Patt Morrison, *Deja Vu All Over Again*, L.A. TIMES, Aug. 29, 1997, at B2.

[6]David Rosenzweig and Tom Gorman, *U.S. Launches Probe of Police in Riverside Civil Rights: Tyisha Miller's Slaying Prompts Investigation of the Department's Use of Force and Treatment of Minorities*, L.A. TIMES, July 9, 1999, at A1.

[7]For examples of lesser-known cases of police brutality and the way in which police officers often lie for each other to cover them up, see Jennifer E. Koepke, *The Failure to Breach the Blue Wall of Silence: The Circling of the Wagons to Protect Police Perjury*, 39 WASHBURN L.J. 211 (2000).

[8]Joel Lefkowitz, *Psychological Attributes of Policemen: A Review of Research and Opinion*, 31 J. SOCIAL ISSUES 3-26 (1975); *see also* Joel Lefkowitz, *Industrial – Organizational Psychology and the Police*, 5 AM. PSYCHOLOGIST 346-64 (1977).

[9]*Id.*

[10]*See, e.g.*, Robert Reiner, *Police Research in the United Kingdom*, in MODERN POLICING, (M. Tonry & N. Morris, eds., University of Chicago Press 1992).

[11]CURT R. BARTOL & ANNE M. BARTOL, PSYCHOLOGY AND LAW 62 (2d ed. 1994).

[12]PETER K. MANNING & JOHN VAN MAANEN (EDS.), POLICING: A VIEW FROM THE STREET 271 (1978).

[13]Sarah E. Waldeck, *Cops, Community Policing, and the Social Norms Approach to Crime Control: Should One Make Us More Comfortable with the Others?*, 34 GA. L. REV. 1253, 1266 (2000).

III. SELECTING POLICE OFFICERS

Behavioral scientists routinely work with law enforcement agencies to select candidates from a pool of applicants. The importance of screening applicants should be self-evident, although screening may not always help select people who will be good police officers. Good screening, however, should help to "screen out" those who should not be police officers. In fact, a failure to conduct a thorough applicant screening may give rise to civil liability for a department or municipality. Since the early 1980s, courts have held that a failure to evaluate, administer, and monitor a psychological testing program to identify violence-prone police officers could constitute negligence or gross-negligence.[14]

The screening of police applicants generally utilizes three procedures: interviews, situational tests, and psychological tests. The primary point of the interview is to exclude candidates manifesting signs of psychopathology.[15] Although *interviews* are extremely poor tools in terms of their reliability and validity, they are nonetheless considered to be an integral part of the process of evaluating a law enforcement applicant since interviews are flexible, inexpensive, build rapport, ease anxiety, and encourage applicant cooperation.[16] Moreover, interviews may help to identify some desirable qualities in applicants, such as maturity, good interpersonal skills, and a sense of humor.[17]

Situational tests simulate various situations a police officer may encounter in the line of duty in order to evaluate the applicant's performance in a given situation. While these have high intuitive appeal, they are expensive, take a lot of time, and have poor predictive validity insofar as they do not predict actual field performance very well.[18]

Psychological testing has the highest predictive validity of any procedures used in the screening of applicants for law enforcement positions, but still leave much to be desired. For example, intelligence tests tend to correlate well with achievement in police training programs, but have poor predictive validity to actual job performance.[19] And personality tests, although better than interviews and situational tests, often produce only a weak to moderate relationship between test performance and job performance, as you will see below.[20]

Psychological testing is routine today, but it was not always the case. Psychological testing of police applicants appears to have begun in 1916 when Lewis Terman, the Stanford professor who updated Alfred Binet's intelligence test, administered his revised test to police and fire department applicants.[21] He, like others after him, found below-average intelligence scores in the

---

[14]E.g., Bonsignore v. The City of New York, 683 F.2d 635, 637 (2d Cir. 1982); Hild v. Bruner, 496 F. Supp. 93, 99 (D.N.J. 1980).

[15]J.M. Silverstein, *The Psychologist as a Panel Member*, 11 SOCIAL ACTION & L. 72-74 (1985).

[16]THEADORE H. BLAU, PSYCHOLOGICAL SERVICES FOR LAW ENFORCEMENT (New York, NY: Wiley 1994).

[17]Silverstein, *supra* note 15; *see also* JAMES THOMAS CHANDLER, MODERN POLICE PSYCHOLOGY (Springfield, IL: Charles C. Thomas 1990).

[18]R.B. Mills, R.J. McDevitt, & S. Tonkin, *Situational Tests in Metropolitan Police Recruit Selection*, 57 J. CRIM. L., CRIMINOLOGY & POLICE SCI. 99-104 (1966); E.C. Diliman, *Role-Playing as a Technique in Police Selection*, 24 PUB. PERSONNEL REV. 116-118 (1963).

[19]BARTOL & BARTOL, *supra* note 11, at 45-46.

[20]*Id.* at 45.

[21]Lewis Terman, *A Trial of Mental and Pedagogical Tests in a Civil Service Examination for Police and Firemen*, 1 J. APPLIED PYSCHOL. 17-29 (1917).

police applicant pool and recommended that no one with an IQ of less than 80 be hired.[22] In contrast to the time of Terman's research, police work today attracts people of at least average intelligence.[23] And, in those jurisdictions that require their law enforcement officers to have a college education, they attract applicants of above-average intelligence.[24]

In spite of the increasing use of intelligence tests around World War II, especially in the military, psychological testing of police applicants was not a routine part of the selection process until the 1980s. In fact, in 1955, "only fourteen cities with populations over 100,000 had officially adopted psychological testing as part of their processes for hiring police. . . . By 1990, . . . 64 percent of state police departments and 73 percent of municipal police departments requir[ed] their incoming candidates to take at least one psychological test as a condition of employment."[25] Today, it is routine in nearly all police departments.

The purpose of administering psychological tests is to weed out those people who seem likely to react to the stress of being a law enforcement officer in a manner inconsistent with the goals of policing. Put more bluntly, the tests attempt to identify violence-prone applicants.[26]

The MMPI is the most widely used tool for the psychological assessment of law enforcement applicants. Nearly 60 percent of all state and city police agencies used the MMPI, up from 19.2 percent in 1972.[27] The California Personality Inventory (CPI), another objective personality test fashioned after the MMPI, is also widely used.[28] In spite of their widespread use, numerous studies have found little evidence to support their use as an accurate predictor of police performance."[29] Other studies have been more positive, demonstrating accurate predictive validity of 69 percent of 55 officers in a study using profiles developed from the MMPI and CPI.[30] Such evidence should be viewed with skepticism for two important reasons. First, neither test was designed to identity potentially violent personalities from nonviolent ones. Second, the studies finding significant levels of predictive validity have been methodologically flawed.[31]

---

[22]*Id.; see also* L.L. THURSTONE, PRIMARY MENTAL ABILITIES (Psychometric Monograph No. 1) (Chicago, IL : University of Chicago Press 1938).

[23]BARTOL & BARTOL, *supra* note 11, at 43.

[24]*Id.*

[25]Michelle A. Travis, *Psychological Health Tests for Violence-Prone Police Officers: Objectives, Shortcomings, and Alternatives*, 46 STAN. L. REV. 1717, 1719 (1994) (citing Philip Ash, Karen B. Slora & Cynthia F. Britton, *Police Agency Officer Selection Practices*, 17 J. POLICE SCI. & ADMIN. 258, 263 (1990); Eric Ostrov, *Police/Law Enforcement and Psychology*, 4 BEHAV. SCI. & L. 353, 353 (1986)).

[26]*E.g.*, Joyce I. McQuilkin, Vickey L. Russell, Alan G. Frost & Wayne R. Faust, *Psychological Test Validity for Selecting Law Enforcement Officers*, 17 J. POLICE SCI. & ADMIN. 289, 290 (1990).

[27]Ash et al., *supra* note 25, at 260-64.

[28]*Id.*

[29]Travis, *supra* note 25, at 1733 (citing Marcia C. Mills & John G. Stratton, *The MMPI and the Prediction of Police Job Performance*, FBI L. ENFORCEMENT BULL., Feb. 1982, at 10, 13; *see also* T.R. Holland, R.B. Heim & N. Holt, *Personality Patterns Among Correctional Officer Applicants*, 32 J. CLINICAL PSYCH. 786, 786-91 (1976); L.S. Schoenfeld, J.L. Kobos & I.R. Phinney, *Screening Police Applicants: A Study of Reliability with the MMPI*, 47 PSYCH. REP. 419, 419-25 (1980); D. Lester, S.D. Babcock, J.P. Cassisi & M. Brunella, *Hiring Despite the Psychologists' Objections*, 7 CRIM. JUST. & BEHAV. 41, 41-49 (1980); R.J. Levy, *Predicting Police Failures*, 58 J. CRIM. L., CRIMINOLOGY & POLICE SCI. 265, 265-76 (1967)).

[30]George E. Hargrave & Deirdre Hiatt, *Law Enforcement Selection with the Interview, MMPI, and CPI: A Study of Reliability and Validity*, 15 J. POLICE SCI. & ADMIN. 110, 111 (1987); *see also* George E. Hargrave, Deirdre Hiatt & Tim W. Gaffney, *An MMPI Measure of Aggression in Law Enforcement Officers and Applicants*, 16 J. POLICE SCI. & ADMIN. 268, 272 (1988); George E. Hargrave, *Using the MMPI and CPI to Screen Law Enforcement Applicants: A Study of Reliability and Validity of Clinicians' Decisions*, 13 J. POLICE SCI. & ADMIN. 221, 221 (1985).

[31]Travis, *supra* note 25, at 1734-37 and notes cited therein.

Accordingly, the usefulness of using the MMPI and the CPI for screening police applicants is questionable.[32]

A relatively new objective personality test was designed specifically for measuring the "behavioral patterns and personality traits of law enforcement candidates," called the **Inwald Personality Inventory** (IPI).[33] It is the third most popular psychological test used in screening police applicants.[34] It contains 310 true–false questions constructed by Inwald after more than 2500 interviews with police.[35] It "ranks the candidate along twenty-six scales that measure such qualities as stress reaction, deviant behavior patterns, interpersonal difficulties, antisocial behaviors, suspiciousness, anxiety, and rigidity."[36] Like the MMPI, though, it does not identity violence-prone applicants, although it does identify personality characteristics that are particularly relevant to police work. To date, several studies have validated the use of the IPI to predict future job performance,[37] especially when used in combination with the MMPI.[38]

One of the newest psychological tests used to test law enforcement applicants is the **Officer at Risk Examination** (ORE). Unlike the other widely used personality tests, the ORE is a 143 multiple-choice question test designed by clinicians working with law enforcement officers to specifically identify violence-prone police officers.[39] The test is still new enough that an insufficient body of data testing its validity and reliability is available.[40]

A final thought on the screening of police applicants is warranted. In addition to the psychological screening process described above, applicants for positions as law enforcement officers typically undergo an extensive background check. In addition to verifying educational credentials, prior work experience, and military history, applicants normally are screened via a number of other methods including checks on the applicants credit, driving record, and criminal history; interviews with spouses, family members and personal references; and polygraph examinations.[41]

---

[32]MARK SHERMAN, PERSONALITY: INQUIRY AND APPLICATION 185 (1979).

[33]Travis, *supra* note 25, at 1727.

[34]*Id.* (citing Ash et al., *supra* note 25, at 262).

[35]*Id.*

[36]*Id.*; *see also* Elizabeth J. Shusman, Robin E. Inwald & Hilary F. Knatz, *A Cross-Validation Study of Police Recruit Performance as Predicted by the IPI and MMPI*, 15 J. POLICE SCI. & ADMIN. 162, 163 (1987).

[37]Elizabeth J. Shusman and Robin E. Inwald, *Predictive Validity of the Inwald Personality Inventory*, 18 CRIM. JUST. & BEHAV. 419-26 (1991).

[38]Elizabeth J. Shusman and Robin E. Inwald, *A Longitudinal Validation Study of Correctional Officer Job Performance as Predicted by the IPI and MMPI*, 19 CRIM. JUST. & BEHAV. 173-80 (1991); José M. Cortina, Mary L. Doherty, Neil Schmidt, *The Five Big Personality Factors in the IPI and MMPI: Predictors of Police Performance*, 45 PERSONNEL PSYCHOL. 119-40 (1992). Forrest Scogin, Joseph Schumacher, & Jennifer Gardner, *Predictive Validity of Psychological Testing in Law Enforcement Settings*, 26 PROFESSIONAL PSYCHOL. RESEARCH & PRACT. 68-71 (1995).

[39]Travis, *supra* note 25, at 1728 (citing William Barnhill, *Early Warnings: Identifying Violence-Prone Police Officers*, WASH. POST, Aug. 11, 1992, at B5).

[40]*Id.*

[41]Thomas H. Wright, *Pre-Employment Background Investigations*, 60 FBI LAW ENFORCEMENT BULL. 16 (1991).

IV. POLICE TRAINING

"The first efforts at professionalization of the police began with the formation of the International Association of Chiefs of Police, in 1893."[42] By the 1950s, the American Bar Association had drafted the Model Police Training Act.[43] National standards for police training were developed in the 1960s and 1970s and have been continually revised over the last thirty years. Police training today is very different than it was even just a generation ago.[44] After applicants are screened and selected as described in the preceding section:

> Recruits in major municipalities typically undergo substantial . . . training prior to serving on a police force. This . . . training includes . . . complete full-time basic training in police science and general education requirements. Experienced officers undertake specialized and/or refresher training periodically, receive substantial training for supervisory positions, and perform under chain of command and supervision models which attempt to ensure order within departments.[45]

And, as a rule, mental health professionals are routine participants in many facets of law enforcement officer training.[46]

Over 95 percent of police forces require applicants for law enforcement positions to have completed high school[47]; less than one percent of law enforcement officer do not have a high school diploma.[48] In last twenty years of the twentieth century, more and more police departments have added the requirement that its recruits have some college-level education. And although many jurisdictions do not require recruits to have earned a college degree, nearly half of law enforcement officers have completed at least two years of college, and over 25 percent are college graduates.[49] And these numbers continue to increase in the wake of data that show a decrease in complaints against or about police as educational levels of the force increase which, in turn, has led to increased educational standards for accreditation of a police training program.[50]

The length of police training varies considerably, from only a few weeks in small jurisdictions, to several months in major U.S. cities and in certain state police academies.[51] In addition to classroom training in criminal law, criminal procedure, evidence, and investigations, police recruits undergo a wide variety of specialized training, ranging from physical training with

---

[42]Contributing Authors, *Revocation of Police Officer Certification: A Viable Remedy for Police Misconduct?*, 45 ST. LOUIS L.J. 541m 550 (2001).

[43]*Id.*

[44]BLAU, *supra* note 16. at 69-162.

[45]Hazel Glenn Beh, *Municipal Liability for Failure to Investigate Citizen Complaints Against Police*, 25 FORDHAM URB. L.J. 209, 213-14 (1998) (internal citations omitted).

[46]*Id.*; *see also* Wright, *supra* note 41.

[47]Alan Vodicka, *Educational Requirements for Police Recruits*, 42 LAW & ORDER 91, 93 (1994).

[48]Thomas J. Deakin, *Police Professionalism: the Renaissance of American Law Enforcement* 272-73 (1988).

[49]Vodicka, *supra* note 47 , at 93; *see also* Larry Armstrong & Clinton Longenecker, *Police Management Training: A National Survey*, 61 FBI LAW ENFORCEMENT BULL. 22, 22, 26 n.2 (1992); David L. Carter & Allen D. Sapp, *College Education and Policing: Coming of Age*, 61 FBI LAW ENFORCEMENT BULL. 8 (1992).

[50]Vodicka, *supra* note 47 , at 93; *see also* Blau, *supra* note 16, at 2; Raymond E. Arthurs, Jr., *Accreditation: A Small Department's Experience*, 59 FBI LAW ENFORCEMENT BULL. 1 (1990).

[51] Albert A. Apa & Thomas J. Jurkanin, *Police Officer Standards & Training Commissions: Three Decades of Growth*, 57 THE POLICE CHIEF 27, 30 (1990).

firearms and combat techniques to diversity sensitivity training.[52] The National Advisory Commission on Criminal Justice Standards and Goals recommends at least 400 hours of police training, as presented in Table 11.1. Police chiefs and criminal justice educators generally agree with these recommendations, but see a need for more instruction in law and in communications, both orally and in writing.[53]

Behavioral scientists play particularly important roles in teaching law enforcement officers the material in the human values and problems curriculum. Moreover, they play an important part in specialized police training in crisis intervention that goes beyond the basic curriculum outlined above. The next three subsections deal with three specialized areas of crisis intervention: interacting with the mentally ill; responding to domestic violence calls; and hostage negotiations.

A. Police and the Mentally Ill Citizen

Since the deinstitutionalization movement of the 1970s, police have increasingly had to deal with mentally ill people on a daily basis. In 1976, for example, New York City police took approximately 1000 "emotionally disturbed people" into hospitals for psychiatric evaluation.[54] A generation later in 1998, the New York City police reported 64,424 encounters with "emotionally disturbed people," 24,787 of whom were brought to hospitals for evaluation.[55] Most of these encounters usually involve bizarre but noncriminal behavior, or involve petty offenses "such as trespassing, disorderly conduct, and vagrancy."[56] Police often makes arrests for these crimes, especially if they believe it will involve less paperwork than effectuating a hospitalization.[57] Given the surge of mentally ill people in the criminal justice system, due largely to the "deinstitutionalization" movement of the 1960s and 1970s,[58] the economic shift from mental health spending to correctional spending in the 1980s and 1990s,[59] the lack of insurance coverage for the mentally ill,[60] and "aggressive prosecution and incarceration for

---

[52]E.g., Stephen M. Hennessey, *Achieving Cultural Competence*, 60 The Police Chief 46 (1993).

[53]Meadows, *supra* note 2.

[54]E. Fuller Torrey, Out of the Shadows 73-74 (1997).

[55]Ken Kress, *An Argument for Assisted Outpatient Treatment for Persons with Serious Mental Illness Illustrated with Reference to a Proposed Statute for Iowa*, 85 Iowa L. Rev. 1269, 1355 (2000) (citing Elizabeth Bumiller, *In the Wake of Attack, Giuliani Cracks Down on Homeless*, N.Y. Times (late ed.), Nov. 20, 1999, at A1).

[56]*Id.* at 1355.

[57]E.g., Arthur R. Matthews, *Observations on Police Policy an Procedures for Emergency Detention of the Mentally Ill*, 61 J. Crim. L., Criminology, & Police Sci. 283-95 (1970).

[58]T. Howard Stone, *Therapeutic Implications of Incarceration for Persons with Severe Mental Disorders: Searching for Rational Health Policy*, 24 Am. J. Crim. L. 283, 291 (1997) (citing Mary L. Durham, *The Impact of Deinstitutionalization on the Current Treatment of the Mentally Ill*, Int'l J. L. & Psychiatry 117, 123-24 (1989)); *see also* Fox Butterfield, *Asylums Behind Bars: A Special Report; Prisons Replace Hospitals for the Nation's Mentally Ill*, The New York Times, Mar. 5, 1998, at A1.

[59]Stone, *supra* note 58 (citing Robert D. Miller, *Economic Factors Leading to Diversion of the Mentally Disordered Offender from the Civil to the Criminal Commitment Systems*, 15 Int'l J. L. & Psychiatry 1 (1991)).

[60]Jeffrey Rubin, *Paying for Care: Legal Developments in the Financing of Mental Health Services*, 28 Hous. L. Rev. 143, 162-64 (1991).

drug-related offenses,"[61] some have labeled the phenomenon the "criminalization" of being mentally ill.[62]

Table 11.1: Recommended Hours of Police Training

Subject Area	Percentage of Training Time	Hours
Introduction to the Criminal Justice System Overview of courts, policing, and corrections with an emphasis on role of police	8%	32
Law Focus on criminal law, criminal procedure, constitutional law, law of evidence, and judicial processes	10%	40
Human Values and Problems Criminology; conflict-management and resolution; mediation; cultural awareness and diversity training; public relations	22%	88
Patrol and Investigation Procedures Traffic management; investigation techniques; reporting; arrest and detention procedures; conducting interviews and interrogations; case preparation	33%	132
Police Proficiency Driver training; physical training; emergency medical training; training on use of force for self-defense, defense of others, effectuating arrests, and control of crowds, prisoners, etc.	18%	72
Administration Policies, rules, regulations, and procedures; police organization; personnel issues	9%	36

Source: National Advisory Commission on Criminal Justice Standards and Goals, *Report on Police* 394 (1973).

What highlights the need for police training in dealing with the mentally ill beyond the mere numbers of people encountered is the fact that mentally ill people are much more likely to be hurt or killed in encounters with law enforcement officers.[63] And, after arrest, those with mental illness often find themselves treated more harshly for the same offenses then defendants without a history of mental illness.[64] While these problems are not necessarily caused by law enforcement as much as they are by a failure of good public policy in dealing with the mentally ill in society, certainly better police training in handling mentally ill people can help.

[61] Stone, *supra* note 58, at 291.

[62] *E.g.*, Linda A. Teplin, *The Criminalization of the Mentally Ill: Speculation in Search of Data*, in MENTAL HEALTH AND CRIMINAL JUSTICE 63-85 (Linda A. Teplin, ed., Newberry Park, CA: Sage 1984).

[63] Kress, *supra* note 55, at 1355, 1363-64.

[64] Ellen Hochstedler Steury, *Specifying "Criminalization" of the Mentally Disordered Misdemeanant*, 82 J. CRIM. L. & CRIMINOLOGY 334 (1991).

B. Police and Domestic Violence

Police spend more time responding to domestic violence calls than to homicide, rape, and assault calls combined. And these domestic violence situations pose the greatest danger to law enforcement officers. In fact, police are more like to be assaulted or killed responding to a domestic violence call than to any other type of disturbance.[65] Contrary to popular belief, domestic violence is not overwhelmingly male on female; studies have found that women and men abuse their domestic partners in roughly equal rates.[66] The major difference is that when women are victimized by battering men, they tend to be hurt much more severely than men who are victimized by women.[67]

Regardless of the gender of the victim, for decades police conceptualized acts of assault and/or battery that occurred between intimate partners as private matter.[68] This often led to police failing to respond to domestic violence calls.[69] Even when they did respond, the view that domestic violence was a private matter "fostered and encouraged the police to attempt to help the parties rather than arrest the abusers."[70] Only between 3 and 10 percent of domestic violence calls resulted in an arrest.[71] One study showed that even when the victim was bleeding, police made an arrest in only 15 percent of the cases.[72] Consider this except from a 1974 police training manual:

> In dealing with family disputes the power of arrest should be exercised as a last resort. The officer should never create a police problem when there is only a family problem existing. . . . In family dispute interventions the most important tool the officer has at his command is the technique of being a good listener. . . . The intervening officer, by demonstrating his ability to listen, may well have transmitted this quality to the participants. Thus, the officer has instilled in the family group the importance of being able to listen.[73]

Other training manuals went as far as to encourage the responding officer to lie to the victim, stating that court was not in session, or that no judge was available to hear this kind of dispute.[74]

---

[65]THOMAS KETTERMAN & MARJORIE KRAVITZ, POLICE CRISIS INTERVENTION: A SELECTED BIBLIOGRAPHY (Washington, D.C.: Gov't Printing Office 1978) (reporting that nearly 25 percent of police deaths and assaults occur during response to domestic violence situations); *see also* DEBORAH L. RHODE, JUSTICE AND GENDER: SEX DISCRIMINATION AND THE LAW 239 (1989) (reporting that roughly one-third of all police injuries occur during response to domestic violence calls).

[66]Daniel G. Saunders, *Wife Abuse, Husband Abuse, or Mutual Combat?, in* FEMINIST PERSPECTIVES ON WIFE ABUSE 95 (Kersti Yllo & Michele Bograd eds., 1988) (citing Murray Straus, Richard Gelles & Susan Steinmetz, BEHIND CLOSED DOORS: VIOLENCE IN AMERICAN FAMILIES 43-44 (1980)).

[67]*Id.*

[68]Douglas R. Marvin, *The Dynamics of Domestic Abuse, Law Enforcement Bulletin* (posted July 1997) <http://www.fbi.gov/library/leb/1997/july973.htm>.

[69]ALAN JAY LINCOLN & MURRAY A. STRAUSS, CRIME AND THE FAMILY 136 (1985).

[70]Jennifer R. Hagan, *Can We Lose the Battle and Still Win the War?: The Fight Against Domestic Violence after the Death of Title III of the Violence Against Women Act*, 50 DEPAUL L. REV. 919, 936 (2001).

[71]LINCOLN & STRAUSS, *supra* note 69, at 136.

[72]*Id.* (citing Lisa M. Fitzgerald, *The Violence Against Women Act: Is It An Effective Solution?*, 1 HOW. SCROLL 46, 47 (1993)).

[73]Paula Finley Mangum, *Reconceptualizing Battered Woman Syndrome Evidence: Prosecution Use of Expert Testimony on Battering*, 19 B.C. THIRD WORLD L.J. 593, 596 n.19 (1999) (citing CRISIS INTERVENTION AND THE POLICE: SELECTED READINGS 111, 117, 118 (Richard W. Kobetz ed., 1974)).

[74]Amy Eppler, *Battered Women and the Equal Protection Clause: Will the Constitution Help Them When the Police Won't?*, 95 YALE L.J. 788, 790 n.12 (1986) (quoting Eisenberg & Micklow, *The Assaulted Wife: Catch 22 Revisited*, 3 WOMEN'S RTS. L. REV. 138, 156-57 (1977)).

The law has responded in several ways, ranging from allowing warrantless arrests of people when probable cause exists to believe an act of domestic violence or the breach of a restraining order has occurred, to mandatory arrest statutes in such situations.[75] But changes in the law do not necessarily change police attitudes and behavior. For many police officers uneducated in the psychological, sociological, and economic factors that often keep a woman in an abusive relationship, they believe that "battered women love what they get and they deserve it."[76] Psychology has assisted in helping law enforcement personnel transcend its old-time views and help officers not only see domestic violence for the crime it is, but also to understand the reasons why a victim might stay in an abusive relationship, refuse to press charges against an abuser, and even feel responsible for a battering incident.[77]

Through training and education programs, police have become better educated to view domestic violence as any other crime of violence.[78] From counseling the victim to gathering evidence at the scene to allow for prosecution without the victim's cooperation, specialized domestic violence training programs have decreased the rate of domestic violence in many cities throughout the county.[79] For example, the San Francisco Family Violence Prevention Fund trains officers to respond to domestic violence calls using hypothetical fact patterns.

> For example, because a battered woman is often reluctant to turn against her batterer, the curriculum teaches the officer to ask precise, direct questions when interviewing her about the battery. Recognizing the financial and emotional ties common between abuser and victim, the officer learns to turn reluctance into cooperation by stressing the availability of probation and counseling. By integrating domestic violence theory and the practical challenges of law enforcement, the curriculum shows how a police reaction tailored to the domestic violence dynamic is necessary for successful intervention.[80]

In spite of the progress made both in substantive law and police training, it is questionable whether perpetrators of domestic violence crime are ever really brought to justice. One study found that 95 percent of men arrested on assault or battery charges stemming from a domestic situation in Milwaukee were not prosecuted, and only 1 percent were convicted.[81] Another study in Connecticut, a state that extensively trains its police and mandates the arrest of offenders upon probable cause, demonstrated that 80 percent of domestic violence cases are either dismissed or are disposed of via a no-contest plea such that virtually none of the cases result in a felony conviction.[82] Clearly, behavioral scientists have a large role to play in not only police training,

---

[75]LAWRENCE W. SHERMAN, JANELL D. SCHMIDT & DENNIS P. ROGAN, POLICING DOMESTIC VIOLENCE: EXPERIMENTS AND DILEMMAS 111, 112 (1992).

[76]Jennifer R. Adler, *Strengthening Victims' Rights in Domestic Violence Cases: an Argument for 30-day Mandatory Restraining Orders in Massachusetts,* 8 B.U. PUB. INT. L.J. 303, 318 n.113 (1999) (citing Rai Kowal, *Working Luncheon on Domestic Violence,* (Sept. 30, 1991) in CTR. FOR HEALTH COMMUNICATION, HARV. INST. OF PUB. HEALTH 4 (1991)).

[77]Peter G. Jaffee et al., *in* LEGAL RESPONSES TO WIFE ASSAULT: CURRENT TRENDS AND EVALUATION 62-95 (N. Zoe Hilton, ed., (Sage 1993)

[78]*See generally* PATRICIA G. BARNES (ED.), DOMESTIC VIOLENCE: FROM A PRIVATE MATTER TO A FEDERAL OFFENSE (1998).

[79]Hagan, *supra* note 70.

[80]The Harvard Law Review, *Developments in the Law – Legal Responses to Domestic Violence: Iv. Making State , Institutions More Responsive,* 106 HARV. L. REV. 1551, 1555 (1993).

[81]Joan Zorza, *The Criminal Law of Misdemeanor Domestic Violence, 1970-1990,* 83 J. CRIM. L. & CRIMINOLOGY 46, 71 (1992).

[82]Evan Stark, *Re-presenting Woman Battering: From Battered Woman Syndrome to Coercive Control,* 58 ALB. L. REV. 973, 978 n.27 (1995) (citing 1991 Conn. State Police Fam. Violence Intervention Unit Ann. Rep. 4).

but also in educating prosecutors, judges, juries, and other actors in the justice system about the realities of domestic violence.

C. Hostage Negotiations

Specialized hostage negotiations units were first started in 1972 by the New York City Police Department.[83] The FBI built on the NYPD's foundation starting in 1973,[84] and by 1978, the FBI began to train an elite group of special agents to be hostage negotiators. This was in direct response to several hostage situations, ranging from international incidents such as the killing of eleven Israeli athletes by Palestinian terrorists at the 1972 Olympics in Germany and of Iranian extremists taking hostages at the U.S. Embassy in Iran, to domestic incidents like the Aryan Nation created barricade on Whidbey Island, Washington in 1984. In 1985, the Crisis Management Unit of the FBI "formed the Critical Incident Negotiation Team (CINT), a small, highly trained and mobile group of experienced FBI crisis negotiators."[85] The FBI's approach has become the model upon which many police departments train their own hostage negotiators. In fact, a 1992 survey of hostage negotiators found that the FBI had done the initial training of at least 40 percent of team members.[86] And while the FBI's image undoubtedly has been tarnished in the wake of the mismanagement of the situation with the Branch Dividians in Waco, Texas and the anti-government Freemen in Montana,[87] they continue to handle negotiations under federal jurisdiction and provide "around-the-clock consultation to state and local law enforcement agencies."[88]

The FBI classifies hostage-taking into one of four broad categories.[89] Each category of hostage-taker differs not only in their psychological motivations, but also in how they are to be resolved. The largest of the four groups is the ***mentally disordered persons*** group.[90] Some research suggests that this group accounts for more than half of all hostage incidents.[91] These hostage-takers often behave irrationally and/or become suicidal. Their goal in taking hostages is usually ***expressive***—to make a psychological point. "Expressive offenders generally feel that they have little control over events in their lives. They want to be important, and they believe the media coverage accompanying their hostage taking will help them active this goal."[92]

Common criminals often take hostages when they are caught committing a crime. Such acts are ***instrumental*** insofar as there is a recognizable goal concerning some material gain. Common criminals tend to be more predictable than mentally disturbed hostage-takers, due, in large part,

---

[83]Gary W. Noesner, *Negotiation Concepts for Commanders*, 68 FBI L. ENFORCEMENT BULL. 6-14 (1999).

[84]*Id.*

[85]James M. Botting, Frederick J. Lanceley & Gary W. Noesner, *The FBI's Critical Incident Negotiation Team*, 64 FBI L. ENFORCEMENT BULL. 12-15 (1995).

[86]Mitchell R. Hammer, Clinton R. Van Zant & Randell Rogan, *Crisis-Hostage Negotiation Team Profile*, 63 FBI L. ENFORCEMENT BULL. 8-11 (1994).

[87]*See, e.g.,* David B. Kopel & Paul M. Blackman, *Can Soldiers Be Peace Officers? The Waco Disaster and the Militarization of American Law Enforcement*, 30 AKRON L. REV. 619 (1997).

[88]Botting et al., *supra* note 85, at 12.

[89]G. Dwayne Fuselier & Gary W. Noesner, *Confronting the Terrorist Hostage Taker*, 59 FBI L. ENFORCEMENT BULL. 6-11 (1990).

[90]Randy Borum & Thomas Strentz, *The Borderline Personality: Negotiation Strategies*, 61 FBI L. ENFORCEMENT BULL. 1-26 (1992).

[91]*Id.*

[92]CURT R. BARTOL, CRIMINAL BEHAVIOR: A PSYCHOSOCIAL APPROACH 342 (Prentice Hall 5th ed. 1999).

to the simple fact that they tend to be more rational. This is evidenced by the fact that in 95 percent of cases in which criminals have taken hostages, negotiators have been able to secure the safe release of the hostages.

Prisoners comprise the third type of hostage-takers. Sometimes prison riots are planned, and the purpose of taking hostages is clearly instrumental. Other times, prison revolts are less planned and the initial acts were expressive; instrumental goals then tend to be developed by inmate leaders as the situation unfolds.

The most well-known type of hostage-taker are *terrorists.* The purpose of an act of terrorism is to gain and focus attention regarding some cause, making such acts both expressive and instrumental. A terrorist incident is defined by the U.S. government several ways, ranging from "a distinct criminal act committed or threatened to be committed by a group or single individual in order to advance a political objective, and greatly endangering safety or property,"[93] to "unlawful use or threatened use of force or violence . . . for coercing or intimidating governments or societies often for achieving political, religious, or ideological objectives."[94] Contrary to popular beliefs, terrorists are rarely sophisticated. Then tend to be young, from disadvantaged socioeconomic backgrounds, and with little, if any, formal training in terrorism.[95] Given their backgrounds, coupled with the fact that they tend to believe so deeply in the underlying cause motivating the act of terrorism, they are considered to be among the most dangerous of all hostage-takers. After all, terrorists are often more than willing to kill the innocent people they have seized as hostages.

Regardless of type of hostage-taker, the negotiation strategies used to deal with hostage situations is remarkably consistent.[96] Law enforcement personnel, as opposed to mental health professionals, lead hostage negotiations. "Although input from mental health professionals may be invaluable during a crisis, their role should be limited to consultation. Most professionals will readily admit that they are trained to work in clinical settings and are not prepared for the extreme stress and adverse conditions that unfold during hostage situations."[97] That being said, nearly 40 percent of all law enforcement hostage negotiation teams use a mental health professional as a consultant to the negotiation team, offering insights on the perpetrator's mental status, motives, personality, and stress level, and fatigue level.[98] And doing so seems to pay off; agencies using a mental health professional consultant report more incidents ending by negotiated surrender and fewer incidents resulting in the serious injury or death of a hostage.[99]

Joseph Betz outlined five police response strategies to hostage situations. They were: (1) attack without any attempt at negotiation; (2) neither attack nor negotiate, but wait it out; (3) negotiate without concession; (4) negotiate with concessions; and (5) negotiate and lie about

---

[93]Dep't of Defense Directive 3025.12, *Employment of Military Resources in the Event of Civil Disturbances*, para. IV B (Aug. 19, 1971).

[94]Dep't of Defense Directive 2000.12, *Protection of DOD Personnel and Resources Against Terrorist Acts*, para. C 4 (July 16, 1986).

[95]Fuselier & Noesner, *supra* note 89, at 10.

[96]*Id.*

[97]Francis V. Burke, Jr., *Lying During Crisis Negotiations: A Costly Means to Expedient Resolution*, 14 CRIM. JUST. ETHICS 49-62 (1995).

[98]William M. Butler, Harold Leitenberg, & G. Dwayne Fuselier, *The Use of Mental Health Professional Consultants to Police Hostage Negotiation Teams*, 11 BEHAV. SCI. & L. 213-21 (1993).

[99]*Id.*

concessions.[100] When negotiation of the hostage situation is the route chosen by law enforcement, the last option—lying—is not the preferred method.[101] Dr. Thomas Fagan, the former director of clinical training for the Federal Bureau of Prison's Psychology Services Branch and coordinator of its Hostage Negotiation Training Program, suggests a six-step approach to hostage negotiations, which are reproduced in the left column of Table 11.2.[102] The right column of Table 11.2 contains important tactics identified by Fuselier and Noesner for successful hostage negotiations.[103]

Table 11.2: Steps and Guidelines to Hostage Negotiations

Steps	Guidelines
1: Establish Contact and Open a Line of Communication	Stabilize and contain the situation.
2: Restore Calmness to the Situation	Do not rush; take time. Do not use the term "hostages" to refer to the victims. Do not direct attention to the victims.
3: Gather Information	Listen to the hostage-taker; good listening skills are far more important than talking.
4: Develop a Plan or Negotiation Strategy	Do not offer anything. Be as honest as possible, avoiding deceptive tricks. Do not dismiss a request as trivial. Never say "no." Do not set a deadline and avoid accepting one.
5: Sell the Plan to the Perpetrator	Do not make alternative suggestions. Do not introduce others into the negotiations process. Do not allow any exchange of hostages, especially a negotiator for a hostage.
6: Prepare for Surrender	

Sources: Thomas J. Fagan, *Negotiating by the Numbers*, 62 Corrections Today 132–136 (2000); G. Dwayne Fuselier and Gary W. Noesner, *Confronting the Terrorist Hostage Taker*, 59 FBI L Enforcement Bull 6–11 (1990).

One of the more interesting phenomena that can occur during hostage situations is the development of a traumatic bonding between the captor and the hostage, known as the **Stockholm effect** (also known as Stockholm syndrome). The development of this bizarre kinship was named after a 1973 hostage-taking incident in a bank in Stockholm, Sweden after which the victims expressed a "strong attachment to their captors, to the point of refusing to testify against

---

[100]Joseph Betz, *Moral Considerations Concerning the Police Response to Hostage-Takers*, in Ethics, Public Policy, and Criminal Justice 110-32 (F. Elliston, ed. 1982).

[101]*See* Burke, *supra* note 97.

[102]Thomas J. Fagan, *Negotiating by the Numbers*, 62 Corrections Today 132-36 (2000).

[103]G. Dwayne Fuselier & Gary W. Noesner, *Confronting the Terrorist Hostage Taker*, 59 FBI L. Enforcement Bull. 6-11 (1990); *see also* G. Wayne Fuselier, *A Practical Overview of Hostage Negotiations*, 50 FBI L. Enforcement Bull. 2-7, 10-15 (1981).

them."[104] The syndrome is typically seen in male captives. A 1982 study reported that Stockholm syndrome developed in half of all of the recent victims of hostage cases, underscoring its pervasiveness.[105] Consider this quote from a passenger on TWA Flight 847 when it was hijacked to Beirut: "They weren't bad people. They let me eat, they let me sleep, they gave me my life."[106]

Four conditions are necessary for development of Stockholm syndrome: "the hostage is threatened with death by the captor and believes that the captor can carry out the threat if he so desires; the hostage cannot escape and is dependent on the captor; the hostage is isolated from others and is only exposed to the perspective of the captor; and the hostage perceives some degree of kindness from the captor."[107] The hostage identifies with the hostage-taker who, having the power to kill the hostage, comes to be perceived favorably for allowing the hostage to live.[108] "The victims' need to survive is stronger than his impulse to hate the person who has created his dilemma."[109] Successful hostage negotiators try to use the odd relationship between captor and captive by becoming a part of the dynamic themselves. "They attempt to become a psychological member of the hostage group who maintains important ties to the outside world"[110]—contacts they can use to negotiate a peaceful resolution of the conflict.

V. STRESS AND ADAPTATION

A. Causes of Police Stress

Without argument, law enforcement work is stressful. Police routinely have to deal with violence, death, fatal accidents, hostility, and situations where their lives are at risk. Accordingly, law enforcement has routinely been presumed to be one of the most stressful occupations.[111] One police psychologist described the profession as "high in psychic battering."[112] Yet, the degree to which law enforcement it is stressful is widely disputed in the literature. Several studies have

---

[104]Marshall D. Beall, *Hostage Negotiations*, in CONTEMPORARY TERRORISM, (John D. Elliott & Leslie K. Gibson eds.) 229-230 (1978).

[105]David A. Soskis & Frank M. Ochberg, *Concepts of Terrorist Victimization*, in VICTIMS OF TERRORISM 105-35 (Frank M. Ochberg & David A. Soskis eds., 1982)).

[106]Stockholm Syndrome <http://www.syntac.net/hoax/stock.php>.

[107]Hope Toffel, *Crazy Women, Unharmed Men, and Evil Children: Confronting the Myths about Battered People Who Kill Their Abusers, and the Argument for Extending Battering Syndrome Self-defenses to All Victims of Domestic Violence*, 70 SO. CAL. L. REV. 337, 353 (1996) (citing Dee L.R. Graham, Edna Rawlings & Nelly Rimini, *Survivors of Terror: Battered Women, Hostages, and the Stockholm Syndrome*, in FEMINIST PERSPECTIVES ON WIFE ABUSE 217, 220-21 (Kersti Yllo & Michele Bograd eds., 1988)).

[108]*Id.* at 353-54.

[109]Borum & Strentz, *supra* note 90.

[110]LAWRENCE S. WRIGHTSMAN, MICHAEL T. NIETZEL & WILLIAM H. FORTUNE, PSYCHOLOGY AND THE LEGAL SYSTEM 145 (4th ed. 1998).

[111]*E.g.*, R.T. Sigler & C.N. Wilson, *Stress in the Work Place: Comparing Police Stress with Teacher Stress*, 16 J. POLICE SCI. & ADMIN. 151-162 (1988); Nancy Norvell et al., *Perceived Stress Levels and Physical Symptoms in Supervisory Law Enforcement Personnel*, 16 J. POLICE SCI. & ADMIN. 75, 75 (1988).

[112]David F. Machell, *The Recovering Alcoholic Police Officer and the Danger of Professional Emotional Suppression*, 6 ALCOHOLISM TREATMENT Q. 85, 86 (1989).

found that police work is no more stressful than other jobs.[113] These studies find that moments of very high stress are extremely rare and, even when experienced, are often positive stressors for police officers who enjoy the excitement of the job.[114] But overall, these data suggest that "police officers seem to experience about the same level of stress as other people."[115]

1. Non-Task Related Stressors

Police stress research has focused on four categories of stressors: (1) external, (2) internal, (3) task-related, and (4) individual.[116]

> External stressors include disillusionment with the justice system as a whole, particularly the perceived leniency of court decisions, negative media coverage, and disapproval of decisions arising out of government and administrative bodies. Internal stressors encompass departmental problems, ranging from poor police training and below-average equipment to unclear reward incentives and career development guidelines. Task-related stressors include traditional problems erroneously viewed as the most frequent source of stress on the job, such as fear, danger of physical harm, exposure to the violence, and unmanageable work loads. Individual stressors embrace an officer's personal fears regarding individual performance and success.[117]

Contrary to popular belief, the internal factors are the most frequent cause of police stress, with external factors such as negative media attention a close second.[118] The task-related stressors they encounter on the street often rank as the least-cited stressors.[119] Scholars believe that officers become desensitized and/or detached from the danger they encounter every day, allowing them to cope well with task-related stressors.[120]

In contrast, the internal stressors have been demonstrated to be significant occupational stressors for police. Specific factors contributing to internal occupational stress include: the autocratic "quasi-paramilitaristic model; hierarchical structure; poor supervision; lack of employee input into policy and decision making; excessive paperwork; lack of administrative support; role conflict and ambiguity; inadequate pay and resources; adverse work schedules; boredom; and unfair discipline, performance evaluation and promotion practices."[121]

---

[113]Peter M. Hart & Alexander J. Wearing, *Police Stress and Well-Being: Integrating Personality, Coping and Daily Work Experiences*, 68 J. OCCUPATIONAL & ORGANIZATIONAL PSYCHOL. 133-57 (1995); Richard H. Anson & Mary E. Bloom, *Police Stress in an Occupational Context*, 16 J. POLICE SCI. & ADMIN. 231, 231 (1988).

[114]Jerome E. Storch & Robert Panzarella, *Police Stress: State-Trait Anxiety in Relation to Occupational and Personal Stressors*, J. CRIM. JUST., Mar.-Apr. 1996, at 106.

[115]*Id.*

[116]W. Clinton Terry III, *Police Stress: The Empirical Evidence*, 9 J. POLICE SCI. & ADMIN. 61, 67 (1981);

[117]Marquette Law Review, *Workers' Compensation and High Stress Occupations: Application of Wisconsin's Unusual Stress Test to Law Enforcement Post-traumatic Stress Disorder*, 77 MARQ. L. REV. 147, 153 (1993).

[118]Jerome E. Storch & Robert Panzarella, *Police Stress: State-trait Anxiety in Relation to Occupational and Personal Stressors*, 24 J. CRIM. JUST. 99-107 (1996); John P. Crank & Michael Caldero, *The Production of Occupational Stress in Medium-Sized Police Agencies: A Survey of Line Officers in Eight Municipal Departments*, 19 J. CRIM. JUST. 339, 343 (1991).

[119]Storch & Panzarella, *supra* note 118, at 106 Crank & Caldero, *supra* note 118, at 349; Terry, *supra* note 116, at 64 n.5.

[120]Terry, *supra* note 116, at 64.

[121]R.M. AYRES, PREVENTING LAW ENFORCEMENT STRESS: THE ORGANIZATION'S ROLE 1 (Washington, D.C.: U.S. Bureau of Justice Assistance 1990).

2. Task-Related Critical Incident Stressors

Several task-related incidents have been repeatedly demonstrated to be intense stressors for law enforcement officers. These incidences that expose officers to trauma are called *critical incident stressors.* Such events include "a line-of-duty death or serious injury of a coworker, a police suicide, an officer-involved shooting in a combat situation, a life-threatening assault on an officer, a death or serious injury caused by an officer," and other situations in which an officer is exposed to something highly traumatic.[122] These intense task-related stressor rank low in comparison to internal and external stressors for most police officers because they occur so infrequently in comparison to internal and external ones. For example, few police officers are actually killed in the line of duty. For example, "of the 523,262 officers employed in . . . police agencies [nationwide] in 1990, only [66] officers were feloniously killed in the line of duty."[123] The use of the word "only" in the previous sentence should not be misconstrued, as any officer lost in the line of duty is tragic. The point is, though, that the occurrence of such a loss is relatively rare. When it does happen, however, it can take a tremendous toll on fellow officers, causing a post-traumatic stress response in law enforcement officers.

Post-traumatic stress disorder (PTSD) is a psychological disorder that can be triggered as a response to an event that involved "actual or threatened death or serious injury, or a threat to the physical integrity of self or others" that caused the person experiencing the event to react with "fear, helplessness, or horror."[124] Given the fact that law enforcement officers, by the nature of their work, can encounter such a situation at any time, the law has been slow to accept the PTSD diagnosis in law enforcement personnel.[125] Mental health professionals play an important role in the diagnosis of PTSD when it occurs. One of situations in which PTSD has been clearly identified in law enforcement personnel involves *post-shooting trauma.* Most police officers go through their careers without ever firing a weapon in the line of duty. "Law enforcement personnel kill about 600 criminal suspects yearly, shoot and wound another 1,200, and fire at and miss an additional 1,800."[126]

> In [the 1990s], American police officers have killed over 350 persons annually and wounded numerous others. . . . Studies have demonstrated that the rate of police shootings vary greatly from city to city. In 1992, for example, Los Angeles police shot ten people per every 1,000 officers whereas New York police shot three people per every 1,000 officers. Another study found that the frequency of police shootings varied from 0.5 to 2.5 persons killed per every 100,000 people. Variations in shooting rates may well be the result of differing organizational policies concerning the use of force.[127]

---

[122]Arthur W. Kureczka, *Critical Incident Stress In Law Enforcement*, 65 FBI L. ENFORCEMENT BULL. 10-16, 11 (1996).

[123]Travis, *supra* note 25, at 1089 (citing 1990 FBI Uniform Crime Rep. V, at 237).

[124]AMERICAN PSYCHIATRIC ASSOCIATION, DIAGNOSTIC AND STATISTICAL MANUAL OF MENTAL DISORDERS 427-29 (4th ed. 1994).

[125]*See, e.g.,* cases discussed in Marquette Law Review, *supra* note 117.

[126]Irene Prior Loftus, G. David Porter, J. Robert Suffoletta, Jr., & Deanne M. Tomse, *The "Reasonable" Approach to Excessive Force Cases under Section 1983*, 64 NOTRE DAME L. REV. 136, 140 (1989) (citing Geller, Deadly Force, NATIONAL INSTITUTE OF JUSTICE CRIMINAL FILE STUDY GUIDE 3 (1990)); *see also* HARRY W. MORE, SPECIAL TOPICS IN POLICING (Anderson Publishing 1991).

[127]Robert M. Myers, *Code of Silence: Police Shootings and the Right to Remain Silent*, 26 GOLDEN GATE U.L. REV. 497, 502-04 (1996) (citing, *inter alia,* WILLIAM A. GELLER & MICHAEL SCOTT, DEADLY FORCE: WHAT WE KNOW 100 (1992); Lorie Fridell, *Justifiable Use of Measures in Research on Deadly Force*, 17 J. CRIM. JUST. 157, 160 (1989); Lawrence W. Sherman & Robert H. Langworthy, *Measuring Homicide by Police Officers*, 70 J. CRIM. L. & CRIMINOLOGY 546 (1979); Gerald F. Uelman, *Varieties of Police Policy: A Study of Police Policy Regarding the Use of Deadly Force in Los Angeles County*, 6 LOY. L.A. L. REV. 1, 59 (1973)).

Police officers who kill in the line of duty often experience common psychological problems. One of the most common post-shooting experiences is some kind of perceptual disturbance during the shooting incident. Time distortions occur the most frequently, with 83 percent of officers in one study of eighty-six officers feeling as if time "slowed down" or "stood still."[128] More than half of these officers also reported visual disturbance, such a "tunnel vision" in which nothing else seemed to exist other than the object on which the officer's attention was focused (e.g., the gun in the suspect's hand). More than half also reported auditory distortions, such as not having heard shots being fired.[129] After such incidents, officers reported a wide variety of symptoms and a complete range of intensity of these symptoms, including "a heightened sense of danger, anger, sleep difficulties, isolation/withdrawal, and flashbacks."[130]

B. Adaptational Risks

Unfortunately, police often fail to deal with their stress appropriately. Police "have a strong sense of self-sufficiency and insist that they can solve their own problems."[131] They often fear that admitting stress may be adversely affecting their performance will result in them being viewed as weak, unprofessional, or inadequate.[132] "The most common method of dealing with work-related stress [i]s keeping problems to one's self and working hard," rather than seeking help.[133] Failure to properly deal with stress can lead to any number of negative consequences. A central tenet of organizational/industrial psychology holds that as stress level increases, job performance decreases.[134] Empirical data supporting that general proposition as applied to policing is notably absent in the literature since other factors, most notably experience, affect job performance.[135] Job performance aside, several important risks face law enforcement officers who fail to develop good coping mechanisms to deal with job stress, ranging from burnout, addictions, to depression and suicide.

1. Burnout

Police ***burnout*** is one of the most common results of failing to deal properly with stress.[136] Burnout is defined as "the result of constant or repeated emotional pressure associated with an intense involvement with people over long periods of time."[137] More simply, people suffering from burn out are worn out from giving so much of their time and energy. It is a combination of

---

[128]Roger M. Solomon & James M. Horn, *Post-Shooting Traumatic Reactions: A Pilot Study, in* PSYCHOLOGICAL SERVICES FOR LAW ENFORCEMENT (James T. Reese & Harvey A. Goldstein, eds., Washington, D.C.: U.S. Gov't Printing Office 1986).

[129]*Id.*

[130]BARTOL & BARTOL, *supra* note 11, at 81 (citing *id.*).

[131]Kureczka, *supra* note 122, at 15.

[132]Mark H. Anshel, *A Conceptual Model and Implications for Coping with Stressful Events in Police Work*, 27 CRIM, JUST. & BEHAV. 375-400 (2000).

[133]*See generally* DAVID A. ALEXANDER, LESLIE G. WALKER, GEORGE INNES, POLICE STRESS AT WORK (1993); WILLIAM H. KROES, BROKEN COPS: THE OTHER SIDE OF POLICING (1988).

[134]JOHN B. MINER, INDUSTRIAL ORGANIZATIONAL PSYCHOLOGY 156 (1992).

[135]*See* BARTOL & BARTOL, *supra* note 11, at 75 (summarizing conflicting studies).

[136]*See generally* Gerald Loren Fishkin, POLICE BURNOUT: SIGNS, SYMPTOMS AND SOLUTIONS (1987).

[137]Tod M. Burke, *Dispatcher Stress*, 64 FBI L. ENFORCEMENT BULL. 1-6 (1995) (citing AYALA M. PINES, ELLIOT ARONSON, & DITSA KAFRY, BURNOUT: FROM TEDIUM TO PERSONAL GROWTH 15 (New York: Free Press, 1981)).

psychological, behavioral, and physical symptoms that characterize an apathetic work attitude.[138] Burnout has a three-stage onset. In the first phase, called *emotional exhaustion,* the person feels tired of their work, having lost the enthusiasm that once was there.[139] In the second phase, *depersonalization* sets in, often leaving the person feeling cynical, insensitive or uncaring, and underappreciated.[140] The final phase is the full onset of burning out, in which the person comes to a "painful realization" that he or she can "no longer can help people in need" and that he or she has "nothing left in them to give."[141] Accordingly, the burned out person just stops trying.

2. Alcohol and Drug Abuse

Alcohol and drug abuse are another problem for stressed-out law enforcement officers. During any given shift, a police officer is likely to encounter drugs or alcohol in dealing with a homeless person, a driver, or in confronting a criminal. Moreover, police culture is "particularly conducive to coping by drinking."[142] Given that policing is male-dominated and styled after the military, it is not surprising to find that blowing off stream with peers over drinks—something Joseph Wambaugh called "choirpractice"— is a widespread practice.[143] Moreover, undercover work, especially in vice and narcotic squads, often necessitates a police officer's apparent use of drugs or alcohol to maintain credibility. Given these and other contributing factors, research suggests that anywhere from 10 to 40 percent of law enforcers may be alcoholic.[144]

> One survey of 2200 officers in twenty-nine police departments reported that 23 percent had serious drinking problems. Forty percent of Chicago officers responding to a survey reported drinking on-duty. Another study reported that 53 percent of officers came to work with a hangover and that an "average" officer in the study drank on-the-job about eight days in every six-month period.[145]

3. Depression and Suicide

Depression is a mood disorder whose symptoms produce debilitating psychological, behavioral, and physical reactions. Changing schedules that interfere with getting proper rest, as well as drug or alcohol use, can cause biochemical imbalances in the body that produce *endogenous depression.* But most police depression is *reactive depression*—depression that is a reaction to any of the external stressors described above. But it does not take a critical incident to lead to depression. Bartol and Bartol cite the research of Paul McLean in support of the theory that omnipresent *microstressors* in life are largely responsible for reactive depression.[146] Six sources

---

[138]Alan M. Goodman, *A Model for Police Officer Burnout*, 5 J. BUS. & PSYCHOL. 85-99 (1990).

[139]*See* BARTOL & BARTOL, *supra* note 11, at 80.

[140]*Id.*

[141]Pines et al., *supra* note 137, at 15.

[142]Sally Gross-Farina, *Fit for Duty? Cops, Choirpractice, and Another Chance for Healing*, 47 U. MIAMI L. REV. 1079, 1091 (1993).

[143]JOSEPH WAMBAUGH, THE CHOIRBOYS (1975).

[144]Farina, *supra* note 142, at 1091.

[145]*Id.* (citing CRIMINAL JUSTICE CENTER, SAM HOUSTON STATE UNIV., ALCOHOL AND DRUG PREVENTION STRATEGIES FOR LAW ENFORCEMENT 13-15 (1991); Ronald C. Van Raalte, *Alcohol as a Problem Among Officers*, POLICE CHIEF, Feb. 1979, at 38)).

[146]BARTOL & BARTOL, *supra* note 11, at 83 (citing Peter D. McLean, *Depression as a Specific Response to Stress*, in STRESS AND ANXIETY, Vol. 3 (I.G. Sarasuri & Charles D. Speilberger, eds., Washington, D.C.: Hemisphere Publishing 1976)).

of microstress in particular may produce reactive depression: a reduction of productivity; lack of effective interpersonal communications; lack of realistic goals; inadequate social interactions; difficulties making decisions or solving problems; and lack of self-control.[147] Given the fact that many of these microstressors are part and parcel of police work, depression is a palpable threat to law enforcement officers.

Given the problems of alcohol use and depression, it should come as no surprise to find that *suicide* is another maladaptive reaction in policing. Among suicide victims in general, between 20 and 36 percent had a history of alcohol abuse or were drinking before killing themselves.[148] The alcohol–suicide link appears to be particularly strong in policing. For example, one study of twenty-one Chicago police officers who killed themselves in the three year period from 1977 to 1979 found that fifteen had problems with alcohol.[149] More recent studies in Los Angeles, California[150] and Queensland, Australia[151] found a similar correlation between officer suicide and alcoholism. The Australia study also found a "striking" proximity in time of disciplinary events and suicides.[152]

Any study of police suicide rate must be put in context with the suicide rate for the general population. When that is done, some studies have found that suicide rates for police officers are higher than they are for the general population.[153] Other studies have replicated this finding, but report that the apparent significance of the job disappears when controls are introduced for socioeconomic variables.[154] And some of the more recent studies fail to show any statistically significant difference in police suicide rates from those in the general population.[155] Accordingly, there is insufficient data upon which to conclude that police are at higher risk for suicide than people in other professions.[156] The good news is that police suicide rates appear to be decreasing in the last twenty years or so.[157] Perhaps the recognition of police stress, alcoholism, and depression as serious problems and the corresponding increase in services available to officers suffering from these problems has helped.

C. Coping with Police Stress

To help cope with police stress, organizational structures must "monitor officers' use of maladaptive coping (e.g., excessive drinking, high absenteeism) and the lack of adaptive coping

---

[147]*Id.* at 83-84.

[148]U.S. Dep't of Health and Human Servs., 7th Special Report to the U.S. Congress on Alcohol and Health xxvi (1990).

[149]Marcia Wagner & Richard J. Brzeczek, *Alcoholism and Suicide: A Fatal Connection*, 52 FBI L. Enforcement Bull. 14 (1983).

[150]Rose Lee Josephson & Martin Reiser, *Officer Suicide in the Los Angeles Police Department: A Twelve Year Follow-up*, 17 J. Police Sci. & Admin. 227, 228 (1990).

[151]Christopher Henry Cantor, Ruth Tyman, & Penelope Joy Slater, *A Historical Survey of Police Suicide in Queensland, Australia, 1843-1992*, 25 Suicide & Life-Threatening Behav. 499-507 (1995).

[152]*Id.*

[153]*E.g.,* Wagner & Brzeczek, *supra* note 149; A. Schmidtke, S. Fricke & D. Lester, *Suicide Among German Federal and State Police Officers*, 84 Psychol. Reports 157-66 (1999).

[154]Steven Stack & Thomas Kelley, 13 Am. J. Police 73-90 (1994).

[155]Josephson & Reiser, *supra* note 150.

[156]*See, e.g.,* Bartol & Bartol, *supra* note 11, at 85; Clinton W. Terry, *Police Stress: The Empirical Evidence*, 9 J. Police Sci. & Admin. 61-75 (1981).

[157]*E.g.,* Wagner & Brzeczek, *supra* note 149; Cantor et al., *supra* note 151.

(e.g., physical exercise), and to encourages continued access to stress management training."[158] A 1988 study reported that 53 percent of police agencies regularly used counseling services for their officers, and roughly one-third hired mental health professionals to conduct workshops and seminars to teach successful mechanisms for coping with police stress.[159] In the decade following that study, as recognition of police stress as a serious problem has increased, so did resources available to law enforcement officers. At least 80 percent of 380 police agencies nationwide participating in a recent study reported offering counseling, employee assistance programs, workout facilities, training in domestic violence, and insurance that covered mental health treatment.[160]

These attempts to decrease police stress appear to be paying off. As noted above, it appears that police suicide are down. And studies examining the effects of psychological interventions after critical incidents have demonstrated the positive effects of these interventions. For example, a study of FBI agents that compared those who had benefit serving at a time when post-shooting debriefing and treatment was available with those agents who did not have such services at the time of a shooting incident found that those receiving treatment readjusted to life better than those who did not.[161]

Today, mental health clinicians routinely perform *fitness for duty* evaluations of law enforcement officers—psychological screenings designed to ensure that police officers are not suffering from a pathological amount of stress and/or one of the related disorders that are a function of high stress. Sometimes these fitness-for-duty examinations are routine, occurring at specified time intervals; sometimes they are required when an officer faces a critical incident stressor; other times they are required when some question as to the officer's fitness arises in the form of a poor assessment by a superior officer or in the form of a complaint from a citizen. When these are conducted, they should be performed by a licensed clinician who is familiar with police psychology, but is *not* related with any mental health professional who routinely provides counseling services or educational seminars for a police department.[162] Moreover, fitness for duty evaluations should be comprehensive, involving all of the procedures discussed in the chapter on forensic clinical assessment—including a physical examination, clinical interviews, a battery of psychological tests, and a complete case history (including information gathered from co-workers and family members).[163]

VI. CONCLUSION

Stereotypes of police being authoritarian and conservative exist for good reasons, although the existence of an over-arching "police personality" has not been supported by research. Police come from many backgrounds today and face a variety of stressors. The most intense stressors

---

[158]Anshel, *supra* note 132, at abstract.

[159]Robert P. Delprino & Charles Bahn, *National Survey of the Extent and Nature of Psychological Services in Police Departments*," 19 PROF. PSYCHOL.: RES. & PRAC., 421-25 (1988).

[160]ROBERT P. DELPRINO, KAREN O'QUIN, CHERYL KENNEDY, IDENTIFICATION OF WORK AND FAMILY SERVICES FOR LAW ENFORCEMENT PERSONNEL, (Washington, D.C.: Police Research and Education Project, U.S. National Institute of Justice 1997).

[161]John Henry Campbell, *A Comparative Analysis of the Effects of Post-Shooting Trauma on Special Agents of the Federal Bureau of Investigation*, Dissertation, Michigan State University (1992).

[162]John T. Super, *Select Legal and Ethical Aspects of Fitness for Duty Evaluations*, 25 J. CRIM. JUST. 223-29 (1997).

[163]*See generally* Chapter Four; *see also id.*; Blau, *supra* note 16, at 134-42.

appear to be organizational in nature, not caused by the actual duties of performing law enforcement tasks. Yet, the combination of both microstressors and macrostressors can lead to burnout, alcohol and chemical dependencies, depression, health problems, and even suicide, although there are no reliable data to support that these occur in police with any more frequency than they do in the general population. Monitoring police stress and assisting law enforcement officers in developing coping mechanisms for stress is one of the best ways of preventing dysfunctional adaptation, thereby leading to happier, healthier, and more productive officers.

CHAPTER TWELVE
IDENTIFICATIONS, INTERROGATIONS, AND CONFESSIONS

I. IDENTIFICATIONS AND EYEWITNESS TESTIMONY

You have undoubtedly heard the phrase "seeing is believing." Juries accept this adage as a truism when they consider the testimony of an eyewitness. But there are serious problems with the accuracy of eyewitness identifications.

Unreliability of eyewitness identification testimony may have many causes. First, of course, it is possible that an eyewitness is lying. Concerns about the truthfulness of what someone alleges to have seen can be traced back to the time of Moses: "Thou shalt not bear false witness against thy neighbour."[1] Yet, juries are expected to assess the veracity of all witnesses, and cross-examination is presumed to reveal when eyewitnesses have motivation to lie, just as it would with any other witness. The more troubling situation is the eyewitness who honestly believes his or her testimony is the truth but is incorrect. Even back in Ancient Greece, Plato cautioned, "have sight and hearing any truth in them? Are they not, as the poets are always telling us, inaccurate witnesses?"[2]

There is no truly accurate way to know how frequently mistaken identifications result in wrongful convictions. But decades of research on the topic have consistently found that mistaken identification is the leading cause of wrongful convictions.[3] In fact, it is so common that it practically rivals the sum of all other errors that lead to wrongful conviction.[4] For example, between 75 and 85 percent of the convictions overturned by DNA evidence have involved a mistaken eyewitness.[5] This is likely due to the fact, as the Supreme Court has observed, that "despite its inherent unreliability, much eyewitness identification evidence has a powerful impact on juries . . . . All evidence points rather strikingly to the conclusion that there is almost nothing more convincing than a live human being who takes the stand, points a finger at the defendant, and says, 'That's the one!'"[6] Yet, studies have repeatedly shown a roughly 40 percent rate of

---

[1]   Exodus 20:16 (King James).

[2]   PLATO, PORTRAIT OF SOCRATES, BEING THE APOLOGY, CRITO, AND PHAEDO OF PLATO 99 (R.W. Livingstone, ed., Oxford Univ. Press 1938).

[3]   William David Gross, *The Unfortunate Faith: A Solution to the Unwarranted Reliance Upon Eyewitness Testimony*, 5 TEX. WESLEYAN L. REV. 307, 313 (1999) (*citing* SIEGFRIED L. SPORER ET AL., PSYCHOLOGICAL ISSUES IN EYEWITNESS IDENTIFICATION, 3 (1966)); *see also* Aldert Vrij, *Psychological Factors in Eyewitness Testimony*, *in* PSYCHOLOGY AND LAW: TRUTHFULNESS, ACCURACY, AND CREDIBILITY 105-19 (Amina Memon, Alder Vrij, & Ray Bull eds., McGraw–Hill 1998); C. RONALD HUFF, ARYE RATTNER, EDWARD SAGARIN, CONVICTED BUT INNOCENT : WRONGFUL CONVICTION AND PUBLIC POLICY,66, 83-104 (Thousand Oaks, CA: Sage Publications 1996).

[4]   *See* Arye Rattner, *Convicted But Innocent: Wrongful Conviction and the Criminal Justice System*, 12 LAW & HUM. BEHAV. 283, 287-91 (1988).

[5]   *Compare* The Innocence Project, Mistaken Eyewitness Identifications, *available online at* http://www.innocenceproject.org/causes/mistakenid.php (reporting that 125 of 163, or 76.69%, of post-conviction DNA exonerations in the U.S. involved mistaken eyewitness identification); *with* Barry Scheck, Peter Neufeld, & Jim Dwyer, ACTUAL INNOCENCE: FIVE DAYS TO EXECUTION, AND OTHER DISPATCHES FROM THE WRONGLY CONVICTED (2000) (mistaken eyewitnesses factor in 84% of 67 wrongful convictions); Edward Connors, Thomas Lundregan, Neal Miller & Tom McCain, Convicted by Juries, Exonerated by Science: Case Studies in the Use of DNA Evidence to Establish Innocence after Trial (Department of Justice, 1996) (86% of 28 cases studied involved mistaken eyewitness identification), *available online at* http://www.ncjrs.gov/txtfiles/dnaevid.txt.

[6]   Watkins v. Sowders, 449 U.S. 341, 352 (1981).

mistaken identifications.[7] In spite of this, nearly 80,000 suspects are targeted every year based on an eyewitness identification.[8]

Given the many of causes of misidentification, the United State Supreme Court has held that identifications that occur under questionable circumstances should not be admitted at trial. "[R]eliability is the linchpin in determining the admissibility of identification testimony. . . ."[9] The Supreme Court's demand for reliability in identification procedures is a result of its conclusion that "the vagaries of eyewitness identification are well-known; the annals of criminal law are rife with instances of mistaken identification."[10] To prevent such misidentifications, the Court in *Manson v. Brathwaite* reiterated its belief in the criteria for examining the reliability of identifications set down in *Neil v. Biggers*.[11] The criteria includes "the opportunity of the witness to view the criminal at the time of the crime, the witness' degree of attention, the accuracy of the witness' prior description of the criminal, the level of certainty demonstrated by the witness at the confrontation, and the length of time between the crime and the confrontation."[12] While all of these legal factors seem straight-forward enough, in reality, they depend on complex psychological issues pertaining to perception and memory that we will now explore.

A. Perception

Putting aside the issue of intentional deception, inaccuracy of eyewitness testimony stems from the fact that memories are not exact recordings of events.[13] First and foremost, memory is dependent on perception. We tend to think of perception in terms of our basic senses—sight, hearing, touch, taste, and smell. But **perception** is really a process—"the total amalgam of sensory signals received and then processed by an individual at any one time."[14] This process is highly selective and is as dependent upon psychological factors as it is on physical senses because it is an "interpretive process."[15] The "actual" sensory data we perceive is "processed in light of experience, learning, preferences, biases, and expectations."[16]

One of the most important factors affecting our ability to perceive is the volume of sensory stimulation. "Perception is highly selective because the number of signals or amount of information impinging upon the senses is so great that the mind can process only a small fraction

---

7   Vrij, *supra* note 3, at 106.

8   A.G. Goldstein, J. E. Chance, & G.R. Schneller, *Frequency of Eyewitness Identification in Criminal Cases: a Survey of Prosecutors*. 27 BULL. PSYCHOLOGIC SOC'Y 71-74 (Jan. 1989).

9   Manson v. Brathwaite, 432 U.S. 98, 114 (1977).

10   *Id.* at 119 (*quoting* United States v. Wade, 388 U.S. 218, 228 (1967)).

11   409 U.S. 188, 199-200 (1972).

12   *Id.*

13   Peter J. Cohen, *How Shall They Be Known? Daubert v. Merrell Dow Pharmaceuticals and Eyewitness Identification*, 16 PACE L. REV. 237, 242 (1996); *see generally* Richard C. Atkinson & Richard M. Shiffrin, *Human Memory: A Proposed System and its Control Processes, in* KENNETH W. SPENCE AND JANET T. SPENCE, THE PSYCHOLOGY OF LEARNING AND MOTIVATION: ADVANCES IN RESEARCH AND THEORY, Vol. 2 89-195 (Academic Press, 1968).

14   Steven I. Friedland, *On Common Sense and the Evaluation of Witness Credibility*, 40 CASE W. RES. L. REV. 165, 181 (1990); *see generally* STANLEY COREN, LAWRENCE M. WARD, & JAMES T. ENNS, SENSATION AND PERCEPTION 356 (6th ed., Wiley & Sons, 2003).

15   Robert Buckhout, *Psychology and Eyewitness Identification*, 2 L. & PSYCHOL. REV. 75, 76 (1976); *see also* Friedland, *supra* note 14; Coren et al., *supra* note 14.

16   Frederick E. Chemay, *Unreliable Eyewitness Evidence: The Expert Psychologist and the Defense in Criminal Cases*, 45 LA. L. REV. 721, 724 (1985); *see also* Fredrik H. Leinfelt, *Descriptive Eyewitness Testimony: The Influence of Emotionality, Racial Identification, Question Style, and Selective Perception*, 29 CRIM. JUST. REV. 317 (2004).

of the incoming data."[17] This means we focus on certain stimuli while filtering out others. This results not only in incomplete acquisition of sensory data, but also in differential processing (i.e., interpretation) of events.[18] Even when lighting and distance conditions are good for observation, a person may still experience incomplete acquisition if he or she is "overwhelmed with too much information in too short a period of time,"[19] a function of differential processing referred to as *sensory overload*.

Another important factor affecting perception is how humans fill gaps caused by incomplete sensory acquisition.[20] When these gaps are filled, the details often fit logically, but inaccurately.[21] The type of stimuli involved also affects perception. In particular, people are poor perceivers of duration (we tend to overestimate how long something takes), time (it "flies by" or "drags on"), speed, distance, height, and weight.[22] It is important to keep in mind that people are not aware of their individual variations in the process of perception. In other words, how we perceive and synthesize sensory data are unconscious processes.

B. The Three Phases of Memory

Memory, like perception, is an unconscious process.[23] It is dependent upon three critical stages— acquisition/encoding, retention, and recall/retrieval. All three steps are affected by a number of physical and psychological factors that can taint the accuracy of a memory.[24] Even someone's mood can taint accuracy of a memory.[25] Yet, juries often fail to comprehend the complexities of memory when assessing the testimony of an eyewitness, which can, in turn, lead to conviction of an innocent person.

1. Acquisition Phase

The first stage in the development of memory is the *acquisition, or encoding, stage*. During this first stage in the development of memories, sensory data, as perceived by the individual, are encoded in the appropriate areas of the cerebral cortex.[26] Accordingly, the acquisition of memories is dependent upon perception. Since perception itself is a process dependent on a number of individualized factors, this stage in the process of developing memories is affected by those same factors. Sensory overload is particularly important since it can lead to so many gaps

---

[17] Friedland, *supra* note 14, at 181 (*quoting* Chemay, *supra* note 16, at 723); *see generally* Nelson Cowan, *The Magical Number 4 in Short-Term Memory: A Reconsideration of Mental Storage Capacity*, 24 BEHAVIORAL & BRAIN SCIENCES 87 (2000) (discussing sensory overload as one of the many factors that affect perception and memory).

[18] *See* CURT R. BARTOL & ANNE M. BARTOL, PSYCHOLOGY AND LAW 219 (2d ed. 1994).

[19] Chemay, *supra* note 16, at 726.

[20] *Id.*

[21] *Id.* at 724 (*citing* Buckhout, *supra* note 15, at 5, 6); *see generally* Andrew Roberts, *The Problem of Mistaken Identification: Some Observations on Process*, 8 INT'L J. EVID. & PROOF 100 (2004).

[22] Friedland, *supra* note 14, at 181 (*citing* ELIZABETH F. LOFTUS, EYEWITNESS TESTIMONY 22 (1979)).

[23] Friedland, *supra* note 14, at 182; Chemay, *supra* note 16, at 724.

[24] Cohen, *supra* note 13, at 242-43.

[25] Joseph P. Forgas, Simon M. Laham & Patrick T. Vargas, *Mood Effects on Eyewitness Memory: Affective Influences on Susceptibility to Misinformation*, 41 J. EXPERIMENTAL SOCIAL PSYCHOL. 574 (2005).

[26] *See generally* Ralph N. Haber & Lyn Haber, *Experiencing, Remembering and Reporting Events: The Cognitive Psychology of Eyewitness Testimony,* 6 PSYCHOL, PUB. POL'Y & L. 1057 (2000).

in memory that *confabulation*—"the creation or substitution of false memories through later suggestion"[27]—can occur.

Perceptual variability aside, another important factor that affects memory acquisition is a person's expectations, which influence the way in which details about an event are encoded. An observer tends to seek out some information and avoid other information, an effect called the *confirmation bias*.[28] What gets encoded is, therefore, partially dependent on what the observer was looking for.

2. Retention Phase

The *retention, or storage, phase* follows the encoding phase in the memory process. During this phase, the brain stores the memory until it is called upon for retrieval. How much data is being encoded and retained obviously affects this phase. The greater the amount of data presented, especially in shorter periods of time, the less that will be retained. The other obvious factor is the retention interval—how much time passes between storage of the memory and retrieval of it. But a third, far less obvious factor than the amount of data or the retention interval, has the most potentially negative effect on memory retention: the *post-event misinformation effect*. Exposure to subsequent information affects the way in which memories are retained.[29] Therefore, exposure to post-event misinformation can lead to an eyewitness accepting misinformation as if it were an accurate account.[30]

> For example, a witness to a traffic accident may later read a newspaper article which stated that the driver had been drinking before the accident. "Post-event information can not only enhance existing memories but also change a witness' memory and even cause nonexistent details to become incorporated into a previously acquired memory." When witnesses later learn new information which conflicts with the original input, many will compromise between what they saw and what they were told later on.[31]

---

[27] Chemay, *supra* note 16, at 726; *see also* Giuliana A.L. Mazzoni, L.; Manila Vannucci & Elizabeth F. Loftus, *Misremembering Story Material*, 4 LEGAL & CRIMINOLOGICAL PSYCHOL. 93 (1999).

[28] D. Michael Risinger, Michael J. Saks, William C. Thompson,& Robert Rosenthal, *The Daubert/Kumho Implications of Observer Effects in Forensic Science: Hidden Problems of Expectation and Suggestion*, 90 CALIF. L. REV. 1, 7 (2002); *see also* Karl Ask & Pär Anders Granhag, *Motivational Sources of Confirmation Bias in Criminal Investigations: The Need for Cognitive Closure*, 2 J. INVESTIG. PSYCH. OFFENDER PROFIL. 43 (2005); Greg O. Niemeyer, *The Function of Stereotypes in Visual Perception*, 106 DOCUMENTA OPHTHALMOLOGICA 61 (Jan. 2003); John M. Darley & Paget H. Gross, *A Hypothesis-Confirming Bias in Labeling Effects*, 44 J. PERSONALITY & SOC. PSYCH. 20 (1983); Anthony G. Greenwald, *The Totalitarian Ego: Fabrication and Revision of Personal History*, 35 AM. PSYCHOLOGIST 603, 606 (1980).

[29] Cohen, *supra* note 13, at 246 (*citing* Loftus, *supra* note 22, at 35, 54); *see also* Helen M. Patterson & Richard I. Kemp, *Co-witnesses Talk: A Survey of Eyewitness Discussion*, 12 PSYCHOL., CRIME & L. 181 (2006); Carl Martin Allwood, Jens Knutsson & Pär Anders Granhag, *Eyewitnesses Under Influence: How Feedback Affects the Realism in Confidence Judgements*, 12 PSYCHOL., CRIME & L. 25 (. 2006).

[30] *See generally* John C. Brigham, Adina W. Wasserman & Christian A. Meissner, *Disputed Eyewitness Identification Evidence: Important Legal and Scientific Issues*, 36 CT. REV. 12, 15 (1999); *see also* Patterson & Kemp, *supra* note 29; Allwood, et al., *supra* note 29; John S. Shaw, Sena Garven, & James M. Wood, *Co-Witness Information Can Have Immediate Effects on Eyewitness Memory Reports*, 21 LAW & HUM. BEHAV. 503 (1997); Felicity Jenkins & Graham Davies, *Contamination of Facial Memory through Exposure to Misleading Composite Pictures*, 70 J. APPLIED PSYCH. 164 (1985).

[31] Cohen, *supra* note 13, at 246-47.

3. Retrieval Phase

Finally, the ***retrieval phase*** occurs when "the brain searches for the pertinent information, retrieves it, and communicates it."[32] This process necessarily occurs when eyewitnesses describe what they observed to police, when they participate in lineup or photo array identifications, and when they testify in court. Time is a very important factor in memory retrieval. As a rule, the longer the time period between acquisition, retention, and retrieval, the more difficulty we have retrieving the memory.[33]

In addition to the passage of time, it has been repeatedly demonstrated that retrieval of memories can be affected by a process known as ***unconscious transference***. In this phenomenon, different memory images may become combined or confused with one another.[34] This can manifest itself when an eyewitness, accurately recalling an innocent bystander at the scene of a crime, incorrectly identifies that bystander as the perpetrator.[35]

C. Estimator Variables (Non-Systemic Variables) Impacting Perception and Memory

In addition to the perceptual differences discussed earlier, memory is also impacted by a number of phenomena that collectively are referred to as ***estimator variables***—those variables over which the criminal justice system has no control. Estimator variables can be broken down into two categories: "event factors" and "witness factors." ***Event factors*** include "lighting conditions, changes in visual adaptation to light and dark, duration of the event, speed and distance involved, and the presence or absence of violence."[36] ***Witness factors*** include stress, fear, physical limitation on sensory perception (e.g., poor eyesight, hearing impairment, alcohol or drug intoxication), expectations, age (the very young and very old have unique problems), and gender.[37] We will examine each of the major event and witness factors in turn.

---

[32] Chemay, *supra* note 16, at 725 (*quoting* CURT BARTOL, PSYCHOLOGY AND AMERICAN LAW 171 (1983); *see also* Haber & Haber, *supra* note 26; BARTOL & BARTOL, *supra* note 18, at 219).

[33] BARTOL & BARTOL, *supra* note 18, at 220.

[34] Brigham, Wasserman & Meissner, *supra* note 30, at 15; *see also* Mark R. Phillips, R. Edward Geiselman, David Haghighi & Cynthia Lin, *Some Boundary Conditions for Bystander Misidentification*, 24 CRIM. JUST. & BEHAV. 370-90 (1997); R. Edward Geiselman, David Haghighi & Ronna Stown, *Unconscious Transference and Characteristics of Accurate and Inaccurate Eyewitnesses*, 2 PSYCHOL., CRIME & L. 197 (1996); Elizabeth F. Loftus, *Unconscious Transference*, 2 LAW & PSYCH. REV. 93 (1976).

[35] Timothy J. Perfect & Lucy J. Harris, *Adult Age Differences in Unconscious Transference: Source Confusion or Identity Blending?*, 31 MEMORY & COGNITION 570 (2003); Christian A. Meissner, Self-Generated Misinformation: the Influence of Retrieval Processes in Verbal Overshadowing (Unpublished master's thesis, Florida State Univ., 1998); J. Don Read, Patricia Tollestrup, Richard Hammersley, & Eileen McFadzen, *The Unconscious Transference Effect: Are Innocent Bystanders Ever Misidentified?*, 4 APPLIED COGNITIVE PSYCH. 3 (1990).

[36] Cohen, *supra* note 13, at 242 (*citing* Elizabeth F. Loftus et al., *The Psychology of Eyewitness Testimony, Psychological Methods, in* CRIMINAL INVESTIGATION AND EVIDENCE 6-13 (David C. Raskin ed., 1989)); *see also* Haber & Haber, *supra* note 26; *see generally,* BRIAN L. CUTLER & STEPHEN D. PENROD, MISTAKEN IDENTIFICATIONS: THE EYEWITNESS, PSYCHOLOGY, AND LAW (New York: Cambridge Univ. Press, 1995).

[37] *Id.* (*citing* ELIZABETH LOFTUS & JAMES M. DOYLE, EYEWITNESS TESTIMONY: CIVIL AND CRIMINAL 36, 45 (2d ed. 1992)); *see also* Haber & Haber, *supra* note 26; CUTLER & PENROD, *supra* note 36.

1. Time as an Event Factor

Both common sense and our own experience inform us about temporal effects on memory. First and foremost, the longer one has to examine something, the better the memory formation will be and the more accurate recall will be.[38] Conversely, the less time someone has to witness an event, the less complete, and therefore less accurate, both perception and memory will be.[39] Closely related to the duration of time for observation is the rate at which events happen. Given the limitations of human perception, when things happen very quickly, memory can be negatively affected. This is true even when an eyewitness has a reasonable period of time to observe an event, since attention is focused on processing a fast-moving series of events, rather than on a particular aspect of the occurrence.[40]

We all know that memory declines over time. Research has confirmed that time delay impacts the accuracy of identification, but to a much smaller degree than might be expected.[41] This may be due to the fact that memory does not fade away in increments over time, but rather fades fairly rapidly immediately following the event – a phenomenon referred to as the *forgetting curve*.[42] After the initial fade, there is a greater likelihood of confabulation. Such filling and/or alteration of memory by post-event discussions has a much more powerful negative impact on the accuracy of recall than does the passage of time alone.[43].[44]

2. Event Significance and Violence as Event Factors

Overall event significance plays a significant role in the accuracy of memory recall. When people fail to perceive that a significant event is transpiring, their attention is not focused on the event, and the lack of attention leads to poorer perception and memory of the event.[45] But, when people are aware that a significant event is taking place, their attention is better focused and, correspondingly, perception and memory of the event is improved.[46] In terms of eyewitness accuracy, this often translates into high levels of inaccuracy in identifications for the perpetrator of a petty theft, and higher rates of accuracy for a more significant non-violent crime.[47]

---

[38] Amina Memon, Lorraine Hope, & Ray Bull, *Exposure Duration: Effects on Eyewitness Accuracy and Confidence*, 94 BRITISH J. PSYCHOL. 339 (2003); BARTOL & BARTOL, *supra* note 18, at 220 (*citing, inter alia,* Geoffrey R. Loftus, *Eye Fixations and Recognition Memory*, 3 COGNITIVE PSYCHOL. 164-66 (1979)); Stephen D. Penrod, Elizabeth F. Loftus, & J.D. Winkler, *The Reliability of Eyewitness Testimony: A Psychological Perspective, in* THE PSYCHOLOGY OF THE COURTROOM 119 (Norbert L. Kerr & Robert M. Bray eds., 1982).

[39] *See* BARTOL & BARTOL, *supra* note 18; Memon, et al., *supra* note 38; Penrod, Loftus & Winkler, *supra* note 38.

[40] BARTOL & BARTOL, *supra* note 18, at 221; Haber & Haber, *supra* note 26, at 1060.

[41] Vrij, *supra* note 3, at 111.

[42] Friedland, *supra* note 14, at 183 (*citing* LOFTUS, *supra* note 22, at 53; H. EBBINGHAUS, MEMORY: A CONTRIBUTION TO EXPERIMENTAL PSYCHOLOGY (1964)); *see also* Haber & Haber, *supra* note 26, at 1060-1061; *see generally* Sverker Sikstrom, *Forgetting Curves: Implications for Connectionist Models*, 45 COGNITIVE PSYCHOL. 95 (2002).

[43] *Id.* (*citing* LOFTUS, *supra* note 22, at 54-78); Penrod, Loftus & Winkler, *supra* note 38, at 134-38; Haber & Haber, *supra* note 26.

[44] *Id.* (citing Loftus, *supra* note 36, at 54-78); Penrod, Loftus & Winkler, *supra* note 38, at 134-38.

[45] *See* Michael R. Leippe, Gary L. Wells, & Thomas M. Ostrom, *Crime Seriousness as a Determinant of Accuracy in Eyewitness Identification*, 63 J. APPLIED PSYCHOL. 345-51 (1978)(the more serious the crime, the more likely the witness will identify the correct criminal).

[46] *Id.*; *see also* Chemay, *supra* note 16, at 728.

[47] Chemay, *supra* note 16, at 728.

The use of the limiting phrase "non-violent crime" in the previous sentence is important because the seriousness of the crime in and of itself is not a determinative factor of event significance and the corresponding attention being paid to the event. The violence level of the crime is also important. Even when witnesses understand that they are watching a significant event, "the more violent the act, the lower will be the accuracy and completeness of perception and memory."[48] This is a function of the negative impact high levels of arousal and stress can produce as discussed in the next section.

3. Arousal and Stress as Event Factors

Contrary to the popular belief that stress heightens perception and memory, research suggests that perception and memory acquisition function most accurately when the subject is exposed to a moderate amount of stress.[49] This is often referred to as the ***Yerkes-Dodson Law,*** which holds that when stress levels are too low, people do not pay sufficient attention, and when stress levels are too high, the ability to concentrate and perceive are negatively impacted.[50]

The Yerkes-Dodson law has a strong effect on people's ability to perceive and remember certain details of an event. Detail significance refers to the minutia of a crime scene, as opposed to its overall significance. When people are concerned about personal safety, they tend to focus their attention on the details that most directly affect their safety, such as "blood, masks, weapons, and aggressive actions."[51] While focusing on these details, they pay less attention to the other details of the crime scene, such as characteristics of the perpetrator (e.g., facial features, hair color and style, clothing, height, weight, etc.), the crime scene, and other important details.[52] This phenomenon manifests itself particularly when a weapon is present.[53] The so-called ***weapons effect*** describes crime situations in which a weapon is used and witnesses spend more time and psychic energy focusing on the weapon rather than on other aspects of the event.[54] The weapons effect results in incomplete or inaccurate information about the crime scene and the perpetrator.[55] This effect is magnified when the use of a weapon comes as a surprise to a witness.[56]

---

[48]   *Id.* (*citing* Clifford, *Eyewitness Testimony: The Bridging of a Credibility Gap, in* PSYCHOLOGY, LAW AND LEGAL PROCESSES 167, 176-77 (David P. Farrington, Keith Hawkins, Sally M. Lloyd-Bostock eds., 1979)).

[49]   *Eyewitness Testimony, in* Psychology, Law and Legal Process, *supra* note 51, at 243 (*citing* LOFTUS, *supra* note 22, at 33); *see also* Linda S. Katz & J. Reid, *Expert Testimony on the Fallibility of Eyewitness Identification,* 1 CRIM. JUST. J. 177, 184-86 (1977).

[50]   Robert M. Yerkes & J.D. Dodson, *The Relation of Strength of Stimulus to Rapidity of Habit Formation,* 18 J. COMPAR. NEUROLOGY & PSYCHOL., 459-82 (1908); Elizabeth F. Loftus, *Ten Years in the Life of an Expert Witness,* 10 LAW & HUM. BEHAV. 241, 254-55 (1986).

[51]   BARTOL & BARTOL, *supra* note 18, at 221.

[52]   *E.g.,* Kenneth A. Deffenbacher, Brian H. Bornstein, Steven D. Penrod, E. Kiernan McGorty, *A Meta-Analytic Review of the Effects of High Stress on Eyewitness Memory* 28 L. & HUM. BEHAV. 687 (2004); Charles A. Morgan, et al., *Accuracy of Eyewitness Memory for Persons Encountered during Exposure to Highly Intense Stress* , 27 INT'L J. PSYCHIATRY & THE L. 265 (2004).

[53]   Deffenbacher, et al., *supra* note 52; Morgan, et al., *supra* note 52; Kerri L. Pickel, *The Influence of Context on the "Weapon Focus" Effect,* 23 L. & HUM. BEHAV. 299 (1999).

[54]   Cohen, *supra* note 13, at 244 (*citing* Loftus & Doyle, *supra* note 37, at 34).

[55]   Nancy Mehrkens Steblay, *A Meta-Analytic Review of the Weapon Focus Effect,* 16 LAW & HUM. BEHAV. 413 (1992); ELIZABETH F. LOFTUS, EYEWITNESS TESTIMONY 35-36 (2d ed. 1996).

[56]   Pickel, *supra* note 53, at 299-311.

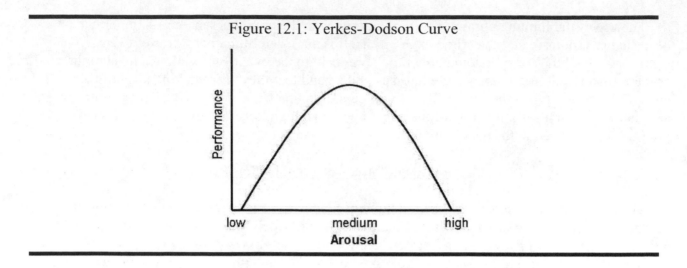

Figure 12.1: Yerkes-Dodson Curve

4. Expectancies and Stereotypes as Witness Factors

"A person's expectations and stereotypes can also affect both perception and memory: what he perceives and encodes is, to a large extent, determined by cultural biases, personal prejudices, effects of training, prior information, and expectations induced by motivational states, among others."[57] Whether the hunter is looking for deer, or one is searching for Bigfoot or the Loch Ness Monster, what one expects to see clearly influences what one thinks has been seen.[58] Unfortunately, stereotypes affect expectations in terms of who looks like a criminal.[59] For example,

> in one experiment a "semi-dramatic" photograph was shown to a wide variety of subjects, including whites and blacks of varying backgrounds. The photograph showed several people sitting in a subway car, with a black man standing and conversing with a white man, who was also standing, but holding a razor. Over half of the subjects reported that the black man had been holding the razor, and several described the black man as "brandishing it wildly." Effectively, expectations and stereotypes cause people to see and remember what they want or expect to see or to remember. This phenomenon should be of concern to the criminal justice system as "[t]here is evidence that some people may in fact incorporate their stereotype of 'criminal' in their identification of suspects. . . ."[60]

5. Age and Gender as Witness Factors

Age is an important factor affecting witnesses' memories. Children usually fail to retain as many details as adults, but the percentage of "correct" information that children are able to recall is proportionally similar to that of adults.[61] In terms of making accurate identifications, pre-

---

[57] Chemay, *supra* note 16, at 726-27 (*citing* Penrod, Loftus & Winkler, *supra* note 38, at 129-30); *see also* sources cited *supra* at notes 16 & 26-30.

[58] BARTOL & BARTOL, *supra* note 18, at 227; *see also* sources cited *supra* at notes 16 & 26-30.

[59] Penrod, Loftus & Winkler, *supra* note 38, at 129-30; Michael R. Leippe, *Effects of Integrative Memorial and Cognitive Processes on the Correspondence of Eyewitness Accuracy and Confidence*, 4 L. & HUM. BEHAV. 261-274 (1980).

[60] Chemay, *supra* note 16, at 727 (*citing* Loftus, *supra* note 22, at 37-39).

[61] Brigham, Wasserman & Meissner, *supra* note 30, at 16; Joanna D. Pozzulo & R.C.L. Lindsay, *Identification Accuracy of Children Versus Adults: A Meta-Analysis*, 22 LAW & HUM. BEHAV. 549 (1998).

schoolers are much less likely than adults to make a correct identification.[62] But once children attain the age of five or six, they do not differ significantly from adults in their ability to make an accurate identification.[63] However, children up to the age of thirteen are more likely than adults to correctly reject a target-absent lineup.[64] In contrast, elderly witnesses are much less reliable than younger ones.[65] The elderly frequently believe events they imagined were actually perceived, a mistake known as a *reifying error*.[66] And both children and the elderly are particularly "susceptible to the effects of suggestive questioning or post-event misinformation."[67]

Gender has much less significance on memory accuracy than age. Some studies suggest that women might have slightly higher accuracy rates in facial recognition,[68] and other studies suggest that recall is consistent with gender stereotypes.[69] For example, a woman might pay more attention to clothing, while a man might take notice of the make of a car.[70] These gender differences, however, are generally considered to have little significance on the overall accuracy of eyewitness identifications.[71]

6. The Cross-Over Factors Concerning Characteristics of the Offender

An eyewitness is much more likely to identify accurately someone of his or her own race than someone of a different race.[72] The same is true, although arguably to a lesser extent, for cross-ethnic identifications.[73] Because of cross-racial bias, people apply more lenient criteria in identifying someone of a different race or ethnicity, while using more stringent requirements for making an identification of someone of the same racial or ethnic group.[74] The result of cross-

---

[62]   Pozzulo & Lindsay, *supra* note 61.

[63]   *Id.*; Gail S. Goodman & Rebecca S. Reed, *Age Differences in Eyewitness Testimony*, 10 LAW & HUM. BEHAV. 317 (1986).

[64]   Pozzulo & Lindsay, *supra* note 61, at 563.

[65]   A. Daniel Yarmey, *The Elderly Witness, in* PSYCHOLOGICAL ISSUES IN EYEWITNESS IDENTIFICATION, 259 (Siegfried Ludwig Sporer, Roy S. Malpass, & Guenter Koehnken, eds., Mahwah, NJ: Lawrence Erlbaum Associates 1996).

[66]   Amina Memon, Lorraine Hope, James Bartlett, & Ray Bull, *Eyewitness Recognition Errors: The Effects of Mugshot Viewing and Choosing in Young and Old Adults*, 30 MEMORY & COGNITION 1219 (2002); *see also* Amina Memon & Fiona Gabbert, *Improving the Identification Accuracy of Senior Witnesses: Do Prelineup Questions and Sequential Testing Help?*, 88 J. APPLIED PSYCHOL. 341 (2003); Gillian Cohen & Dorothy Faulkner, *The Effects of Aging on Perceived and Generated Memories, in* EVERYDAY COGNITION IN ADULTHOOD AND LATE LIFE 222-43 (Leonard W. Poon, David C. Rubin, & Barbara A. Wilson, eds., New York: Cambridge University Press, 1989).

[67]   Pozzulo & Lindsay, *supra* note 61, at 16; Goodman & Reed, *supra* note 63.

[68]   Torun Lindholm & Sven Ake Christianson, *Gender Effects in Eyewitness Accounts of a Violent Crime*, 4 PSYCHOL., CRIME & L. 323 (1998).

[69]   Douglas J. Herrmann, Mary Crawford & Michelle Holdsworth, *Gender-Linked Differences in Everyday Memory Performance*, 83 BRITISH J. PSYCHOL. 221 (1992).

[70]   *See* Elizabeth F. Loftus, Mahzarin R. Banaji, Jonathan W. Schooler, & Rachael A. Foster, *Who Remembers What? Gender Differences in Memory*, 26 MICH. QTRLY. REV. 64 (1987).

[71]   Vrij, *supra* note 3, at 108.

[72]   Heather M. Kleider & Stephen D. Goldinger, *Stereotyping Ricochet: Complex Effects of Racial Distinctiveness on Identification Accuracy*, 25 L. & HUM. BEHAV. 605 (2001); Alexandra J. Golby, John D.E. Gabrieli, Joan Y. Chiao, & Jennifer L. Eberhardt, *Differential Responses in the Fusiform Region to Same-Race and Other-Race Faces*, 4 NATURE-NEUROSCIENCE 845 (2001); Michael R. Leippe, *The Case for Expert Testimony About Eyewitness Memory*, 1 PSYCH. PUB. POL. & L. 909, 917 (1995).

[73]   Siegfried Ludwig Sporer, *Recognizing Faces of Other Ethnic Groups: an Integration of Theories*, 7 PSYCHOL., PUB. POL'Y & L. 36 (2001).

[74]   *See* Kleider & Goldinger, *supra* note 72; Golby et al., *supra* note 72. Leippe, *supra* note 72; Sporer, *supra* note 73.; *see also* James M. Doyle, *Discounting the Error Costs: Cross-Racial False Alarms in the Culture of Contemporary Criminal Justice*, 7 PSYCHOL., PUB. POL'Y & L. 253 (2001).

racial bias is a higher rate of false positive identifications, especially when a Caucasian eyewitness identifies an African-American suspect.[75] A combination of event factors (e.g., duration and conditions of viewing) interact with cross-racial bias to further inhibit the reliability of cross-racial identifications.[76] Courts have begun to take notice of this significant limitation on identification accuracy. The Supreme Court of New Jersey, for example, has mandated that juries be instructed on the risks of inaccuracies in cross-racial identifications when an "identification is a critical issue in the case, and an eyewitness's cross-racial identification is not corroborated by other evidence giving it independent reliability."[77]

Another variable that affects the accuracy of an eyewitnesses' identification of a suspect is the facial distinctiveness of the suspect. Suspects with faces that an eyewitness perceives as either highly attractive or highly unattractive are much more likely to be remembered accurately than faces that lack distinctiveness.[78] A complicating matter, however, is that some characteristics of facial distinctiveness are easily changed. For example, a suspect can disguise himself or herself during the perpetration of a crime, or change his/her appearance after it by altering hair style, hair color, the presence or absence of facial hair, the wearing of glasses, and so on.[79] Accordingly, while some distinctive facial features might increase subsequent recognition of a person, to be accurate, the two comparisons must use non-malleable characteristics. That is easier said than done.

D. Systemic Factors Impacting Perception and Memory

In addition to the various witness and situational factors affecting the accuracy of identifications, a number of factors within the criminal justice system itself impact the reliability of eyewitness identifications. **Showups**—the presentation of only the suspect to a witness—are highly suggestive and, accordingly, produce high levels of false identifications.[80] Moreover, showups have a biasing effect on any subsequent identification at a lineup or in court.[81] Showups should, therefore, not be used absent some extenuating circumstance that prevents a photo array or lineup from being used. But even when a photo array or a lineup is conducted, a number of systemic factors can affect the reliability of these processes.

---

[75] Doyle, *supra* note 74; *see also* Golby, et al., *supra* note 72.

[76] Otto H. MacLin, M. Kimberly MacLin & Roy S. Malpass, *Race, Arousal, Attention, Exposure and Delay: An Examination of Factors Moderating Face Recognition*, 7 PSYCHOL., PUB. POL'Y & L. 134 (2001).

[77] New Jersey v. Cromedy, 727 A.2d 457, 467 (N.J. 1999).

[78] Julie A. Sarno & Thomas R. Alley, *Attractiveness and the Memorability of Faces: Only a Matter of Distinctiveness?*, 110 AM. J. PSYCHOL. 81 (1997); John C. Brigham, *Target Person Distinctiveness and Attractiveness as Moderator Variables in the Confidence-Accuracy Relationship in Eyewitness Identifications*, 11 BASIC & APPLIED SOC. PSYCHOL. 101 (1990); Peter N. Shapiro & Steven D. Penrod, *Meta-Analysis of Facial Identification Studies*, 100 PSYCHOL. BULL. 139, 145 (1986).

[79] Vrij, *supra* note 3, at 109; *see also* John W. Shepherd, & Hadyn D. Ellis, *Face Recall – Methods and Problems*, in PSYCHOLOGICAL ISSUES IN EYEWITNESS IDENTIFICATION 87-115 (Siegfried Ludwig Sporer, Roy S. Malpass, et al., eds. 1996).

[80] Vrij, *supra* note 3, at 115; *see also* A. Daniel Yarmey, *Person Identification in Showups and Lineups*, in EYEWITNESS MEMORY: THEORETICAL AND APPLIED PERSPECTIVES 131-54 (Charles P. Thompson & Douglas J. Herrmann eds., Mahwah, NJ: Lawrence Erlbaum 1998).

[81] Bruce W. Behrman & Lance T. Vayder, *The Biasing Influence of a Police Showup: Does the Observation of a Single Suspect Taint Later Identification?*, 79 PERCEPTUAL & MOTOR SKILLS, 1239 (1994).

1. Lineup or Array Fairness

It should be self-evident that for a lineup or photo array to be fair, the actual suspect should not stand out from the other participants (called "foils") in a lineup or photo array.[82] But constructing a truly fair lineup or photo array can be difficult. While the participants should not be clones of each other, they should generally be of the same race,[83] should be similarly dressed (although preferably not in clothing matching witnesses' descriptions of clothing worn by the culprit),[84] should not be of substantially differing height and weight,[85] and should not have visible distinctive features (e.g., all should have similar or absent facial hair; either all of none should have tattoos, etc.).[86]

The number of foils presented along with the suspect is also important to lineup or photo array fairness. The more people who participate in a lineup, the less likely a suspect will be identified merely by chance. The same is true of photo arrays; the more photographs presented to the witness, the less likely it is the suspect will be identified by chance. Accordingly, most experts recommend that at least six people be in a lineup or photo array.[87] To decrease chance identifications, England routinely uses nine or ten people and Canada uses twelve.[88]

2. Administration of and Instructions for Lineups and Photo Arrays

Both who administers a lineup or photo array and how that person does so affect the reliability of an identification. First, the procedure should be double-blind. That is, neither the witness nor the person administering the lineup or photo array should know who the suspect is and who the foils are.[89] The procedure greatly reduces, if not eliminates, suggestive questioning by the administrator and other possibilities of the administrator unduly influencing the witness, either consciously or unconsciously.[90]

Second, eyewitnesses should be explicitly informed that the suspect may not be in the lineup or array. This should reduce the pressure on the witness to make an identification, thereby

---

[82] Gary L. Wells & Eric P. Seelau, *Eyewitness Identification: Psychological Research and Legal Policy on Lineups*, 1 PSYCHOL., PUB. POL'Y & L. 765, 779 (1995).

[83] *Id.*; *see also* Donald P. Judges, *Two Cheers for the Department of Justice's Eyewitness Evidence: A Guide for Law Enforcement*, 53 ARK. L. REV. 231, 254 (2000).

[84] A. Daniel Yarmey, Meagan J. Yarmey, A. Linda Yarmey, *Accuracy of Eyewitness Identifications in Showups and Lineups*, 20 L. & HUM. BEHAV. 459 (1996).

[85] Wells & Seelau, *supra* note 82, at 779; Judges, *supra* note 83, at 254.

[86] *See* Wells & Seelau, *supra* note 82; Judges, *supra* note 83; Yarmey et al., *supra* note 84.

[87] Gary L. Wells, Mark Small, Steven D. Penrod, Roy S. Malpass, Solomon M. Fulero & C.A.E. Brimacombe, *Eyewitness Identification Procedures: Recommendations for Lineups and Photospreads*, 22 LAW & HUM. Behav. 603, 633 (1998); Avaraham M. Levi, *Are Defendants Guilty If They Were Chosen in a Lineup?*, 22 LAW & HUM. BEHAV. 389 (1998); Garl L. Wells, Eric P. Seelau, Sheila M. Rydell and C.A. Elizabeth Luus, *Recommendations for Properly Conducted Lineup Identification Task* in DAVID FRANK ROSS, J. DON READ, MICHAEL P. TOGLIA. (EDS.), ADULT EYEWITNESS TESTIMONY: CURRENT TRENDS AND DEVELOPMENTS (N.Y.: Cambridge Univ. Press 1994) at 229 ("A lineup should contain at least five appropriate distractors for every one suspect.").

[88] Avraham M. Levi & R.C.L. Lindsay, *Lineup and Photo Spread Procedures: Issues Concerning Policy Recommendations*, 7 PSYCH. PUB. POL. & L. 776, 787 (2001).

[89] Wells & Seelau, *supra* note 82, at 775-78.

[90] *Id.* at 776; *see also* Nancy Mehrkens Steblay, *Social Influence in Eyewitness Recall: A Meta-Analytic Review of Lineup Instruction Effects*, 21 L. & HUM. BEHAV. 283 (1997).

decreasing the risk that the witness will make a questionable identification by selecting "the person who best resembles the culprit relative to the others in the lineup" or array.[91]

A third issue with lineup or photo array administration concerns the presentation of the participants. Historically, all of the participants in a photo array or lineup were presented to the witness at the same time—a practice that continues to this day. But research has demonstrated that sequential viewing of photographs or lineup participants one after another, rather than simultaneous viewing of all participants, is preferable. As with the previous precaution, this procedure reduces a witness' use of relative decision-making by encouraging a witness to use an absolute threshold.[92] "Critical tests of this hypothesis have consistently shown that a sequential procedure produces fewer false identifications than does a simultaneous procedure with little or no decrease in rates of accurate identification."[93]

Finally, when sequential viewing is used, witnesses should be asked how certain they are of an identification. Obtaining a statement of confidence level before other information can prevent contamination of a witness' judgment, thereby increasing the reliability of an identification.[94] Since confidence level at the time of initial identification is a powerful force in determining both the admissibility of an out-of-court identification[95] and the weight accorded to it by the trier-of-fact,[96] it should be self-evident why an uncontaminated statement of high confidence should be obtained at the time of an initial identification.[97] But the importance of initial confidence goes beyond the obvious in light of a phenomenon called ***confidence malleability.*** Confidence malleability is "the tendency for an eyewitness to become more or less confident in his or her identification as a function of events that occur after the identification."[98]

E. Reform of Problematic Systemic Variables

In light of the empirical research demonstrating systemic problems with eyewitness identification, the American Psychology and Law Society and the U.S. Department of Justice both published guides for reforming the way the criminal justice system approaches eyewitness evidence.[99] In 2001, New Jersey became the first state to require two of the primary safeguards

---

[91] *Id.* at 778-79.

[92] *Id.* at 772; *see also* Levy & Lindsay, *supra* note 88; Steblay, *supra* note 90.

[93] Wells & Seelau, *supra* note 82, at 772 (*citing* Siegfried Ludwig Sporer, *Eyewitness Identification Accuracy, Confidence, and Decision Times in Simultaneous and Sequential Lineups*, 78 J. APPLIED PSYCHOL. 22 (1993); Brian L. Cutler & Steven D. Penrod, *Improving the Reliability of Eyewitness Identification: Lineup Construction and Presentation*, 73 J. APPLIED PSYCHOL. 281 (1988)).

[94] *Id.* at 780-81.

[95] Manson v. Brathwaite, 432 U.S. 98, 114 (1977); Neil v. Biggers, 409 U.S. 188, 199-200 (1972).

[96] Steven M. Smith, R.C.L. Lindsay & Sean Pryke, *Postdictors of Eyewitness Errors: Can False Identifications Be Diagnosed?*, 85 J. APPLIED PSYCHOL. 542 (2000); Michael R. Leippe, Andrew P. Manion & Ann Romanczyk, *Eyewitness Persuasion: How and How Well Do Fact Finders Judge the Accuracy of Adults' and Children's Memory Reports?*, 63 J. PERSONALITY & SOC. PSYCHOL. 181 (1992); Michael R. Leippe, Andrew P. Manion & Ann Romanczyk, *Eyewitness Memory for a Touching Experience: Accuracy Differences Between Child and Adult Witnesses*, 76 J. APPLIED PSYCHOL. 367 (1991); Gary L. Wells & Michael R. Leippe, *How Do Triers of Fact Infer the Accuracy of Eyewitness Identifications? Using Memory for Peripheral Detail Can Be Misleading*, 66 J. APPLIED PSYCHOL. 682 (1981).

[97] *See, e.g.,* Allwood, et al., *supra* note 29; Nathan Weber & Neil Brewer, *Positive Versus Negative Face Recognition Decisions: Confidence, Accuracy, and Response Latency*, 20 APPLIED COGNITIVE PSYCHOL. 17 (2006).

[98] Wells & Seelau, *supra* note 82, at 774; *see also* Steven D. Penrod & Brian L. Cutler, *Witness Confidence And Witness Accuracy: Assessing Their Forensic Relation*, 1 PSYCHOL. PUB. POL'Y & L. 817 (1995).

[99] Gary L. Wells et al., *supra* note 87, at 603; U.S. Dep't of Justice, Eyewitness Evidence: A Guide for Law Enforcement (Oct. 1999), avail. at www.ncjrs.org/pdffiles1/nij/178240.pdf.).

recommended in those reports: blind administration of photo arrays and lineups, and sequential lineups.[100] "The use of blind procedures prevents an investigator from accidentally providing suspect information to a witness, thereby significantly decreasing the likelihood of misidentification based upon memory contamination."[101] The confidence of identification procedures is likewise increased by sequentially showing an eyewitness a single photo or person at a time, helping to reduce the chance of an eyewitness making a relative judgment between the choices presented, "thereby encouraging the use of the absolute judgment process."[102]

Following New Jersey's lead, several other states began to examine how identification procedures can be conducted to minimize many of the systemic variables that negatively affect memory. For example, North Carolina implemented blind administration and sequential lineup procedures in 2003.[103] Also in 2003, the Illinois state legislature enacted a law requiring that all lineups be "'photographed or otherwise recorded,' and such photographs must be given to defense during discovery, along with all photographs of suspects shown to the eyewitness during the photo spread."[104] Additionally, eyewitnesses participating in lineups must sign a consent form that informs them that "the suspect might not be in the lineup; the eyewitness is not obligated to make an identification; and the eyewitness 'should not assume that the person administering the lineup or photo spread knows which person is the suspect in the case.'"[105] Massachusetts is considering not only sequential administration of photos or people in lineups and blind administration procedures but is also studying other safeguards such as "electronic recording of statements made by suspects whenever possible and practical; [and] providing an attorney for every suspect who participates in a live lineup."[106]

While reform of eyewitness identification procedures can have a very positive effect on minimizing misidentification of a suspect due to systemic variables, these policy enhancements have no effect on any of the non-systemic estimator variables described earlier. Since the many estimator variables described above have a strong effect on memory acquisition, encoding, and retention, there remains a need for jurors to understand the complex ways in which these factors can influence eyewitness identifications.

F. The Role of Forensic Psychologists as Experts Dealing with Eyewitness Evidence

Bio-psycho-social factors affecting perception and memory are not within the common knowledge of the average juror. Expert testimony regarding these factors would therefore "assist the trier of fact to understand" the unreliable nature of eyewitness identifications, and, therefore, such expert testimony should be admissible under Federal Rule of Evidence 702 and state

---

[100] Winn S. Collins, *Safeguards for Eyewitness Identification*, 77-MAR. WIS. LAW. 8, 11 (2004) (*citing* Letter from John J. Farmer Jr., New Jersey Attorney General, to County Prosecutors et al. 1-2 (Apr. 18, 2001), avail. at www.state.nj.us/lps/dcj/agguide/photoid.pdf.).

[101] *Id.* at 11 (*citing* Wells et al., *supra* note 87, at 627).

[102] *Id.* at 11 (*citing* U.S. Dep't of Justice, Eyewitness Evidence: A Trainer's Manual for Law Enforcement 38 (Sept. 2003), avail. at www.ncjrs.org/nij/eyewitness/188678.pdf.).

[103] Collins, *supra* note 100, at 49 (*citing* Letter from I. Beverly Lake Jr., Chief Justice, Supreme Court of North Carolina, to Scott Perry et al., Director, Criminal Justice Training & Standards, North Carolina Department of Justice (Oct. 9, 2003)).

[104] Scott Ehlers, *Eyewitness Identification: State Law Reform*, 29-Apr. CHAMPION 34 (2005) (*citing* 725 ILL. COMP. STAT. 5/107A-5(a)).

[105] *Id.* (*citing* 725 ILL. COMP. STAT. 5/107A-5(b)).

[106] National District Attorneys Association, *Task Force Recommendations on Eyewitness Identification*, 39-Apr. PROSECUTOR 16 (2005).

evidence codes.[107] Not only would that expert testimony be proper under Rule 702, but it would also be "extremely helpful in combating the false image of accuracy that confident witnesses often possess."[108] "Expert testimony has been proven to improve juror knowledge, sensitize jurors to witnessing and identification factors, and desensitize them toward witness confidence."[109] Yet some courts do not recognize the value of the testimony.[110]

Courts have inconsistently admitted expert testimony on the reliability of eyewitness identifications. The overwhelming majority of courts have excluded such expert testimony.[111] The reason most frequently cited by courts for excluding expert testimony is that expert testimony regarding the accuracy of identifications usurps the role of the jury as the sole judge of the credibility of witnesses.[112] Other reasons given for refusing to allow such expert testimony include: the testimony would not assist the trier of fact;[113] the testimony would be misleading to the jury;[114] and cross-examination of the eyewitness in conjunction with jury instructions would address the substance of the proffered testimony.[115] But these conclusions are belied by the empirical data.[116] For example, in *United States v. Smith*,[117] the defendant was convicted of stealing guns from a gun shop. Several lay witnesses testified they saw the defendant running out of the store with the guns. At trial, the defendant proffered expert testimony regarding eyewitness reliability. The expert would have explained the "circumstances that give rise to inaccurate memories,"[118] as well as the phenomenon of an eyewitness' false confidence in the identification of a suspect. The appellate court concluded that the district court had properly excluded the proffered expert testimony. The circuit court explained that "in the instant case, the

---

[107] Fed. R. Evid. 702; *see also* Bert Black, *Evolving Legal Standards for the Admissibility of Scientific Evidence*, 239 SCIENCE 1508, 1512 n.1 (1988).

[108] Brooke Whisonant Patterson, *The "Tyranny of the Eyewitness,"* 28 LAW & PSYCHOL. REV. 195, 202 (2004) (*citing* Leippe, *supra* note 72, at 909-10 (advocating eyewitness expert testimony to inform jurors about psychological processes and the variable affecting the accuracy of eyewitness testimony).

[109] *Id.* at 202, n. 77 (*citing* Penrod & Cutler, *supra* note 98, at 841).

[110] For an excellent roadmap designed to guide attorneys in raising issues regarding perception and memory, see Lisa Steele, *Trying Identification Cases: an Outline for Raising Eyewitness ID Issues*, 28-Nov. CHAMPION 8 (2004).

[111] *See generally* Paul C. Giannelli & Edward J. Imwinkelried, Scientific Evidence ' 9.2(C), at 434-39 (3d ed. 1999); David L. Faigman et al., Science in the Law: Social Behavioral Science Issues ' 8-1.1, at 370 n.3 (2002).

[112] United States v. Lumpkin, 192 F.3d 280, 289 (2d Cir. 1999); United States v. Hall, 165 F.3d 1095, 1107 (7th Cir. 1999) ("the credibility of eyewitness testimony is generally not an appropriate subject matter for expert testimony because it influences a critical function of the jury determining the credibility of witnesses."), *cert. denied*, 527 U.S. 1029 (1999).

[113] United States v. Hall, 165 F.3d 1095, 1102 (7th Cir. 1999); United States v. Smith, 156 F.3d 1046 (10th Cir. 1998); United States v. Walton, 1997 WL 525179 (9th Cir. 1997); United States v. Smith, 122 F.3d 1355, 1358 (11th Cir. 1997); United States v. Kime, 99 F.3d 870, 884 (8th Cir. 1996); United States v. Brien, 59 F.3d 274, 277 (1st Cir. 1995); United States v. Rincon, 28 F.3d 921, 925 (9th Cir. 1994).

[114] United States v. Walton, 1997 WL 525179 (9th Cir. 1997); *Smith*, 122 F.3d at 1358; *Kime*, 99 F.3d at 884 (8th Cir. 1996); United States v. Brien, 59 F.3d 274, 277 (1st Cir. 1995); *Rincon*, 28 F.3d at 925; United States v. Burrous, 934 F. Supp. 525, 528 (E.D.N.Y. 1996).

[115] United States v. Crotteau, 218 F.3d 826, 832 (7th Cir. 2000).

[116] Mark S. Brodin, *Behavioral Science Evidence in the Age of* Daubert*: Reflections of a Skeptic*, 73 U. CIN. L. REV. 867, 890-91 (2005); *see also* Newsome v. McCabe, 319 F.3d 301 (7th Cir. 2003); Crotteau, 218 F.3d at 832; United States v. Walton, 1997 WL 525179 (9th Cir. 1997); *compare Smith*, 122 F.3d 1355 with *Rincon*, 28 F.3d at 925.

[117] 156 F.3d 1046 (10th Cir. 1998).

[118] *Id.* at 1052.

proffered testimony touches 'on areas of common knowledge.' Thus, . . . the testimony would not assist the trier of fact."[119]

Courts' refusal to admit expert testimony on the unreliability of eyewitness testimony is ironic, because it is "the form of social science evidence which is most solidly based in 'hard' empirical science.[120]

> Expert testimony concerning the limitations and weaknesses of eyewitness identification is firmly rooted in experimental foundation, derived from decades of psychological research on human perception and memory as well as an impressive peer review literature. Like [battered women's syndrome or rape trauma syndrome] evidence, this testimony purports to educate the fact-finder about reasons a witness at trial should be believed or disbelieved. The expert is prepared to testify about the factors that adversely affect accuracy (for example, stress, "weapon focus," and confusion of post-event information) and to contradict assumptions likely to be shared by jurors, such as the equation of the witness's level of certainty with the accuracy of the identification.[121]

Some judges have demonstrated an understanding of the psychological research on unreliability of eyewitness identifications and the associated false confidence that eyewitnesses can have in mistaken identifications.[122] Recognizing that these phenomena are not within the common knowledge of jurors, some courts permit experts to address these issues at trial.[123] The following excerpt from *United States v. Hines*[124] illustrates one judge's understanding of the purpose of expert testimony in eyewitness identification cases:

> While jurors may well be confident that they can draw the appropriate inferences about eyewitness identification directly from their life experiences, their confidence may be misplaced, especially where cross-racial identification is concerned. . . . Nor do I agree that this testimony somehow usurps the function of the jury. The function of the expert here is not to say to the jury— "you should believe or not believe the eyewitness." All that the expert does is provide the jury with more information with which the jury can then make a more informed decision.[125]

Finally, assuming that expert testimony on the reliability of eyewitness identifications will be accepted by a court, it is essential under *Daubert* that the testimony being offered is based upon research supported by appropriate methodologies and proper statistical analysis.[126]

---

[119] *Id.* at 1053; *see also* McMullen v. Florida, 714 So. 2d 368, 372 (Fla. 1998) (*quoting* Johnson v. Florida, 438 So. 2d 774, 777 (Fla. 1983) ("a jury is fully capable of assessing a witness' ability to perceive and remember, given the assistance of cross-examination and cautionary instructions, without the aid of expert testimony.").

[120] Brodin, *supra* note 116, at 889; *see also* Saul M. Kassin, V. Anne Tubb, Harmon M. Hosch & Amina Memon, *On the "General Acceptance" of Eyewitness Testimony Research: A New Survey of the Experts*, 56 AM. PSYCHOLOGIST 405 (2001).

[121] Brodin, *supra* note 116, at 890.

[122] Brian L. Cutler, Steven D. Penrod, & T.E. Stuve, *Juror Decision Making in Eyewitness Identification Cases*, 12 LAW & HUM. BEHAV. 41 (1988) (concluding that laypersons do not know about or understand the factors influencing perception and memory outlined in Section II of this Article).

[123] Newsome, 319 F.3d at 305-07; United States v. Smithers, 212 F.3d 306, 316 (6th Cir. 2000) ("Today, there is no question that many aspects of perception and memory are not within the common experience of most jurors, and in fact, many factors that affect memory are counter-intuitive."); United States v. Hines, 55 F. Supp.2d 62 (D. Mass. 1999); United States v. Norwood, 939 F. Supp. 1132, (D.N.J. 1996).

[124] 55 F. Supp.2d 62 (D. Mass. 1999).

[125] *Id.* at 71-72.

[126] Henry F. Fradella, Adam Fogarty & Lauren O'Neill, *The Impact of* Daubert *on the Admissibility of Behavioral Science Testimony*, 30 PEPPERDINE L. REV. 403 (2003).

II. INTERROGATIONS AND CONFESSIONS

A. Confession Evidence

A **confession** is an admission of guilt. Even at early English common law, out-of-court confessions were recognized to be weak evidence. Blackstone, the English legal commentator and scholar, wrote of such confessions that they were "the weakest and most suspicious of all testimony; even liable to be obtained by artifice, false hopes, promises of favor, or menaces; seldom remembered accurately, or reported with due precision; and incapable in their nature of being disproved by other negative evidence."[127] The suspiciousness of confessions obtained as a result of police interrogations waned for a period in U.S. history, but resurfaced in the 1930s as courts began to take note of the often brutal police tactics that were used against criminal suspects.[128] In fact, a federal commission investigating police conduct used the term "the third degree" to describe their tactics.[129] They defined the term as "the inflicting of pain, physical or mental, to extract confessions or statements."[130]

> The Commission documented the use of a litany of sadistic practices, including beating with fists, blackjacks, rubber hoses, and telephone books; the use of hot lights; confinement in airless and fetid rooms; and hanging from windows. The Commission was also concerned with psychologically abusive tactics, such as incommunicado detention, prolonged relay questioning, stripping the suspect of clothing, and the deprivation of sleep and food.[131]

The U.S. Supreme Court began citing the Wickersham Commission's report on police brutality in obtaining confessions as evidence that confessions were often involuntary and/or unreliable.[132]

When people are facing physical or psychological torture, it should be self-evident why they might confess to something they did not do. U.S. history is replete with examples of false confessions in the wake of such tactics.

> Many colonists falsely confessed to being witches in Salem, Massachusetts, in 1692. The trials resulted in at least nineteen executions before they stopped. When the nineteen month-old baby of Charles Lindbergh was kidnapped and murdered in 1932, over 200 innocent people came forward to confess to the crime. Even today, Mohammed Saddiq Odeh, a prime suspect in the bombings of the United States embassies in Kenya and Tanzania on 7 August 1998, claims Pakistani investigators used coercion to obtain a false confession from him about his involvement in the bombings.[133]

---

[127] 4 William Blackstone, Commentaries *357.

[128] Steven Penney, *Theories of Confession Admissibility: A Historical View*, 25 Am. J. Crim. L. 309, 335-36 (1998).

[129] *Id.* at 336 (citing Wickersham Commission, National Commission on Law Observance and Enforcement, Pub. No. 11, Report on Lawlessness in Law Enforcement 158-60 (1931)).

[130] *Id.*

[131] *Id.*

[132] See, e.g., Culombe v. Connecticut, 367 U.S. 568, 572-76 (1961); Haley v. Ohio, 332 U.S. 596, 605-06 (1944) (Frankfurter, J., concurring); Stein v. New York, 346 U.S. 156, 201-02 & n.* (1953) (Frankfurter, J., dissenting); Ashcraft v. Tennessee, 322 U.S. 143, 150 nn.5-6, 153 n.8 (1944); Chambers v. Florida, 309 U.S. 227, 238 n.11, 240 n.15 (1940).

[133] James R. Agar, II, *The Admissibility of False Confession Expert Testimony*, 1999 Army Law. 26, 26 (1999).

The seminal case excluding confessions on constitutional grounds was *Bram v. United States.*[134] *Bram* marked the first time the Supreme Court relied on the Fifth Amendment privilege against self-incrimination as a basis for holding that confessions had to be made voluntarily. In the years following *Bram,* however, the Court turned to the Due Process Clause of the Fourteenth Amendment as a justification for excluding confessions that were not voluntarily given. Under this approach, exemplified in *Brown v. Mississippi*, the "totality of the circumstances" of each confession had to be examined to determine both the voluntariness of a confession and its overall reliability.[135] Under this approach, confessions that were beaten out of suspects were clearly inadmissible, just as they had been under *Bram*, albeit under a different constitutional rationale.[136] Tactics falling shy of such levels of brutality proved more difficult to analyze under a due process framework. In the wake of numerous examples of confessions that were inappropriately obtained, the Supreme Court decided *Miranda v. Arizona* in 1966.[137]

Miranda established a new "bright-line" rule. It held that any pre-trail statements made by a suspect who was subjected to custodial interrogation by police were inadmissible at trial unless the suspect had been informed of certain constitutional rights and then made a knowing, intelligent, and voluntary waiver of those rights.[138] Moreover, the burden of persuasion of proving such a waiver would fall on the prosecution. Underlying the Court's reasoning in *Miranda* was the fact that anyone being interrogated while in police custody was being subjected to an inherently coercive process that could "subjugate the [suspect] to the will of [the] examiner," thereby interfering with the Fifth Amendment right against self-incrimination.[139] The Supreme Court assumed that the prophylactic step of informing a suspect of his or rights would decrease the likelihood that a confession was obtained involuntarily.

The immediate reaction to *Miranda* was that it would impede the police in solving crimes, and thereby negatively affect the conviction rate.[140] Yet, most researchers who have studied this question empirically have concluded that *Miranda* appears to have had no such effect.[141] A minority of researchers, however, question this body of research and assert that *Miranda* has "resulted in a lost confession in one out of every six cases"[142] But this statistic is disputed by many researchers who call into question the selection of cases used in the research,[143] and who point out that between 78 to 96 percent of suspects still waive their *Miranda* rights and submit to police interrogation.[144] These statistics call into question the validity of the Supreme Court's assumption about the prophylactic nature of *Miranda* warnings.

---

[134] 168 U.S. 532 (1897).

[135] 297 U.S. 278 (1936).

[136] *Id.*

[137] 384 U.S. 436, 444 (1966).

[138] *Id.* at 492; *see* Chapter Five for a complete analysis of the capacity to confess.

[139] *Id.* at 457-58.

[140] Patrick A. Malone, *"You Have the Right to Remain Silent"*: Miranda *After Twenty Years*, 55 AM. SCHOLAR 367 (1986).

[141] *Id.* at 367-68; *see also* Richard A. Leo, *Inside the Interrogation Room*, 86 J. CRIM. L. & CRIMINOLOGY 266-303 (1996).

[142] Paul G. Cassell, Miranda's *Social Costs: An Empirical Reassessment*, 90 NW. U. L. REV. 387, 417 (1996); Paul G. Cassell & Bret Hyman, *Police Interrogation in the 1990s: An Empirical Study of the Effects of* Miranda, 43 U.C.L.A. L. REV. 839, 871 (1996).

[143]   Steven J. Schulhofer, Miranda *and Clearance Rates*, 91 NW. U. L. REV. 278, 278-79 (1996).

[144] Amanda L. Prebble, *Manipulated by* Miranda: *A Critical Analysis of Bright Lines and Voluntary Confessions under* United States v. Dickerson, 68 U. CIN. L. REV. 555 , 579 (citing Leo, *supra* note 141); George C. Thomas, *Plain Talk About the* Miranda *Empirical Debate: A Steady-State" Theory of Confessions*, 43 U.C.L.A. L. REV. 933-59 (1996); Richard Leo, Miranda *and the Problem of False Confessions*, in THE MIRANDA DEBATE 271-82 (1998)).

In spite of the inconclusive nature of the empirical research studying the impact of *Miranda*, it remains the law today. It was called into question by a Fourth Circuit case in 1999 that held Congress has legislatively overruled *Miranda* when it enacted 18 U.S.C. ' 3501—a provision that allowed confessions to be admissible, even if *Miranda* rights had been violated by law enforcement, so long as the confession was still deemed to be voluntary.[145] The Supreme Court, however, reversed the Fourth Circuit's holding and reaffirmed *Miranda*, stressing the constitutional nature of the rule.[146] So if *Miranda* is violated, the exclusionary rule will usually act to keep the suspect's statements out of evidence. But what if *Miranda* is not violated? Certainly informing a suspect of his or her rights and then obtaining a waiver from the suspect does not necessarily mean the goal of *Miranda* has been satisfied. A confession obtained without a *Miranda* violation can still violate due process if the confession was coerced.[147]

B. Interrogation and False Confessions

Interrogation is the questioning of a suspect. Interrogation has two primary goals: "the exploration and resolution of issues" in a case,[148] and obtaining a confession from a suspect. It is the latter goal that differentiates a true interrogation from an interview, as an interrogation is designed to elicit an incriminating response from a suspect.[149]

> Skilled interrogators know that every suspect has a weakness. As the standard police manuals explain, the purpose of interrogation techniques is to exploit that weakness. The most widely used manual, *Criminal Interrogation and Confessions,* by Fred E. Inbau, John E. Reid, and Joseph P. Buckley . . . states that "an individual will confess (tell the truth) when he perceives the consequences of a confession as more desirable than the continued anxiety of deception." Thus, when interrogating a suspect who is strongly believed to be guilty, an interrogator aims to "decrease the suspect's perception of the consequences of confessing, while at the same time increasing the suspect's internal anxiety associated with his deception."[150]

Playing on these weaknesses, police are highly skilled at eliciting incriminating statements from suspects. And there is good reason for police to interrogate suspects vigorously. Research has demonstrated that a confession is the most damaging evidence that can be presented against a defendant at trial.[151] Police eagerness to obtain the ever-damning confession has led to the development of a number of interrogation tactics that are highly questionable in light of core values in *Miranda*. There exists a real likelihood of false confessions in light of some of these tactics,[152] as well as due to reasons that have nothing to do with the inherently coercive nature of custodial interrogations. We will address the three major types of false confessions in turn.

---

[145] United States v. Dickerson, 166 F.3d 667, 673 (4th Cir. 1999), rev'd, 530 U.S. 428 (2000).

[146] 530 U.S. 428, 438 (2000).

[147] *E.g.*, Frazier v. Cupp, 394 U.S. 731 (1969).

[148] R.F. ROYAL & S.R. SCHUTT, THE GENTLE ART OF INTERVIEWING AND INTERROGATION: A PROFESSIONAL MANUAL AND GUIDE 25 (Prentice Hall 1976).

[149] Rhode Island v. Innis, 46 U.S. 291 (1980); Brewer v. Williams, 430 U.S. 387 (1977).

[150] Welsh S. White, *False Confessions and the Constitution: Safeguards Against Untrustworthy Confessions*, 32 HARV. C.R.-C.L. L. REV. 105, 118 (1997).

[151] Saul M. Kassin, *The Psychology of Confession Evidence*, 52 AM. PSYCHOLOGIST 221 (1997).

[152] Richard A. Leo & Richard J. Ofshe, *The Consequences of False Confessions: Deprivations of Liberty and Miscarriages of Justice in the Age of Psychological Interrogation*, 88 J. CRIM. L. & CRIMINOLOGY 429 (1998).

Before doing so, however, it should be noted that we have poor empirical research in the area of false confessions. The main problem with studies examining false confessions has to do with sampling procedures. We study those cases in which we come to find out someone was wrongfully convicted. The purposeful sampling necessarily means that case selection of the exceptional cases masks those cases about which we have no data. Accordingly, we have no reliable, systematic measures of how frequently people falsely confess. Estimates range from a low of two to three dozen per year[153] to a high of over 600 per year in the United States.[154] Accordingly, the true extent of the problem of false confessions is not known. What is clear, however, is that false confessions do occur. And they generally fall into one of the three following categories, although sometimes there is overlap between them, so they should not be viewed as mutually exclusive categories.[155]

1. Voluntary False Confessions

Some people confess to crimes they did not commit without anyone having every questioned them, let alone coerced them. Such confessions are totally voluntary. As Wrightsman has pointed out, "they may be instigated by a desire of publicity or by generalized guilt, or they may reflect some form of psychotic behavior." The more than 200 false confessions to the kidnapping of the Lindbergh baby are examples of such confessions.

2. Coerced-Internalized False Confessions

Coerced-internalized false confessions occur when an innocent suspect confesses to a crime he or she did not commit but has come to believe they did, in fact, commit the crime. In other words, they internalize the false belief that they are guilty, even though they are not. How does this occur? Research indicates that some police interrogation tactics are so highly stressful and confusing for a suspect that the truth becomes confused with what the police are telling the suspect, rendering the suspect "hopelessly confused."[156]

Certainly low intelligence and high suggestibility are very important factors in having a suspect become so confused during interrogation that they falsely come to believe their own guilt and confess accordingly. But there are other factors as well, as illustrated by the case of Peter Reilly. At age 18, he confessed to killing his mother and was convicted accordingly. But on appeal, exculpatory evidence demonstrated that it was factually impossible for Reilly to have committed the killing, and his conviction was reversed.[157] The interrogation of Reilly occurred at 6:30 a.m., approximately nine hours after he had learned of his mother's death. After four hours of questioning, he submitted to a polygraph test and was told that the test indicated he was lying. Even though Reilly kept insisting that he "didn't do it," the interrogator kept emphasizing the "infallibility" of a lie detector test.[158] The police continued to interrogate him for six more hours during which time they suggested motives for the crime to Peter and even encouraged him to

---

[153] Cassell, *supra* note 142.

[154] Huff, Rattner, & Sagarin, *supra* note 3.

[155] Gisli H. Gudjonsson, The Psychology of Interrogations, Confessions and Testimony 258 (1992).

[156] H. H. Foster, *Confessions and the Station House Syndrome*, 18 DePaul L. Rev. 683, 690-91 (1969).

[157] Reilly v. State, 355 A.2d 324, 329 (Conn. Super. Ct. 1976).

[158] White, *supra* note 150, at 126.

visualize the steps taken to have killed his mother. Throughout the time, Reilly continued to deny any memory of killing his mother, "yet tried with almost pathetic eagerness to supply details that would please his interrogator."[159]

On appeal, psychologists asserted that Reilly falsely confessed due to his "youth, his low self-esteem, his trust of authority, and the fact that he had recently undergone a traumatic experience."[160] The interrogator's having preyed on Reilly's unusual suggestibility in terms of the alleged infallibility of the polygraph test further contributed to Reilly having made a coerced-internalized confession.

3. Coerced-Compliant False Confessions

Confessions that suspects make knowing themselves to be innocent but given to stop law enforcement interrogation are called ***coerced-compliant false confessions.*** The situation described earlier in *Bram v. United States* in which suspects were physically tortured until they confessed is an example of this type of false confession. Confessions made in response to third-degree tactics described earlier are also examples of this type of confession. Although it would be nice if the most egregious third-degree tactics were simply remnants of a dark period in police history, such wishful thinking would be naive,[161] as the repeated use of a stun gun during an interrogation by New York police in the mid-1980s illustrates. Although the third degree appears from time to time, albeit rarely, the much more prevalent form of police coercion in modern times is psychological, often involving deception ranging from "sympathy for the suspect, to exaggerating the strength of the evidence against the suspect, to falsely alleging that a witness has identified the suspect."[162] Although some police tactics are highly circumspect, it is clear that "*Miranda* forbids coercion, not mere strategic deception . . . . Ploys to mislead a suspect or lull him into a false sense of security that do not rise to the level of compulsion or coercion to speak are not within *Miranda's* concerns."[163] Whether these ploys are merely acts of deception or they rise to the level of police coercion is a question of fact that must be examined on a case-by-case basis using what is known as "the totality of the circumstances test."

C. Deception vs. Coercion Under the Totality of the Circumstances Test

The central question in evaluating whether a suspect knowingly, intelligently, and voluntarily waived *Miranda* rights is "whether, in the totality of the circumstances, law enforcement officials obtained the evidence by overbearing the will of the accused."[164] Two distinct lines of inquiry need to be made to answer this question. The first involves the police conduct at issue; the second involves the capacity of the suspect to have resisted the police tactics used.[165] Even if

---

[159] *Id.*

[160] *Id.* at 127 (citing GUDJONSSON, *supra* note 155, at 235-40, 252-56).

[161] Confession at Gunpoint? (ABC News Television Broadcast, Mar. 29, 1991).

[162] Laurie Magid, *Deceptive Police Interrogation Practices: How Far Is Too Far?:c Deceptive Police Interrogation Practices: How Far Is Too Far?*, 99 MICH. L. REV. 1168, 1174-75 (2001).

[163] Illinois v. Perkins, 496 U.S. 292, 297 (1990).

[164] Robert S. Seigal & Matthew J. Warren, *Thirtieth Annual Review of Criminal Procedure: Introduction and Guide for Users: I. Investigation and Police Practices: Custodial Interrogations*, 89 Geo. L.J. 1193, 1211 (2001) (citing Haynes v. Washington, 373 U.S. 503, 513-14 (1963)).

[165] *E.g.*, Mincey v. Arizona, 437 U.S. 385, 399-401 (1978).

the will of a suspect is particularly weak, due to low intelligence, youth, disability, or otherwise, it is clear that there must be some police misconduct in the first line of inquiry for a constitutional violation to be found to have occurred.[166]

When does permissible police deception cross the line to become impermissible police coercion? Trickery by the police has repeatedly been held to be constitutionally permissive. For example, in *Frazier v. Cupp*,[167] police falsely told a suspect that his cousin, who had been his accomplice in the crime, had already given a full confession.[168] In the face of that material lie, and partially based on the police falsely portraying their sympathy for the suspect, the suspect gave a full confession.[169] The Court stressed that while deception was relevant to examining the voluntariness of a *Miranda* waiver and subsequent confession, it was not dispositive.[170] The Court upheld the confession. *Frazier v. Cupp* nicely illustrates how the Supreme Court has "repeatedly declined the opportunity to place any specific limits on the use of deception during interrogation."[171]

Since deceptive tactics are a part of the totality of the circumstances test, but are not dispositive factors, the question then turns to examining the other that must be considered. Those most commonly assessed in the totality of the circumstances test are:

> (1) the location of the questioning; (2) whether *Miranda* warnings were given; and (3) whether the accused initiated contact with law enforcement officials. An accused's personal characteristics, such as youth, drug problems, psychological problems, physical condition, and inexperience with the criminal justice system are also factors in this totality test, but have not been held individually sufficient to render a confession involuntary. Courts generally have held the following practices insufficiently coercive to constitute a Fifth Amendment violation: (1) promises of leniency or psychiatric treatment; (2) confrontation of the accused with other evidence of guilt; (3) an interrogator's appeal to the defendant's emotions; and (4) an interrogator's false or misleading statements.[172]

In contrast to trickery or tactics of mere deception that are accepted by the courts, police are not permitted to use coercive means. Certainly anything approaching third-degree tactics—including the use of force (whether actual or threatened), torture, or physical abuse—are now constitutionally barred.[173] So are "threats (even implicit ones) of harm or punishment; prolonged isolations or deprivations of food or sleep; . . . and the failure to notify the suspect of his or her *Miranda* rights."[174] And, although promises of leniency are frowned upon, they rarely will invalidate a confession unless the police lie that the suspect will not be prosecuted if he or she confesses.

---

[166] Colorado v. Connelly, 479 U.S. 157, 170 (1986) (upholding the confession of a mentally ill suspect since the suspect approached police to make a confession without the police having done anything coercive).

[167] *Id.* at 1176.

[168] 394 U.S. 731 (1969).

[169] *Id.* at 738.

[170] *Id.*

[171] Magid, *supra* note 162, at 1176.

[172] Seigal & Warren, *supra* note 164, at 1211-13 (internal citations omitted).

[173] *Id.* at 1214.

[174] Lawrence S. Wrightsman, Forensic Psychology 156 (2001).

In spite of the distinction between deception and coercion, telling the difference between the two is not always easy. For example, in *Welch v. Butler*,[175] a confession was held to be voluntary although it was induced by a lengthy prayer session conducted by a born-again Christian police officer who talked to the suspect about the nature of divine forgiveness and salvation. In contrast, *People v. Phelps*[176] held a rape confession to be involuntary when police officers had indicated that a lack of cooperation on the suspect's part would lead to a painful penile swab procedure to obtain evidence. The threat of imposition of pain was key to the court's decision.

D. The Role of Forensic Psychologists as Experts Dealing with Interrogations and Confessions

Testimony by psychologists and psychiatrists regarding false confessions is generally accepted by the courts, but in two distinct ways. First, testimony regarding empirical research into the phenomenon of false confessions is permitted if the expert offers only generalized information. They are permitted to testify that false confessions occur. They can also explore the traits associated with those who may falsely testify. However, such experts are not permitted to testify about anything specifically relating to the defendant on trial, such as stating that the defendant's mental impairments increase the likelihood of that individual falsely confessing. In contrast, though, psychologists and psychiatrists who have performed a clinical evaluation of the defendant are permitted to testify about the specific likelihood of a false confession from a defendant based upon their evaluation of the defendant, provided they have used generally accepted methods of clinical assessment.[177]

III. CONCLUSION

Eyewitness identifications and confessions by suspects to police are two of the most important types of evidence in a criminal trial. They are highly influential insofar as juries are swayed to find guilt beyond a reasonable doubt when these types of evidence are introduced at trial. Yet, both eyewitness identifications and confessions are types of evidence that are fraught with potential for serious error. In addition to problems with perception that can negatively impact eyewitness identifications, a number of situational and systemic factors can affect the reliability of an identification, even when the eyewitness has a high degree of confidence in his or her identification. Similarly, confessions may be inaccurate or totally false for a number of reasons ranging from purposeful lying by a suspect to deceptive police interrogation tactics that lead to incriminating statements being made by a truly innocent suspect.

The behavioral sciences have much to offer the justice system in terms of empirical evidence that helps the legal system understand the phenomena of mistaken identifications and false confessions. Moreover, the insights that psychology has been able to share with the law have resulted in improvements to identification and interrogation processes. Yet, many suggestions for improvements remain that have yet to be acted upon by the justice system. Until they are, the behavioral sciences can help to educate juries on mistaken identifications and false confessions through expert testimony. But that requires courts to admit such testimony under either the *Frye* test or the *Daubert* test, depending on the rule applicable in a particular jurisdiction. Since judges

---

[175] 835 F.2d 92 (5th Cir. 1988).

[176] 456 N.W.2d 290 (Neb. 1990).

[177] See Fradella, Fogarty & O'Neill, *supra* note 126 (citing United States v. Hall, 974 F. Supp. 1198, 1205 (C.D. Ill. 1997); United States v. Hall, 93 F.3d 1337 (7th Cir. 1996)).

have been ruling inconsistently on whether such expert testimony is necessary, there remains legal barriers to helping jurors understand both phenomenon. Until those barriers are removed, there remains a very real possibility of wrongful convictions when questionable eyewitness identifications or confessions evidence is used.

CHAPTER THIRTEEN
PSYCHOLOGY AND JURIES

I. JURY SELECTION

The jury is most frequently the trier-of-fact in the trial process. According to the Sixth Amendment to the U.S. Constitution, "In all criminal prosecutions, the accused shall enjoy the right to a speedy and public trial by an impartial jury of the States and district wherein the crime shall have been committed . . ."[1] The Seventh Amendment provides for "the right of trial by jury" in civil cases.[2] Most state constitutions contain similar guarantees.[3]

In order to assemble a jury, potential jurors receive a **summons** in the mail ordering them to appear in court at a specified time and date. The people who are so summoned comprise the **"venire"**, the prospective jurors for cases. The summons is usually accompanied by a juror-questionnaire that is used to make sure the recipient is qualified to serve as a member of the venire panel. In a run-of-the mill case, forty or fifty people might be summoned in order to select a twelve person jury. In a high profile case, hundreds might be called for jury service.

Of course, just because someone was summoned to jury service, does not mean they will respond to the summons. Any number of factors might prevent someone who has been summoned from responding. First, some people simply never receive a summons, since they are transient. This, of course, most effects disenfranchised minority populations and has the secondary effect of limiting the representation of the venire.[4] However, even when people do receive a summons, between 20 and 45 percent simply disregard them, leaving as little as 55 percent who actually appear for service.[5]

A. Representativeness of a Jury

A jury is supposed to be representative of society as a whole. This does not mean that either the venire or the actual petit jury must be, "a perfect mirror of the community or accurately reflected the proportionate strength of every identifiable group."[6] It does mean, that "all defendants are entitled to be tried by jurors drawn from a pool representing a fair cross-section of the community ,[7] although the actual jury, eventually impaneled, need not."[8] In reality, this foundation of constitutional law has proven to be more aspiring than effective. Historically, venire panels were not representative of a community. Middle-aged to older white men were over-represented for decades. There were many ways of picking a venire. They ranged from

---

[1]U.S. Const. amend. VI.

[2]U.S. Const. amend. VII.

[3]See Albert W. Alschuler & Andrew G. Deiss, *A Brief History of the Criminal Jury in the United States*, 61 U. CHI L. REV. 867 (1994); Stephen Landsman, *The Civil Jury in America: Scenes from an Unappreciated History*, 44 HASTINGS L.J. 579 (1993).

[4]*See, e.g.*, Deborah Ramirez, *Affirmative Jury Selection: A Proposal to Advance Both the Deliberative Ideal and Jury Diversity*, 1998 U. CHI. LEGAL F. 161, 169-70 (1998).

[5]Kurt M. Saunders, *Race and Representation in Jury Service Selection*, 36 DUQ. L. REV. 49, 64 (1997) (citing STEPHEN J. ADLER, THE JURY: TRIAL AND ERROR IN THE AMERICAN COURTROOM 243 (1994)).

[6]Swain v. Alabama, 380 U.S. 202, 208 (1965).

[7]Saunders, *supra* note 5, at 55 (citing Taylor v. Louisiana, 419 U.S. 522 (1975); Theil v. Southern Pacific Co., 328 U.S. 217, 220 (1946)).

[8]*Id.* (citing Fay v. New York, 332 U.S. 261 (1947)).

exclusive use of voter-registration lists to selecting "retired or unemployed men who hung around the courthouse all day."[9]

As time went on, we began to recognize that an unrepresentative jury was problematic for the justice system. Homogeneity led, not only to blatant discrimination (all white male juries consistently refusing to convict a fellow white man of murdering a black man),[0] but also to more subtle forms of discrimination. Yet, it was not until the late 1960s that we began to even consider the impact that the systematic exclusion of minorities from jury service had on the justice system.

Professor Ramirez[11] articulately sets forth three distinct reasons why juries need to be diverse.

> [First] when a jury is racially mixed, the verdict it reaches is more likely to be seen as fair, considered, and impartial than one reached by a verdict emerging from a racially homogenous jury. . . . [Second], a racially diverse jury is likely to deliberate differently and more fairly than a homogenous jury . . . . [T]he presence of even one minority juror is likely to suppress the direct expression of racial bias or stereotypes and to mute any positive reinforcement of such views if they were expressed. . . . [A] racially diverse jury can sometimes affirmatively reduce or eliminate the racial prejudices and stereotypes that accompany jurors to the courtroom. At least one study has shown that with a racially mixed jury, jurors are more likely to respect different racial perspectives and to confront their own prejudice and stereotypes when such beliefs are recognized and addressed during deliberations. This prejudice reduction effect is yet another reason to believe that racially mixed juries enhance the truthseeking function of jury deliberations. [And third,] racially diverse juries bring to their deliberations a broader range of life experiences that allow them to use their common sense more effectively when they evaluate the facts presented at trial.[12]

In spite of the benefits of a diverse venire, there are numerous systemic barriers to a truly representative jury, which therefore, impact negatively on their psychology. The most common contributor to this problem is the way in which the venire is selected. As mentioned earlier, voter registration is one of the most prevalent means in selecting the people to whom a jury summons would be mailed. Because minorities tend to be under-represented on voter registration lists, this method contributes to venire homogeneity. Venire diversity can also be increased by using telephone lists, motor vehicle or driver's license rolls, and welfare and unemployment lists— processes that have been implemented in many U.S. jurisdictions from the mid-1980s through the late 1990s.[13]

The jury questionnaire used to screen the venire is another factor contributing to the exclusion of people who might comprise a more diverse venire, thereby increasing the representativeness of the jury pool. For example, the visually or hearing impaired were

---

[9]LAWRENCE S. WRIGHTSMAN, EDIE GREENE, MICHAEL T. NIETZEL, & WILLIAM H. FORTUNE, PSYCHOLOGY AND THE LEGAL SYSTEM 386 (5th ed. 2002).

[10]Albert W. Alschuler, *Racial Quotas and the Jury*, 44 DUKE L.J. 704, 706 (1995).

[11]Ramirez, *supra* note 4.

[12]*Id.* at 163-65 (internal citations omitted).

[13]*Id.* at 169-70.

prohibited from serving on juries, as were those who did not speak English, those convicted of felonies, and those who were not U.S. citizens.[14] While those who are deaf or do not speak English have begun to serve on juries, their ability to do so depends on the services of translators who may or may not be available in any given jurisdiction. Felons are permanently excluded from jury service in more than half the states and in the federal justice system, and the remaining states place various restrictions on jury service for convicts, including restrictions for those people on probation or parole.[15] Given the fact that one out of every three black males between the ages of twenty and twenty-nine is currently under some form of correctional supervision, this bar against jury service for those who have been convicted of a crime further serves to exclude people who might contribute to the diversity of the jury.

Another impediment to a representative jury is the way in which jurors are compensated for their time. Jurors are often paid only a nominal amount for their service. Since minorities are over-represented in low-paying jobs, they are disproportionately excluded from jury service on the grounds that serving would cause them an "economic hardship."[16]

And finally, the remaining exclusions or exemptions from jury service also work to prevent a truly diverse jury from being assembled. Public officials, including police and fire department employees, are excluded by federal law.[17] Full-time students, teachers, clergy members, and lawyers have also traditionally been exempted from service or, alternatively, have been given the opportunity to exempt themselves from jury service.[18] While the same holds true today for full-time students, since they cannot "make up" lost time in school, teachers, lawyers, and physicians are no longer exempted from jury service in many jurisdictions. Police, fire-fighters, and emergency medical personnel (i.e., paramedics) continue to be in light of the essential roles they perform each day.

B. The *Voir Dire* Process

The process of summoning venire people and excluding those whose juror questionnaires reveal disqualifying information is only the first step in the jury selection process. Once qualified venire persons are assembled in a courtroom, the actual process of selecting a jury from the venire panel begins. This process is known as ***voir dire***, a Latin term meaning "to speak the truth."[19]

Although it may not seem so intuitively, selecting the right people from the venire to sit on the petit jury is one of the most important parts of the trial process—so much so that experts generally agree that "85 percent of the cases litigated are won or lost when the jury is selected!"[20] Given this fact, it is not surprising that behavioral scientists from a variety of disciplines (e.g., sociology, psychology, marketing, communications, etc.) are hired as jury

---

[14]WRIGHTSMAN, ET AL., *supra* note 9, at 389.

[15]Kathleen M. Olivares, Velmer S. Burton, Jr., & Francis T. Cullen, *The Collateral Consequences of a Felony Conviction: A National Study of Legal Codes 10 Years Later*, 60 FED. PROBATION 10, 13 (Sept .1996).

[16]HIROSHI FUKURAI, EDGAR W. BUTLER & RICHARD KROOTH, RACE AND THE JURY: RACIAL DISENFRACHISEMENT AND THE SEARCH FOR JUSTICE 52 (Plenum 1993).

[17]28 U.S.C. § 1863(b)(5).

[18]ADLER, *supra* note 5, at 219

[19]BLACK'S LAW DICTIONARY 1575 (6th ed. 1990).

[20]*E.g.*, Herald P. Fahringer, "*Mirror, Mirror On The Wall...*," 64 N.Y. ST. B.J. 22 (1992).

consultants to assist in jury selection.[21] These social scientists attempt to engage in a process commonly referred to as *scientific jury selection*—an attempt "to compile and implement the 'ideal' juror profile."[22] The factors most frequently considered in assembling the ideal jury include "juror occupation, gender, race/ethnicity, demeanor and appearance, wealth and social status, religion, marital status, and age."[23] The merit of scientific jury selection, however, is contested in both scholarly research and by legal practitioners.[24]

The main purpose of *voir dire* is to weed out those members of the venire who would not be fair and impartial jurors.[25] In addition, *voir dire* should accomplish four other goals:

(1) Establish credibility and rapport with the panel for you and your client, if you are the defense attorney;
(2) Elicit information from the panel to determine which members are the most and least likely to accept your theory of the case;
(3) Educate and sell members on your theory of the case; and,
(4) Neutralize or highlight problem areas in the case.[26]

Accomplishing these tasks is achieved through asking questions to the people in the venire. But how that process is conducted varies greatly from courtroom to courtroom, as the judge controls the entirety of the *voir dire* process, which ranges from who questions the venire, what questions will be asked, and the wording of questions to whether questions will be asked individually or to the whole venire panel simultaneously as a group and how long the whole process will be permitted to go on.[27] In most federal courts, and increasingly in state courts, judges conduct *voir dire* even though most lawyers would prefer to conduct *voir dire* themselves.[28]

1. The Accuracy of *Voir Dire*

In contrast to scientific jury selection, which can be quite expensive, traditional *voir dire* is generally considered to be "a convenient, cheap, and administratively efficient way to detect bias" even though it may not be "a particularly accurate approach."[29] One of the main factors

---

[21]Soloman M. Fulero & Steven D. Penrod, *The Myths and Realities of Attorney Jury Selection Folklore and Scientific Jury Selection: What Works?*, 17 OHIO N.U. L. REV. 229, 229-30 (1990).

[22]Jeremy W. Barber, *The Jury is Still Out: The Role of Jury Science in the Modern American Courtroom*, 31 AM. CRIM. L. REV. 1225, 1234 (1994).

[23] Jim Goodwin, *Articulating the Inarticulable: Relying on Nonverbal Behavioral Cues to Deception to Strike Jurors During Voir Dire*, 38 ARIZ. L. REV. 739, n.6 (1996) (citing Fulero & Penrod, *supra* note 21, at 229-37.

[24]*Id.* at 170 (citing Fulero & Penrod, *supra* note 21, at 229; Robert Plutchik & Alice K. Schwartz, *Jury Selection: Folklore or Science?*, 1 CRIM. L. BULL. 3, 5 (1965)); compare Victor Gold, *Covert Advocacy: Reflections on the Use of Psychological Persuasion Techniques in the Courtroom*, 65 N.C. L. REV. 481 (1987) (rejecting scientific jury selection), with J. Alexander Tanford & Sarah Tanford, *Better Trials Through Science: A Defense of Psychologist-Lawyer Collaboration*, 66 N.C. L. REV. 741 (1988) (advocating scientific jury selection).

[25]Goodwin, *supra* note 23, at 745.

[26]Julie Hasdorff, *The Art of Trial Advocacy: Voir Dire: What's the Point?*, 2001 ARMY LAW. 17, 17 (2001).

[27]Goodwin, *supra* note 23, at 746 (citing James W. McElhaney, *Jury Voir Dire: Getting the Most Out of Jury Selection*, 79 A.B.A. J. 78, 78 (1993)); Toni M. Massaro, *Peremptories Or Peers?– Rethinking Sixth Amendment Doctrine, Images, and Procedures*, 64 N.C. L. REV. 501, 506 (1986); Arthur J. Stanley & Robert G. Begam, *Who Should Conduct Voir Dire?*, 61 JUDICATURE 70 (1977).

[28]Goodwin, *supra* note 23, at 746.

[29]*Id.* at 750 (citing ABA STANDARDS FOR CRIMINAL JUSTICE 8-3.5 (3d ed. 1992) (commentary)).

contributing to the inaccuracy of the problem is whether jurors answer the questions posed to them honestly. Although the venire is sworn under oath to answer truthfully, they clearly do not always do so.[30] Sometimes they simply refuse to admit to facts or thoughts they find embarrassing to share during the judicial process such as a prior conviction for a crime or prior victimization of a crime for either themselves or a close family member. Other times it is less personal, but still not something a venire member will admit even though under oath. For example:

> Research indicates that 90% of a juror's decisions are formed before jury deliberation begins, that roughly two-thirds of jury panels are biased against the accused, that roughly 25% of jurors entertain the opinion, from the outset, that the accused must be guilty or he would not have been charged with the offense, and that although 86% of the jury pool maintains a fixed opinion about the accused's guilt, less than 20% of the actual panel will admit it. [31]

Even when venirepersons are not deliberately concealing what they might perceive to be embarrassing information, most jurors want to please the court and the attorneys by being "good" jurors.[32] Accordingly, jurors may purposefully or unconsciously lie during *voir dire* to conceal their biases or prejudices in an attempt (again, whether conscious or not) "to be correct, positive, and pleasing."[33]

The questions asked during *voir dire* are designed to detect juror bias, especially in the face of venire dishonesty about the existence of such bias. But lawyers have vastly differing abilities in this area.[34] It is undisputed, though, that some attorneys who are highly skilled in the *voir dire* process have a particular knack for detecting jury bias.[35] The methods at their disposal to do so include "ranking scales, community attitudinal surveys, survey-based statistical modeling, juror investigations, in-courtroom ratings of authoritarianism, group dynamic analysis, focus groups, mock trials, shadow juries, in-court assessment of juror non-verbal communication, and even psychics."[36] Most attorneys, however, do not go to such lengths as part of *voir dire*. Rather, they tend to rely on their own personal beliefs about jurors that are often based upon "superstition, general attitudes about people, or stereotypes."[37]

In contrast to traditional *voir dire*, scientific jury selection tries to measure juror bias. Two distinct areas are usually probed in an attempt to do so: authoritarianism and pro-prosecutor or pro-defense orientation. Research suggests that the more authoritarian a prospective juror is (i.e., "conventional, conservative, power-oriented, and deferential to authority"[38]), the more likely the

---

[30]Margaret Covington, *Jury Selection: Innovative Approaches to Both Civil and Criminal Litigation*, 16 ST. MARY'S L.J. 575, 580-81 (1985).

[31]*Id.* at 580-81.

[32]*Id.* at 581.

[33]*Id.*; *see also* Barber, *supra* note 22, at 1243; Dale W. Broeder, *Voir Dire Examinations: An Empirical Study*, 38 S. CAL. L. REV. 503, 528 (1965).

[34]Goodwin, *supra* note 23, at 750.

[35]*Id.*

[36]*Id.* (citing Massaro, *supra* note 27, at 523 n.109; Barber, *supra* note 22, at 1225).

[37]*Id.* (citing Massaro, *supra* note 27, at 522 n.108; E. Hawrish & E. Tate, *Determinants of Jury Selection*, 39 SASK. L. REV. 285, 285 (1975)).

[38]Dennis J. Devine, Laura D. Clayton, Benjamin B. Dunford, Rasmy Seying, & Jennifer Pryce, *Jury Decision Making: 45 Years of Empirical Research on Deliberating Groups*, 7 PSYCH. PUB. POL. AND L. 622, 674 (2001).

juror is to convict. Other factors are examined to determine whether a prospective juror may be pro-prosecution (or pro-plaintiff in a civil case) or pro-defense. For example, demographic characteristics of jurors on certain factors "interact with defendant characteristics to produce a bias in favor of defendants who are similar to the jury in some salient respect" such as race, gender, socio-economic status[39] Case specific issues also play a role. For example, jurors who feel there has been a "litigation explosion" are hostile to delivering verdicts for civil plaintiffs. Conversely, hostility toward corporations or the medical establishment might bias a juror toward a plaintiff.

2. Clues Used to Detect Venire Bias and/or Deception

Most lawyers focus on verbal responses from jurors to detect bias.[40] Skilled attorneys, however, also pick up on *leakage cues*—non-verbal responses that indicate deception.[41] Leakage cues come in three forms: "verbal (the words which are actually spoken, along with their syntactical arrangement), paralinguistic (aspects of speech—such as breathing, pauses and latencies, pitch and tone of voice, and speech disturbances—that are not actually concerned with the content of the message), and kinesic (body language, such as facial expressions, body movements, body orientation, eye contact, and hand movements)."[42] Problematically, though, many lawyers are unskilled at focusing on the important leakage clues, often paying unnecessary attention to the least telling ones (e.g., crossed feet or arms, poor posture, covered mouths, etc.).[43]

The leakage cues that have been scientifically associated with deception are:

> (1) pupil dilation, (2) speech errors, (3) increased vocal pitch, (4) increased use of adaptors [e.g., running a hand through one's hair, scratching an elbow, biting a lip, placing a finger over the mouth, and playing with a pencil], (5) decreased smiling in general and [felt/genuine] . . . smiles in particular, (6) increased use of masking smiles, (7) increased speech hesitations/response latencies, (8) decreased use of illustrators [e.g., pointing, pictorial enactment, rhythmic movements, or kinetic actions such as using a chopping motion with the hand to simulate the movements of an ax, pointing a finger at someone and pretending to shoot them, or shaking a fist at an antagonist], (9) heightened arousal, (10) negative affect displays, (11) increased pauses, and (12) decreased message duration.[44]

Goodwin points out that it is not just the presence or absence of these factors that should be paid attention to, but also changes or shifts in such behaviors between the period of general *voir dire* questioning and specific questions designed to get at bias. For example, "if a juror used numerous hand movements to illustrate responses during the initial questioning period, but suddenly ceases doing so during the subsequent questioning phase, he should be regarded with

---

[39]*Id.* at 673.

[40]Edward J. Imwinkelried, *Demeanor Impeachment: Law and Tactics*, 9 AM. J. TRIAL ADVOC. 183, 187 (1985).

[41]Paul Ekman & Wallace Friesen, *Nonverbal Leakage and Clues to Deception*, 32 PSYCHIATRY 88 (1969).

[42]Goodwin, *supra* note 23, at 752 (citing David Suggs & Bruce D. Sales, *Using Communication Cues to Evaluate Prospective Jurors During the Voir Dire*, 20 ARIZ. L. REV. 629, 630-31 (1978)).

[43]*Id.* at 753-54.

[44]*Id.* at 754; 757 (citing Jim C. Goodwin, Veracity Judgments in the Field: Police Officers' Beliefs About Lie Detection 126 (March 7, 1994) (unpublished M.A. thesis, Colorado State University)) (other internal citations omitted).

skepticism."[45] Similarly, high voice pitch during specific questioning in contrast to general questioning indicates deception.[46] Speech pauses and speech errors (i.e., "tripping over one's words) are not necessarily indicative of deception in and of themselves, but the truthful venire person will not show an increase in speech pauses or errors when responding to specific bias questions in comparison to when responding to general *voir dire* questions.[47] And changes in affect—especially those evidenced by changes in facial expressions "for each of some seven primary affect states: happiness, anger, fear, surprise, sadness, disgust, and interest" during critical periods of questioning can indicate deception.[48]

3. Strikes for Cause

As stated earlier, the goal of *voir dire* is to purge from the jury those prospective jurors who are unable to render a fair and impartial verdict. In response to both substantive verbal and non-verbal responses to questions, a venire person may be struck from the jury pool either for demonstrable cause, or for impalpable reasons.

   Strikes for cause have existed since the dawn of the jury system in the late 1100s and early 1200s in England, although back then, the only reasons recognized as good cause to strike a potential juror was if he was related to the defendant by "blood, marriage or economic interest."[49] As it was in ancient Rome and Greece, in early English common law a venire person's inability to be impartial was not recognized as good cause to strike him.[50] These juries were presentational, not final decision-makers. In other words, their function was to investigate a crime and make a formal accusation, not decide on guilt. "Once the presentment juries accused a defendant of a crime, they turned him or her over to the ruler for trial and punishment."[51] It was not until the 1500s when English common law juries had become the firmly established triers-of-fact.[52] Once juries were acting in this decision-making role, there was a real need for impartial jurors, and strikes for cause became commonplace.[53]

   Under the Sixth Amendment to the U.S. Constitution, a criminal defendant is guaranteed a fair and impartial jury.[54] Through the operation of the Fourteenth Amendment Due Process Clause, this guarantee is made applicable to the states.[55] Accordingly, every state and the federal court system all recognize the right of exercising strikes for cause by both sides in case.[56] Modern strikes for cause generally fall into one of two categories: principal challenges and fact-partial challenges. ***Principal challenges*** involve strikes of potential jurors because they have some relationship to one of the "principals" or participants in the case. They are presumed to be

---

[45]*Id.* at 757.

[46]*Id.*

[47]*Id.*

[48]*Id.*

[49]William T. Pizzi & Morris B. Hoffman, *Jury Selection Errors on Appeal*, 38 AM. CRIM. L. REV. 1391, 1406 (2001).

[50]*Id.* at 1406-07.

[51]*Id.* at 1407.

[52]*Id.* at 1407-08.

[53]*Id.* at 1408.

[54]Duncan v. Louisiana, 391 U.S. 145, 149 (1968).

[55]Pizzi & Hoffman, *supra* note 49, at 1409 (citing FRANCIS H. HELLER, THE SIXTH AMENDMENT TO THE CONSTITUTION OF THE UNITED STATES 71 (1951)).

[56]*Id.*

partial on account of this relationship.[57] ***Fact-partial challenges*** involve strikes of potential jurors because the subject matter of the dispute presents issues on which the potential juror is biased, prejudiced, or predisposed to a particular outcome because of their belief system or experiences.[58] For example, someone who had a family member killed by a drunk driving accident would not be a fair and impartial juror in a criminal driving-under-the-influence case, even if the venire person knew no one involved in the case. The person's background would predispose him or her to be biased against the defendant, rendering the venire person fact-partial. Both sides to a case (plaintiff and defendant in a civil case, or prosecution and defendant in a criminal case) have an unlimited number of strikes for cause to ensure the most fair and impartial jury possible.

4. Peremptory Challenges

Peremptory strikes occur when a party seeks to strike a venire person when there is not good cause to do so. Peremptory strikes first appeared in English common law in the latter part of the thirteenth century, but they could only be exercised by prosecutors and only in capital, criminal cases.[59] As common law evolved, a finite number of peremptory strikes (first, twenty-five, later, twenty, then seven, then three) were granted to criminal defendants, first in capital cases, and later in all felony cases.[60] The practice was embraced in the United States and was statutorily granted as a right to criminal defendants in capital cases in 1790.[61] In 1856, Congress granted ten peremptory strikes to criminal defendants in non-capital felony trials, and two to prosecutors.[62] In 1872, Congress granted prosecutors an additional peremptory strike, and also granted both sides in a civil dispute three peremptory strikes each.[63] The numbers were tinkered with from time to time. As of the writing of this text, the version in place in the federal system grants both sides twenty peremptory strikes in capital cases; "the prosecution gets six and the defendant ten in non-capital felony cases; and each side gets three in misdemeanor and civil cases."[64] Most states have similar rules.[65]

Regardless of the number of peremptory strikes each side has, the purpose of these strikes is usually the same. Originally, they were designed and used for a curative purpose—to correct the mistake of a judge for failing to strike a juror for cause.[66] And they are still used in that manner today. But they are also used to by lawyers to exclude from the jury those people whom they believe to be hostile to their side of the case, even if not so hostile that the venireperson in question would be struck for cause. In other words, attorneys use peremptory strikes to eliminate the jurors they think might not vote for their side during the jury deliberations process "even

---

[57]*Id.*

[58]*Id.*

[59]*Id.* at 1412.

[60]*Id.* at 1413.

[61]*Id.* at 1414.

[62]*Id.*

[63]*Id.* at 1415.

[64]*Id.*; *see also* Fed. R. Crim. P. 24(b) (for criminal); 28 U.S.C. § 1870 (for civil).

[65]*Id.* at 1416.

[66]United States v. Martinez-Salazar, 528 U.S. 304, 318-19 (2000) (Scalia, J., concurring).

without being able to assign a reason for . . . his dislike."[67] Counsel must be careful, however, not to run afoul of the federal constitution when they are exercising their peremptory challenges.

In 1986, the U.S. Supreme Court decided *Batson v. Kentucky*.[68] A jury comprised of all Caucasians convicted an African-American male of burglary. The prosecution used four of its six peremptory challenges to strike African-Americans from the venire. The Supreme Court held that the prosecution's actions violated the equal protection guarantee of the constitution when it used its peremptory strikes to eliminate people on the basis of race.[69] The Supreme Court extended its holding in *Batson* to cover strikes based on gender in *J.E.B. v. Alabama ex rel. T.B.* in 1994.[70]

A *Batson* challenge to a peremptory strike occurs in three phases. First, the party suspecting a peremptory strike has been exercised by opposing counsel in violation of *Batson* must object and make a showing that the juror in question is "a member of a racial group capable of being singled out for differential treatment."[71] The objecting party bears the burden of persuasion in establishing a prima facie case of impermissible discrimination. Once that is done, the side seeking to exercise the peremptory strike must respond to the objection by offering a non-discriminatory reason for wanting to strike the particular juror. "The reason need not rise to the justification of a challenge for cause, but cannot be a mere denial of discriminatory purpose . . . [;] the . . . explanation need not be persuasive, . . . but need only have a 'facial validity.'"[72]

The principle of non-discrimination at the core of *Batson* and *J.E.B.* has not yet been extended by the Supreme Court to other categories, such as ethnicity, religion, or sexual orientation. But some lower federal courts have done so on their own. For example, a federal court in New York upheld the application of *Batson* to strikes against Italian-Americans.[73] But the Supreme Court refused to do so in a case involving Spanish-speaking Latinos.[74] And while California law prohibits striking jurors on the basis of sexual orientation, the courts that have examined this issue have generally declined to apply *Batson* to that characteristic on the basis that doing so might pry too intimately into the private lives of the venire, potentially threatening to "out" gay, lesbian, or bisexual jurors during the *voir dire* process.[75] The reasoning proffered for not extending *Batson* on religious grounds was explained in *State v. Davis*,[76] nicely summarized by Johnstone as follows:

> The *Davis* court found that, although "a juror's religious beliefs are inviolate . . . they are the basis for a person's moral values," and therefore a peremptory strike based on religion does not manifest a "pernicious religious bias." In other words, concerns about reinforcing impermissible stereotypes do not weigh as heavily

---

[67]WILLIAM M. BLACKSTONE, 4 COMMENTARIES ON THE LAWS OF ENGLAND 347 (Chicago 1979).

[68]476 U.S. 79 (1986).

[69]*Id.*; see also Powers v. Ohio, 499 U.S. 400 (1991) (holding equal protection rights fo jurors are violated when they are struck on the basis of their race, regardless of the race of the defendant).

[70]511 U.S. 127 (1994).

[71]*Batson*, 476 U.S. at 94.

[72]A. C. Johnstone, *Peremptory Pragmatism: Religion and the Administration of the* Batson *Rule*, 1998 U. CHI. LEGAL F. 441, 446 (1998) (quoting Pucket v. Elem, 514 US 765 (1995)).

[73]United States v Biaggi, 853 F.2d 89, 96 (2d Cir. 1988).

[74]Hernandez v New York, 500 U.S. 352 (1991).

[75]Johnson v Campbell, 92 F.3d 951, 953 (9th Cir 1996).

[76]504 N.W.2d 767 (Minn. 1993).

with religion as with race, because a juror's religion may determine his views in a way that the law, the other jurors, and the juror himself can recognize as legitimate. This legitimacy mitigates cynicism among jurors, while striking jurors on the basis that religion correlates to moral values promotes impartiality.[77]

II. PROBLEMS FOR THE JURY PROCESS

A. The Invalidity of the *Tabula Rasa* Theory

In every case, whether civil or criminal, a jury is supposed to base its verdict on the evidence presented at trial. That necessarily means that juries are not supposed to consider any ***extra-legal information***—information they have other than the evidence presented to them at trial.[78] But can they do so? The law assumes juries can. But there is empirical evidence that suggests they cannot.

> The entire effort of our trial procedure is to secure . . . jurors who do not know . . . anything of either the character [of the parties] or events [on trial] . . . . The zeal displayed in this effort to empty the minds of the jurors . . . [is a sign] that the jury . . . is an impartial organ of justice.[79]

The sentiment expressed in the preceding quote is known as the ***tabula rasa***—Latin for "clean slate." But jurors do not actually come to court with an "empty mind." And if they did, would we really want them on a jury? Mark Twain commented on this paradox after he observed jury selection in a murder case. Twain noted several intelligent potential jurors were dismissed since they had read newspaper accounts of the case even though each of them said they would be able to put aside the information they had read and decide the case fairly and impartially on the evidence. Twain concluded "ignoramuses alone could mete out unsullied justice."[80]

Media attention is not the only factor that interferes with the tabula rasa theory. Even in run-of-the-mill cases that have received no media attention, jurors will inevitably still bring their own knowledge and experiences to the deliberation process. "All adults have beliefs, values, and prejudices which make impartiality in the tabula rasa sense impossible."[81] Kalven and Zeisel reported that jurors are less likely to convict a defendant on a charge involving conduct in which the jurors had personally engaged in the past, such as gambling or reckless driving.[82] Even such irrelevant factors such as the defendant's attractiveness or how sympathetic the defendant appears to the jury have both been found to be significant factors in juror's determinations of guilt.[83] And demographic characteristics affect juror decision making as well:

---

[77]Johnstone, *supra* note 72, at 451.

[78]Patterson v Colorado, 205 US 454, 462 (1907).

[79]Jeffrey Abramson, *Two Ideals of Jury Deliberation*, 1998 U. Chi. Legal F. 125, 143 (1998) (quoting United States v Parker, 19 F. Supp. 450, 458 (D.N.J. 1937).

[80]Mark Twain, 2 Roughing It 56-57 (Harper & Brothers 1913).

[81]James J. Gobert, *In Search of the Impartial Jury*, 79 J. Crim. L. & Criminology 269, 271 (1988).

[82]Harry Kalven & Hans Zeisel, The American Jury 291, 326 (1966).

[83]*Id.* at ch. 15; see also Sigall & Ostrove, *Beautiful But Dangerous: Effects of Offender Attractiveness and Nature of the Crime on Juridic Judgment*, 31 J. Personality & Soc. Psychol. 410 (1975).

Numerous studies now suggest a correlation between juror attitudes and such variables as occupation, sex, race, and socioeconomic status. In addition, a juror's family, social, political, and personal associations may all affect the juror's decision making. Unfortunately, jurors are often unaware of these factors or the degree to which they are affected by them.[84]

Keep in mind, though, that lawyers are usually not seeking jurors with empty minds during *voir dire;* they aren't even seeking jurors with "open minds"![85] Trial attorneys are actually seeking out potential jurors who are favorable to their side of the case. How effective they are at doing so, whether using traditional or scientific jury selection methods, is a topic a great debate with empirical evidence to support both sides in the debate over the usefulness of either approach.

B. Evidentiary Problems Impacting Jury Functioning

1. Opening Statements

Both criminal and civil trials begin with the lawyers for both sides making ***opening statements*** to the jury. The party with the burden of persuasion makes its opening statement first. Thus, the plaintiff in a civil case or the prosecution in a criminal case goes first. Defense counsel usually makes its opening statement immediately following the plaintiff or prosecution. Some judges, however, will allow defense counsel to wait until the close of the case-in-chief against them, and then make their opening statement before putting on the defense's case-in-chief. Empirical research suggests the former is the better practice from the defense strategy, as waiting until later in the case allows the other side to bond with the jury without ever having heard from the defense.[86]

Opening statements are not evidence.[87] The lawyers are not sworn; they are not giving testimony. Nor are they permitted to argue the strength of the evidence they plan to introduce. Opening statements are simply a roadmap of what they lawyers expect to happen during the course of the trial. They are, in effect, outlines of the case the lawyers plan to present. In spite of the fact that opening statements are not evidence, we know they have a profound impact on the jury. They are the first chance attorneys have to present a "powerful, compelling story" that might get the jury to bond with them.[88]

In addition to the rule that argument is not permitted in opening statements, a host of other rules are designed to ensure opening statements do not unduly taint the jury before evidence is actually admitted during the trial.

---

[84]*Id.* at 322 (internal citations omitted).

[85]*Id.* at 142.

[86]Gary L. Wells, Lawrence S. Wrightsman & Peter K. Miene, *The Timing of the Defense Opening Statement: Don't Wait until the Evidence Is In*, 15 J. APPLIED SOC. PSYCHOL. 758 (1985).

[87]LEONARD DECOF, THE ART OF ADVOCACY 1.06[1] (1992); James R. Lucas, *Opening Statement*, 13 U. HAW. L. REV. 349, 351 (1991).

[88]L. Timothy Perrin, *From O.J. to Mcveigh: The Use of Argument in the Opening Statement*, 48 EMORY L.J. 107, 108 (1999); E. Allen Lind & Gina Y. Ke, *Opening and Closing Statements, in* THE PSYCHOLOGY OF EVIDENCE AND TRIAL PROCEDURE 229, 229-52 (Saul M. Kassin & Lawrence S. Wrightsman eds. 1985).

The rules preclude discussion of inadmissible evidence or evidence of doubtful admissibility during the opening statement. The advocate may only discuss evidence that he has a good faith belief will be introduced during the trial. Moreover, the lawyer may not discuss the law beyond a brief or cursory mention, and may not express personal opinions about the evidence or the case. These limits share universal acceptance among lawyers and judges. Some courts also prohibit any discussion of the opposing side's evidence in the case.[89]

In spite of these rules, lawyers routinely disregard these rules. Why? Because advocacy in opening statements is highly effective. A detailed and well-organized opening statement presents the jury with a *schema*—a thematic framework through which to view the trial.[90] Psychological research has repeatedly demonstrated that even though jurors are admonished not to make up their minds until the conclusion of trial after having given fair and impartial consideration to the evidence, many jurors appear to make a preliminary decision with regard to the outcome of the case after hearing opening statements.[91] In fact, according to some studies, up to 80 percent of jurors "irrevocably" make up their minds after opening statements."[92] Lawyers know this, and they act accordingly. They know opening statements are their opportunity to make an effective connection with the jurors.[93]

The fact that lawyers often break the rules regarding the scope of opening statement should invite the question, "How can they get away with it?" First and foremost, it is difficult to tell where the line between persuasive advocacy and impermissible argument should be drawn. Secondly, opposing counsel is highly hesitant to object for several reasons. First, it is considered poor form or bad lawyering etiquette to interrupt another lawyer's opening statement.[94] Second, if opposing counsel does object, they fear alienating the jury. Jurors, hopefully engrossed in the story being told to them, do not appreciate having the story interrupted. They might conclude that opposing counsel is objecting in an attempt to hide evidence from them and therefore draw negative inferences from the fact that an objection was made. Third, some lawyers will not object in the hopes that if they permit some argumentation in their opponent's opening statement, the courtesy will be returned to them when they make their opening statement.[95] And fourth, there is little deterrence from engaging in some misbehavior during opening statements. If an objection is made and sustained, the lawyer just moves ahead, often with nothing more than a mere admonition from the judge. And since opening statements are not evidence, misconduct during opening statements rarely forms the basis of a successful appeal.[96]

---

[89]Perrin, *supra* note 88, at 111 (internal citations omitted).

[90]Nancy Pennington & Reid Hastie, *A Cognitive Theory of Juror Decision Making: The Story Model*, 13 CARDOZO L. REV. 519, 520 (1991); John Lingle & Thomas Ostrom, *Principles of Memory and Cognition in Attitude Formation, in* COGNITIVE RESPONSES IN PERSUASION 399 (Timothy Brock et al., eds. 1981).

[91]*Id.* at 115 (citing Michael F. Colley, *The Opening Statement: Structure, Issues, Techniques*, TRIAL (Nov. 1982), at 54; Kalven & Zeisel, *supra* note 82; Lucas, *supra* note 87, at 351).

[92]James F. McKenzie, *Eloquence in Opening Statement*, TRIAL DIPL. J. (Spring 1987), at 32.

[93]E.g., Thomas A. Pyszczynski & Lawrence S. Wrightsman, *The Effects of Opening Statements on Mock Jurors' Verdicts in a Simulated Criminal Trial*, 11 J. APPLIED SOC. PSYCHOL. 301 (1981).

[94]Perrin, *supra* note 88, at 125 (citing KENNEY F. HEGLAND, TRIAL AND PRACTICE SKILLS 199 (2d ed. 1994)).

[95]*Id.*

[96]*Id.* at 125-26; *see also* Bennett L. Gershman, *Why Prosecutors Misbehave*, 22 CRIM. L. BULL. 131-43 (1986).

2. Inadmissible Evidence

When jurors receive inadmissible evidence, it is clear it has an effect on them. The *voir dire* process is supposed to screen out those jurors who have been tainted by pretrial publicity. And jurors are supposed to avoid the media while sitting on jury duty as a preventive measure for post-*voir dire* media exposure. Just because they are supposed to do so, however, does not mean they actually will. But even assuming they follow the judicial directives to avoid the media during the pendency of a trial, jurors might still be exposed to inadmissible evidence in court due to attorney mistake or misconduct.

When something is said in court that is inadmissible under the rule of evidence, judges give what is known as ***curative instructions***—a directive to the jury to disregard the evidence that should not have come out in court. But jurors cannot "unhear" what they have already heard.[97] They will be influenced by having heard the inadmissible evidence,[98] although the degree to which it impacts their ultimate verdicts is unclear.[99] Similarly, there are situations in which judges give ***limiting instructions***—instructions to use evidence for only one purpose, but not for others. For example:

> If a defendant testifies during a trial, the judge may allow evidence to be admitted that the defendant has a prior record of convictions. Jurors are instructed to limit their use of this evidence to determine the credibility of the defendant's testimony and not to use that information to infer that the defendant has committed an act, has negative traits, or has a criminal disposition. Similarly, a judge may allow prior conviction information to show that a defendant had a motive, an opportunity, specific knowledge, or has used a common pattern, but again jurors are instructed not to infer negative traits about the defendant. When limited-use evidence is used for unintended purposes, it is considered prejudicial to the defendant. With few exceptions, empirical research has repeatedly demonstrated that both types of limiting instructions are unsuccessful at controlling jurors' cognitive processes.[100]

While curative or limiting instructions work to a certain degree,[101] they potentially can make matters worse. By telling a jury to disregard evidence or use it for only a limited purpose, the judge is actually calling greater attention to the matter. This is known as the ***backfire effect.***[102] The more prejudicial the material, the more likely it is that the material will have a substantial impact on their ultimate decision-making. Examples of such unduly prejudicial materials include hearing the defendant confessed to the crime even though the confession was subsequently ruled inadmissible, or hearing a defendant failed a lie detector test even though such results are inadmissible due to their scientific unreliability. When errors of such magnitude occur, the judge might have to declare a mistrial and start again with a jury that has not been tainted with the inadmissible evidence.

---

[97]Joel D. Lieberman & Jamie Arndt, *Understanding the Limits of Limiting Instructions: Social Psychological Explanations for the Failures of Instructions to Disregard Pretrial Publicity and Other Inadmissible Evidence*, 6 PSYCH. PUB. POL. AND L. 677 (2000).

[98]REID HASTIE, STEVEN D. PENROD & NANCY PENNINGTON, INSIDE THE JURY 232 (1983).

[99]*Id.*; *see also* Divine et al., *supra* note 38, 686-87.

[100]Lieberman & Arndt, *supra* note 97 at 685.

[101]*Id.*

[102]*Id.* at 689 (citing M. Cox & S. Tanford, *Effects of Evidence and Instructions in Civil Trials: An Experimental Investigation of Rules of Admissibility*, 4 SOC. BEHAV. 31 (1989)).

The ineffectiveness of curative or limiting instructions may be based, in part, on several psychological phenomenon. **Belief perseverance** is one of these reasons. Once an individual forms a belief, it "becomes highly resistant to change and influences how [he or she] perceive[s] and construct[s] future information."[103] But belief perseverance is only a partial explanation since we know from research that at least some beliefs can be changed by curative instructions. Take, for example, the research of Kassin and Sommers[104] in which jurors were played an audiotape in which the defendant confessed to the murder with which he was charged. After hearing the tape, jurors' beliefs about the defendant's guilt increased significantly. But once the judge gave them an instruction to disregard the evidence, the beliefs about the defendant's guilt did not persist. Belief perseverance, then, cannot totally explain the backfire effect.

Reactance theory is another explanation for the backfire effect. Reactance theory hypothesizes that psychological arousal increases when someone perceives a threat to their free-choice in decision-making. If jurors perceive a curative or limiting instruction as impinging on their ability to freely make a decision, then they "may be motivated to assert that freedom and attend more strongly to the evidence that is ruled inadmissible."[105]

Another possible explanation for the backfire effect is the theory of *ironic processes of thought suppression.* When people are told not think of something, it actually increases their tendency to do what they were asked not to do.[106] Interestingly, this theoretical explanation runs contrary to reactance theory. Reactance theory posits that the focus on the inadmissible material is an intentional assertion of juror autonomy. The ironic processes model posits just the opposite insofar as it holds that people, wanting to be good jurors, attempt to comply with the curative or limiting instruction and, in doing so, wind up ironically focusing on that which they are trying not to focus on.

It is likely that these causes interact with each other.[107] But regardless of what actually causes of the backfire effect, it appears there are some steps that can be taken to mitigate its effect. To avoid reactance and thought suppression effects, judicial admonitions to the jury should be gentle rather than stern.[108] Further, explaining *why* something should be disregarded might also help in preventing reactance since a rational understanding as to why something should not be considered might make jurors feel less threatened that their decision-making freedom is being encroached upon.[109]

C. Problems with Jury Instructions

The American justice system vests considerable power in juries, especially in criminal cases where acquittals are not reviewable on appeals and convictions are given great deference on

---

[103]*Id.* at 691.

[104]S.M. Kassin & S.R. Sommers, *Inadmissible Testimony, Instructions to Disregard, and the Jury: Substantive Versus Procedural Considerations*, 23 PERSONALITY & SOC. PSYCHOL. BULL. 1046-1054 (1997).

[105]Lieberman & Arndt, *supra* note 97, at 697.

[106]*Id.* at 697-700; see also D.M. Wegner, *Ironic Processes of Mental Control*, 101 PSYCHOL. REV. 34-52 (1994).

[107]*Id.* at 703 (citing A.E. Kelly & M.M. Nauta, *Reactance and Thought Suppression*, 23 PERSONALITY & SOC. PSYCHOL. BULL. 1123-1132 (1997)).

[108]*Id.* at 704.

[109]*Id.* (citing L. Eichorn, *Social Science Findings and the Jury's Ability to Disregard Evidence Under the Federal Rules of Evidence*, 52 L. & CONTEMP. PROB. 341-353 (1989)).

appeal.[110] To guide them in arriving at verdicts, juries are given instructions by judges. These instructions are essential to the judicial process since they are designed to inform the jury of the law they are supposed to apply during their deliberations. "Juries should follow the law that is enacted by the legislature and construed by the courts, rather than pursuing their own notions of how a case ought to be decided or making up the rules as they proceed."[111] Such was not always the case, however. Juries at early English common law were not given instructions. Instead, they were supposed to do what they thought best under the facts as they had come to understand the evidence from the trial.[112] In other words, they were supposed to apply common sense.[113] Given the arbitrary nature of such decision-making, however, judges in England eventually began to instruct the jury. But even today, they do so only orally and quite informally.[114]

In the United States, judges originally followed the early common law tradition of not instructing juries.[115] But as the U.S. evolved from an organic to a mechanical society, legal disputes grew more complex. By the late 1800s, judges were no longer permitted to summarize the facts for a jury at the conclusion of trial.[116] Their sole job was to determine the governing law and communicate that law to the jury who was then to act as the sole trier-of-fact.[117] This, however, brought another set of problems. Parties often fought extensively over how a jury should be instructed. The process often became akin to reinventing the wheel with each trial. But worse yet, judges were inconsistent in the way they defined the governing law for juries. Reversal on appeal for errors in jury instructions were commonplace.[118]

To address these problems, in 1935, a trial court judge in Los Angeles suggested that a committee of lawyers and judge be formed to draft a uniform set of civil jury instructions.[119] These rules were published as the *Book of Approved Jury Instructions*. A set of uniform instructions for California criminal cases was published soon thereafter. The success of these books resulted in many other jurisdictions publishing their own sets of uniform jury instructions for both civil and criminal cases.[120] Because the language of the approved jury instructions were taken from statutes and judicial opinions, they minimized inconsistencies and dramatically reduced the number of reversals on appeals for instructional error.[121] But statutes and judicial opinions are not written for the layperson; they are written for judges and lawyers. Accordingly, they may not have helped jurors understand the law. Once this issue began to be studied by social scientists in the early 1970s, it became clear that jurors frequently misunderstood jury

---

[110] *See* Jackson v. Virginia, 443 U.S. 307, 318-19 (1979)

[111] Peter Tiersma, *The Rocky Road to Legal Reform: Improving the Language of Jury Instructions*, 66 BROOK. L. REV. 1081, 1081 (2001).

[112] *Id.* at 1082.

[113] *Id.*

[114] *Id.* at 1083.

[115] *Id.*

[116] *Id.*

[117] *Id.*

[118] *Id.*

[119] *Id.* (citing ROBERT G. NIELAND, PATTERN JURY INSTRUCTIONS: A CRITICAL LOOK AT A MODERN MOVEMENT TO IMPROVE THE JURY SYSTEM 6 (1979)).

[120] *Id.* 1083-84.

[121] *Id.* at 1084.

instructions and, as a result, juries failed to follow the instructions given to them.[122] In fact, one of the seminal studies of the original California civil jury instructions conducted by Robert and Veda Charrow found that mock jurors understood only half of the instructions![123] Their findings were replicated in many other jurisdictions by other researchers.[124] These researchers identified several contributing causes to this problem.

First, jurors may simply not remember the details of the jury instructions told to them in court.[125] Some courts have addressed this problem by providing juries with written jury instructions.

Even when written jury instructions are provided, the language of the instructions often promotes juror misunderstanding. At best, jury instructions are "stereotyped, antiseptic statements of abstract rules."[126] At worst, they are downright incomprehensible.[127] *Psycholinguistic* studies (the study of how people understand language) have concluded that long, complex sentences containing abstract concepts and foreign vocabulary are the primary culprits of incomprehensible jury instructions.[128] This research has also demonstrated, though, that jury understanding of jury instructions increases when the instructions are rewritten in shorter sentences and provide a factual context for their application and synonyms for obscure or specialized vocabulary words.[129] Unfortunately, the law has not reformed pattern jury instructions based on this research.

Third, when juries ask judges for clarification on the instructions they have received, it is commonplace for judges to simply tell the jury to go back and re-read the instruction as given to them, something that is totally unhelpful.[130] Perhaps judges are hesitant to clarify instructions for political reasons.

> Because jury instructions are standardized, judges are very reluctant to declare that a particular instruction was poorly drafted, especially in criminal cases, because there might be dozens or hundreds of prisoners in the jurisdiction who were convicted on the same instruction. Judges

---

[122]*Id.*; Paul H. Robinson, *Are Criminal Codes Irrelevant?*, 68 S. Cal. L. Rev. 159, 170-75 (1994); Lawrence J. Severance & Elizabeth F. Loftus, *Improving the Ability of Jurors to Comprehend and Apply Criminal Jury Instructions*, 17 Law & Soc'y Rev. 153 (1982).

[123]Tiersma, *supra* note 111, at 1084-85 (citing Robert Charrow & Veda Charrow, *Making Legal Language Understandable: A Psycholinguistic Study of Jury Instructions*, 79 Colum. L. Rev. 1306 (1979)).

[124]Amiram Elwork et al., Making Jury Instructions Understandable (1982); Phoebe C. Ellsworth, *Are Twelve Heads Better Than One?*, 52 Law & Contemp. Probs. 205 (1989); Geoffrey P. Kramer & Dorean M. Koenig, *Do Jurors Understand Criminal Jury Instructions? Analyzing the Results of the Michigan Juror Comprehension Project*, 23 U. Mich. J.L. Reform 401 (1990); Bradley Saxton, *How Well Do Jurors Understand Jury Instructions? A Field Test Using Real Juries and Real Trials in Wyoming*, 33 Land & Water L. Rev. 59 (1998); Joel D. Lieberman & Bruce D. Sales, *What Social Science Teaches Us About the Jury Instruction Process*, Psych., Pub. Pol'y & L. 589 (1997); Shari Seidman Diamond, *Instructing on Death: Psychologists, Juries and Judges*, 49 Am. Psychol. 425 (1993); J. Alexander Tanford, *Law Reform by Courts, Legislatures, and Commissions Following Empirical Research on Jury Instructions*, 25 L. & Soc'y Rev. 155 (1991); J. Alexander Tanford, *The Law and Psychology of Jury Instructions*, 69 Neb. L. Rev. 71 (1990); Saul M. Kassin & Lawrence S. Wrightsman, The American Jury on Trial (1988); Severance & Loftus, n *supra* note 122; David U. Strawn & Raymond W. Buchanan, *Jury Confusion: A Threat to Justice*, 59 Judicature 478 (1976).

[125]Vicki L. Smith, *When Prior Knowledge and Law Collide: Helping Jurors Use the Law*, 17 Law & Hum. Behav. 507, 508-11 (1993).

[126]Lawrence M. Friedman, A History of American Law 137 (1973).

[127]*E.g.*, Severance & Loftus, *supra* note 122, at 183; Kassin & Wrightsman, *supra* note 124, at 141-63.

[128]*See* sources *supra* note 124.

[129]*See* sources *id.*; see also Walter M. Steele, Jr. & Elizabeth G. Thomburg, *Jury Instructions: A Persistent Failure to Communicate*, 67 N.C.L. Rev. 77, 83 (1988).

[130]Tiersma, *supra* note 111, at 1086-87.

understandably fear opening the floodgates to massive amounts of litigation. If the case involves the death penalty, the stakes are even higher, and the political pressure to let sleeping dogs lie is even more intense.[131]

But in spite of this unhelpfulness of simply referring a jury back to the original instruction without giving clarification, the U.S. Supreme Court has refused to find the practice reversible error.[132]

III. CONCLUSION

There is probably no such thing as the perfect jury. Jury selection using the *voir dire* process is flawed for a number of reasons. And once a jury is selected, a number of problems present themselves during trial that make it difficult for a jury to render a fair and impartial verdict under the law. The problems range from juror biases that were not properly screened out during *voir dire* to the prejudicial effect of juror exposure to inadmissible evidence. Finally, even if a trial were truly error-free in the presentation of evidence, the likelihood of juries actually understanding all of the evidence presented, and then properly applying the law to the facts, is low in light of the problems with the way jury instructions are written.

Given these rather significant problems, why do we hold on to the jury system? Some have called for the abolition of juries altogether. As far back as 1872, Mark Twain wrote, "The jury system puts a ban on intelligence and honesty, and a premium upon ignorance, stupidity and perjury. It is a shame that we must continue to use a worthless system because it was good a thousand years ago."[133] But the reasons we tend to hold on to the institution of lay juries may be due in large part to our history and philosophy regarding the entrustment of power to government.[134] Simply put, juries act as a check on governmental power. The fate of people in terms of their lives, liberty, and property lies not in the hands of a governmental official, but with a group of fellow citizens. Moreover, the jury process represents egalitarian values—ordinary people sitting in judgment not only of each other, but also of public figures. "Despite some flaws, it serves the cause of justice very well. For over 700 years it has weathered criticism and attack, always to survive and to be cherished by the peoples who own it."[135]

Since we continue to use the jury as the ultimate decision maker under the law, it is clear that there are steps that can be taken to improve the quality of jury decision-making. Some calls for reform have already been enacted.[136] Jurors are now routinely given notebooks in which they record their impressions during trial.[137] Written jury instructions are often provided to juries.[138] Sometimes, pre-instructions are given at the start of trial to reinforce important legal concepts to jurors. But other suggestions for improvements, like plain-language jury instructions—have yet to be fully implemented.

---

[131]*Id.* at 1088.

[132]Weeks v. Angelone, 528 U.S. 225, 234 (2000).

[133]Mark Curriden, *Putting the Squeeze on Juries*, A.B.A. J. 52, 52 (August 2000) (quoting Mark Twain 1872).

[134]E.g., Beacon Theatres, Inc. v. Westover, 359 U.S. 500, 501 (1959); Austin Wakeman Scott, *Trial by Jury and the Reform of Civil Procedure*, 31 HARV. L. REV. 669, 767 (1918).

[135]VALERIE P. HANS & NEIL VIDMAR, JUDGING THE JURY 251 (1986).

[136]Tom M. Dees, III, *Juries: on the Verge of Extinction? A Discussion of Jury Reform*, 54 S.M.U.L. REV. 1755 (2001).

[137]*Id.* at 1773.

[138]*Id.* at 1778-79.

There have been several radical proposals for jury reform, some of which have been ignored, such as using professional juries—groups of people with specialized knowledge pertinent to the particulars of a case. Other proposals—such as allowing jurors to ask questions of witnesses during trial—may never be universally implemented, but small trial applications of this procedure have been implemented in a handful of progressive jurisdictions like Arizona, California, Colorado, New York, Illinois, and the District of Columbia.[139] In 1995, jurors in Arizona were permitted to discuss the case amongst themselves throughout the trial. This was a radical departure from the tradition rule of allowing discussions on the evidence only after the conclusion of trial. Behavioral scientists suggested this process would improve both juror comprehension and recollection, as well as improve jury cohesion, thereby positively influencing the deliberations process.[140] Although there were concerns about jurors reaching premature judgments without having heard all of the evidence, most jurors who participated in some pre-deliberation discussions reported favorably on the process.[141] Clearly, the behavioral science have much to contribute towards the improvement of our jury system.

---

[139]*Id.* at 1774-78.

[140]Valerie P. Hans, Paula L. Hannaford, & G. Thomas Munsterman, *The Arizona Jury Reform Permitting Civil Jury Trial Discussion: The Views of Trial Participants, Judges, and Jurors*, 32 U. MICH. J.L. REFORM 349 (1999).

[141]*Id.*

CHAPTER FOURTEEN
THE PSYCHOLOGY OF SENTENCING

What do you think of when you hear the term ***criminal punishment***? There are many forms it can take. The formal punishments most closely associated with criminal law include fines, restitution, probation, community service, intensive monitoring, home arrest, imprisonment, and even death. Informal forms of punishment also go along with the formal criminal sanction, such as the social stigma of having been labeled a criminal. This label might not only hold one out for scorn, shame, or other form of disapproval, but also might be a barrier to future employment, result in the loss of voting privileges, and subject the actor to the risk of enhanced punishments for a future offense. This chapter explores how criminal punishments are imposed in the sentencing process and how they are carried out by the correctional system.

I. THEORETICAL CONCERNS REGARDING PUNISHMENT

A. <u>Punishment, Human Agency and the Social Contract</u>

Much of the theoretical underpinnings of modern theories of punishment are based on what is known as the ***Classical School of Criminology.*** The Classical School is primarily founded upon the work of Cesare Beccaria[1] and Jeremy Bentham.[2] Their views on crime were founded upon a notion of human nature rooted in utilitarian principle of free agency. People are viewed as rational beings, empowered by free will to maximize pleasure and minimize pain. Thus, people are agents of self-determination who can choose how to act based on the hedonistic principle of pleasure seeking and pain avoidance.[3]

Classical theory developed at a time when the criminal justice system was characterized by a focus on the value of social order over procedure, even at the expense of rights.

> [There were] many laws against morality, victimless crimes, social order, and the state. It assume[d] the accused guilty rather than innocent and use[d] any means, often torture, to obtain convictions, believing rules of procedure impede[d] swift convictions. It [wa]s concerned with general rather than individual deterrence and use[d] publically administered, severe sentences to symbolically punish arbitrarily selected offenders to instill fear in others.[4]

Beccaria and Bentham were concerned with arbitrariness and cruelty of the criminal justice system of the time. They viewed society as having been formed as part of a consensual social contract.[5] Given their view of man as a rational thinker, the functioning of the crime control

---

[1]Cesare Beccaria, *On Crimes and Punishment* (1764), *reprinted in* CRIMINOLOGICAL THEORY 7-19 (Frank P. Williams & Marilyn McShane eds., Anderson Publishing Co. 1993).

[2]Jeremy Bentham, *An Introduction to the Principles of Morals and Legislation* (1822) *in* ETHICAL THEORY AND SOCIAL ISSUES 118-26 (David T. Goldberg, ed., 2d ed., Harcourt, Brace & Co., 1995).

[3]The notion of pure rationality in classical theory is problematic, but a critique of classical theory is beyond the scope of the chapter.

[4]WERNER EINSTADTER & STUART HENRY, CRIMINOLOGICAL THEORY: AN ANALYSIS OF ITS UNDERLYING ASSUMPTIONS 43 (Harcourt Brace College Publishers, 1995).

[5]THOMAS HOBBES, LEVIATHAN (1651), *reprinted* ETHICAL THEORY AND SOCIAL ISSUES 58-64 (David T. Goldberg, ed., 2d ed., Harcourt, Brace & Co. 1995); JOHN LOCKE, TWO TREATISES OF GOVERNMENT (Cambridge University Press 1964) (originally published 1690).

model then functioning in society was incompatible with having voluntarily and rationally given up freedom to become a part of a social order in which torture and arbitrariness was the rule. As reformists, they articulated a view of the state in which it played a highly limited role and in which it was "accorded only that power necessary to protect individuals' rights and liberties . . . based on a consensus between rational citizens."[6]

The consensus upon which the classical school is based is often referred to as the *social contract*—a hermeneutic concept formulated to explain the legitimacy of the state, the exercise of its civil and criminal regulatory power, and the source of political obligation.[7] Social contract theory begins with humans in what Hobbes and Locke called the *state of nature*.[8] In this state, all humans are equal and have complete autonomy; no person has authority over another person.[9] The state of nature is a dangerous place since, with no person having authority over the next, it is a ruleless, chaotic environment in which every person is out only to protect him or herself. Our basic human needs—such as food, water, shelter, and sleep—are all sought after by people in the state of nature with the autonomy to take what they want when they want it. When two people want the same thing and cannot use or enjoy it at the same time, "they become enemies; and in the way to their End ... endeavour to destroy or subdue" each other."[10]

Given this violence and the need for self-preservation, the logical end of existing in the state of nature is the extinction of the species unless some form of cooperation is developed to avoid that end. Keeping in mind the premise of rationale decision-making, social contract theorists posit that humankind opted to relinquish some of their autonomy so that they could not only avoid death, but also pursue other things in life protected from the chaos in the state of nature.[11] In doing so, they formed the state. They gave up the power to do anything at any cost in exchange for the government to provide stability and peace. To avoid going back to the state of nature, each person has a obligation to obey the rules set forth by the state. Correspondingly, the state has an obligation to protect its citizens by honoring their freedoms and protecting their interests.

The role of law in this social contract is to "insure the greatest happiness to be shared by the greatest number."[12] Not only, then, should law represent the wishes of the majority, but also should insure compliance with that consensus via punishment.[13] Punishing those who violate the rules of the social contract (i.e., the law) avoids descent back into the state of nature in two ways.

---

[6]Jock Young, *Thinking Seriously About Crime: Some Models of Criminology*, *in* CRIME AND SOCIETY: READINGS IN HISTORY AND THEORY 257 (Mike Fitzgerald, Gregor McLennan & Jennie Pawson. eds., Routledge and Kegan Paul 1981).

[7]RICHARD KRAUT, SOCRATES AND THE STATE 91-114 (1984).

[8]*See* sources cited *supra* at note 5.

[9]Edward A. Harris, *From Social Contract to Hypothetical Agreement: Consent and the Obligation To Obey the Law*, 92 COLUM. L. REV. 651, 657 (1992) (citing THOMAS HOBBES, LEVIATHAN 63-66 (I, 13), 105 (II, 20) (J.M. Dent & Sons Ltd. 1914) (1651); John Locke, *The Second Treatise of Government: An Essay Concerning the True Original, Extent, and End of Civil Government*, *in* TWO TREATISES OF GOVERNMENT, 265, 315, 330-51 (§§ 73, 95-126) (Peter Laslett ed., student ed. 1988) (3d ed. 1698)).

[10]April L. Cherry, *Social Contract Theory, Welfare Reform, Race, and the Male Sex-Right*, 75 OR. L. REV. 1037, 1045 (1996) (quoting THOMAS HOBBES, LEVIATHAN *in* INTRODUCTION TO THOMAS HOBBES 183 (C.B. MacPherson, ed. 1981) 1981) (originally published 1651)).

[11]JEAN-JACQUES ROUSSEAU, THE SOCIAL CONTRACT 49-58 (Maurice Cranston trans., Penguin Classics 1968) (originally published 1762). It should be noted that Rousseau did not see the state of nature as wild and chaotic in the way Hobbes and Locke did. Instead, he saw it as lonely and unfair. The human needs to bond with others, to love, to pity, and to protect each other from those who would take advantage of others – were Rousseau's reasons for agreeing to the social contract.

[12]Beccaria, *supra* note 1, at 8.

[13]*Id.* at 8-10.

First, the law as representative of social contract consensus builds internal social controls.[14] Secondly, punishment represents coercive social control and is therefore justified in being used to maintain the social order.[15]

Classical theory's reliance on a model of rational thought through hedonistic calculus is rejected by a number of schools of criminological thought that have been largely influenced by the varying psychological paradigms. For example, some biological positivists would argue that criminal behavior is a function of genetic makeup and cannot be control via threat of punishment.[16] Certain psychologists would argue that humans are controlled through "largely unconscious thought that impel him to act quite without regard to any rational principle of pleasure-seeking."[17] In spite of the wealth of data from the behavioral sciences that cast doubt upon the assumptions of the Classical School of Criminology, there is little doubt that the law still relies on its views of human agency. Moreover, the ways in which we deal with crime and punishment both theoretically and practically continue to be based on many of the principles of the Classical School.

B. Justifying Punishment

Under the utilitarian views of the Classical School, "the purpose of punishment is to contribute to the greater good of society, understood as an aggregation of the good of individuals."[18] Accordingly, punishment is only justified when the benefits to be gained from inflicting criminal punishment on the wrongdoer outweigh the harm caused to the criminal offender *and* to society at large. As we explore the four primary theoretical justifications for criminal punishment, ask yourself which ones appear to be based on this utilitarian principle in theory, and which ones, if any, actually live up to this utilitarian goal.

1. Retribution

The first major theory of punishment is *retribution* theory. It holds that the criminal justice system should exact deserved suffering on the wrongdoer because of his or her breach of the social contract by having committed a crime. It is often referred to as getting one's "just desserts."

> Retributivism denotes a family of philosophies, versions of which were embraced by Greek and Roman thinkers as well as by the Jewish and Christian traditions. . . . The root idea or metaphor of retributivism is that transgression creates an imbalance that must be restored by the . . . suffering . . . of the wrongdoer. The idea was found in cosmological form in the pre-Socratics, and was fundamental in classical Greek and stoic ethics. The role of retribution, divine and civil, in

---

[14]*See* Chapter Two (citing EDWARD ALSWORTH ROSS, SOCIAL CONTROL: A SURVEY OF THE FOUNDATIONS OF ORDER (MacMillian 1901)).

[15]*See* Chapter Two (citing JOHANNES ANDENAES, PUNISHMENT AND DETERRENCE (Univ. Mich. Press 1974)).

[16]*E.g.,* C. Ray Jeffery, *Biological and Neuropsychiatric Approaches to Criminal Behavior, in* VARIETIES OF CRIMINOLOGY: READINGS FROM A DYNAMIC DISCIPLINE 15-28 (G. Barak ed., Praeger, 1994); C. RAY JEFFERY, ATTACKS ON THE INSANITY DEFENSE: BIOLOGICAL PSYCHIATRY AND NEW PERSPECTIVES ON CRIMINAL BEHAVIOR (Thomas 1985).

[17]HERBERT PACKER, THE LIMITS OF THE CRIMINAL SANCTION 41 (Stanford Univ. Press 1968) (citing WALTER BROMBERG, CRIME AND THE MIND: A PSYCHIATRIC ANALYSIS OF CRIME AND PUNISHMENT (Macmillan 1965); GREGORY ZILBOORG, THE PSYCHOLOGY OF THE CRIMINAL ACT AND PUNISHMENT (Harcourt, Brace 1954)).

[18]Deirdre Golash & James P. Lynch, *Public Opinion, Crime Seriousness, and Sentencing Policy,* 22 AM. J. CRIM. L. 703, 708 (1995).

Jewish and Christian traditions is undeniable, although crosscut and permeated with the redemptive themes of the imperfection and unity of human nature in all subjects and roles—transgressor and victim, offender and judge.[19]

Retribution is most commonly justified from three standpoints. The first is *revenge*—making the criminal suffer for his or her crimes to diffuses both societal anger and the anger of the victim and the victim's next-of-kin. Revenge as a basis for punishment has it roots in ancient times. In fact, the doctrine of *lex talionis* in which there is "an eye for an eye, a tooth for a tooth" appeared in the Code of Hammurabi between 1792 and 1750 B.C.E.[20] By officially inflicting deserved suffering via formal criminal punishment, the exacting of vigilante justice by aggrieved individuals was discouraged, thereby helping to maintain the status quo under the social contract.[21]

Closely related to revenge is *restitution*—the notion that the wrongdoer give back to the victim so as to make the victim whole again. "Those who take more liberty than the norm allows and more than others take will, finally, be disgorged of their loot. Crime does not pay; observing the law does."[22] Financial compensation is one form of restitution, but "doing one's time" to "pay back one's debt to society" also encompasses a notion of restitution.

Finally, retribution can also be justified under a theory of *expatiation*. Expatiation means atoning for sin. Under this approach, which stems from Judeo-Christian values, the suffering experiences via the infliction of criminal punishment acts as a penance which helps the wrongdoer atone for his or her crime, thereby become morally reformed.[23]

2. Deterrence

The second major approach to criminal punishment is *deterrence* theory. Classical deterrence theory rejects the notion of retributive justice on the grounds that punishment as an end in and of itself cannot be justified.[24] Instead, deterrence theory is predicated on the utilitarian notion that the criminal law should be used as a tool to control rational decision-making.[25] A rational decision-maker, who theoretically would not like the criminal punishment that would be inflicted upon the actor if he or she committed the crime, is supposed to conclude that it would be in his or her best interests *not* to do the crime, thereby avoiding the unpleasant consequences that would come with criminal punishment.

Deterrence theory suggests that the criminal justice system can effectuate two types of deterrence: general and specific. The *general deterrent* goal of criminal law presumes that the

---

[19]Elizabeth Rapaport, *Symposium on Law, Psychology, and the Emotions: Retribution and Redemption in the Operation of Executive Clemency*, 74 CHI.-KENT. L. REV. 1501, 1511 (2000).

[20]Laws of Hammurabi 196-97, 200, *in* LAW COLLECTIONS FROM MESOPOTAMIA AND ASIA MINOR 121 (Martha T. Roth trans., 1995).

[21]For a comprehensive review of ancient laws designed to control crime, see James Lindgren, *Why the Ancients May Not Have Needed a System of Criminal Law*, 76 B.U.L. REV. 29 (1996).

[22]*See, e.g.,* Gerard V. Bradley, *Retribution and the Secondary Aims of Punishment*, 44 AM. J. JURIS. 105, 107 (1999); Martha C. Nussbaum, *Equity and Mercy*, 22 PHIL. & PUB. AFF. 83, 86 (1993); FEODOR DOSTOYEVSKY, CRIME AND PUNISHMENT (Swetlana A. Geier, trans., 1994) (originally published 1866).

[23]*E.g.,* ROBERT NOZICK, PHILOSOPHICAL EXPLANATIONS 371-74 (1981); R.A. DUFF, TRIALS AND PUNISHMENTS 254-62 (1986); Jean Hampton, *The Moral Education Theory of Punishment*, 13 PHIL. & PUB. AFF. 208, 223 (1984).

[24]*See, e.g.,* Beccaria, *supra* note 1.

[25]*See generally* Jeremy Bentham, *Principles of Penal Law (Rationale of Punishment)*, in 1 THE WORKS OF JEREMY BENTHAM 365-98 (John Bowring, ed., 1962) (originally published 1830).

threat of punishment will prevent the general population from engaging in the proscribed conduct. The *specific deterrent* goal of criminal law postulates that those for whom the general deterrent of law was insufficient to prevent them from having engaged in the proscribed conduct should be subjected to punishment so that they are likely to be discouraged from engaging in the proscribed conduct again.

Both Beccaria and Bentham in their classical deterrence models argued several factors will influence the effectiveness of punishment as a general deterrent. Much scholarly research has demonstrated that the effectiveness of law as a deterrent is dependent upon three primary factors: severity, certainty, and celerity (i.e., swiftness). *Severity* is concerned with how severe the punishment is. The theory postulates that the more severe the punishment, the less likely the actor is to engage in the proscribed conduct. The second factor, *certainty,* is concerned with how likely the actor is to get away with the crime as opposed to being caught. According to deterrence theory, the more likely the actor is going to be caught, the less likely he or she is to engage in the conduct. Finally, *celerity* is the factor that looks at the swiftness of punishment. The theory suggests that the faster the punishment is inflicted after the offense, the less likely the person is to engage in the proscribed conduct. Conversely, the later or further off the punishment, the less likely the person is to be deterred.

Scholars continue to argue which of the three is the most important for criminal law to be an effective deterrent.[26] But as evidenced by the trend of ever-increasing sanctions and the continuing call for harsher sentences, legislatures have seized on severity as key. But the focus on severity may be improperly placed from a theoretical standpoint.[27] After all, even if the punishment were quite severe, if you had a near perfect chance of not being caught (i.e., "getting away with it"), might you not risk it?

3. Rehabilitation

The third major approach to criminal punishment is *rehabilitation* theory. It advocates that the proper aim of the criminal justice system should be to reform the criminal so that he or she can become part of the general social order.[28] The very notion of criminal "corrections" connotes "correcting" the criminal wrongdoer along the lines of rehabilitation theory.

The rehabilitative model is derived in large part from the works of Plato,[29] St. Thomas Aquinas,[30] and Hegel.[31] While popular in the 1960s and 1970s and arguably still an important consideration from the viewpoint of correctional system personnel, rehabilitation as justification for imposing criminal punishment fell out of favor with legislators and much of the public-at-large in the 1980s when the "get tough on crime" attitude became prevalent. This punitive

---

[26] DERYCK BEYLEVELD, A BIBLIOGRAPHY ON GENERAL DETERRENCE RESEARCH (Saxon House 1980); Daniel Nagin, *Methodological Issues in Estimating the Deterrence Effect of Sanctions*, 12 L. & SOC'Y REV. 341-366 (1978).

[27] *See, e.g.,* Harold G. Grasmick & Donald Green, *Legal Punishment, Social Disapproval, and Internalization as Inhibitors of Illegal Behavior*, 71 J. CRIM. L. & CRIMINOLOGY 325-35 (1980); Charles R. Tittle, *Sanction, Fear, and the Maintenance of Social Order*, 55 SOCIAL FORCES 579-95(1977).

[28] PACKER, *supra* note 17, at 53.

[29] 2 M. PLOSCOWE, CRIME AND CRIMINAL LAW 293 (1939); *see also* PHILIP BEAN, PUNISHMENT: A PHILOSOPHICAL AND CRIMINOLOGICAL INQUIRY (Martin Robertson 1981).

[30] ST. THOMAS AQUINAS, 1 SUMMA THEOLOGICA Q. 92 Art. 2 Reply Obj. 4 (Fathers of the English Dominican Province trans. 1947); *see also* BEAN, *supra* note 29.

[31] Markus Dirk Dubber, *Rediscovering Hegel's Theory of Crime and Punishment*, 92 MICH. L. REV. 1601-21 (1994); *see also see also* BEAN, *supra* note 29.

attitude toward criminal punishment embraces retribution and deterrence, and, arguably, the fourth main approach to punishment: incapacitation.

4. Incapacitation

Incapacitation theory rejects the ideals of retribution, deterrence, and rehabilitation as either illegitimate or unworkable. Instead, it holds that we simply incapacitate criminals by removing them from society, thereby protecting society from the danger posed by evil-doers.[32] Incapacitation is accomplished by getting criminals off the streets and incarcerating them away from where they can do harm to the law-abiding members of society.

C. Limiting Punishment

When the American Law Institute drafted the Model Penal Code between 1954 and 1962, it specified deterrence, rehabilitation, and incapacitation as the goals of criminal punishment; retribution was omitted.[33] Since that time, it is clear that rehabilitation has significantly declined as a modern justification for criminal punishment and retribution is "back with a vengeance."[34] In spite of the more punitive nature of criminal sanctions since approximately 1980, there are a number of principles that continue to limit criminal punishment.

1. Due Process vs. Crime Control

Striking an appropriate balance between the benefits and harms of punishment is one of the inherent tensions in our criminal justice system. Arguably this tension is most evident in balancing substantive and procedural criminal law. In his classic text *The Limits of the Criminal Sanction,*[35] Herbert Packer articulated two competing models that incorporate this struggle for balance. "Many have attempted to replace or add to Packer's models, but none have enjoyed his success and durability."[36]

On one hand, in what Packer dubbed the ***crime control model,*** the criminal law has as its main focus the repression of criminal conduct.[37] Laws prescribe norms. When societal norms expressed in criminal law are broken, the police and prosecutors operate the criminal justice system in an "assembly-line conveyor belt" fashion.[38] Their job is to investigate crimes, screen out the innocent, and secure "as expeditiously as possible, the conviction of the rest, with a minimum of occasions for challenge, let alone post-audit."[39] This model recognizes that law enforcement has limited resources, so it places a high "premium on speed and finality" once offenders are caught and brought into the criminal justice system.[40] The core value within this

---

[32]PACKER, *supra* note 17, at 48.

[33]AMERICAN LAW INSTITUTE, MODEL PENAL CODE § 1.02 cmt. 15 (1985).

[34]Michele Cotton, *Back with a Vengeance: The Resilience of Retribution as an Articulated Purpose of Criminal Punishment*, 37 AM. CRIM. L. REV. 1313 (2000).

[35]PACKER, *supra* note 17 (expanding up Herbert Packer, *Two Models of the Criminal Process*, 113 U. PA. L. REV. 1 (1964)).

[36]Kent Roach, *Four Models of the Criminal Process*, 89 J. CRIM. L. & CRIMINOLOGY 671, 676 (1999).

[37]PACKER, *supra* note 17, at 158.

[38]*Id.* at 159.

[39]*Id.* at 160.

[40]*Id.* at 159.

model is efficiency in the criminal process. Punishment under the crime control model focuses on incapacitation, deterrence, and retribution.

In contrast, the ***due process model*** is concerned with "the formal structure of the law" with a focus on "the reliability of the fact-finding process."[41] The core value within this model is the protection of individual rights. It asserts that granting too much leeway to law enforcement officials will result in losses of rights and freedoms. Careful consideration of each case, with multiple layers of checks and balances to guard against the infringement of individual rights and liberties, even at the expense of speedy processing of offenders, is emphasized. Punishment under the due process model focuses on rehabilitation.

There is some common ground between the crime control and due process models, such as stability, continuity, a separate process for defining that which is criminal and those who are criminals, and some notion of an adversarial process, although the crime control model de-emphasizes its role while "the due process model tends to make it central."[42] Beyond these few similarities, these two views on the criminal process are fairly at odds with each other. There is little doubt that both repressing crime and safeguarding due process rights are core values of the U.S. justice system. Due process rights, both substantive and procedural, limit the criminal sanction. Three utilitarian principles in particular underlie some of our more important due process limitations: legality, proportionality, and culpability.

2. Legality

The ***principle of legality*** is the at the heart of notions of due process and fairness. Packer described the principle of legality as the first and most important limitation on the criminal sanction. "Conduct may not be treated as criminal unless it has been so defined by an authority having the institutional competence to do so before it has taken place."[43] In other words, before someone is criminally punished for violating the law, they should have fair notice of what is criminally proscribed by an act of a legislative body. Without knowledge that something is illegal, no person can engage in rationale decision-making (using hedonistic calculus) regarding the conduct. The principle of legality does not require that a person have ***actual knowledge*** of the law, or a correct understanding of it. All that is required is that a person have ***constructive knowledge***—a fair opportunity to have discovered the existence of the legal rule proscribing the conduct in terms that are reasonably clear.[44]

The principle of legality is achieved in several ways. First and foremost, criminal laws must be legislatively enacted and published as part of a jurisdiction's penal laws (i.e., criminal code). These law must be publically available. They must be specific enough to convey what conduct is not allowed, otherwise, they will be held to be invalid by a court as being unconstitutionally vague. And if reasonable people could differ as to the application of a criminal law to the conduct at issue in the case, the statute must be given a strict construction, and the benefit of the doubt must be given to the defendant.[45]

---

[41]*Id.* at 163.

[42]*Id.* at 157.

[43]PACKER, *supra* note 17, at 79-80.

[44]Steven B. Duke, *Criminal Law: Commentary: Legality in the Second Circuit*, 49 BROOKLYN L. REV. 911, 912 (1983).

[45]*See id.* at 913-16.

3. Culpability

The second principle is ***culpability.*** According to this principle, we should punish only those who are responsible for their conduct. Conversely we do not punish those persons who commit an act when they are without legal fault for their conduct. At the heart of this concept are the notions of "free will" and "autonomy." While these constructs are open to attack both philosophically, psychologically, and empirically, the criminal law accepts these as givens—not necessarily because the law takes them as being "true," but rather because the law operates better if they are accepted as if they were true. Given this view of human nature, the doctrine of culpability posits that it is fair to punish those who, having been given fair notice that certain conduct is criminally proscribed, nonetheless *choose* to disobey the law.[46] The limiting factor of the principle of culpability comes into play when this element of choice is not present. Accordingly, the criminal law does not seek to punish involuntary acts or acts that were not a product of free will, such as actions committed under duress or actions committed by mistake. Nor does the law seek to punish even the deliberate acts of those who are mentally incapable of having chosen to violate the law. The defenses of insanity and diminished capacity discussed in Chapters Six and Seven respectively are examples of how the law limits punishment via the principle of culpability.

4. Proportionality

The third limiting principle is referred to as the principle of ***proportionality***. It posits that punishment should be proportional to the offense. Unfortunately, there is no magic formula to judging the proportionality of crime or punishment. We differentiate what is more severe as compared to what is less severe often using nothing more than common sense. Legislatures do this when the designate offenses as violations, misdemeanors, and felonies. They further differentiate the severity of an offense from other offenses when they designate a crime at a certain level of offense, such a felony in the first degree as opposed to a felony in the third degree. And, finally, legislatures differentiate the severity of a crime in their sentencing schemes. One hopes, however, that the exercise of reasoned judgment in making these determination are guided by certain moral principles.

Consistent with his utilitarian beliefs that the moral thing to do is that which promotes the greatest good for the greatest number of people, Jeremy Bentham argued that the law must be effective in order to be justifiable. Accordingly, he asserts that the law should punish, and can only effectively punish, when three main criteria are met. First, closely related to the principles of legality and culpability, there must be ***grounds*** for punishment. Where there is no mischief for the law to punish, why punish at all? Second, the punishment must be ***effective.*** Why bother to punish when punishment will not be effective in stopping the mischievous conduct? Finally the punishment must be ***profitable.***[47] Why bother to punish when the results of punishment produce greater harm that the act being punished itself?

> Bentham's approach to proportionality is summed up in his belief that punishing someone more than is necessary, even to achieve desirable goals, is "evil without justification." Although this focus on utilitarian necessity is not the same thing as proportionality between punishment and crime, it is a recognition of the importance of punishment limitation. Further, along with classical

---

[46] *Id.* at 912; PACKER, *supra* note 17, at 73-87.

[47] 1 THE WORKS OF JEREMY BENTHAM 399-402 (J. Bowring ed. 1843).

punishment theorist Cesare Beccaria, Bentham realized that if crimes of unequal gravity were punished equally, the public would lose the important ability to distinguish serious wrongs from more trivial ones.[48]

In short, the principle of proportionality is the embodiment of the notion that the punishment should "fit the crime." Doing so not only serves the retributive notion of revenge, but also serves to safeguard the offender from excessive or arbitrary punishment. Toward these ends, some states have specifically provided for the notion of proportionality as part of their penal codes. However, the extent to which, if any, the doctrine of proportionality is embedded in U.S. constitutional and criminal law is open to debate. As a rule, legislatures and courts do not engage in some Benthamite calculus of the profitability of punishment that would involve the weighing of harms. They tend to be guided by common sense judgment and the holdings of a series of U.S. Supreme Court decisions dealing with the proportionality doctrine.

Courts are called to engage in a proportionality analysis from time to time when criminal defendants challenge their sentences under the Eighth Amendment's Cruel and Unusual Punishments Clause. In the 1910 case *Weems v. United States*,[49] the U.S. Supreme Court first signaled that the doctrine of proportionality was a part of Eighth Amendment jurisprudence. In *Weems*, the defendant was convicted of falsifying a cash book for a small amount of money. He was sentenced to a fine and fifteen years of punishment called a "cadena temporal"— imprisonment in shackles at the ankles and hands while being forced to perform hard labor.[50] The Supreme Court sided with Mr. Weems, finding his sentence was disproportionately lengthy in light of the offense he committed and, further, that is was "cruel and unusual because of its harsh and oppressive nature."[51] Decades later, in *Rummel v. Estelle*,[52] the Court explained that it was not the length of Weem's incarceration that rendered his sentence violative of the Eighth Amendment, but rather it was the "unique nature" of the cadena punishment that was cruel and unusual.

Other important Supreme Court cases identified the doctrine of proportionality as being a part of Eighth Amendment jurisprudence. In *Gregg v. Georgia*,[53] the Supreme Court made it clear "that excessiveness alone, without regard to the barbaric nature of the punishment, was sufficient to invalidate a sentence."[54] In the year after the *Gregg* decision year, the Court decided *Coker v. Georgia*.[55] It held that the death penalty for the crime of rape was unconstitutionally cruel and unusual punishment in light of the disproportionate nature of the offense to the punishment, again signaling that the excessiveness of a sentence was in and of itself a sufficient basis to render a criminal sanction unconstitutional.[56] Yet, the *Rummel* Court dismissed both of

---

[48]Steven Grossman, *Proportionality in Non-Capital Sentencing: The Supreme Court's Tortured Approach to Cruel and Unusual Punishment*, 84 KY. L.J. 107, 167 (1995).

[49]217 U.S. 349 (1910).

[50]*Id.* at 364.

[51]Grossman, *supra* note 48, at 111.

[52]445 U.S. 263 (1980).

[53]428 U.S. 153 (1976).

[54]Grossman, *supra* note 48, at 113.

[55]433 U.S. 584, 592 (1977) (plurality opinion).

[56]Coker, 433 U.S. at 592.

these decisions as being "'of limited assistance' in deciding the constitutionality of terms of imprisonment" since they involved sentences of death, not imprisonment.[57]

The dismissive approach the Supreme Court took in *Rummel* toward the principle of proportionality was further solidified in *Hutto v. Davis*.[58] The defendant was sentenced in Virginia to forty years imprisonment and a fine of $20,000 for possession with intent to distribute nine ounces of marijuana. In upholding the sentence, the Supreme Court reiterated its pronouncement in *Rummel* that the cases requiring an Eighth Amendment proportionality analysis were limited to death penalty cases, while any "assessment of the excessiveness of a prison term was inherently subjective and therefore 'purely a matter of legislative prerogative.'"[59]

Surprisingly, the Supreme Court breathed new life into the principle of proportionality just six years after deciding *Hutto* when it rendered its decision in *Solem v. Helm*.[60] The defendant had been convicted of offering a forged check, a felony under applicable state law that carried a maximum penalty of five years incarceration and a $5,000 fine. But the defendant already had three prior felony convictions, so he was sentenced under a recidivist statute to life in prison without the possibility of parole.[61] In vacating the defendant's sentence as being excessive and, therefore unconstitutional under the Eighth Amendment's cruel and unusual punishment clause, the Supreme Court set forth three factors to guide courts when wrestling with questions of proportionality: (1) the proportionality between the severity of the crime and the severity of the sentence; (2) the proportionality of sentence imposed in other jurisdictions for the crime at issue in a case; and (3) the proportionality of the sentence imposed in the jurisdiction at issue in the given case on other criminals who commit similar or more series crimes.[62] When weighing these factors, the *Solem* Court noted that "there are generally accepted criteria for comparing the severity of different crimes."[63] These criteria reflect back to utilitarian ideals such as the "harm caused or threatened to the victim or society" and the relative culpability of the defendant in terms of his or her level of *mens rea*.[64] Decisions of the Supreme Court after *Solem*, however, have cast serious doubt on the validity of these factors in proportionality challenges, even though *Solem* has not yet been expressly overruled.

Obviously, the decisions of the Supreme Court discussed above sent "a mixed and confusing message with respect to . . . the requirement of proportional sentencing."[65] This confusion led the Court to issue another pronouncement on the role of the proportionality principle in Eighth Amendment jurisprudence in *Harmelin v. Michigan*.[66] The defendant in *Harmelin* was convicted of possession 672 grams of cocaine. Under Michigan law, anyone possessing more than 650 grams of cocaine received a mandatory sentence of life in prison without the possibility of parole. The highly fractured Court appeared to agree on very little. A majority of five justices

---

[57]Grossman, *supra* note 48, at 113 (citing Rummel, 445 U.S. at 272).

[58]454 U.S. 370 (1982) (per curiam).

[59]Grossman, *supra* note 48, at 122 (citing *Hutto*, 454 U.S. at 373, and quoting *Rummel*, 445 U.S. at 274).

[60]463 U.S. 277 (1983).

[61]*Id.* at 282.

[62]*Id.* at 291-92; *see also* David S. Mackey, *Rationality Versus Proportionality: Reconsidering the Constitutional Limits on Criminal Sanctions*, 51 Tenn. L. Rev. 623, 628 (1984).

[63]*Id.* at 294.

[64]*Id.* at 292-94.

[65]Grossman, *supra* note 48, at 141.

[66]501 U.S. 957 (1991).

agreed the sentence was not disproportionate to the offense, so they affirmed his sentence. But two justices — Chief Justice Rehnquist and Justice Scalia — wrote a concurring opinion to emphasize their view that the Cruel and Unusual Punishment Clause contains no guarantee of proportional punishment.[67] Justice Thomas later echoed their views when he wrote in *Ewing v. California*,[68] "that the proportionality test announced in *Solem v. Helm* . . . is incapable of judicial application," and that "the Cruel and Unusual Punishments Clause of the Eighth Amendment contains no proportionality principle."[69]

Since the Court's decision in *Harmelin*, most proportionality-based appeals have failed, although a handful have succeeded.[70] It appears the lower courts have embraced Justice Kennedy's conclusion regarding the proportionality principle in his concurring opinion in *Harmelin*. "The Eighth Amendment does not require strict proportionality between crime and sentence. Rather, it forbids only extreme sentences that are 'grossly disproportionate' to the crime."[71] The Supreme Court cited Justice Kennedy's concurrence in *Harmelin* favorably in its two most recent pronouncements on proportionality. In *Ewing v. California*,[72] the Court upheld California's "three strikes and you're out" sentencing scheme. The defendant in that case had been sentenced to life in prison for having shoplifted three golf clubs valued at approximately $1,200. He had several prior misdemeanor and felony convictions, including one for robbery and three for residential burglary which served as the triggering crimes for application of the three strikes rule. In affirming his sentence, the Court found Ewing's life sentence was not unconstitutionally disproportionate to the theft, but rather that it reflected "a rational legislative judgment, entitled to deference, that offenders who have committed serious or violent felonies and who continue to commit felonies must be incapacitated."[73] Using the same logic, the Court reached an identical result in *Lockyer v. Andrade*,[74] in which it upheld two consecutive life sentences under California's three-strikes law for a defendant who had stolen approximately $150 worth of videotapes. Thus, it appears that the principle of proportionality has little relevance today to Eighth Amendment jurisprudence other than in death penalty cases.

II. SENTENCING

A. Shared Control of Sentencing

Sentencing is technically a part of the judicial process.[75] The responsibility for sentencing, however, is shared with both the legislative and executive branches of government. Legislatures that set the parameters for criminal sentences when they designate crimes at a particular level of

---

[67]Grossman, *supra* note 48, at 143 (citing *Harmelin*, 501 U.S. at 961).

[68]539 U.S. 11 (2003).

[69]*Id.* at 32.

[70]Stephen T. Parr, *Symmetric Proportionality: A New Perspective on the Cruel and Unusual Punishment Clause*, 68 TENN. L. REV. 41, 58 (2000) (citing STEPHEN A. SALTZBURG & DANIEL J. CAPRA, AMERICAN CRIMINAL PROCEDURE: CASES AND COMMENTARY 1319 (6th ed. 2000)).

[71]*Harmelin*, 501 U.S. at 1001 (Kennedy, J., concurring) (quoting *Solem v. Helm*, 463 U.S. 277, 288 (1983)).

[72]539 U.S. 11 (2003).

[73]*Id.* at 32.

[74]538 U.S. 63, 72 (2003).

[75]*E.g.* DAVID W. NEUBAUER, AMERICA'S COURTS AND THE CRIMINAL JUSTICE SYSTEM 376 (Wadsworth 6th ed. 1999).

offense, and designate the permissible punishments for those offenses.[76] The executive branch controls the imposition of sentence through two mechanisms, the most important of which is the parole system. ***Parole*** is the early release of a prisoner from incarceration after having served a portion of a sentence. Parole decisions are made by parole boards, comprised of people appointed by the executive branch of government, most frequently, the governor of a state.[77] Parolees remains under supervision upon release and can be returned to prison for the balance of their unexpired term for violating the conditions of their parole or committing any new crimes.[78] A much less frequently used tool to control criminal sentences, the chief executive (i.e., the governor of a state or the president of the United States) can grant executive clemency, called a ***pardon*** in which the inmate is "forgiven" for his crime and has sentences commuted accordingly.

B. The Sentencing Hearing

Within the statutory sentencing framework set by a legislature, it is the judge who usually imposes sentence on a criminal defendant. Sentence is imposed at a ***sentencing hearing.*** The judge presides over this hearing at which the prosecutor and defense attorney both make arguments to the court to convince the judge to impose what each believes to be an appropriate sentence. The defendant may make a plea on his or her own behalf, hoping to influence the judge favorably. In some jurisdictions, the victims of crime (or their next-of-kin if the victim is dead or unable to speak on his or her own behalf) is also allowed the make a statement to the court. The hearing is quick compared to the other phases in the criminal process. Sentencing hearings generally take less than twenty minutes and often last only five or ten minutes.[79]

1. Judicial Discretion in Sentencing

The sentencing process is designed to impose criminal punishment within the theoretical framework described in Section I of this chapter. Doing so, of course, is no easy task. Moreover, how it is accomplished will often be dependent upon the individual philosophy of the sentencing judge when there is some discretion to be exercised. For example, Hogarth found that Canadian magistrates who favored the deterrence model favored the imposition of prison sentences over other sentencing alternatives.[80] Similarly, Gottfredson et al., found that a judge's predisposition toward the rehabilitative was evident in the imposition of sentences designed to treat the offender.[81] But the amount of discretion a judge has to exercise in sentencing varies greatly depending on the type of sentencing scheme that is in place in a particular jurisdiction.

---

[76]*Id.* at 377-378.

[77]*Id.* at 380.

[78]*Id.*

[79]VLADIMIR J. KONECNI & EBBE B. EBBESEN (EDS.), THE CRIMINAL JUSTICE SYSTEM: A SOCIAL-PSYCHOLOGICAL ANALYSIS (W.H. Freeman & Co. 1982).

[80]JOHN HOGARTH, SENTENCING AS A HUMAN PROCESS (Univ. Toronto Press 1971).

[81]Don M. Gottfredson, Stephen D. Gottfredson & Catherine Conly, *Stakes and Risk: Incapacitative Intent in Sentencing Decisions*, 7 BEHAV. SCI. & L. 91, 103-04 (1989).

2. Indeterminate Sentences

The level of judicial sentencing discretion today is quite different than it was some years ago. From the 1940s through the 1950s, the rehabilitative model was the dominant philosophical justification behind criminal sentencing.[82] Accordingly, sentences were supposed to be tailored by judges to the needs of a particular offender insofar as their punishments were supposed to "change the characters, attitudes, and behavior of offenders, both to benefit them and to make them less of a threat to society."[83] This approach involved what is called *indeterminate sentencing*. Legislatures prescribed a range of permissible sentences, usually setting a minimum sentence, but leaving the maximum up to the discretion of the judge.[84] Other jurisdictions with an indeterminate sentencing scheme had legislatures that set a minimum and maximum range, but left the judge free to impose sentence as he or she saw fit. The judge could use any criteria "considered relevant without any checks or accountability on his [or her] discretion."[85] And during the serving of a criminal sentence, corrections officials—usually parole boards—were free to release inmates at any time if they believed them to be rehabilitated.

3. Presentence Investigation and Reports

In order to tailor a sentence that was appropriate for a particular offender, the judge needed information about the defendant that would not be garnered during the course of trial, if there was one. Since most criminal cases are plea bargained rather than tried, the need for personal information about a defendant who plead guilty was even greater. The gathering of this information is called *presentence investigation* (PSI).[86] Probation officers conduct PSIs, investigating the "individual and social history of the offender, his personality, his mental and moral characteristics."[87] This typically involves reviewing a defendant's prior criminal background, educational and employment history, relationships with family and friends, use of alcohol and/or controlled substances, and a psychological evaluation if warranted.[88] After a PSI is completed, the investigating probation officer prepares a *presentence investigation report* (PSIR) for the sentencing judge containing all of the relevant information gathering during the PSI. The report often concludes with a sentencing recommendation, including any "special conditions of probation, plans for treatment, and an assessment of community resources available to facilitate rehabilitation."[89]

How judges use PSIRs is debated in the literature. Some studies have found that judges rely heavily on PSIRs.[90] Others report that judges skim PSIRs and read only those sections they deem

---

[82]Francis A. Allen, The Decline of the Rehabilitative Ideal (Yale Univ. Press 1981).

[83]G. Alan Tarr, Judicial Process and Judicial Policymaking (Wadsworth 2nd ed. 1999) (citing Allen, *supra* note 82).

[84]Cotton, *supra* note 34, at 1316.

[85]Andrew J. Fuchs, *The Effect of* Apprendi v. New Jersey *on the Federal Sentencing Guidelines: Blurring the Distinction Between Sentencing Factors and Elements of a Crime*, 69 Fordham L. Rev. 1399, 1413 (2001).

[86]Neubauer, *supra* note 75, at 401.

[87]Fuchs, *supra* note 85, at 1414 (quoting Lester B. Orfield, Criminal Procedure from Arrest to Appeal 544 (1947)).

[88]Neubauer, *supra* note 75, at 401.

[89]*Id.* at 401-02.

[90]James R. David, The Sentencing Dispositions of New York City Lower Court Criminal Judges (1980) (unpublished Ph.D. dissertation, New York University) (Ann Arbor, MI: University Microfilms International).

most important.[91] It does seem, however, that judges tend impose sentence in accordance with the recommendations of a PSIR even though they are not bound to do so.[92] The concordance rate is particularly high—as high as 95 percent in one study—for first-time offenders for whom probation is recommended.[93] The same study yielded a concordance rate of 88 percent agreement when the PSIR recommended against probation. A more recent study replicated these results with respect to first-time offenders, but found that probation officers recommended incarceration for recidivists almost twice as often as judges imposed it.[94]

4. Judicial Bias in Sentencing

A growing concern "over unconstrained judicial discretion and sentence disparities for similar crimes" started in the 1970s and continued through the early 1980s.[95] "Factors ranging from judicial idiosyncrasy and strategic behavior by lawyers, to 'invidious discrimination on the basis of race, class, gender, and the like,' were blamed for sentencing disparities."[96] Consider the following story.

> [A] judge in Dallas justified the lenient sentence he imposed on . . .an eighteen-year-old who had murdered two gay men, by stating, "I put prostitutes and gays at about the same level, and I'd be hard put to give somebody life for killing a prostitute." The judge implied that the victims had invited their own murders when he said, "These two guys that got killed wouldn't have been killed if they hadn't been cruising the streets picking up teen-age boys. I don't care much for queers cruising the streets. I've got a teen-age boy." The judge insinuated that the victims were at fault despite the fact that no conclusive evidence was presented at trial that the victims had solicited sex and despite witnesses' testimony that Bednarski and a group of friends "had set out to harass homosexuals and entered the men's car with the intent of beating them."[97]

Discrimination need not be of the invidious nature demonstrated by the Dallas judge quoted above. Sometimes such biases are caused by systematic inculcation of stereotypes in society. The best example of this is the gender bias that is pervasive in the law. "Stereotyped thinking about the nature and roles of the sexes, devaluation of women and what is perceived as women's work, and myths and misconceptions about the social and economic realities of women's and men's lives are as prevalent in the justice system as in the other institutions of society."[98] This has manifested itself in women receiving smaller shares of marital assets in divorce proceedings[99];

---

[91]Michael D. Norman & Robert C. Wadman, *Utah Presentence Investigation Reports: User Group Perceptions of Quality and Effectiveness*, 64 FED. PROBATION 7-12 (2000).

[92]Christina Rush & Jeremy Robertson, *Presentence Reports: the Utility of Information to the Sentencing Decision*, 11 L. HUM. BEHAV. 147-155 (1987); NEUBAUER., *supra* note 75, at 402.

[93]Robert H. Carter & Leslie T. Wilkins, 58 J. CRIM. L., CRIMINOLOGY, AND POLICE SCI. 503-514 (1967).

[94]Curtis Campbell, Candace McCoy & Chimezie Osigweh, *The Influence of Probation Recommendations on Sentencing Decisions and Their Predictive Accuracy*, 54 FED. PROBATION 13-21 (1990).

[95]Rachel Konforty, *Efforts to Control Judicial Discretion: the Problem of Aids and Sentencing*, 1998 ANN. SURV. AM. L. 49, 50 (1998).

[96]*Id.*

[97]Lu-in Wang, *The Complexities of Hate*, 60 OHIO ST. L.J. 799, 879 (1999) (quoting Lisa Belkin, *Anti-Gay Comments Spark Dallas Furor/Judge Defends Leniency for Teen Killer*, HOUS. CHRON., Dec. 17, 1988, at 29; Larry Rowe, *Gays Discouraged by Report Clearing Dallas Judge of Bias*, DAILY TEXAN, Nov. 2, 1989, at 8).

[98]Donald C. Nugent, *Judicial Bias*, 42 CLEV. ST. L. REV. 1, 35 (1994).

[99]*Id.* at 36-37.

receiving preference in child custody proceedings over men[100]; being perceived as the party responsible for being victimized, especially in rape and domestic violence cases[101]; being paternalistically treated in courtrooms as witnesses, litigants, and attorneys[102]; and more lenient criminal sentences than men for the same crimes.[103]

Other types of discrimination that have been well documented in the literature include racial and ethnic bias, most notably against minorities[104]; regional bias against those not from the area[105]; and economic bias as documented in the critically acclaimed book *The Rich Get Richer and the Poor Get Prison*.[106] Less obvious factors that often have nothing to do with the defendant but rather with the judge's own background also play a factor in the way judicial discretion is exercised in the sentencing process. Such factors include the judge's age and years of experience; whether the judge was previously employed as a prosecutor or defense attorney; the judge's politics—especially party affiliation in jurisdictions that elect judges; and the judge's own views on the behavior of the defendant both in relation to the criminal conduct and conduct in the courtroom.

5. Determinate Sentencing to Reduce Bias

In response to the concerns over disparate sentencing, Congress passed the Sentencing Reform Act of 1984.[107] Under the provisions of the Act, Congress created the United States Sentencing Commission and empowered it to create a uniform set of federal sentencing guidelines that would greatly reduce judicial sentencing discretion in a manner designed to reduce sentencing disparities and to realistically project the needs of the federal correctional system.[108] The Sentencing Commission promulgated the Federal Sentencing Guidelines which went into effect on November 1, 1987, officially moving the federal sentencing schema from an indeterminate one to a ***determinate sentencing*** structure—one in which the sentence is fixed or predetermined for a given offensive, with only minor adjustments, if any, being permissible based on the specific facts of a case.

The Federal Sentencing Guidelines set the sentence judges to impose based primarily on two factors: the offense level and the defendant's criminal history.

> The Criminal History Category of the Guidelines measures the defendant's prior convictions of felonies and misdemeanors, while the Offense Level measures the seriousness of the instant crime through the (1) base offense level; (2) specific offense characteristics; and (3) additional adjustments. A judge applies the Guidelines by finding the intersection on the Sentencing Table Grid of the appropriate Criminal History Category on the horizontal axis and the Offense Level on the vertical axis. The intersection designates the number of months in the defendant's sentencing

---

[100]*Id.* at 40.

[101]*Id* at 41-43.

[102]*Id.* at 43-45.

[103]*See* JOANNE BELKNAP, THE INVISIBLE WOMAN: GENDER, CRIME, AND JUSTICE (Wadsworth 1996).

[104]Wang, *supra* note 97, at 45-48.

[105]*Id.* at 48.

[106]JEFFREY REIMAN, THE RICH GET RICHER AND THE POOR GET PRISON: IDEOLOGY, CLASS, AND JUSTICE (Allyn & Bacon 1995).

[107]William W. Wilkins, Jr. & John R. Steer, *The Role of Sentencing Guideline Amendments in Reducing Unwarranted Sentencing Disparity,* 50 WASH. & LEE L. REV. 63, 87 (1993).

[108]Paul J. Hofer, Kevin R. Blackwell, & R. Barry Ruback, *The Effect of the Federal Sentencing Guidelines on Inter-Judge Sentencing Disparity,* 90 J. CRIM. L. & CRIMINOLOGY 239, 254 (1999).

range within the statutory penalty range for the crime. The judge retains only minimal discretion because he is limited to imposing a sentence within that narrow sentencing range.[109]

At the time the guidelines went into effect though 2005, the Federal Sentencing Guidelines were mandatory.

> Judges resented the fact that the Guidelines removed most of the judicial discretion and many concerned observers held the view that the Guidelines system failed to achieve the original goals: "Efforts to eliminate disparity in sentencing have resulted in an incursion on the independence of the federal judiciary, a transfer of power from the judiciary to prosecutors and a proliferation of unjustifiably harsh individual sentences." The most obvious result of the Guidelines has been harsher sentences, many with an adverse racial impact. Long prison sentences have become the norm in the federal system with little diversion to alternative punishment options. Essentially, judges simply did not have the flexibility to adjust sentences to alternative punishments, and instead were directed through the Guidelines structure to send offenders to prison.[110]

Some states, like California, adopted mandatory guidelines similar to the Federal Sentencing Guidelines. But most of the nearly 20 states that a adopted sentencing guidelines opted for a voluntary guideline system wherein judges may sentence a defendant outside the guideline range as the facts of a case may warrant in their discretion.[111] Federal judges gained the same prerogative in January of 2005 when the U.S. Supreme Court invalidated the Federal Sentencing Guidelines in the companion cases of *United States v. Booker* and *United States v. Fanfan*.[112] *Booker* declared that the Federal Sentencing Guidelines were unconstitutional "because they permitted a sentencing judge to impose a sentence based on facts found by a judge, not a jury," and therefore violated the Sixth Amendment's guarantee to have a jury decide factual issues under the proof beyond a reasonable doubt standard.[113] The Court, however, did not invalidate the Guidelines in their entirety. Rather, the Court's remedy was to excise the portions of federal law mandating the use of the Guidelines, thereby rendering them advisory. Federal courts now use the Sentencing Guidelines to help establish presumptively reasonable sentences from which sentencing judges and appellate courts can vary if they are unreasonable in light of the facts of a particular case.[114]

6. The Impact of Determinate Sentencing

One of the more controversial aspects of determinate sentencing is the notion of the ***minimum mandatory sentence.*** Such sentences are set by legislatures and required a defendant to serve a statutorily set minimum period of incarceration if convicted of a particular offense. Judges very much dislike these sentences since it deprives them of the ability to fashion a sentence appropriate to the facts of a particular case; all offenders are sentenced the same way without regard to individual circumstances. These types of sentences have been adopted in many states

---

[109]Fuchs, *supra* note 85, at 1417-18.

[110]Sandra D. Jordan, *Have We Come Full Circle? Judicial Sentencing Discretion Revived in* Booker *and* Fanfan, 33 PEPP. L. REV. 615, 626 (2006).

[111]TARR, *supra* note 83, at 206.

[112]543 U.S. 220 (2005).

[113]Jordan, *supra* note 110, at 628..

[114]*Id.* at 633.

and in the federal system for drug offenses; the commission of crimes using a firearm; and for repeat felony offenders (e.g., "Three Strikes and You're Out" laws). Some states have even designed minimum mandatory sentences for first-time misdemeanor offenders of drunk driving laws.[115] It is generally agreed up that minimum mandatory sentences have been a large contributor to the tremendous increase in prison population in the last two decades of the twentieth century. Prison inmates increased by 237 percent and jail inmates by 174 percent between 1980 and 1995,[116] more than doubling incarceration rate to 615 per 100,000 people in 1996.[117] By the year 2000, 6.31 million people in the United States were in jail, prison, or on parole.[118]

In addition to contributing to the skyrocking number of people being incarcerated, it appears that determinate sentences have not achieved their intended goal of eradicating sentence disparities. This is due to a number of factors. First, the guidelines themselves set differential sentencing schemes that contain inherent biases that are unrelated to the exercise of judicial discretion. The most egregious example of this is the different mandatory minimum sentences to be imposed for possession of cocaine hydrochloride—the white powder from cocaine that is snorted—and crack cocaine—the much less expensive, solid rock form of the drug that smoked. Possessing five grams of the power form of the drug is a misdemeanor punishable by less than a year in jail. Possessing the same amount of crack is a felony offense carrying a mandatory minimum sentence of five years in prison.[119] This sentencing disparity has the practical effect of creating a 100 to 1 ratio for the possession of power cocaine to crack, a disparity that manifests itself racially. "Because crack is more often sold by blacks, and powder by whites, the harshest penalties were largely experienced by blacks."[120] In fact, African-Americans comprise roughly 26 percent of crack users, but have been convicted of nearly 93 percent of federal crack offenses.[121]

Second, determining sentence schemes did not eliminate sentencing discretion; they merely shifted the discretion from the judge to the prosecutor. "Prosecutors have circumvented the laws when they believed them unduly harsh, often with the approval of judges and police, usually be refusing to charge arrestees with offenses that carry a mandatory sentence."[122]

And third, unless convicted of a crime carrying a mandatory minimum sentence, judges have the power to make adjustments under the sentencing guidelines that can greatly affect the permissible range. These adjustments are called ***upward departures*** or ***downward departures,*** depending on whether the range is being increased or decreased. Mustard found that "large differences in the length of sentence exist on the basis of race, gender, education, income, and citizenship. These disparities occur in spite of explicit statements in the guidelines that these

---

[115]*See, e.g.,* Henry F. Fradella, *Minimum Mandatory Sentences: Arizona's Ineffective Tool for the Social Control of DUI*, 11 CRIM. JUST. POL'Y REV. 113-35 (2000).

[116]*See* BUREAU OF JUSTICE STATISTICS, U.S. DEP'T OF JUSTICE. CORRECTIONAL POPULATIONS IN THE UNITED STATES, 1980-1995, [available online] <http://www.ojp.usdoj.gov/bjs/glance/corr2.txt>.

[117]*See* CHRISTOPHER J. MUMOLA & ALLEN J. BECK, U.S. DEP'T OF JUSTICE, PRISONERS IN 1996, at 2 tbl.1 (showing rate change from year-end 1985 to mid-year 1996).

[118]*See* BUREAU OF JUSTICE STATISTICS, U.S. DEP'T OF JUSTICE. CORRECTIONAL POPULATIONS IN THE UNITED STATES, 1999 [available online] <http://www.ojp.usdoj.gov/bjs/glance/corr2.txt>.

[119]*See* 21 U.S.C. 841(b)(1)(A)(ii), (iii); U.S. Sentencing Commission Guideline Manual 2D1.1 (1997).

[120]Kathleen Daly & Michael Tonry, *Gender, Race, and Sentencing*, 22 CRIME & JUST. 201, 230 (1997).

[121]Andrew N. Sacher, *Inequities of the Drug War: Legislative Discrimination on the Cocaine Battlefield*, 19 CARDOZO L. REV. 1149, 1164 (1997).

[122]TARR, *supra* note 83, at 206.

characteristics should not affect the sentence length."[123] These factors have tremendous impact on whether a judge granted an upward or downward departure; in fact, they accounted for over half of the sentencing disparities found in Mustard's comprehensive study.[124]

C. Special Considerations in Sentencing Juveniles

What should we do with children who commit crimes? Until 1899, juveniles were processed through the same criminal justice system that handled adults.[125] Convicted children were either jailed with adults, or were institutionalized with other youth in what amounted to be "juvenile prisons, with prison bars, prison cells, prison garb, prison labor, prison punishments, and prison discipline."[126]

In 1899, Illinois set up the first juvenile justice system in the United States.[127] Within twenty years, all but two states followed suit, and by the end of World War II, every state has a separate juvenile court system.[128] In philosophy, if not in practice, juvenile court proceedings were designed to be "benign, nonpunitive, and therapeutic" with rehabilitation as its "fundamental goal."[129] Proceedings were not designed to be adversarial, but rather were lax—without formal criminal procedures and often without lawyers![130] Proceedings were not designed to determine the guilt of a child, but rather to how to best help a child in need. "Dispositions, therefore, were indeterminate, non-proportional, and individualized."[131]

Given the noncriminal nature of juvenile proceedings, children in the juvenile court system were routinely deprived of the constitutional protections that were guaranteed to adults in criminal courts.[132] By the 1960s, however, children's rights advocates pushed for reforms. While some procedural due process protections were granted to juveniles by the U.S. Supreme Court in *Kent v. United States*,[133] it was the 1967 landmark case of *In re Gault*[134] that extended a wide range of constitutional protections to children in the juvenile justice system. The court held that whenever a juvenile's liberty was at risk due to the possibility of incarceration, certain due process rights were guaranteed to them. These include "adequate, timely, written notice of the allegations; assistance of counsel; an opportunity to confront and cross-examine witnesses under oath; and a privilege against self-incrimination."[135] Later, in the case of *In re Winship*, the court

---

[123]David B. Mustard, *Racial, Ethnic, and Gender Disparities in Sentencing: Evidence from the U.S. Federal Courts*, 44 J. LAW & ECON. 285, 311 (2001); DOUGLAS C. MCDONALD & KENNETH E. CARLSON, SENTENCING IN THE FEDERAL COURTS: DOES RACE MATTER? 177 (1993).

[124]*Id.* at 311-12.

[125]Andrew Walkover, *The Infancy Defense in the New Juvenile Court*, 31 UCLA L. REV. 503, 509 (1984).

[126]Robert W. Sweet, Jr., *Deinstitutionalization of Status Offenders: In Perspective*, 18 PEPP. L. REV. 389, 391-92 (1991) (quoting HASTINGS HART, PREVENTIVE TREATMENT OF NEGLECTED CHILDREN 11 (1910)).

[127]JOHN C. WATKINS, JR., THE JUVENILE JUSTICE CENTURY: A SOCIOLEGAL COMMENTARY ON AMERICAN JUVENILE COURTS 43 (1998).

[128]*Id.* at 45.

[129]Brenda Gordon, *A Criminal's Justice or a Child's Injustice? Trends in the Waiver of Juvenile Court Jurisdiction and the Flaws in the Arizona Response*, 41 ARIZ. L. REV. 193, 197 (1999).

[130]*Id.* at 198.

[131]*Id.*

[132]*Id.* at 199.

[133]383 U.S. 541 (1966).

[134]387 U.S. 1 (1967).

[135]Gordon, *supra* note 129, at 202 (citing *Gault*, 387 U.S. at 33, 36-37, 55, 57).

extended the requirement of proof beyond a reasonable doubt to juveniles due to the risk of wrongful conviction when using a less stringent standard.[136] The right to a trial by jury, however, has never been recognized for juveniles.[137]

Although the juvenile justice system has retained its rehabilitative focus, there is no doubt that a more punitive stance has come into play in the 1980s and 1990s.[138] This may be due, in part, to the fact that the juvenile crime rate increased 35 percent between 1988 and 1997.[139] It is also likely due to the fact that the public perceived juvenile crime to have become more violent and destructive than it had been in the past.[140] The public believed that juvenile justice system was itself partly to blame, feeling it coddled youthful offenders and failed to rehabilitate them.[141] The public overwhelming felt that serious juvenile offenders should be treated no differently than their adult counterparts.[142] Legislatures responded to these concerns by cracking down on juvenile crime by treating incorrigible or particularly violent juveniles as adults using *juvenile waivers*.[143] Waivers take juveniles out of the jurisdiction of the juvenile justice system and allow them to be prosecuted in adult court.

There are three types of juvenile waivers, one or more types of which exist in every state.[144] Nearly all states grant juvenile court judges the authority to transfer jurisdiction from themselves to adult court. This is called *judicial waiver.* When deciding whether to transfer a juvenile, the judge "engages in a case-by-case clinical assessment of not only the youth's best interest, but also the best interest of the public, which reflects the individualized sentencing discretion characteristic of juvenile courts."[145]

Judicial waivers have been criticized for a number of reasons. First, juvenile judges "exercise broad, standardless discretion" using "amorphous and contradictory substantive factors" such as amenability to treatment or dangerousness.[146] And there are data which suggest judicial waiver decisions are often arbitrary, often taking into account factors such as race, ethnicity, and gender.[147] Moreover, it appears one of the most important determinants of whether a transfer will be authorized concerns the length of time from the child's age at the time of the offense to the jurisdictional age limit of the court. If the offense is serious enough that the length of the

---

[136]In re Winship, 397 U.S. 358, 363, 368 (1970).

[137]McKeiver v. Pennsylvania, 403 U.S. 528 (1971).

[138]Gordon, *supra* note 129, at 203-04.

[139]Federal Bureau of Investigation, U.S. Dep't of Justice, Crime in the United States – 1997: Uniform Crime Reports for the United States tbl.32 (1998).

[140]Gordon, *supra* note 129, at 203.

[141]Ralph A. Rossum, *Holding Juveniles Accountable: Reforming America's "Juvenile Injustice System*," 22 Pepp. L. Rev. 907, 907-09 (1995)

[142]Gordon, *supra* note 129, at 203 n.94 (citing Sarah Glazer, *Juvenile Justice: Should Violent Youths Get Tougher Punishments?*, CQ Researcher, Feb. 25, 1994, at 171).

[143]Marcy Rasmussen Podkopacz & Barry C. Feld, *Judicial Waiver Policy and Practice: Persistence, Seriousness and Race*, 14 Law & Ineq. J. 73, 75 (1995).

[144]Lisa A. Cintron, *Rehabilitating the Juvenile Court System: Limiting Juvenile Transfers to Adult Criminal Court*, 90 Nw. U. L. Rev. 1254, 1263 nn.72-73 (1996).

[145]Gordon, *supra* note 129, at 204-05.

[146]Marcy Rasmussen Podkopacz & Barry C. Feld, *The End of the Line: An Empirical Study of Judicial Waiver*, 86 J. Crim. L. & Criminology 449, 453 (1996).

[147]Joel Eigen, *The Determinants and Impact of Jurisdictional Transfer in Philadelphia*, in Readings in Public Policy 339-40 (John C. Hall et al., eds., 1981); Donna M. Hamparian et al., Youth in Adult Court: Between Two Worlds 104-05 (1982).

sentence warranted is greater than the jurisdictional age limit, judges are very likely to transfer the case.[148]

Even with such unpredictability in the decision-making process of judicial waivers, studies have documented the "crucial role that probation recommendations and psychological evaluations play in the 'individualized' waiver process. . . [as their] recommendations to the court to retain or refer a youth significantly affect the eventual judicial waiver decision."[149]

About half of the states have attempted to regulate the unpredictable nature of judicial waivers by removing the waiver decision from the hands of juvenile court judges, whether only under certain circumstances, or always. ***Legislative waivers*** mandate the transfer of juveniles to adult court when a child commits one or more enumerated offenses, thereby statutorily excluding such offenders from the jurisdiction of juvenile courts.[150] Approximately half of the states have such waivers for children between the ages of 12 and 18 if they commit such offenses as murder, rape, armed robbery, car jacking, aggravated assault and battery, and even drug dealing in some states.[151] In doing so, these laws prevent the exercise of judicial discretion from keeping a violent offender from being criminally processed through the adult criminal justice system.

Other states have given the power to prosecutors to decide if a juvenile should be transferred to adult court. Like legislative waivers, ***prosecutorial waivers*** take the determination of whether a juvenile should be tried as an adult out of the discretion of a juvenile court judge. Discretion, however, is still a part of the process insofar as the prosecutor has the power to decide whether to send a case to juvenile court or adult court. Some have condemned this practice as vesting too much power in prosecutors who are "often punitive and retributive."[152] Others have praised this mechanism, arguing "that prosecutors are more neutral, balanced, responsive, and objective gatekeepers than either 'totally child-oriented' juvenile court judges or 'get tough' legislators."[153]

The entire concept of juvenile waivers raises difficult philosophical questions. Simply switching to a punitive and incapacitative model may take care of the problem short term, but it is not a long-term solution. Consider the thoughts of the great American jurist Skelly Wright:

> There is no denying the fact that we cannot write these children off forever. Some day they will grow up and at some point they will have to be freed from incarceration. We will inevitably hear from [them] again, and the kind of society we have in the years to come will in no small measure depend upon our treatment of them now.[154]

D. Special Considerations for Sentences of Death

The death penalty is considered to be the ultimate form of punishment. While it remains controversial, 56 percent of U.S. residents favor the imposition of the death penalty for a murder

---

[148]Jeffrey Fagan & Elizabeth Piper Deschenes, *Determinants of Judicial Waiver Decisions for Violent Juvenile Offenders*, 81 J. CRIM. L. & CRIMINOLOGY 314 (1990); Podkopacz & Feld, *supra* note 146, at 492.

[149]Podkopacz & Feld, *supra* note 146, at 492.

[150]Barry C. Feld, *The Transformation of the Juvenile Court*, 75 MINN. L. REV. 691, 707 (1991).

[151]Cintron, *supra* note 144, at 1269 nn.98-99.

[152]Gordon, *supra* note 129, at 205.

[153]*Id.* at 207 (quoting Francis B. McCarthy, *The Serious Offender and Juvenile Court Reform: The Case for Prosecutorial Waiver of Juvenile Court Jurisdiction*, 38 ST. LOUIS U. L.J. 629, 664-65 (1994)).

[154]United States v. Bland, 472 F.2d 1329, 1349 (D.C. Cir. 1972).

conviction over 38 percent who favor a sentence of life imprisonment without the possibility of parole.[155] Overall, 75.7 percent of Americans favor the death penalty.[156]

The death penalty was routine at English common law.[157] All but nine U.S. states had a death penalty in 1970.[158] In 1972, the U.S. Supreme Court decided the landmark case of *Furman v. Georgia*[159] in which it invalidated all of these laws. Three of the five justices in the majority decided the manner in which the death penalty was imposed was arbitrary and capricious and therefore was unconstitutional.[160] The other two justice voting with the majority believed the death penalty itself was cruel and unusual punishment and therefore was unconstitutional no matter how it was administered.[161]

Four years later in *Gregg v. Georgia*,[162] seven justices on the Supreme Court made it clear that they did not consider the death penalty to be unconstitutional per se. They did, however, invalidate the mandatory imposition of the death penalty since such statutes failed to take into account the particular facts and circumstances of a given case.[163]

The United States is one of the few democracies in the world that has a death penalty. The only other NATO country to have a death penalty is Turkey, and no one has been executed under their law since 1984.[164] Turkey is expected to join Russia, Poland, and other former Soviet-bloc countries that abolished the death penalty in the 1990s in the hopes of becoming members of the Council of Europe.[165] The United States is therefore in a unique position with respect to its support for the death penalty.

1. The Bifurcated Trial Process

Death penalty cases are handled in a **bifurcated process.** In the first phase, called the guilt phase, the guilt of the defendant is considered in the same manner any criminal trial is conducted.[166] If the defendant is found not guilty, the case is over. If convicted, however, the case then proceeds to the second phase, often called the penalty phase, in which the decision whether to impose a sentence of death is made by a jury.

The goal fo *Furman* was to limit the amount of discretion in the penalty phase in such as way as to prevent "unbridled jury discretion."[167] To meet that mandate, death penalty statutes set for

---

[155]BUREAU OF JUSTICE STATISTICS, 1998 SOURCEBOOK OF CRIMINAL JUSTICE STATISTICS 131 (1999).

[156]*Id.* at 133.

[157]NEUBAUER, *supra* note 75, at 388.

[158]*Id.*

[159]408 U.S. 238 (1972).

[160]*Id.* at 242-43 (Douglas, J., concurring).

[161]*Id.* at 305, 369 (Brennan & Marshall, JJ., concurring).

[162]428 U.S. 153, 206-07 (1976) (plurality opinion).

[163]Woodson v. North Carolina, 428 U.S. 280, 305 (1976).

[164]Stephen B. Bright, *Will the Death Penalty Remain Alive in the Twenty-first Century?: International Norms, Discrimination, Arbitrariness, and the Risk of Executing the Innocent*, 2001 WIS. L. REV. 1, 3 (2001) (citing Amnesty International, *The Death Penalty Worldwide; Developments in 1999*, at 11 (May 12, 2000), available at <http://web.amnesty.org>).

[165]*Id.*

[166]*See generally*, DAVID W. NEUBAUER, AMERICA'S COURTS AND THE CRIMINAL JUSTICE SYSTEM (8th ed., Belmont, CA: Wadsworth, 2005).

[167]*Woodson*, 428 U.S. at 302.

specific aggravating and mitigating circumstances the jury must consider when deciding whether to impose the death penalty. As a rule, all mitigating factors the defense wishes to introduce may be considered.[168] On the other hand, aggravating factors must be clearly defined. For example, a Georgia aggravating factor allowed for the imposition of a death sentence if the nature of the offense was "outrageously or wantonly vile, horrible and inhuman."[169] The Supreme Court invalidated this factor on the basis that it was so vague that it did not restrain the arbitrary and capricious infliction of the death penalty.[170] A similar outcome was reached in *Maynard v. Cartwright*[171] when the Court invalidated a provision allowing for the imposition of the death penalty upon a finding that the offense was "especially heinous, atrocious, or cruel."[172]

2. Deterrence and Brutalization

At the dawn of the twenty-first century, the U.S. federal government and thirty-eight states have laws allowing for imposition of the death penalty; the jurisdictions without the death penalty are Alaska, the District of Columbia, Hawaii, Iowa, Maine, Massachusetts, Michigan, Minnesota, North Dakota, Rhode Island, Vermont, West Virginia, and Wisconsin.[173] Since the decision of the U.S. Supreme Court in *Coker v. Georgia*[174] invalidating the imposition of the death penalty for rape, its use has been reserved for the crime of murder.

The continued use of the death penalty is often justified for its retributive punishment, its incapacitation of the offender, and for its deterrent effect. Yet the deterrent effect of the death penalty is highly questionable.[175] For example, one recent study examined [176] executions in Texas between 1984 and 1997. It was hypothesized that if deterrent effect were to exist, it would be found in Texas due to the high number of death sentences and executions within the state. But no evidence of a deterrent effect was found. Quite the contrary, the study concluded that the number of executions was unrelated to murder rates and felony rates in general. Similar findings with regard to the lack of deterrent effect were found in 1998 study in Oklahoma.[177] In fact, that study found a significant increase in stranger killings and non-felony stranger killings after Oklahoma resumed executions after a twenty-five-year moratorium. And ten of the twelve states

---

[168]Eddings v. Oklahoma, 455 U.S. 104 (1982).

[169]Godfrey v. Georgia, 446 U.S. 420, 433 (1980).

[170]Kimberly A. Orem, *Evolution of an Eighth Amendment Dichotomy: Substantive and Procedural Protections within the Cruel and Unusual Punishment Clause in Capital Cases*, 12 Cap. Def. J. 345, 349 (2000) (citing *id.*).

[171]486 U.S. 356, 360-66 (1988).

[172]*Id.*

[173]NAACP Legal Defense and Educational Fund, Inc., *Death Row U.S.A.*, (last modified January 1, 2001) <http://www.deathpenaltyinfo.org/firstpage.html#with>.

[174]433 U.S. 584, 592 (1977) (plurality opinion).

[175]*See, e.g.,* Ernie Thompson, *Effects of an Execution on Homicides in California*, 3 Homicide Studies 129-150 (1999); Keith Harries & Derral Cheatwood, The Geography of Execution: The Capital Punishment Quagmire in America (Rowman & Littlefield 1997); Michael Radelet & Ronald L. Akers, *Deterrence and The Death Penalty: The Views of Experts*, 87 J. Crim. L. & Criminology 1-16 (1996); Scott H. Decker & Carol W. Kohfeld, *A Deterrence Study of the Death Penalty in Illinois, 1933-1980*, 12 J. Crim. Just. 367-377 (1984); William C. Bailey, *Disaggregation in Deterrence and Death Penalty Research: The Case of Murder in Chicago,* 74 J. Crim. L. & Criminology 827-859 (1983).

[176]John Sorenson, Robert Wrinkle, Victoria Brewer, & James Marquart, *Capital Punishment and Deterrence: Examining the Effect of Executions on Murder in Texas*, 45 Crime & Delinquency 481-93 (1999).

[177]William Bailey, *Deterrence, Brutalization, and the Death Penalty: Another Examination of Oklahoma's Return to Capital Punishment*, 36 Criminology 711-33 (1998).

without the death penalty have homicide rates below the national average, whereas half of the states with the death penalty have homicide rates above.

The data suggesting that the executions may actually increase the homicide rate has been used to support what is called the ***brutalization hypothesis***. It proposes that executions legitimize violence "by modeling the very abhorrent behavior it wishes to discourage in others."[178]

3. Nontheoretical Criticisms of the Death Penalty

Critics of the death penalty not only point out that it may not deter serious violent crime, but actually have the opposite effect due to the brutalization hypothesis, and also point to the overwhelming amount of evidence that the death penalty is not fairly applied. For example, considerable controversy surrounds the execution of juveniles, the mentally ill, and the mentally challenged/retarded.[179] Even when these special considerations are not present, the "pro-death" composition of juries and the racially biased manner in which juries apply the death penalty are two of the most cited problems with the administration of the death penalty.

Since juries decide whether to impose the death penalty, inquiring about prospective juror's views on the death penalty seems both appropriate and arguably necessary. Since the Supreme Court's 1968 decision in *Witherspoon v. Illinois*, it has become routine to excuse those jurors who are so morally opposed to the death penalty that they could not vote to impose it under any circumstances.[180] This process led defendants to challenge this procedure on the basis that these ***"death qualified juries"*** were predisposed to impose a death sentence. Though supported by both common sense and a wealth of psychological data,[181] constitutional challenges on these grounds have been rejected for more than thirty years.[182]

Another leading criticism of the death penalty is the racially disparate way in which it is applied. The leading case on racism in the death penalty is *McCleskey v. Kemp*.[183] McCleskey was an African-America man who was sentenced to death for killing a white police officer during the commission of a robbery. At trial, McCleskey attempted to challenge the death penalty as violative of the Fourteenth Amendment's equal protection clause and as violative of the Eighth Amendment's cruel and unusual punishment clause. He did so by introducing evidence from a comprehensive study by Baldus et al., that indicated "defendants charged with killing white victims were 4.3 times as likely to receive a death sentence as defendants charged with killing blacks."[184] The evidence McCleskey presented was "[s]upported by the most

---

[178] ALBERT BANDURA, SOCIAL FOUNDATIONS OF THOUGHT AND ACTION: A SOCIAL COGNITIVE THEORY 333 (Prentice Hall 1986).

[179] *See generally* Lyn Entzeroth, *Putting the Mentally Retarded Criminal Defendant to Death: Charting the Development of a National Consensus to Exempt the Mentally Retarded from the Death Penalty*, 52 ALA. L. REV. 911 (2001); Bryan Lester Dupler, *Another Look at Evolving Standards: Will Decency Prevail Against Executing the Mentally Retarded?*, 52 OKLA. L. REV. 593 (1999); Carol Steiker & Jordan Steiker, *ABA's Proposed Moratorium: Defending Categorical Exemptions to the Death Penalty: Reflections on the ABA's Resolutions Concerning the Execution of Juveniles and Persons with Mental Retardation*, 61 LAW & CONTEMP. PROB. 89 (1998).

[180] Witherspoon v. Illinois, 391 U.S. 510, 512 (1968).

[181] *See id.* at 517; Craig Haney, *On the Selection of Capital Juries: The Biasing Effects of the Death-Qualification Process*, 8 LAW & HUM. BEHAV. 121 (1984).

[182] *Witherspoon*, 391 U.S. at 512; Lockhart v. McCree, 476 U.S. 162 (1986).

[183] 481 U.S. 279 (1987).

[184] *Id.* at 287; *see* Baldus, Pulaski & Woodworth, *Comparative Review of Death Sentences: An Empirical Study of the Georgia Experience*, 74 J. CRIM. L. & CRIMINOLOGY 661 (1983).

comprehensive statistical analysis ever done on the racial demographics of capital sentencing in a single state."[185]

The validity of the Baldus study upon which McCleskey relied was reviewed in detail by the district court and rejected.[186] The court even stated that the study did not represent "good statistical methodology."[187] The district judge's findings regarding the Baldus study were rendered moot on appeal when both the court of appeals and the Supreme Court assumed the validity of the study, but held that McCleskey's claims failed under the applicable law: McCleskey had failed to prove "the existence of purposeful discrimination" which had "a discriminatory effect on him."[188]

Before examining what the Supreme Court did in its decision, it is important to note that many scholars have commented on the validity of the Baldus study. For example, a member of the National Academy of Sciences' Committee on Sentencing Research testified that the Baldus study had "very high credibility" and was "far and away the most complete and thorough analysis of sentencing that [had] ever been done."[189] Others have since commented that the Baldus investigation was "among the best empirical studies on criminal sentencing ever conducted."[190]

McCleskey's Eighth Amendment challenge relied on prior Supreme Court precedent that held the death penalty could "not be imposed under sentencing procedures that create a substantial risk that the punishment will be inflicted in an arbitrary and capricious manner."[191] Under this authority, a defendant does not have to prove that race affected his particular sentencing decision, but rather that race impacts that "sentencing system as a whole."[192]

One would think that McCleskey's statistical proof would have been well-suited to establish the requisite pattern of arbitrary and capricious sentencing since it demonstrated that the rate of capital sentencing in a white-victim case was 120 percent greater than the rate in a black victim case. The majority, however, rejected the perspective of the prior case law which interpreted the Eighth Amendment as concerned with the risk of arbitrary and capricious decisions in the system as a whole. Instead, it looked to see if racial considerations affected McCleskey's particular case, rendering the statistical evidence next-to-useless. In doing so, the Court "shifted the precedent's system-wide perspective, which encouraged scientific research, to a particularized perspective that rendered the research conducted irrelevant."[193] Accordingly, although it seems clear that the death penalty is applied in a racist manner, the Supreme Court has yet to rule that this fact violates the U.S. Constitution.

---

[185]Randall L. Kennedy, McCleskey v. Kemp: *Race, Capital Punishment, and the Supreme Court*, 101 Harv. L. Rev. 1388 (1988).

[186]McCleskey v. Zant, 580 F. Supp. 338, 356-61 (N.D. Ga. 1984), *rev'd*, 753 F.2d 877 (11th Cir. 1985), *aff'd*, 481 U.S. 279 (1987).

[187]*Id.* at 379.

[188]McCleskey v. Kemp, 481 U.S. at 292.

[189]Kennedy, *supra* note 185, at 1399-1400 (quoting Federal Trial Transcript at 1740, McCleskey v. Zant, 580 F. Supp. 338 (N.D. Ga. 1984)).

[190]*Id.* (citing Brief Amici Curiae for Dr. Franklin M. Fisher, Dr. Richard O. Lempert, Dr. Peter W. Sperlich, Dr. Marvin E. Wolfgang, Professor Hans Zeisel & Professor Franklin E.
Zimring in Support of Petitioner Warren McCleskey at 3).

[191]Godfrey v. Georgia, 446 U.S. 420, 427 (1980) (citations omitted).

[192]Gregg v. Georgia, 428 U.S. 153, 200 (1976).

[193]David L. Faigman, *Normative Constitutional Fact-Finding: Exploring the Empirical Component of Constitutional Interpretation*, 139 U. Pa. L. Rev. 541, 600 (1991).

A final issue is worth noting before closing our discussion of the death penalty. Since 1973, one hundred people in twenty-two states have been released from death row with evidence of their innocence.[194] The American Bar Association has called for a moratorium on executions in light of the number of innocent people being freed from death row in the wake of DNA analysis and heightened scrutiny.[195] But most states have not enacted legislation allowing for DNA testing after a conviction. This state of affairs has even led to a Supreme Court Justice Sandra Day O'Connor to go on record as saying, "If statistics are any indication, the system may well be allowing some innocent defendants to be executed."[196] Justice O'Connor also pointed out the economic disparities evident in death sentencing. Defendants with more money get better legal defense teams and thereby avoid death sentences. In contrast, Justice O'Connor pointed to Texas where "people represented by court-appointed lawyers were 28 percent more likely to be convicted than those who hired their own lawyers. If convicted, they were 44 percent more likely to be sentenced to death."[197] In the wake of such criticisms, combined with international pressure from Amnesty International and foreign governments, some commentators have suggested that the end of the death penalty in the U.S. cannot be too far off.[198]

---

[194]Death Penalty Information Center, *Innocence and the Death Penalty* <http://www.deathpenaltyinfo.org/innoc.html>; Rhonda McMillion, *Pulling the Plug on Executions: ABA's Call for Death Penalty Moratorium Sparks Debate in Congress*, 86 A.B.A.J. 99 (2000).

[195]*See, e.g.,* McMillion, *supra* note 194, at 99; Mark Hansen, *More for Moratorium: Aba Conference Bolsters Momentum to Halt Executions*, 86 A.B.A.J. 92 (2000).

[196]*O'Connor Questions Death Penalty*, N.Y. TIMES, July 4, 2001, at A-9.

[197]*Id.*

[198]*E.g.,* Jonathan Alter, *Why The Mess Really Matters*, NEWSWEEK May 21, 2001, at 29; Michael P. Seng, *Reflections on When "We, the People" Kill*, 34 J. MARSHALL L. REV. 713 (2001); Samuel R. Gross, *A Multifarious Look at Capital Punishment: Keynote Address: Still Unfair, Still Arbitrary-But Do We Care?*, 26 OHIO N.U.L. REV. 517 (2000).

CHAPTER FIFTEEN
CORRECTIONAL PSYCHOLOGY

I. AN OVERVIEW OF THE CORRECTIONAL SYSTEM

When we speak of the correctional system, we are actually referring to a "set of interrelated organizations, agencies, and programs that hold, treat, and sometimes punish those persons known or strongly believed to have committed a crime."[1] Rates of imprisonment were relatively stable through the 1970s—enough so that some commentators wrote of the "end of imprisonment"[2] and "crime of punishment."[3] But as "tough on crime" attitudes grew, so did attitudes towards more punitive criminal sentences.[4] As a result, the number of people under correctional supervision in the United States has skyrocketed from 1.84 million people in 1980 to 4.35 million in 1990 and nearly 7 million by 2005, representing a 45.3 percent increase in just the 1990s alone.[5] These numbers include the people on probation, in jails and prisons, and on parole.[6]

Jails are local correctional facilities usually run by municipalities or counties. They are designed to hold people two types of people: (1) those convicted of misdemeanors (crimes for which the period of incarceration is generally less than one year), and (2) those who have been denied bail while awaiting disposition of criminal charges.[7] In contrast, *prisons* are run either by state governments or the federal government and are designed to incarcerate people who have been convicted of felonies (crimes for which the period of imprisonment is greater than one year).[8] These dichotomies are not always clear in practice, however. For example, some states incarcerate low-level felons for eighteen to twenty-four months in county jails, while others use a combined jail–prison system.[9]

In addition to incarceration in jails and prisons, the probation and parole systems also are mechanisms of criminal corrections. *Probation* is a sentence which allows a defendant to avoid incarceration, yet still places him or her under the jurisdiction of the correctional system in such a way that allows for the monitoring of the defendant's compliance with special restrictions placed upon him or her as a part of sentencing (e.g., abstaining from using drugs and/or alcohol; obeying all laws; participating in educational, psychological, or addiction counseling; supporting dependents; physically staying within a restricted geographical area).[10] Probation can be as lax as requiring a probationer to check-in with a supervising probation officer once per month at a

---

[1]RICHARD A. TEWSKSBURY, INTRODUCTION TO CORRECTIONS 3 (3d ed. McGraw–Hill 1997).

[2]ROBERT SOMMER, THE END OF IMPRISONMENT (Oxford University Press 1976); JESSICA MITFORD, KIND AND USUAL PUNISHMENT: THE PRISON BUSINESS. (Vintage 1971).

[3]KARL MENNINGER, THE CRIME OF PUNISHMENT (Penguin 1968).

[4]TODD R. CLEAR, HARM IN AMERICAN PENOLOGY: OFFENDERS, VICTIMS, AND THEIR COMMUNITIES (SUNY Press 1994).

[5]BUREAU OF JUSTICE STATISTICS, *Table 6.1: Adults on Probation, in Jail or Prison, and on Parole 1980-1999*, *in* SOURCEBOOK OF CRIMINAL JUSTICE STATISTICS 1999, at 484.

[6]*Id.*

[7]TEWKSBURY, *supra* note 1, at 281.

[8]*Id.* at 83-99.

[9]CURT R. BARTOL & ANNE M. BARTOL, PSYCHOLOGY AND LAW 346 (2d ed. 1994).

[10]TEWKSBURY, *supra* note 1, at 327.

designated time.[11] At the other extreme, probation can be as intensive as maintaining both scheduled and random daily contacts between the probationer and a supervision probation officer,[12] or electronically monitoring a probationer twenty-four hours per day.[13] If the offender does not comply with any of the special terms of probation, a court can revoke the sentence of probation and resentence the defendant to a term of incarceration.[14]

Between the sanctions of incarceration and probation are a wide range of criminal sentences referred to as *intermediate sanctions* such as house-arrest or required living in a *community-based correctional facility* such as a halfway house, a boot camp, a work furlough camp, etc. These facilities are designed to hold people for part of each day, allowing them to maintain employment or attend school during applicable hours, while keeping them under correctional supervision at other times.[15] These sanctions may be coupled with forms of intensive supervision by a probation officer or via electronic monitoring while a defendants is out of one's home or community-based facility for work or school reasons.

Parole is a lot like probation except it is granted to a prisoner after he or she has served some time incarcerated in a jail or prison. It is a conditional release prior to the expiration of the full-length of the sentence term that requires the parolee to be supervised by a parole officer upon release from an institution in much the same way a probationer is supervised by a probation officer.[16] Parole is most frequently granted to prisoners as a reward for good conduct while incarcerated.[17] Like with probation, special conditions of release can be imposed on a parolee requiring the convict to do certain things and refrain from doing other things. The violation of any of these special terms of release can result in the revocation of parole, thereby requiring the parolee to return to prison to serve out the balance of his or her original sentence.[18]

II. EFFECTS OF IMPRISONMENT

A. The Sociological Data

Jails and prisons are total institutions. *Total institutions* are places "of residence and work where a large number of like-situated individuals, cut off from the wider society for an appreciable period of time, together lead an enforced, formally administered round of life."[19] Boarding schools, psychiatric institutions, military barracks, and religious monasteries are all examples of total institutions. Living life in a total institution inevitably causes some psychological effects ranging from the subtle to the profound, depending on the type of total institution. The psychological effects experienced by those sentenced to live life in penal total institutions are undoubtedly quite different from those experienced by someone who voluntarily enters a

---

[11]*Id.* at 328.

[12]*Id.* at 329.

[13]*Id.* at 331.

[14]*Id.* at 341-42.

[15]*Id.* at 330.

[16]*Id.* at 355.

[17]*Id.* at 359.

[18]*Id.* at 369-73.

[19]MICHAEL HARALAMBOS & MARTIN HOLBORN, SOCIOLOGY: THEME AND PERSPECTIVES 305 (4th ed. Collins Educational 1995).

religious order.[20] Most of the research on the psychological effects of prison life has been conducted by sociologists who have portrayed the life in penal total institutions as "brutal, mortifying, and damaging."[21] The most famous of these sociologists was the pioneering work of Erving Goffman and Gresham Sykes.

The loss of liberty upon entering a penal total institution is probably the most obvious deprivation of incarceration.[22] Freedom of movement, freedom of speech, and freedom of association are often highly restricted. Life is isolating, cutting people off from their families, their friends, their work, and all of the conveniences, goods, and services of the outside world.[23] This isolation results in "lost emotional relationships, loneliness, and boredom."[24] It further serves as a constant reminder that the offender is morally condemned by society for his or her actions, something Sykes asserted was quite damaging to the inmate's sense of self-worth.[25]

The loss of freedom engenders secondary losses which also cause psychological pain. Inmates are deprived of their ability to engage in their normal sexual relationships. Involuntary celibacy causes psychological and sexual frustration. This, in turn, can lead to violence of both a physical and sexual nature. And even if violence is avoided, inmates must often cope with omnipresent homosexual sexual outlets that can be threatening to an inmate's sense of sexuality.[26]

The loss of freedom also deprives prisoners of their autonomy. Routine daily activities, such as when to eat, sleep, shower, exercise, work, and so on are all dictated by an inflexible daily schedule set for the inmate. Sykes thought the loss of autonomy caused further self-esteem damage since it reduces an inmate to "the weak, helpless, dependent status of childhood."[27]

Finally, inmates are deprived of feelings of safety and security that accompanied their lives outside of the penal total institution. They live in fear of physical and/or sexual assault from violent inmates.[28] In the words of a long-time inmate, "everyone is afraid. It is not an emotional or psychological fear. It is a practical matter. If you don't threaten someone at the very least, someone will threaten you . . . . Many times you have to 'prey' on someone, or you will be 'preyed' on yourself."[29]

The combined effects of these deprivations can take a substantial toll on an inmate.[30] Johnson claimed that the combination of psychological deprivations lead to a "destruction" of the "human personality."[31] Many term the loss of personal identity ***deindividualization.*** People often cope with the loss of individual identity by fitting in to the pre-existing subculture within

---

[20]*See generally*, JAMES B. JACOBS, STATEVILLE: THE PENITENTIARY IN MASS SOCIETY (Univ. Chicago Press 1977).

[21]Alison Liebling, *Prison Suicide and Prisoner Coping*, 26 CRIME & JUST. 283, 285 (1999).

[22]GRESHAM SYKES, THE SOCIETY OF CAPTIVES 63-78 (Princeton Univ. Press 1958).

[23]*Id.*; ERVING GOFFMAN, ASYLUMS (Anchor 1961).

[24]Liebling, *supra* note 21, at 285.

[25]SYKES, *supra* note 22, at 65-66.

[26]*Id.* at 71-72.

[27]*Id.* at 75.

[28]*Id.* at 77-78.

[29]ROBERT JOHNSON & HANS TOCH (EDS.), THE PAINS OF IMPRISONMENT 86 (Sage 1982).

[30]SYKES, *supra* note 22, at 69-72; Nicolette Parisi, *The Prisoner's Pressures and Responses, in* COPING WITH IMPRISONMENT 9-26 (Nicolette Parisi ed., Sage Publications 1982).

[31]ROBERT JOHNSON, HARD TIME: UNDERSTANDING AND REFORMING THE PRISON (Wadsworth 1996).

the prison. But adapting to the customs and mores of inmate life, a process known as *prisonization,* might explain the psychological data on the effects of incarceration.

B. The Psychological Data

The sociological research discussed above has been criticized both methodologically and in terms of ideological bias.[32] Psychological studies have not confirmed sociologists' findings. In fact, one of the leading scholars on the psychological effects of imprisonment points to the research done in prisons by psychologists as having "done much to deflate the sweeping exaggerations—chiefly by sociologists—about the ill effects of normal incarceration."[33] Most of the psychological studies have concluded the effects of imprisonment are minimal after a period of initial adjustment.[34] Yet, psychological studies have demonstrated "fear, anxiety, loneliness, trauma, depression, injustice, powerlessness, violence, rejection, and uncertainty are all part of the experience of prison."[35]

One of the most profound studies of the psychological effects of incarceration is called the *Stanford Prison Experiment.* It was conducted by the psychology department at Stanford University in 1971.[36] It was supposed to last for two weeks, but it was called off after just six days.

After placing an advertisement in a local newspaper, researchers tested seventy applicants who had volunteered to participate in a study on the psychological effects of imprisonment. After screening out those with "psychological problems, medical disabilities, or a history of crime or drug abuse," they were left with twenty-four male college students who were "healthy, intelligent, and middle-class."[37] By the flip of a coin, half of the participants were assigned to be prison guards, while the other half were assigned the roles of prison inmates.[38] A simulated prison was constructed in the basement of the building housing the psychology department that looked remarkably real, including having small cells with steel bars and cell numbers.[39]

Guards were given no instructions other than "to do whatever they thought was necessary to maintain law and order in the prison and to command the respect of the prisoners."[40] They were dressed in khaki guard uniforms; issued billy-clubs, whistles, and handcuffs; and all wore mirrored sun-glasses to hide both their emotions and identities from the inmates.[41] All guards were explicitly prohibited from using physical punishment or aggression against the prisoners.

---

[32]*E.g.,* R. Sapsford, *Life Sentence Prisoners,* 18 BRITISH J. CRIMINOLOGY 128-45 (1978); Nigel Walker, *The Unwanted Effects of Long-Term Imprisonment, in* PROBLEMS OF LONG-TERM IMPRISONMENT (Anthony E. Bottoms & Roy Light, eds., Gower 1987).

[33]Walker, *supra* note 32.

[34]Liebling, *supra* note 21, at 284 (citing, *inter alia,* Walker, *supra* note 32; EDWARD ZAMBLE & FRANK J. PORPORINO, COPING, BEHAVIOR, AND ADAPTATION IN PRISON INMATES (Springer-Verlag 1988).

[35]*Id.* at 341.

[36]Craig Haney, W. Curtis Banks, & Philip Zimbardo, *Interpersonal Dynamics in a Simulated Prison,* 1 INT'L J. CRIMINOLOGY & PENOLOGY 69-97 (1973); *see also* Stanford Prison Experiment Slide Show [available online] </http://www.prisonexp.org> [hereinafter "Online Show"].

[37]Online Show, *supra* note 36, at slide 4 <http://www.prisonexp.org/slide-4.htm>.

[38]*Id.*

[39]*Id.* at slide 5 <http://www.prisonexp.org/slide-5.htm>.

[40]*Id.* at slide 12 <http://www.prisonexp.org/slide-12.htm>.

[41]*Id.* at slide 13 <http://www.prisonexp.org/slide-13.htm>.

The mock-prisoners were unexpectedly "arrested" by the real police officers at their homes. They were taken into custody, booked at the police station, and taken blindfolded to the mock-prison, being told they were in a real jail.[42] Upon arriving at the jail, they were stripped searched, sprayed with a deodorant spray they were told was a delousing spray, and left to stand alone and naked for a short while.[43] They were issued a uniform—rubber sandals and a dress-like smock with a prisoner identification number on it, which they were forced to wear without any underwear beneath it, thereby creating extra humiliation and a sense of emasculation.[44] They were issued a stocking cap as a substitute for having their heads shaved. And they were chained at their feet.

Early in the experiment, the prisoners did not take things too seriously. The first day passed without incident, but by the second day, the inmates revolted by removing their sticking caps, ripping off their prisoner identification numbers, and barricading themselves into a cell by pushing their cots against the cell doors.[45] The guards, however, quelled the revolt using force. First, the called for backup from "off-duty" guards. Then, they used a fire extinguisher to shoot "a stream of skin-chilling carbon dioxide" at the prisoners.[46] This allowed the guards to gain entrance to the cells, whereupon they "stripped the prisoners naked, took the beds out, forced the ringleaders of the prisoner rebellion into solitary confinement, and generally began to harass and intimidate the prisoners."[47]

The three inmates who were the least involved in the revolt were given special privileges. They got their clothes and beds back, as well as special food they were allowed to eat in the sight of other prisoners who were being denied food.[48] The following day, however, the guards mixed and mingled the "good" prisoners and the "bad" ones, intentionally causing confusion as a means of exercising psychological control over the inmates by breaking prisoner alliances.[49] The revolt, and the guards response to it, had the effect of causing the guards to bond. No longer was this a simple simulation for them. They viewed the inmates as trouble-makers and even feared for their own safety which, in turn, led them to increase their levels of control, surveillance, and aggression.[50] They even denied prisoners permission to use bathroom facilities, forcing prisoners to use a bucket in their cells. This led to the permeation of the smell of urine and feces.[51]

By the third day, one of the inmates had to be released. He was suffering from "acute emotional disturbance, disorganized thinking, uncontrollable crying, and rage."[52] Yet, at first, he was not believed. Both the guards and the researchers thought he was trying to "con" his way out of incarceration.

---

[42]*Id.* at slide 7 <http://www.prisonexp.org/slide-7.htm>.

[43]*Id.* at slides 8-9 <http://www.prisonexp.org/slide-8.htm> & <http://www.prisonexp.org/slide-9.htm>.

[44]*Id.* at slide 10 <http://www.prisonexp.org/slide-10.htm>.

[45]*Id.* at slide 16 <http://www.prisonexp.org/slide-16.htm>.

[46]*Id.* at slide 17 <http://www.prisonexp.org/slide-17.htm>.

[47]*Id.* at slide 18 <http://www.prisonexp.org/slide-18.htm>.

[48]*Id.* at slide 19 <http://www.prisonexp.org/slide-19.htm>.

[49]*Id.* at slide 20 <http://www.prisonexp.org/slide-20.htm>.

[50]*Id.*

[51]*Id.* at slide 21 <http://www.prisonexp.org/slide-21.htm>.

[52]*Id.* at slide 22 <http://www.prisonexp.org/slide-22.htm>.

In the days that followed, it was rumored than an escape was being planned by the inmates. Based on this rumor, the guards took steps to prevent an escape with the cooperation of the researchers who, according to their own statements, ceased to act like experimental social psychologists and instead responded with "concern over the security of [their] prison."[53] They even tried to get the Palo Alto Police to allow their mock-prisoners to be transported to a real jail to prevent escape—a request which was, of course, denied.[54] Instead, they formulated a secondary plan which involved chaining the prisoners together, putting bags over their heads, and transporting them to a storage room elsewhere in the building until after the anticipated break in occurred. While they were in this room, one of the lead researchers waited in the mock-prison area for the alleged co-conspirators, planning to tell them the experiment was over. Of course, no one ever came, as the jail-break was nothing more than a rumor. However, a colleague from the psychology department did stop by to speak with the researcher as he waited for the co-conspirators. After explaining the study and what was going on at that time, the colleague asked him what the independent variable of the study was.

> To my surprise, I got really angry at him. Here I had a prison break on my hands. The security of my men and the stability of my prison was at stake, and now, I had to deal with this bleeding-heart, liberal, academic, effete dingdong who was concerned about the independent variable! It wasn't until much later that I realized how far into my prison role I was at that point—that I was thinking like a prison superintendent rather than a research psychologist.[55]

After the jail-break attempt failed to materialize, the guards increasingly harassed the prisoners. A Catholic priest who had been a prison chaplain was called in to assess the situation. He interviewed each prisoner individually. In what the researchers called a "Kafkaesque" development, half of the inmates introduced themselves by their prisoner identification number rather than by their name![56] One of the inmates did not want to meet with the priest, but rather was asking for a physician. After some coaxing, he finally agreed to meet with the priest during which time "he broke down and began to cry hysterically."[57] When the other prisoners heard his crying, they taunted him. Other prisoners experienced similar symptoms after a mock parole board had denied their request for parole.[58] One even developed a psychosomatic rash.[59]

Meanwhile, the guards had developed distinct personalities, some being thought of as "good guards" given their relatively humane treatment of the inmates, while others had become militaristic,[60] and others were even sadistic[61]—engaging in "pornographic and degrading abuse of the prisoners."[62] This fact, coupled with visits from family members that prompted them to contact lawyers to get their sons "out of prison," led the researchers to the realization that they had to stop the study. They had inadvertently created an unacceptable situation.

---

[53]*Id.* at slide 25 <http://www.prisonexp.org/slide-25.htm>.

[54]*Id.*

[55]*Id.* at slide 27 <http://www.prisonexp.org/slide-27.htm>.

[56]*Id.* at slide 29 <http://www.prisonexp.org/slide-29.htm>.

[57]*Id.* at slide 30 <http://www.prisonexp.org/slide-30.htm>.

[58]*Id.* at slide 35 <http://www.prisonexp.org/slide-35.htm>.

[59]*Id.*

[60]*Id.* at slide 37 <http://www.prisonexp.org/slide-37.htm>.

[61]*Id.*

[62]*Id.* at slide 38 <http://www.prisonexp.org/slide-38.htm>.

> By the end of the study, the prisoners were disintegrated, both as a group and as individuals. There was no longer any group unity; just a bunch of isolated individuals hanging on, much like prisoners of war or hospitalized mental patients. The guards had won total control of the prison, and they commanded the blind obedience of each prisoner.[63]

The Stanford Prison Experiment shows the devastating psychological effects the incarceration setting can have—not only on inmates, but also on otherwise well-adjusted guards. Yet, because the study lacks external validity, it may not be generalizable to "real" prisoners and guards.[64] And for what should be obvious ethical considerations, no one has ever attempted to replicate the study.[65]

While the state of research on the psychological effects of incarceration still leaves much to be desired, it is generally accepted in the psychological literature that there is a U-shaped pattern adjustment "with the strongest emotional stress reactions occurring at the beginning of the sentence, and the end, as the time to be released approaches.[66] While incarceration in prison can cause a number of psychological effects that can be quite devastating—some of which are obvious, others of which are more impalpable, it appears these are temporally limited so that no "permanent harm to the psychological well-being of inmates" is caused.[67]

C. Special Considerations for Overcrowding and Solitary Confinement

There are several exceptions to the general findings that no long-term psychological damage is caused by imprisonment. The two most prominent ones are prison overcrowding and isolation.

Overcrowding increases inmate and staff tension levels, resulting in higher rates of disciplinary infractions and corresponding higher rates of lock-up procedures.[68] It can result in inhumane living conditions in which inmates sleep on the floors of cells and common areas.[69] Increased levels of noise and decreased levels of privacy lead to increased levels of psychological problems, violence, illness, complaints, and even inmate deaths.[70] Anxiety, depression, headaches, high blood pressure, and other cardio-vascular problems can be both short- and long-term complications of sharing too little space with too many people.[71]

---

[63]*Id.* at slide 35 <http://www.prisonexp.org/slide-35.htm>.

[64]*See, e.g.*, JOHN MONAHAN & LAURENS WALKER, SOCIAL SCIENCE AND LAW: CASES AND MATERIALS (2d ed. Foundation Press 1990).

[65]For a more comprehensive discussion of both the ethical considerations raised by the Stanford Prison Experiment and the practical implications of it, see Craig Haney and Philip G. Zimbardo, *The Past and Future of U.S. Prison Policy: Twenty-five Years after the Stanford Prison Experiment*, 53 AM. PSYCHOLOGIST 709-27 (1988).

[66]BARTOL & BARTOL, *supra* note 198, at 366.

[67]ZAMBLE & PORPORINO, *supra* note 223, at 149.

[68]James Austin, *Using Early Release to Relieve Prison Crowding: A Dilemma in Public Policy*, 32 CRIME & DELINQ. 404, 412 (1986).

[69]Jason S. Ornduff, *Releasing the Elderly Inmate: A Solution to Prison Overcrowding*, 4 ELDER L.J. 173, 176-77 (1996) (citing Monmouth County Correctional Institution Inmates v. Lanzaro, 595 F. Supp. 1417, 1421 (D.N.J. 1984)).

[70] Austin, *supra* note 68, at 412; Liebling, *supra* note 21, at 284-85 (citing Gerald G. Gaes, *The Effects of Overcrowding in Prison, in* 6 CRIME AND JUSTICE: AN ANNUAL REVIEW OF RESEARCH (Michael Tonry & Norval Morris eds., University of Chicago Press 1985)).

[71]PAUL B. PAULUS, VERNE C. COX & GARVIN MCCAIN, PRISON CROWDING: A PSYCHOLOGICAL PERSPECTIVE (Springer-Verlag 1988).

Isolation, whether done for disciplinary purposes or for protective custody reasons, is common in prisons. Some people respond well to isolation, even enjoying the solitude away from the many stressors of daily prison life.[72] Others, however, respond very negatively to isolation evidencing:

> 1) sensory disturbances: perceptual distortions and loss of perceptual constancy, in some cases without hallucinations; 2) ideas of reference and paranoid ideation short of overt delusions; 3) emergence of primitive aggressive fantasies, which remained ego-dystonic and with reality-testing preserved; 4) disturbances of memory and attention short of overt disorientation and confusional state; and 5) derealization experiences without massive dissociative regression.[73]

The earlier studies that found a lack of negative effects have been criticized methodologically for using college students in simulation exercises, or inmate who volunteered to be placed in solitary confinement. Today, nearly all of the modern studies on solitary confinement conclude that "even in the absence of physical brutality or unhygienic conditions, [it] can produce emotional damage, declines in mental functioning and even the most extreme forms of psychopathology, such as depersonalization, hallucination and delusions."[74] Moreover, because inmates often leave solitary confinement "more resentful, antagonistic and violence-prone" than when they entered, its legitimate penological usefulness is questionable.[75]

III. CLINICAL CARE OF THE MENTALLY ILL IN CORRECTIONAL SETTINGS

A. Minimal Standards of Care

Estimates of the percentage of incarcerated people with serious mental disorders range from a conservative 7.2 percent[76] to 20 percent in certain metropolitan jails.[77] Other studies show a range of 15 to 40 percent of inmates with "moderate" mental illnesses.[78] Both empirical research and common sense tell us that the mentally ill criminal offender often does not receive adequate treatment while incarcerated. "The lack of adequate mental health resources exacerbates existing

---

[72]Peter Suedfeld, *Reactions and Attributes of Prisoners in Solitary Confinement,* 9 Crim. Just. & Behav. 303 (1982); Richard H. Walters, *Effect of Solitary Confinement on Prisoners,* 19 Am. J. Psychiatry. 771 (1963).

[73]Christine Rebman, *The Eighth Amendment and Solitary Confinement: The Gap in Protection from Psychological Consequences,* 49 DePaul L. Rev. 567, 580 (1999) (citing See Stuart Grassian, *Psychopathological Effects of Solitary Confinement,* 140 Am. J. Psychiatry 1450 (1983); Craig Haney, *Infamous Punishment: The Psychological Consequences of Isolation,* 3 Nat'l Prison Proj. J. 6-7 (1993)).

[74]Thomas B. Benjamin & Kenneth Lux, *Solitary Confinement as Psychological Punishment,* 13 Cal. W. L. Rev. 265, 268 (1977).

[75]Edward Kaufman, *The Violation of Psychiatric Standards of Care in Prisons,* 137 Am. J. Psychiatry, 566, 569 (1980).

[76]T. Howard Stone, *Therapeutic Implications of Incarceration for Persons with Severe Mental Disorders: Searching for Rational Health Policy,* 24 Am. J. Crim. L. 283, 291 (1997) (citing E. Fuller Torrey et al., Criminalizing the Seriously Mentally Ill: The Abuse of Jails as Mental Hospitals 13 (1992)).

[77]Fox Butterfield, *Asylums Behind Bars: A Special Report; Prisons Replace Hospitals for the Nation's Mentally Ill,* The New York Times, Mar. 5, 1998, at A1; *see also* Stone, *supra* note 76, at 288-89 (*citing* Linda A. Teplin, *Psychiatric and Substance Abuse Disorders Among Male Urban Jail Detainees,* 84 Am. J. Pub. Health 290, 292 (1994) (reporting range from 6.2% - 9.4%)).

[78]Sheilagh Hodgins, *Assessing Mental Disorder in the Criminal Justice System: Feasibility versus Clinical Accuracy,* 18 Int'l J. L. & Psychiatry 15-28 (1995).

serious mental conditions for inmates, resulting in decompensation in inmate mental and physical health, inmate suicides, and related complications in inmate management for correctional officials."[79]

Scholars have repeatedly demonstrated that the mentally ill inmate fails to adapt to life in jail or prison on every measure of psychological adaptation.[80] This fact often manifests itself in significantly higher rates of disciplinary infractions[81] and suicide rates[82] for mentally ill inmates than for inmates who are not mentally ill. What can be done about this situation?

Given that offenders are brought to jail after arrest, one of the more pressing needs of the correctional system is to screen inmates upon their entrance to a jail to identify and manage those persons who pose a risk of danger to themselves or others.[83] And while the same is also necessary in the prison setting, prisons must also have programs to monitor inmates with mental illnesses throughout their period of incarceration. Moreover, one would hope that beyond simple management, we would also seek to treat mentally ill prisoners, not only from a humanitarian vantage point, but also because doing so helps to protect other inmates and correctional personal while someone is incarcerated, and society as a whole upon that person's release.[84]

It is doubtful that there is a constitutional right to treatment when someone is involuntarily civilly committed.[85] In the correctional setting, the right is even more nebulous, as the Supreme Court has never ruled on whether (and to what extent, if any), inmates have the right to mental health assessment and treatment. In *Estelle v. Gamble*,[86] however, the Court ruled that correctional officials cannot be "deliberately indifferent to the serious medical needs" of a prisoner without running afoul of the Eighth Amendment's ban on cruel and unusual punishment.[87] This amorphous standard requires three distinct showings to be made before a right to treatment is triggered.

First, a prisoner's mental illness would have to constitute a "serious medical need" to trigger the application of the *Estelle* standard. It is clear that:

> "routine" illnesses that might produce some minor discomfort are not included in the definition of serious medical need. Thus, with respect to mental illness, minor episodes of clinical depression or the like may not require treatment. However, many disorders classified under Axis I of the Diagnostic and Statistical Manual of Mental Disorders would fall into the category of serious medical needs.[88]

Second, the "deliberate indifference" standard has been interpreted by the Supreme Court in *Farmer v. Brennan*[89] to require a subjective state of mind on behalf of correctional officials that

---

[79]Stone, *supra* note 76, at 285.

[80]*Id.* at 299 (citing HANS TOCH ET AL., COPING: MALADAPTATION IN PRISONS 42, 50-54 (1989)).

[81]*Id.* (citing TOCH et al., *supra* note 80, at xvii, xix).

[82]*Id.* (citing TORREY ET AL., *supra* note 76, at 60-61).

[83]James R.P. Ogloff, Ronald Roesch, & Stephen D. Hart, *Mental Health Services in Jails and Prisons: Legal, Clinical, and Policy Issues*, 18 LAW & PSYCHOL. REV. 109, 111 (1994).

[84]*Id.* at 112.

[85]Youngberg v. Romero, 457 U.S. 307 (1982).

[86]429 U.S. 97 (1976).

[87]*Id.* at 104-05.

[88]Ogloff et al., *supra* note 83, at 120-21.

[89]511 U.S. 825 (1994).

is akin to criminal recklessness— a conscious disregard of a known risk.[90] "Isolated negligence or malpractice is insufficient to state an *Estelle* claim. Deliberate indifference exists when action is not taken in the face of a 'strong likelihood, rather than a mere possibility' that failure to provide care would result in harm to the prisoner."[91]

Third, a constitutional infraction would occur only if the deliberate indifference to a prisoner's serious mental health needs resulted in the "unnecessary and wanton infliction of pain"—the standard for an Eighth Amendment violation.[92] Thus, the consequences to the untreated inmate would have to be substantial.

Although the Supreme Court has not weighed in on the specifics of applying the *Estelle* standards to mentally ill inmates, some lower federal courts have done so. In *Bowring v. Godwin*,[93] the Fourth Circuit held that mentally ill inmates were:

> entitled to psychological or psychiatric treatment if a physician or other health care provider, exercising ordinary skill and care at the time of observation, concludes with reasonable medical certainty (1) that the prisoner's symptoms evidence a serious disease or injury; (2) that such disease or injury is curable or may be substantially alleviated; and (3) that the potential for harm to the prisoner by reason of delay or the denial of care would be substantial.[94]

The court was clear to limit the right to treatment based on the medical necessity of treatment, "not simply that which may be considered merely desirable.[95] A federal district court fleshed out the standard in more detail in the 1980 case of *Ruiz v. Estelle*.[96] In that case, the court set forth the six specific guidelines presented in Table 15.1 for a constitutionally acceptable mental health treatment program in the Texas penal system. It is important to keep in mind that other jurisdictions have not adopted these standards as a matter of constitutional law, but they are helpful nonetheless is explaining the minimal standards that might be required under the Eighth Amendment for inmates with mental illnesses.

---

[90]*Id.* at 839-40.

[91]Ogloff et al., *supra* note 83, at 121 (citing Guglielmoni v. Alexander, 583 F. Supp. 821, 826 (D. Conn. 1984)).

[92]*Id.*

[93]551 F.2d 44 (1977).

[94]*Id.* at 47.

[95]*Id.* at 48.

[96]503 F. Supp. 1265 (S.D. Tex. 1980), *aff'd in part & rev'd in part*, 679 F.2d 1115 (5th Cir. 1982), *cert. denied*, 460 U.S. 1042 (1983).s

Table 15.1: Minimum Standards for Mental Health Care in Prisons

1. There must be a systematic program for screening and evaluating inmates in order to identify those who require mental health treatment;

2. Treatment must entail more than segregation and close supervision of the inmate patients;

3. Treatment requires the participation of trained mental health professionals, who must be employed in sufficient numbers to identify and treat in an individualized manner those treatable inmates suffering from serious mental disorders;

4. Accurate, complete, and confidential records of the mental health treatment process must be maintained;

5. Prescription and administration of behavior-altering medications in dangerous amounts, by dangerous methods, or without appropriate supervision and periodic evaluation, is an unacceptable method of treatment; and

6. A basic program for the identification, treatment, and supervision of inmates with suicidal tendencies is a necessary component of any mental health treatment program.

Source: *Ruiz v. Estelle,* 503 F. Supp. 1265, 1339 (S.D. Tex. 1980).

B. Intake and Ongoing Screening of Inmates

Within twenty-four hours of arrival at a correctional institution, an intake screening should be performed.[97] Ideally, such a screening would be performed by a mental health clinician, but the realities of correctional administration often dictate that such screening be done by a trained paraprofessional, such as a nurse, social worker, or specially trained correctional officer.[98] A semi-structured interview such as the mental status examination is usually used to "detect serious mental disorder requiring rapid management, treatment, or further evaluation."[99] Accordingly, the intake screening process is designed to assessment immediate mental health needs, not long-term treatment.

Those inmates requiring immediate mental health services may need to be transferred out of the correctional institution. The determination to divert a prisoner to a mental health facility is usually made in two steps. If an intake screening identifies someone who has more serious or acute needs than can be met in the correctional institution, a mental health specialist is usually called upon to do a more comprehensive psychological or psychiatric examination of the inmate.[100] If diversion is warranted in the clinician's opinion, then the inmate is entitled to a transfer hearing before a neutral judicial officer to ensure due process.[101] If the opinion of the clinician after assessment is that diversion is not warranted, the clinician should devise a plan of treatment for the inmate to be implemented within the correctional institution.[102]

---

[97]Ogloff et al., *supra* note 83, at 127-28.

[98]*Id.*

[99]*Id.*

[100]James R.P. Ogloff et al., *Screening, Assessment, and Identification of Services for Mentally Ill Offenders in Prisons, in* MENTAL ILLNESS IN AMERICA'S PRISONS (Henry J. Steadman & Joseph Cocozza, eds. 1993).

[101]Vitek v. Jones, 445 U.S. 480, 494 (1980).

[102]Ogloff et al., *supra* note 83, at 126.

Of course, not all mental disorders will be evident upon intake screening. Correctional institutions need to have a system in place that allows for the continual monitoring of the mental status of inmates. This is usually accomplished in two primary ways. First, a self-referral process should be in place where an inmate experiencing psychological difficulties can go for help.[103] Second, correctional staff, especially correctional officers, "should be trained to recognize signs of mental disorder."[104] And third, although more of an ideal than a plan in routine practice, "a formal process for ensuring that inmates are periodically assessed" should also be in place.[105]

C. Treatment

Opportunities for treatment during a period of incarceration differ greatly depending on the type of facility. As a rule, jails are too small and underfunded to do more than screen inmates and dispense medications.[106] However, medium and large jails—especially those in metropolitan areas, can offer treatment programs.[107] In contrast, prisons offer much better opportunities for treatment.[108] Behavioral cognitive therapies are quite popular.[109] And many prisons have developed programs to treat specific disorders, such as depression, alcohol and chemical dependencies, and aggression/anger management, to comprehensive programs to treat specific types of offenders, such a sex offenders and psychopaths.[110] That being said, an overwhelming number of correctional facilities—both jails and prisons—lack:

> adequate mental health resources to effectively provide the treatment required by persons with severe mental disorders. The lack of adequate mental health resources exacerbates existing serious mental conditions for inmates, resulting in decompensation in inmate mental and physical health, inmate suicides, and related complications in inmate management for correctional officials.[111]

Numerous books and articles have been published on the lack of treatment of mentally ill jail and prison inmates. Many such scholarly works not only point out the empirical evidence that we

---

[103]*Id.* at 128.

[104]*Id.* (citing P. Randall Kropp et al., *The Perceptions of Correctional Officers Toward Mentally Disordered Offenders*, 12 Int'l J. L. & Psychiatry 181, 187-88 (1989)).

[105]*Id.*

[106]*Id.* at 130 (citing, *inter alia,* The Mentally Ill in Jail: Planning for Essential Services (Henry J. Steadman et al. eds., 1989); Carole H. Morgan, *Developing Mental Health Services for Local Jails*, 8 Crim. Just. & Behav. 259 (1981)).

[107]*Id.*

[108]Marnie E. Rice & Grant T. Harris, *Treatment for Prisoners with Mental Disorder, in* Mental Illness in America's Prisons (Henry J. Steadman & Joseph J. Cocozza, eds. 1993); Christopher D. Webster et al., *Treatment Programmes for Mentally Ill Offenders, in* Clinical Approaches To The Mentally Disordered Offender (Kevin Howells & Clive R. Hollin, eds. 1993).

[109]Gisli H. Gudjonnson, *Psychological Treatment for the Mentally Ill Offender*, 16 Issues in Crim. Leg. Psychology 15 (1990); Joseph D. Bloom & John M. Bradford, *An Overview of Psychiatric Treatment Approaches to Three Offender Groups,* 39 Hosp. & Community Psychiatry 151 (1988).

[110]Ogloff et al., *supra* note 83, at 131-32 (citing, *inter alia,* Gudjonnson, *supra* note 109; Bloom & Bradford, *supra* note 109; Richard F. Ramsay & Bryan L. Tanney, *Suicide Prevention in High-Risk Prison Populations*, 29 Can. J. Crim. 295 (1987); Marnie E. Rice, *An Evaluation of a Maximum Security Therapeutic Community for Psychopaths and Other Mentally Disordered Offenders*, 16 Law & Hum. Behav. 399 (1992); Henry J. Steadman & Edward J. Holohean, *Estimating Mental Health Needs and Service Utilization Among Prison Inmates*, 19 Bull. Am. Acad. Psychiatry & L. 297 (1991); Joel A. Dvoskin & Henry J. Steadman, *Chronically Mentally Ill Inmates: The Wrong Concept for the Right Services*, 12 Int'l J. L. & Psychiatry 203 (1989)).

[111]Stone, *supra* note 76, at 285.

have a national crisis in dealing with mentally ill inmates but also conduct a detailed examination of inmate's rights in their calls for reform, covering legal arguments from substantive and procedural due process rights and equal protection to the application of the American with Disabilities Act[112] and Section 504 of the Rehabilitation Act of 1973.[113] Yet the conditions inmates with untreated mental illness face often prevent them "from obtaining access to prison programs or rehabilitation plans which could facilitate release and improve post-release success. As a result, inmates with severe mental disorders are virtually condemned to a cycle of criminal offending."[114] Thus, mentally ill inmates may serve longer sentences because of their inability to qualify for early release, and, upon their release, are likely to find themselves yet again involved with the criminal justice system.

IV. REHABILITATION OF THE CRIMINAL OFFENDER

Separate and apart from the issue of caring for the mentally ill while incarcerated is the issue of rehabilitating the criminal. Does the correctional system "correct"? In other words, are we successful in rehabilitating offenders? There are certainly many people who feel "nothing works," and this is supported by both the high overall recidivism rate in the United States, as well as empirical scholarship. But Gaes et al. have taken issue with this conclusion and argued that "most correctional treatments for adult prisoners probably have modest positive effects" while "juvenile interventions seem to have stronger effects."[115]

Gaes et al. have identified six principles for effective correctional treatment based on a meta-analysis of many studies.[116] First, treatment interventions must be linked to "criminogenic characteristics"—those psychological shortcoming that are directly related to an individual's propensity to commit crimes.[117] Examples of such traits include "pro-criminal attitudes, pro-criminal associates, impulsivity, weak socialization, below average verbal intelligence, a taste for risk, weak problem-solving and self-control skills, early onset of antisocial behavior, poor parental practices, and deficits in educational, vocational, and employment skills."[118]

Second, treatment programs should be multi-modal, addressing all criminogenic deficits, not just select ones. This may require sequencing of therapies, addressing basic cognitive and/or emotional deficits first before proceeding to higher-level criminogenic needs.[119]

Third, as we know from educational and developmental psychology, people have different learning styles. Having a treatment program that assumes all people with a particular need will respond to a particular therapy violates this principle. Accordingly, treatment programs must be

---

[112]*E.g.*, Stone, *supra* note 76 (citing, *inter alia*, 42 U.S.C. §§ 12101-213 (1990)).

[113]*Id.* (citing 29 U.S.C. § 794 (1973)).

[114]Stone, *supra* note 76, at 357.

[115]Gerald G. Gaes, Timothy J. Flanagan, Laurence L. Motiuk, and Lynn Stewart, *Adult Correctional Treatment*, 26 CRIME & JUST. 361 (1999).

[116]*Id.* at 363-66.

[117]*Id.* at 363.

[118]*Id.* (citing Donald Arthur Andrews, *The Psychology of Criminal Conduct and Effective Treatment*, *in* WHAT WORKS: REDUCING REOFFENDING – GUIDELINES FROM RESEARCH AND PRACTICE (James McGuire, ed., Wiley 1995)).

[119]*Id.* at 364.

responsive to the particular needs of offenders, matching an inmate's learning style with the teaching style of the professional providing treatment.[120]

Fourth, offenders need to be differentiated by risk. "Higher-risk clients are more likely to benefit from treatment than are lower-risk clients." Targeting the intensity of a treatment program to those who are in the most need and who are most likely to benefit from it should be a part of the implementation of treatment programs.[121]

Fifth, treatment program must provide coping skills—skills that allow offenders to gain both an understanding into anti-social behaviors and mechanisms to resist them. Skills-oriented behavioral-cognitive treatments designed to model and shape pro-social behaviors are among the most effective therapies.[122]

Sixth, there must be continuity of care. "The best intervention will fail if there are insufficient funds or if there is a lack of commitment from treatment staff, administrators, or support staff."[123] This includes the necessity of continuing treatment during and after the period of incarceration. Of course, doing so is challenging, to say the least, but increased coordinated efforts with community care organizations and post-release monitoring is essential for insuring continuity of care. Moreover, post-release treatments will be the most effective "if it is a continuation of the type of treatment delivered in the institutional setting."[124]

Seventh, interventions should be comprehensive and of sufficient duration. This requires monitoring an individual's progress and being responsive to his or her evolving needs. While this is often routine in monitoring dosages of medications, it is much less common in monitoring the sufficiency of ongoing therapies.

With these principles in mind, there are certain therapies that have proven to be more successful in the rehabilitation of inmates than others. The Table 15.2, prepared by Lipsey et al.,[125] compares types of treatments and their effectiveness with juveniles. Similar findings have been found with adults, but it should be noted that the majority of research on the efficacy of therapeutic interventions with convicts has been conducted on juveniles.[126]

---

[120]*Id.*

[121]*Id.*

[122]*Id.*

[123]*Id.* at 364-65.

[124]*Id.* at 365.

[125]Mark W. Lipsey, David B. Wilson & Lynn Cothern, *Effective Intervention For Serious Juvenile Offenders* (U.S. Dept. of Justice, Office of Juvenile Justice and Delinquency Prevention 2000) [available online] <http://www.ncjrs.org/pdffiles1/ojjdp/181201.pdf>.

[126]*See* Gaes et al, *supra* note 115.

Table 15.2: Comparison of Treatment Types in Order of Effectiveness

Types of Treatment Used With Noninstitutionalized Offenders	Types of Treatment Used With Institutionalized Offenders
Positive effects, consistent evidence	
Individual counseling Interpersonal skills Behavioral programs	Interpersonal skills Teaching family homes
Positive effects, less consistent evidence	
Multiple services Restitution, probation/parole	Behavioral programs Community residential Multiple services
Mixed but generally positive effects, inconsistent evidence	
Employment related Academic programs Advocacy/casework Family counseling Group counseling	Individual counseling Guided group counseling Group counseling
Weak or no effects, inconsistent evidence	
Reduced caseload, probation/parole	Employment related Drug abstinence Wilderness/challenge
Weak or no effects, consistent evidence	
Wilderness/challenge Early release, probation/parole Deterrence programs Vocational programs	Milieu therapy

Source: Mark W. Lipsey, David B. Wilson & Lynn Cothern, *Effective Intervention For Serious Juvenile Offenders* (U.S. Dept. of Justice, Office of Juvenile Justice and Delinquency Prevention 2000) [available online] <http://www.ncjrs.org/pdffiles1/ojjdp/181201.pdf>.

V. CONCLUSION

At the dawn of the 21st century, criminal punishment clearly focuses on retribution, deterrence, and incapacitation. But even though rehabilitation of criminal offenders has become less important to society (especially in terms of criminal law and sentencing), it remains a concern within the correctional system. Yet, correctional resources are insufficient to rehabilitate criminal offenders. At the same time, though, if offender-specific treatments that focus on cognitive-behavioral therapy and skills-building are put into place, there is reason to be hopeful that incarceration can rehabilitate criminal offenders.

Rehabilitation, however, is difficult to achieve within the correctional setting for many reasons, not the least of which is that jails and prisons are often unsafe for both inmates and correctional staff. The perils of life in a penal institution are exacerbated by the presence of mentally ill inmates. While most prisoners adapt to prison fairly well, the same cannot be said for those will mental disorders, as they are more likely to be in trouble within the correctional disciplinary system while incarcerated and, as a result, are more likely to be detained longer within the correctional setting—a fact which may worsen their symptoms while incarcerated and doom them to repeat encounters with the law upon release.

Behavioral scientists can help to change the plight of the criminal offender (and thereby help not only the offender, but society as a whole) by developing better treatment programs for the incarcerated. Resources to do so, however, must be provided to them by both the states and federal governments.

Moreover, society can help the incarceration crises in the U.S. by recognizing that the warehousing of criminals without providing treatment and rehabilitative services is, at best, a temporary fix for a serious problem. The development of community-based alternatives to incarceration and better public policies for dealing with the mentally ill hold the most promise for changing the unsettling course of corrections in the United States.

APPENDIX A: SELECTED MENTAL DISORDERS IN THE DSM-IV

I. AN OVERVIEW OF THE DSM

A. Introduction to the DSM and Its Multiaxial Classification System

Mental health professionals use a classification system to describe and diagnose mental disorders. The system is laid out in the American Psychiatric Association's *Diagnostic and Statistical Manual of Mental Disorders*,[1] now in its fourth edition. It is commonly referred to as the DSM. As stated in Chapter Two, the DSM was first created in 1952 and has been through four majors revisions since then. The DSM-IV contains diagnostic criteria for 410 mental disorders.[2]

According the DSM-IV, a *mental disorder* is a:

> clinically significant behavioral or psychological syndrome or pattern that occurs in an individual and that is associated with present distress (e.g., a painful symptom) or disability (i.e., impairment in one or more important areas of functioning) or with a significantly increased risk of suffering death, pain, disability, or an important loss of freedom. In addition, this syndrome or pattern must not be merely an expectable and culturally sanctioned response to a particular event. Whatever its original cause, it must currently be considered a manifestation of a behavioral, psychological, or biological dysfunction in the individual.[3]

The DSM-IV systematically describes a range of disorders subgrouped into sixteen major diagnostic classes (e.g., Substance-Related Disorders, Mood Disorders, Anxiety Disorders, Personality Disorders). Classification within this system extends beyond simply labeling individuals with disorders; assessment also includes a five-tier, multiaxial approach that organizes and communicates additional clinical information.

First introduced in the DSM-III, the DSM-IV uses a classification system that rates an individual on five separate axes (the plural of axis). The principal diagnosis occurs on either Axis I or Axis II. Axis I is specifically reserved for reporting any clinical disorders (e.g., schizophrenia) or conditions from one or more of the diagnostic classes except for personality disorders and mental retardation, both of which are classified as Axis II disorders. The remaining axes are not necessary to make a diagnosis. Rather, they are used to assess other variables that should be taken into account during the clinical assessment of a patient.

Axis I contains all of the major mental disorders that do not fall into the realm of personality disorders or mental retardation. The categories of Axis I disorders are presented in Table A.1. Some of the more prevalent Axis I disorders seen in the forensic context are discussed in detail later in this chapter. Axis II, as mentioned above, includes mental retardation and the personality disorders. The personality disorders specifically included in Axis II are presented in Table A.2.

---

[1] AMERICAN PSYCHIATRIC ASSOCIATION, DIAGNOSTIC AND STATISTICAL MANUAL OF MENTAL DISORDERS (4th ed. 1994) [hereinafter DSM-IV].

[2] Steven I. Friedland, *on Treatment, Punishment, and the Civil Commitment of Sex Offenders*, 70 U. COLO. L. REV. 73, 134 & n.340-42 (1999) (citing ARIZ Sharon Begley, *Is Everybody Crazy?*, NEWSWEEK, Jan. 26, 1998, 52); *see also* Jeanne Louise Carriere, *Reconstructing the Grounds for Interdiction*, 54 LA. L. REV. 1199, 1225 (1994); Phil Brown, *The Name Game: Toward a Sociology of Diagnosis*, 11 J. MIND & BEHAV. 385, 397-99 (1990).

[3] DSM-IV, *supra* note 1, xxi-ii.

Axis III is for reporting current medical conditions that are relevant to understanding and/or managing of the mental disorder. Some such general medical conditions may be parasitic diseases; diseases of the blood, nervous, circulatory, respiratory, or digestive systems; injuries, or poisoning.

Axis IV is reserved for reporting psychosocial and environmental problems that may be influential factors on diagnosis or treatment. These problems are grouped together in nine categories that are presented in Table A.3.

Axis V is reserved for reporting an individual's overall global assessment of functioning. Clinicians determine this by using the Global Assessment of Functioning (GAF) Scale. The scale ranges from 1, usually corresponding to an immediate suicide threat, to 100, indicating the possession of positive qualities and superior functioning. The GAF is valuable in tracking an individual's progress over time, such as from admission to discharge, or from first to last day of treatment. The rating scale is reproduced in Table A.4.

Table A.1: Axis I Disorders

Axis I Category	Diagnoses Included
Disorders Usually First Diagnosed in Infancy, Childhood, or Adolescence	Learning disorders (e.g., dyslexia); motor skill disorders; communication disorders (e.g, stuttering); pervasive developmental disorders (e.g., autism); attention-deficit and disruptive behavior disorders (e.g., ADHD); feeding and eating disorders (e.g., pica); tic disorders (e.g, Tourette's); elimination disorders (e.g, enuresis); and other disorders (e.g., separation anxiety and selective mutism).
Delirium, Dementia, and Amnestic and Other Cognitive Disorders	Delirium (i.e., disturbances of consciousness and cognitive functioning); dementia (i.e, multiple cognitive disorders that includes memory impairment); amnesia; post-concussional disorders following head trauma.
Mental Disorders Due to a General Medical Condition	Any mental disorder (e.g., delirium, dementia, amnesia, psychosis, mood disorders, anxiety disorders, sexual dysfunction) that are the direct physiological consequence of a general medical condition classified on Axis III (previously known as "organic" in nature).
Substance-Related Disorders	Any mental disorder related to the taking of alcohol, drugs (over-the-counter, prescribed, or illicit), or to toxic exposure (e.g., heavy metals, poisons, etc.).
Schizophrenia and Other Psychotic Disorders	Schizophrenia (including paranoid, disorganized, catatonic, undifferentiated, and residual subtypes); schizophreniform disorder; schizoaffective disorder, delusional disorder; brief and/or shared psychotic disorders; substance-induced psychosis.
Mood Disorders	Major depression; dysthymic disorder; bipolar disorder; mania
Anxiety Disorders	Panic attacks; specific phobias; social phobias; obsessive-compulsive disorder; post-traumatic stress disorder; acute stress disorder; generalized anxiety disorder

Axis I Category	Diagnoses Included
Somatoform Disorders	Somatization disorder (i.e., hysteria); conversion disorder; hypochondriasis; and body dysmorphic disorder.
Factitious Disorders	Any disorder the symptoms of which are intentionally produced or feigned to assume the sick role (as opposed to malingering motivated by an external incentive).
Dissociative Disorders	Dissociative amnesia; dissociative fugue; dissociative identity disorder (multiple personality disorder); and depersonalization disorder.
Sexual and Gender Identity Disorders	Hypoactive sexual desire disorder; paraphilias (e.g., exhibitionism, fetishism, frotteurism, pedophilia, sexual sadism or masochism, transvestic fetishism, voyeurism); gender identity disorders.
Eating Disorders	Anorexia nervosa; bulimia nervosa.
Sleep Disorders	Dyssomnias (e.g., insomnia, hypersomnia, narcolepsy, sleep apnea, circadian rhythm sleep disorder); and parasomnias (e.g., nightmare disorder, sleep terror disorder, sleepwalking)
Impulse-Control Disorders Not Elsewhere Classified	Intermittent explosive disorder; kleptomania; pyromania; pathological gambling; and trichotillomania (i.e., recurrent pulling out of one's hair).
Adjustment Disorder	Any clinically significant emotional or behavioral symptom that is a result of an identifiable psychosocial stressor such as the termination of a relationship, getting fired, going away to college, etc. Does not include bereavement.

Table A.2: Axis II Personality Disorders

Personality Disorder	Brief Description
Paranoid Personality Disorder	A pattern of distrust and suspiciousness such that others' motives are interpreted as malevolent.
Schizoid Personality Disorder	A pattern of detachment from social relationships and a restricted range of emotional expression.
Schizotypal Personality Disorder	A pattern of acute discomfort in close relationships, cognitive or perceptual distortions, and eccentricities of behavior.
Antisocial Personality Disorder	A patter of disregard for, and violation of, the rights of others.
Borderline Personality Disorder	A pattern of instability in interpersonal relationships, self-image, affect (moods), and marked impulsivity.
Histrionic Personality Disorder	A pattern of excessive emotionality and attention-seeking.
Narcissistic Personality Disorder	A pattern of grandiosity, need for admiration, and lack of empathy.
Avoidant Personality Disorder	A pattern of social inhibition, feelings of inadequacy, and hypersensitivity to negative evaluations.
Dependent Personality Disorder	A pattern of submissive and clinging behavior related to an excessive need to be taken care of.
Obsessive-Compulsive Personality Disorder	A pattern of preoccupation with orderliness, perfectionism, and control.

Adapted from: DSM-IV at 629.

Table A.3: Axis IV Categories

Problem Category	Examples
Problems with primary support group	Death of a family member; health problems in the family; divorce; marriage; remarriage; birth of a sibling; sexual, physical, or verbal abuse;
Problems related to the social environment	Living alone, discrimination, death or loss of a friend, adjustment to life cycle transition.
Educational problems	Illiteracy, academic problems, discord with teachers or classmates, inadequate school environment.
Occupational problems	Unemployment, threat of job loss, stressful working schedule, job dissatisfaction, job, change, discord with boss or coworkers.
Housing problems	Homelessness, inadequate housing, unsafe neighborhood.
Economic problems	Poverty, inadequate finances, insufficient welfare support.
Problems with access to health care services	Inadequate health care services, unavailable transportation to health care facilities, insurance problems.
Problems related to interaction with the legal system	Arrest, victimization, incarceration, litigation.
Other psychosocial and environmental problems	Exposure to disasters, war, unavailability of social services, discord with nonfamily caregivers.

Table A.4: Global Assessment of Functioning (GAF) Scale

Consider psychological, social, and occupational functioning on a hypothetical continuum of mental health-illness. Do not include impairment in functioning due to physical (or environmental) limitations.

Code	(Note: Use intermediate codes when appropriate, e.g., 45, 68, 72.)
100	Superior functioning in a wide range of activities, life's problems never seem to get out of hand, is
91	sought out by others because of his or her many positive qualities. No symptoms.
90	Absent or minimal symptoms (e.g., mild anxiety before an exam), interested and involved in a
81	wide range of activities, effective, generally satisfied with life, no more than everyday problems or concerns (e.g., an occasional argument with family members).
80	If symptoms are present, they are transient and expectable reactions to psychosocial stressors
71	(e.g., difficulty concentrating after family argument); no more than impairment in social occupational or school functioning (e.g., temporarily falling behind in schoolwork).
70	Some mild symptoms (e.g., depressed mood and mild insomnia) OR some difficulty in social,
61	occupational, or school functioning (e.g., occasional truancy, or theft within the household), but generally functioning pretty well, has some meaningful interpersonal relationships.
60	Moderate symptoms (e.g., flat affect and circumstantial speech, occasional panic attacks) OR
51	moderate difficulty in social occupational or school functioning (e.g. few friends, conflicts with peers or coworkers).
50	Serious symptoms (e.g., suicidal ideation, severe obsessional rituals, frequent shoplifting) OR any
41	serious impairment in social occupational, or school functioning (e.g., no friends, unable to keep a job).
40	Some impairment in reality testing or communication (e.g., speech is at times illogical, obscure, or
31	irrelevant) OR major impairment in several areas, such as work or school, family relations, judgment, thinking, or mood (e.g., depressed man avoids friends, neglects family, and is unable to work; child frequently beats up younger children, is defiant at home, and is failing at school).
30	Behavior is considerably influenced by delusions or hallucinations OR serious impairment in
21	communication or judgment (e.g., sometimes incoherent, acts grossly inappropriately, suicidal preoccupation) OR inability to function in almost all areas (e.g., stays in bed all day; no job, home, or friends).
20	Some danger of hurting self or others (e.g., suicide attempts without clear expectation of death;
11	frequently violent; manic excitement) OR occasionally fails to maintain minimal personal hygiene (e.g., smears feces) OR gross impairment in communication (e.g., largely incoherent or mute).
10	Persistent danger of severely hurting self or others (e.g., recurrent violence) OR persistent inability
01	to maintain minimal personal hygiene OR serious suicidal act with clear expectation of death.
00	Inadequate information

Source: DSM-IV at 32.

B. Use of the DSM in Forensic Settings

When the DSM-IV is used in forensic settings, there is a risk that it will be "misused or misunderstood."[4] First, a DSM diagnosis does not require any information regarding the etiology of a mental disorder. Determining someone to be schizophrenic, for example, says nothing about what may have caused the condition. Moreover, a diagnosis carries no implications concerning an individual's degree of control over behaviors associated (and not associated) with a particular disorder. Even if impulse control is a part of the diagnosed disorder, that does not necessarily mean that the individual could not have controlled himself or herself at the particular time in question. That is just one example of the broader principle that a diagnosis does not, in and of itself, establish any causal link between the disorder and the behaviors about which the law might be concerned. Finally, and most importantly, clinical diagnoses do not translate into answers to the questions posed by the law. While a clinical diagnosis may or may not be ultimately helpful in determining whether an individual meets a specified legal standard (e.g., insanity, incompetency, disability), such determinations require thorough forensic assessment beyond the arrival at a diagnosis.

II. THE PSYCHOSES

The term *psychosis* is used to describe the most serious of mental disorders in which the person suffering from psychosis is impaired so severely that he or she is out-of-touch with reality. The most prominent of the psychoses is schizophrenia, but other psychotic disorders are often subsumed under the label schizophrenic disorders.

A. Schizophrenia

Schizophrenia in a psychotic disorder characterized by severely disturbed thinking, emotions, and perceptions that drastically impair functioning for a time period of at least six months. First conceptualized by Emil Kraepelin as *dementia praecox,* schizophrenia has been described as "arguably the worst disease affecting mankind."[5]

The word schizophrenia is taken from the Greek, "schizo" for split, and "phreno" for mind. Despite the word origin, schizophrenia does not involve what is commonly referred to as a split or multiple personality. Rather, the "split mind" refers to the state of having one's emotions and thoughts split, not only from each other, but from reality as well. [6]

1. Onset and Course

Schizophrenia is a complex disorder for which there is no known cure. Contrary to popular belief, it is a fairly common disorder, with one out of every hundred people in the United States being affected with it.[7] Symptoms of schizophrenia usually begin in the early 20s for men and

---

[4]DSM-IV, *supra* note 1, at xxiii.

[5]Editorial, *Where Next with Psychiatric Illness?*, NATURE, Nov. 10, 1988, at 95.

[6]*See* E. FULLER TORREY, SURVIVING SCHIZOPHRENIA: A FAMILY MANUAL 3 (rev. ed. 1988) (finding 64% of respondents in a survey erroneously thought schizophrenia had to do with multiple personalities).

[7]Anne J. Ryan, Note*: True Protection for Persons with Severe Mental Disabilities, Such as Schizophrenia, Involved as Subjects in Research? A Look and Consideration of the "Protection of Human Subjects,"* 9 J.L. & HEALTH 349, 368 (1994/1995); *see also* TORREY, *supra* note 6, at 3.

late 20s for women.[8] Diagnosed schizophrenics are two to three times more likely to have either never been married, or to be divorced or separated.[9] They are "less likely to have earned a college degree or to be employed . . . ."[10] And although schizophrenia appears in all races and socioeconomic strata, it is "five times more prevalent in lower socioeconomic groups as compared to higher socioeconomic groups."[11]

There is great variability in the course of schizophrenia.

> Some individuals display periodic exacerbations and remissions of the disease while others remain chronically ill. Complete remission, however, is uncommon in this disorder and a substantial number of patients continue to manifest symptoms of schizophrenia throughout their lives. The negative symptoms of the disease are particularly persistent over the course of the illness.[12]

2. Symptoms

Clinicians have grouped the symptoms of schizophrenia into three categories: positive symptoms, negative symptoms, and psychomotor symptoms.

The ***positive symptoms*** of schizophrenia are so termed because they concern pathologically excessive distortions of thinking, perception, language, communication, and behavior monitoring. They include delusions, hallucinations, and disorganized speech (characterized by tangentiality, loose associations, derailment, and incoherence, as well as abnormal speech content, such as perseveration, neologisms, clang associations, and word salad).

The ***negative symptoms*** "reflect a dimunition or loss of normal functions."[13] One of the most common negative symptoms is inappropriate, blunted, or flattened affect. Another common negative symptom is ***alogia***—a poverty of speech characterized by an individual's brief, empty replies or patterns of speech. Many schizophrenics display ***avolition***—a lack of energy. As a result, they often lack the motivation to engage in goal-motivated behavior of even the most routine types, such as eating, maintaining proper hygiene, dressing appropriately, and doing basic chores. ***Asociality*** is often observed in schizophrenics, characterized by "few friends, poor social skills, and little interest in being with other people."[14] ***Anhedonia***, the inability to experience pleasure, is another common negative symptom. It involves a loss of interest in activities that were formerly pleasurable.

The ***psychomotor symptoms*** are impairments of movement. Losing spontaneity of movement, making odd grimaces and facial expressions, and acting in childlike mannerisms are all examples of disorganized behavior. At one extreme, a person might fail to react to environmental stimuli normally. This is known as ***catatonia.*** It includes echopraxia (i.e., imitated movements) and waxy flexibility (i.e., posturing). In its most severe form, known as ***catatonic stupor,*** a patient sits silent and motionless in near complete nonresponsiveness to the

---

[8]DSM-IV, *supra* note 1, at 282.

[9]Office of Technology Assessment, 102d Cong., The Biology of Mental Disorders, Doc. No. OTA-BA-538, 51 (Sept. 1992).

[10]Ryan, *supra* note 7, at 366 (citing *id.*).

[11]*Id.*

[12]*Id.* at 365.

[13]DSM-IV, *supra* note 1, at 274.

[14]Gerald C. Davison & John M. Neale, Abnormal Psychology 268 (7th ed. 1998).

environment. At the other extreme, *catatonic excitement* might occur—"purposeless and unstimulated excessive motor activity."[15]

3. Diagnostic Criteria

The DSM-IV requirements for diagnoses are presented in Table A.5. As should be evident from a review of the table, two or more of the positive, negative, or psychomotor symptoms must be present for a significant period of time over the course of a one-month period (see Criterion A). An exception is made if only one positive symptom is present, so long as that one symptom is either bizarre delusions or hallucinations.

The presence of Criterion A symptoms is not enough for diagnosis. For a significant amount of time since the onset of symptoms, there must be a level of dysfunction that interferes with work, social relations, or self-care (see Criterion B). Additionally, some symptomology must be present for longer that a six-month period (see Criterion C). Finally, symptoms cannot be a consequence of some other mental disorder, substance abuse, developmental disorder, or other general medical condition (see Criteria D-F).

---

[15]DSM-IV, *supra* note 1 at 276.

Table A.5: Diagnostic Criteria for Schizophrenia

A.   Characteristic Symptoms: Two (or more) of the following, each present for a significant portion of time during a 1-month period (or less if successfully treated):
- (1)   delusions
- (2)   hallucinations
- (3)   disorganized speech (e.g., frequent derailment or incoherence)
- (4)   grossly disorganized or catatonic behavior
- (5)   negative symptoms, i.e., affective flattening, alogia, or avolition

        Note: Only one Criterion A symptom is required if delusions are bizarre or hallucinations consist of a voice keeping up a running commentary on the person's behavior or thoughts, or two or more voices conversing with each other.

B.   Social/Occupational Dysfunction: For a significant portion of the time since the onset of the disturbance, one or more major areas of functioning such as work, interpersonal relations, or self-care are markedly below the level achieved prior to the onset (or when the onset is in childhood or adolescence, failure to achieve expected level of interpersonal, academic, or occupational achievement).

C.   Duration: Continuous signs of the disturbance persist for at least six months. This six-month period must include at least one month of symptoms (or less if successfully treated) that meet Criterion A (i.e., active-phase symptoms) and may include periods of prodromal or residual symptoms. During these prodromal or residual periods, the signs of the disturbance may be manifested by only negative symptoms or two or more symptoms listed in Criterion A present in an attenuated form (e.g., odd beliefs, unusual perceptual experiences).

D.   Schizoaffective and Mood Disorder Exclusion: Schizoaffective Disorder and Mood Disorder With Psychotic Features have been ruled out because either (1) no Major Depressive, Manic, or Mixed Episodes have occurred concurrently with the active-phase symptoms; or (2) if mood episodes have occurred during active-phase symptoms, their total duration has been brief relative to the duration of the active and residual periods.

E.   Substance/General Medical Condition Exclusion: The disturbance is not due to the direct physiological effects of a substance (e.g., a drug of abuse, a medication) or a general medical condition.

F.   Relationship to a Pervasive Developmental Disorder: If there is a history of Autistic Disorder or another Pervasive Developmental Disorder, the additional diagnosis of Schizophrenia is made only if prominent delusions or hallucinations are also present for at least a month (or less if successfully treated).

Source: DSM-IV at 285-86.

Once the diagnostic criteria for schizophrenia are met, the disorder can be further classified as one of five subtypes: paranoid, disorganized, catatonic, residual, or undifferentiated.

The essential feature of ***paranoid schizophrenia*** is the dominant presence of one or more delusions or auditory hallucinations almost to the exclusion of all other symptoms. Delusions are most often of the persecutory or grandiose type and hallucinations tend to gravitate towards the same delusional theme. "Associated features include anxiety, anger, aloofness, and argumentativeness."[16]

Those individuals diagnosed with ***disorganized schizophrenia*** (formally called hebephrenic schizophrenia) have three main symptoms present: "disorganized speech, disorganized behavior, and flat or inappropriate affect."[17] ***Catatonic schizophrenia*** is the subtype characterized by any two of the following symptoms: motoric immobility (catatonia); excessive motor activity;

---

[16]*Id.* at 287.

[17]*Id.*

extreme negativism or mutism; peculiarities of voluntary movement (e.g., bizarre postures); and echolalia or echopraxia. ***Residual schizophrenia*** is diagnosed when someone was diagnosed with full-blown schizophrenia in the past, but currently the condition is notably missing positive symptoms (e.g., prominent delusions, hallucinations, disorganized speech, and grossly disorganized or catatonic behavior), yet severe negative symptoms persist. Finally, ***undifferentiated schizophrenia*** is an appropriate subtype diagnosis where the qualifying criteria for a diagnosis of schizophrenia are met, but the criteria are not met for the paranoid, disorganized, catatonic type, or residual subtypes.

B. Schizophrenic-Like Psychoses

The DSM-IV made substantial revisions to the definition of schizophrenia. In narrowing the definition of the disorder, the DSM clarified how schizophrenia differs from other psychoses. All of the following disorders, like schizophrenia, cannot be diagnosed if the symptoms are the direct physiological effects of a drug or a general medical condition. If psychotic symptoms are by the former, the appropriate diagnosis is ***substance-induced psychosis;*** if by the latter, ***psychotic disorder due to general medical condition*** is the diagnosis. Baring these causes, the following psychoses are recognized in the DSM-IV.

Schizophreniform disorder is identical to schizophrenia except for two important distinctions. The Criterion C requirement of symptomology for at least six months is not required for this diagnosis. The Criterion B requirement of impaired social or occupational functioning is also not required, although it may be present. Therefore, so long as the diagnostic requirements of Criteria A, D, and E are met (e.g, active symptoms present for at least one month and are not otherwise explained by other disorders), the diagnosis is appropriate.[18]

Schizoaffective disorder is a disease in which the active symptoms of schizophrenia exist (Criterion A symptoms met), while there is either a major depressive episode, a manic episode, or a mixed episode during which time depressed mood is present.[19] These affective (or mood) disorders will be explained later in this chapter.

If a patient suffers from nonbizarre delusions (defined by the DSM as "situations that occur in real life, such as being followed, poisoned, infected, loved at a distance, deceived . . . "),[20] but the other Criterion A symptoms of schizophrenia are not present, the appropriate diagnosis is called ***delusional disorder.*** Functioning, although impaired to some degree, is not severely impaired, nor is behavior "obviously odd or bizarre."[21] Hallucinations, especially tactile and olfactory ones, may be present if they are not prominent and they are related to the subject of the delusions.

A ***brief psychotic disorder***, formerly known as a brief reactive psychosis, is one in which one or more of the active symptoms of schizophrenia (i.e., Criterion A symptoms) have an acute onset that last anywhere from one to thirty days, after which the person returns to normal functioning. Onset may or may not be due to an intense stressor, although that is common, as is post-partum onset.[22]

---

[18] *Id.* at 290-91.

[19] *Id.* at 295.

[20] *Id.* at 301

[21] *Id.*

[22] *Id.* at 302.

III. MOOD DISORDERS

Mood is defined as "prolonged emotion that colors the whole psychic life."[23] Everyone's moods change during the course of week, a day, or even an hour. As a part of life, we all experience intense natural highs and, unfortunately, we all get a case of the blues from time to time. Such mood changes are normal. They are different from **mood disorders** (formerly known as **affective disorders**). All are Axis I disorders that can be quite debilitating. What differentiate any one of them from "normal" changes in mood are (1) the extremeness of the emotions experienced; and (2) the sustained period of time over which they persist.[24]

A. Major Depression

Major depression is one of the most common of mental disorders. One of the earliest terms was "melancholia," literally meaning "black bile." It dates back to the time of Hippocrates in Ancient Greece. Each of us has experienced periods of depression associated with the loss of a loved one, the break-up of a romantic relationship, or some unexpected serious setback. What differentiates that type of common depression, often referred to as **dysphoria,** from major clinical depression is the intensity of the depressive feelings and how long they last. Dysphoric states are "less pervasive and run a more time-limited course" than major depression.[25]

1. Onset and Course

Depression can strike anyone at anytime, although some people are at much greater risk of depression than others. It is one of the most common forms of disability worldwide.[26] It has a "life-time prevalence rate of about 17 percent. It is about twice as common in women as in men; it occurs more frequently among members of lower socioeconomic classes, and most frequently among young adults."[27]

The National Institute of Health estimates that more than 17.6 million Americans suffer from some type of depression.[28] Between 70 and 80 percent of patients treated with antidepressant drugs will experience relief from depression.[29] If untreated, symptoms usually remit within eight or nine months, but subsequently reoccur in nearly 90 percent of cases.[30] Between 70 and 80 percent of those affected with depression will experience a recurrence of the disorder, usually

---

[23]DONALD W. GOODWIN & SAMUEL B. GUZE, PSYCHIATRIC DIAGNOSIS 3 (4th ed. 1989).

[24]*Id.*

[25]*Adults and Mental Health: Mood Disorders in* UNITED STATES PUBLIC HEALTH SERVICE, MENTAL HEALTH: A REPORT OF THE U.S. SURGEON GENERAL, Ch. 4, § 3 (Government Printing Office Stock No. 017-024-01653-5) (available on-line at <http://www.surgeongeneral.gov/library/mentalhealth/chapter4/sec3.html>).

[26]Christopher J.L. Murray J., & Alan D. Lopez, *Evidence-Based Health Policy — Lessons from the Global Burden of Disease Study*, 274 SCI. 740–743 (1996).

[27]DAVISON & NEALE, *supra* note 14, at 227.

[28]Douglas A. Blair, *Employees Suffering from Bipolar Disorder or Clinical Depression: Fighting an Uphill Battle for Protection Under Title I of the Americans with Disabilities Act*, 29 SETON HALL L. REV. 1347 (1999) (citing Kenneth E. Young & William H. Foster III, *Stress and Mental Disorders in the Workplace: Increased Focus Under the Americans With Disabilities Act*, 8 S.C. LAW. 33, 33 (July/Aug., 1996)).

[29]Robert Michels & Peter M. Marzuk, *Progress in Psychiatry*, 329 NEW ENG. J. MED. 628, 628-29 (1993).

[30]Michael E. Thase & L.R. Sullivan, L. R., *Relapse and Recurrence of Depression: A Practical Approach for Prevention*, 4 CNS DRUGS 261–277 (1995).

within three to five years; it will be chronic for 15 percent of all depression patients.[31] And 10 to 15 percent of patients who are hospitalized for depression eventually commit suicide.[32] Major depressive disorders account for about 20 to 35 percent of all deaths by suicide.[33]

2. Symptoms of a Major Depressive Episode

A *major depressive episode* is characterized by a depressed mood, a loss of motivation, and/or anhedonia (i.e., loss of interest in pleasurable activities).[34] The feelings must last most of the day, nearly every day for at least two weeks. People who are depressed generally feel intensely sad and report feelings of emptiness, worthlessness, and/or despair. Crying spells are also quite common, and at times an individual might vocalize somatic complaints (e.g., body aches or pains, feeling sick-like, or overly fatigued). Also common, although mostly in children and adolescents, a major depressive episode might produce irritability, or feelings of anxiousness, anger, or frustration.[35]

Depressed individuals lose the desire to participate in daily activities.[36] Most report a lack of drive or initiative, and must force themselves to engage in the activities necessary for functioning (e.g., working, eating, exercising, and/or maintaining hygiene), if they can muster the ability to do so.[37] Friends or family members might notice that the individual is socially withdrawn, and no longer finds interest in formally pleasurable pastimes, often including sex.

Appetite changes in both directions usually occur, often with corresponding weight loss or gain (e.g., a change of more than 5 percent of body weight in a month). Depressed individuals spend more time in bed and experience hypersomnia or insomnia nearly every day. Some might initially have trouble falling to sleep, returning to sleep after waking up during the night or waking up too early, or even waking up at all. Psychomotor functioning is also disturbed. Some individuals might become overly agitated, not being able to sit still or continually pacing, while others might exhibit slowed or retarded speech, thinking and/or body movements. Decreases in energy and fatigue are common, even in the absence of any physical exertion. Depressed people often feel that even small tasks require too much energy to be accomplished.[38]

Certain cognitive distortions are present during a major depressive episode. There may be feelings of excessive worthlessness or inappropriate guilt. Depressed individuals hold negative evaluations of their self-worth and believe the future to be bleak and empty. Such individuals might also blame themselves for uncontrollable occurrences or misinterpret trivial day-to-day events as unchanging character flaws or defects. Sometimes the feelings of worthlessness and guilt can be so severe as to be characterized as delusional and may even be accompanied by mood-congruent hallucinations.[39] Further distortions might include a depressed person's "inability to think, concentrate, or make decisions."[40] At the extreme, both memory and other

---

[31]*Id.*

[32]Jules Angst et al., *Suicide Risk in Patients with Major Depressive Disorder*, 60 J. CLINICAL PSYCHIATRY 57–62 (1999).

[33]*Id.*

[34]DSM-IV, *supra* note 1, at 320.

[35]*Id.*; *see also* DAVISON & NEALE, *supra* note 14, at 226; GOODWIN & GUZE, *supra* note 23, at 15.

[36]DSM-IV, *supra* note 1, at 321.

[37]*Id.*

[38]*Id.*

[39]GOODWIN & GUZE, *supra* note 23, at 16.

[40]DSM-IV, *supra* note 1, at 322.

cognitive functioning may be impaired, although they are often imagined by the individual and they disappear after the depression lifts.

A common component of a major depressive disorder is the recurrent thought of death or suicide. Thoughts could range from just feeling "that others would be better off if the person were dead, to transient [1 to 2 minute] but recurring [once or twice per week] thoughts of suicide, to actual specific plans of how to commit suicide."[41] Motivations behind suicide thoughts and attempts are usually do the feelings of hopelessness associated with insurmountable life problems or obstacles.

3. Diagnostic Criteria for Major Depressive Episode

The requirements for a diagnosis of major depression are presented in Table A.6. Criterion A lists the emotional and behavioral symptoms from which a diagnosis may be made. Criterion B requires the absence of manic symptoms for a diagnosis of major depression. Criterion C is the standard requirement that the symptoms interfere with normal social or occupational functioning. Criterion D mirrors the requirement of all of the major Axis I disorders by indicating diagnosis is not appropriate if Criterion A factors are a result of the ingestion of drugs or a general medical condition. Finally, Criterion E limits the applicability of the diagnosis for those grieving the loss of a loved one.

---

[41] *Id.*

Table A.6: Diagnostic Criteria for Major Depressive Episode

A.   Five (or more) of the following symptoms have been present during the same two-week period and represent a change from previous functioning; at least one of the symptoms is either (1) depressed mood or (2) loss of interest or pleasure.

Note: Do not include symptoms that are clearly due to a general medical condition, or mood-incongruent delusions or hallucinations.

    (1)   depressed mood most of the day, nearly every day, as indicated by either subjective report (e.g., feels sad or empty) or observation made by others (e.g., appears tearful). Note: In children and adolescents, can be irritable mood.

    (2)   markedly diminished interest or pleasure in all, or almost all, activities most of the day, nearly every day (as indicated by either subjective account or observation made by others).

    (3)   significant weight loss when not dieting or weight gain (e.g., a change of more than 5 percent of body weight in a month), or decrease or increase in appetite nearly every day. Note: In children, consider failure to make expected weight gains.

    (4)   insomnia or hypersomnia nearly every day.

    (5)   psychomotor agitation or retardation nearly every day (observable by others, not merely subjective feelings of restlessness or being slowed down).

    (6)   fatigue or loss of energy nearly every day.

    (7)   feelings of worthlessness or excessive or inappropriate guilt (which may be delusional) nearly every day (not merely self-reproach or guilt about being sick).

    (8)   diminished ability to think or concentrate, or indecisiveness, nearly every day (either by subjective account or as observed by others).

    (9)   recurrent thoughts of death (not just fear of dying), recurrent suicidal ideation without a specific plan, or a suicide attempt or a specific plan for committing suicide.

B.   The symptoms do not meet criteria for a Mixed Episode.

C.   The symptoms cause clinically significant distress or impairment in social, occupational, or other important areas of functioning.

D.   The symptoms are not due to the direct physiological effects of a substance (e.g., a drug of abuse, a medication) or a general medical condition (e.g., hypothyroidism).

E.   The symptoms are not better accounted for by bereavement, (i.e., after the loss of a loved one, [unless] the symptoms persist for longer than two months [after the loss of a loved one] or are characterized by marked functional impairment, morbid preoccupation with worthlessness, suicidal ideation, psychotic symptoms, or psychomotor retardation.

Source: DSM-IV at 327.

4. Relation to Major Depressive Disorders

When one or more major depressive episodes occur over a relatively short period of time, an individual most likely can be diagnosed with a pattern of unipolar depression. A diagnosis of **major depressive disorder** requires the presence of one or more major depressive episodes. In contrast, **recurrent major depressive disorder** is diagnosed when there is a presence of two or more major depressive episodes with at minimum of two months between each episode. Unipolar depression can also be seasonal and fluctuate with the weather, or it can be postpartum and follow the birth of a child.

Individuals who display a more chronic, but less debilitating pattern of depression might receive a diagnosis of **dysthymic disorder.** Dysthymia is a chronic mood disturbance characterized by a loss of interest or pleasure in most activities of daily life but not meeting the full criteria for a major depressive episode. The diagnosis of dysthymia requires mild to moderate mood depression most of the time for a duration of at least two years.

B. Mania

Mania is, in an odd way, the opposite of depression. It comes from a French word meaning "frenzied."[42] The symptoms of mania affect the same areas of functioning as do the symptoms of depression, but they do so in drastically different ways. A *manic episode* is defined by a period of time (lasting at least one week) during which "an abnormally and persistently elevated, expansive, or irritable mood" is present.[43] The euphoria experienced must be disproportionate to what is actually going on in the individual's life.

1. Symptoms of a Manic Episode

A manic individual may become overly enthusiastic for everyday interpersonal, social, or other areas of functioning. This over-enthusiasm is often accompanied by hyperactivity, talkativeness, flight of ideas, distractibility, and impracticality.[44] Some manic individuals can become overly irritable and angry especially when things do not goes as they planned. Regardless, usually three or more of the following symptoms must be present to a significant degree in order to qualify the diagnosis of a manic episode.

A manic individual typically experiences inflated self-esteem "ranging from uncritical self-confidence to marked grandiosity [that may even] reach delusional proportions" in which the individual might believe he or she is "larger than life" or have more a reason to exist than the average human being.[45] When this symptom is present, an individual may feel like they are an expert on everything, even in areas in which experience or talent is objectively lacking.

A decreased need for sleep is a hallmark of mania. After sleeping only a few hours, the manic individual may be full of energy and show no signs of sleep deprivation. In more extreme cases, an individual may stay awake for days, requiring no sleep to keep functioning without feeling tired.[46]

The behavior, including speech, of an individual having a manic episode is very active. People with mania generally move very quickly and race from task to task as if always in a hurry. Typically, their speech is characterized as being rapid, loud, and often difficult to understand given the rapid rate of speech and the flight of ideas in speech content.[47] Sometimes, manics can talk nonstop for hours, often becoming theatrical, with dramatic and flamboyant mannerisms and movements.

As with depression, cognitive impairment may also be present. Not only do the thoughts of the manic person often race, but they are also subject to easy distractibility. And judgment is frequently impaired, especially with regard to the consequences of one's actions. For example, manics often get themselves involved with dangerous activities, reckless sexual encounters, risky

---

[42]Surgeon General on Mental Health, *supra* note 25.

[43]DSM-IV, *supra* note 1, at 328.

[44]Davison & Neale, *supra* note 14, at 226.

[45]DSM-IV, *supra* note 1, at 328.

[46]*Id.*

[47]*Id.* at 329.

business deals, and other activities that provide a "rush" or make the person the center of attention. Shopping sprees during which the manic has no concern for the financial consequences of his or her spending are also quite common. Hospitalization is often necessary to protect the person from his or her own recklessness.

There is usually an increase in goal-directed behaviors in educational, occupational, or sexual spheres.[48] And, almost always, there is an increase in social functioning. And while social interaction with someone on a manic high might be briefly enjoyable (i.e., an infectiously good mood), their need to be the center of constant social interaction will usually produce social interactions in which they are overbearing, domineering, and demanding in nature. This often makes it unpleasant for close family and friends to be around the manic person, although the manic individual will likely not notice this, or, if they do, they will likely not understand it.

2. Diagnostic Criteria for a Manic Episode

The DSM criteria for diagnosis of a manic episode are presented in Table A.7. Criterion A defines the mood required for diagnosis. Criterion B lists the feelings or behaviors from which three or more must have been persistent during the week of elevated, expansive, or irritable mood required under Criterion A. Criteria C, D, and E require, as most Axis I disorders do, that the mood disturbance impair social, occupational, or education functioning, and that the symptoms are not due to drugs, alcohol, a general medical condition, or other pathological condition.

---

[48]*Id.*

Table A.7: Criteria for Manic Episode

A.   A distinct period of abnormally and persistently elevated, expansive, or irritable mood, lasting at least one week (or any duration if hospitalization is necessary).

B.   During the period of mood disturbance, three (or more) of the following symptoms have persisted (four if the mood is only irritable) and have been present to a significant degree:

   (1)   inflated self-esteem or grandiosity.

   (2)   decreased need for sleep (e.g., feels rested after only three hours of sleep).

   (3)   more talkative than usual or pressure to keep talking.

   (4)   flight of ideas or subjective experience that thoughts are racing.

   (5)   distractibility (i.e., attention too easily drawn to unimportant or irrelevant external stimuli).

   (6)   increase in goal-directed activity (either socially, at work or school, or sexually) or psychomotor agitation.

   (7)   excessive involvement in pleasurable activities that have a high potential for painful consequences (e.g., engaging in unrestrained buying sprees, sexual indiscretions, or foolish business investments).

C.   The symptoms do not meet criteria for a Mixed Episode.

D.   The mood disturbance is sufficiently severe to cause marked impairment in occupational functioning or in usual social activities or relationships with others, or to necessitate hospitalization to prevent harm to self or others, or there are psychotic features.

E.   The symptoms are not due to the direct physiological effects of a substance (e.g., a drug of abuse, a medication, or other treatment) or a general medical condition (e.g., hyperthyroidism).

Source: DSM-IV at 332.

3. Hypomania

A *hypomanic episode* (*hypomania*) is a less severe version of a manic episode. Like mania, it requires "a distinct period of abnormally and persistently elevated, expansive, or irritable mood."[49] It also requires at least three other symptoms from the list under Criterion B for mania. But unlike mania, the symptoms need to last for only four days, as opposed to the week required for a manic episode diagnosis. More importantly, the symptoms cannot be severe enough to have caused marked impairment in social, occupational, or educational functioning, even though they were observable by others. Hence, hypomania is not associated with marked impairments in judgment or performance, nor is it associated with any psychotic symptoms (e.g., grandiose delusions).[50] In fact, it is often associated with great creativity.

Hypomania is a transitional phase into full mania for about half of the people who experience the disorder; the other half never experience full-blown mania.[51] It is also seen as a side-effect in people being treated for a major depressive episode with antidepressant drugs.[52]

---

[49]*Id.* at 335.

[50]*See* Frederick K. Goodwin & Kay Redfield Jamison, Manic-Depressive Illness (1990).

[51]*Id.*

[52]*Id.*

C. Mixed Episodes

Mixed episodes are diagnosed when an individual has experienced symptoms qualifying for both a major depressive episode and a manic episode. The diagnostic criteria for both mood disturbances must be met with the exception of duration. Instead, the criteria for both disorders has to have occurred during a one-week period.

D. Bipolar Disorders

Bipolar Disorder is a mood disorder in which a history of major depression is combined with reoccurrences of manic or hypomanic episodes. It used to be known as "manic depression." Depending on the combination of the underlying episodes, bipolar disease is classified as either Bipolar I (prior manic episode) or Bipolar II (prior hypomanic episode). In other words, a diagnosis of *Bipolar I* is appropriate if the patient has experienced one or more major depressive episodes, as well as either one or more manic episodes, or one or more mixed episodes. *Bipolar II* disorders are characterized by the presence of one or more major depressive episodes accompanied only by a history of hypomanic, not full-blown manic or mixed episodes.

> About 1.1 percent of the adult population suffers from the type I form, and 0.6 percent from the type II form. Episodes of mania occur, on average, every 2 to 4 years, although accelerated mood cycles can occur annually or even more frequently. The type I form of bipolar disorder is about equally common in men and women, unlike major depressive disorder, which is more common in women.[53]

Despite the milder manic symptoms in Bipolar II, "the prognosis for patients with bipolar type II disorder is poorer than that for recurrent (unipolar) major depression, and there is some evidence that the risk of rapid cycling (four or more episodes each year) is greater than with bipolar type I."[54]

IV. ANXIETY DISORDERS

Anxiety disorders are diagnosed when a person suffers from a pathological level of anxiety. Pathological anxiety is not the same level of nervousness or anxiousness that everyone feels from time to time when facing a stressful situation. Rather, *pathological anxiety* is concerned with "intense apprehension, fearfulness, or terror, often associated with a sense of impending doom."[55]

A. Panic Attacks and Agoraphobia

The DSM-IV lists any number of diagnostic causes of anxiety. They all, however, share something in common. The anxiety causes either panic attacks or agoraphobia, or both.

---

[53]Surgeon General on Mental Health, *supra* note 25 (citing GOODWIN & JAMISON *supra* note 50; Raymond G. Kessler et al., *Lifetime and 12-month Prevalence of DSM-III-R Psychiatric Disorders in the United States. Results from the National Comorbidity Survey*, 51 ARCH. GEN. PSYCHIATRY 8–19 (1994)).

[54]Surgeon General on Mental Health, *supra* note 25 (citing William Coryell et al., *Rapidly Cycling Affective Disorder: Demographics, Diagnosis, Family History, and Course*, 49 ARCH. GEN. PSYCHIATRY 126–131 (1992)).

[55]DSM-IV, *supra* note 1, at 393.

1. Panic Attacks

A *panic attack* is a "discrete period of intense fear or discomfort that is accompanied by" four or more panic symptoms.[56] Panic attacks appear suddenly (also called sudden onset) and usually peak within ten minutes. They are accompanied by an intense urge to escape or flee because of some imagined or perceived imminent danger. They can be totally unexpected, coming "out of nowhere"; be situationally bound or cued (i.e., invariably occurring "on exposure to or in anticipation of" the triggering cue; or situationally predisposed (i.e., more likely to occur in a given context, but not invariably triggered by the cue).[57]

The criteria for a panic attack are presented in Table A.8. It is important to note that it is inappropriate to diagnosis a panic attack in and of itself. Instead, it is diagnosed in the context of some other anxiety disorder (e.g., panic disorder, either with or without agoraphobia).

Table A.8: Criteria for Panic Attack

A discrete period of intense fear or discomfort, in which four or more of the following symptoms developed abruptly and reached a peak within ten minutes:

    (1)   palpitations, pounding heart, or accelerated heart rate

    (2)   sweating

    (3)   trembling or shaking

    (4)   sensations of shortness of breath or smothering

    (5)   feeling of choking

    (6)   chest pain or discomfort

    (7)   nausea or abdominal distress

    (8)   feeling dizzy, unsteady, lightheaded, or faint

    (9)   derealization (feelings of unreality) or depersonalization (being detached from oneself)

    (10) fear of losing control or going crazy

    (11) fear of dying

    (12) paresthesias (numbness or tingling sensations)

    (13) chills or hot flushes

Source: DSM-IV at 395.

---

2. Agoraphobia

Agoraphobia is a condition that causes an individual extreme "anxiety about being in places or situations from which escape might prove difficult (or embarrassing) or in which help may not be available in the event of having a panic attack . . . or panic-like symptoms."[58] Individuals with agoraphobia avoid the places or situations that trigger the panic. The criteria for diagnosis are presented in Table A.9. It can be diagnosed in association with another anxiety disorder (e.g., panic disorder with agoraphobia), or on its own when there is no history of a panic disorder (e.g,

---

[56]*Id.* at 394.

[57]*Id.* at 394-95.

[58]*Id.* at 396.

when "the focus of fear is on the occurrence of incapacitating or extremely embarrassing panic-like symptoms or limited-symptom attacks, rather than full panic attacks").[59]

Table A.9: Criteria for Agoraphobia

A. Anxiety about being in places or situations from which escape might prove difficult (or embarrassing) or in which help may not be available in the event of having an unexpected or situationally predisposed panic attack or panic-like symptoms. Agoraphobia hears typically involve characteristic clusters of situations that include being outside the home alone; being in a crowd or standing in line; being on a bridge; and traveling in a bus, train, or automobile. Note: Consider the diagnosis of specific phobia is the avoidance is limited to one or only a few specific situations, or social phobia if the avoidance is limited to social situations.

B. The situations are avoided (e.g., travel is restricted) or else are endured with marked distress or with anxiety about having a panic attack or panic-like symptoms, or require the presence of a companion.

C. The anxiety or phobic avoidance is not better accounted for by another mental disorder, such as social phobia (e.g., avoidance limited to social situations because of fear of embarrassment), specific phobia (e.g., avoidance limited to a single situation like elevators), obsessive-compulsive disorder (e.g., avoidance of dirt in someone with an obsession about contamination), posttraumatic stress disorder (e.g., avoidance of stimuli associated with a severe stressor), or separation anxiety disorder (e.g, avoidance of leaving home or relatives).

Source: DSM-IV at 396-97.

B. Panic Disorder

A *panic disorder* is characterized by the presence of "recurrent, unexpected Panic Attacks" followed by at least one month of one of the following: (a) "persistent concern about having additional attacks"; (b) "worry about the possible implications or consequences of the attack (e.g., losing control, having a heart attack, 'going crazy'")", or (c) "a significant behavioral change related to the attacks."[60] As with other diagnoses, the attacks cannot be due to alcohol, drugs, or a general medical condition, nor can they be better accounted for by another diagnosis. Panic disorders can occur with or without agoraphobia.

C. Specific Phobia

A *specific phobia* is defined as "marked and persistent fear that is excessive or unreasonable, cued by the presence or anticipation of a specific object or situation (e.g., flying, heights, animals, receiving an injection, seeing blood) . . . [that] almost invariably provokes an immediate anxiety response which may take the form of a situationally-bound or situationally predisposed Panic Attack."[61] The trigger cannot be fear of a socially embarrassing situation (since that is a social phobia) or of being in a public place (since that is agoraphobia).

Adolescents and adults with a specific phobia realize that their fears are excessive or unreasonable, but nonetheless remain fearful and avoid the phobia situation or object at all costs. Such avoidance must interfere with daily, occupational, social, or academic performance.

Included in the diagnosis for specific phobia are categories of specific types of feared objects or situations. The *animal type,* primarily having an onset in childhood, usually involves the fear

---

[59]*Id.* at 403.

[60]*Id.* at 402.

[61]*Id.* at 410.

of animals (zoophobia) or insects (entomophobia). The **natural environment type,** also generally having an onset in childhood, includes fears of objects in the natural environment such as heights (acrophobia), water (hydrophobia), or wind (anemophobia). The **blood-injection-injury type** is specified by a fear of blood (hematophobia), injury or illness (nosemaphobia), or injections (trypanophobia). The situational type should be specified in the diagnosis if fear is caused by a situations such as flying (aerophobia), crossing a bridge (gephyrophobia), travel (hodophobia), and/or enclosed spaces (claustrophobia). Finally, the "*other type*" includes fears about other nonspecified stimuli including choking (pnigophobia), noise or loud talking (phonophobia), and sleeping (hypnophobia).

D. Social Phobia

Social phobia (otherwise known as social anxiety disorder) is characterized by "a marked and persistent fear of one or more social or performance situations in which the person is exposed to unfamiliar people or to possible scrutiny by others. The individual fears that he or she will act in a way (or show anxiety symptoms) that will be humiliating or embarrassing."[62] The person might not be physically able to speak due to persistent hand shaking, voice shaking, or other panic symptoms associated with the disorder.

As with other anxiety disorders, "exposure to the feared social situation almost invariably provoked anxiety."[63] Accordingly the situations are either avoided or endured with intense distress, the result of which is interference with social, occupational, or academic functioning. As with specific phobias, this diagnosis is only warranted if the individual knows his or her fear is unreasonable or excessive, yet avoids the situation anyway.

E. Obsessive-Compulsive Disorder

The hallmark of **Obsessive-Compulsive Disorder** (OCD) is the presence of obsessions, compulsions, or both. **Obsessions** are intrusive, recurrent thought, impulses, and images that come unbidden to the mind[,] appear irrational and uncontrollable to the individual experiencing them[,] . . . [and] interfere with normal functioning."[64] **Compulsions** are repetitive behaviors or mental acts "that the person feels driven to perform in order to reduce the distress caused by obsessive thoughts or to prevent some calamity from happening."[65] Often, compulsive behaviors have little or nothing to do with the obsessions, or are clearly excessive reactions to them.

1. Diagnostic Criteria

OCD is a debilitating illness. The "thoughts, impulses, and images are not simply excessive worries about real-life problems."[66] Quite the contrary, they are often unrelated to the ordinary difficulties of everyday life. Moreover, they cause marked distress that can severely impair functioning in a variety of spheres. They might occupy hours of a person's day, interfering with the ability to meet social, occupation, and academic responsibilities. They may even cause other

---

[62]*Id.* at 416.

[63]*Id.* at 417.

[64]Davison & Neale, *supra* note 14, at 142.

[65]*Id.*

[66]DSM-IV, *supra* note 1, at 418.

medical problems. For example, someone might wash their hands so many times per day that they bleed. The person suffering from OCD has some insight (the level varies) into the fact that their thoughts and behaviors are excessive or unreasonable but are without the ability to stop the obsessions and/or compulsions in spite of such insight.

Table A.10: Criteria for Obsessive-Compulsive Disorder

A.   Either obsessions or compulsions:

Obsessions as defined by (1), (2), (3), and (4):

    (1)   recurrent and persistent thoughts, impulses, or images that are experienced, at some time during the disturbance, as intrusive and inappropriate and that cause marked anxiety or distress;

    (2)   the thoughts, impulses, or images are not simply excessive worries about real-life problems;

    (3)   the person attempts to ignore or suppress such thoughts, impulses, or images, or to neutralize them with some other thought or action;

    (4)   the person recognizes that the obsessional thoughts, impulses, or images are a product of his or her own mind (not imposed from without as in thought insertion).

Compulsions as defined by (1) and (2):

    (1)   repetitive behaviors (e.g., hand washing, ordering, checking) or mental acts (e.g., praying, counting, repeating words silently) that the person feels driven to perform in response to an obsession, or according to rules that must be applied rigidly;

    (2)   the behaviors or mental acts are aimed at preventing or reducing distress or preventing some dreaded event or situation; however, these behaviors or mental acts either are not connected in a realistic way with what they are designed to neutralize or prevent or are clearly excessive.

B.   At some point during the course of the disorder, the person has recognized that the obsessions or compulsions are excessive or unreasonable. Note: This does not apply to children.

C.   The obsessions or compulsions cause marked distress, are time consuming (take more than one (1) hour a day), or significantly interfere with the person's normal routine, occupational (or academic) functioning, or usual social activities or relationships.

D.   If another Axis I disorder is present, the content of the obsessions or compulsions is not restricted to it (e.g., preoccupation with food in the presence of an Eating Disorder; hair pulling in the presence of Trichotillomania; concern with appearance in the presence of Body Dysmorphic Disorder; preoccupation with drugs in the presence of a Substance Use Disorder; preoccupation with having a serious illness in the presence of Hypochondriasis; preoccupation with sexual urges or fantasies in the presence of a Paraphilia; or guilty ruminations in the presence of Major Depressive Disorder).

E.   The disturbance is not due to the direct physiological effects of a substance (e.g., a drug of abuse, a medication) or a general medical condition.

Specify Type as "With Poor Insight" if, for most of the time during the current episode, the person does not recognize that the obsessions and compulsions are excessive or unreasonable.

Source: DSM-IV at 422-23.

2. Relationship to Other Disorders

Although obsessive-compulsive disorder and obsessive compulsive personality disorder have similar names, the clinical manifestations of these disorders are quite different. Obsessive-compulsive personality disorder is not characterized by the presence of obsessions or compulsions, bur rather involves a pervasive pattern of preoccupation with orderliness, perfectionism, and control and must begin by early adulthood. If an individual manifests symptoms of both obsessive-compulsive disorder and obsessive-compulsive personality disorder, both diagnoses can be given.

Other behaviors that are frequently confused with OCD involve "compulsive" eating, gambling, sexual activity, drinking, and the like. Even though people describe "irresistible urges" to engage in such activities, they are not true compulsions because they bring pleasure to the individual. In contrast, true compulsions are engaged in due to anxiety, and are often disconcerting to the person experiencing them.[67]

F. Posttraumatic Stress Disorder

Posttraumatic Stress Disorder (PTSD) is the diagnosis given to those people who suffer anxiety symptoms after they are exposed to an extremely traumatic stressor that involved actual death or serious bodily injury, or the real threat of either. The diagnostic criteria for the disorder are presented in Table A.11.

Table A.11: Criteria for Posttraumatic Stress Disorder

A.   The person has been exposed to a traumatic event in which both of the following were present:

   (1)   the person experienced, witnessed, or was confronted with an event or events that involved actual or threatened death or serious injury, or a threat to the physical integrity of self or others

   (2)   the person's response involved intense fear, helplessness, or horror. Note: In children, this may be expressed instead by disorganized or agitated behavior

B.   The traumatic event is persistently reexperienced in one (or more) of the following ways:

   (1)   recurrent and intrusive distressing recollections of the event, including images, thoughts, or perceptions. Note: In young children, repetitive play may occur in which themes or aspects of the trauma are expressed.

   (2)   recurrent distressing dreams of the event. Note: In children, there may be frightening dreams without recognizable content.

   (3)   acting or feeling as if the traumatic event were recurring (includes a sense of reliving the experience, illusions, hallucinations, and dissociative flashback episodes, including those that occur on awakening or when intoxicated). Note: In young children, trauma-specific reenactment may occur.

   (4)   intense psychological distress at exposure to internal or external cues that symbolize or resemble an aspect of the traumatic event.

   (5)   physiological reactivity on exposure to internal or external cues that symbolize or resemble an aspect of the traumatic event.

C.   Persistent avoidance of stimuli associated with the trauma and numbing of general responsiveness (not present before the trauma), as indicated by three or more of the following:

   (1)   efforts to avoid thoughts, feelings, or conversations associated with the trauma.

   (2)   efforts to avoid activities, places, or people that arouse recollections of the trauma.

   (3)   inability to recall an important aspect of the trauma.

   (4)   markedly diminished interest or participation in significant activities.

   (5)   feeling of detachment or estrangement from others.

   (6)   restricted range of affect (e.g., unable to have loving feelings).

---

[67]Davison & Neale, *supra* note 14, at 143.

(7)   sense of a foreshortened future (e.g., does not expect to have a career, marriage, children, or a normal life span).

D.   Persistent symptoms of increased arousal (not present before the trauma), as indicated by two or more of the following:

     (1)   difficulty falling or staying asleep.

     (2)   irritability or outbursts of anger.

     (3)   difficulty concentrating.

     (4)   hypervigilance.

     (5)   exaggerated startle response.

E.   Duration of the disturbance (symptoms in Criteria B, C, and D) is more than one (1) month.

F.   The disturbance causes clinically significant distress or impairment in social, occupational, or other important areas of functioning.

Specify if:

Acute: if duration of symptoms is less than three months; Chronic: if duration of symptoms is three months or more

With Delayed Onset: if onset of symptoms is at least six months after the stressor

Source: DSM-IV at 427–429.

V. DISSOCIATIVE DISORDERS

The *dissociative disorders* all share the symptom of *dissociation* in common. Dissociation has been defined as a "psycho-physiological process whereby information – incoming, stored, or outgoing—is actively deflected from integration with its usual or expected associations."[68] Whether sudden or gradual, short-term or chronic, dissociation results in "disruption in the usually integrated functions of consciousness, memory, identity, or perception of the environment.[69] There are four main dissociative disorders.

Dissociative amnesia is the "inability to recall important personal information, usually of a traumatic or stressful nature, that is too extensive to be explained by ordinary forgetfulness."[70] The memory loss nearly always surrounds the period during and immediately after the traumatic event (having witnessed the death of a loved one is a common one), but in rare cases it continues from the event forward to the present, or can even cover periods from earlier in life.[71]

Dissociative fugue "is characterized by sudden, unexpected travel away from home or one's customary place of work, accompanied by an inability to recall one's past and confusion about personal identity or the assumption of a new identity."[72] When a new identity is assumed, it can be a completely different life than the one the person lived before the onset of fugue state,

---

[68]Louis J. West, *Dissociative Reactions*, in COMPREHENSIVE TEXTBOOK OF PSYCHIATRY 890, 890 (A.M. Freedman & H.I. Kaplan eds., 1967).

[69]DSM-IV, *supra* note 1, at 477.

[70]*Id.* at 477.

[71]DAVISON & NEALE, *supra* note 14, at 167.

[72]DSM-IV, *supra* note 1, at 477.

involving different jobs, social networks, and even different personality characteristics.[73] These states tend be last for relatively short periods of time and recovery is usually complete.[74]

In contrast to the two above disorders which involve impairment of both memory and reality testing, if one is in touch with reality and memory functions properly, yet the patient still experiences feelings of detachment from self and thought processes, then the proper diagnosis is **depersonalization disorder.** These "out-of-body experiences" can involve seeing oneself at a distance, feeling mechanical, or going through life as if it were not a real experience.[75] Many people experience nonpathological forms of this. Daydreaming, for example, can briefly dissociate oneself from reality such that we fail to hear the phone or what someone was saying to us. "Highway hypnosis" is another example—those times when we seem to drive on autopilot "not really concentrating on our driving . . . but we nevertheless obeyed all traffic rules and arrived safely at our destination with little, if any, memory of how we got there or what occurred along the way."[76]

By far, the most interesting and controversial of the disorders in this Axis I category is **Dissociative Identity Disorder** (DID), formerly known as multiple personality disorder. The disease "reflects a failure to integrate various aspects of identity, memory and consciousness."[77] The diagnostic criteria for the disorder is presented in Table A.12.

Table A.12: Criteria for Dissociative Identity Disorder

A. The presence of two or more distinct identities or personality states (each with its own relatively enduring pattern of perceiving, relating to, and thinking about the environment and self).

B. At least two of these identities or personality states recurrently take control of the person's behavior.

C. Inability to recall important personal information that is too extensive to be explained by ordinary forgetfulness.

D. The disturbance is not due to direct physiological effects of a substance (e.g., blackouts or chaotic behavior during alcohol intoxication) or general medical condition (e.g., complex partial seizures). Note: In children, the symptoms are not attributable to imaginary playmates or other fantasy play.

Source: DSM-IV at 487.

Like the other dissociative disorders, DID is thought to be caused by trauma. It is most frequently experienced by victims of "severe, recurrent traumatic experiences usually occurring during childhood or early adolescence . . . [during which] . . . dissociation is a normal process that is initially used defensively by [the] individual to handle traumatic experiences and evolves . . . into a maladaptive or pathological [disorder.]"[78] In other words, the dissociation acts as a sort of "protective amnesia" so that the person does not have to cope with the trauma.[79] Case

---

[73]DAVISON & NEALE, *supra* note 14, at 169.

[74]*Id.*

[75]*Id.* at 170.

[76]Mark Anthony Miller, *The Unreliability of Testimony From a Witness With Multiple Personality Disorder (MPD): Why Courts Must Acknowledge the Connection Between Hypnosis and MPD and Adopt a "Per Se" Rule of Exclusion for MPD Testimony,* 27 PEPP. L. REV. 193, 199 (2000) (citing FRANK W. PUTNAM, DIAGNOSIS AND TREATMENT OF MULTIPLE PERSONALITY DISORDER 10 (1989)).

[77]DSM-IV *supra* note 1, at 484.

[78]PUTNAM, *supra* note 76, at 8-9.

[79]EUGENE L. BLISS, MULTIPLE PERSONALITY, ALLIED DISORDERS, AND HYPNOSIS 143 (1986).

histories have demonstrated that 97 percent of patients in two extensive studies all suffered from such childhood trauma, usually of a sexually abusive nature.[80] Due to this evidence, some mental health professionals think of MPD as a type of posttraumatic stress syndrome.[81]

The multiple personalities experienced by someone with DID can be subtle differences in character traits.[82] But the personalities can also be so different that it is impossible to believe that the same physical being could exhibit such dramatically differing traits. The personalities often speak in their own unique voices, sometimes using a different accent, or even a foreign language. They are often different-handed, wear glasses with different prescriptions, have different intelligent quotients, perform differently on cognitive functioning tests, use different vocabulary, have different genders and/or sexual orientations, and even have different blood pressures, electro-encephalogram, and galvanic skin responses.[83]

For this diagnosis to apply, there must be at least two personalities. But having only two is quite rare—a fact that is often used to detect malingering. Most people develop several distinct personalities. It is not uncommon for there to be between ten and twenty, although in rare cases, upwards of a hundred have been reported.[84] Some of the personalities may be aware of the existence of others, while others are completely unaware that anything out-of-the ordinary transpires with them other than the fact that they sometimes "lose time."

Diagnosis of DID is difficult, taking, on average, more than six and a half years to diagnose. Problems with diagnosis range from symptomology, which might be misdiagnosed as a psychosis, to hesitance to make a DID diagnosis. Such hesitance often stems from the fact that hypnosis is usually needed to both diagnose and treat DID, yet, by its nature, is highly suggestive and often unreliable.[85]

VI. THE PERSONALITY DISORDERS

A. Personality Disorders in General

The personality disorders classified on Axis II were presented earlier in this chapter in Table A.2. As a review of that table should make clear, the personality disorders contain a varied mix of mental disorders. A *personality disorder* is defined as "an enduring pattern of inner experiences and behavior that deviates markedly from the expectations of the individual's culture; is pervasive and inflexible; has an onset in adolescence or early adulthood; is stable over time; and leads to distress or impairment."[86] The general criteria for diagnosing any personality disorder is presented in Table A.13.

The DSM-IV has divided the personality disorders into clusters—groups of disorders that have some common theme running through them. Cluster A, also called the "odd/eccentric" cluster, includes disorders in which strange or bizarre behaviors not rising to the level of

---

[80]Elyn R. Saks, *Multiple Personality Disorder and Criminal Responsibility*, 25 U.C. DAVIS L. REV. 383, 394 n.34 (1992) (citing Richard P. Kluft, *An Update on Multiple Personality Disorder*, 38 HOSP. & COMMUNITY PSYCHIATRY 363, 366 (1987)).

[81]*Id.* at 395 (citing Kluft, *supra* note 80, at 364).

[82]Sabra McDonald Owens, *The Multiple Personality Disorder (MPD) Defense*, 8 Md. J. Contemp. L. Issues 237, 242 (1997).

[83]*See generally* Sacks, *supra* note 80.

[84]SANDRA J. HOCKING, SOMEONE I KNOW HAS MULTIPLE PERSONALITIES 70 (1994).

[85]*See generally, e.g.*, Owens, *supra* note 82; Miller, *supra* note 76; Jacqueline R. Kanovitz, et al., *Witnesses With Multiple Personality Disorder*, 23 PEPP. L. REV. 387 (1996).

[86]DSM-IV, *supra* note 1, at 629.

psychosis are classified. Cluster B is called the "dramatic/erratic" cluster. It contains disorders in which variable types of behavior not rising to the level of a mood or somatoform disorder are classified. And Cluster C is called the "anxious/fearful" cluster, which contains disorders in which behaviors not meeting the diagnostic criteria for a full-blown anxiety disorder are classified.

It is important to differentiate personality traits from personality disorders. All of us have certain quirks or idiosyncracies that make us who we are. Many of such traits will mirror the diagnostic criteria for one or more of the Axis II personality disorders. For example, most good professors (i.e., those who are engaging, funny, inspiring, and good at both communicating their knowledge and at motivating students to learn) display histrionic and narcissistic personality traits. What distinguishes such professors from those suffering from the associated personality disorders is the intensity, duration, and effects of their personality traits. The personality disorders involve extremes in traits that are inflexible, maladaptive, persistent across time and situations, and cause impairment in life functioning.[87]

It should also be noted that many personality disorders are ***comorbid*** with Axis I disorders. ***Comorbidity*** means that two or more disorders exist together and, can even contribute to one and other. With these qualifications in mind, we now turn to the specifics of selected personality disorders.

Table A.13: General Diagnostic Criteria for a Personality Disorder

A.   An enduring pattern of inner experience and behavior that deviates markedly from the expectations of the individual's culture. This pattern is manifested in two or more of the following areas:

         (1)   cognition (i.e., ways of perceiving and interpreting self, other people, and events)

         (2)   affectivity (i.e., the range, intensity, and appropriateness of emotional response)

         (3)   interpersonal functioning

         (4)   impulse control

B.   The enduring pattern is inflexible and pervasive across a broad range of personal and social situations.

C.   The enduring pattern leads to clinically significant distress or impairment in social, occupational, or other important areas of functioning.

D.   The pattern is stable and of long duration and its onset can be traced back at least to adolescence or early adulthood.

E.   The enduring pattern is not better accounted for as a manifestation or consequence of another mental disorder.

F.   The enduring pattern is not due to the direct physiological effects of a substance (e.g., a drug of abuse, a medication) or a general medical condition (e.g., head trauma).

Source: DSM-IV at 633.

---

[87] *Id.*

B. The Odd/Eccentric Cluster of Personality Disorders

1. Paranoid Personality Disorder

As you might recall from our earlier review of psychoses, a number of Axis I disorders may involve ***paranoia***, a "pervasive distrust and suspiciousness of others such that their motives are interpreted as malevolent."[88] ***Paranoid personality disorder*** also concerns paranoia, but it differs from psychoses in that there is an absence of psychotic symptoms, such as hallucinations and delusions. To be diagnosed with this disorder, the paranoia must meet the general criteria for a personality disorder and have at least four of the following symptoms:

> (1) suspects, without sufficient basis, that others are exploiting, harming, or deceiving him or her; (2) is preoccupied with unjustified doubts about the loyalty or trustworthiness of friends or associates; (3) is reluctant to confide in others because of unwarranted fear that the information will be used maliciously against him or her; (4) reads hidden demeaning or threatening meanings into benign remarks or events; (5) persistently bears grudges, (i.e., is unforgiving of insults, injuries, or slights); (6) perceives attacks on his or her character or reputation that are not apparent to others and is quick to react angrily or to counterattack; [and] (7) has recurrent suspicions, without justification, regarding fidelity of spouse or sexual partner.[89]

2. Schizoid Personality Disorder

Schizoid refers to detachment from social relationships and a restricted range of expression of emotions in interpersonal settings. One with ***schizoid personality disorder*** manifests schizoid traits in accordance with the general requires for all personality disorders and experiences at least four of the following symptoms:

> (1) neither desires nor enjoys close relationships, including being part of a family; (2) almost always chooses solitary activities; (3) has little, if any, interest in having sexual experiences with another person; (4) takes pleasure in few, if any, activities; (5) lacks close friends or confidants other than first-degree relatives; (6) appears indifferent to the praise or criticism of others; [and] (7) shows emotional coldness, detachment, or flattened affectivity.[90]

As with paranoid personality disorder, a lack of psychotic symptoms is required for this diagnosis. If psychotic symptoms are present, an Axis I psychosis is the more appropriate diagnosis.

---

[88] *Id.* at 637.

[89] *Id.* at 637-38.

[90] *Id.* at 641.

3. Schizotypal Personality Disorder

This disorder is conceptually one of the more difficult personality disorders because its diagnostic criteria is quite similar to those of some Axis I psychoses. Like with schizoid personality disorder, the **schizotypal personality** will be detached from social relationships and have a reduced capacity for close relationships. Additionally, though, the schizotypal personality will also manifest cognitive and behavioral distortions. Five or more of the following symptoms are required for diagnosis:

> (1) ideas of reference (excluding delusions of reference); (2) odd beliefs or magical thinking that influences behavior and is inconsistent with subcultural norms (e.g., superstitiousness, belief in clairvoyance, telepathy, or "sixth sense"; in children and adolescents, bizarre fantasies or preoccupations); (3) unusual perceptual experiences, including bodily illusions; (4) odd thinking and speech (e.g., vague, circumstantial, metaphorical, overelaborate, or stereotyped); (5) suspiciousness or paranoid ideation; (6) inappropriate or constricted affect; (7) behavior or appearance that is odd, eccentric, or peculiar; (8) lack of close friends or confidants other than first-degree relatives; [and] (9) excessive social anxiety that does not diminish with familiarity and tends to be associated with paranoid fears rather than negative judgments about self.[91]

C. The Dramatic/Erratic Cluster

1. Antisocial Personality Disorder

Arguably, no other diagnosis in the DSM has provoked as much controversy at **antisocial personality disorder** (ASPD). This diagnosis epitomizes the medicalization of deviance insofar as it classifies delinquent and/or criminal behavior as a mental illness. As you will see throughout this book, the law has steadfastly rejected this diagnosis as a qualifying mental illness for the purposes of incapacity to stand criminal trial,[92] insanity,[93] diminished capacity,[94] civil commitment,[95] and a wide variety of civil competencies.[96] A review of the diagnostic criteria presented in Table A.14 might illustrate why the law is so hostile to this diagnosis.

Before reviewing the diagnostic criteria for ASPD, two caveats should be made. First, as with all of the personality disorders, care should be taken not to confuse some anti-social personality traits with the full-blown psychiatric disorder. Second, special care must be taken when conducting a clinical assessment of someone who may be anti-social personality disordered. They may omit key facts during assessment, exaggerate or completely fabricate other facts, or select their words so carefully as to intentionally mislead the evaluator.[97] Accordingly, a complete case history is of paramount importance since the clinical interview may be unreliable in light of the nature of the disorder.

---

[91]*Id.* at 645.

[92]See Chapter Four.

[93]See Chapter Six.

[94]See Chapter Seven.

[95]See Chapter Eight.

[96]See Chapter Nine.

[97]William H. Reid, *Antisocial Personality, Psychopathy, and Forensic Psychiatry*, 14 J. Psychiatric Prac. 55 (2001).

Table A.14: Criteria for Antisocial Personality Disorder

A.   There is a pervasive pattern of disregard for and violation of the rights of others occurring since age 15 years, as indicated by three or more of the following:

    (1)   failure to conform to social norms with respect to lawful behaviors as indicated by repeatedly performing acts that are grounds for arrest.

    (2)   deceitfulness, as indicated by repeated lying, use of aliases, or conning others for personal profit or pleasure.

    (3)   impulsivity or failure to plan ahead.

    (4)   irritability and aggressiveness, as indicated by repeated physical fights or assaults.

    (5)   reckless disregard for safety of self or others.

    (6)   consistent irresponsibility, as indicated by repeated failure to sustain consistent work behavior or honor financial obligations.

    (7)   lack of remorse, as indicated by being indifferent to or rationalizing having hurt, mistreated, or stolen from another.

B.   The individual is at least age 18 years.

C.   There is evidence of conduct disorder with onset before age of fifteen (15) years

    [Note: Conduct disorder includes aggression to people and animals (bullying, threatening, initiating fights, using a weapon, robbery, forcing sexual activity); destruction of property (including by fire); deceitfulness or theft (including break & entering, shoplifting); and serious rule violations (truancy or running away).]

D.   The occurrence of antisocial behavior is not exclusively during the course of Schizophrenia or a Manic Episode.

Source: DSM-IV at 649–650.

There was a time when antisocial personality disorder was simply the clinical term used to described "psychopaths," but today, largely due to the work of Dr. Robert Hare, behavioral scientists tend to differentiate between true *psychopathy* and ASPD. Psychopathy is reserved for people meeting the more stringent criteria set forth in Hare's Psychopathy Checklist-Revised (PCL-R).[98] The PCL-R is a twenty-item instrument used primarily to detect psychopathy in males in a forensic setting. It is administered by a trained evaluator after engaging in a semi-structured interview with an evaluee and after having reviewed his institutional file.[99] Not only has research demonstrated the validity of PCL-R, it has also revealed its usefulness as a predictor of dangerousness.[100]

Unlike the DSM-IV, which focuses mainly on behaviors, psychopathy is also concerned with the affective and interpersonal dimensions of behavior. Psychopaths are egocentric, selfish, liars, callous, and are devoid of a moral conscience by societal standards.[101] Yet, the true psychopath "is neither neurotic, psychotic, nor emotionally disturbed, as commonly believed."[102] Instead, the psychopath often exhibits superficial charm, appears friendly and outgoing, and is above-average

[98]Robert D. Hare, The Hare Psychopathy Checklist—Revised Manual (North Tonawanda, NY: 1991).

[99]*Id.*; Curt Bartol, Criminal Behavior: A Psychosocial Approach 94 (6th ed., Prentice Hall 2002).

[100]Mairead Dolan & M. Doyle, *Violence Risk Prediction: Clinical and Actuarial Measures and the Role of the Psychopathy Checklist*, 177 British J. Psychiatry 303-11 (2000).

[101]Bartol, *supra* note 99, at 81.

[102]*Id.* at 88.

in intelligence, although psychopaths may come across as being more intelligent than they really are.[103] Some of the differences between ASPD and psychopathy are presented in Table A.15.

Table A.15: Comparing Antisocial Personality Disorder and Psychopathy

Antisocial Personality Disorder	Psychopathy
Broader, more inclusive	Narrower, more severe, more likely to be reflected in criminality
Primarily behavior-based approach to diagnosis (i.e., persistent violations of social norms, including lying, stealing, truancy, inconsistent work behavior and traffic arrests)	Based on both behaviors and personality deficits, most especially egocentricity, deceit, shallow affect, manipulativeness, selfishness, and lack of empathy, guilt or remorse
Focuses on antisocial behaviors	Includes many behaviors associated with other personality disorders as well, including narcissistic, histrionic, paranoid, and borderline

Adapted from William H. Reid, *Antisocial Personality, Psychopathy, and Forensic Psychiatry*, 14 J Psychiatric Prac 55, 56 (2001), and Robert D. Hare, *Psychopathy and Antisocial Personality Disorder: A Case of Diagnostic Confusion*, 13 Psychiatric Times (2003).

In spite of the criminal conduct that is often associated with ASPD, not all criminals suffer from ASPD. In fact, most studies estimate that between 50 and 80 percent of the prison inmate population qualify for an ASPD diagnosis.[104] In contrast, only about one-third would qualify for diagnosis as a true psychopath.[105] The psychopath, however, is a category of offender who is far more dangerous to society.[106] One of the primary reasons for this is that ASPD offenders tend to "age out" of their criminal conduct, but psychopaths do not.[107] In fact, psychopathy is considered to be a critical factor in the assessment of risk of future dangerousness and its diagnosis, and therefore, "can affect decisions involving civil commitment, parole from prison, access to treatment, detention under dangerous offender legislation, and even capital sentencing."[108]

---

[103]*Id.* at 90; Hervey Cleckley, The Mask of Sanity (6th ed., Mosby 1988).

[104]Reid, *supra* note 97, at 56 (citing T.A. Widiger & E. Corbitt, *Antisocial Personality Disorder*, in The DSM-IV Personality Disorders 103-34 (W.J. Livesley, ed., New York: Guilford, 1995).

[105]*Id.*

[106]*Id.*

[107]*E.g.,* Ray DeV Peters, Robert J. McMahon & Vernon L. Quinsey (eds.), Aggression and Violence Throughout the Life Span (Sage Publications 1992); Stephen D. Hart, *Psychopathy and Risk for Violence*, in Psychopathy: Theory, Research, and Implications for Society 355-73 (D.J. Cooke, A.E. Forth, & R.D. Hare, eds. 1998).

[108]James Hemphill & Stephen D. Hart, *Forensic and Clinical Issues in the Assessment of Psychopathy*, in 11 Handbook of Psychology: Forensic Psychology 86 (Alan M. Goldstein, ed., John Wiley & Sons, Inc. 2003).

2. Borderline Personality Disorder

The **borderline personality** is an unstable one. The disorder requires "a pattern of instability in interpersonal relationships, self-image, and affects, and marked impulsivity."[109] This is manifested by the persistence of five or more of the following:

> (1) frantic efforts to avoid real or imagined abandonment (do not include suicidal or self-mutilating behavior covered in Criterion 5); (2) a pattern of unstable and intense interpersonal relationships characterized by alternating between extremes of idealization and devaluation; (3) identity disturbance: markedly and persistently unstable self-image or sense of self; (4) impulsivity in at least two areas that are potentially self-damaging (e.g., spending, sex, substance abuse, reckless driving, binge eating) (do not include suicidal or self-mutilating behavior covered in Criterion 5); (5) recurrent suicidal behavior, gestures, or threats, or self-mutilating behavior; (6) affective instability due to a marked reactivity of mood (e.g., intense episodic dysphoria, irritability, or anxiety usually lasting a few hours and only rarely more than a few days); (7) chronic feelings of emptiness; (8) inappropriate, intense anger or difficulty controlling anger (e.g., frequent displays of temper, constant anger, recurrent physical fights); [and] (9) transient, stress-related paranoid ideation or severe dissociative symptoms.[110]

3. Histrionic Personality Disorder

The **histrionic personality** exhibits a pattern of excessive emotionality and attention seeking behaviors. This pattern is indicated by the presence of five or more of the following symptoms:

> (1) is uncomfortable in situations in which he or she is not the center of attention; (2) interaction with others is often characterized by inappropriate sexually seductive or provocative behavior; (3) displays rapidly shifting and shallow expression of emotions; (4) consistently uses physical appearance to draw attention to self; (5) has a style of speech that is excessively impressionistic and lacking in detail; (6) shows self-dramatization, theatricality, and exaggerated expression of emotion; (7) is suggestible, i.e., easily influenced by others or circumstances; [and] (8) considers relationships to be more intimate than they actually are.[111]

4. Narcissistic Personality Disorder

The **narcissistic personality** is one where there is a pattern of grandiosity (in fantasy or behavior), a need for admiration, and a lack of empathy. For diagnosis, the pattern must be evidenced by five or more of the following:

> (1) has a grandiose sense of self-importance (e.g., exaggerates achievements and talents, expects to be recognized as superior without commensurate achievements); (2) is preoccupied with fantasies of unlimited success, power, brilliance, beauty, or ideal love; (3) believes that he or she is "special" and unique and can only be understood by, or should associate with, other special or high-status people (or institutions); (4) requires excessive admiration; (5) has a sense of entitlement, i.e., unreasonable expectations of especially favorable treatment or automatic compliance with his or her expectations; (6) is interpersonally exploitative (i.e., takes advantage of others to achieve his or her own ends); (7) lacks empathy: is unwilling to recognize or identify with the feelings and needs of others; (8) is often envious of others or believes that others are envious of him or her; [and] (9) shows arrogant, haughty behaviors or attitudes.[112]

---

[109]DSM-IV, *supra* note 1, at 654.

[110]*Id.*

[111]*Id.* at 657-58.

[112]*Id.* at 661.

D. The Anxious/Fearful Cluster

1. Avoidant Personality Disorder

The *avoidant personality* is socially inhibited, feels inadequate, and is hypersensitive to negative evaluation. Four or more of the following are required for diagnosis:

> (1) avoids occupational activities that involve significant interpersonal contact, because of fears of criticism, disapproval, or rejection; (2) is unwilling to get involved with people unless certain of being liked; (3) shows restraint within intimate relationships because of the fear of being shamed or ridiculed; (4) is preoccupied with being criticized or rejected in social situations; (5) is inhibited in new interpersonal situations because of feelings of inadequacy; (6) views self as socially inept, personally unappealing, or inferior to others; [and] (7) is unusually reluctant to take personal risks or to engage in any new activities because they may prove embarrassing.[113]

2. Dependent Personality Disorder

A *dependent personality* needs to be taken care of to an excess. Characterized by submissive and clinging behavior and fear of separation, the disorder requires five or more of the following for diagnosis:

> (1) has difficulty making everyday decisions without an excessive amount of advice and reassurance from others; (2) needs others to assume responsibility for most major areas of his or her life; (3) has difficulty expressing disagreement with other because of fear of loss of support or approval (note: do not include realistic fears of retribution); (4) has difficulty initiating projects or doing things on his or her own (because of a lack of self-confidence in judgment or abilities rather than a lack of motivation or energy); (5) goes to excessive lengths to obtain nurturance and support from others, to the point of volunteering to do things that are unpleasant; (6) feels uncomfortable or helpless when alone because of exaggerated fears of being unable to care for himself or herself; (7) urgently seeks another relationship as a source of care and support when a close relationship ends; [and] (8) is unrealistically preoccupied with fears of being left to take care of himself or herself.[114]

3. Obsessive-Compulsive Personality Disorder

The *obsessive-compulsive personality* is one preoccupied with orderliness, perfectionism, and control. Such preoccupation is at the expense of flexibility, openness, and efficiency. For diagnosis, four or more of the following criteria must be met:

> (1) is preoccupied with details, rules, lists, order, organization, or schedules to the extent that the major point of the activity is lost; (2) shows perfectionism that interferes with task completion (e.g., is unable to complete a project because his or her own overly strict standards are not met); (3) is excessively devoted to work and productivity to the exclusion of leisure activities and friendships (not accounted for by obvious economic necessity); (4) is overconscientious, scrupulous, and inflexible about matters of morality, ethics, or values (not accounted for by cultural or religious identification); (5) is unable to discard worn-out or worthless objects even when they have no sentimental value; (6) is reluctant to delegate tasks or to work with others unless they submit to exactly his or her way of doing things; (7) adopts a miserly spending style

---

[113]*Id.* at 664-65.

[114]*Id.* at 668-69.

toward both self and others; money is viewed as something to be hoarded for future catastrophes; [and] (8) shows rigidity and stubbornness.[115]

VII. ORGANIC COGNITIVE IMPAIRMENTS

A number of mental disorders significantly impair cognition and memory functioning. The etiology of several of these disorders is known to be due to a medical condition or to a toxic substance. The two most important cognitive impairments for forensic psychology are delirium and dementia. "A *delirium* is characterized by a disturbance of consciousness and a change in cognition that develop over a short period of time"; "a *dementia* is characterized by multiple cognitive deficits that include impairment in memory."[116]

Although memory impairment is typically more pronounced in dementia (that is especially the case with long-term memory impairment), memory dysfunction is common to both diagnoses. The key difference between the two disorders is the disturbance in consciousness that occurs in delirium, but not in dementia.

A. Delirium

A *delirium* is a disturbance of consciousness marked by "reduced clarity of awareness of the environment, with reduced ability to focus, sustain, or shift attention."[117] It comes from the Latin meaning "out-of-track."[118] It is coupled by a change in cognition, such as memory deficit (especially short-term memory), disorientation (especially to time and place), language disturbances, and/or perceptual disturbances not better accounted for by dementia.[119] Delirium is often acute (setting in over the course of only hours or days) and is usually reversible.

Delirium can affect people of any age, although it is most commonly seen in children and in older adults.[120] Delirium affects "10 percent of all hospitalized patients, 20 percent of burn patients, 30 percent of ICU patients, and 30 percent of hospitalized AIDS patients."[121] It affects between 10 and 26 percent in the general surgical population, "with significantly higher rates in certain surgical subpopulations, particularly the elderly, patients who have undergone orthopaedic procedures, and patients undergoing eye surgery or cardiotomy."[122] And the mortality rate for delirium is quite high, with approximately 40 percent of patients dying from either the underlying condition or from exhaustion.[123]

---

[115]*Id.* at 672-73.

[116]*Id.* at 123.

[117]*Id.* at 129, 131, 132.

[118]DAVISON & NEALE, *supra* note 14, at 460.

[119]DSM-IV, *supra* note 1, at 129, 131, 132.

[120]DAVISON & NEALE, *supra* note 14, at 461.

[121]Robert L. Herting, Jr. & Nora R. Frohberg, *Neurology: Delirium, in* UNIVERSITY OF IOWA FAMILY PRACTICE HANDBOOK Chapter 14 (Mark A. Graber et al., eds., 3d ed. 1999) <http://www.vh.org/Providers/ClinRef/FPHandbook/Chapter14/03-14.html>.

[122]*Drug-Induced Delirium: Diagnosis, Management, and Prevention,* 10(3) DRUGS & THERAPY PERSPECTIVES 5-9 (Alison J. Forbes ed., 1997) [hereinafter "Drug Induced Delirium"] <http://surgery.medscape.com/adis/DTP/1997/v10.n03/dtp1003.2/dtp1003.2.html>

[123]DAVISON & NEALE, *supra* note 14, at 461.

1. Causes of Delirium

There are a number of causes of delirium. By far, the most common cause of delirium is drugs. Nearly any drug can cause delirium, but the most common ones to do so include: opiate and salicylate analgesics, antiarrhythmics (e.g., lidocaine, procainamide); certain antibiotics; anti-convulsants (especially primidone and phenobarbital); anti-hypertensives (especially methyldopa); anti-inflammatory drugs (especially steroids); anti-Parkisonisms (especially L-DOPA); anti-depressants; barbiturates; benzodiazepines; neuroleptics; hallucinogens; sympathomimetics (especially cocaine, amphetamines, and phenylephrine); and bromides.[124]

Systemic infections, fever, and shock are among the most common causes of delirium. Acute metabolic disorders (e.g., acidosis, electrolyte disturbances, hepatic or renal failure, dehydration, hyperthermia or hypothermia, and trauma—especially head trauma) are other common causes of delirium. Pathology of the central nervous system (e.g., hemorrhages, seizures, strokes, tumors); hypoxia (due to anemia, hypotension, pulmonary and/or cardiac failure, and pulmonary embolisms); vitamin and mineral deficiencies; and endocrinopathies (e.g., thyroid dysfunction, adrenal dysfunction, hyper- or hypoglycemia); and toxic exposure (especially to heavy metals like lead manganese, and mercury) are also all causes of delirium.[125]

2. Symptoms of Delirium

The primary symptoms of delirium include: impaired attention and concentration; disorganized thinking; reduced levels of consciousness; perceptual disturbances (visual and auditory hallucinations, as well as paranoid delusions are quite common, although not required for diagnosis)[126]; altered behavior and mood (especially mood swings); poor judgment and insight; inability to problem solve; profound changes in sleep patters; disorientation; and marked increase or decrease in motor activity.

3. Levels of Delirium

Because delirium involves impairment of low-level functioning, all higher-ordered functioning of the brain is impaired. The level of impairment is often assessed on a three-tiered scale. Level I impairment is concerned with consciousness. Level I functioning is assessed on a four-point continuum from being alert to comatose. If the patient is awake, aware, interacting, and responsive to stimuli, although not necessarily attentive, he or she is said to be *alert.* If the patient can be aroused, but does not maintain arousal, the patient is said to be *lethargic.* The patient is *stuporous* if he or she can only be slightly aroused with intense stimulation. And finally, if the patient is *comatose,* arousal, even with the most painful of stimuli, is not possible.

Level II impairment is concerned with attention and concentration. It is assessed by monitoring the patient's ability to be task-oriented while obtaining the case history and conducting the mental status examination. Scores of 24 and below on the Folstein MMSE indicate significant cognitive impairment. Level III impairment is concerned with behavior. It is

---

[124]Drug-Induced Delirium, *supra* note 122.

[125]David A. Casey et al., *Delirium: Quick Recognition, Careful Evaluation, and Appropriate Treatment*, 100 Postgraduate Medicine 121 (1996); Herting & Frohberg, *supra* note 121.

[126]Davison & Neale, *supra* note 14, at 461.

assessed by observing appearance and dress; motor activity; facial expression; mood and affect; and overall behavior during the clinical interview.

B. Dementia

Declines in memory and cognitive abilities are a normal consequence of aging.[127] But severe impairment of both short- and long-term memory are not a part of normal aging nor is disintegration of personality due to impaired insight and judgment. When such symptoms occur, a person is much more likely to be experiencing some form of *dementia*—a chronic, progressive, and usually nonreversible loss of higher mental functions affecting memory, cognition, and ability to function independently.

1. Causes of Dementia

There are more than seventy types of dementia, but between 80 and 90 percent of all dementias are caused either by Alzheimer's disease (due primary to deterioration of brain tissue) or vascular dementia (formerly known as "multi-infarct dementia," a type of dementia caused by cardiovascular disease, primarily due to multiple vascular lesions in the cerebral cortex of the brain).[128] The DSM-IV includes diagnostic criteria for several types of dementia: Dementia of the Alzheimer's Type, Vascular Dementia, Dementia due to HIV Disease, Dementia due to Head Trauma, Dementia due to Parkinson's Disease, Dementia due to Huntington's Disease, Dementia due to Pick's Disease, Dementia due to Creutzfeldt-Jakob Disease, Dementia due to Other General Medical Conditions, Substance-Induced Persisting Dementia, as well as Dementia due to Multiple Etiologies.

2. Symptoms of Dementia

Cognitive deficits, especially in short- and long-term memory, are the hallmarks of dementia. Memory impairment, affecting either the ability to learn new information or the ability to recall previously learned information, or both, is a requirement for diagnosis.[129] In early stages, this may manifest itself by misplacing valuables, getting lost, and forgetting to complete routine tasks like cooking, cleaning, etc. As the disease progresses, however, memory impairment can be severe, including the inability to recall one's own name and family members.[130] Unlike with delirium, dementia does not involve impairment of consciousness, attention, or concentration until late in the course of disease.

Memory impairment alone is insufficient for a diagnosis of dementia. At least one of the following other important cognitive disturbances must coexist with the memory impairment: (a) aphasia (i.e., language disturbances, such as difficulty in producing the names of individuals or objects, or excessive use of generalized words such as "it" or "thing")[131]; (b) apraxia (i.e.,

---

[127]FERGUS I.M. CRAIK & TIMOTHY SALTHOUSE (EDS.), HANDBOOK OF AGING AND COGNITION (1992).

[128]Robert L. Herting, Jr. & Nora R. Frohberg, *Neurology: Dementia, in* UNIVERSITY OF IOWA FAMILY PRACTICE HANDBOOK Chapter 14 (Mark A. Graber et al., eds., 3d ed. 1999) <http://www.vh.org/Providers/ClinRef/FPHandbook/Chapter14/02-14.html>.

[129]DSM-IV, *supra* note 1, at 142.

[130]*Id.* at 134.

[131]*Id.*

impaired ability to carry out motor activities despite intact motor function, such as combing hair, brushing teeth, dressing, writing, and drawing)[132]; (c) agnosia (failure to recognize or identify objects despite intact sensory function); or (d) disturbance in executive functioning (i.e., planning, organizing, sequencing, abstracting).[133] These cognitive deficits must impair social or occupational functioning; represent a decline from a previous level of functioning; and not be better accounted for by either a delirium or an Axis I disorder.[134]

Dementia also typically involves changes in the patient's personality. Mood swings, aggressive outbursts, suspiciousness, marked irritability (may even seem to be inappropriate affect in later stages of the disease), apathy or indifference, and anxiety and depression may be present as the disease progresses.[135]

VIII. THE PARAPHILIAS

Paraphilia is a generic term used to broadly refer to a group of inappropriately deviant sexual activities or sexual thoughts. According to the DSM, the essential features of the paraphilias are "recurrent, intense sexually arousing fantasies, sexual urges, or behaviors that involve unusual objects, activities, or situations and cause clinically significant distress or impairment in social, occupational, or other important areas of functioning."[136] The objects of sexual attraction in the paraphilias are either inappropriate people, such as children, those impaired in a manner such that they cannot consent to sex, or the dead, or to inappropriate objects, such as articles of clothing.

A. Types of Paraphilias

There are several common types of paraphilia. The DSM names eight of them specifically. *Fetishism* involves sexual attraction to either an inanimate object like shoes or a vacuum cleaner, or, alternatively, to a particular source of "tactile stimulation, such as rubber," latex, or leather.[137] When the particular fetish involves wearing clothing associated with the opposite sex, it is called *transvestic fetishism. Frotteurism* involves touching or rubbing against a nonconsenting person for sexual gratification.

Voyeurism occurs when someone watches another person undressing, being naked, or engaged in sexual conduct in order to become sexually aroused while the person being observed has no knowledge they are being watched. Voyeurs are often referred to in common parlance as "peeping Toms." In contrast, when someone achieves sexual arousal because they are exposing themselves to other nonconsenting people, they have the paraphilia known as *exhibitionism.*

Sexual arousal and gratification involving the infliction of pain and/or humiliation forms the basis of two paraphilias. People who enjoy inflicting the pain or humiliation are properly

---

[132]*Id.* at 134-35.

[133]*Id.* at 135.

[134]*Id.* at 142-43.

[135]*Id.* at 134-39; *see also* Mayo Clinic On-Line, *Geriatric Medicine: Dementia* <http://www.mayo.edu/geriatrics-rst/Dementia.I.html#RTFToC1>.

[136]American Psychiatric Ass'n, Diagnostic and Statistical Manual of Mental Disorder 566 (4th ed., text rev. 2000) [hereinafter DSM-IV-TR].

[137]David H. Barlow & V. Mark Durand, Abnormal Psychology: An Integrative Approach 323-24 (2nd ed., Wadsworth 2002).

diagnosed with **sexual sadism.** The flip side involves **sexual masochism**—the enjoyment of having the pain or humiliation inflicted upon themselves. It should be noted that rapist are not considered to have a paraphilia since their patterns of sexual arousal usually do not meet the diagnostic criteria for one of the paraphilias.[138] Some rapists meet the criteria for anti-social personality disorder. But a particular type of rapist called the **sadistic rapist** does suffer from sexual sadism. They take pleasure and gratification in the infliction of pain, suffering, and humiliation on their victims.[139]

Pedophilia is the paraphilia in which someone is sexually attracted to children or very young (prepubescent) adolescents. Pedophiles may be attracted to young boys, girls, or both. And pedophilia may or may not involve **incest,** which involves sexual relations with a relative within a close degree of kinship. "Although pedophilia and incest have much in common, victims of pedophilia tend to be young children, and victims of incest tend to be girls who are beginning to mature physically."[140] And it should noted that although sexual attraction to post-pubescent teenagers is not pedophilia (the term for such attraction is **ephebophilia**, and it is not a mental disorder), sexual conduct with a post-pubescent teen under the age of consent (usually 18, although it varies by jurisdiction) is the crime of statutory rape.

In addition to the eight named paraphilias, the DSM has a category for "Paraphilias Not Otherwise Specified."[141] Frequently included in this catch-all category are: **necrophilia,** an erotic attraction to corpses;[142] **telephone scatologia,** sexual excitement by making obscene phone calls, **zoophilia,** sexual attractiion to animals (which may lead to **bestiality,** actual sexual contact with an animal); **coprophilia** (referred to as "scat"), sexual attraction to feces; **klismaphilia,** sexual excitation by enemas; and **urophilia** (referred to as "water sports"), sexual excitation by urine.[143]

B. Legal Significance of Paraphilias

The law has generally taken the view that the paraphilias, like anti-social personality disorder and impulse control disorders, are not true mental illnesses, but rather are labels applied by the behavioral sciences through the medicalization of deviance. This is so because these types of disorder are "marked primarily by abnormalities of desire, conduct, and pervasive behavioral or affective style, rather than by relatively discrete, severe abnormalities of cognition, perception, and affect.[144] Moreover, the abnormalities embodied in the paraphilias do not correspond to any notion of criminal nonresponsibility. Pedophiles, for example, know the nature and quality of their acts and know their conduct is criminal. They know better than to molest a child in view of a responsible third party.[145] Accordingly, the paraphilias generally do not qualify as bona-fide "mental disease or defects" for insanity or diminished capacity purposes.[146] But since people

---

[138]*Id.* at 325.

[139]*See generally id.* at 325-26; NICHOLAS A. GROTH, MEN WHO RAPE: THE PSYCHOLOGY OF THE OFFENDER 44 (Plennam Press 1979).

[140]BARLOW & DURAND, *supra* note 137, at 326.

[141]DSV-IV *supra* note 1, at 532.

[142]*Id.* at 522-23.

[143]*Id.* at 532; see also Tyler Trent Ochoa & Christine Newman Jones, *Defiling the Dead: Necrophilia and the Law*, 18 WHITTIER L. REV. 539, 540-41 (1997).

[144]Stephen J. Morse, *Uncontrollable Urges and Irrational People*, 88 VA. L. REV. 1025, 1045-46 (2002).

[145]*Id.* at 1055.

[146]See Chapters Six and Seven, respectively.

suffering from certain paraphilias are both mentally ill and "dangerous," they have increasingly been subject to involuntary civil commitment.[147]

IX. CONCLUSION

There are hundreds of disorders recognized in DSM-IV. This Appendix provides an overview of the diagnostic criteria for only a select few of them that are often seen in the forensic setting. This Appendix should not be viewed as containing sufficient information upon which any particular diagnosis can be made, especially since information on differential diagnosis has generally been omitted. Also omitted is information from research on the etiology, course, and treatment of many of the diseases. Such research should be consulted for a more complete understanding of the disorders.

---

[147]See Chapter 10; *see also* Morse, *supra* note 144; John M. Fabian, Kansas v. Hendricks *and Beyond: "Mental Abnormality," "Volition," "Dangerousness," and the Debate Between Community Safety and Civil Liberty*, 34 U.W.L.A.L. REV. 529 (2002).